EBSCO 6-30-99

1998
The Supreme Court Review

1998
The

"Judges as persons, or courts as institutions, are entitled to
no greater immunity from criticism than other persons
or institutions . . . [J]udges must be kept mindful of their limitations and
of their ultimate public responsibility by a vigorous
stream of criticism expressed with candor however blunt."
—*Felix Frankfurter*

". . . while it is proper that people should find fault when
their judges fail, it is only reasonable that they should recognize the
difficulties. . . . Let them be severely brought to book,
when they go wrong, but by those who will take the trouble
to understand them."
—*Learned Hand*

THE LAW SCHOOL

THE UNIVERSITY OF CHICAGO

Supreme Court Review

EDITED BY

DENNIS J. HUTCHINSON

DAVID A. STRAUSS

AND GEOFFREY R. STONE

THE UNIVERSITY OF CHICAGO PRESS

CHICAGO AND LONDON

INTERNATIONAL STANDARD BOOK NUMBER: 0-226-36316-3

LIBRARY OF CONGRESS CATALOG CARD NUMBER: 60-14353

THE UNIVERSITY OF CHICAGO PRESS, CHICAGO 60637

THE UNIVERSITY OF CHICAGO PRESS, LTD., LONDON

© 1999 BY THE UNIVERSITY OF CHICAGO, ALL RIGHTS RESERVED, PUBLISHED 1999

PRINTED IN THE UNITED STATES OF AMERICA

The paper used in this publication meets the minimum requirements of American National Standard for Information Sciences–Permanence of Paper for Printed Library Materials, ANSI Z39.48-1984. ⊗

CONTENTS

CORNELIA T. L. PILLARD
AND T. ALEXANDER ALEINIKOFF

SKEPTICAL SCRUTINY OF PLENARY POWER: JUDICIAL AND EXECUTIVE BRANCH DECISION MAKING IN MILLER v ALBRIGHT

In 1996, just a few months after the United States successfully urged the Supreme Court in *United States v Virginia*[1] to invalidate as sex-discriminatory the male-only admissions policy at the Virginia Military Institute, the District of Columbia Circuit in *Miller v Albright*[2] upheld a federal law that used an express, sex-based

Cornelia Pillard is Associate Professor of Law, Georgetown University Law Center. She is currently on leave to work in the U.S. Department of Justice as Deputy Assistant Attorney General, Office of Legal Counsel. T. Alexander Aleinikoff is Professor of Law, Georgetown University Law Center.

AUTHORS' NOTE: We would like to thank Catherine W. Brown, David D. Cole, Walter E. Dellinger III, Edward C. DuMont, Vicki C. Jackson, Edwin S. Kneedler, Martin S. Lederman, David A. Martin, Hiroshi Motomura, Gerald L. Neuman, Donald Patterson, Louis H. Pollak, Susan Deller Ross, Peter H. Schuck, Louis Michael Seidman, Peter J. Spiro, Mark V. Tushnet, Carlos M. Vázquez, and Robin L. West and members of the Georgetown University Law Center faculty workshop for their thoughtful comments regarding earlier drafts of this article. Special thanks also to the Law Center for providing us with summer writing grants, and for enabling us to hire Keri McGrath and Daniel Wadleigh to provide their excellent research assistance. Professor Aleinikoff was General Counsel and Executive Associate Commissioner at the Immigration and Naturalization Service from 1994 to 1997; Professor Pillard was an Assistant to the Solicitor General from 1994 to 1997, where she drafted briefs for the United States in *United States v Virginia*. The views expressed herein are the authors' own views, however, and, except where specifically so stated, should not be understood to express the views of the United States or of any of the persons thanked herein.

[1] 518 US 515 (1996).

[2] 118 S Ct 1428 (1998).

distinction. Section 309(a) of the Immigration and Nationality Act (INA) makes it harder for male U.S. citizens than for female citizens to convey their citizenship to their children if those children were born abroad out of wedlock and the other parent was not a U.S. citizen.[3] Notwithstanding the United States' position in *Virginia* that sex-based classifications are virtually always unconstitutional, the government defended Section 309(a) in the Supreme Court. As the government saw it, *Miller* involved a claim by an alien abroad, so the Constitution did not apply or, at most, the Court should review the claim with extraordinary deference to the political branches. If deferential review applied, rather than *Virginia*'s "skeptical scrutiny," the government believed that the Court should uphold the statute.

When review was granted, the case seemed to present an opportunity for the Court to revisit the larger issue it had addressed two decades earlier in *Fiallo v Bell*:[4] how to reconcile heightened, "skeptical" scrutiny of sex-based classifications with diminished scrutiny of immigration and naturalization measures in a case that seemed to call for both. The Court in *Fiallo* had sustained a sex-based classification in an INA provision closely analogous to Section 309(a), but dealing with eligibility for permanent resident status rather than citizenship. *Fiallo* treated Congress's plenary power over immigration as categorically trumping the otherwise heightened level of scrutiny applicable to sex-based classifications. But virtually the entire body of modern constitutional law on sex discrimination developed after *Fiallo*. The Court decided *Fiallo* in 1977, close on the heels of its 1976 decision in *Craig v Boren*,[5] the first case in which it applied intermediate constitutional scrutiny to a sex-based classification. The two ensuing decades of sex discrimination decisions strengthened and clarified the equal protection standard. The court of appeals in *Miller* had upheld the statute under *Fiallo* over a dissent arguing that the Supreme Court should reconsider *Fiallo* in light of the intervening sex discrimination jurisprudence. The government's brief in opposition to certiorari characterized *Miller* as squarely governed by *Fiallo*, so the Supreme

---

[3] 8 USC § 1409(a).

[4] 430 US 787 (1977).

[5] 429 US 190 (1976).

Court's decision to grant review so soon after *Virginia* suggested that *Fiallo* might be headed for the dustbin.

Instead, the Court issued a decision on nonjusticiability grounds that was so fractured and narrow as to seem almost meaningless. But there is, on closer examination, much that is surprising and significant about *Miller*. The case provides an opportunity for re-examining the nature and justifications for the plenary power doctrine.

We start by analyzing Section 309(a) and explaining why we believe those Justices who concluded that the statute unconstitutionally discriminates based on sex are clearly right. We then argue that judicial deference under the plenary power doctrine is an institutionally rather than substantively based doctrine—meaning, not that sex discrimination is more tolerable in immigration and naturalization than it is domestically, but that sex discrimination norms are judicially underenforced in the former context for reasons relating to the relative institutional competence of the judiciary and the political branches.

We then look at *Miller*'s implications for the future of the plenary power doctrine. Although the Court did not reach the merits, the five separate opinions provide significant clues about the current Justices' thinking on the interplay between plenary power and constitutional rights. A majority of the Justices distinguished Ms. Miller's claim from the immigration claims in *Fiallo* by emphasizing that Miller sought not immigration but citizenship, and suggested that the Court would fully enforce equal protection norms in a citizenship case. The Justices' disinclination to apply plenary power deference to citizenship claims is supported by the importance of citizenship to the individual who claims it, as well as by the lack of persuasive justifications for allowing discriminations against putative citizens abroad that we do not tolerate in the domestic context. Ultimately, however, we show why we do not think that the Court can draw a stable distinction between a claim of *jus sanguinis* (bloodline) citizenship such as Ms. Miller's and an immigration or naturalization claim. *Miller* raises the prospect that the plenary power doctrine is as inappropriate in immigration and nationality law generally as the Justices in *Miller* suggest it is for *jus sanguinis* citizenship claims.

Finally, we discuss the implications for government lawyers of our sex discrimination and plenary power analyses. That discussion has two parts: First, we argue that the underenforced-norms reading of the plenary power cases suggests that the political branches should not use deferential, rational-basis review in conducting their own constitutional review of immigration, nationality, or citizenship measures, but should apply full-fledged constitutional norms. Second, we argue that, after *Miller*, the courts lack adequate justifications for the plenary power doctrine—at least in the absence of a new, substantive rationale for diminished protection of individual rights—in *jus sanguinis* citizenship cases like *Miller*, and, indeed, lack grounds for relying on it in immigration and nationality cases generally.

I. Section 309(a) and the Miller Litigation

There are few sex-based classifications left in federal law, apart from a handful in military statutes[6] and a few in laws governing immigration, naturalization, and bloodline citizenship. Section 309(a) of the INA is one of these increasingly rare laws. Under Section 301(g) of the INA, a child who is born abroad of one alien parent and one U.S. citizen parent is generally deemed to be a citizen of the United States at birth.[7] But if such a child was born out of wedlock and the citizen parent is the father, Section 309(a) imposes several additional conditions, including: that a blood relationship between the child and the father be established by clear and convincing evidence; that the father have agreed in writing to provide financial support for the child until she or he turns eighteen; and that, while the child is under the age of eighteen, the father legitimate the child or acknowledge paternity in writing under oath, or that paternity be established by adjudication.[8] A

---

[6] The Military Selective Service Act, providing for a male-only draft, was upheld against an equal protection challenge in *Rostker v Goldberg*, 453 US 57 (1981). The Act has since been repealed.

[7] Immigration and Nationality Act ("INA") § 301(g), 8 USC § 1401(g).

[8] INA § 309(a), 8 USC § 1409(a), provides:

The provisions of paragraphs (c), (d), (e), and (g) of Section 1401 of this title, and of paragraph (2) of Section 1408 of this title [establishing U.S. citizenship or nationality of certain children born abroad], shall apply as of the date of birth to a person born out of wedlock if—

(1) a blood relationship between the person and the father is established by clear and convincing evidence,

(2) the father had the nationality of the United States at the time of the person's birth,

child born out of wedlock to a U.S. citizen mother is not subject to Section 309(a) but instead "shall be held to have acquired
at birth the nationality status of his mother."[9] In other words, an
unmarried citizen mother's citizenship passes virtually automatically,[10] whereas an unmarried citizen father must not only prove
the parental link that for the mother is assumed, but must also
meet a deadline for establishing a formal legal relationship with
his child and agree to support her financially until she reaches
age eighteen.[11]

There is an additional sex-based distinction in the duration of
U.S. residency required of parents wishing to convey citizenship
to their nonmarital children born abroad. The citizen parent in a
mixed-citizenship couple—whether married or not—generally
must have been a U.S. resident for at least five years before the
child's birth in order to convey citizenship to that child.[12] Citizen
mothers of nonmarital children, however, need only have resided
in the United States for one year in order to convey citizenship.[13]
Congress added the shorter, one-year residency requirement in
1952, apparently based on a concern to avoid statelessness on the
part of nonmarital children of U.S. citizen mothers.[14] The assump-

---

(3) the father (unless deceased) has agreed in writing to provide financial
support for the person until the person reaches the age of 18 years, and
 (4) while the person is under the age of 18 years—
 (A) the person is legitimated under the law of the person's residence or
domicile,
 (B) the father acknowledges paternity of the person in writing under oath,
or
 (C) the paternity of the person is established by adjudication of a competent
court.

[9] INA § 309(c), 8 USC 1409(c).

[10] But see 7 US Dep't of State, *Foreign Affairs Manual* 1131.4, 1131.5-4(b)-(c), 1133.6
(rev 2/15/91) (requiring some evidence of maternity).

[11] Under a transitional provision applicable to Lorelyn Miller, she had the option to elect
a deadline of her twenty-first, not eighteenth, birthday. See note following 8 USC § 1409
(effective date of 1986 amendment); 118 S Ct 1428, 1433 n 3 (Stevens opinion). Ms. Miller's
application was untimely under either deadline, however, and for simplicity we will refer
to the age-eighteen deadline.

[12] The citizen parent must have, before the child's birth, been "physically present in the
United States or its outlying possessions for a period or periods totaling not less than five
years, at least two of which were after attaining the age of fourteen years," with overseas
service in the U.S. military or with certain international organizations counting toward the
residency requirement. INA § 301(g), 8 USC § 1401(g).

[13] INA § 309(c), 8 USC § 1409(c).

[14] The Senate Report describes the purpose of the new, shorter residency requirement
for mothers as "insur[ing] that the child shall have a nationality at birth." S Rep No 1137,
82d Cong, 2d Sess 4 (Jan 29, 1952).

tion behind that concern seems to have been that other countries generally granted citizenship to nonmarital children only through their mothers, potentially leaving nonmarital children born overseas of foreign fathers and U.S. mothers without any nationality at all.[15]

Lorelyn Penero Miller was born in the Philippines in 1970 to Luz Penero, a Filipina, and Charlie Miller, a U.S. soldier stationed in the Philippines. Mr. Miller and Ms. Penero were unmarried. Mr. Miller returned to the United States when his tour of duty ended. He apparently was not much of a letter writer, but as Ms. Miller grew up she corresponded regularly with her paternal grandmother who lived near Mr. Miller in Texas. After her grandmother died some time in the late 1980s, Ms. Miller had more frequent direct communication with her father. Neither of them was aware, however, of the deadline in Section 309(a) for establishing the prerequisites for Ms. Miller's birthright citizenship. As it happened, it was not until shortly after Ms. Miller's twenty-first birthday that her father got a voluntary paternity decree from a Texas court, and Ms. Miller applied for recognition as a U.S. citizen. The State Department rejected the application on the ground that Ms. Miller's father had not formally legitimated her and agreed to provide her financial support before she came of age.[16] Ms. Miller brought suit challenging the constitutionality of Section 309(a), and her father joined as a plaintiff.

Both lower courts upheld the statute. The district court held

---

[15] The differential residency requirements were not at issue in *Miller*, because Mr. Miller satisfied the more stringent requirements applicable to citizen fathers. See *Miller v Albright*, 118 S Ct at 1435 & nn 5–8 (Stevens opinion). The requirement that a blood relationship between the child and the father, but not the mother, be proved by clear and convincing evidence was also not at issue, because the government conceded that petitioner met it. See id at 1436. As for the requirement that the father, but not the mother, agree in writing to provide financial support for the child until she reaches age eighteen, Justice Stevens stated that it was "unclear" whether that provision even applied to petitioner's case in view of her eligibility for an interim provision not applying that requirement, and the State Department's apparent reliance only on Section 309(a)(4) to deny Ms. Miller citizenship. Id at 1436. The focus in *Miller* was thus on the age-eighteen deadline for legally establishing paternity.

[16] Interestingly, it was not at first clear that the statute would be enforced. When Lorelyn Miller initially submitted the Texas court's voluntary paternity decree to the U.S. Embassy in Manila, consular officials responded that "in our opinion, the petition decree legitimizes Lorelyn at birth." See Br for Pet 5. Moreover, at that time a federal court in New Jersey had held that Section 309 unconstitutionally discriminates against illegitimate children, and the government apparently declined to appeal. *LeBrun v Thornburgh*, 777 F Supp 1204, 1210–14 (D NJ 1991).

that *Fiallo* barred the equal protection claims and that Ms. Miller lacked a redressable injury because, under *INS v Pangilinan*,[17] the courts lack power to grant citizenship as a remedy.[18] The court of appeals disagreed that Ms. Miller's injury was judicially nonredressable, but held that, under the deferential standard of review applicable to "rules for the admission and exclusion of aliens," the statute withstood constitutional challenge. The court concluded that the statute rationally served an interest in promoting early ties to the United States and to the citizen parent: "A mother is far less likely to ignore the child she has carried in her womb than is the natural father, who may not even be aware of its existence," and it is therefore "entirely reasonable for Congress to require special evidence of such ties between an illegitimate child and its father."[19] Judge Wald concurred in the judgment because she believed Ms. Miller's claim was foreclosed by *Fiallo*, but she asserted that *Fiallo* is "out of step" with current law and "should be changed by Congress or the Supreme Court."[20]

A. THE GOVERNMENT'S POSITION

The Supreme Court granted Ms. Miller's petition seeking review of the question whether Section 309(a) unconstitutionally discriminates based on sex.[21] Somewhat surprisingly, in view of the United States' recent successful argument in *Virginia* that even largely accurate sex-based generalizations virtually always violate equal protection, the government argued in the strongest terms

---

[17] 486 US 875 (1988) (holding, in response to equal protection and due process challenge, that courts lack power to confer citizenship on group of veterans under long-expired special immigration statute authorizing citizenship by naturalization on Filipino nationals who served with the U.S. Armed Forces during World War II).

[18] *Miller v Christopher*, Civ 6:93CV39 (ED Tex June 2, 1993) (reprinted in App B to Br for Resp *Miller v Albright*, 118 S Ct 1428 (1998) (No. 96-1060)), and 870 F Supp 1, 3 (DDC 1994).

[19] *Miller v Christopher*, 96 F3d 1467, 1472 (DC Cir 1996).

[20] Id at 1477.

[21] The question presented was "is the distinction in 8 USC § 1409 between 'illegitimate' children of US citizen mothers and 'illegitimate' children of U.S. fathers a violation of the Fifth Amendment to the United States Constitution." See *Miller v Albright*, 117 S Ct 1689 (1977) (Mem). The Court amended the grant of certiorari to limit its consideration to that question from among the five that the petitioner presented, which included questions whether the statute unconstitutionally discriminates based on illegitimacy, and whether the Court should give effect to the retroactivity of the state court's paternity determination. Compare id with Pet 1.

that sex-based classifications relating to immigration and nationality should be subject to little or no judicial review.[22] The government argued that *Fiallo* controlled, and that because Congress has
"plenary power" over immigration and nationality, the Court
should review Section 309(a)'s sex-based distinctions with "extraordinary deference," and should uphold the statute "so long as
it was based on a facially legitimate and bona fide reason"—a standard the government described as "more deferential even than the
familiar 'rational basis' standard applied in the context of purely
domestic legislation."[23] Such deference, the government insisted,
"is not a relic of the legal past," but rests on the Constitution's
delegation to Congress of power over naturalization, as well as on
considerations of "national sovereignty, foreign relations, and the
fundamentally political character of immigration and nationality
decisions."[24] Those considerations, it maintained, place claims
such as Ms. Miller's "beyond the institutional competence of the
judiciary."[25] The government also asserted that Ms. Miller, as an
alien outside the United States, had no substantive rights under
the Fifth Amendment.[26] Insofar as the rights of Mr. Miller, a U.S.
citizen, might be implicated, it contended that the Court should
also review his equal protection claim with the kind of deference
ordinarily reserved for immigration matters, because full-fledged
constitutional review of a citizen parent's claim "would vitiate the
rule of deference in the context of acquisition of nationality
through birth abroad."[27]

The government did not, however, rest entirely on the deferential standard of review. It also argued that Section 309(a) should
be sustained even if subjected to heightened scrutiny under *United
States v Virginia*.[28] Section 309(a)'s different treatment of unmar-

---

[22] The government also contended that, as a threshold matter, there was no justiciable
issue presented because Mr. Miller lacked standing. Br for Resp 10–12.

[23] Id at 8–9, 21 (quoting *Fiallo*, 430 US at 792), 34 & n 19.

[24] Id at 8, 12–14, 22.

[25] Id at 22.

[26] Id at 10–12.

[27] Id at 38 n 20. See also id at 42 ("whatever a citizen's interest in the matter, the actual
subject of an immigration or naturalization law like that at issue here is the alien abroad,
who has no right to invoke the heightened scrutiny of gender-based distinctions that is
required in other contexts by the United States Constitution.").

[28] Id at 43 n 22.

ried citizen fathers of foreign-born children as compared with mothers was, in the government's view, "not based on invidious gender stereotypes, but on real differences" in the situation of the citizen mothers and putative citizen fathers of illegitimate children born abroad.[29] The government argued that the statutory require- ments of legally establishing paternity and providing financial sup- port tie the child to the United States by ensuring that the child has a "nexus to a citizen parent."[30] The mother physically bears the child, her maternal relationship typically is legally established immediately by the birth certificate, and her financial support obli- gations flow from that legal relationship. The government thus characterized Sections 309(a)(3) and (4) as placing the out-of- wedlock child of a U.S. citizen father "in a position roughly equiv- alent to that of the typical foreign-born child claiming through an unmarried citizen mother."[31] The government acknowledged that Section 309(a)(4)'s time deadline on proof of paternity cannot be explained as serving the need for reliable proof of a blood relation- ship in view of the separate provision requiring clear and convinc- ing proof of paternity,[32] but speculated that the animating concern might have been to ensure "that citizenship not devolve automati- cally on a foreign-born child who is unlikely to develop, in his or her formative years, substantial personal ties to the United States."[33]

B. THE COURT'S DECISION

As framed, the case seemed poised either to reaffirm the defer- ential plenary power standard applied in *Fiallo* or to strike down the statute based on post-*Fiallo* developments in sex discrimination law. The Court did neither, although, as we explain, it did lay important groundwork for the latter course.

A fractured Court upheld the statute. Justice Stevens rejected the sex discrimination claim on its merits, but his opinion garnered

---

[29] Id at 43.

[30] Id at 24, 26.

[31] Id at 24.

[32] The government's brief pointed out that Congress in 1986 revised the statute to require clear and convincing proof of biological paternity without imposing any time limitation, and the State Department "has never declined to recognize such testing," so long as reliably performed. Id at 27.

[33] Id at 27–28.

only the additional vote of Chief Justice Rehnquist, with four other Justices concurring in the judgment on other grounds.[34] The concurring Justices concluded either that Ms. Miller had no first-party claim and lacked third-party standing to raise her father's claim,[35] or that her injury was not judicially redressable in view of courts' lack of power to confer citizenship as a remedy.[36]

Miller is a peculiar decision because, although the government prevailed, the Court upheld the statute in only the most formal sense, and none of the government's arguments persuaded a majority of the Court. The Court did not validate the statute's constitutionality; in fact, Justice Ginsburg asserted in her dissenting opinion that "a solid majority" of the Court—Justices O'Connor and Kennedy and the three dissenters—believed Section 309(a) unconstitutionally discriminates on the basis of sex.[37] That may be an overstatement in view of Justice O'Connor's limited opinion.[38] But it is certainly accurate that no majority endorsed the statute's constitutionality as a matter of equal protection. There was also no majority for the government's proposition that a deferential standard of review should apply to Ms. Miller's claim; the five Justices who analyzed her claim on the merits at all applied heightened review in light of Ms. Miller's asserted right to citizenship from birth.[39] Not a single Justice embraced the government's suggestion that Ms. Miller was an alien lacking any Fifth Amendment rights.[40] At least where a person outside the United States raises a citizenship claim, as Ms. Miller did, a majority of the Justices viewed her as a rights holder under the Constitution.[41] And the

---

[34] 118 S Ct at 1432–42 (Stevens opinion, joined by Rehnquist); id at 1442–46 (O'Connor, joined by Kennedy, concurring); id at 1446–49 (Scalia, joined by Thomas, concurring).

[35] Id at 1442 (O'Connor, joined by Kennedy, concurring).

[36] Id at 1446 (Scalia, joined by Thomas, concurring).

[37] Id at 1450 (Ginsburg, joined by Souter and Breyer, dissenting).

[38] See text at note 65. Although Justices O'Connor and Kennedy stated that Section 309(a) could not withstand heightened scrutiny, it remains an open question whether they would apply heightened scrutiny or some lower level of review had they believed that the claim of sex discrimination in birthright citizenship was properly before the Court.

[39] 18 S Ct at 1436–42 & n 11 (Stevens opinion); id at 1458–63 (Breyer opinion).

[40] Id at 1436 n 10 (Stevens opinion); id at 1445 (O'Connor concurring); id at 1456–57 (Breyer dissenting); see also id at 1447 n 1 (Scalia concurring).

[41] Seven Justices distinguished *Johnson v Eisentrager*, 339 US 763 (1950), and *United States v Verdugo-Urquidez*, 494 US 259 (1990)—cases in which the Court had held that aliens abroad lacked constitutional rights—as not involving persons abroad claiming U.S. citizenship or nationality. Id at 1436 n 10 (Stevens opinion); id at 1456–57 (Breyer dissenting)

Justices also rebuffed the government's contention that, in the realm of immigration and naturalization, courts should review the constitutional claims of even established citizens such as Charlie Miller with extra deference to the political branches;[42] five Justices applied heightened scrutiny to Ms. Miller's third-party claim that the statute unconstitutionally discriminates between U.S. citizen fathers and their U.S. citizen mother counterparts.[43]

1. *Miller as a justiciability decision*. The *Miller* decision seems anticlimactic at first blush. As noted above, the Court appeared to have granted review to revisit the plenary power doctrine as it affects sex discrimination claims, and perhaps to overrule or limit *Fiallo*. But, as it turned out, the dispositive votes were cast on nonjusticiability grounds, with Justices O'Connor and Kennedy voting to affirm based on a perceived lack of third-party standing, and Justices Scalia and Thomas on the ground that petitioner's injury was not judicially redressable. Neither of those issues had been raised in the government's brief in opposition to the petition for certiorari, and their resolution had not seemed to be the focus of the case when the Court agreed to hear it.[44]

The standing question had a convoluted history in the litigation. On the government's motion, the district court had held that Mr. Miller lacked standing to challenge Section 309(a) because it was his daughter, not he, who suffered the harm of citizenship denial.[45]

("those cases [*Eisentrager* and *Verdugo-Urquidez*], as Justice Stevens points out, are irrelevant, for the matter at issue here is whether or not Lorelyn is a citizen."); id at 1445 (O'Connor concurring) ("[w]hile it is unclear whether an alien may assert constitutional objections when he or she is outside the territory of the United States [citing *Eisentrager* and *Verdugo-Urquidez*], I will assume that petitioner may challenge the constitutionality of § 1409").

Because Justice Scalia concluded that Ms. Miller had standing to raise her father's claim, he found that "there is no need for me to reach the Government's claim . . . that petitioner cannot invoke the Equal Protection Clause on her own behalf because she is not within the jurisdiction of the United States." Id at 1447 n 1 (Scalia concurring).

[42] Br for Resp 38 n 20, 42.

[43] 118 S Ct at 1437–42 (Stevens opinion) (analyzing statute under heightened scrutiny); id at 1454 (Ginsburg, joined by Souter and Breyer, dissenting); id at 1457–58 (Breyer, joined by Souter and Ginsburg, dissenting).

[44] Indeed, the government at the petition stage apparently took the opposite view of the redressability issue from the one it (and Justices Scalia and Thomas) ended up adopting. In its Brief in Opposition, the government stated that "the court of appeals correctly concluded that petitioner could be declared a citizen by virtue of the general rule of section 1408(g) . . . if [the Court] declared the specific rule of Section 1409(a) unconstitutional." Br in Opp 13–14.

[45] See 118 S Ct at 1433.

With Mr. Miller, a Texas resident, out of the case, the federal court in Texas transferred it to the U.S. District Court for the District of Columbia. Mr. Miller did not appeal his dismissal,[46] and the case proceeded with Ms. Miller as the sole plaintiff. Once Charlie Miller was out of the case, however, the government argued to the Supreme Court that the district court had it backwards: It was Charlie Miller, and *not* his daughter, who had been the victim of discrimination, and she lacked third-party standing to raise his claim.

Only Justices O'Connor and Kennedy agreed, but they provided crucial swing votes. Justice O'Connor observed that Section 309 "accords differential treatment to fathers and mothers, not to sons and daughters."[47] Petitioner thus was not herself a victim of sex discrimination; the only sex discrimination claim at issue was the father's claim that he should have the same right as a citizen mother to convey U.S. citizenship to his child.[48] In holding that Ms. Miller lacked standing, Justice O'Connor stressed that third-party standing is "a prudential limitation on the exercise of federal jurisdiction," under which a party injured by a statute may challenge it on behalf of a person to whom she has a close relation only if there is "some hindrance to the third party's ability to protect his or her own interests."[49] Ms. Miller concededly had both a close relation to her father (at least in the abstract) and an injury, but Justice O'Connor did not view the government's erroneous yet successful motion in the district court to dismiss Mr. Miller from the case, nor the transfer of the case away from his home state of Texas to Washington, D.C., as sufficient hindrance to justify third-party standing.[50] As a practical matter, Justice O'Connor's standing

---

[46] The appeal would have required the plaintiffs to litigate on two fronts—in the Fifth Circuit on Mr. Miller's appeal, and in the DC Circuit on Ms. Miller's appeal. Moreover, the plaintiffs' lawyer believed that Ms. Miller's claim was the heart of the case, and that in any event her third-party standing was clear under *Wauchope v United States Department of State*, 985 F2d 1407, 1410–11 (9th Cir 1992). August 27, 1998, telephone conversation with the Millers' counsel, Donald Patterson.

[47] 118 S Ct at 1442.

[48] Id.

[49] Id at 1443 (quoting *Powers v Ohio*, 499 US 400, 411 (1991)).

[50] Id at 1443–45. Notwithstanding that Mr. Miller had been a co-plaintiff, Justice O'Connor believed that the fact that he "never indicated any intent to challenge his dismissal from the suit" suggested a lack of interest in enforcing his rights. In Justice O'Connor's view, "any hindrance to the vindication of Charlie Miller's constitutional rights is ultimately self imposed." Id at 1444.

decision was necessary to the outcome, but as a precedential matter, it lacks force because seven Justices—including four who supported the judgment—disagreed with it.[51]

Thus, a majority of the Justices believed that Ms. Miller had third-party standing to raise her father's claims, and a majority also appears to have thought that Section 309(a) unconstitutionally discriminated against Mr. Miller. Section 309(a) survived at least in part because those views were held by different majorities. But *Miller* placed Section 309(a) on the chopping block. When the right plaintiff comes along, the relevant guidance for the lower courts comes not from the standing analysis, but from the majority of the Justices' views on the merits.[52]

As Justice Scalia pointed out, however, there is another potential justiciability obstacle that the lower courts will have to contend with before ruling for the next citizen-father who sues: whether the courts can redress the injury by granting citizenship to the plaintiff's child.[53] It remains unclear under *Miller* how real that second obstacle is. The three dissenting Justices expressly disagreed with Justice Scalia that any such bar existed,[54] but the four other Justices did not state their views.[55]

Justice Scalia, joined by Justice Thomas, started from the prem-

---

[51] Five of the Justices—Stevens, Souter, Ginsburg, Breyer, and Chief Justice Rehnquist—concluded that Ms. Miller had standing to raise claims on her own behalf as well as third-party standing to assert her father's claim. Id at 1436 (Stevens opinion) (agreeing with the court of appeals' holding as to Ms. Miller's own standing, and holding under *Craig v Boren*, 429 US 190 (1976), that she could raise her father's claims of discrimination); id at 1456–57 (Breyer dissenting) (finding third-party standing on the ground that "the conclusion that the Government 'hindered' Charlie's assertion of his own rights in this case is irresistible," and opining that Ms. Miller had a first-party discrimination claim because "she belongs to a class of children of citizen-fathers, whom the law distinguishes from the class of children of citizen-mothers, solely on the ground of the parent's gender"). Justice Scalia, joined by Justice Thomas, "accept[ed] petitioner's third-party standing." Id at 1447 n 1.

[52] The propriety of lower court judges counting the Justices' votes—rather than limiting consideration to what Professor Caminker has called "unified-majority dispositional rules"—is debatable, but a strong case can be made in favor of judges considering the Court's "fragmented-majority dispositional rules" such as those in the *Miller* opinions. See Evan H. Caminker, *Precedent and Prediction: The Forward-Looking Aspects of Inferior Court Decisionmaking*, 73 Tex L Rev 1 (1994).

[53] 118 S Ct at 1446–50.

[54] Id at 1463–64 (Breyer dissenting).

[55] See id at 1442 (Stevens opinion) ("Because we conclude that there is no constitutional violation to remedy, we express no opinion on this question"); id at 1445 (O'Connor concurring) (referring to "the potential problems with fashioning a remedy for [petitioner's] injury" as a factor weighing against recognition of petitioner's third-party standing).

ise that the Constitution confers birthright citizenship only on persons born in the United States, and that for all others Congress controls the terms of naturalization: "If there is no congressional enactment granting petitioner citizenship, she remains an alien."[56] Ms. Miller acknowledged that she could not meet two statutory preconditions to the acquisition of citizenship—the requirements that (1) her father commit in writing to support her until she reached legal majority,[57] and (2) she be legitimated, or that her father's paternity be adjudicated or acknowledged, before she reached age eighteen.[58] In Justice Scalia's view, that failure ended the matter, because the Court lacked authority to sever the allegedly unconstitutional provisions and grant her citizenship under the remaining statutory terms.

Justices Breyer, Souter, and Ginsburg disagreed; in their view, the Court could remedy the discrimination by striking from the statute the offending provisions. The Court need not grant citizenship, the dissenters asserted, because without the sex-based limitations the statute itself would confer citizenship automatically and "at birth."[59] Congress would have favored such severance, the dissenters reasoned, both because advances in the reliability of proving paternity by DNA testing have overcome concerns that drove the challenged statutory provisions, and because the statute expressly authorizes severance.[60]

While the case was, for all practical purposes, decided on justiciability grounds, the justiciability issues should not mask the real importance of the *Miller* decision. Although the Court formally sustained Section 309(a), we argue below that the reasoning of a majority of the Justices calls into question the viability, not only of the statute, but of the plenary power doctrine and the Court's past approach to individual rights claims in the area of immigration and naturalization. The justiciability flaws in Ms. Miller's case make the decision appear less significant than it is.

2. *Miller as a sex discrimination decision.* Section 309(a) draws a sex-based distinction between male and female unwed U.S. parents

---

[56] Id at 1446.

[57] INA § 309(a)(3), 8 USC § 1409(a)(3).

[58] INA § 309(a)(4), 8 USC § 1409(a)(4).

[59] 118 S Ct at 1457, 1463–64.

[60] Id at 1463–64.

of foreign-born children. Had Mr. Miller been female, his daughter's U.S. citizenship would have been assured, and the lateness of any efforts to establish a legal and financial relationship would not have mattered.[61]

Only Justice Stevens, joined by Justice Rehnquist, defended the statute as nondiscriminatory.[62] He reasoned that the requirement that paternity be established or acknowledged before the child turns eighteen could be justified by three purposes he believed were served by the time limitation on acknowledgment or adjudication of paternity: (1) ensuring reliable proof of a biological relationship between the father and child, (2) encouraging "a healthy relationship between the citizen parent and the child while the child is a minor," and (3) "foster[ing] ties between the foreign-born child and the United States."[63] He found the statute's sex-based classification to be substantially related to those purposes.

Justice Stevens's central contention was that the statute's different treatment of women and men was justified by "real differences" between the sexes. Differences between the biological functions of men and women in procreation mean that "the unmarried father may not even know that his child exists, and the child may not know the father's identity." In the absence of such knowledge, the father and child may lack even "the opportunity . . . to develop a personal relationship." In contrast, a mother will always know that she has borne a child, and "typically will have custody of the child immediately after the birth," giving the child "the opportunity to develop ties with its citizen mother at an early age." Given the fact that male members of the military frequently conceive

---

[61] Although Ms. Miller was not discriminated against based on her *own* sex, Section 309(a) disadvantaged her based on her citizen parent's sex—a distinction that also seems fair to describe as sex-based. Compare *Palmore v Sidoti*, 466 US 429 (1984) (consideration of race of mother's new husband in denying child custody to mother amounts to discrimination based on race). If one accepts this analysis, of course, third-party standing would not be necessary because Ms. Miller would have a first-party claim.

[62] Justice Scalia, joined by Justice Thomas, declined to reach the merits of the sex discrimination issue, 118 S Ct at 1446, and, as discussed below, the other five Justices would have concluded that the statute failed heightened constitutional scrutiny, id at 1445–46 (O'Connor, joined by Kennedy, concurring) (noting that they did "not share Justice Stevens' assessment that the provision withstands heightened scrutiny," but believed that it did survive the rational-basis review that they believed to be appropriate); id at 1457–58 (Breyer, joined by Souter and Ginsburg, dissenting) (concluding that the provision could not withstand heightened scrutiny).

[63] Id at 1438–39.

children abroad and then return home without verifying whether any offspring resulted from their sexual encounters, Justice Stevens believed that Congress had legitimate grounds for concern that out-of-wedlock offspring born abroad of U.S. fathers might lack any ties to the citizen parent and to the United States. In Justice Stevens's view, the additional hurdles imposed on the male citizen parent operate roughly to equalize the likelihood that his child (as compared to the child of a female citizen) will have ties to the citizen parent and hence to the United States. A requirement that a parent seeking to convey citizenship show that there was at least an opportunity for that child to develop such ties "performs a meaningful purpose for citizen fathers, but normally would be superfluous for citizen mothers," and will at least "reduce, rather than aggravate, the disparity between the two classes of children."[64]

Five members of the Court rejected Justice Stevens's conclusion that Section 309(a) could survive heightened scrutiny. Justice O'Connor, joined by Justice Kennedy, did not reach the issue, but nonetheless stated: "I do not share Justice Stevens' assessment that the provision withstands heightened scrutiny," because "[i]t is unlikely . . . that any gender classifications based on stereotypes can survive heightened scrutiny."[65] Justice O'Connor expressed no opinion, however, on whether heightened scrutiny would be the appropriate standard of review for a bloodline citizenship claim. The three dissenting Justices would have applied heightened scrutiny to Ms. Miller's claim whether it was viewed as a first-party or third-party challenge. They argued that sex-based distinctions are subject to a "strong presumption of constitutional invalidity," which was not rebutted by the government's stated purposes for the challenged provisions.[66] In their view, the statute relied on sex as both an over- and underinclusive proxy for parental ties, and, given workable sex-neutral alternatives, the sex-based classification was not justified by any important governmental interest.

In sum, a majority of the Justices in *Miller* stated that statutes based on sex-role stereotypes are unconstitutional under heightened scrutiny, and there is reason to believe that they would apply

---

[64] Id at 1439.

[65] Id at 1445–46.

[66] Id at 1460–63.

such scrutiny to Lorelyn Miller's citizenship claim. As a sex discrimination case, *Miller* signals no retreat from the Court's modern
sex equality doctrine. Part II explains in more detail, not only why
the five Justices who identified a potential equal protection defect
in Section 309(a) were correct, but also why we believe that is the
only plausible view in light of the Court's precedents.

3. *Miller as an immigration and citizenship decision.* Just as *Miller*
initially seemed to be a disappointment for women's rights, it also
appeared to be a loss for proponents of immigrants' constitutional
rights. But in fact, *Miller* is a victory masquerading as a defeat.
Assuming that new plaintiffs can clear the justiciability hurdles,
they should win a challenge to Section 309(a). A majority of the
Justices concluded that because Ms. Miller was a putative citizen-
at-birth, *Fiallo*'s special judicial deference to immigration questions
did not apply. The Court thus rejected the initial framing of the
case as a reprise of *Fiallo*. As Justice Stevens reasoned, "the question to be decided is whether petitioner is such an alien or
whether, as she claims, she is a citizen. Thus, we must address the
merits to determine whether the predicate for this argument is
accurate."[67] The three dissenters agreed that *Fiallo*'s deferential
standard was inapplicable because Ms. Miller claimed that she was
already a citizen. Justice Breyer drew a distinction between *jus sanguinis* citizenship statutes, and immigration or naturalization statutes: The former, "because they confer the status of citizenship
'at birth,' . . . do not involve the transfer of loyalties that underlies
the naturalization of aliens, where precedent sets a more lenient
standard of review."[68]

Justice O'Connor believed that only rational-basis review applied to Ms. Miller's claim, but she relied not on *Fiallo*, or any
characterization of Ms. Miller as an alien, but on her view that
petitioner had no third-party standing, and no first-party discrimination claim to which heightened constitutional scrutiny might

---

[67] Id at 1436 n 10. Justice Stevens also thought that deference was unnecessary in any
event, because Section 309(a) survived even the heightened constitutional scrutiny ordinarily
applicable to sex-based classifications. Id at 1437 n 11.

[68] 118 S Ct at 1458. Justice Breyer pointed out that if lenient review applied in *Miller*,
it would also logically apply when a married American couple travel or work abroad and
bear a child there—thereby producing a child entitled to citizenship not because of birth
on American soil, but because of his parents' citizenship. Justice Breyer thought it would
be anomalous for any statute discriminating against such children to be subject to less than
full judicial review. Id.

apply.[69] Justices Scalia and Thomas alone affirmatively embraced the notion of judicial deference to Congress.[70] They rejected Justice Breyer's distinction between *jus sanguinis* citizenship and acquisition of citizenship through naturalization, noting that Congress has equal constitutional authority to set the terms for both.[71]

The Court's decision, therefore, was hardly a defeat in the effort to get heightened judicial scrutiny of Section 309(a). But the even bigger story is that *Miller* undermines *Fiallo* itself. The Justices in *Miller* distinguished their nondeferential treatment of *jus sanguinis* citizenship from the more deferential stance that the Court has taken on immigration and naturalization claims; *Miller* thus attempts to leave *Fiallo* intact. But the Court's efforts to distinguish *Miller* from *Fiallo* are unstable. As we will argue below in Part III, *jus sanguinis* citizenship claims cannot meaningfully be distinguished from immigration and naturalization claims. That suggests that the Court must move in either of two directions: backtrack and disavow even for *jus sanguinis* claims the more muscular approach outlined in *Miller*, or follow the course that we think is both more sound and more likely and abandon its posture of extreme deference for immigration and naturalization claims as well.

II. Skepticism Well Deserved

Five Justices in *Miller* apparently believed that Section 309(a) would not survive heightened scrutiny. Under modern equal protection doctrine, those five Justices plainly had the better view. Section 309(a) impermissibly uses sex as an inexact proxy for other attributes of unwed parents, fosters stereotypes that "reflect and reinforce historical patterns of discrimination,"[72] and eschews sex-neutral standards that could serve the government's purposes as well or better. The statute is a virtual issue-spotter of equal protection defects.

As the dissenters point out, Justice Stevens's reliance on sex-based generalizations to justify the statute is clear on the face of his own opinion, where he consistently modified his characteriza-

---

[69] Id at 1445.

[70] See id at 1447.

[71] Id at 1446 (Scalia opinion); compare id at 1463–64 (Breyer opinion).

[72] *JEB v Alabama*, 114 S Ct 1419, 1428 (1994).

tions of the circumstances of one sex or the other by referring to what "typically," "normally," or "often" happens to women or men.[73] A core attribute of heightened scrutiny, however, is that it condemns the use of inexact sex-based generalizations. Current "typical" behavior of men as a group and women as a group may itself result from historical sex-based bias, and thus must not be relied on to justify further inscribing those differences into the law.[74] Sex-based generalizations are also prohibited because they deny opportunities to individuals who do not conform to socially defined roles.[75] Thus, even where sex-based generalizations have some factual accuracy, the Court has consistently invalidated legal restrictions based on them.[76] As Justice O'Connor wrote in *JEB v Alabama*, the constitutional determination that sex must not be used as a proxy for attitude or behavior is "a statement about what this nation stands for" even where it may not be "a statement of fact."[77] It is not enough, under equal protection heightened scrutiny, to conclude as Justice Stevens did that an unmarried mother *typically* will have emotional or cultural ties with her biological child, while an unmarried father *often* will not. It is no doubt cur-

---

[73] 118 S Ct at 1438 ("The blood relationship to the birth mother . . . is *typically* established by hospital records and birth certificates"); id at 1439 (mother "*typically* will have custody of the child immediately after birth"; requirement that father take affirmative acts to demonstrate the possibility that their child will develop ties to the U.S. "*normally* would be superfluous for citizen mothers"; mother "*often* has custody at birth").

[74] See *JEB v Alabama*, 114 S Ct at 1428 (law must not "reflect and reinforce patterns of historical discrimination"); *Craig v Boren*, 429 US 190, 202 n 14 (1976) (rejecting proffered justification for different beer-purchase ages for males and females based on higher risk of males having alcohol-related safety problems, the Court reasoned that "[t]he very social stereotypes that find reflection in age differential laws are likely substantially to distort the accuracy of . . . comparative statistics" regarding drinking and driving).

[75] *United States v Virginia*, 518 US 515 (1996); *Mississippi Univ. for Women v Hogan*, 458 US 718, 725 (1982).

[76] Although sex-based generalizations may contain "a measure of truth" or empirical accuracy, heightened scrutiny prohibits using sex as a proxy, unless it is supported by an "exceedingly persuasive" governmental justification for doing so. *Virginia*, 116 US at 2274; *Hogan*, 458 US at 724; *see Craig*, 429 US at 200–201 (invalidating differential beer purchase ages for men and women despite statistics showing that young men presented greater safety risks from drunk driving than did young women); *Weinberger v Weisenfeld*, 420 US 636, 645 (1975) (invalidating sex-based social security survivors' benefits despite "empirical support" for the conclusion that men are more likely than women to be primary breadwinners); *Frontiero v Richardson*, 411 US 677, 688–89 (1973) (plurality opinion) (invalidating presumption of wives' but not husbands' dependency for purposes of benefits determinations despite the "empirical" fact that "wives in our society frequently are dependent on their husbands, while husbands rarely are dependent on their wives").

[77] 114 S Ct at 1432 (O'Connor concurring).

rently true that greater numbers of out-of-wedlock children have more significant ties to their mothers than to their fathers, and that many do not know their fathers at all. But as Judge Wald noted in her concurrence in the court of appeals' decision, "there is a world of difference between noting that men and women often fill different roles in society and using these different roles as the justification for imposing inflexible legal restrictions on one sex and not on the other."[78]

Concrete examples make clear that Section 309(a) is both under- and overinclusive, and show why that poor fit makes the law incompatible with the Supreme Court's sex discrimination decisions. Section 309(a) fails to require proof of a legal relationship or financial support obligations on the part of mothers even when they do not fulfill the statute's underlying assumption of maternal ties. Anyone who has watched the popular film "Secrets and Lies" or read Charles Dickens's *Bleak House* knows that biological mothers do not always develop ties with their biological children or, regrettably, even know that their child has survived. An unmarried U.S. woman might abandon a child she had with a foreign man to whom she was not married because she was ashamed to return to the United States with the child.[79] An unmarried mother might have no interest in child rearing, or might be drug addicted or mentally ill and unable to care for an infant, and thus might abandon it. Section 309(a) is also plainly overinclusive. A nonmarital child raised from infancy by an American father, whether on his own or with help from the foreign mother or other family members, would have precisely the ties to the citizen parent and the United States that Section 309(a) seeks to foster, and yet the father would have to fulfill additional requirements not demanded of a women in his situation in order to convey his citizenship. Finally, even where its requirements are met, Section 309(a)(3) does not assure any tie to a U.S. citizen father, because it permits a biological child to obtain an adjudication of paternity without any affirmative act by the father, and perhaps even over his express objection. A child thus could, at least in theory, obtain U.S. citizenship

---

[78] 96 F3d at 1475 (Wald concurring).

[79] For example, a female member of the armed services with a sweetheart back home might leave the child she conceived with a foreign lover with him or his family in order to return to the United States to pursue her life as she had previously envisioned it.

despite a wholly antagonistic relationship with, or complete alienation from, a U.S. parent.[80] The dissenters correctly characterized the relationship between the statutory requirements and the government's asserted objectives as one of "total misfit."[81]

By assuming away the admittedly atypical cases—the closely involved father and the careless mother—Section 309(a) gives legal weight to restrictive stereotypes about men's and women's parenting roles. Women are assumed to be caretakers of children; men are assumed not to be. Fathers are thought to be breadwinners who should financially support their children, whereas financial support from mothers is beside the point, whether because mothers are believed not to earn significant income or because it is taken for granted that they will behave generously toward their own offspring and voluntarily support them financially.

Those sex-role stereotypes contribute to sex inequality.[82] Because women, not men, are expected to be caretakers of their children, there is generally greater (although still marginal) social and institutional acceptance of women than of men who take parenting leaves, cease outside employment, remain longer in less demanding jobs, or work part time in order to spend time rearing young children.[83] Women as a group disproportionately bear the corresponding costs of being primary caretakers in the form of less compensation, professional advancement, and self-fulfillment through work. And when men are not seriously expected to be primary or significant caretakers of their children, they as a group bear costs in terms of less intimacy with their children and self-fulfillment through parenting. These sex-role stereotypes restrict the individual choices of both sexes.[84] Sex-role stereotypes about parenting,

[80] But see text at notes 88–92.

[81] *Miller*, 118 S Ct at 1461.

[82] The Court has been particularly unwilling to sustain sex-based classifications that reinforce gender stereotypes. See *Hogan*, 458 US at 725 ("[c]are must be taken in ascertaining whether the [government's] objective itself reflects archaic and stereotyped notions."); *Orr v Orr*, 440 US 268, 283 (1979) (alimony for women but not men invalidated in part because it carried "the baggage of sexual stereotypes"); *Stanton v Stanton*, 421 US 7, 15 (1975) (different ages of majority for girls and boys relied on the "role-typing that society has long imposed").

[83] This is not to suggest that fathers do not get disproportionate credit for fulfilling even a small portion of child rearing and household responsibilities, but rather that fathers who take an equal or predominant role in child rearing and make career sacrifices for it are viewed as strange.

[84] The assumption reflected in the text that men's roles in caring for their children affect women includes an assumption that the mother at least potentially shares child rearing with

and the legal and social institutions that reinforce them, are a major remaining obstacle to social and economic equality and choice for both women and men.[85]

Section 309(a) not only builds on traditional parenting roles, but also provides concrete benefits to men that it denies to women, and does so in a way that reflects and reinforces men's, but not women's, sexual irresponsibility. The statute effectively gives U.S. men, but not U.S. women, a choice to disavow the children they conceive with foreign partners. Justice Stevens may be right to characterize as relatively low the hurdles that Section 309(a) places before fathers who are aware of the statute's deadlines and motivated to have their children become U.S. citizens.[86] But his view fails to capture the way the provision may also benefit men by letting fathers, but not mothers, off the hook. Not every unwed U.S.-citizen father will view conveying citizenship to his child as a benefit to himself.[87] A serviceman who has had unprotected sex overseas with a woman to whom he is not married, and who does not want any child conceived in that encounter following him to the United States, claiming him as her father and demanding financial support, may well be relieved that Section 309(a) renders his child's U.S. citizenship less than automatic. As we have

a man. Mothers in lesbian couples, and single mothers who prefer no involvement from the biological father, would obviously not be directly affected by greater male involvement in parenting. See Christine A. Littleton, *Does It Still Make Sense to Talk About "Women"?* 1 UCLA Women's Law J 15, 29–30 (1991). To the extent that more male caretaking might increase the impetus behind social changes such as affordable, high-quality childcare and the normalization of shorter or more flexible working hours, however, such a change would ameliorate some of the economic inequality that female households currently experience. But cf. Littleton, id (characterizing those issues as workers' rights, rather than women's rights, concerns). And breaking down dichotomous, sex-based social expectations is part of freeing all women (and men) to make the choices that match their vision of a good life.

[85] As Professor Martha Fineman has pointed out, "[a]ll women must care about social and legal constructions of motherhood, because, although we may make individual choices not to become a mother, social construction and its legal ramifications operate independent of individual choice," affecting all women, whether they are mothers or not. Martha L. A. Fineman, *Feminist Theory and the Law*, 18 Harv J L & Pub Pol 349, 364 (1995).

[86] See 118 S Ct at 1440. There are, however, many plausible reasons that a motivated father might fail to meet the statute's age-eighteen deadline: He might be unaware of the law. He might not recognize the benefits of U.S. citizenship for the child until the child was over eighteen because, for example, elderly grandparents in the United States only then began to need care and the company of their descendants, or because the reality of limited employment opportunities for noncitizens in the United States only began to seem relevant when the child reached an age when she needed employment.

[87] Some U.S. mothers similarly might not want to convey their citizenship to their nonmarital children born abroad, but the statute does not give operative significance to their ambivalence the way it does for men.

seen, Section 309(a) discriminates *against the caring father* who wants to convey his citizenship but did not know about the law or recognize until too late the importance of U.S. citizenship for his children; but it also discriminates *in favor of the careless father* by making it easier for him to ignore his overseas, out-of-wedlock offspring. In the words of Professor Karen Czapanskiy, it reinforces social treatment of mothers as "draftees" into a parental role and fathers as "volunteers."[88] Those effects, apparently unnoticed by the Justices, are not tolerable under any theory of sex equality.

As a formal matter, Section 309(a)(4)(C) does permit a child to seek a paternity adjudication against an unwilling father, so a father cannot be certain that his decision not to legitimate or acknowledge his child will prevail. As a practical matter, however, his decision will virtually always be definitive. In order to override his preference, a child overseas (or her foreign mother in her behalf) would have to know about the statute, and specifically about her opportunity under Section 309(a)(4)(C), to get a court adjudication, locate the correct state court in the United States, hire a lawyer, and file and win an involuntary paternity action. If she managed to get that far, she would still have to satisfy Section 309(a)(3)'s financial-support prong. It is not at all clear that a child-support order would count as "agree[ing] in writing to provide financial support" under the statute, but even if it did, the child would face similar logistical obstacles to obtaining such an order. And the nonmarital child abroad might have no substantive right to support from a U.S. father if, for example, the law of the place of birth applied and conferred no such right, and if the relevant U.S. domestic law did not apply extraterritorially.

Of course, if statistics regarding paternal nonsupport of nonmarital children are any guide,[89] the very fact that Section 309(a) requires the father to acknowledge his support obligations will likely deter many fathers from taking advantage of Section 309(a) voluntarily to confer citizenship on their children. Justice Stevens im-

---

[88] See Karen Czapanskiy, *Volunteers and Draftees: The Struggle for Parental Equality*, 38 UCLA L Rev 1415 (1991).

[89] One estimate states that only 37 percent of noncustodial fathers of nonmarital children pay any of their court-ordered child support, Melissa Fletcher Stoeltje, *Counting on Child Support*, Houston Chronicle (Jan 26, 1997), and the figure is presumably substantially lower for the vast category of such children for whom no court order has been obtained.

plicitly recognized as much when he asserted that the age-eighteen deadline helps to prevent U.S. males from fraudulently claiming paternity because it requires that the claim be made during the child's legal minority, when the man would risk liability for child support.[90] But Justice Stevens neglected to draw the related conclusion that it is at least equally plausible that a child's biological father would likewise be deterred from making a bona fide paternity claim.[91] As much as we may condemn such irresponsible parental behavior, the truth is that Section 309(a)(3) gives irresponsible U.S. fathers valuable financial freedoms that it denies to U.S. mothers.[92]

Justice Stevens understood his analysis to depend not on stereotypes or generalizations, but on a "real" difference between women, who at least are aware whether they have biological offspring, and men, who may not be. That difference does, to be sure, stem from the fact that biological mothers, by physically bearing children, must be aware of them at birth in a way that fathers need not be. The problem with Justice Stevens's analysis, however, is that the knowledge that comes from giving birth bears only a loose—and constitutionally inadequate—relationship to the interest in family bonds and ties to the United States. The relationship between the mother's unique biological role and the interest in fostering children's ties to their citizen parents depends on the stereotyped generalization that an unmarried mother, as a result of having given birth, can be legally presumed to develop a caring relationship with the child *after* the child's birth during its legal

---

[90] 118 S Ct at 1439 n 15.

[91] Given the ambiguous value to fathers as a class of any decision invalidating Section 309(a), Justice O'Connor's conclusion that Ms. Miller lacked third-party standing is particularly troubling. Although he did not so argue, Mr. Miller or other men in his situation may well be "hindered" from raising constitutional objection to Section 309(a) by the prospect of having their children come to the United States and seek their financial support. And a U.S. citizen mother who seeks the "benefit" of an equal opportunity to ignore her out-of-wedlock offspring born abroad is in no position to sue to challenge Section 309(a).

[92] Allowing U.S. fathers to elect not to convey citizenship on their foreign-born children is also a policy with ugly class and race implications when U.S. fathers conceive children abroad with poor and/or minority women. As noted above, alien children abroad will often be unable to claim financial support from their U.S. fathers. Thus, the option that Section 309(a) protects for U.S. fathers not to convey citizenship to such children gives those fathers more latitude not to take financial responsibility for their nonmarital child born abroad of foreign mothers than they have under domestic law vis-à-vis nonmarital children born in the United States.

minority, while the biological father cannot.[93] As Justice Breyer noted, to the extent that Section 309(a)(4) is merely a means to assure that fathers know of their children's existence just as mothers inevitably do as a result of having given birth,

> [t]he distance between this knowledge and the claimed objectives . . . is far too great to satisfy any legal requirement of tailoring or proportionality. . . . Simple knowledge of a child's existence may, or may not, be followed by the kinds of relationships for which Justice Stevens hopes. A mother or a father, knowing of a child's birth, may nonetheless fail to care for the child or even to acknowledge the child. A father with strong ties to the child may, simply by lack of knowledge, fail to comply with the statute's formal requirements. A father with weak ties might readily comply.[94]

To be sure, knowledge of a child's existence is a prerequisite to developing a relationship with that child, but a sex-neutral alternative to Section 309(a) readily could require that citizenship be conveyed only from biological parents who know their children and demonstrate the kind of familial ties that the government values.

Justice Stevens also fell far from the mark in seeking to justify the statute as a way roughly to equalize the burdens that biological mothers and fathers bear in having children, or to reward mothers for the physical risks, discomfort, and pain of pregnancy and childbirth.[95] The government's stated objective behind Section 309(a) is to ensure that *jus sanguinis* citizens have ties to the United States through their citizen parent; it has never been to reward women for childbirth, or to offset the physical burdens they suffer. Indeed, if that were the objective, it would be strange to pursue it only in the context of unmarried, and not married, mixed-citizenship couples. In any event, because the physical sacrifices biological mothers make before and during birth do not ensure the development of the parental ties the statute seeks to foster, those sacrifices do

---

[93] Id at 1461.

[94] Id at 1462.

[95] Id at 1437 (Stevens opinion) ("If the citizen is the unmarried female, she must first choose to carry the pregnancy to term and reject the alternative of abortion. . . . She must then actually give birth to the child. Section 309(c) rewards that choice and labor by conferring citizenship on her child." In contrast, "all that § [309(a)(4)] requires is that [the biological father] be willing and able to acknowledge his paternity in writing under oath while the child is still a minor. . . . It seems obvious that the burdens imposed on the female citizen are more severe than those imposed on the male citizen").

not substantially relate, any more than mere knowledge of birth, to the statutory objective of fostering ties to the United States.

The stereotypical use of sex as an inexact proxy for parental ties is especially problematic in view of the ready availability of sex-neutral alternative measures to serve the government's stated objectives.[96] The objectives of reliably determining biological parenthood and promoting ties to the United States could be equally well served by sex-neutral requirements applicable to all nonmarital children born abroad of mixed-citizenship unions. The *Miller* dissenters aptly pointed out that Congress "could simply substitute a requirement of knowledge-of-birth for the present subsection (a)(4); or it could distinguish between caretaker and non-caretaker parents, rather than between men and women."[97] Alternatively, ties to the United States could be established by requiring out-of-wedlock children to seek citizenship before they turn eighteen,[98] or by requiring that the caretaker parent have lived in the United States.[99]

The need for reliable proof of biological parenthood can also be met as well or better by sex-neutral measures than by the statute's current requirements. The statute could simply require that both mothers and fathers prove their parenthood by clear and convincing evidence. The additional requirement that only fathers meet a deadline for establishing a formal legal relationship with their children is not needed to ensure accuracy of paternity determinations. The assumptions behind the statutory requirement that fathers but not mothers prove their biological relation to the child are that maternity is universally and reliably established by birth

---

[96] Where governmental purposes are "as well served by a gender-neutral classification as one that gender classifies and therefore carries with it the baggage of sexual stereotypes, the [government] cannot be permitted to classify on the basis of sex." *Orr v Orr*, 440 US 268, 283 (1979).

[97] 118 S Ct at 1463 (Breyer dissenting).

[98] See 8 USC §§ 1431(a)(1), 1432(a)(4) (providing in sex-neutral terms that a foreign-born child who does not become a citizen at birth may in certain circumstances obtain derivative citizenship if one or both parents is a citizen, but only if the child seeks naturalization before age eighteen).

[99] Children born abroad before 1934 of one U.S. citizen parent are U.S. citizens, provided only that their citizen parent—whether male or female—have resided in the United States. See Section 1993 of the Revised Statutes of 1874 (quoted in *Wauchope v United States Department of State*, 985 F2d 1407, 1410 n 1 (9th Cir 1992)) (providing citizenship for children of U.S. fathers); INA § 301(h), 8 USC 1401(h) (equalizing Section 1993 by providing for citizenship of children of U.S. mothers).

itself, whereas paternity is difficult to prove and subject to fraud, especially with the passage of time. Both assumptions are questionable. Recent studies show that one-third of all births abroad occur without birth certificates.[100] That reality, especially when coupled with the increased incidence of adoptions from abroad, suggests a need for proof of maternity by U.S.-citizen putative mothers before the children they assert they bore overseas are recognized as *jus sanguinis* U.S. citizens. As for fathers, the notion that requiring them to undertake a formal act establishing paternity before their child turns eighteen "lessens the risk of fraudulent claims made years after"[101] is no longer true in light of the availability of highly accurate DNA testing, the reliability of which does not wane over time.[102]

Justice Stevens found apparent support for his defense of Section 309(a), however, in *Lehr v Robertson*,[103] an equal protection decision that upheld under heightened scrutiny a sex-based classification grounded in part on the generalization that the birth mother has stronger parental ties than the father. The statute in *Lehr* automatically gave mothers of illegitimate children prior notice of a proposed adoption, but extended the same right to unmarried fathers only if they had taken an affirmative step to claim paternity, such as by entering their names in the state's "putative father registry."[104] A biological father challenged the adoption by the biological mother's husband of a child the father had never supported and rarely seen, arguing that his failure to receive prior notice and a right to veto the adoption violated due process and equal protec-

---

[100] Associated Press, *U.N.: Lack of Birth Papers Harming Millions of Kids*, Chicago Tribune (July 9, 1998) (discussing figures in UNICEF report entitled *The Progress of Nations 1998*).

[101] 118 S Ct at 1440 (Stevens opinion).

[102] Justice Stevens protested that DNA testing may be expensive and more intrusive than the methods of establishing paternity required in Section 309(a). 118 S Ct at 1439 & nn 12–13. DNA testing need not, of course, be the only permissible method of proof, but the fact that it exists and may be used in cases in which other evidence is unavailable or stale alleviates the concern regarding reliable proof that the government asserts in support of Section 309(a). And the costs of DNA testing presumably pale in comparison to the financial support obligations a father must shoulder under Section 309(a)(3).

[103] 463 US 248 (1983); see also *Quilloin v Walcott*, 434 US 246, 252 (1978) (unanimously sustaining against due process challenge a state law that denied biological fathers but not mothers of nonmarital children authority to veto adoption, and affirming adoption by mother's husband who had played paternal role for child for several years before adoption).

[104] 463 US at 251–52.

tion. In rejecting the equal protection claim, the Court, per Justice Stevens, underscored that the father did not "complain of his exemption from the[] responsibilities" of supervising, educating, protecting, and caring for the child.[105] The Court distinguished *Caban v Mohammed*, in which the Court four years earlier had found an equal protection defect in a similar sex-based adoption provision, on the ground that the mother and father in *Caban* were in fact similarly situated, whereas the *Lehr* parents were not.[106] The *Lehr* Court concluded that, "[i]f one parent has an established custodial relationship with the child and the other parent has either abandoned or never established a relationship, the Equal Protection Clause does not prevent a State from according the two parents different legal rights."[107]

Given the availability of sex-neutral mechanisms for assessing whether a custodial or other active parenting relationship has been established, *Lehr*'s tolerance of a state statute that used sex as an inexact proxy for parental ties is hard to square with the rest of the Court's sex discrimination cases.[108] The case might itself be seen as a reaffirmation of the Court's commitment to sex neutrality; after all, the concluding passage in *Lehr* states the issue in gender-neutral terms, underscoring the fairness of treating differently, not men and women, but custodial and noncustodial parents.[109] But a puzzle remains, because the statute in *Lehr* used sex, not those gender-neutral categories, as the basis for distinguishing among parents entitled to notice and those who were not. Under the Supreme Court's other sex equality cases, the *Lehr* result (notice to the custodial parent but not the absentee parent) may well be constitutionally permissible, but the means—the use of a sex-based classification—is not. *Lehr* might be viewed as an as-applied chal-

---

[105] Id at 267.

[106] Id at 267–68, citing *Caban*, 441 US 380 (1979).

[107] 463 US at 267–68.

[108] This is especially so if one credits suggestions that the Court's *Virginia* decision ratcheted up the standard of review of sex-based classifications. See *Virginia*, 116 S Ct at 2294 (Scalia dissenting) (asserting, without contradiction by the majority, that the Court's decision effectively accepted the government's argument that strict scrutiny should apply to sex-based classifications); see generally Babcock, Freedman et al., *August 1996 Professors' Update to Sex Discrimination and the Law: History, Practice, and Theory Second Edition, Materials on the Virginia Military Institute (VMI) Case*, 36–38, 44.

[109] 118 S Ct at 267–68.

lenge, upholding the statute only insofar as the statute's sex-based generalization is accurate. That reading, too, seems inadequate, however, because the equal protection defect inheres in any use of the sex-based classification itself, not only in those applications where it is inaccurate.[110]

In any event, *Miller* is different from *Lehr*, as suggested by the fact that Justice O'Connor joined the majority in *Lehr* but concluded in *Miller* that Section 309(a) would not withstand heightened scrutiny. *Lehr* reflects a special concern that difficulties in verifying the paternity of a putative father could delay an adoption that was in the child's best interests.[111] Such a concern is not applicable in *Miller*, and, as Justice Breyer suggested, it may no longer apply even in the adoption context because the availability of DNA testing can quickly erase doubts about paternity and expedite the process.[112] *Lehr* may more generally be viewed as an expression of the Court's solicitousness toward placement of children with intact nuclear families,[113] a value that does not appear to be directly relevant to the INA's different treatment of unwed mothers and fathers. Finally, *Lehr* may also reflect a related perception that granting a biological, noncaretaker father a right to veto his child's adoption by the mother's new husband would have detracted from

---

[110] See *Northeastern Florida Chapter of Associated General Contractors v Jacksonville*, 508 US 656 (1993) (recognizing standing to challenge a racial classification even where a race-neutral alternative admittedly would have had the same effect on the plaintiff as the challenged classification, because "[t]he 'injury in fact' in an equal protection case of this variety is the denial of equal treatment resulting from the imposition of the barrier, not the ultimate inability to obtain the benefit"); *Heckler v Mathews*, 465 US 728, 739 (1984) (recognizing standing even where remedy could equalize men's and women's benefits by nullifying those afforded to the favored sex, rather than extending them to the disfavored sex, because "discrimination itself, by perpetuating 'archaic and stereotyped notions' or by stigmatizing members of the disfavored group as 'innately inferior' and therefore less worthy participants in the political community, can cause serious noneconomic injuries to those persons who are personally denied equal treatment solely because of their membership in disfavored group"). These cases suggest that the father in *Lehr* suffered an equal protection injury from the mere application of the statute, even if the result was constitutionally permissible in that case.

[111] See 468 US at 257.

[112] See 118 S Ct at 1463 (Breyer dissenting).

[113] Professor Marjorie Schultz analyzes *Lehr* in the context of competing models of biological versus social fatherhood, and characterizes the decision as expressing the Court's "preference for conventional nuclear families over biological connection in certain circumstances." Marjorie Schultz, *Reproductive Technology and Intent-Based Parenthood: An Opportunity for Gender Neutrality*, 1990 Wis L Rev 297, 317–18.

the caretaking mother's ability to carry out her own plans for herself and her child.[114] A sex-neutral INA would not have the same zero-sum effects as between fathers' and mothers' choices. If, for example, Ms. Miller obtained U.S. citizenship, she would not be required to leave her mother and move immediately to the United States to join her father; moreover, Ms. Miller's citizenship could be of substantial benefit to her mother, because it would give Ms. Miller the opportunity eventually to bring her mother to the United States as well.[115] In sum, even assuming that *Lehr* remains valid, Section 309(a) cannot be squared with the Court's established equal protection doctrine prohibiting sex-based classifications that are not supported by "exceedingly persuasive" justifications.[116]

* * *

Viewed without deference, Section 309(a) imposes unconstitutional sex discrimination. Justice Stevens's reasoning to the contrary not only apparently failed to persuade a majority of the Court, but is wrong under established constitutional analysis. As noted above, what allowed Section 309(a) to stand, at least for now, was not that the law was free from equal protection defect, but that Justices O'Connor and Kennedy thought the wrong plaintiff was before the Court.

That brings into focus three issues of continuing importance. The first question—our answer to which follows from the preced-

---

[114] See also *Planned Parenthood of Central Mo. v Danforth*, 428 US 52, 71 (1976) (sustaining statute that gives women's interest in deciding whether to terminate a pregnancy priority over men's in light of "the obvious fact that when the wife and the husband disagree on this decision, the view of only one of the two marriage partners can prevail"). Recognition of a right on the part of biological mothers whether to choose abortion without a corresponding (and potentially conflicting) right of biological fathers derives from the fact that women and men are not similarly situated with respect to the physical and emotional consequences of bearing children. See *Planned Parenthood of Southeastern Pennsylvania v Casey*, 505 US 833, 896 (1992) (invalidating spousal notification requirement, and recognizing that "[i]t is an inescapable biological fact that state regulation with respect to the child a woman is carrying will have a far greater impact on the mother's liberty than on the father's"); *Danforth*, 428 US at 69, 71 (invalidating spousal consent requirement, and commenting that "[i]nasmuch as it is the woman who physically bears the child and who is the more directly and immediately affected by the pregnancy, as between the two, the balance weighs in her favor"). Viewing Section 309(a) as constitutionally problematic does not call into question the validity of women's exclusive right to reproductive choice.

[115] Immediate relatives (including parents) of citizens of the United States may be admitted to the United States without being counted against numerical immigration limitations. INA § 201(b), 8 USC § 1151(b).

[116] *Hogan*, 458 US at 724–25.

ing analysis—is how courts faced with plaintiffs who *do* have standing should evaluate constitutional challenges to Section 309(a). A lower federal court that reads *Miller* and counts votes should understand that the Supreme Court in all probability would, if it reached the merits, review the statute nondeferentially and—if a majority agrees with Justice Breyer rather than Justice Scalia on the remediability point—hold it unconstitutional.[117] Thus, the government's victory in *Miller* is likely to be short-lived, and, indeed, ought not survive the next case.

The second question is whether courts reviewing sex discrimination claims in the area of immigration and nationality generally should continue to apply deferential review to express sex-based classifications. We address this issue in Part III, where we argue that *Miller*'s recognition that the political branches do not require deferential judicial review in the bloodline citizenship context puts great pressure on prevailing doctrine that deference is warranted in the immigration and nationality area generally. As Judge Wald aptly suggested in her concurring opinion in the court of appeals,[118] it is time for the Court to reconsider the plenary power doctrine.

Section 309(a)'s constitutional infirmity under heightened scrutiny also raises a third issue: what the political branches should have done when first faced with the proposed 1986 amendments to Section 309(a), and where the political branches should go from here in dealing with sex-based classifications in immigration law. We argue in Part IV that the political branches have responsibilities to comply with the Constitution that are independent of the Court's willingness (or not) to enforce constitutional norms. Those responsibilities mean that the political branches generally should apply full constitutional scrutiny to immigration and nationality measures and, in particular, that when they amended the INA in 1986 they should have rendered an independent constitutional judgment as to whether Section 309(a)'s sex-based distinctions should have been replaced with sex-neutral alternatives. The executive branch's constitutional responsibilities also suggest that, in light of *Miller* and the arguments we present in Part II, the State

---

[117] See note 52.

[118] *Miller v Christopher*, 96 F3d at 1477 (Wald concurring).

Department should stay its enforcement of Section 309(a) and work with Congress to enact a sex-neutral substitute.

III. PLENARY POWER AND POLITICAL QUESTIONS

A. PLENARY POWER AS JUDICIAL UNDERENFORCEMENT

For more than a century, immigration law has been haunted by the so-called plenary power doctrine, a Court-crafted rule of extreme judicial deference to congressional and executive exercises of the immigration power.[119] The doctrine has never been applied to all cases involving aliens. The Court has made clear that outside the immigration and naturalization context, immigrants (even unauthorized migrants[120]) enjoy most of the constitutional rights afforded citizens;[121] and state regulations that discriminate on the basis of alienage (other than those involving political rights) will be strictly scrutinized.[122] Even within the field of immigration regulation, the Court made an exception to the plenary power doctrine when it nondeferentially applied due process norms to removal proceedings.[123] In the main, however, courts exhibit extraordinary restraint in reviewing substantive immigration and naturalization regulations—specifically, classifications of which aliens shall be entitled to enter and remain in the United States and the terms of their residence—whether or not the regulations establish categories or implicate rights in a manner that normally invokes more active judicial scrutiny.

The cases offer a common theme as the justification for judicial deference. The government's brief in *Miller*, noting that "[d]eferential review of legislation concerning immigration and nationality

---

[119] See Gerald L. Neuman, *Strangers to the Constitution: Immigrants, Borders, and Fundamental Law*, ch 7 (Princeton, 1996); Stephen H. Legomsky, *Immigration and the Judiciary— Law and Politics in Britain and America*, ch 3 (Oxford, 1987); Stephen H. Legomsky, *Immigration Law and the Principle of Plenary Congressional Power*, 1984 Supreme Court Review 255; Hiroshi Motomura, *Immigration Law After a Century of Plenary Power: Phantom Constitutional Norms and Statutory Interpretation*, 100 Yale L J 545, 545, 573–74 (1990).

[120] *Plyler v Doe*, 457 US 202 (1982) (invalidating Texas statute denying public education to undocumented immigrant children).

[121] *United States v Balsys*, 118 S Ct 2218, 2222 (1998); *Wong Wing v United States*, 163 US 228, (1896).

[122] *Graham v Richardson*, 403 US 365, 375 (1971).

[123] *Landon v Plasencia*, 459 US 21, 32 n 7 (1982); *Yamataya v Fisher*, 189 US 86 (1903).

is not a relic of the past," summarized the argument as follows: the power to regulate immigration is "a necessary and inherent attribute of national sovereignty," its exercise implicates U.S. relations with foreign powers, and policies regarding admission to the U.S. and acquisition of citizenship are "uniquely political in character."[124] This, however, is more a laundry list than an exercise in logic. When one separates out the items, one sees that cases decided in the nineteenth century exhibit a judicial strategy distinct from that displayed in the modern cases.

The nineteenth-century cases announced constitutional holdings about the scope of congressional power. Consistent with the categorical judicial style of the day,[125] the Court purported to distinguish separate spheres for the judiciary and the political branches. The judiciary would police those boundaries, but it would not intrude into issues squarely within the province of the nonjudicial branches. Such issues were labeled "political"—meaning, appropriate for resolution by the political branches. In calling a question "political" the Court had already concluded that Congress or the executive was operating within constitutional or statutory limits, and that therefore no further substantive judicial review of the challenged conduct was warranted.[126]

Thus, in *Fong Yue Ting v United States*, the Court noted that, in exercising the power of judicial review, "it behooves the court to be careful that it not undertake to pass upon *political questions*, the final decision of which has been committed by the Constitution to the other departments of government."[127] In more modern terms, we would say that the nineteenth-century Court would not second-guess the legislature or executive branch on issues of policy. That this is the Court's meaning is made clear later in the same opinion:

---

[124] Br for Resp at 22. See *Harisiades v Shaughnessy*, 342 US 580, 588–89 (1952); *Fong Yue Ting v United States*, 149 US 698, 713 (1893); *Chinese Exclusion Case (Chae Chan Ping v United States)*, 130 US 581, 604 (1889) ("If [a nation] could not exclude aliens it would be to that extent subject to the control of another power.").

[125] See Duncan Kennedy, *Toward an Historical Understanding of Legal Consciousness: The Case of Classical Legal Thought in America, 1850–1940*, 3 Res in L & Soc'y 3, 8 (1980).

[126] For example, in *Marbury v Madison*, Chief Justice Marshall separated cases appropriate for judicial resolution from "questions in their nature political"—that is, cases where executive officers "perform duties in which they have a discretion." 5 US (1 Cranch) 137, 170 (1803).

[127] 149 US 698, 712 (1893) (emphasis supplied).

The question whether, and upon what conditions, these aliens shall be permitted to remain within the United States being one to be determined by the political departments of the government, the judicial department cannot properly express an opinion upon the wisdom, the policy or the justice of the measures enacted by Congress in the exercise of the powers confided to it by the Constitution over the subject.[128]

In these cases, the Court concluded, as a matter of substantive constitutional law, that the Constitution has not been violated—either because the Constitution does not speak to the question (we will call this the "no law" position), or because the exercise of authority is clearly within the legitimate domain of the legislature or executive.[129]

The modern cases are structured quite differently, though they cite and quote the late nineteenth-century cases. The Court's categorical reasoning has been replaced by twentieth-century discussions of the appropriate level of scrutiny to be applied to the immigration or nationality regulation at issue. The Court thus talks not about matters being confided to the final judgment of the political branches, but rather of "the need for special judicial deference"[130] and the appropriateness of "narrow review of decisions made by the Congress or the President in the area of immigration and naturalization."[131]

What accounts for the extraordinary deference of the courts in the modern cases? There are two possibilities. The Court may be applying a different set of substantive constitutional rules to immigration and naturalization laws than it would apply to similar distinctions in the domestic context. (We will call this the "substantive norm" position.) Alternatively, the Court may believe that the same substantive norms govern immigration as other matters but that the norm should be partially suspended for institutional reasons going to the appropriateness of the exercise of judicial power (the "institutional deference" position). Institutional deference, in turn, might have two sources. A court may conclude that such deference is constitutionally based, or it may exercise judicial restraint

---

[128] Id at 731.

[129] See Louis Henkin, *Is There a Political Question Doctrine?* 85 Yale L J 597, 601, 610–12 (1976).

[130] *Fiallo v Bell*, 430 US 787, 793 (1977).

[131] *Mathews v Diaz*, 426 US 67, 82 (1976).

for nonconstitutional institutional reasons.[132] In either case, institutional deference signals the existence of what Professor Sager has termed an "underenforced constitutional norm."[133]

Much of the scholarship in the immigration field has seen in the modern cases (regrettable) declarations of substantive constitutional law.[134] To some extent the characterization of the cases as substantive norm decisions may be part of a strategic effort to persuade the courts to abandon the substantive double standard: the idea that the Constitution would not condemn, say, race-based exclusion laws seems so foreign to modern constitutionalism that to assert that the doctrine does so is to undermine it. This reading of the cases finds footing in some of the rather extreme language that the Court has used over the years. What, after all, does one make of the statements that "[w]hatever the procedure authorized by Congress is, it is due process as far as an alien denied entry is concerned,"[135] and "an alien seeking initial admission to the United States requests a privilege and has no constitutional rights regarding his application"?[136] The substantive norm interpretation

---

[132] A mixture of constitutional and prudential considerations is well known in standing doctrine. See *Valley Forge Christian College v Americans United for Separation of Church and State*, 454 US 464, 471–76 (1982).

[133] Lawrence G. Sager, *Fair Measure: The Legal Status of Underenforced Constitutional Norms*, 91 Harv L Rev 1212, 1218–20 (1978).

[134] For example, Charles Gordon, *The Alien and the Constitution*, 9 Cal W L Rev 1, 20–37 (1972); Louis Henkin, *The Court and United States Sovereignty: A Century of Chinese Exclusion and Its Progeny*, 100 Harv L Rev 853, 858–63 (1987); Michael Scaperlanda, *Polishing the Tarnished Golden Door*, 1993 Wis L Rev 965; Linda Kelly, *Preserving the Fundamental Right to Family Unity: Championing Notions of Social Contract and Community Ties in the Battle of Plenary Power versus Aliens' Rights*, 41 Vill L Rev 725, 733–38 (1996); Frank Wu, *The Limits of Borders: A Moderate Proposal for Immigration Reform*, 7 Stan L & Policy Rev 35, 43–46 (1996); Note, *Personhood Under the Due Process Clause: A Constitutional Analysis of the Illegal Immigration Reform and Immigrant Responsibility Act of 1996*, 83 Cornell L Rev 820, 828–32 (1998). One author of this article has, on occasion, succumbed to this characterization of the cases. See T. Alexander Aleinikoff, *Federal Regulation of Aliens and the Constitution*, 83 Am J Intl L 862, 864 (1989) (constitutional norm applied to admission and exclusion powers holds that "as to matters relating to admission and expulsion, Congress possess[es] 'plenary' power virtually unfettered by the Constitution"). See also Stephen Legomsky, *Immigration and the Judiciary* (cited in note 119) (compare 178, 190–91 with 308, 313) (plenary power doctrine described in both substantive norm and institutional deference terms).
We think Gerald Neuman gets it right in concluding that the "more enduring legacy" of the *Chinese Exclusion Case* is not that aliens do not possess rights, but rather that the courts should be wary of enforcing them. Gerald Neuman, *Strangers to the Constitution* at 134 (cited in note 119).

[135] *United States ex rel Knauff v Shaughnessy*, 338 US 537, 544 (1950). See *Shaughnessy v United States ex rel Mezei*, 345 US 206, 212 (1953).

[136] *Landon v Plasencia*, 459 US 21, 32 (1982).

has also been aided by an obiter dictum in *Mathews v Diaz*.[137] In the course of noting that the Constitution does not automatically condemn all distinctions between citizens and aliens—hardly a startling conclusion—Justice Stevens wrote that "[i]n the exercise of its broad power of naturalization and immigration, Congress regularly makes rules that would be unacceptable if applied to citizens."[138]

But there is less to these hints than meets the eye. First, Justice Stevens's comment in *Mathews* has been dramatically overread in support of classifications that discriminate against aliens.[139] As Justice Stevens makes clear in a sentence that follows immediately the oft-cited proposition, he is referring not to regulations that draw distinctions based on alienage but rather to Congress's power to exclude and remove aliens—a power that Congress presumably cannot exercise over citizens.

Second, the statements by the Court in the past half-century that appear to echo the "no law" position of the nineteenth century are primarily found in cases involving the rights of persons arriving at the border for the first time.[140] This exception at the border has a long, if controversial, history in immigration law. It is founded on the fiction that an alien at a port of entry is not inside the territory of the United States, and therefore the Constitution does not apply. Decades of scholarship have decried the fiction. As scholars from Henry Hart to Gerald Neuman have forcefully shown, the claim that the Constitution has nothing to say when the government expels persons who are seeking to enter our territory cannot be squared with the idea of a rule of law.[141] Reversal of these "no law" cases is thus long overdue. In any event, they

---

[137] 426 US 67.

[138] Id at 79–80.

[139] As it was, for example, in *Fiallo*, 430 US at 792.

[140] An exception is Justice Frankfurter's opinion for the Court in *Galvan v Press*, 347 US 522 (1954), which upheld retroactive application of a statute mandating the deportation of any alien who at any time after entry had been a member of the Communist Party. Justice Frankfurter's statement that the formulation of immigration policies is "entrusted exclusively to Congress," id at 531, has been undercut by subsequent Supreme Court holdings that immigration regulations are subject to (albeit limited) judicial review. *Fiallo v Bell*, 430 US at 793 n 5, 795–96 n 6; *Mathews v Diaz*, 426 US at 82.

[141] Henry M. Hart, Jr., *The Power of Congress to Limit the Jurisdiction of Federal Courts: An Exercise in Dialectic*, 66 Harv L Rev 1362, 1389–96 (1953); Neuman, *Strangers to the Constitution* at 118–38 (cited in note 119).

add no obvious support to a substantive norm position with respect to aliens inside the border.[142]

The institutional deference reading of the Court's cases receives strong support in the one modern case in which the Court actually seeks to supply a rationale in support of low-level scrutiny. In *Mathews v Diaz*, Justice Stevens, writing for the Court, provided the following analysis:

> For reasons long recognized as valid, the responsibility for regulating the relationship between the United States and our alien visitors has been committed to the political branches of the Federal Government. Since decisions in these matters may implicate our relations with foreign powers, and since a wide variety of classifications must be defined in light of changing political and economic circumstances, such decisions are frequently of a character more appropriate to either the Legislature or the Executive than to the Judiciary. . . . Any rule of constitutional law that would inhibit the flexibility of the political branches of government to respond to changing world conditions should be adopted only with the greatest caution. The reasons that preclude judicial review of political questions also dictate a narrow standard of review of decisions made by Congress or the President in the area of immigration and naturalization.[143]

The language here is not of a separate set of substantive norms for immigration and nationality cases, but rather the need for judicial caution and attention to role. Particularly revealing is the concluding sentence's reference to the "political question" doctrine—signaling concerns of justiciability rather than the presence of an applicable (lower than normal) substantive constitutional norm.[144] As the Court has noted, "[i]n invoking the political question doctrine, a court acknowledges the possibility that a constitutional provision may not be judicially enforceable. Such a decision is of course very different from determining that specific congressional action does not violate the Constitution."[145]

Justice Stevens is careful to reason by analogy to the political question doctrine, rather than fully to invoke it. A conclusion that

---

[142] See Legomsky, 1984 Supreme Court Review at 276–77 (cited in note 119).

[143] 426 US 67, 81–82 (1976) (emphasis supplied).

[144] See Laurence Tribe, *American Constitutional Law* § 3–13 (Foundation, 2d ed 1988).

[145] *U.S. Dep't of Commerce v Montana*, 503 US 442, 457 (1992) (footnotes omitted).

immigration cases involve nonjusticiable political questions is not consistent with applying even a low level of scrutiny. But Justice Stevens's description of immigration and nationality policies as "decisions . . . [that] may implicate our relations with foreign powers" is an obvious reference to congressional and executive branch actions that have typically been found to constitute nonjusticiable political questions.[146] Reference to the political question doctrine also provides a linkage—albeit in the form of a pun—to the nineteenth-century decisions that saw immigration cases as raising "political questions." As noted above, that terminology in the early cases referred to matters of policy appropriate for congressional resolution, not to the modern political question doctrine of nonjusticiability, nor to the deferential standard of review applied in the modern plenary power cases. But Justice Stevens makes the most of the play on words, using the word "political" four times in the quoted paragraph.[147] Thus, the Court in *Mathews* based the application of low-level scrutiny on an understanding of the appropriate role of the courts, invoking the spirit but not the full force of both the nineteenth-century cases and the modern political question doctrine in crafting a rule of institutional deference.

To be sure, the cases are not examples of ringing clarity on the question of the source of low-level scrutiny. *Fiallo*, for instance, is a muddle of quotations from the old ("no law") cases, references to the "political character" of the immigration power, citations to *Mathews* and other modern deference cases, and a concluding quo-

---

[146] See *Baker v Carr*, 369 US 186, 211–13 (1962). This connection is made even clearer in an earlier opinion, *Harisiades v Shaughnessy*, 342 US 580. There the Court upheld a statute mandating the deportation of persons who had been members of the Communist Party. Justice Jackson, writing for the majority, stated: "[A]ny policy toward aliens is vitally and intricately interwoven with contemporaneous policies in regard to the conduct of foreign relations, the war power, and the maintenance of a republican form of government." Id at 588–89. These references invoked subject areas that had been ruled political questions in the past. See, for example, *Oetjen v Central Leather Co.*, 246 US 297, 302 (1918) (recognition of a foreign government); *Commercial Trust v Miller*, 262 US 51, 57 (1923) (cessation of hostilities); *Luther v Borden*, 48 US (7 How.) 1 (1849) (Guaranty Clause). They thus offered support for Justice Jackson's conclusion that "[s]uch matters are so exclusively entrusted to the political branches of government as to be largely immune from judicial inquiry or interference." Interestingly, despite this "no law" sounding language, Justice Jackson examined the deportation ground under prevailing First Amendment doctrine that the Court applied to domestic legislation. See *Harisiades*, 342 US at 592; Aleinikoff, 83 Am J Intl L at 868–69 (cited in note 134).

[147] See text at note 143.

tation from Justice Frankfurter that immigration matters are "solely for the responsibility of the Congress and wholly outside the power of this Court to control."[148] With this kind of ordnance, the result in the case is, so to speak, overdetermined. And *Mathews* itself can be read as a substantive norm case, despite the Court's invocation of a quasi-political question doctrine. There the Court held that the rule of strict scrutiny for state laws that deny welfare benefits on the basis of alienage is not applicable to federal laws that do the same. One might see in *Mathews*, then, the application of a substantive norm that regulations disfavoring aliens, when adopted by Congress, are not unconstitutional when viewed as an exercise of the immigration power. On this reading, the Court has not refused for prudential reasons to apply the usual nondiscrimination norm; it has crafted a different (fully enforced) nondiscrimination norm for federal laws.[149]

In the end we find the institutional deference reading more persuasive. One can make the decisions fit the substantive law position, but it does not seem to get to the core of the cases. The Court never purports to identify a different substantive norm in immigration cases. Consider *Fiallo*. At issue in the case was a provision in the immigration code that permitted out-of-wedlock children to enter the United States based on a relationship with a U.S. citizen or permanent resident alien mother but not a U.S. citizen or permanent resident alien father. The plaintiffs argued that the "double-barreled discrimination" (sex and illegitimacy) rendered the statute plainly unconstitutional under prevailing law. A majority of the Justices disagreed. The Court adopted a standard of virtual judicial abdication—that the statute will be sustained if based on a "facially legitimate and bona fide reason."[150] But it did not do so by announcing a substantive norm for immigration cases; it did not make arguments that discrimination on these bases was less offensive in the immigration area, that immigrants may not

---

[148] 430 US at 792–96. The Court does not indicate that the Frankfurter quotation, taken from *Harisiades v Shaughnessy*, is located in a concurring opinion. 342 US at 597 (Frankfurter concurring).

[149] *Mathews* can, with equal plausibility, be read as consistent with the institutional deference position: the reasons that caution against judicial intervention in immigration regulations apply in cases of federal regulation; but because the immigration power is exclusively federal, no similar deference is warranted in cases involving state regulation of aliens.

[150] 430 US at 794–95.

invoke equal protection principles, or that those principles must be differently interpreted when applied to immigrants. Instead, the Court reiterated several times that it had "no judicial authority to substitute our political judgment for that of the Congress."[151] To us, this is the language of institutional deference amounting to underenforcement, not the rendering of a substantive judgment on the meaning of equal protection in immigration cases.[152]

* * *

How the plenary power doctrine is understood has important implications for all three branches of government. If the plenary power cases are examples of underenforced constitutional norms, then Congress and the executive have a constitutional duty to take the norms seriously in writing and implementing immigration and nationality statutes.[153] Furthermore, as we argue immediately below, a majority of the Justices in *Miller* implicitly concluded that institutional reasons do not foreclose full constitutional scrutiny of sex-based *nationality* statutes—that is, statutes providing for the granting of citizenship. Thus, *Miller* moves nationality cases from an underenforced to an enforced norm category. It therefore necessitates a shift in the approaches of lower courts to such cases.

B. MILLER V ALBRIGHT: UNDERCUTTING UNDERENFORCEMENT

The underenforced norm reading is the best interpretation of the pre-*Miller* precedent. But *Miller*, we believe, has fundamentally changed the rules, as much by what it did not say as by what it did. As we noted, the court of appeals opinions and the parties' briefs were largely about *Fiallo*. Indeed, Judge Wald "regretfully" concurred in the panel's decision based on her belief that *Fiallo* "foreclose[d]" a conclusion that the statute was unconstitutional.[154] If the Supreme Court had been of the same view, then its opinion would have been short and simple. Indeed, there would have been

---

[151] Id at 798.

[152] A conclusion that the immigration cases embody the substantive norm position would put the burden on the government to provide a substantive theory as to why such regulations are subject to an exceedingly low standard of review. For persuasive analysis and rejection of such substantive theories, see Neuman, *Strangers to the Constitution*, ch 7 (cited in note 119) and Legomsky, 1984 Supreme Court Review at 260–78 (cited in note 119).

[153] See Sager, 91 Harv L Rev at 1227 (cited in note 133).

[154] 96 F3d at 1473 (Wald concurring).

little reason for the Court to take the case for review if it thought that it clearly fell within the ambit of *Fiallo*.

But opinions in *Miller* representing a majority of the Justices read like sex discrimination opinions, not like the usual opinions in immigration cases. Other than in Justice Scalia's opinion, we do not find the paragraphs that typically begin immigration and naturalization cases, reciting the cases establishing plenary congressional power and mandating judicial deference. Justice Stevens's opinion (joined by the Chief Justice) includes a passing reference to *Mathews v Diaz* in a footnote,[155] but the style and tenor of his text are far more consistent with his opinions in sex discrimination cases than in immigration cases.[156] And the opinions of Justices Breyer and Ginsburg (both joined by Justice Souter) show no sign of deference based on subject matter. In short, *Miller* (but for the justiciability obstacles) is a case of *full* enforcement of a constitutional norm. While the Justices disagreed over whether the statute passes scrutiny under the test usually applied in sex discrimination cases (and whether that claim is properly before the Court), there is little doubt that a majority believed that the statute ought to be judged under the usual sex discrimination standard. The case is therefore of singular importance for the field of nationality law.

There is language in several of the opinions that might suggest that the Court's new-found willingness to apply usual constitutional norms begins and ends with citizenship statutes. Justice Breyer's three-Justice dissenting opinion purported to distinguish citizenship-at-birth cases from immigration and naturalization cases. Statutes that confer citizenship at birth, he wrote, "do not involve the transfer of loyalties that underlies the naturalization of aliens, where precedent sets a more lenient standard of review. *See Fiallo v Bell*[.]"[157] Justice Stevens, while putting aside the question

---

[155] 118 S Ct at 1437 n 11 (Stevens opinion).

[156] Compare the opinions Justice Stevens wrote for the Court in *Lehr v Robertson*, 463 US 248 (1983), and *Mathews v Diaz*, 426 US 67 (1976).

[157] 118 S Ct at 1458 (Breyer dissenting). Bryer later noted:

> In sum, the statutes that automatically transfer American citizenship from parent to child "at birth" differ significantly from those that confer citizenship on those who originally owed loyalty to a different nation. To fail to recognize this difference, and consequently to apply an unusually lenient constitutional standard of review here, could deprive the children of millions of Americans, married and unmarried, working abroad, traveling, say, even temporarily to Canada or Mexico, of the most basic kind of constitutional protection.

Id at 1460.

whether *Fiallo* "dictates the outcome of this case," distinguished *Fiallo* as involving "the claims of several aliens to a special immigration preference, whereas here the petitioner claims that she is, and for years has been, an American citizen."[158] And Justice Scalia's opinion applied the policy of deference to the statute in *Miller;* a fortiori, he is unlikely to apply any higher level of scrutiny to immigration cases.

Thus, a surface reading of the opinions cuts against the idea that *Miller* signaled a shift in immigration jurisprudence generally, as opposed to citizenship cases alone.[159] But it is not obvious that *Miller* can be so easily limited to nationality cases. The question is whether the line drawn between citizenship-at-birth cases (such as *Miller*) and immigration and naturalization cases (such as *Fiallo*) can be sustained.

The Constitution, of course, provides citizenship at birth only to persons born in the United States. It says nothing explicit about the power of Congress to provide citizenship *jure sanguinis* (by bloodline) to persons born overseas. In confronting this conundrum, the Court has determined that such statutes must be exercises of the naturalization power.[160] This conclusion finds support in the first federal citizenship statute, adopted in 1790. Entitled "An Act to establish an uniform Rule of Naturalization," its single section provided qualifications for admission to citizenship of aliens residing inside the United States and for the birthright citizenship of children born to U.S. citizen fathers outside the United States.[161] Thus, citizenship by descent—"not covered by the Fourteenth Amendment" and "necessarily left to proper congressional action"[162]—is bestowed only upon those who meet specific statutory requirements. In this way it bears a closer resemblance to

---

[158] 118 S Ct at 1434 (Stevens opinion).

[159] It is noteworthy, however, that the Justices failed to respond to Judge Wald's opinion below urging the Court to reconsider *Fiallo*. 96 F3d at 1477 (Wald concurring). Had they sought to draw a sharp line between citizenship and immigration cases they could have done so by expressly affirming *Fiallo*. Such language would deter other lower court judges from sending the Court pointed invitations to overturn its precedents. But the Court didn't do so. The Justices simply put *Fiallo* to one side.

[160] *Rogers v Bellei*, 401 US 815, 830 (1971), quoting *United States v Wong Kim Ark*, 169 US 649, 688 (1898).

[161] Act of March 26, 1790, § 1, 1 Stat 103. Today, the immigration code does not categorize citizenship by descent as a form of naturalization. See note 168.

[162] *Rogers*, 401 US at 830.

other membership decisions established by statute—naturalization and admission as an immigrant—than to the automatic conferral of citizenship by birth in the United States.

In these three statutory areas—citizenship by descent, naturalization, and immigration—the Court has recognized Congress's broad power to establish categories and prerequisites. To our shame, racial and gender classifications have littered these areas of regulation since the earliest days of the nation.[163] No Supreme Court case (prior to the opinions in *Miller*) had suggested that classifications permitted in one area would be unacceptable in the others; and no Supreme Court case has ever invalidated such a classification. It is therefore not surprising that the court of appeals in *Miller* concluded,[164] and the government's brief to the Supreme Court asserted,[165] that the plenary power doctrine of the immigration cases applied in similar fashion to challenges to *jus sanguinis* statutes.

Citizenship by birth in the territory of the United States has generally been viewed in a different light. The Fourteenth Amendment fixed *jus soli* citizenship in the Constitution, to make permanent the rejection of Justice Taney's opinion in *Dred Scott*. The power of the principle was affirmed by the Court's striking decision in *United States v Wong Kim Ark*,[166] which held that children born in the United States to Chinese immigrant parents were citizens at birth—even though federal law prohibited their parents from seeking or obtaining naturalization.

History and precedent have thus tended to place constitutional membership decisions in one category and congressional membership decisions in another.[167] This schema puts *jus soli* citizenship

---

[163] See Act of March 26, 1790, § 1, 1 Stat 103 (limiting *jus sanguinis* citizenship to the children of U.S. citizen fathers; restricting naturalization to "free white" persons). Racial bars to naturalization were not fully extirpated until 1952. See Ian F. Haney López, *White by Law: The Legal Construction of Race* 42–47 (NYU, 1996). The first major federal immigration statutes provided for the exclusion of Chinese. Act of May 6, 1882, ch 126, 22 Stat 58.

[164] 96 F3d at 1470–71.

[165] Br for Resp 21–23.

[166] 169 US 649 (1898).

[167] *Rogers v Bellei*, 401 US 815 (1971), should be considered in this light. The case considered the constitutionality of the (now repealed) requirement that *jus sanguinis* citizens born abroad take up residence in the United States for five years between the ages of fourteen and twenty-eight in order to preserve their citizenship. Under the statutory scheme, a child was held to be a citizen at birth, but was deemed to lose his or her citizenship if the residency requirement was not met in time. The dissenting Justices analogized the operation

in one category, while *jus sanguinis* citizenship, naturalization, and immigration are placed in another. If *Miller* is read as fully enforcing constitutional norms for *jus sanguinis* citizenship, then arguably the conceptual categories have shifted. This is the explicit project of Justice Breyer's dissent, which went to lengths to explain why both varieties of birthright citizenship—*jus soli* and *jus sanguinis*—fit under the full enforcement rubric, while naturalization and immigration regulations do not.[168] Under this reformulated schema, one category encompasses citizens-at-birth (both constitutional and statutory); the other includes citizens-by-naturalization and immigrants (exclusively statutory).

Can this classification be sustained? Or does shifting the statutory benefit of *jus sanguinis* citizenship into the fully enforced norms category tend to bring along other statutory benefits in the immigration and citizenship field?

One argument for separating birthright citizenship from naturalization and immigration might arise from the strong preference, in international and domestic law, for avoiding statelessness.[169] On this account, denying birthright citizenship in situations that can occasion statelessness is more troubling than denying naturalization or an immigration status because one may assume that persons in the latter two categories have a preexisting citizenship to fall back on. Justice Breyer signaled this concern when he noted that under discriminatory *jus sanguinis* rules "many . . . children, lacking

---

of the condition subsequent to a deprivation of citizenship, which would have triggered the strict rules of *Afroyim v Rusk*, 387 US 253 (1967) (permitting loss of citizenship only if citizen affirmatively intended to relinquish it). But the majority had little trouble sustaining the challenged provision, finding that it was a reasonable way to deal with problems of dual nationality. 401 US at 831–36. The holding in *Bellei* does not coincide exactly with the constitutional/statutory line described in text because the rule of *Afroyim* would apply to naturalized as well as birthright citizenship. But the ease with which the Court sustained the condition subsequent demonstrates its view that congressional decisions regulating the acquisition of citizenship *jure sanguinis* are largely free from judicial restraint.

[168] 118 S Ct at 1458–60 (Breyer dissenting). Breyer quoted a provision of the INA that supports this distinction. Id at 1460. The statute defines "naturalization" as "the conferring of nationality of a state upon a person after birth, by any means whatsoever," INA § 101(a)(23), 8 USC § 1101(a)(23), thereby separating *jus sanguinis* birthright citizenship from naturalization (and immigration) regulations. But this statutory line is surely not determinative of the constitutional issue.

[169] As we note in text at notes 14–15, concerns about statelessness may account in part for the sex-based distinction in the statute under challenge in *Miller*. We argue here that the issue of statelessness does not justify applying constitutional standards to immigration statutes that are different from those that are applied to citizenship statutes.

citizenship, would be placed outside the domain of basic constitutional protections."[170]

This is a legitimate concern, but one with little purchase in today's world. Lorelyn Miller is unlikely to be born stateless if she is born in the country of which her mother is a citizen; and even if she were born outside her mother's country of citizenship, she would not be stateless unless that country had a rule that barred transmission of citizenship *jure sanguinis* in such a case *and* the country in which she is born is not a *jus soli* state. This result was far more likely in earlier days when citizenship was largely transmitted by the father.[171] But virtually everywhere today birth to a mother in her home country transmits citizenship; and most states permit transmission of the mother's citizenship even when the birth occurs outside the mother's state of citizenship.

Perhaps Justice Breyer's concern was not so much statelessness as a child's lack of *U.S.* citizenship (whether or not he or she has citizenship in another country). The Court has frequently noted the extraordinary value placed on U.S. citizenship, describing it as "a most precious right" regarded by many as "the highest hope of civilized men."[172] A desire to avoid discriminatory distribution of such a highly valued right (and the opportunities that accompany it) might be seen as justification for placing birthright citizenship in a class by itself. But if it is the significance of U.S. citizenship that triggers full enforcement of constitutional norms, then it is hard to see why *naturalization* regulations would be left on the other side of the line.

Justice Breyer sought to distinguish naturalization from *jus sanguinis* citizenship by noting that naturalization involves "a transfer of loyalties" rather than acquisition of a status at birth.[173] But the significance of that distinction is unclear, and he did not elaborate on it. Perhaps it is intended to signal the nature and depth of a citizen's attachment to the United States: for birthright citizens,

---

[170] 118 S Ct at 1458 (Breyer dissenting).

[171] These are the statutes and practices referred to in Justice Ginsburg's dissent. 118 S Ct at 1450–53.

[172] *Kennedy v Mendoza-Martinez*, 372 US 144, 159 (1963); *Schneiderman v United States*, 320 US 118, 122 (1943).

[173] 118 S Ct at 1458 (Breyer dissenting).

U.S. nationality may be a core aspect of identity whose nonrecognition or deprivation may inflict serious harm. This characterization may well be accurate for persons born in the United States or for children born to U.S. citizens who are traveling abroad.[174] But it is not necessarily an apt description of all *jus sanguinis* citizens. Under the law, citizenship by descent may be asserted by someone who has never resided in the United States nor resided with a U.S. citizen until almost the age of majority. To be eligible for naturalization, however, an immigrant usually must have been residing in the United States as a lawful permanent resident for at least five years.[175] At the time of naturalization, most aliens are fully-functioning members of U.S. society. From this perspective, the naturalizing citizen is likely to be as much a part of the American polity as the person asserting birthright citizenship from abroad.[176]

Consideration of the importance of U.S. citizenship, then, may nudge naturalization into the same category as birthright citizenship. But such reasons do not obviously reach immigration regulations. On what basis, then, might it be argued that *Miller*'s reasoning casts a shadow on *Fiallo?* Curiously enough, Justice Stevens's opinion provides grounds for thinking that it might. Although, as noted above, Justice Stevens purported to distinguish *Fiallo* as involving "a special immigration preference" rather than a claim to U.S. citizenship,[177] he later seemed to undo the distinction in a footnote:

> Though petitioner claims to be a citizen from birth, rather than claiming an immigration preference, citizenship does not pass by descent. . . . Thus she must still meet the statutory requirements set by Congress for citizenship. . . . Deference to the political branches dictates "a narrow standard of review

---

[174] Id at 1460.

[175] INA § 316(a), 8 USC § 1427(a). Spouses of U.S. citizens may naturalize after three years' residence. INA § 319(a), 8 USC § 1430(a).

[176] Interestingly, although we usually think of the Fourteenth Amendment as affirming the principle of *jus soli*, it in fact recognizes the citizenship of "persons born *or naturalized* in the United States." The Amendment, as noted, is silent as to citizenship by descent. In *Rogers v Bellei*, Justice Black's dissent argued that *jus sanguinis* citizens come within the protection of the Fourteenth Amendment because the Amendment's coverage of persons "naturalized in the United States" should be read to mean "naturalized *into*" the United States. 401 US at 839–43 (Black dissenting).

[177] Id at 1434 (Stevens opinion).

of decisions made by the Congress or the President in the area
of immigration and naturalization." *Mathews v Diaz*[.][178]

The footnote successfully answered Breyer's analysis: *jus sanguinis* citizenship and immigration classifications are creatures of federal statute. But the footnote equally undermined Justice Stevens's
attempt to put *Fiallo* aside. Citizenship-at-birth for some children
born overseas is as much a "special . . . preference" as immigration
for some classes of children.

It may be hard to see these kinds of citizenship decisions as
pretty much the same as immigration decisions. Our usual mental
image of the immigration process is of an alien arriving on our
shore, attaining full membership after a number of years, and
thereby bestowing American citizenship on his or her children and
subsequent generations. From this perspective, there appears to be
a significant difference between immigration and citizenship; it is
the distinction we draw between probationary and tenured workers, between guests and members of the family.

But the rules and practices that define the American system of
membership do not map on to this "straight-line model." Immigration, naturalization, and birthright citizenship provide overlapping, sometimes anomalous, modes of access to membership. For
example, while the straight-line model is likely to view membership decisions as the province of full members, the combination
of the *jus soli* principle and immigration means that nonmembers
can "create" full members (by having children in the United
States). And while the straight-line model might suppose that *jus
sanguinis* citizenship would be recognized at birth, with the child
living in an "American" home (even if overseas), in fact such citizenship may be asserted long after birth by a person who has established relatively few ties to this country. In such cases, the recognition of U.S. citizenship may serve as an efficient method of
acquiring residence in the United States—rather more akin to admission as an immigrant than to the affirmation of a long-standing
sense of identity.

Finally, it is important to see that immigration classifications do
more than decide which persons living beyond our borders shall
be invited to join us as "guests." Because a large number of immi-

---

[178] Id at 1436 n 11.

grants are granted permanent resident status based on their relationship to a U.S. citizen,[179] such classifications necessarily draw
lines among full members.[180] Justice Marshall made this discrimination among U.S. citizens the focal point of his dissent in *Fiallo*.[181]
Justice Powell's response, relegated to a footnote in the majority
opinion, avoids rather than answers the argument. While accepting
Justice Marshall's reasoning as "facially plausible," Justice Powell
asserted that its "fallacy . . . is rooted deeply in the fundamental
principles of sovereignty."[182] But why the plenary power cases should
be read to justify discrimination among citizens is never explained.

In sum, despite our intuition that birthright citizenship is quali-
tatively different from naturalization or admission as an immigrant,
it is difficult to construct a persuasive case for limiting the application of usual constitutional norms solely to *jus sanguinis* statutes.
Upon reflection, perhaps this should not surprise us. The Constitution is a document fundamentally concerned with creating and
limiting the powers of government, not on behalf of citizens, but
on behalf of persons.[183] Importantly, this is not to say that for all
purposes aliens and citizens are entitled to similar treatment. The
point is that the usual constitutional norms are not suspended for
immigration regulations, even if these norms tolerate differences

---

[179] In fiscal year 1996, 52 percent of the 787,335 immigrants admitted to the United
States for permanent residence entered on the basis of a close family relationship with a
U.S. citizen. (These numbers do not include persons who entered the United States as
refugees or were granted political asylum here.) U.S. Dept of Justice, INS, *1996 Statistical
Yearbook of the Immigration and Naturalization Service*, table B (Oct 1997).

[180] See Wu, 7 Stan L & Policy Rev at 49–50 (cited in note 134); Kelly, 41 Vill L Rev
at 778–80 (cited in note 134). See also Hiroshi Motomura, *Whose Immigration Law? Citizens,
Aliens, and the Constitution*, 97 Colum L Rev 1567, 1582–83 (1997) (reviewing Gerald Neu-
man, *Strangers to the Constitution*); Hiroshi Motomura, *Whose Alien Nation? Two Models
of Constitutional Immigration Law*, 94 Mich L Rev 1927, 1942–52 (1996) (reviewing Peter
Brimelow, *Alien Nation*).
The Court seems to have understood this relationship of sponsor to beneficiary in *Miller*.
Irrespective of its ruling as to Lorelyn Miller's standing, the Justices agreed that Charlie
Miller—had he remained a party—could have contested the differential treatment accorded
U.S. citizen mothers and fathers who sought to confer citizenship on out-of-wedlock chil-
dren. Indeed, Justice O'Connor thought that Mr. Miller was the only person who had
standing to assert the constitutionality of the sex-based classification in the statute. 118 S
Ct at 1442–43 (O'Connor concurring). Immigration laws that create classes of U.S. citizens
entitled to sponsor close family members should similarly be seen from the perspective of
the sponsoring citizen as well as the would-be immigrant.

[181] 430 US 787, 806–09 (Marshall dissenting).

[182] Id at 795–96 n 6. See Wu, 7 Stan L & Policy Rev at 45–46 (cited in note 134).

[183] See Alexander M. Bickel, *The Morality of Consent* ch 2 (Yale, 1975).

between citizens and aliens. For example, there is general agreement that U.S. citizens may not be banished or exiled; yet no one doubts the existence of a federal deportation power. So, too, procedural due process norms may call for different procedures for adjudicating claims to citizenship than claims to immigrant status.[184] But these differences in treatment do not turn on the nonapplication of norms to immigration decisions. Rather, they turn on differential explication of existing norms based on criteria relevant to the norms. For example, in determining what process is due under the Fifth Amendment, the prevailing analysis looks to the individual's stake in the proper outcome of an adjudication[185]—a test that might well place more value on citizenship claims than claims to enter as an immigrant. Thus, a conclusion that immigration regulations are not immune from usual constitutional norms does not mean that we cannot continue to place a high value on U.S. citizenship.

C. THE COLLAPSE OF INSTITUTIONAL DEFERENCE
AND THE ECLIPSE OF PLENARY POWER

We have argued that *Miller*'s full enforcement of constitutional norms cannot easily be limited to citizenship-by-descent statutes. But this gets us only halfway to full enforcement in naturalization and immigration cases. Because underenforcement is a function of the inappropriateness of judicial intervention, we must consider whether there might be grounds for institutional deference in the immigration area—even if the Court has cast them aside for citizenship statutes. We conclude that the reasons usually offered for deference in immigration and nationality cases appear quite weak after *Miller*.

We have noted above that the Court has explained its stance of deference in quasi-political-question terms.[186] But, as others have shown,[187] it takes little more than a glance at the *Baker v Carr* factors[188] to recognize their inapplicability to most constitutional

---

[184] See INA § 242(b)(5), (7)(B), 8 USC § 1252(b)(5), (7)(B) (special procedures for determinations of claims to U.S. nationality that arise in the course of a removal proceeding).

[185] *Mathews v Eldridge*, 424 US 319 (1976).

[186] See text at notes 130–52.

[187] We make the arguments in this section cursory because they have received full and persuasive treatment in Neuman, *Strangers to the Constitution*, ch 7 (cited in note 119) and Legomsky, 1984 Supreme Court Review at 261–69 (cited in note 119).

[188] 369 US 186, 217 (1962).

questions involving immigration and naturalization. These areas of federal power are no more or less demonstrably committed to another branch than other federal powers such as the commerce or tax and spending powers. (Indeed, the immigration power is not specifically mentioned anywhere in the Constitution.) When the challenges are based on the Due Process and Equal Protection Clauses (as most are), there is no basis for finding a lack of judicially discoverable or manageable standards; these are mainstays of modern constitutional law. Nor it is likely that a court decision invalidating an immigration or naturalization classification or procedure would "express a lack of respect due coordinate branches" or unduly create "the potentiality of embarrassment from multifarious pronouncements by various departments on one question"[189]—at least no more than a holding that an exercise of the commerce power exceeds Congress's authority.[190]

Immigration regulations are frequently said to implicate the foreign relations of the United States—an area courts have largely left to the political branches. But *Baker v Carr* properly notes that "it is error to suppose that every case or controversy which touches foreign relations lies beyond judicial cognizance."[191] As Professor Legomsky has sensibly suggested, nothing would prevent the court from staying its hand in a case that truly called for application of the political question doctrine[192]—for example, a declaration by the President barring entry to the United States of citizens of a country with which the United States is at war.[193]

A variant of the quasi-political-question ground for institutional deference focuses on the nature of immigration and nationality regulations as "membership decisions." As the government argued in its brief to the Court in *Miller*:

> [P]olicies toward the admission to this country, and most especially to full citizenship therein, of those not born here are uniquely political in character, dealing as they do with the threshold question of who is entitled to any share in the bene-

---

[189] Id.

[190] See *United States v Lopez*, 115 S Ct 1624 (1995).

[191] 369 US at 211.

[192] Legomsky, 1984 Supreme Court Review at 268–69 (cited in note 119).

[193] See INA § 212(f), 8 USC § 1182(f) (authorizing President to suspend entry of classes of aliens whose admission would be "detrimental to the interests of the United States").

fits, protections, and responsibilities of the democratic compact that the Constitution represents.[194]

Michael Walzer has similarly argued that admission policies "suggest the deepest meaning of self-determination," helping to constitute "historically stable, ongoing associations of men and women with some special commitment to one another and some special sense of their common life."[195] To some degree, these statements are true—although in the American context appeals to deep notions of membership have as frequently accompanied racist and nativist policies as they have policies of inclusiveness and tolerance.[196] But more often the classification of aliens and the establishment of procedures for their entry and removal constitute decisions that are grounded in everyday judgments about family ties, efficiency, fraud- and crime-prevention, and economic impact. To be sure, such policies have important social, economic, and political consequences for the United States. But so do a host of other federal regulations that the Court would not hesitate to analyze under prevailing constitutional norms.[197]

Miller's application of usual constitutional norms to such decisions is therefore less remarkable than we might initially suppose. But what *is* remarkable about *Miller* is that the norms are applied to the set of membership decisions—citizenship rules—that arguably call for the greatest degree of institutional deference. The endowment of citizenship is how the United States creates full members, entitled—at least in theory—to the full array of rights and opportunities possessed by other citizens and entitled to participate in the governing of the state. From an institutional deference perspective, then, one might imagine that the Court would be more hesitant to intervene in decisions granting full membership rights than in decisions regulating temporary access to U.S. soil. On this account, *Miller* and *Fiallo* are a curious pair of cases. The Court has fully enforced a norm in an area likely to be

---

[194] Br for Resp 22.

[195] Michael Walzer, *Spheres of Justice: A Defense of Pluralism and Equality* 62 (Basic Books, 1983).

[196] See Rogers M. Smith, *Civic Ideals: Conflicting Visions of Citizenship in U.S. History* (Yale, 1997).

[197] See T. Alexander Aleinikoff, *Citizens, Aliens, Membership and the Constitution*, 7 Const Comm 9, 32–34 (1990).

deemed more fundamental by the political branches. Once that bridge has been crossed, arguments for deference to immigration decisions seem much harder to sustain.[198]

The Court already knows that the government can live with constitutional scrutiny in the immigration field. For nearly a century it has applied due process norms to procedures for the removal of aliens within the United States.[199] There is no evidence that these rulings have unduly hobbled federal efforts at enforcement of the immigration laws. This point may be generalized. It seems clear that rejecting the plenary power doctrine will not leave the United States weak, unprotected, or vulnerable. In *Miller*, a holding that the citizenship statute violated the Constitution would not have injured relations with the Philippines, harmed the U.S. economy, or placed the United States in a disadvantageous position on the world stage. And none of the various opinions in *Miller* made even a gesture at suggesting that dire consequences would flow from a decision in Miller's favor. Indeed, some might say that it would make this country stronger by showing to the world a nation willing to take its most fundamental commitments seriously across the board. But for us, it is enough that the Court has shown the way in *Miller*: that respect for constitutional principles can and should now outweigh institutional reasons for judicial deference in immigration and citizenship matters.

In this way, *Miller* may well come to be seen as the *Baker v Carr* of immigration law, rendering fully justiciable what had earlier been seen as beyond judicial competence. In the pre–*Baker v Carr* days, it was argued that the Court's intervention in the "political thicket"[200] of reapportionment would be improvident and unwise. History now tells a different story. Democratic norms have been promoted without any diminution of respect for the Court.[201] Chief among the naysayers was Felix Frankfurter, whose dissent in *Baker* is a monument to the perils of dire predictions. His call

---

[198] Of course, from the individual's perspective, citizenship may be viewed as a more significant benefit than a green card. But the traditional position of judicial deference flows not from the relative value placed on the benefit by the individual, but rather from institutional considerations.

[199] *Yamataya v Fisher*, 189 US 86 (1903).

[200] *Colgrove v Green*, 328 US 549, 556 (1946) (Frankfurter opinion).

[201] See Peter Schuck, *The Thickest Thicket: Political Gerrymandering and Judicial Regulation of Politics*, 87 Colum L Rev 1325, 1380–81 (1987).

for judicial nonintervention in the reapportionment cases echoes his statements in the immigration cases. The utterances, which still figure prominently in the Court's decisions and in the government's briefs, seem increasingly sterile with the years. In a concurring opinion in *Harisiades* (which no other member of the Court joined), he declared that regulation of immigration is a matter "solely for the responsibility of the Congress and wholly outside the power of this Court to control."[202] Thus, "whether immigration laws have reflected xenophobia in general or anti-Semitism or anti-Catholicism," it is up to Congress, not the courts, to correct them.[203] Three years later, Justice Frankfurter wrote the majority opinion in *Galvan v Press*, a case upholding the retroactive application of a deportation statute ordering the removal of any person who at any time had been a member of the Communist Party. Had he been "writing on a clean slate," Justice Frankfurter reported, he might have concluded that the law violated due process and the Ex Post Facto Clause. But the slate was not clean: "[t]hat the formulation of [immigration] policies is entrusted exclusively to Congress has become about as firmly embedded in the legislative and judicial tissues of our body politic as any aspect of our government."[204] These words were written in the same year that *Brown v Board of Education* invalidated the deeply ingrained legal and social system of segregation.

The Court took the right turn in *Baker v Carr*, laying Justice Frankfurter's rhetoric to the side. *Miller* shows that Justice Frankfurter's concerns in immigration and nationality cases carry little weight today. It is time to lay them to rest too.

IV. MILLER AND THE ROLES OF GOVERNMENT LAWYERS

A. THE OBLIGATIONS AND PERILS OF UNDERENFORCEMENT

Although the Court arrived at many of the right conclusions in *Miller*, the case never should have reached the Court in the form in which it did. Under the underenforcement regime that was in place before *Miller*, the political branches have the primary respon-

---

[202] 342 US at 597 (Frankfurter concurring).

[203] Id.

[204] 347 US 522, 530–31 (1954).

sibility for interpreting the Constitution. It appears that they did not carry out that responsibility in connection with the statute at issue in *Miller*. We now reexamine the political branches' approach to immigration law in that light.[205]

1. *The obligations.* The executive branch's usual approach to constitutional decision making in immigration matters is exemplified by a recent regulation establishing procedures for the detention and release of criminal aliens.[206] One aspect of the regulation authorizes the United States to detain for deportation any permanent resident alien who has in the past been convicted of certain crimes, without making an individualized determination that the particular permanent resident alien poses a risk of flight or danger to the community. In describing the INS's view that such a procedure is consistent with due process, the regulation's preamble relies heavily on the plenary power doctrine. Liberally quoting from the plenary power cases, including *Mathews v Diaz* and *Fiallo v Bell*, the INS notes that responsibility over immigration "has been committed to the political branches of the Federal Government."[207] The agency explains that, "[o]nce a facially legitimate and bona fide reason is found, courts will neither look behind the exercise of discretion, nor test it by balancing its justification against the constitutional interest asserted by those challenging the statute."[208] The entire constitutional argument is framed in terms of how the *courts* review the political branches' treatment of aliens. The INS predicts, based on prior judicial decisions sustaining analogous immigration measures, that the courts would sustain the detention regulation against constitutional challenge.[209]

Our reading of the modern plenary power cases as establishing a regime of judicially underenforced constitutional norms suggests, however, that simply forecasting the Court's reaction is inadequate. If the judiciary partially suspends its own enforcement of constitutional norms (such as procedural fairness or, as in *Miller*,

---

[205] The following analysis uses executive-branch illustrations, but the point could be similarly developed regarding the obligations of Congress.

[206] 8 CFR Parts 3 and 236 (1998).

[207] 63 FR 27441, 27444 (1998).

[208] Id, quoting *Campos v INS*, 961 F2d 309, 316 (1st Cir 1992).

[209] 63 FR at 27444–27446.

sex equality) for institutional rather than substantive reasons,[210] it is inappropriate for the political branches themselves to mimic the Court's restraint for purposes of their constitutional evaluation. Doing so amounts to the kind of "circular buck-passing" that Professor David Strauss has identified.[211] The current Court applies lenient review under the plenary power doctrine as a way of deferring to the political branches. The assumption behind that deference is not that the political branches will also be lenient with themselves, but that those branches require flexibility in foreign affairs that would be hampered by judicial review. If the political branches parrot the courts' lenient scrutiny, everyone has deferred to everyone else, and nobody has done the full-fledged constitutional analysis. The premise of the plenary power doctrine that the political branches will do a full constitutional review thus remains unfulfilled. In our view, institutional limits on judicial review should be irrelevant to the political branches' own constitutional calculus, since they do not share the judiciary's institutional constraints.

That understanding of the political branches' approach to their own constitutional decision making in the immigration area helps to explain how the current version of the sex-based distinctions in Section 309(a) of the INA was adopted as recently as 1986 and enforced against Charlie and Lorelyn Miller, even after the Court's latest and strongest condemnations of sex-based classifications.[212] Congress has included sex-based variants of these provisions in every version of the INA since it was first enacted in 1940.[213] In the early years, of course, express sex-based classifications were common, and the Court would have applied only rational-basis review to sustain them against equal protection challenges.[214] The INA's

---

[210] See Sager, 91 Harv L Rev at 1213–28 (cited in note 133); Brest, *The Conscientious Legislator's Guide to Constitutional Interpretation*, 27 Stan L Rev 585, 589 (1975).

[211] Strauss, *Presidential Interpretation of the Constitution*, 15 Cardozo L Rev 113, 128–29 (1993).

[212] The 1986 amendments added subsections 309(a)(4)(B) and 309(a)(4)(C), permitting acknowledgment or adjudication of paternity to suffice in place of legitimation, imposed the subsection 309(a)(1) requirement that paternity, but not maternity, be shown by clear and convincing proof, and added the subsection 309(a)(3) requirement that the father promise financial support until the child turns eighteen. See Act of Nov 14, 1986, § 13, 100 Stat 3657.

[213] See 118 S Ct at 1453 (Ginsburg dissenting).

[214] See, for example, *Goesart v Cleary*, 335 US 464 (1948).

initial different treatment of fathers and mothers probably raised
no constitutional eyebrows. When the political branches as late as
1986 opted not to change course and adopt sex-neutral, rather than
sex-based, provisions, they might perhaps have concluded (erroneously, we think) that the provisions would survive heightened
scrutiny; but there is no suggestion in the legislative record that
Congress or the executive even considered the potential unconstitutionality of the sex-based classification.[215] The underenforced-
norms reading of the plenary power doctrine would require, however, that the political branches do their own constitutional analysis under heightened scrutiny.[216] Plenary power, on this understanding, does not give the political branches a blank check to do
as they please, but leaves them with a special responsibility to comply with constitutional norms in view of a diminished judicial
backstop.

Suggesting that the political branches should do a constitutional
analysis, and not merely piggyback on their predictions of the
courts' underenforcement, does not answer the question *how* those
branches should do their "own" constitutional analysis. That
question cannot be answered without reference to some theory
of the political branches' role in constitutional interpretation.
There is, for example, a wide range of views regarding whether
the political branches should consider themselves bound by Supreme Court opinions, or only by Supreme Court judgments in
cases to which the government was a party, or something in
between.[217]

Depending on the political branches' views of how much autonomy they have in interpreting the Constitution, there may be a

---

[215] See Legislative History of 1986 Amendments to the Immigration and Nationality Act,
reprinted at 1986 USCCAN 6182–83 (House Report); id at 6184 (letter from James W.
Dyer, Acting Assistant Secretary, Legislative and Intergovernmental Affairs, U.S. Department of State, urging enactment of the amendments). The State Department evidently
requested the 1986 amendments to Section 309(a) in order to "reduce the administrative
burdens involved in ascertaining paternal domiciles and keeping track of widely variant
requirements for formal legitimation." See *Miller*, Br for Resp 20.

[216] To the extent that one might assume that they concluded that the amendments were
constitutional under *Lehr*, we believe that should not have been a basis for endorsing the
bill. See text at notes 111–16.

[217] See generally *Symposium, Executive Branch Interpretation of the Law*, 15 Cardozo L Rev
43–174 (1993).

significant range of answers to the question of how Congress and the executive should have reviewed Section 309(a) and its amendments in a non-buck-passing manner. Adherents of the opinions-as-binding approach would insist that the political branches apply heightened equal protection scrutiny as the Court's cases have defined it. Under this approach, the political branches should have amended Section 309(a) to make it sex-neutral in order to cure its constitutional defect before it ever got to the Supreme Court in *Miller*. Adherents of the full-autonomy approach would consider the political branches not to be bound by the Supreme Court's sex discrimination precedents and would suggest that they be followed only insofar as the political branches find them persuasive. They thus might contend that the 1986 amendment contained no constitutional problem that needed fixing. If, for example, the political branches disagreed with the Court and believed that the Equal Protection Clause, properly understood, requires only rational-basis review of sex-based classifications across the board,[218] they might for that reason, and not through any "circular buck-passing," have seen no need to amend or to refrain from enforcing Section 309(a).

We do not purport to resolve here the complex questions regarding the appropriate scope of the political branches' power to interpret the Constitution.[219] What is clear, however, is that the underenforced-norms thesis requires the political branches to take the laboring oar in evaluating the constitutionality of legislation and deciding whether to enforce it. As noted above, however, there is no sign in the legislative record that the equal protection issues were considered at all. In the absence of either a persuasive analysis that Section 309(a) satisfies equal protection, or a substantive rationale for concluding that sex-based classifications are somehow more acceptable in immigration and nationality decisions than elsewhere, Congress should have replaced the different treatment of mothers and fathers in the statute with sex-neutral terms, or

---

[218] See, for example, *United States v Virginia*, 116 S Ct at 2295–96 (Scalia dissenting).

[219] One theory that we do find persuasive is that an executive branch constitutional decision maker should regard judicial precedent in the way a sitting Supreme Court Justice would—that is, with a healthy regard for stare decisis, but with authority to stray from past decisions where reasons favoring a new constitutional interpretation outweigh stare decisis concerns. See Strauss, 15 Cardozo L Rev at 127 (cited in note 211).

the President should have vetoed, or at least registered his objection to, a bill that failed to do so.[220]

There is a risk—which *Miller* illustrates—that the political branches will not remove a constitutional defect in a statute, and that the question will therefore arise for government litigators, and the Solicitor General in particular, of whether and how to defend the statute in light of the underenforced-norms thesis. That risk is enhanced if one accepts that the underenforced-norms thesis places additional responsibility on the political branches that those branches may fail to acknowledge.

Under the prevailing view of the Solicitor General's role, he should not defend a statute that is "patently unconstitutional," even if doing so requires him to confess error and forfeit a lower-court victory.[221] There is reason to construe the confession-of-error authority narrowly to guard against the temptation to make such decisions as "a form of post-enactment veto of legislation that the current administration did not like."[222] Indeed, if the presumption is that the enactment of the legislation expresses the judgment of Congress and the President that it is constitutional, then the Solicitor General's ordinary role is to defend that judgment, even where he suspects the courts might properly disagree with it; thus, the burden is on the Solicitor General to explain any decision to override the political branches' constitutional judgment by declining to defend the statute.[223] Generally, the Solicitor General should

---

[220] There are examples. See H. Jefferson Powell, *The Province and Duty of the Political Departments,* 65 U Chi L Rev 365, 383 (1998) (discussing President's public declaration that a statute excluding all HIV-positive personnel from the military was unconstitutional and should be repealed, and observing that, "[i]n evaluating the constitutionality of [the HIV military-exclusion provision], the president applied the basic norm of equal protection without the screens of deference the courts employ").

[221] Drew S. Days, *In Search of the Solicitor General's Clients: A Drama with Many Characters,* 83 Ky L J 485, 500, 503 (1995) (quoting Representation of Congress and Congressional Interests in Court: Hearings Before the Subcommittee on Separation of Powers of the Senate Committee on the Judiciary, 94th Cong, 2d Sess 9 (1975) (statement of Rex Lee); Letter from Griffin Bell to Senator Robert Byrd, at 2 (May 8, 1979) (declining to defend statute where "reasonable arguments cannot be advanced to defend the challenged statute")).

[222] Days, 83 Ky L J at 502.

[223] See Michael McConnell, *The Rule of Law and the Role of the Solicitor General,* 21 Loyola L Rev 1105, 1117 (1988) (suggesting that, in evaluating the constitutionality of acts of Congress, the Solicitor General should take particular care in light of the effect of such a decision on "the scope of authority of a separate and independent branch of government").

largely leave to the Court the role of reviewing constitutional judgments of the political branches.[224]

The argument for a very narrow role for confessions of error assumes the existence of full judicial enforcement of constitutional norms. But for the same reasons that political-branch lawyers in an advisory role bear greater responsibilities in areas of judicial underenforcement, the Solicitor General should also act with greater constitutional vigilance in those areas. That need for vigilance suggests that the Solicitor General should modify that general approach in the underenforced-norms context and be more willing to acknowledge a statute's constitutional defect.

The underenforcement thesis shows, for example, that a stance typical for Solicitors General in the domestic context is inappropriate for underenforced norms: Faced with an immigration or nationality measure that the Solicitor General believes contains a constitutional defect, he must not (1) choose to defend the statute on the ground that the Court, not the Solicitor General or any other executive branch official, is the appropriate final arbiter of constitutional questions, and then (2) argue that the Court should uphold the statute under a diminished level of judicial scrutiny as a matter of deference to the political branches.[225] The ordinary reasoning—that the courts, because of their relative impartiality, are in a superior position to decide constitutional issues—does not apply when, as a matter of relative institutional competence, the courts have determined that they will not fully enforce the relevant

---

[224] It may seem odd to conclude that, in a full-enforcement context, the Solicitor General should confess error only in cases in which a constitutional defect in the government's position is patent, because those are the cases in which the Court is most likely to rule against the government in any event. In borderline cases, in contrast, the Solicitor General's advocacy is more likely to tip the balance in the government's favor (and against what the Solicitor General in fact believes is the better view), but the traditional view assumes that in such cases the Solicitor General would forcefully argue in favor of the constitutionality of the government act. Thus, the traditional view actually may increase the risk of circular buck-passing. That view is thus justified less as a concomitant of the Solicitor General's duty to uphold the Constitution than as a reflection of his obligations as an officer of the Court not to present a frivolous argument and force an adversary to litigate where the adversary's victory is certain, especially where confessing error presumably would not adversely affect the outcome his client would expect in any event.

[225] See, for example, Days, *The Interests of the United States, the Solicitor General and Individual Rights*, 41 SLU L J 1, 7 (1996) (arguing that courts rather than the Solicitor General should decide difficult constitutional issues in immigration and military contexts, and also asserting that courts should act deferentially toward the political branches in those contexts).

constitutional norms, but will leave it to the political branches to decide how best to do so. A decision to defend an apparently (but not patently) unconstitutional statute presents less risk in a full-enforcement context; the Solicitor General can assume that, if the statute is unconstitutional, the Court will so declare. In the context of judicial underenforcement, however, the same stance is another version of circular buck-passing. In *Miller* itself, the Solicitor General should have sought to obviate that problem by confessing error in the brief in opposition to the petition for certiorari and expressing the executive branch's intention of working with Congress to enact a sex-neutral substitute.

The Court might grant review even in the face of the Solicitor General's confession of error and then uphold the statute under plenary power deference.[226] But the government's independent duties would be unaffected by such a judicial decision, and the political branches should not view it as giving the statute an imprimatur of constitutionality. Whether or not the Court reviews a statute and sustains it under the plenary power doctrine, the executive should seek to work with Congress to fix any constitutional defect to the point where it would withstand undiluted constitutional review.

2. *Perils of accepting the underenforcement model.* Our view—that the political branches should take greater responsibility for ensuring that immigrants' constitutional rights are protected—honors the institutional concerns that drive the plenary power doctrine but closes a troubling constitutional gap left by the political branches' current approach to constitutional review of immigration measures. It also has the potential for enriching constitutional dialogue in the immigration area by seriously involving actors other than the courts in the project of elaborating constitutional rights.[227]

---

[226] If the Solicitor General confesses error, the Court can appoint an amicus to make the argument in favor of the statute's constitutionality, or Congress can persist in disagreeing with the Solicitor General and represent itself. See 2 USC 288 (1988).

[227] See generally Michael J. Sandel, *Democracy's Discontent: America in Search of a Public Philosophy*, 107–08 (Harvard, 1996) (court-centered constitutionalism has come to limit the terms of political discourse in the United States); Thomas W. Merrill, *Judicial Opinions as Binding Law and as Explanations for Judgments*, 15 Cardozo L Rev 43, 77 (1993) ("an executive branch that grows accustomed to taking its cues from courts may lose the capacity to engage in imaginative interpretation of the sort often needed to resolve difficult problems of administration"); Robin West, *Progressive and Conservative Constitutionalism*, 88 Mich L Rev 641, 718 (1990) ("[I]f progressives were to reorient progressive constitutional debate

It may seem quixotic to ask the political branches to shoulder a greater constitutional duty to protect immigrants' individual rights. Doing so would require the political branches to act against their institutional interests, curtailing their own prerogatives in order to respect individual rights. In areas of full judicial enforcement, Congress and the executive may be relatively effective at constitutional self-restraint, but in those areas—unlike the plenary power area—they act with the knowledge that, if they overstep the Court's established constitutional bounds, the Court will correct their errors.

There is some basis for optimism. The political branches clearly have not, up to now, been recognizing their responsibilities under an underenforced-norms conception of the plenary power doctrine. It is possible that, if the courts more clearly communicated that conception, the political branches would learn that, whereas in areas of fully enforced norms they can track judicial reasoning and rely on the courts to correct their mistakes, they must reason differently in a regime of underenforcement, themselves applying heightened or strict scrutiny even where the courts would not. Government lawyers are typically highly role-sensitive, seeking to make only those decisions and exercise only those powers that come within their constitutionally and statutorily defined province. The first step, then, is to establish clearly that a different model of constitutional decision making applies under the plenary power doctrine than in contexts where rights are fully enforced by the courts. Given such a clear understanding, congressional and executive branch counsel might respond adequately to the challenge to interpret and enforce constitutional rights.

But the perils of asking the political branches to shoulder a greater constitutional duty remain, and they are substantial. Not only are there grounds for concern that the political branches, faced with scant judicial check, will take lightly any responsibility they have to protect immigrants' rights, but there is also cause to worry that general acceptance of the underenforced-norms reading of the plenary power cases would, from immigrants' perspective, actually make the situation worse. As we noted

---

toward legislative politics rather than adjudicative law, they would invigorate and enrich the terms and the stakes of public debate. . . . We have, in effect, alienated the responsibility for public morality to the courts").

above, some scholars have argued that the plenary power doctrine represents not mere judicial underenforcement, but a substantive lower standard applicable to immigration claims. We reject that view as inconsistent with the cases' language, and as unsupported by the kind of logic that such a reading would require. But one virtue of the substantive-norms reading is that it brings to the surface the unfulfilled demand for substantive justification of diminished rights protection: It openly asserts that immigrants get lower levels of constitutional protection in various ways because that is all they deserve, and thereby arguably presses the courts either persuasively to justify the lower levels of protection, or to raise them.

The underenforced-norms thesis, in contrast, may have the effect of releasing that pressure on the courts without improving immigrants' constitutional rights protection. As a practical matter, the underenforced-norms thesis points to the political branches as the place where the constitutional buck stops. But, as we have acknowledged, the political branches may be ill-suited and unlikely to act against their own turf interests to fully enforce immigrants' individual rights. The net result might well be a stronger normative justification for judicial abdication, accompanied by a precatory, unenforceable, and unheeded obligation on Congress and the executive.

The risk that judicial deference leads to unjustified incursions into individual rights provides additional reason for courts to curtail that deference and to fully enforce constitutional norms. We have outlined two parallel and distinct theories of *Miller:* First, we argue that, given the underenforced constitutional norms reading of the plenary power cases, the political branches themselves should have fully enforced constitutional sex discrimination norms when they amended Section 309(a); second, we argue that the Court's decision in *Miller* points the way to full judicial enforcement of constitutional norms for citizenship and immigration matters alike. If one concludes that constitutional enforcement of individual rights by the political branches against their own institutional habits and interests is an awkward and unlikely proposition, then full enforcement by the judiciary seems more attractive. Faced with a clear constitutional norm that overbroad sex-based classifications are unconstitutional in the absence of an "exceedingly persuasive" governmental justification,[228] Congress in 1986 added and the President approved new sex-based classifications in the INA even though sex-neutral provisions would have worked as well. There is no evidence that the political branches played the role the underenforced-norms theory gives them. The 1986 amendments to Section 309(a) illustrate the risk that, if courts do not enforce the constitutional rights of people like the Millers, nobody will.

B. GOVERNMENT LAWYERING UNDER FULLY ENFORCED NORMS: SECTION 309(A) AND IMMIGRATION LAW

The preceding discussion addresses some consequences for government lawyering of the underenforced-norms thesis. But we argued in Part III that the judiciary, in light of *Miller*, has bases for fully enforcing constitutional norms in immigration, nationality, and citizenship. The prospect of full enforcement raises new issues for government lawyers. There likely is another U.S. serviceman who has a child born overseas to a noncitizen mother. Suppose that serviceman seeks to challenge the constitutionality of the statute left standing—barely—in *Miller*. What position should government lawyers and policy-makers take in such a case?

If the case reached a court, it would not be inappropriate for the government to argue that *Miller* did not hold Section 309 unconstitutional—Justice O'Connor's strong intimation is properly classified as dicta. But it would be inappropriate—in the post-*Miller* world—for the government to trot out the plenary power cases and argue for extreme deference. *Miller* suggests that the usual norms of constitutional law will apply, at the very least, to *jus sanguinis* citizenship cases. Thus the government must decide what its substantive position is on the question of the explicit sex-based rule in the statute. Once Justice Frankfurter's crutch of deference is gone, what would be the government's reason for asserting that its successful argument in *United States v Virginia* for significantly heightened scrutiny should not apply in citizenship cases? Of course, the government would be free to argue, as it did in *Miller*, that the statute satisfies heightened scrutiny. But it seems

---

[228] *Hogan*, 458 US at 725.

clear that a majority of the Justices rejected that view—and rightly so, according to our earlier analysis.

Because the logic of *Miller* is not limited to *jus sanguinis* statutes, the requirement that a government advocate present a substantive theory of government power justifying diminished scrutiny ought also to apply in immigration cases. Assume, for example, a legal challenge to provisions in the immigration code that permit parents of U.S. citizens to obtain immigrant status in the United States but do not provide similar benefits to parents of resident aliens.[229] Even conceding a new era of full enforcement, the government might well wish to argue for a low level of judicial scrutiny. Such an argument could be based on the substantive claim that distinctions between citizens and aliens are constitutionally tolerable. But the theoretical architecture of such an argument could not be based on the quasi-political question foundation of the plenary power cases; rather, the government would have to come forward with a plausible constitutional account of why norms of equal protection do not condemn this instance of discrimination based on alienage.[230]

Government legal advisers are in a slightly different position. Their duty is not to try to defend an existing, duly enacted statute, regulation, or other governmental act. Rather, their job is to inform the client of the legality of planned conduct under their best view of the prevailing law. (Of course, this might include a judgment of where the law is likely to go and how the government might edge it along in that direction.)

Consider, then, how the State Department ought to treat the next application for registration as a U.S. citizen by a person in Lorelyn Miller's situation. The conscientious government adviser ought to read *Miller v Albright* as giving last rites to the statutory provision. That reading, coupled with the government's position in *Virginia*, ought to lead the conscientious adviser to conclude that the statute cannot constitutionally be applied to deny citizenship to the applicant.

---

[229] See INA § 201(b), 8 USC § 1151(b).

[230] Once shorn of the old plenary power language, the justifications become remarkably thin. See John W. Guendelsberger, *The Right to Family Unification in French and United States Immigration Law*, 21 Cornell Intl L J 1 (1988); T. Alexander Aleinikoff, *The Tightening Circle of Membership*, 22 Hastings Const L Q 915, 921–22 (1995).

But that is only half a solution. It tells the State Department that it cannot *deny* citizenship in such a case, but it does not demonstrate that the applicant must be *granted* citizenship. The question is whether—and if so, how—the offending provision might be severed from the other provisions regulating *jus sanguinis* citizenship. At first blush it might be suggested that the State Department simply treat Section 309 as a nullity, thereby permitting the out-of-wedlock applicant to be recognized as a citizen under Section 301(g) if the U.S. citizen father had met the statutory U.S. residency requirements. But, as we explore in the paragraphs that follow, the statutory structure is complicated enough to give a conscientious government decision maker pause before simply registering the applicant as a citizen.

First recall the rules for children born in wedlock to a U.S. citizen parent and a noncitizen parent. Under INA Section 301(g), such children are citizens at birth provided that the U.S. citizen parent had been "physically present in the United States . . . for a period or periods totaling not less than five years, at least two of which were after attaining the age of fourteen years."[231] The rules for children born out of wedlock, defined in INA Section 309, are different for children of U.S. citizen mothers as compared to children of U.S. citizen fathers. (This, of course, was the issue in *Miller*.) Out-of-wedlock children of U.S. citizen mothers obtain citizenship at birth if the mother has "previously been physically present in the United States . . . for a continuous period of one year."[232] The rules for nonmarital children born to U.S. citizen fathers were what was under scrutiny in *Miller*—requiring five years' U.S. residency plus a special showing regarding paternal ties.

Thus the residency requirements for out-of-wedlock children born to a U.S. parent are importantly different from the standards applied to children born in wedlock to a U.S. citizen parent and a noncitizen parent—and different in a somewhat peculiar way. Compared to the five-year residency requirements for parents of in-wedlock children, out-of-wedlock children born abroad to U.S. citizen fathers face tougher rules: they must meet the five-year parent-residency rule of Section 301(g) as well as the special rules of Section 309(a). But nonmarital children born to U.S. citizen moth-

---

[231] INA § 309(g), USC § 1401(g).

[232] INA § 309(c), 8 USC § 1409(c).

ers face easier rules: They obtain citizenship at birth if their mother was physically present in the United States for one year prior to their birth.[233]

It is thus far from clear exactly how the conscientious policy-maker at the State Department ought to proceed in ensuring sex equality under the statute. Justice Breyer's dissent proposes that the government simply treat the offending provisions as nullities, effectively deleting the support and legitimation/acknowledgment elements of Section 309(a) from the code.[234] But this approach would leave in place Section 309(c), which establishes the more favorable residency rule for U.S. citizen mothers of nonmarital children.[235] It thus does not render the statute sex-neutral.[236]

Another alternative would be to consider Section 309 a nullity in its entirety. Out-of-wedlock children would thereby be able to obtain citizenship directly under Section 301's requirements. But this solution produces the curious result of adopting a less favor-able rule for out-of-wedlock children born to U.S. citizen mothers than is currently the case (i.e., mothers of these children would now have to have resided in the United States for five years rather than the current requirement of one year). This may be a sensible result—the current favorable treatment may be a relic of the past.[237] But it is not clear that the State Department has the au-thority to deny citizenship to a class of persons currently entitled to citizenship under federal statutes.[238] Moreover, for more than

---

[233] As noted earlier (note 14), the favorable treatment accorded nonmarital children of U.S. citizen mothers was motivated primarily by a desire to avoid statelessness. Because the citizenship of a nonmarital child usually followed the citizenship of the mother, a child of a U.S. citizen mother and a noncitizen father born in the father's home country was likely to be stateless unless the child was recognized as a U.S. citizen. Accordingly, U.S. law adopted a relaxed standard for nonmarital children born to U.S. mothers abroad. Non-marital children of U.S. citizen fathers did not usually require special treatment in order to be a citizen somewhere: They likely acquired the citizenship of the non-U.S. mother at birth. See *Wauchope v U.S. Dep't of State*, 985 F2d at 1414.

[234] 118 S Ct at 1463–64 (Breyer dissenting).

[235] Thus we are mystified—as was Justice Breyer—by Justice Scalia's assertion that Justice Breyer's remedy would favor fathers over mothers. See id at 1449 (Scalia concurring); 1464 (Breyer dissenting).

[236] As noted, such favorable treatment of mothers was originally justified on grounds of avoiding statelessness. But there is no reason that such a provision cannot be sex-neutral.

[237] See note 171. But see Br for Resp 33–34 n 18, reporting the views of the State Depart-ment that concern about statelessness are still applicable to out-of-wedlock children born to U.S. citizen mothers in Germany, Great Britain, South Korea, and Vietnam.

[238] Compare *Califano v Westcott*, 443 US 76, 92 (1979) (rejecting state's proposed sex-neutral remedy for unconstitutional sex discrimination in a welfare statute that would have

fifty years Congress has had separate *jus sanguinis* rules for out-of-wedlock and in-wedlock children. Eliminating that difference might be a good thing. But it seems likely that Congress would seek to maintain it in some form, albeit with sex-neutral catego-ries.[239] Thus, if the goal of the conscientious decision maker is to devise a sex-neutral policy consistent with the intent and structure of the underlying statute, treating Section 309 as a nullity appears to be an inappropriate response.

Another strategy would be to try to render Section 309 (govern-ing nonmarital children) sex-neutral, either by (1) applying the rules for mothers to fathers, (2) applying the rules for fathers to mothers, or (3) crafting a new set of rules that would apply to both (e.g., a rule that would grant citizenship where the U.S. citizen could demonstrate a caretaker parent role). The last alternative—which appears sensible to us—seems consistent both with congres-sional intent (assuming that the invalid sex-based rule was based on concern about the existence of a parent-child relationship) and with the structure of the statute (by maintaining different rules for out-of-wedlock and in-wedlock children). But, as with the strategy of simply treating Section 309 as a nullity, a new rule such as this would deny citizenship to some children who are currently granted citizenship by the current statute—that is, out-of-wedlock children of U.S. mothers whose mother cannot meet the new standard. If the executive concludes that this is a result Congress would wish to avoid, then it rules out both this alternative and the second alternative of applying the rule for fathers to mothers.

We are therefore left with the first alternative of applying the rule for mothers in Section 309(c) to fathers. But this would pro-duce the curious result of treating the out-of-wedlock children of one U.S. citizen parent and one noncitizen parent more favorably than the in-wedlock children born to a similarly mixed-citizenship couple: The father of an out-of-wedlock child would have to estab-lish U.S. residency of only a year (under a sex-neutral Section

---

had the effect of terminating eligibility for benefits of some families currently receiving them).

[239] Differential treatment might be based on the perception that parents are less likely to have close relationships with out-of-wedlock children. We express no view on the consti-tutionality of such an assumption in a post-*Miller* world, for example, under constitutional decisions prohibiting discrimination based on illegitimacy—but it would behoove the gov-ernment to assess its constitutionality before adopting a policy based on such an assumption.

309(c)), while the father of an in-wedlock child would have to establish U.S. residency of five years (under Section 301(g)). Furthermore, the rule would require no showing of any established parent-child relationship, a result that seems distinctly contrary to congressional intent.

In the somewhat analogous situation of a court attempting to remedy the unconstitutionality of an underinclusive statute, the Supreme Court has stated that the judge must "measure the intensity of [Congress's] commitment to the residual policy and consider the degree of potential disruption of the statutory scheme that would occur by extension as opposed to abrogation."[240] Under this analysis, the Department of State has no good option. Congress's commitment to the "residual policy" of wanting assurance of a parent-child relationship in the case of out-of-wedlock children appears strong; and the crafting of sex-neutral rules, either by extending the treatment afforded U.S. citizen mothers to U.S. citizen fathers or by abrogating Section 309 altogether, seems to disrupt significantly the statutory scheme. So the Department of State faces a real quandary: Denying recognition of the citizenship of our hypothetical applicant would be an unconstitutional act; but there is no obvious way to anticipate how Congress would choose among the various feasible sex-neutral rules for recognition of citizenship. What, then, should the conscientious policy-maker do?

The overriding duty of the State Department is to act in conformity with the Constitution. Thus, it may not deny citizenship to our hypothetical applicant on the basis of INA Section 309(a). Beyond this, the answer remains unclear. Any plausible rule that the Department might craft to overcome the constitutional problem would appear either to deny citizenship to persons who would be eligible for it under the current statute or to entitle persons to citizenship in a manner inconsistent with congressional intent. The State Department could, we suppose, do its best at guessing how Congress would have answered the question if it had known that the current rules were unconstitutional. But given the complexity of the materials here, such a guess would have all the appearance of a coin toss. In such a case, we believe the wisest course of action is for the State Department (1) not to deny citizenship to

---

[240] *Heckler v Mathews*, 465 US 728, 739 n 5 (1984), quoting *Welsh v United States*, 398 US 333, 365 (1970) (Harlan concurring).

out-of-wedlock children of U.S. citizen fathers, and (2) to propose legislation that remedies the unconstitutionality of the present statute.[241]

V. Conclusion

But for want of the proper plaintiff, one of the few remaining sex-based distinctions in immigration and nationality law would be history. Unfortunately, the Court's recognition that fully enforced norms apply in citizenship cases came without the help of the Solicitor General—indeed, in the face of a brief that argued not only that Lorelyn Miller had no rights to assert but further that, even if she did, the law passed constitutional muster under the heightened scrutiny test applied to sex-based statutes. Neither position of the government is tenable, and a majority of the Justices properly rejected both.

Under our reading of the plenary power doctrine, of course, the issue never should have reached the Court. Institutionally based judicial deference to the political branches places the responsibility with Congress and the executive to apply full-fledged constitutional norms even when the courts will not. If the political branches had been doing their part, they would have amended the INA provisions governing *jus sanguinis* citizenship for nonmarital children born abroad of mixed-citizenship parentage to make them sex-neutral. The political branches instead have treated the plenary power doctrine like a blank check, leaving them free to do whatever the courts will allow. But *Miller* suggests that, where the political branches abdicate, the courts may now step in.

---

[241] There is a precedent for doing just that. One example occurred in case that is a close cousin to *Miller*. *Wauchope v U.S. Dep't of State*, 985 F2d 1407 (9th Cir 1993), considered a constitutional challenge to earlier *jus sanguinis* rules that had permitted U.S. citizen fathers but not mothers to pass citizenship by descent. Although the law was made sex-neutral in 1934, its discriminatory effects lingered because the statutory changes were not made retroactive. Thus, children born overseas to U.S. citizen mothers before 1934 were not recognized as citizens at birth. The court of appeals upheld the lower court's finding of an equal protection violation, and it rejected the government's argument that the district court erred in declaring the plaintiffs U.S. citizens. The United States decided not to appeal, based on the conclusion that the Ninth Circuit's ruling was consistent with modern-day sex discrimination norms. Instead, it proposed legislation, subsequently adopted by Congress, that retrospectively remedied the sex-based inequality. Immigration and Nationality Technical Corrections Act of 1994, § 1, Pub L 103–416, 108 Stat 4305, 4306. See Drew S. Days III, *The Solicitor General and the American Legal Ideal*, 49 SMU L Rev 73, 81 (1995).

Miller does more than cast doubt on sex-based citizenship laws. It forces fundamental reconsideration of the underpinnings of the plenary power doctrine. This means that the government is no longer entitled to argue for extreme judicial deference in immigration and nationality cases; rather, it must come up with a substantive constitutional theory regarding the extent of and limits upon the federal immigration power. That theory, to be consistent with *Miller* and true to the government's position in *United States v Virginia*, should begin with the premise that sex-based rules in immigration and nationality laws are presumptively unconstitutional.

Miller v Albright is a case with the wrong plaintiff seeking relief that cannot easily be granted by a court or the executive branch. Yet sometimes hard cases make good law.

MATTHEW D. ADLER
AND SETH F. KREIMER

THE NEW ETIQUETTE OF
FEDERALISM: NEW YORK, PRINTZ,
AND YESKEY

A majority of the Supreme Court once more believes that state autonomy is a fundamental, constitutional value and has set out to develop that proposition from case to case. As a result, the Tenth Amendment and its penumbrae have recently generated a series of intricate, judicially declared limitations on federal power. The jurisprudence of federalism has been bedecked with formalistic distinctions that provide law professors rich opportunity to chase law students down a series of hypotheticals and into contradictions. While this may be good fun for professors, and occasionally for students, one suspects that the new federalism doctrines quickly will drive political actors, judges, and practicing lawyers to distraction. The area lacks a fabric of constitutional law sufficiently coherent and well-justified to last.

This article focuses on the proposition that the federal government may not "commandeer" state officials, and the attendant doctrines announced by the Court. The anticommandeering doctrines are of interest not only because they have impelled the

Matthew Adler is Assistant Professor, University of Pennsylvania Law School. Seth Kreimer is Professor, University of Pennsylvania Law School.

AUTHORS' NOTE: We thank Ed Baker, Evan Caminker, Jonathan Entin, Barry Friedman, Frank Goodman, and Rick Hills for their incisive comments and criticisms; and Samantha Fisherman, Kathy Scobey, and Mary Sigler, for their excellent research assistance. Of course, we alone are responsible for any mistakes and oversights in this article."

Court to invalidate two federal statutes in the last seven years, but because they are both unspecified and potentially explosive.[1] If developed expansively, they threaten to undermine the supremacy of federal law.

The doctrines, as announced by the Court in *Printz v United States*[2] and *New York v United States*,[3] and reaffirmed last Term in *Pennsylvania Department of Corrections v Yeskey*,[4] create a regime of dichotomous boundaries. Like the federalism jurisprudence set forth, a generation ago, in *National League of Cities v Usery*,[5] the new jurisprudence of commandeering purports to define an area of total state (and local) immunity from federal intervention.[6] Neither the magnitude of the federal interest nor the degree of interference with state prerogatives is relevant. Rather, the doctrinal boundaries constitute what Justice Kennedy calls "the etiquette of federalism," and a federal trespass across those boundaries is per se invalid.[7]

---

[1] As Professor Tushnet has observed, "[O]ne can use the word 'commandeer' to refer to almost anything that affects a state's ability to pursue the substantive policies it prefers." Mark Tushnet, *Keeping Your Eye on the Ball: The Significance of the Revival of Constitutional Federalism*, 13 Ga St U L Rev 1065, 1067 (1997). For examples of the potential reach of the anticommandeering principle, see *Condon v Reno*, 155 F3d 453 (4th Cir 1998) (invalidating Driver's Privacy Protection Act, which prohibited dissemination of information contained in state motor vehicle records, as a commandeering); *West v Anne Arundel County*, 137 F3d 752, 760 (4th Cir 1998) (entertaining claim that application of the Fair Labor Standards Act to state subdivision was a commandeering; rejecting only as a matter of stare decisis); *Burbank-Glendale-Pasadena Airport Auth. v City of Burbank*, 136 F3d 1360, 1364–65 (9th Cir 1998) (Kozinski concurring) (arguing that empowering state officials to bring a preemption claim in federal court might be commandeering). The anticommandeering doctrines have already attracted considerable scholarly attention. See, in particular, Evan H. Caminker, *Printz, State Sovereignty, and the Limits of Formalism*, 1997 Supreme Court Review 199; Evan H. Caminker, *State Sovereignty and Subordinacy: May Congress Commandeer State Officers to Implement Federal Law?* 95 Colum L Rev 1001 (1995); Roderick M. Hills, Jr., *The Political Economy of Cooperative Federalism: Why State Autonomy Makes Sense and "Dual Sovereignty" Doesn't*, 96 Mich L Rev 813 (1998); Vicki C. Jackson, *Federalism and the Uses and Limits of Law: Printz and Principle?* 111 Harv L Rev 2180 (1998).

[2] 117 S Ct 2365 (1997).

[3] 505 US 144 (1992).

[4] 118 S Ct 1952 (1998).

[5] 426 US 833 (1976), overruled, *Garcia v San Antonio Metropolitan Transit Auth.*, 469 US 528 (1985).

[6] Although the Tenth Amendment refers simply to "States," not localities, and although the parallel reference to "State[s]" in the Eleventh Amendment has been read by the Court solely to immunize states, not localities, from suit, the anticommandeering doctrines protect both state and local governments. See *Printz*, 117 S Ct at 2382 n 15. For the remainder of this article, we generally use "state" to mean "state or local."

[7] *United States v Lopez*, 514 US 549, 583 (1995) (Kennedy concurring) (citing *New York* as a case "where the etiquette of federalism has been violated by a formal command from

In such a regime, a great deal hinges on the exact contours of the area protected from federal infringement. If they are to be consistent with precedent, the doctrinal boundaries that define this area must map onto the outcomes of prior cases. If they are to be workable, the boundaries must be intelligible and coherent. And if they are to be at all intellectually persuasive, the boundaries cannot be simple result-oriented gerrymanders. Unfortunately, the anticommandeering doctrines seem headed for trouble in all three dimensions. In this article we seek to clarify as sympathetically as possible the doctrinal boundaries between permissible federal regulation and impermissible commandeering, to assess those boundaries in light of the justifications for judicially enforced federalism, and to explore the possibility of an expressive justification for the boundaries that cannot be otherwise justified.[8]

Part I lays out our understanding of the basic pieces of the puzzle: the explicit lines of demarcation that the Court has drawn in *Printz, New York,* and *Yeskey,* and the values that constitutional federalism might be understood to realize. Part II argues that behind the explicit lines must lie a more basic distinction, alluded to by the Court in *Printz,* between impermissible commandeering and the permissible federal preemption of state law. We flesh out the preemption/commandeering distinction, but conclude that the distinction is only poorly justified by the values of constitutional federalism.

Parts III and IV engage in the same exercise for the lines of demarcation explicitly set forth by the case law. Part III addresses the three distinctions adopted in *New York* and *Printz:* between commandeering and conditional funding or preemption, between generally applicable and targeted federal statutes, and between commandeering of state officials exercising the judicial function and commandeering of other officials. In each case, the boundaries in question seem to us both normatively insupportable and practically unworkable. Part IV goes to the issue addressed in the most recent commandeering case, *Yeskey*—whether an anticommandeering

---

the National Government directing the state to enact a certain policy . . . or to organize its governmental functions in a certain way").

[8] *Printz* also sketched out a unitary executive argument for the anticommandeering doctrine. See 117 S Ct at 2378. We have nothing to add to Professor Caminker's persuasive criticism of that argument, see 1997 Supreme Court Review at 223–33 (cited in note 1), and thus focus here on the federalism argument.

prohibition should include an exemption for federal legislation adopted to enforce the Reconstruction Amendments. We conclude that the answer should be "yes," both as a matter of the case law and as a matter of federalism values, but also suggest that the task of delineating a clear and workable exemption will be a difficult one.

Finally, in Part V we explore, with skepticism, the possibility of an expressive justification for the anticommandeering doctrines here described.

I. Five Lines of Demarcation in Search of a Rationale

A. DOCTRINE: LINES OF DEMARCATION

In dissenting from the Court's 1985 decision to cease enforcing state sovereignty constraints on the national government, Justices O'Connor and Rehnquist each announced a hope and expectation that the Court would return to the fray.[9] In fact, federalism doctrine was reinvigorated six years later when *Gregory v Ashcroft* introduced a "plain statement rule"[10] for congressional action that interferes with "the authority of the people of the States to determine the qualifications of their most important government officials."[11] But it was not until the next year, in *New York v United States*, that the Court actually held a federal statute unconstitutional on federalism grounds.

In *New York*, the majority invalidated one part of a federal scheme seeking to induce states to make provision for the disposal of low-level nuclear waste, and sustained two others. The Court drew a line of demarcation between legitimate conditional exercises of the federal spending or preemption power, on the one hand, and illegitimate "commandeer[ing]," on the other.[12] The de-

---

[9] See *Garcia v San Antonio Metropolitan Transit Auth.*, 469 US 528, 580 (1985) (Rehnquist dissenting); id at 589 (O'Connor dissenting).

[10] 501 US 452, 461 (1991).

[11] Id at 463. The scope of the plain statement rule has proved elusive. Compare *City of Edmonds v Oxford House, Inc.*, 514 US 725, 732 n 5 (1995) (land use regulation was not " 'a decision of the most fundamental sort for a sovereign entity' ") (quoting *Gregory v Ashcroft*, 501 US at 460) with *BFP v Resolution Trust Corp.*, 511 US 531, 544 n 8 (1994) ("essential sovereign interest in the security and stability of title to land" triggered plain statement rule). The Court's opinion in *Yeskey*, discussed below, does not clarify matters.

[12] 505 US at 161 ("Congress may not simply commandeer the legislative processes of the States by directly compelling them to enact and enforce a federal regulatory program")

gree of justification or public necessity was held to be irrelevant; commandeering was an irredeemable constitutional violation, while conditional spending or preemption was per se consistent with constitutional constraints. The *New York* Court drew a second line of demarcation by affirming prior cases upholding the imposition of federal duties upon state judges; the Court reasoned that, as a matter of the text of the Supremacy Clause, judicial officials were peculiarly subject to federal demands.[13] Finally, the Court suggested that the prohibition on federal commandeering would not cover "generally applicable" statutes.[14]

Two Terms ago, in *Printz*, the Court went one step further. It applied the prohibition on commandeering not only to federal statutes which mandated policy-making by legislative officials, but to the Brady Act, a federal statute that merely imposed on state law enforcement officials the obligation to "'make a reasonable effort'"[15] to determine whether certain pending firearm purchases would be illegal. *Printz* reiterated the suggestion that statutes of general applicability fell outside the coverage of the anticommandeering principle.[16] The Court reaffirmed that this principle did not apply to statutes imposing federal duties on state judges, and clarified that any state official performing judicial functions was also subject to commandeering.[17] And the majority in *Printz* did not take issue with the proposition, articulated by the dissent,[18] that Congress could induce action by state officials through conditional federal spending or preemption.[19]

(internal quotation omitted); see id at 161–69 (distinguishing between commandeering and conditional spending or preemption).

[13] See id at 178–79.

[14] Id at 177–78.

[15] 117 S Ct at 2369 (quoting Brady Act).

[16] See id at 2383.

[17] See id at 2371, 2381 and n 14. It probably would be unwarranted to conclude that every directive to state judges and state officials exercising a judicial function, otherwise within Congress's Article I powers, is constitutionally permissible. See, for example, *Howlett v Rose*, 496 US 356, 372 (1990) ("The requirement that a state court of competent jurisdiction treat federal law as the law of the land does not necessarily include within it a requirement that the State create a court competent to hear the case in which the federal claim is presented"). However, *Printz* and *New York* clearly exempt judges and state officials exercising a judicial function from the generic prohibition on commandeering.

[18] See id at 2396–97 (Stevens dissenting).

[19] The majority opinion itself seems explicitly to acknowledge the constitutional legitimacy of cooperative federalism programs in the course of its unitary executive discussion. See id at 2378 n 12.

Pennsylvania Dept of Corrections v Yeskey offered the opportunity to clarify matters. The Court reviewed the applicability of the Americans with Disabilities Act (ADA) to the operation of a state prison system. The *Yeskey* petitioners and amici argued before the Court not only that the ADA failed the "plain statement" requirement of *Ashcroft*, but that application of the statute to prisons would be at odds with *Printz*, since the statute imposed duties of "reasonable accommodation" which could be far more intrusive than the Brady Act.[20] A unanimous Court, however, saw no need to reach the constitutional question.

Justice Scalia's opinion took the position that even if a "plain statement rule" applied, it was "amply met" by the terms of the ADA.[21] The opinion went on to avoid the question whether the ADA was barred by *Printz*, on the ground that the question had not been raised before the lower courts.[22] *Yeskey* was, however, illuminating in one way. The opinion suggested more directly what had been implicit in *New York* and *Printz:* the limits imposed by those cases do not apply to congressional enactments rooted in Section 5 of the Fourteenth Amendment.[23]

Thus, by the end of last Term, the Court had erected an enclave of state sovereignty explicitly bounded by four lines of demarcation. In addition, as we will argue below, these four demarcations presuppose a fifth, implicit distinction between federal preemption and commandeering. A federal requirement will be judged per se unconstitutional if:

1) the requirement commandeers state officials, rather than merely preempting state law; and

2) it does so directly rather than as a condition for federal spending, or for nonpreemption of state law; and

3) the requirement is targeted at state officials, rather than being generally applicable to state officials and private persons alike; and

4) the officials commandeered are exercising legislative or executive rather than judicial functions; and

5) the requirement is grounded in the Commerce Clause or

---

[20] See Brief for the Petitioners 23–25; Brief Amicus Curiae of the Criminal Justice Legal Foundation 23–24.

[21] 118 S Ct at 1954.

[22] See id at 1956.

[23] See id. See Part IV for a discussion of the Section 5 exception.

Congress's other Article I powers, rather than in the grants of power to Congress in the Reconstruction Amendments.

A great deal turns on the placement of these boundaries. We will suggest that they are both unclear and (with the exception of the last) unjustified by the values of federalism that the Court has invoked. We begin with a brief review of those values.

B. THE RATIONALES: THE VALUES OF FEDERALISM

What are the arguable values of constitutional federalism? More robustly, why might there be good reason to constitutionalize federalism guarantees and have these guarantees enforced by the Supreme Court,[24] as in such recent cases as *United States v Lopez*,[25] *Seminole Tribe of Florida v Florida*,[26] *City of Boerne v Flores*,[27] and the cases of most interest for us, *New York* and *Printz?* In this Part, we briefly summarize the values or functions that enforceable constitutional federalism might be understood to serve, with specific reference to the Court's own defense of this feature of our constitutional system. This summary should not be taken as an endorsement. Rather, our claim is conditional: on the assumption that constitutional federalism does serve important values, those values are poorly tracked by the anticommandeering doctrines set forth in *New York* and further developed by *Printz.* The critique of *New York* and *Printz* advanced here is an internal critique, which assumes without endorsing the basic normative presuppositions upon which those cases rest.[28]

What, then, are the presuppositions of the Court's federalism cases and, more generally, of constitutional federalism? To begin,

---

[24] For discussion of the values that constitutional federalism, and federalism doctrine, arguably serve, see Barry Friedman, *Valuing Federalism*, 82 Minn L Rev 317, 386–405 (1997); Jackson, 111 Harv L Rev at 2213–28 (cited in note 1); Deborah Jones Merritt, *The Guarantee Clause and State Autonomy: Federalism for a Third Century*, 88 Colum L Rev 1, 3–10 (1988); Michael W. McConnell, *Federalism: Evaluating the Founders' Design*, 54 U Chi L Rev 1484, 1491–1511 (1987); Andrzej Rapaczynski, *From Sovereignty to Process: The Jurisprudence of Federalism after Garcia*, 1985 Supreme Court Review 341, 380–414; David L. Shapiro, *Federalism: A Dialogue* 75–106 (Northwestern U Press, 1995). A critical survey is provided by Edward L. Rubin and Malcolm Feeley, *Federalism: Some Notes on a National Neurosis*, 41 UCLA L Rev 903 (1994).

[25] 514 US 549 (1995).

[26] 517 US 44 (1996).

[27] 117 S Ct 2157 (1997).

[28] For an external critique, see Rubin and Feeley, 41 UCLA L Rev at 903–52.

federalism might be justified in light of the geographic diversity of one or more variable V_i to which policy is appropriately responsive:[29] the geographic diversity of citizen preferences, needs, or interests; or, alternatively, of physical, social, or economic conditions; or even, perhaps, of the ethical norms and goals that undergird governmental policy. The simplest, static version of the argument says this: the values of some V_i are in fact different in different geographic regions; these variations are significant, that is, large enough to make different policies optimal for different regions; therefore a governmental regime that permits policy to vary by region, rather than requiring a single national policy, is optimal. As the Court crisply stated in *Gregory v Ashcroft*, federalism "assures a decentralized government that will be more sensitive to the diverse needs of a heterogeneous society."[30] The geographic diversity argument can also be put, more elaborately, in dynamic rather than static form: if separate governments defined by geographic region exist, then citizens will migrate to different regions depending on, say, their needs, interests, or ethical views, such that over time geographic regions characterized by different values of some V_i will emerge. The dynamic version of the geographic diversity argument is, in effect, the argument famously advanced some forty years ago by Charles Tiebout, and since developed at great length in the economics literature on federalism.[31]

A different argument for federalism stresses governmental innovation rather than geographic diversity.[32] As with the diversity argument, the innovation argument can be formulated either statically or dynamically. The static formulation is that proposed by Justice Brandeis in his oft-quoted dissent to *New State Ice Co. v Liebmann:* "To stay experimentation in things social and economic is a grave responsibility. . . . It is one of the happy incidents of the federal system that a single courageous State may, if its citizens choose, serve as a laboratory; and try novel social and economic

---

[29] See, for example, Friedman, 82 Minn L Rev at 401–02; Merritt, 88 Colum L Rev at 8–9; McConnell, 54 U Chi L Rev at 1493–94.

[30] 501 US at 458.

[31] See Charles M. Tiebout, *A Pure Theory of Local Expenditures*, 64 J Pol Econ 416 (1956); Rubin and Feeley, 41 UCLA L Rev at 918 n 62 (citing literature).

[32] See, for example, *Ashcroft*, 501 US at 458; Friedman, 82 Minn L Rev at 397–400; Merritt, 88 Colum L Rev at 9; McConnell, 54 U Chi L Rev at 1498–99; Shapiro, *Federalism* at 138–39.

experiments without risk to the rest of the country."[33] The notion here is that the efficacy of novel governmental policies is uncertain, and thus that, quite apart from the geographic diversity of needs, interests, and so on, it makes sense to create a mechanism by which to test novel policies on a subnational scale. That way, policy testing occurs more quickly, and the harmful effects of poor policies are confined to particular regions rather than spread nationwide. One objection here is that state governments have an incentive to underinvest in policy innovation, as compared with the federal government, since each state realizes within its boundaries only a portion of the benefits from successful innovation, but bears all the costs of failure.[34] A partial response to this objection holds that successful states will induce immigration (with concomitant benefits, such as tax dollars) by the residents or firms of less successful states. Thus is delineated a dynamic version of the innovation argument for federalism which, like the different kind of dynamic argument proposed by Tiebout, has been popular among economists.[35]

Yet a third value arguably served by federalism is one that might be termed "tyranny prevention."[36] It is this value that has figured most prominently in the recent case law. As the majority in *New York* explained:

> [T]he Constitution divides authority between federal and state governments for the protection of individuals. State sovereignty is not just an end in itself. Rather, federalism secures to citizens the liberties that derive from the diffusion of sovereign power. Just as the separation and independence of the coordinate branches of the Federal Government serve to prevent the accumulation of excessive power in any one branch, a healthy balance of power between the States and the Federal Government will reduce the risk of tyranny and abuse from either front.[37]

---

[33] 285 US 262, 311 (1932) (Brandeis dissenting).

[34] See Susan Rose-Ackerman, *Risk Taking and Reelection: Does Federalism Promote Innovation?* 9 J Legal Stud 593 (1980) (questioning, on various grounds, incentive of states to innovate).

[35] See Rubin and Feeley, 41 UCLA L Rev at 920–21 nn 68–69 (citing sources for and against the thesis that interstate competition is beneficial).

[36] Rapaczinski argues at length that federalism serves a "tyranny prevention" function. See 1985 Supreme Court Review at 380–95. For other scholarly accounts that, in name or substance, defend a tyranny-prevention view, see Friedman, 82 Minn L Rev at 402–04; Jackson, 111 Harv L Rev at 2218–20; Merritt, 88 Colum L Rev at 3–7; McConnell, 54 U Chi L Rev at 1500–07.

[37] 505 US at 181 (internal quotations and citations omitted).

Printz heartily seconded this line of argument: "This separation of the two spheres [state and federal] is one of the Constitution's structural protections of liberty."[38] The claim, very roughly, is that the amount of tyranny in a unitary regime (that is, the total tyranny at the level of the national government) is greater than the amount of tyranny in a federal regime (that is, the total tyranny at the level of the national government plus the total tyranny at the level of the state governments). Place to one side, for the moment, the interesting problem of how to make commensurate different kinds of tyranny, or tyranny at different levels of government. (For example, if the move from a unitary regime to a federal regime weakens the hold of powerful interest groups on the national government, but creates compact states, each with its government dominated by a homogenous majority of in-state citizens, has overall tyranny decreased or increased?) The more basic question is what one means by "tyranny." Broadly speaking, we suggest, "tyranny" can be understood as the unjustified responsiveness of governmental policies, or actions, or decisions, to particular groups or persons.[39]

There are plausible arguments that constitutional federalism helps to mitigate tyranny so defined. In particular, we will take as true the claim that constitutional federalism serves to reduce the interest-group dominance that would obtain in a unitary regime, because the collective-action problems that hinder political activity

---

[38] 117 S Ct at 2378.

[39] A narrower definition of tyranny would require unjustified governmental responsiveness to governmental officials. Classically, of course, the "tyrant" was someone who held formal office—indeed, was the head of state—rather than simply being a powerful person. But the narrower definition entails that talk of the "tyranny of the majority," or of "interest group tyranny," is confused. We see no confusion here. These kinds of governmental pathologies, like classic tyranny, or "legislative tyranny" (the responsiveness of government to the interests of legislators, such as their interest in entrenching themselves in office), or "bureaucratic tyranny," are all instances of the same general phenomenon, namely, the unwarranted control of government by powerful groups or individuals—whether those persons hold formal office or not.

Tyranny is, at a minimum, unjustified responsiveness to particular groups or persons, not mere responsiveness; if, for example, it truly is the case that governments justifiably give greater weight to the interests of citizens as opposed to noncitizens, that hardly counts as "tyranny." We will not pursue the issue whether further qualifiers are needed, e.g., "oppressive" or "liberty-infringing" unjustified responsiveness, because we do not think it plausible that such qualifiers materially change our argument. See, for example, Part II.C. (considering whether tyranny, as here defined, is more problematic when it ensues in governmental action rather than inaction).

by diffuse, unorganized groups at the national level are less difficult to overcome in the smaller world of state politics.[40] We will also accept, for purposes of our internal critique, the standard view that constitutional federalism undermines tyranny in the narrower and more traditional sense of "tyranny by national officials," whether legislators, bureaucrats, judges, or the President.[41] We do find it quite implausible that constitutional federalism reduces tyranny along *all* dimensions. For example, the claim that (1) the national government is more likely than state governments to be dominated by a majority of the citizenry, to the detriment of the minority, is in obvious tension with the claim that (2) the national government is more likely than state governments to be dominated by well-organized interest groups, to the detriment of the majority. This returns us to the problem, alluded to above, of how to make commensurate different kinds of tyranny. Rather than take a stance on that problem, we will generally advance a critique of *Printz* and *New York* that is robust across different methods of commensuration, and across the different types of tyranny (interest-group tyranny, official tyranny, and others) that constitutional federalism might possibly mitigate.[42]

The final value arguably served by constitutional federalism is one that we shall term "political community."[43] It is a shibboleth of the literature endorsing federalism that states facilitate a kind or degree of political participation by citizens that does not occur at the national level.[44] We will assume that (*a*) democratic politics (including citizen involvement) has *intrinsic* value or importance,[45] and (*b*) the realm of state politics, if and only if adequately protected by the right sort of constitutionalized federalism guarantees,

---

[40] See Rapaczynski, 1985 Supreme Court Review at 386–88.

[41] See id at 388–91.

[42] But see Part III.C.

[43] The Court did not rely upon the value of political community in *Printz* and *New York*, but it did do so in another case that figures importantly in current federalism jurisprudence, *Gregory v Ashcroft*. See *Ashcroft*, 501 US at 460–64.

[44] See, for example, Friedman, 82 Minn L Rev at 389–94; Jackson, 111 Harv L Rev at 2221; Merritt, 88 Colum L Rev at 7–8; McConnell, 54 U Chi L Rev at 1507–11; Rapaczynski, 1985 Supreme Court Review at 395–408; Shapiro, *Federalism* at 139; S. Candice Hoke, *Preemption Pathologies and Civic Republican Values*, 71 BU L Rev 685, 701–14 (1991).

[45] See Matthew D. Adler, *Judicial Restraint in the Administrative State: Beyond the Counter-majoritarian Difficulty*, 145 U Pa L Rev 759, 796–806 (1997) (elaborating this idea).

can realize this intrinsic value in a manner, or to a degree, that a unitary regime cannot.[46]

II. PREEMPTION VERSUS COMMANDEERING: THE BACKGROUND DEMARCATION

Printz and *New York* clearly adopt three lines of demarcation: (1) between coercive directives to state officials, on the one hand, and "cooperative federalism" statutes (conditional spending or preemption) on the other; (2) between coercive directives to state officials exercising a legislative or executive function, and coercive directives to state officials exercising a judicial function; and (3) between targeted coercive directives to state legislators or executives, and coercive directives that are generally applicable both to state officials and to private persons. In addition, the Supreme Court, in cases prior to *New York* and *Printz*, as well as in the *Yeskey* decision, has articulated a fourth demarcation line: (4) between coercive directives to state officials that are promulgated by Congress pursuant to its ordinary Article I powers, and coercive directives promulgated pursuant to Section 5 of the Fourteenth Amendment and the parallel enforcement provisions in the Thirteenth and Fifteenth Amendments.[47]

Do these four demarcations together define the Court's new state sovereignty jurisprudence? We think not. The four lines of demarcation just described are, we believe, overlaid upon a fifth and much more basic one: the demarcation between *preemption* and *commandeering*. *Printz* and *New York* barely recognize this point. Nonetheless, we shall now claim, those decisions are best interpreted, in the context of wider case law, as standing for the proposition that the federal government may impose certain duties on state officials, even though the officials are nonjudicial, even though the duties are coercive and targeted in the strongest sense,

---

[46] The first assumption, (*a*), makes the concept of "political community" stronger than and distinct from the weaker view that democratic politics has merely instrumental importance in increasing the quality of governmental *outcomes*. We take it that the proponents of "political community" mean to endorse the stronger view. Indeed, if state politics is construed to have merely weak, instrumental significance, then the line between the political-community value of federalism and the others discussed above, particularly tyranny prevention, becomes quite blurred. Presumably, the main instrumental (outcome-enhancing) as opposed to intrinsic role of democratic involvement is to reduce certain kinds of tyranny: interest-group dominance as well as official entrenchment.

[47] See Parts III, IV (discussing these four demarcations).

and even though federal action is grounded merely upon the Commerce Clause or another Article I power rather than upon the Reconstruction Amendments.[48]

In this Part, we defend this interpretive claim. Then we discuss how the preemption/commandeering distinction should be fleshed out. Our suggestion will be that the distinction is most plausibly and sympathetically construed as a distinction between inaction and action—between the negative duties that (albeit targeted, coercive, and directed to nonjudicial officials) are a permissible accompaniment of the federal power to preempt, and the affirmative duties that are not. Finally, we argue that the preemption/commandeering distinction, even when construed in this plausible and sympathetic way, is not strongly justified by the values of constitutional federalism.

A. IS THERE A PREEMPTION/COMMANDEERING DISTINCTION?

The federal government, where acting within the scope of its authority under the Commerce Clause and the other powers set forth in Article I, Section 8 of the Constitution, has the power to define the legal positions of private parties: to accord private parties federal rights, duties, liberties, powers, liabilities, and other legal positions, and to nullify the state-law rights, duties, etc. that physically or logically conflict[49] with the federal positions.[50] As the Court has explained:

---

[48] For a dramatic, recent failure to understand this point, see *Condon v Reno*, 155 F3d 453 (4th Cir 1998), where the Court invalidated the Driver's Privacy Protection Act—which merely required state motor vehicle departments to refrain from disclosing information in motor vehicle records—on the grounds that the Act was neither generally applicable nor an exercise of Congress's Section 5 power and was therefore unconstitutional under *New York* and *Printz*. By contrast, the courts in *Oklahoma v United States*, 161 F3d 1266 (10th Cir 1998) and *Travis v Reno*, 163 F3d 1000 (7th Cir 1998) upheld the Act against the claim that it impermissibly commandeered state governments.

[49] "Physical conflict" is meant to cover the case where it is physically impossible for persons to comply with both federal- and state-law positions, e.g., where federal law imposes a duty to perform action *A* and state law imposes a duty to refrain from action *A*. "Logical conflict" is meant to cover the case where having the federal position entails—as a matter of the logic of Hohfeldian positions—that the person not have the state law position, e.g., where federal law grants a liberty to perform *A*, and state law imposes a duty to refrain from *A*. Stephen Gardbaum, in a recent, revisionary piece on preemption, agrees that the federal government has the power to override state law in both cases of conflict, but would (in effect) place the case of physical conflict under the Supremacy Clause and the case of logical conflict under the Necessary and Proper Clause. See *The Nature of Preemption*, 79 Cornell L Rev 767 (1994).

[50] More precisely, it is unquestioned that the federal government has the power to define the federal positions of private persons, and to preempt conflicting state-law positions, just

A wealth of precedent attests to congressional authority to displace or pre-empt state laws regulating private activity affecting interstate commerce when these laws conflict with federal law. Moreover, it is clear that the Commerce Clause empowers Congress to prohibit all—and not just inconsistent—state regulation of such activities. Although such congressional enactments obviously curtail or prohibit the States' prerogatives to make legislative choices respecting subjects the States may consider important, the Supremacy Clause permits no other result.[51]

These propositions are explicitly endorsed by *Printz* and *New York*, and understandably so;[52] to deny them would be to eviscerate the Supremacy Clause and two centuries of precedents.

Note, however, that the unquestioned power of the federal government to define the legal positions of private parties, and to pre-empt conflicting state-law positions, does not entail a federal power to define or change the legal positions (particularly the legal duties) of state legislators and enforcement officials. In theory, it is possible to imagine a regime of constitutional federalism in which the federal government has the power under the Commerce Clause (1) to define the legal positions of private parties, and (2) to impose a duty upon federal officials to respect, support, or enforce the rights, duties, etc. of private parties, as defined by the federal government, and also (3) to impose a duty upon state judges and adjudicators to respect, support, or enforce the rights, duties, etc. of private parties, as defined by the federal government,

---

insofar as the federal positions of private persons do not entail duties by state officials. Obviously, it is *not* unquestioned that the federal government can give private persons a claim-right against state officials.

[51] *Hodel v Virginia Surface Mining & Reclamation Ass'n, Inc.*, 452 US 264, 290 (1981) (citations omitted).

[52] See *New York*, 505 US at 178 ("The Constitution . . . gives Congress the authority to regulate matters directly and to pre-empt contrary state regulation"); *Printz*, 117 S Ct at 2374 (stating that "all state actions [obstructing federal law] are *ipso facto* invalid" and citing *Silkwood v Kerr-McGee Corp.*, 464 US 238 (1984), for the proposition that federal law pre-empts conflicting state law). See also *FERC v Mississippi*, 456 US 742, 766–67 (1982) (stressing federal power to define legal positions of private persons, and to preempt conflicting state law); *National League of Cites v Usery*, 426 US 833, 840–45 (1976) (same, but also distinguishing between federal power over private persons and federal power over states themselves), overruled, *Garcia v San Antonio Metropolitan Transit Auth.*, 469 US 528 (1985); *Fry v United States*, 421 US 542, 552 (1975) (Rehnquist dissenting) ("Congress may pre-empt state regulatory authority in areas where both bodies are otherwise competent to act. But this well-recognized principle of the Supremacy Clause is traditionally associated with federal regulation of persons or enterprises, rather than with federal regulation of the State itself. . . .").

but *not* the power to impose any duty at all[53] upon nonjudicial state officials. That is, it is in theory possible to imagine a constitutional regime in which, notwithstanding the federal power to define the legal position of private parties, state legislators and enforcement officials would remain free to act as if federal statutes had not been enacted, and the only governmental officials who would incur duties in virtue of a federal statute (under the Commerce Clause) would be federal officials and state judges and adjudicators. Indeed, a regime of constitutional federalism without federal power to impose duties upon state officials is precisely what an earlier Supreme Court endorsed in an 1861 decision, *Kentucky v Dennison*.[54] As the *Dennison* Court put it: "[W]e think it clear, that the Federal Government, under the Constitution, has no power to impose on a State officer, as such, any duty whatever, and compel him to perform it."[55]

Should *Printz* and *New York* be read as reintroducing the *Dennison* doctrine into constitutional jurisprudence—more specifically, as reintroducing *Dennison* with respect to targeted federal statutes that are addressed to nonjudicial state officials, and that are grounded upon the Commerce Clause or Congress's other Article I powers? We think not. Note, to begin, that the Court, in *FERC v Mississippi*—a state sovereignty case preceding *Printz* and *New York*—specifically disavowed *Dennison* as "not representative of the law today," and stated that the federal power to define the legal positions of private parties encompassed an ancillary power to impose some duties upon (nonjudicial as well as judicial) state officials: "[s]tate legislative [as well as] judicial decisionmakers must give preclusive effect to federal enactments concerning nongovernmental activity."[56] More important, to read *Printz* and *New York* as denying federal power to impose any targeted, coercive duties on nonjudicial state officials would be to read them as undermining the large and long-standing body of preemption case law in which, time and again, the Court has either explicitly authorized or at least not questioned the entry of declaratory or injunctive relief against state enforcement officials, prohibiting the officials from

---

[53] By "duty," here, we mean a legal, sanction-backed duty.

[54] 65 US 66 (1861), overruled, *Puerto Rico v Branstad*, 483 US 219 (1987).

[55] 65 US at 107.

[56] 456 US at 761, 766.

enforcing preempted state laws (specifically, state laws preempted by federal law that is grounded in the Commerce Clause or another Article I power, and not in the Reconstruction Amendments), under threat of civil or criminal contempt. (Such a duty of nonenforcement is clearly targeted; only state officials, not the population at large, have the power to enforce state law.[57]) To give but one example, in *Morales v Trans World Airlines, Inc.*, with Justice Scalia (the author of *Printz*) writing for the majority, the Supreme Court held that state guidelines governing airline fare advertising were preempted by the federal Airline Deregulation Act, and sustained the district court's entry of that portion of a permanent injunction against the Attorney General of Texas which obliged him not to enforce the preempted guidelines against the airlines.[58] The Court in *Printz* and *New York* surely did not intend to call into question *Morales* and the numerous other cases like it.[59]

Indeed, a brief passage in *Printz* seemingly acknowledges that the federal government, by virtue of the Supremacy Clause, *does* have the power to impose targeted legal duties on state legislators and enforcement officials, not merely state adjudicators. This acknowledgment comes in the course of the Court's discussion of a passage from Federalist 27.

> These problems [in Justice Souter's interpretation of the passage] are avoided, of course, if [the passage is] taken to refer to nothing more (or less) than the duty owed to the National Government, on the part of *all* state officials, to enact, enforce,

---

[57] More precisely, only state officials typically have the power to enforce state law in the sense of bringing civil or criminal enforcement actions, or undertaking investigatory activities, in the name of the state. And in the cases referred to here, it is typically state officials alone who are made subject to the declaration or injunction enjoining enforcement. See also *South Carolina v Baker*, 485 US 505, 514 (1988) (suggesting that federal statute which "seek[s] to control or influence the manner in which States regulate private parties" is not "generally applicable") (internal quotation omitted).

[58] 504 US 374 (1992); see id at 380–82 (explicitly authorizing injunctive relief under *Ex parte Young*, 209 US 123 (1908)). For similar cases, see, for example, *Barnett Bank v Nelson*, 517 US 25 (1996); *Livadas v Bradshaw*, 512 US 107 (1994); *Gade v Nat'l Solid Wastes Management Ass'n*, 505 US 88 (1992); *Schneidewind v ANR Pipeline Co.*, 485 US 293 (1988); *Capital Cities Cable, Inc. v Crisp*, 467 US 691 (1984); *Shaw v Delta Air Lines, Inc.*, 463 US 85 (1983); *New Mexico v Mescalero Apache Tribe*, 462 US 324 (1983); *Washington v Washington State Commercial Passenger Fishing Vessel Ass'n*, 443 US 658 (1979); *Douglas v Seacoast Products, Inc.*, 431 US 265 (1977); *Ray v Atlantic Richfield Co.*, 435 US 151 (1978); *Jones v Rath Packing Co.*, 430 US 519 (1977); *City of Burbank v Lockheed Air Terminal Inc.*, 411 US 624 (1973).

[59] Surely, too, the Court did not intend to overrule the line of cases authorizing suit under Section 1983 to enforce federal statutory rights. See *Maine v Thiboutot*, 448 US 1 (1980); *Golden State Transit Corp. v City of Los Angeles*, 493 US 103 (1989).

and interpret state law in such fashion as not to obstruct the operation of federal law, and the attendant reality that all state actions constituting such obstruction, even legislative acts, are *ipso facto* invalid.[60]

This passage is hardly crystalline. But, interpreted in the context of *Morales* and the preemption decisions that *Morales* epitomizes, the passage should be understood to confirm the existence of a demarcation additional to those explicitly set forth by *Printz* and *New York*: the demarcation between preemption and commandeering.

The question remains whether Congress has the power to impose targeted duties on nonjudicial state officials directly, or whether instead it must always do so indirectly, via the federal courts. On the "indirect" view, Congress can pass a statute changing the legal position of private parties, but until a federal court imposes concomitant duties on state officials through some kind of judicial directive, those officials remain free to act as if the federal statute had never been enacted. Surprising as this view might seem, there is real textual support for it in a passage from the *New York* opinion:

> Additional cases cited by the United States [to demonstrate the federal power to issue directives to state governments] discuss the power of federal *courts* to order state officials to comply with federal law. Again, however, the text of the Constitution plainly confers this authority on the federal courts, the "judicial Power" of which "shall extend to all Cases, in Law and Equity, arising under this Constitution. . . ." The Constitution contains no analogous grant of authority to Congress. Moreover, the Supremacy Clause makes federal law paramount over the contrary positions of state officials; the power of federal courts to enforce federal law thus presupposes some authority to order state officials to comply.
>
> In sum, the cases relied upon by the United States hold only that federal law is enforceable in state courts and that federal courts may in proper circumstances order state officials to comply with federal law, propositions that by no means imply any authority on the part of Congress to mandate state regulation.[61]

---

[60] 117 S Ct at 2374. The language from *New York* discussed immediately below, see 505 US at 179, also constitutes a recognition by the Court that at least some federal governmental entities—namely, the federal courts—can impose certain duties upon nonjudicial state officials.

[61] 505 US at 179 (citations omitted). This language, in turn, seems to trace back to Justice O'Connor's opinion in *FERC v Mississippi*. See 456 US at 784 n 13 (O'Connor concurring in the judgment in part and dissenting in part).

What is striking here is both the Court's distinction between judicial and nonjudicial federal directives, and its failure to describe
any category of directives that federal bodies other than the federal
courts can issue to state (legislative and executive) officials. One
of the Court's tasks in future federalism cases will be to provide
a definitive gloss on this language from *New York*, and a definitive
answer to the problem of direct versus indirect duties.

Our own conclusion is that *Printz* and *New York*, together with
other existing lines of federalism cases, are best interpreted as rejecting the indirect view. Congress can, we think, directly issue
preemption commands to state legislators or executives and back
up such commands with the threat of civil or criminal sanction,
quite apart from the power of the federal courts (acknowledged in
New York) to do so. Consider the substantial body of federal criminal law applicable to state officials, and the multiple Supreme
Court cases upholding the prosecution and conviction of state officials pursuant to these statutes.[62] The indirect view would eviscerate or at least gravely disrupt this jurisprudence. Or consider the
well-established doctrine that, where a preempted state law has
wrongly been enforced by the state, injured parties may sue for
damages under Section 1983.[63] The indirect view would require
that state officials or state subdivisions never be made defendant
to such suits, at least prior to a judicial injunction, declaration, or
other directive against them.[64]

In sum, *New York* and *Printz* are best interpreted, in the wider
context of relevant case law, to mean the following: Congress can-

---

[62] A recent example is *Salinas v United States*, 118 S Ct 469 (1997). As the Court has
explained: "[T]he cases in this Court which have recognized an immunity from civil suit
for state officials have presumed the existence of federal criminal liability as a restraining
factor on the conduct of state officials." *United States v Gillock*, 445 US 360, 372 (1980).

[63] See *Golden State Transit Corp. v City of Los Angeles*, 493 US 103 (1989).

[64] A further, significant piece of evidence is the Court's opinion in *Printz* itself, which
fails to mention *New York*'s distinction between federal judicial and non-judicial directives.
Finally, as a matter of constitutional interpretation, the indirect view seems tenuous. The
power to issue a sanction-backed directive is hardly a uniquely judicial power, at least where
the directive is issued to a class of persons ("all state law enforcement officers," etc.), rather
than a named individual. The Court's reasoning in the passage from *New York* implies the
conclusion that a federal statute that is addressed to private persons, and that otherwise
lies within Congress's Article I powers, cannot be accompanied by a penalty provision
threatening those persons with sanction for noncompliance. But since this conclusion is
clearly wrong—since, in truth, there is nothing uniquely judicial about the "authority to
order [persons] to comply" with federal law—then there is no Article III basis for reserving
to the federal courts the unique power to direct compliance by state officials.

not commandeer either state legislators or state executive officials, but it can directly impose some targeted, coercive duties on state executive officials and state legislators[65] pursuant to its power to define the legal positions of private persons. This leads us to the next question: What kind of targeted, coercive duties for state officials are permissible under *New York* and *Printz*, and what kind constitute impermissible commandeering?

B. NEGATIVE VERSUS AFFIRMATIVE DUTIES

Existing scholarship on *Printz* and *New York* has tended to assume, without much discussion, the proposition for which we have just argued at some length: that the federal power of preemption includes a power to impose certain duties on state officials. Moreover, existing scholarship has tended to assume, without argument, the separate proposition that the category of permissible duties are negative duties, duties of inaction, as opposed to positive duties, duties of action.[66] Notably, however, the Court in *Printz* and *New York* does not articulate an action/inaction distinction—not surprisingly, given the Court's failure to confirm, with any clarity, the more basic and logically prior demarcation between commandeering and preemption. We agree with other scholars that the commandeering/preemption distinction is most plausibly and sympathetically fleshed out in terms of (some version of) the action/inaction distinction. But a fair bit of conceptual, interpretive, and normative work is required to accomplish the mapping from preemption onto negative duties, and from commandeering onto affirmative ones.

Let us begin with a paradigm. Paradigmatically, Congress may

---

[65] Although the Court in *Tenney v Brandhove*, 341 US 367 (1951), and its sequelae, see *Bogan v Scott-Harris*, 118 S Ct 966 (1998); *Supreme Court of Va. v Consumers Union*, 446 US 719 (1980); *Lake Country Estates, Inc. v Tahoe Regional Planning Agency*, 440 US 391 (1979), has repeatedly held that state legislators are absolutely immune from suit under Section 1983, we take it that this immunity is statutory, not constitutional. Congress can, under the rubric of preemption, impose duties upon state legislators as well as executive officials. See *United States v Gillock*, 445 US 360 (1980) (finding no state legislative immunity in federal criminal prosecution). Notably, the Court in *Printz* took great pains to deny the import of the legislator/executive distinction, see 117 S Ct at 2380–81, and nowhere suggested that the scope of duties constitutionally imposable upon state executives was wider than that imposable upon legislators.

[66] See Jackson, 111 Harv L Rev at 2201–02; Hills, 96 Mich L Rev at 870–71; Caminker, 1997 Supreme Court Review at 235–36 (all cited in note 1).

oblige state executive officers not to enforce a statute or regulation that creates duties for private persons—this is what is at stake in garden-variety preemption cases—and, we take it, Congress also has the constitutional power to require state legislators (or state agency officials with rule-making power) not to enact a state statute or regulation that creates duties for private persons.[67] For short, we'll call this the "Preemption Paradigm." Conversely, the federalism doctrine set forth in *Printz* and *New York* prohibits Congress from obliging state officials to enact or enforce a statute or regulation that creates duties for private persons. As the Court explained, in the concluding paragraph of the *Printz* opinion:

> We held in *New York* that Congress cannot compel the States to enact or enforce a federal regulatory program. Today we hold that Congress cannot circumvent that prohibition by conscripting the State's officers directly. The Federal Government may neither issue directives requiring the States to address particular problems, nor command the States' officers, or those of their political subdivisions, to administer or enforce a federal regulatory program.[68]

For short, we'll call this paradigmatic case of impermissible federal duties the "Commandeering Paradigm." What is the distinction between the duties imposed upon state officers in the Preemption Paradigm, and the duties imposed upon them in the Commandeering Paradigm?

Some apparent distinctions either are implausible or fail to sort between the two paradigms at all. For example, although *Printz* and *New York* repeatedly state that Congress may not "compel the States to enact or enforce a federal regulatory program," or words to that effect,[69] there surely can be federal statutes that do not literally do that—that do not require state officers to enact or enforce *duties* for private persons—but nonetheless constitute impermissible commandeering. Imagine a federal statute (backed by the

---

[67] See note 65 (discussing legislative immunity).

[68] 117 S Ct at 2384.

[69] See, for example, *Printz*, 117 S Ct at 2369 ("the Brady Act purports to direct state law enforcement officers to participate . . . in the administration of a federally enacted regulatory scheme"); id at 2380 ("[*New York* involved] a federal statute that . . . required the States to enact or administer a federal regulatory program"); id at 2383 (" '[t]he Federal Government may not compel the States to enact or administer a federal regulatory program' ") (quoting *New York*, 505 US at 188).

threat of sanctions for noncomplying states or state officials) that unconditionally requires the state to enact and administer an entitlement program, rather than a program of regulation. We doubt that the Court would uphold a federally required entitlement program of this kind. There is no connection, even an apparent or intuitive one, between federalism values and the regulation/entitlement distinction.[70]

A second distinction between the Preemption Paradigm and the Commandeering Paradigm that can quickly be rejected is the distinction between federal duties that negatively affect the level of state resources and those that do not.[71] For this distinction fails even to observe the boundaries between the two paradigms. Some cases that fall within the Commandeering Paradigm will have very little resource impact, if any, upon the state—consider a federal requirement that the state legislature simply enact a particular duty-creating law, with this law to be implemented by private suit rather than official prosecution. Conversely, cases that fall within the Preemption Paradigm—most obviously, the federal preemption of state taxes[72]—can diminish state resources considerably.

A third unworkable distinction between the Commandeering Paradigm and the Preemption Paradigm is the distinction between a federal requirement that obliges the state to depart from the status quo, and a federal requirement that does not. The problem here is defining the state of affairs that constitutes "the status quo" in a way that is noncircular and nonarbitrary and yet observes the boundary between the two paradigms.[73] Why not say that the state of affairs in which the state enacts and enforces a regulatory program is the status quo, and thus that the Commandeering Paradigm requires no state departure from this baseline? Clearly, to say that the status quo cannot involve federal commandeering

---

[70] See *Printz*, 117 S Ct at 2370–71 (distinguishing early federal statute that required state courts to record applications for citizenship, and similar statutes, with reference to judicial/ nonjudicial demarcation, not by exempting entitlement commandeering from scope of anti-commandeering rule).

[71] See *National League of Cities v Usery*, 426 US at 846 (relying, in part, on substantial costs imposed by Fair Labor Standards Act upon states and subdivisions to justify invalidating the statute), overruled, *Garcia v San Antonio Metropolitan Transit Auth.*, 469 US 528 (1985).

[72] See, for example, *Aloha Airlines, Inc. v Director of Taxation*, 464 US 7 (1983).

[73] For a discussion of various possible definitions of the status quo baseline, see Seth F. Kreimer, *Allocational Sanctions: The Problem of Negative Rights in a Positive State*, 132 U Pa L Rev 1293, 1351–74 (1984).

would be viciously circular; we are here trying to define commandeering by reference to the status quo. Alternately and noncircu-
larly, one might define the status quo as (*a*) the state of affairs that
would have ensued, absent federal intervention, or (*b*) the state of
affairs that the federal government is authorized to effect or aim
at, consistent with its constitutional powers (and with individual
rights), apart from the anticommandeering doctrine. But using
baseline (*a*) means that only a subset of otherwise-constitutional
commandeerings covered by the Commandeering Paradigm—the
subset where the commandeered regulatory program is one that
the state itself would not have enacted, absent federal intervention—are unconstitutional. And using baseline (*b*) means that *no*
otherwise-constitutional commandeerings covered by the Commandeering Paradigm are unconstitutional (in short, that the
anticommandeering doctrine does no constitutional work at all).

This leads us, finally, to the action/inaction distinction. At the
outset, we stress that the distinction is a contested one. What, precisely, makes some person's (or some official's) behavior an "action," as opposed to a mere failure to act, has been and remains
a topic of considerable controversy in the philosophical literature.[74]
But there are at least some philosophically respectable versions of
the distinction that will count the duty imposed upon state officials
in the Commandeering Paradigm as an affirmative duty—a duty
of action—and the duty imposed in the Preemption Paradigm as
a merely negative duty of inaction. For example, one prevalent
account construes the action/inaction distinction as a distinction
between physical movement and immobility.[75] On this account, it
is roughly the case that P "acts" just in case she moves her body
(P's body is voluntarily moved by P), and that otherwise there is
inaction or failure to act by P. And, indeed, one of the differences
between the Commandeering Paradigm and the Preemption Paradigm *is* the difference between movement and immobility. The
enactment and enforcement of a duty-creating statute does indeed
require physical movements by state legislators and enforcement
officers. Some state legislators must open their mouths or raise
their hands to vote "yea" for the statute; and state enforcement

---

[74] See generally Jonathan Bennett, *The Act Itself* (Clarendon, 1995).

[75] See, for example, Michael S. Moore, *Act and Crime: The Philosophy of Action and Its
Implications for Criminal Law* (Clarendon, 1993).

officers must raise their pens, or touch their fingers to computer keyboards, so as to issue arrest warrants, subpoenas, indictments, and so on. By contrast, state officials can not-enact or not-enforce a duty-creating statute by remaining entirely immobile. Note further that the movement/immobility distinction correctly categorizes the case of a federally required entitlement program as a case of commandeering—at least where the entitlement (say, an entitlement to state monies) would not exist absent the enactment of a statute or other positive law by the state, since once again the enactment of positive law requires physical movements by the enactors.

So the action/inaction distinction (at least certain versions of it) can do the conceptual work of sorting between the Commandeering Paradigm and the Preemption Paradigm. Further, the conceptual mapping from preemption onto inaction, and commandeering onto action, has some interpretive plausibility, given the role that the action/inaction distinction has played in other parts of the Court's jurisprudence—specifically, in defining the content of constitutional rights. For example, in the *DeShaney* case, where it denied a due process claim brought by an abused child whom governmental social workers had failed to protect, the Court quite clearly and definitively stated that the Due Process Clause generally imposes only negative duties on government officials, not affirmative duties.[76] There are also some textual hints in the state sovereignty jurisprudence itself (although not much more than that) that the preemption versus commandeering distinction does indeed map onto inaction versus action.[77]

Finally, we suggest that there is a plausible or apparent link between the action/inaction distinction, and at least some of the normative considerations undergirding constitutional federalism. Two of the federalism values we described in Part I—the value of tyranny prevention, and the value of political community—seem to implicate, or plausibly implicate, the distinction. As for tyranny prevention: just as there is considerable philosophical support for the "deontological" view that the action/inaction distinction has

---

[76] *DeShaney v Winnebago County Dept. of Social Services*, 489 US 189, 195–97 (1989).

[77] See *FERC v Mississippi*, 456 US at 762–63 n 27, 765, 767–68 n 30 (noting permissibility of even certain "affirmative" federal obligations for state officials); *Printz*, 117 S Ct at 2374 (noting obligation of state officials "not to obstruct" the operation of federal law).

general moral significance,[78] so it seems plausible that governmental action is worse than governmental inaction, and specifically that tyrannical governmental action is worse than tyrannical governmental inaction. Indeed, this apparent link between action/inaction and the value of tyranny prevention underlies the Court's reasoning in *De Shaney*.

As for the value of political community, it seems plausible that federal statutes compelling a particular subcategory of state action—a subcategory we shall call "authoritative utterances"—do indeed infringe upon the state's functioning as a political community in a distinctive and emphatic way. By "authoritative utterance," we mean a law-producing action: an action by a state official that is an instance of some legal power of hers to define legal rights, duties, and other legal positions.[79] Classic authoritative utterances include the legislative action of enacting a statute, the executive action of issuing a command (e.g., an order to produce information, or an order placing some person under arrest), and the judicial action of imposing a sanction upon, or issuing an injunction to, a particular person.

A requirement that state legislators enact a particular statute seems, somehow, to be more of an interference with state autonomy than a requirement that they refrain from enacting a particular statute. For in the case of the affirmative requirement, there is a discrete, authoritative utterance—the enactment of the statute—that the legislators have been compelled to produce. By contrast, in the case of the negative requirement, it is not (or may not be) true of any utterance that the legislators have produced, that it was thus compelled. It is not (or may not be) true of any entry in the set of legislative utterances (the *Statutes at Large*) that the legislators were obliged by external, federal compulsion to produce that utterance. Similarly, it seems, a requirement that state executives

---

[78] For an overview of the debate between deontologists and consequentialists, see Shelly Kagan, *Normative Ethics* (Westview, 1998).

[79] Notably, however, the statute invalidated in *Printz* did not compel authoritative utterances; state officers were simply required to investigate the legality of gun sales. The "take title" provision invalidated in *New York* did not compel authoritative utterances either, at least insofar as that provision simply required the states to take physical possession of the nuclear waste; however, since such possession, or "title" apart from possession, might lead to judgments against the state, which the state would then be obliged to pay, "authoritative utterances" were arguably involved in *New York*. See 505 US at 154–55, 174–77 (quoting and discussing "take title" provision).

perform an authoritative utterance, of whatever kind, intrudes more sharply on political-community values than a requirement that they refrain from such performance.

In short, we believe that there is a good conceptual, interpretive, and normative case for construing the preemption/commandeering distinction as a distinction between inaction and action. *If* the Court is to craft a jurisprudence that prohibits commandeering, but permits the kind of federal duties for state officials that the preemption case law has long recognized, *then* it should define impermissible commandeering as a targeted, coercive duty for state legislative or executive officials that *requires action* on the part of the officials, and permissible preemption as a duty (perhaps targeted, perhaps coercive, and perhaps addressed to nonjudicial officials) that *does not require official action.*[80] For the remainder of the article, both in .this Part and in subsequent Parts, we use the commandeering/preemption distinction and the action/inaction distinction interchangeably. We shall now argue that the commandeering/preemption distinction—even cashed sympathetically as action versus inaction—is not truly justified by the values of constitutional federalism.

C. PREEMPTION, COMMANDEERING, AND THE VALUES OF
CONSTITUTIONAL FEDERALISM

It seems clear that the preemption/commandeering distinction has little to do with the first two federalism values we described in Part I: the value of responsiveness to geographic diversity, and the value of innovation. A federal statute requiring inaction by state officers (permissible preemption) can dampen interjurisdictional policy variation, no less than a federal statute requiring official action (impermissible commandeering).[81] Indeed, neither in *Printz* nor in *New York* did the Court seek to defend the

---

[80] There is, however, at least one way in which a straight action/inaction distinction is too crude a construal of the commandeering/preemption distinction. Presumably Congress can impose certain affirmative remedial duties upon state officials who breach their negative federal duties. Some such remedial duties, albeit affirmative, will not (we assume) constitute commandeering. See *Golden State Transit Corp. v City of Los Angeles*, 493 US 103 (1989) (upholding Section 1983 damages action against city, for breach of statutory duties under National Labor Relations Act). Undoubtedly, further refinements to the basic distinction between action and inaction will emerge if the Court explicitly adopts that distinction and persists in the anticommandeering jurisprudence.

[81] See Caminker, 95 Colum L Rev at 1078–79 (cited in note 1).

preemption/commandeering distinction with reference to the values of geographic diversity and innovation. Rather, those values are appropriately protected (if at all) through straight Commerce Clause doctrine plus the doctrines governing the scope of Congress's other Article I powers. These doctrines curb national uniformity, and thereby protect the values of diversity and innovation, by limiting the power of Congress to preempt *or* commandeer.

More plausibly, we have already suggested, there is a link between the preemption/commandeering distinction and the value of political community. In the case of federal directives compelling state actions—specifically, in the case of federal directives compelling authoritative utterances by state officials—there is a particular utterance (a particular state statute, say) that the federal government has compelled the state to perform. That surely seems worse for democratic self-governance than the case in which state officials merely have been compelled to refrain from certain utterances. Is it truly worse? We think not, and will now argue to the contrary.

The political-community defense of constitutional federalism rests upon the premise that it is intrinsically valuable for citizens to participate in governance. Democratic procedures and institutions are premised to have intrinsic value, apart from their instrumental value in improving the quality of governmental outcomes. It is further claimed that a federal regime (by virtue of the smaller size of state governments) instantiates this intrinsic value more fully than a unitary regime. How does commandeering undermine that? Commandeering, it must be stressed, does not change the participatory or democratic structure of state government. Although state legislators are now obliged to enact a statute, or state executives are now obliged to issue a directive, it remains the case that legislators are elected by majority vote at regular elections, that executives either are elected themselves or appointed by elected officials, and that state citizens retain whatever rights they otherwise would have to learn about, comment upon, criticize, and challenge the choices of state legislators and executives.

Rather, commandeering undermines self-governance by limiting the set of options that state legislators and executives have. The choice whether to perform the commandeered utterance is no longer a choice that is open to the officials and, derivatively, the citizenry; it is no longer a choice that is responsive to the exercise of electoral and other democratic rights by those citizens. But, of course, the same is true of preemption. Preemption, too, limits the choices of state legislators and executives, and in a precisely complementary way. While commandeering reduces the official's choice set from C_0 (perform the authoritative utterance, not-perform the utterance) to C_1 (perform the utterance), preemption reduces the choice set from C_0 (perform the authoritative utterance, not-perform the utterance) to C_2 (not-perform the utterance). In each case, some opportunity for state legislators, executives, and, derivatively, the state citizenry to shape the content of state law has been removed from them.[82]

To put the point another way: the total corpus of state law is defined both by the authoritative utterances that legislators and executives perform, and by the utterances that legislators and executives refrain from performing. By coercing performances *or* refrainings, commandeering *or* preemption constrains the content of state law and in that way reduces the extent to which state law can be shaped by intrinsically valuable procedures or institutions, thereby undermining the value of political community. But it is not the case that this value is especially or asymmetrically undermined by commandeering.

Why not say that affirmative shaping and negative shaping are differentially valuable—that the reduction of the state's choice set from C_0 to C_1 diminishes political community more than the reduction of the choice set from C_0 to C_2? We think this claim indefensible. The intrinsic value of political community, such as it may be, inheres in responsible decision making by state citizens, and in associated virtues such as deliberation, dialogue, open-mindedness, and impartiality. Qua the opportunity for decision making, there is no difference between the two reductions in choice sets. To explain why affirmative shaping and negative shaping are differentially valuable, one would need to appeal, not to the intrinsic value of decisionmaking, but to something else—say, the intrinsic value, for a state citizen, of *identifying* with the community of state citizens and its laws. The citizen identifies most strongly—or so it might be claimed—with the utterances that her legislators and

---

[82] Professor Caminker makes a similar point, id at 1077–78. In Part III.A. we qualify somewhat the claim that commandeering diminishes choice, but the qualification applies symmetrically to preemption.

executives have performed, not the utterances that they have refrained from performing. Therefore, compelled performance interferes with political community more gravely than compelled refraining. But even if there is something like such an identification
value realized by political communities, apart from the value of
responsible decision making, we do not see why citizens ought to
identify with affirmative utterances (as opposed to the overall corpus of state law), nor do we know of any empirical work to demonstrate that they do in fact thus identify.[83]

Finally, we come to the fourth value of federalism, and the one
explicitly invoked in *Printz* and *New York:* tyranny prevention.
Both commandeering and preemption may be tyranny-enhancing,
along some dimensions, as compared to straight federal or state
directives to private persons—we will not try to deny that here—
but we do deny that commandeering is especially tyranny-enhancing, as compared to preemption.

Consider again the choice set we called C_0: the choice between a
state official's performance of an authoritative utterance (or, more
generally, of an action) and her nonperformance of that utterance
(or, more generally, of that action). Let us assume that federalism
is tyranny-preventing, along a given dimension. That is, the federal
government's resolution of C_0 is more likely to be unjustifiably
responsive to the interests of the given group (economic interest
groups, officials of the relevant government, a homogeneous majority of the relevant citizenry) than the state's resolution of C_0.
If the federal government is permitted to decide whether the state
official should perform the action, then—we will imagine—that
decision is more likely to be tyrannical (in the given way) than a
simple decision by the state official, herself, whether to perform
the action. Why might this obtain? It might obtain because of the
kind of "accountability" considerations adduced by the Court in
Printz and *New York.*

> [W]here the Federal Government compels States to regulate,
> the accountability of both state and federal officials is dimin-
> ished. . . . [I]t may be state officials who will bear the brunt

---

[83] Indeed, we can readily imagine counterexamples to the claim that the state's authoritative utterances have a greater role in characterizing the state, and in fostering identification
(or disassociation) by state citizens, than state decisions to refrain from authoritative utterances. Imagine a state that refrains from proscribing marijuana use or assisted suicide, or
from regulating abortion.

of public disapproval, while the federal officials who devised
the regulatory program may remain insulated from the electoral ramifications of their decision. Accountability is thus diminished when, due to federal coercion, elected state officials
cannot regulate in accordance with the views of the local electorate in matters not pre-empted by federal regulation.[84]

But, again, this is not an argument against commandeering, as
such, because both commandeering and preemption shift C_0 from
the state level to the federal level. When federal officials preempt
a state statute, they can be confident—if the accountability story
is correct—that state rather than federal officials will be held accountable for the nonenactment of the statute. Similarly, when
federal officials commandeer a state statute, they can be confident—following the same story—that state rather than federal officials will be held responsible for the enactment of the statute.
Pace the Court's argument in *New York*,[85] we see no asymmetry
here. The choice between state action and state inaction may be
less accountable to the electorate, where that choice is directed by
a federal statute rather than resolved by state officials themselves,
but, if so, this is true whether the federal directive compels action
or inaction.[86]

What about the claim that tyranny is more problematic when
state action, as opposed to inaction, ensues? The defender of the
preemption/commandeering line might try to reformulate the
Court's accountability argument in *New York* and *Printz*; the point,
she might argue, is not that compelled state inaction is more likely
to be accountable to the electorate than compelled action, but
rather that unaccountable state inaction is simply less troubling.
But is it really? To begin, it bears emphasis that the anticommandeering rule becomes nonsuperfluous just where it involves commandeered state actions that do not violate constitutional rights.
The federal statutes in *Printz* and *New York* did not coerce state
officials to perform actions that violated the First Amendment, the
Takings Clause, the Due Process Clause, the Equal Protection

---

[84] *New York*, 505 US at 168–69. See *Printz*, 117 S Ct at 2377.

[85] See 505 US at 168–69.

[86] For similar skepticism about the Court's accountability rationale, with respect either
to preemption/commandeering or to the cooperative federalism demarcation, see Caminker, 96 Colum L Rev at 1061–74; Hills, 96 Mich L Rev at 824–30; Jackson, 111 Harv
L Rev at 2200–05 (all cited in note 1).

Clause, or any other part of the Bill of Rights; if the federal statutes *had* commandeered rights-violating state action, the Court would not have needed to invoke state sovereignty to justify invalidating those statutes. So the anticommandeering rule (in its non-superfluous portion) involves state action that lies within the zone of permissible action sketched out by the Bill of Rights.

We doubt that state action, at least state action within this zone, is more likely to produce significant harm to the interests or welfare of the citizenry, or of some portion thereof, than state inaction. To see the point, consider the harm to a person P that ensues when P dies. We'll assume, arguendo, that a state government (in some way) produces a graver harm to P's interests or welfare when governmental officials intentionally and directly kill P than when they merely fail to prevent P's death. Yet it violates the Bill of Rights for the state government to intentionally and directly kill P.[87] Conversely, where the state governmental action commandeered by federal statute is constitutionally permissible under the Bill of Rights—and thus the anticommandeering rule comes into play—we see no reason to think that such action is worse per se for P than state governmental inaction. For example, state governmental inaction causes P's death when government fails to regulate the polluters who emit carcinogens into the air that P breathes.[88] State governmental action causes P's death when government prohibits firms from selling P the medication that would cure the cancer. Is P's death worse for him or anyone else when Congress requires state governments to prohibit firms from selling P the medication than when Congress requires state governments to leave the carcinogen-emitting polluters unregulated? We think not.[89]

---

[87] More precisely, it violates the Bill of Rights for state government to intentionally, directly, and unjustifiably kill P. See *Sacramento v Lewis*, 118 S Ct 1708, 1718 (1998) ("It is . . . behavior at the other end of the culpability spectrum [from negligence] that would most probably support a substantive due process claim; conduct intended to injure in some way unjustifiable by any government interest is the sort of official action most likely to rise to the conscience-shocking level."). The qualification for justifiable killing, here, does not materially change our argument. Arguably, a justifiable governmental killing of P is no worse for him than a governmental failure to prevent his death. And even if this is not true, the case of a justifiable killing is a special one; direct and intentional killings by government will generally violate the Bill of Rights. Indeed, insofar as the proponent of *Printz* and *New York* is focused on tyrannical governmental action—action unjustifiably responsive to particular groups or persons—such action will by definition be unjustified.

[88] On inaction as causal, see Bennett, *The Act Itself* at 126–30 (cited in note 74).

[89] What about the claim that, in general, commandeered state action causes serious welfare setbacks, like death, illness, and poverty, while commandeered state inaction will cause

Clearly, there are large, normative issues here that this article cannot hope to resolve definitively.[90] Someone who believes in the asymmetry of governmental action and inaction is unlikely to be persuaded otherwise by our brief discussion. The most we can really accomplish here is to clarify the normative issues raised by the preemption/commandeering distinction. We suggest that the best defense for that distinction rests upon the value of tyranny prevention, rather than the other federalism values of diversity-responsiveness, innovation, and political community. So the Court in *Printz* and *New York* was correct to invoke that value, as opposed to these other three. But the Court went astray in suggesting that differential accountability could explain the distinction. Rather, the claim would have to be that unaccountable action and unaccountable inaction are differentially problematic. And we have tried to undermine that claim, insofar as it is relevant here. Federal commandeering, insofar as it compels state actions that do not violate the Bill of Rights, is not more problematic, we think, than federal preemption.[91]

---

less serious setbacks? If commandeered action and inaction are indeed equally accountable, or unaccountable, as we argued above, we see no reason for this asymmetry.

It has been suggested to us that the anticommandeering doctrine is tyranny-reducing, not in the short-run sense that particular acts of commandeering are particularly likely to be unaccountable or problematic, but in the long-run sense that commandeering enfeebles the states as institutions capable of resisting the national government. Given the host of ways in which preemption and commandeering can symmetrically enfeeble states, for example, by diminishing interstate diversity, by reducing state options and the concomitant intrinsic value of state politics, or by diminishing state resources, we are skeptical about this long-run argument as well.

[90] One standard philosophical justification for the action/inaction distinction, the one we have just addressed insofar as it bears on *Printz* and *New York*, is that certain actions are morally worse than parallel inaction. See, for example, Kagan, *Normative Ethics*, at 70–78 (cited in note 78). Another standard philosophical justification is that affirmative duties are more "demanding"—they interfere more with a person's own life plan—than negative duties. See, for example, Bennett, *The Act Itself*, at 143–63 (cited in note 74). We doubt, however, that this latter justification applies to governmental actors as opposed to private individuals.

[91] Professor Hills develops a different argument for the preemption/commandeering distinction. The argument is subtle, but we take it that Hills, centrally, is willing to concede the harm to federalism values caused by preemption. Rather, he claims, the commandeering power is uniquely unnecessary for the attainment of national goals. Where Congress needs state governments to act, it can purchase action through voluntary agreement with the states; by contrast, intergovernmental bargaining is insufficient to secure warranted preemption, because states would "hold out" for large payments by the federal government. See 96 Mich L Rev at 855–900 (cited in note 1). We are not persuaded, at least insofar as this differential holdout argument is meant to justify the doctrines set forth in *Printz* and *New York*. First, Hills seems to equate commandeering with a federal duty to regulate, and preemption with a federal duty not to regulate. This is not correct, on our reading of *Printz* and *New York*; rather, commandeering equals a federal duty to act, and preemption equals

III. The Explicit Demarcations: Cooperative Federalism, General Applicability, and Adjudication

In this Part, we discuss the three lines of demarcation between permissible and impermissible federal statutes that the Court explicitly set forth in both *New York* and *Printz* and that have been the main focus of scholarly writing in this area: the demarcations concerning cooperative federalism, general applicability, and adjudication. As we see it, these are demarcations *within the set of* affirmative federal duties, since the federal government may permissibly impose negative duties upon state officials as an accompaniment to its power to preempt state law. Thus understood, the three demarcations—like the more basic and implicit distinction between preemption and commandeering—are not justified by the values of constitutional federalism.

A. COOPERATIVE FEDERALISM

The cooperative federalism demarcation distinguishes between so-called "conditional spending" or "conditional preemption" and straight commandeering. Congress may not "compel" the states

---

a federal duty to refrain from action. If, for example, the federal government obliges a state legislature to *repeal an existing regulation*, then that counts as commandeering—because the legislature has been obliged to take the action of repeal—on our understanding of the preemption/commandeering distinction. (There is a possible refinement to the action/inaction interpretation mentioned in note 80, for affirmative remedial duties, but a federal duty to repeal an existing regulation is not necessarily remedial; it might just be deregulatory.) Why should there be lesser holdout problems in securing a state's repeal of an existing regulation than in securing agreement not to enact the regulation in the first place?

Even leaving this point aside, we are not convinced by Hills's argument. *Printz* and *New York* concern the federal power to impose duties upon state legislatures and executives, not the federal power to impose duties upon (*a*) private persons, (*b*) federal officials, or (*c*) state adjudicators. Call the regime in which the federal government only has the power to impose duties upon (*a*), (*b*), and (*c*) the "Baseline Regime." What Hills needs to show, to justify *Printz* and *New York*, is that (1) the Baseline Regime must be supplemented by a federal power to oblige state legislators and executives to refrain from action (paradigmatically, to refrain from regulation), because of insuperable holdout problems otherwise; but (2) the Baseline Regime need not be supplemented by a federal power to oblige state legislators and executives to act, because of the absence of significant holdout problems here. We do not think Hills has demonstrated that, or even focused on the problem in this way. Note that, in the Baseline Regime, state legislatures could enact regulations that conflict with federal law, and state enforcement officials could prosecute violators, but state and federal adjudicators would not impose penalties on the violators. Further, the federal government could enact its own regulations and enforce them through the federal courts. This is the baseline from which the federal government would need to purchase state legislative or executive action or inaction; relative to that baseline, we are not convinced that differential holdout problems afflict the two kinds of purchases.

to "enact or enforce a federal regulatory program"[92] (on our interpretation, to perform actions), but it may "encourage"[93] the states to do so, either by (1) making the payment of federal monies to a state conditional upon the state's performance of the actions, or (2) making nonpreemption of state law conditional upon the state's performance of the actions. This demarcation was integral to the holding of *New York*, where the Court struck down one provision of the federal statute at stake, but upheld two others (corresponding to the two permissible subcategories of conditional spending and conditional preemption); and it was implicitly reaffirmed by the Court in *Printz*.[94]

A fair bit of doctrinal work remains to be done in fleshing out the precise content of the commandeering/cooperative federalism distinction. We take it that commandeering occurs where Congress induces state officials to perform actions by threatening a sanction for nonperformance.[95] The problem then becomes distinguishing between the impermissible threat of a "sanction" and a permissible threat to terminate federal funding or initiate federal preemption unless the action is performed. The Court's basic understanding of this distinction, at least the basic understanding that emerges in *New York*, seems to be this: If Congress threatens state officials with some outcome O, conditional on their failure to perform the actions, where it would be *unconstitutional for Congress to impose O unconditionally*, then that counts as commandeering. By contrast, if Congress threatens state officials with some outcome O', conditional on their failure to perform the actions, where it would be constitutional for Congress to impose O' unconditionally, that counts as permissible "encouragement."[96] Conditional spending and preemption statutes fall on the permissible side of this demarcation (because Congress can unconditionally deny federal funds to the States, and can unconditionally preempt state law). By contrast, the following cases, all of which seem intuitively

---

[92] *Printz*, 117 S Ct at 2384.

[93] *New York*, 505 US at 166.

[94] See notes 18–19 and accompanying text.

[95] If the imposition of an affirmative but unenforced federal duty upon the states were sufficient to constitute commandeering, the Court's frequent references to "compulsion" and "coercion" would be otiose. See, for example, *Printz*, 117 S Ct at 2371 n 2, 2375, 2379, 2383, 2384; *New York*, 505 US at 149, 161, 165, 168, 174, 175, 188.

[96] See, for example, *New York*, 505 US at 175–77.

to be cases of commandeering, are indeed classified that way by the basic test here described: (1) Congress threatens that, unless the actions are performed, the state itself will be "fined," that is, state tax dollars (untraceable to previous federal grants) will be confiscated by federal officers;[97] (2) Congress threatens that, unless the actions are performed, state officers will be personally fined; (3) Congress threatens that, unless the actions are performed, state officers will be jailed.

Note, however, that this basic approach may need to be amended if the anticommandeering doctrine is to have practical significance. For, given the wide range of outcomes that Congress can unconditionally impose, this approach seemingly enables Congress to circumvent the anticommandeering doctrine with ease. The problem of "unconstitutional conditions" looms, here as elsewhere in constitutional law. For example, what is to prevent Congress from making the payment of highway funds to the states conditional upon state enactment of legislation restricting abortion, homosexual sodomy, and the possession of guns near schools?[98] What is to prevent Congress from threatening that, where a state fails to enact and enforce a particular program to regulate nuclear waste, all waste-disposal laws (or all environmental laws!) in that state will be preempted?[99] Either the commandeering/cooperative federalism distinction will be refined by the Court, such that certain action-inducing threats will count as commandeering, notwithstanding the fact that the threatened outcome could be imposed unconditionally; or, seemingly, the no-commandeering prohibition will become a formality.[100]

We doubt that the Court will succeed in refining the commandeering/cooperative federalism demarcation in a coherent and workable fashion. In the area of conditional spending, there

---

[97] See *New York v United States*, 326 US 572 (1946) (indicating that Congress cannot levy tax falling only upon the States).

[98] See, for example, *South Dakota v Dole*, 483 US 203 (1987) (upholding federal statute that conditioned highway funds upon state adoption of 21 as the drinking age); *Virginia v Browner*, 80 F3d 869 (4th Cir 1996) (upholding federal statute that conditioned highway funds upon acceptable state air-pollution plan).

[99] See, for example, *FERC v Mississippi*, 456 US at 764–70 (upholding conditional-preemption statute, threatening sweeping preemption of state law).

[100] See Lynn A. Baker, *Conditional Federal Spending after Lopez*, 95 Colum L Rev 1911 (1995) (discussing risk that Congress's conditional spending power may moot federalism constraints on regulation).

is in fact a refinement already on the books, one briefly mentioned by the Court in *New York:* the so-called *Dole* test, which requires that a spending condition be "germane[]," that is, "reasonably related to the purpose of the expenditure."[101] But the Court has never, in fact, invalidated a conditional spending program for failing the "germaneness" requirement—in particular, it did not do so either in *Dole* or in *New York* itself—and with good reason: the germaneness requirement, in its current form, is vacuous. Consider three possible conditions upon the granting of federal highway funds to the state: (*a*) that the state maintain the highways in good physical repair, (*b*) that the state raise the drinking age to 21, and (*c*) that the state prohibit gun possession in school yards. Intuitively, the first condition is germane, the second (actually upheld by the Court in *Dole*) is a boundary case, and the third is nongermane. But can the intuition be justified? To do so, we need a nonvacuous criterion for individuating purposes, one that the Court has as yet failed to provide. The third condition is nongermane if the purpose of the federal grant is "highway safety." But why not say that its purpose is "physical safety," including both highway safety *and* safety from gun violence? In theory, an individuation criterion might require that a spending condition be germane to the "maximally narrow" (but still constitutional) construal of the purpose behind the spending program, apart from the condition. Even assuming the notion of "maximally narrow" is coherent, it is clear that this kind of criterion is much too restrictive to permit the spending programs upheld in *Dole* or, for that matter, *New York.* The permissible purpose of "maintaining the physical condition of highways" is narrower than the purpose the Court needed to invoke in *Dole*, namely, highway safety. So some lumping of narrow purposes is permissible—but the Court has as yet provided absolutely no clue as to the boundary between permissible and impermissible lumping.

As for the area of conditional preemption, the Court has yet even to announce a doctrinal refinement analogous to the *Dole* "germaneness" test—let alone a workable and coherent one. *New*

---

[101] *South Dakota v Dole*, 483 US at 208; *New York*, 505 US at 172. The other parts of the four-pronged *Dole* test are not responsive to the problem of unconstitutional conditions raised here. Although *Dole* further suggests that a spending statute satisfying the test might nonetheless be unconstitutionally "coercive," see 483 US at 211, it gives no explanation what that means.

York simply stated that "where Congress has the authority to regulate private activity under the Commerce Clause, we have recognized Congress's power to offer States the choice of regulating that activity according to federal standards or having state law preempted by federal regulation";[102] and *Printz* added nothing to this formulation. This unrefined formulation is problematic, as Professor Rick Hills has explained: "If there are no limits on Congress's power to use conditional preemption, then *New York* is a meaningless formality, because the national government could always require that state and local governments either make policy according to federal standards or disband themselves [i.e., have all state and local law within the scope of federal power preempted]."[103] Indeed, the Court in *FERC v Mississippi*, the pre–*New York* decision from which conditional preemption doctrine stems, held that Congress could induce state electricity and gas regulatory commissions to adopt certain federal policies by means of a sweeping threat of federal preemption. (The permissible threat was that, if the commissions failed to adopt the policies, state regulation of electric and gas utilities would be preempted.)

In sum, the constitutional permissibility of conditional spending and conditional preemption threatens to make the anticommandeering rule of *Printz* and *New York* a practical nullity. But even on the assumption that the anticommandeering rule (as eventually refined by the Court) turns out to be coherent, workable, and practically important, we propose a normative critique of the rule: like the background demarcation between duties of inaction and duties of action, the further distinction between state action secured through commandeering versus state action secured through conditional spending or conditional preemption is a distinction poorly justified in light of the values that lie behind constitutional federalism.

Once again, the values of innovation and responsiveness to diversity can be dispensed with fairly quickly. Straight commandeering seems no more likely to produce national uniformity than conditional spending or preemption. One might object that, because Congress must *pay* for uniformity when it purchases state regulation, through conditional spending, the overall degree of

---

[102] 505 US at 167.

[103] Hills, 96 Mich L Rev at 921 (cited in note 1).

uniformity (or of unjustified uniformity) is lower than if both conditional spending and commandeering were permissible. Note,
however, that Congress funds its conditional payments to the
states through the taxation of resources that would otherwise be
available for state taxation and for the (geographically variable)
state programs that state taxation could fund; so the net effect of
conditional spending as opposed to commandeering on overall
uniformity is, at best, speculative. As for conditional preemption,
the cost for the federal government of converting a straight, sanction-backed directive to state officials into a directive backed by
the threat of preemption for noncompliance seems to be sufficiently low that the demarcation between conditional preemption
and straight commandeering cannot be justified on uniformity
grounds.[104]

Here, as with the preemption/commandeering distinction, it
strikes us that a more plausible argument for the Court's new jurisprudence of federalism rests upon the value of political community. Is it not the case that, when Congress compels state legislators or executives to perform an action—in particular, an
authoritative utterance—Congress has reduced the set of choices
available to those officials, derivatively to the state citizenry, and
has thereby diminished the intrinsic values of democratic participation and deliberation? By contrast, is it not true that, in the case
of a conditional spending or preemption program, the state's
choice set is simply shifted rather than reduced? Prior to the
threat, the choice set was (perform, not-perform); subsequent to
the threat, the choice set becomes (perform and receive monies,
not-perform) or (perform, not-perform and incur preemption). Is
there not less of an intrusion on the scope of state choice here
than with straight commandeering?

In responding to this objection, we will focus on the case of
conditional spending. (Our analysis carries over, mutatis mutandis,
to the case of conditional preemption; so as to avoid repetition,
we will not duplicate the analysis for that case, but rather leave
the details to the reader.) Technically, commandeering does not
reduce the state official's choice set. It remains physically possible

---

[104] See Michael C. Dorf and Charles F. Sabel, *A Constitution of Democratic Experimentalism*,
98 Colum L Rev 267, 419–32 (1998) (arguing that conditional federal spending and preemption, like commandeering, threaten interstate variation).

for the official to refrain from performing the commandeered utterance. But if the mandate to perform is backed by the threat of a harsh sanction, to be imposed personally upon the official, then, for purposes of political-community values, the effect on official choice is virtually equivalent to a physical constraint. That is, the choice for the official shifts from (perform, not-perform) to (perform, not-perform and go to jail) or (perform, not-perform and pay a large personal fine). Given the large personal stakes for the official, it is unlikely that she will choose between the options in a manner that advances intrinsic political values—by giving equal weight to the interests of each citizen, with no special weight for her own interest, and relatedly by sincerely responding to citizen proposals and challenges framed in terms of the public good. As the Court explained in the *Spallone* case, where it distinguished between sanctions directed at a municipality and personal sanctions directed against municipal legislators:

> The imposition of sanctions on individual legislators is designed to cause them to vote, not with a view to the interest of their constituents or of the city, but with a view solely to their own personal interests. Even though an individual legislator took the extreme position—or felt that his constituents took the extreme position—that even a huge fine against the city was preferable to [complying with a federal court directive], monetary sanctions against him individually would motivate him to vote to enact the ordinance simply because he did not want to be out of pocket financially. Such fines thus encourage legislators, in effect, to declare that they favor an ordinance not in order to avoid bankrupting the city for which they legislate, but in order to avoid bankrupting themselves.
> This sort of individual sanction effects a much greater perversion of the normal legislative process than does the imposition of sanctions on the city for the failure of these same legislators to enact an ordinance.[105]

Indeed, it would be unfair to ask that an official, faced with jail or a large personal fine, sacrifice self-concern and thereby permit the process of impartial public deliberation to carry on. Conversely, in the unlikely event that an official were to assume a superhuman attitude of impartial public spiritedness in the face of grave personal threat, and treat that decision as no different from

---

[105] *Spallone v United States*, 493 US 265, 279–80 (1990).

the ordinary decision C_0 between (perform, not-perform), then—
we want to claim—the values of political community would *not* be
diminished.

Consider now a case of commandeering that does not involve
large personal stakes for the official decisionmaker. Congress directs state legislators, say, to enact a particular statute, and threatens to impose a $10 million fine—to be paid from the state trea-
sury—for each year that the legislation is not in force for the entire
year. Let us call this the Fine Case. Contrast that with what we
shall call the Payment Case: Congress conditions a yearly payment
of $10 million to the state upon the statute's being in force for
the entire year. It is December 31. In the Fine Case, the state
legislator faces a choice between (enact the statute, not-enact the
statute and deplete the state fisc by $10 million). In the Payment
Case, a case of permissible conditional spending, the state legislator faces a choice between (enact the statute and receive a $10
million federal payment, not-enact the statute). One might say
that, in the Fine Case, "extraneous" considerations have been introduced into the pre-threat choice between (enact, not-enact),
and that the intrinsic value of the pre-threat choice has been diminished. We deny that this is true; the federal government, by
its own actions and utterances, constantly changes the effective
choice sets available to state legislators, and unless the federal actions and utterances are independently unconstitutional (say, under
ordinary Commerce Clause doctrine), we fail to see how their oc-
currence amounts to the introduction of "extraneous" or "value-
reducing" considerations into state choice-sets. But even if it *were*
true, our point here is that precisely symmetrical considerations
are introduced into state deliberations in the Payment Case. The
state, in that case, no longer faces the baseline choice between (enact, not-enact), but the new choice between (enact and receive
funds, not-enact). The two cases differ only in this: in the Fine
Case, but not the Payment Case, the federal action in response to
the legislators' choice is not an action that the federal government
could take unconditionally. But we do not see how, from the perspective of political-community values, that bears on the value or
importance of state legislators having this choice to make.

The upshot of this analysis is that the doctrinal line between
commandeering and cooperative federalism fails to track the value
of political community. Commandeering, as such, no more under-

mines state autonomy—specifically, it no more reduces the scope and value of the choices open to state officials and state citizens— than conditional spending or conditional preemption. What does (or may) track that value is a *cross-cutting* distinction—between threats to the state itself, and personal threats to state officials— that the Court has elsewhere recognized (as in *Spallone*) but specifically rejected in *Printz*.[106]

Finally, with respect to the value of tyranny prevention, we concur in Professor Hills's analysis. As Professor Hills crisply puts it, "[E]rosion of political accountability is endemic to all forms of cooperative federalism."[107] Although cooperative federalism statutes and straight commandeering statutes may both reduce accountability, relative to ordinary federal or state statutes directly regulating private persons, the demarcation between cooperative federalism and commandeering cannot be justified in terms of accountability.[108]

B. GENERAL APPLICABILITY

In both *New York* and *Printz*, the Court intimated that the inflexible prohibition on commandeering would not extend to federal laws of general applicability. Some such distinction is necessary if the prohibition on commandeering is not to immunize states and state subdivisions from Commerce Clause regulation even more broadly than did the regime of *National League of Cities*, which preceded *Garcia* and protected only integral state functions.[109] An unlimited anticommandeering principle would preclude federal antipollution mandates for municipal trash haulers, minimum wage requirements for state universities, or application of environmental regulations to the furnaces of local police stations.

The distinction between laws of general applicability and those

---

[106] See 117 S Ct at 2382 (declining to distinguish between federal statute directed at state itself, and federal statute directed at state officers, at least insofar as actions directed are official).

[107] Hills, 96 Mich L Rev at 828 (cited in note 1).

[108] Nor, of course, can it be justified (à la *De Shaney*) in terms of the differential moral significance of state action and state inaction, because, to reiterate, the very point of the Court's exemption for cooperative-federalism schemes is to create a permissible mechanism by which Congress can induce state officials to perform actions.

[109] See *Garcia*, 469 US at 537 (summarizing *National League of Cities* regime).

which are directed at a protected area of state sovereignty echoes other lines of demarcation drawn in constitutional law. The Court's negative Commerce Clause doctrine is centrally focused on the differential treatment of interstate commerce;[110] the Free Exercise Clause, as currently construed, is almost exclusively concerned with discrimination against religious actors, and permits their activities to be burdened by generally applicable laws;[111] "content discrimination" triggers heightened scrutiny under the Free Speech Clause.[112] Indeed, in wrestling with the comparable issue of state immunity from federal taxation, Justice Frankfurter championed the position that the primary determination should turn on whether the taxes were of general applicability.[113]

But the easy availability of a doctrinal tool does not prove its propriety. The exception for laws of general applicability harbors both difficulties of definition and of justification.

First, the concept of "general applicability" is not pellucid. Is a generally applicable statute simply one written broadly enough to encompass private as well as public entities? In an era of rampant privatization, it is hard to identify many governmental functions that are not carried out by at least some private entities. A law regulating "prisons" would encompass some public and some private entities; likewise a statute regulating "adjudicators." If the Brady Act had applied to "entities with easy access to information about criminal records," rather than "chief law enforcement officer[s],"[114] thereby including credit bureaus and private investigators, would that have saved the statute?

The Court could avoid such difficulties by identifying essentially governmental functions: a federal statute targeting such functions, even if it included some private actors, would then be taken as falling within the scope of the anticommandeering prohibition. In-

---

[110] See, for example, *Camp Newfound/Owatonna, Inc. v Town of Harrison*, 520 US 564 (1997).

[111] See *Employment Division v Smith*, 494 US 872 (1990).

[112] See, for example, *Boos v Barry*, 485 US 312 (1988).

[113] *New York v United States*, 326 US 572 (1946) (opinion of Frankfurter). See also *M'Culloch v Maryland*, 17 US 316, 435–36 (1819); *South Carolina v Baker*, 485 US 505, 514–15 (1988). It is somewhat awkward for the defender of *Printz* and *New York* to rely upon the Frankfurter opinion in view of the fact that Justice Rehnquist's opinion for the Court in *National League of Cities* disparaged it as lacking authority. See 426 US at 843 n 13.

[114] See 117 S Ct at 2369 (quoting Act).

deed, Justice Scalia's opinion in *Printz* steers toward this approach.[115] But distinguishing between governmental and nongovernmental functions is a notoriously tricky business. The Court's difficulties in specifying conceptually or historically "public" activities led to its abandonment of the line in intergovernmental tax immunity cases,[116] and constituted one ground for abandoning *National League of Cities*.[117] *Printz* itself hardly seemed to involve an essentially governmental function; the chief law enforcement officers purportedly commandeered by the Brady Act were simply required to check their records.

In the alternative, the distinction might turn on whether the federal regulation in question specifically identified the objects of regulation as governmental actors. But here again difficulties abound. The rule in *Gregory v Ashcroft* requires that when Congress seeks to include certain state activities in a regulatory scheme, it must clearly so state.[118] Does such a statutory statement make the statute targeted rather than generally applicable? If not, then what about a federal statute that covers both private and public entities, but specifies different duties for the different players?[119] Or a statutory amendment that includes state officials in a scheme that formerly excluded them?[120]

Second, it is far from clear why a regulation of general application should be less problematic in terms of the standard federalism values than a targeted regulation. Commentators who are sympathetic to the anticommandeering principle acknowledge that the line between generally applicable and targeted laws is difficult to

---

[115] See id at 2383 n 17 ("The Brady Act does not merely require CLEOs to report information in their private possession. It requires them to provide information that belongs to the State and is available to them only in their official capacity; and to conduct investigation in their official capacity, by examining databases and records that only state officials have access to. In other words, the suggestion that extension of this statute to private citizens would eliminate the constitutional problem posits the impossible.").

[116] See *Garcia*, 469 US at 540–43 (discussing tax-immunity cases).

[117] See id at 537–47.

[118] See notes 10–11 and accompanying text.

[119] See, for example, the Americans with Disabilities Act, 42 USC §§ 12131 et seq (1994) (duties applicable to public entities); id §§ 12181 et seq (duties applicable to private entities that operate public accommodations or services).

[120] See, for example, *Maryland v Wirtz*, 392 US 183 (1968) (upholding amendment to Fair Labor Standards Act that removed exemption for certain government employers).

defend.[121] An imposition uniformly applied to public and private sectors can suppress innovation, impair responsiveness to geographic diversity, and so on, quite as effectively as one precisely targeted at governmental entities.

Nor are more indirect arguments persuasive. The passage of a generally applicable regulation, it might be argued, could signal the existence of a national interest sufficiently important to justify infringing whatever federalism values might obtain. But this argument overlooks the fact that the federal legal system regularly and in wholly noninvidious circumstances imposes duties on public entities that it omits for private parties. Public entities may not discriminate against federally protected labor arrangements either in their provision of benefits or in regulatory advantages;[122] private entities may choose their own agendas. Persons acting "under color of any [law] of any State" may be sued for violating federal statutory mandates in circumstances where no comparable action is available against private parties.[123] Extortion by public officials constitutes a distinct crime.[124] A variety of considerations, ranging from the unique ability of state officials to frustrate or further national policy, to a desire to acknowledge state priorities, to the unwillingness of state courts to grant relief against public officials, justify this special treatment.

Reciprocally, it could be claimed that generality of application provides the protection of virtual representation; majorities and powerful interests who must themselves live with the results of a

---

[121] See Hills, 96 Mich L Rev at 916–21 (cited in note 1); Deborah Jones Merritt, *Republican Governments and Autonomous States: A New Role for the Guarantee Clause*, 65 U Colo L Rev 815, 826–27 and n 57 (1994) (arguing that concept of general applicability can be linked to Guarantee Clause, but also stating that "a Supreme Court ruling based squarely on the Guarantee Clause is preferable to one maintaining the distinction *New York* suggested between 'generally applicable laws' and laws aimed specifically at a state").

[122] See, for example, *Livadas v Bradshaw*, 512 US 107 (1994) (state government may not refuse to prosecute claims of workers who are governed by arbitration clause); *Golden State Transit Corp. v Los Angeles*, 475 US 608 (1986) (local government may not condition franchise renewal upon firm's settlement of strike); *Wisconsin Dept. of Industry, Labor and Human Relations v Gould Inc.*, 475 US 282 (1986) (state government may not refuse to do business with firms that violate federal labor law).

[123] See, for example, *Wilder v Virginia Hospital Ass'n*, 496 US 498 (1990) (Section 1983 action for failure to comply with federal reimbursement laws); *Golden State Transit Corp. v Los Angeles*, 493 US 103 (1989) (Section 1983 action for local action that was preempted by NLRA).

[124] See *Evans v United States*, 504 US 255, 261 (1992) (extortion defined as obtaining property inter alia " 'under color of official right' " pursuant to 18 USC § 1951).

law will be reluctant to permit the federal government to impose onerous regulations. As the Court put the matter in the context of intergovernmental tax immunities, "[W]here a government imposes a nondiscriminatory tax, . . . the threat of destroying another government can be realized only if the taxing government is willing to impose taxes that will also destroy itself or its constituents."[125] This, indeed, has been the argument of some of the commentators who support the distinction between targeted and generally applicable laws.[126] But the argument from virtual representation is of dubious value in this context, for the evil that the anticommandeering doctrine purports to prevent is not the total destruction of state governments (they would be useless to enforce federal policy if they were destroyed) but rather their subservience to national policy. Federal regulation can undermine the values that state governments serve—tyranny prevention, political community, innovation and diversity—without literally "destroying" those governments or, more generally, without imposing requirements sufficiently onerous to trigger the generalized outrage posited by virtual representation theorists. To put the point more concretely, we fail to see why a federal requirement that state governments properly find obnoxious would necessarily trigger hostility from private entities who are brought within the scope of the requirement. Indeed, in the case where federal regulation hinders the responsiveness of state governments to geographically diverse citizen preferences, beliefs, etc., one might well expect businesses to be less attuned to the local enthusiasms than public officials.[127]

Finally, in other areas of constitutional law, general-applicability requirements are defended as prophylactic measures to screen out problematic governmental motivation.[128] At some points, the

---

[125] *South Carolina v Baker*, 485 US 505, 525–26 n 15 (1988).

[126] See, for example, D. Bruce La Pierre, *Political Accountability in the National Political Process—the Alternative to Judicial Review of Federalism Issues*, 80 Nw U L Rev 577, 648–51 (1985); Edward A. Zelinsky, *Unfunded Mandates, Hidden Taxation, and The Tenth Amendment: On Public Choice, Public Interest, and Public Services*, 46 Vand L Rev 1355, 1385, 1411–12 (1993).

[127] Thus, for example, Professor Lessig recounts that many southern white business owners in fact supported the Civil Rights Act of 1964 as a means of allowing them to maximize profits without offending local norms of racial subordination. Lawrence Lessig, *The Regulation of Social Meaning*, 62 U Chi L Rev 943, 965–66 (1995).

[128] The content-discrimination component of free speech doctrine is defended this way. See, for example, Geoffrey R. Stone, *Content Regulation and the First Amendment*, 25 Wm & Mary L Rev 189, 227–33 (1983).

Court in *Printz* seems to defend the general applicability component of anticommandeering doctrine this way.[129] But the degree to which federal regulations infringe upon the values of federalism seems to be wholly independent of the motives or intentions of the officials who adopt the regulations. At best, motive or intention may be relevant within an expressive account of the anticommandeering doctrine—an account that we consider in Part V below.

C. ADJUDICATION

The third demarcation explicitly drawn by the Court in *Printz* and *New York* concerns the nature of the commandeered function. The federal government may permissibly commandeer the performance of judicial functions by state officials, but it may not compel them either to legislate or to undertake the variety of tasks best understood as executive rather than judicial (e.g., the investigative tasks at issue in *Printz* itself). *Printz* made clear that the line lay between adjudication and other functions, not between legislation and other functions: "*Testa [v Katt]* stands for the proposition that state courts cannot refuse to apply federal law—a conclusion mandated by the terms of the Supremacy Clause ('the Judges in every State shall be bound [by federal law]'). . . . [T]hat says nothing about whether state executive officers must administer federal law."[130] Although the investigative, law-enforcement function commandeered by the Brady Act in *Printz* was not legislative, neither was it judicial, and therefore directing state officials to perform that function was unconstitutional. *Printz* also stated explicitly that the line was a functional one: state officials who were not judges were nonetheless subject to commandeering, insofar as they performed adjudicatory functions.

> It is within the power of the States, as it is within the power of the Federal Government, to transfer some adjudicatory functions to administrative agencies, with opportunity for subsequent judicial review. But it is also within the power of Congress to prescribe, explicitly or by implication (as in the legisla-

---

[129] "But where, as here, it is the whole object of the law to direct the functioning of the state executive, and hence to compromise the structural framework of dual sovereignty, such a 'balancing' analysis is inappropriate." *Printz*, 117 S Ct at 2383.

[130] Id at 2381 (second alteration in original).

tion at issue in FERC [v Mississippi]), that those adjudications must take account of federal law.[131]

Evan Caminker, a prominent scholarly critic of *Printz*, has denied a textual warrant for the Court's distinction between judicial and nonjudicial functions.[132] Professor Caminker has argued, persuasively, that there is no specific basis in the Supremacy Clause for the judicial/nonjudicial distinction, and we would add that there is no specific textual basis for that distinction anywhere else in the Constitution.[133] On the other hand, Caminker has not shown, nor does he purport to show, that the text of the Constitution specifically precludes this demarcation. If, for example, the demarcation were justified in light of certain federalism values, then that demarcation could be constitutionally justified, insofar as those values figure in constitutional adjudication (say, via the Tenth Amendment).

Can the judicial/nonjudicial line be thus defended, in light of some or all of the values we described in Part I? Consider two alternate federal statutes. One statute, *D*, directs a state regulatory agency (e.g., an environmental agency, or a health-and-safety agency) to enact and enforce certain rules in a particular area, and preempts all other rules and all private causes of action in that area. A counterpart statute, *D'*, directs the agency to entertain specified causes of action, which are granted to private citizens (e.g., to persons harmed by pollution, or to injured workers), and preempts all rules and all other causes of action in that area. If *Printz* had declined to draw a demarcation between judicial and nonjudicial functions, then both *D* and *D'* would count as unconstitutional commandeering. *D* imposes an affirmative obligation upon state regulators, and so does *D'*. For *D* unconditionally requires the regulators to issue rules and initiate prosecutions, while *D'* unconditionally requires them to issue adjudicative orders conferring benefits (damages or injunctive relief) upon successful

---

[131] Id at 2381 n 14 (citation omitted).

[132] See Caminker, 1997 Supreme Court Review at 212–15 (cited in note 1).

[133] In particular, the fact that Article III permits Congress to refrain from establishing lower federal courts may lend textual support to the exclusion of state judges from the anticommandeering rule, but not to the further exclusion of state officials who are not judges but exercise the judicial function, such as the regulators in *FERC*. See *Printz*, 117 S Ct at 2371 (relying upon Article III to justify imposition of federal obligations upon state judges).

federal claimants, whose claims the regulators are, in turn, unconditionally required to adjudicate. But, we take it, D' is now
constitutionally permissible.[134]

Does statute D, in fact, offend federalism values more gravely
than statute D'? We think not. Statute D imposes a federal policy
upon the states, by a combination of preemption plus a requirement that the agency issue and enforce certain rules. Statute D'
imposes a federal policy upon the states, by a combination of preemption plus a requirement that the agency entertain certain
causes of action. It is very hard to see how D and D' differ, ceteris
paribus, with respect to the values of responsiveness to diversity
and innovation. If, for example, the provisions of D' defining the
commandeered causes of action are quite open-ended, then there
will be a fair bit of room for interstate variation here. Then again,
if the provisions of D defining the commandeered rules are quite
open-ended, there will be analogous room for variation. To put
the point another way: Commandeering statutes such as D and D'
differentially facilitate interstate variation insofar as they differentially delegate authority to the states; but it is hard to see how two
statutes that delegate an equal amount of authority should differentially facilitate variation just by virtue of the function (legislative
or executive versus judicial) that the statutes commandeer.[135]

Consider next the tyranny-prevention function of federalism.
Here, the distinction between judicial and nonjudicial functions
cuts the wrong way, at least with respect to certain kinds of tyran-
nies: the tyranny of organized groups, and official tyranny. There
is a well-developed literature, both theoretical and empirical, for
the proposition that agency policy-making through adjudication is

---

[134] D' is, in fact, loosely based on the statute upheld in *FERC v Mississippi*. See 456 US
at 759–61. Insofar as D' simply instructs an existing agency with adjudicatory authority to
entertain federal causes of actions where the agency has jurisdiction over "analogous" state
claims, it would not (we take it) be constitutionally impermissible despite the fact that it
constitutes commandeering. See note 17; *FERC*, 456 US at 760 (upholding requirement
that state regulatory commissions can comply with by adjudicating claims, over challenge
by Mississippi Public Service Commission, because "[t]he Mississippi Commission has jurisdiction to entertain claims analogous to those granted by [the federal statute], and it can
satisfy [the statutory] requirements simply by opening its doors to claimants").

[135] Notably, the Court in *Printz* declined to draw a demarcation, either way, along the
dimension of delegation. See 117 S Ct at 2382 (rejecting argument that "requiring state
officers to perform discrete, ministerial tasks specified by Congress does not violate the
principle of *New York* because it does not diminish the accountability of state or federal
officials").

less salient to the general public, and thus more likely to facilitate the "capture" of agencies by organized groups or bureaucratic interests, than the relatively high-visibility process of rule making.[136] The rules impermissibly commandeered by statute D will be more salient, not less salient, than the adjudicatory orders permissibly commandeered by statute D'.

The defender of *Printz* might object here that just because the rules are more salient, they are more likely to (unjustifiably) reflect majority interests within the state. The judicial/nonjudicial distinction cuts the wrong way with respect to interest-group and official tyranny, but the right way with respect to majoritarian tyranny—or so the defense of *Printz* might go. While there is some plausibility to this line of argument, we think that it faces two difficulties: (*a*) the difficulty of making commensurate different tyranny types that we mentioned in Part I, and (*b*) the difficulty that the tyranny types most relevant to constitutional doctrines that limit national power would seem to be official or minoritarian tyranny, not majoritarian tyranny, since a unitary national government is particularly prone to the first two types of tyranny, not the last.[137]

Finally, consider the value of political community. Do D and D' differ with respect to this value? Note, crucially, that in each case the commandeered officials are state agency officials—that is, officials who are typically unelected. Thus it is hard to see how D and D' differentially impede the flourishing of a state political community—at least on the standard view that it is via electoral politics, paradigmatically, via the lawmaking activities of elected state legislators, that intrinsic political values are fostered by constitutional federalism. To be sure, the state agency rule makers and prosecutors in D are formally and informally subject to elected officials (the state governor and the state legislators), but the same is true, or may be true, of the state agency adjudicators in D'. Notably, nothing in *Printz* restricts the applicability of the judicial-function category to politically insulated adjudicators. For example, it is constitutionally permissible for the federal government

---

[136] See Richard J. Pierce, Jr., *Seven Ways to Deossify Agency Rulemaking*, 47 Admin L Rev 59, 59–60 (1995) (summarizing benefits of rule making).

[137] See Rapaczynski, 1985 Supreme Court Review at 385–86 (arguing that federalism is not tyranny-reducing with respect to majoritarian tyranny, except for the oppression by the national government of geographically defined minorities) (cited in note 24).

to require that state commissioners adjudicate federal claims and defenses—as indeed the federal government did in the statute upheld in *FERC v Mississippi*—and *Printz* explicitly preserves this aspect of *FERC*, even though commissioners are notoriously not insulated from electoral politics.[138]

IV. THE SOURCE OF FEDERAL POWER: THE RECONSTRUCTION AMENDMENTS AS BOUNDARIES

The cases in which the Court has enunciated and elaborated the anticommandeering principle have exclusively concerned statues adopted under the Commerce Clause. As a result, there is as yet no authoritative guidance concerning how that principle applies to statutes grounded in other grants of congressional power. Prior commentators have generally viewed this as an open question, though the majority position has been a tentative conclusion that statutes adopted pursuant to the Thirteenth, Fourteenth, and Fifteenth Amendments will fall outside of the prohibition on commandeering.[139]

In our view, the hesitancy of the commentators is misplaced, for a demarcation between federal statutes grounded on the Reconstruction Amendments, and federal statutes grounded on the Commerce Clause or other Article I powers—unlike the demarcations discussed in Parts II and III—is well grounded in constitutional history, judicial doctrine, and legislative practice, as well as being justified by the values of constitutional federalism. We believe, however, that the fuzziness of this demarcation—tied as it is to the Court's fuzzy doctrine, articulated in the *Boerne* case, concerning the scope of the power granted to Congress by the Reconstruction Amendments—will make the demarcation, like its less theoretically satisfying cognates, a shaky foundation for a workable federalism jurisprudence.

---

[138] A classic article is Barry R. Weingast and Mark J. Moran, *Bureaucratic Discretion or Congressional Control? Regulatory Policymaking by the Federal Trade Commission*, 91 J Pol Econ 765 (1983).

[139] See Caminker, 95 Colum L Rev at 1006 n 13, 1087 n 325; Hills, 96 Mich L Rev at 888–89 (both cited in note 1); Merritt, 88 Colum L Rev at 45–46 (cited in note 24); Merritt, 65 U Colo L Rev at 832 (cited in note 121). Professor Caminker appears recently to have gained confidence in the view that the anticommandeering principle is bounded by Section 5 of the Fourteenth Amendment as well by the parallel enforcement provisions of the Thirteenth and Fifteenth Amendments. See Caminker, 1997 Supreme Court Review at 238–42 (cited in note 1).

A. HISTORY, DOCTRINE, AND PRACTICE

The proposition that the Reconstruction Amendments are exceptional, for federalism purposes, is not newly minted for the anticommandeering cases. The Supreme Court has long held that legislation adopted pursuant to the Reconstruction Amendments stands on a uniquely strong ground vis-à-vis the claims of federalism.

The issue was fully ventilated in *Ex Parte Virginia*,[140] where a decisive majority of the Court rejected claims that the enforcement power of Congress under Section 5 of the Fourteenth Amendment was constrained by considerations of state autonomy. The case involved a Virginia judge who had been indicted and arrested pursuant to a federal statute for excluding African Americans from service as grand and petit jurors, and who filed a petition for writ of habeas corpus. Joined by a similar petition by the state of Virginia itself, the judge claimed that the statute unconstitutionally intruded on state autonomy in violation of "the rights of the state of Virginia."[141] The argument persuaded two justices, Field and Clifford, who—relying on antebellum conceptions of federalism and cases such as *Kentucky v Dennison*—argued that nothing

> could have a greater tendency to destroy the independence and autonomy of the states; reduce them to a humiliating and degrading dependence upon the central government . . . than the doctrine asserted in this case, that Congress can exercise coercive authority over judicial officers of the states in the discharge of their duties under state laws. It will be only another step in the same direction towards consolidation, when it assumes to exercise similar coercive authority over governors and legislators of the States.[142]

Seven members of the Court, however, rejected the attack on the federal statute. They did not deny the previous constraints of fed-

---

[140] 100 US 339 (1879).

[141] Id at 341.

[142] Id at 358 (Field dissenting). Justice Field continued, in language reminiscent of some contemporary commentators, "No legislation would be appropriate [under Section 5] which should . . . conflict with the implied prohibitions upon Congress. They are as obligatory as the express prohibitions. The Constitution, as already stated, contemplates the existence and independence of the States in all their reserved powers." Id at 361. Justices Field and Clifford reiterated their position in dissent from *Strauder v West Virginia*, 100 US 303 (1879).

eralism, but recognized that the framing and ratification of the Reconstruction Amendments had effected a large change in federal-state relations. According to the Court:

> [It does not] make any difference that such legislation is restrictive of what the State might have done before the constitutional amendment was adopted. The prohibitions of the Fourteenth Amendment are directed to the States, and they are to a degree restrictions of State power. It is these which Congress is empowered to enforce, and to enforce against State action, however put forth, whether that action be executive, legislative, or judicial. Such enforcement is no invasion of State sovereignty . . . . Indeed, every addition of power to the general government involves a corresponding diminution of the governmental power of the States. It is carved out of them.[143]

This conception of the Reconstruction Amendments as a pro tanto diminution of the immunities otherwise accorded to the states has remained firm in the face of succeeding waves of enthusiasm for states' rights. *Ex Parte Virginia* has been regularly invoked by the Court in support of the proposition that the existence or threat of violations of those amendments justifies federal infringement of state sovereignty.[144] Most recently, during the last period of revival of enforceable federalism constraints on the national government—the *National League of Cities* period—the Court repeatedly confirmed that constraining doctrines would be qualified by the Reconstruction Amendments. In school desegregation and other institutional reform cases, federal decrees intruded into the prerogatives of state officials in ways that would seemingly[145] constitute commandeering: the officials were commanded affirmatively to exercise their sovereign authority. The Court, however, rejected Tenth Amendment challenges to such decrees.[146]

---

[143] 100 US at 346.

[144] See, for example, *Mitchum v Foster*, 407 US 225, 240, 242 (1972); *South Carolina v Katzenbach*, 383 US 301, 325–27 (1966).

[145] We say "seemingly," given the possible exception from the anticommandeering doctrine for certain affirmative remedial duties. See note 80.

[146] See *Missouri v Jenkins*, 495 US 33, 55 (1990) ("The Fourteenth Amendment . . . was avowedly directed against the power of the States, and so permits a federal court to disestablish local government institutions that interfere with its commands.") (internal quotations and citations omitted); *Milliken v Bradley*, 433 US 267, 291 (1977) ("[T]here is no merit to petitioners' claims that the relief ordered here violates the Tenth Amendment and general principles of federalism."); *Monell v Department of Social Services*, 436 US 658, 690 n 54 (1978) ("There is certainly no constitutional impediment to municipal liability [under Section 1983 for a violation of the Fourteenth Amendment] . . . . *National League of Cities v Usery* is irrelevant to our consideration of this case.").

Similarly, despite increasingly solicitous regard for "the Eleventh Amendment, and the principle of state sovereignty which it embodies,"[147] the Court has remained clear that in the exercise of its power under the Reconstruction Amendments, Congress may impose otherwise impermissible liability on the states in federal courts. In *Fitzpatrick v Bitzer*, Justice Rehnquist, writing for seven members of the Court, quoted *Ex Parte Virginia* at length to support the holding that the Fourteenth Amendment constituted an "expansion of Congress' powers—with the corresponding diminution of state sovereignty" sufficient to permit Congress to impose damage liability on states notwithstanding the Eleventh Amendment.[148] The power of Congress under Section 5 to impose liability on states has since remained a staple of the Supreme Court's Eleventh Amendment jurisprudence.[149]

Under settled doctrine, Congress may invade state sovereignty by appropriate legislation designed to protect against violations of the Reconstruction Amendments. The leading case is *City of Rome v United States*,[150] where the Court reviewed the application of the preclearance provisions of the Voting Rights Act to changes in municipal governance, though the changes did not in themselves (the Court assumed) violate the Fifteenth Amendment. The City of Rome argued that *National League of Cities* precluded federal intervention into the integral state function of self-government by popular election, and indeed it is difficult to imagine what function lies closer to the heart of state autonomy. Yet the Supreme Court rejected the claim on the basis of *Ex Parte Virginia* and *Fitzpatrick v Bitzer*.[151]

---

[147] *Fitzbatrick v Bitzer*, 427 US 445, 456 (1976).

[148] Id at 455.

[149] See *Idaho v Coeur d'Alene Tribe*, 117 S Ct 2028, 2039 (1997) (opinion of Kennedy); *Seminole Tribe of Fla. v Florida*, 517 US 44, 59, 65 (1996); *Missouri v Jenkins*, 491 US 274, 279 (1989); *Dellmuth v Muth*, 491 US 223, 227 (1989); *Will v Michigan Dept of State Police*, 491 US 58, 66 (1989); *Atascadero State Hosp. v Scanlon*, 473 US 234, 238 (1985); *Pennhurst State School & Hosp. v Halderman*, 465 US 89, 99 (1984); *Maher v Gagne*, 448 US 122, 132 (1980); *Hutto v Finney*, 437 US 678, 693 (1978); *Pennsylvania v Union Gas Co.*, 491 US 1, 41 (1989) (Scalia concurring and dissenting), overruled, *Seminole Tribe of Fla. v Florida*, 517 US 44 (1996).

[150] 446 US 156 (1980).

[151] Id at 178–80. The dissenters in *City of Rome* did not disagree with the proposition that Congress may infringe state autonomy so as to vindicate rights under the Reconstruction Amendments, but rather rejected the majority's view of the scope of Congress's enforcement power. See id at 200–05 (Powell dissenting); id at 209–19 (Rehnquist dissenting).

. . . *Fitzpatrick* stands for the proposition that principles of federalism that might otherwise be an obstacle to congressional
authority are necessarily overriden by the power to enforce the
Civil War Amendments "by appropriate legislation." Those
Amendments were specifically designed as an expansion of federal power and an intrusion on state sovereignty. Applying this
principle, we hold that Congress had the authority to regulate
state and local voting through the provisions of the Voting
Rights Act.[152]

The Court has since reiterated that "when properly exercising its
power under § 5 [of the Fourteenth Amendment], Congress is not
limited by the same Tenth Amendment constraints that circum-
scribe the exercise of its Commerce Clause powers."[153]

It is true that the Court, in our newest period of revived federalism constraints, has not squarely held that the Reconstruction
Amendments constitute an exception to the current, constraining
doctrines—namely, the anticommandeering doctrines announced
by *Printz* and *New York*. But last Term's opinion in *Yeskey* clearly
suggests as much. The Court's language in *Yeskey* implies that the
anticommandeering doctrines limit only legislation adopted pursuant to the Commerce Clause, and are inapplicable to a federal statute appropriately grounded in the Fourteenth Amendment.[154]

---

[152] Id at 179–80.

[153] *EEOC v Wyoming*, 460 US 226, 243 n 18 (1983). See id at 259 (Burger dissenting);
Hodel v Virginia Surface Mining & Reclamation Ass'n, 452 US 264, 287 n 28 (1981). To be
sure, in *Gregory v Ashcroft*, the Court observed that "this Court has never held that the
Amendment may be applied in complete disregard for a State's constitutional powers," 501
US at 468, but *Yeskey* reads *Ashcroft* as a case involving canons of statutory construction.
See 118 S Ct at 1954. The Court's most recent word on the subject is to reaffirm that:
"Legislation which deters or remedies constitutional violations can fall within the sweep
of Congress' enforcement power even if in the process it prohibits conduct which is not
itself unconstitutional and intrudes into 'legislative spheres of autonomy previously reserved
to the States.'" *Boerne*, 117 S Ct at 2163 (quoting *Fitzpatrick v Bitzer*, 422 US at 455). As
this article went to press, the Supreme Court, in a Voting Rights Act case, reiterated the
position that the "Reconstruction Amendments by their nature comtemplate some intrusion
into areas traditionally reserved to the States" and repeated the language quoted above
from *Boerne*. *Lopez v Monterrey County*, 119 S Ct 693, 703–4 (1999).

[154] In declining to address the merits of the constitutional challenge to the ADA, the
Court commented: "We do not address another issue presented by petitioners: whether
application of the ADA to state prisons is a constitutional exercise of Congress's power
under either the Commerce Clause, compare *Printz v United States* with *Garcia v San Antonio Metropolitan Transit Authority*, or § 5 of the Fourteenth Amendment, see *City of Boerne
v. Flores*." 118 S Ct at 1956 (citations omitted). A fair implication of the comment is that
Printz limits legislation adopted pursuant to the Commerce Clause, while legislation
adopted pursuant to the Fourteenth Amendment is exempt from that limit if appropriate
under the standards of *Boerne*. To be sure, however, a dictum articulated in the process of
refusing to address a substantive issue is not binding precedent.

Given the deep roots of this position, and the reliance of the Court in *Printz* on "historical understanding and practice, . . . the structure of the Constitution, and . . . the jurisprudence of this Court"[155] as the elements used to identify the " 'essential postulate[s]' "[156] of federalism, there is every reason to believe that the Court will confirm this suggestion in a definitive holding when the issue is squarely presented.

A skeptic might respond that interventions under the Fourteenth Amendment do not require commandeering of the sort condemned by *New York* and *Printz*. One might argue that, since the Constitution protects only against government action rather than government inaction, the only legislation required to implement the Fourteenth Amendment will impose negative duties and will thus be a permissible exercise of the federal preemption power. But such a response fails to account both for the scope of well-settled constitutional doctrine and for the legitimacy of congressional action under the Fourteenth Amendment to prevent, as well as to remedy, constitutional violations.

The point is clear with respect to the Equal Protection Clause. An invidious refusal to provide protection or benefits is as much an invasion of the constitutional mandate as an invidious imposition of punishment. In theory, the former refusal can be cured by refusing to provide benefits to anyone; but in practice, such a refusal may be out of the question. Thus equality norms will often, in effect, require affirmative action by the state. To take one example of particular salience to the framers of the Fourteenth Amendment: the Reconstruction Congress was concerned with the differential failure to enforce state laws against the Ku Klux Klan.[157] Obviously, a state will not come into compliance with the Fourteenth Amendment and its implementing statutes by refusing to enforce state laws against anyone; rather, state officials will be required to take affirmative and authoritative action to protect African Americans and Union sympathizers.[158]

---

[155] 117 S Ct at 2370.

[156] Id at 2376 (quoting *Principality of Monaco v Mississippi*, 292 US 313, 322 (1934)) (alteration in original).

[157] See *Monroe v Pape*, 365 US 167, 171–83 (1961) (describing this concern), overruled on other grounds, *Monnell v Department of Social Services*, 436 US 658 (1978).

[158] This analysis depends in part on a matter the Court has not yet addressed: the tightness of the connection between the federal directive and action by state officials, necessary to constitute commandeering. It is as yet unclear whether a directive constitutes impermissible

With respect to the Due Process Clause and incorporated rights, the objection has somewhat greater force. But even in the area of due process, constitutional doctrine not infrequently requires state actors to take affirmative measures to live up to constitutional norms,[159] and in such cases an exception for Fourteenth Amendment obligations will be necessary. Moreover, in all areas, it is entirely plausible that Congress may legitimately impose some prophylactic affirmative obligations.[160]

The Court's failure to recognize a Reconstruction-Amendment exception to the anticommandeering principle would disrupt large segments of our current legal structure. A wide array of federal legislation is premised on the proposition that, in implementing the Reconstruction Amendments, Congress can impinge on the way that state entities choose to structure their internal processes. Some of this legislation is contained in conditional grants like Title VI (although even here the capacity of Congress to allow damage actions in defiance of the Eleventh Amendment is of some relevance).[161] But much other legislation—most prominently Title VII[162] and the voting rights legislation sustained in *City of Rome*, as well as municipal responsibility for deliberate indifference to constitutional violations[163]—also requires the states to take affir-

---

commandeering only if it logically entails state action, or more broadly if such action is effectively compelled. The facts of both *Printz* and *New York* suggest the broader view, which would give the anticommandeering doctrine wider scope and require more insistently the exception for equal protection norms.

[159] Thus, for example, due process can obligate a state to provide medical services to individuals in state custody, see *West v Atkins*, 487 US 42 (1988); *City of Revere v Mass. General Hosp.*, 463 US 239 (1983); *Youngberg v Romeo*, 457 US 307 (1982); *Estelle v Gamble*, 429 US 97 (1976) (Eighth Amendment, applied against states via due process component of Fourteenth Amendment); and to provide retroactive relief to entities from which unlawful taxes have been collected, see *Reich v Collins*, 513 US 106 (1994); *McKesson Corp. v Division of Alcoholic Beverages and Tobacco*, 496 US 18 (1990). Although the federal imposition of certain affirmative remedial obligations upon the states arguably constitutes permissible preemption, quite apart from any special exception from the anticommandeering doctrine for statutes grounded upon Section 5 of the Fourteenth Amendment, see note 80, a Section 5 exception would surely be needed to accommodate the *Youngberg* line of cases.

[160] Although the Court in *Boerne*, discussed in Part IV.C., limited the scope of congressional power under Section 5, *Boerne* also affirmed that some prophylactic legislation is authorized by that provision. See, for example, 117 S Ct at 2163–64.

[161] 42 USC § 2000d-7 authorizes damage actions against state entities under various federal civil rights statutes including Title VI, notwithstanding the strictures of the Eleventh Amendment. See *Franklin v Gwinnett County Public Schools*, 503 US 60, 72 (1992).

[162] See *Fitzpatrick v Bitzer*, 427 US 445, 448 n 2 (1976) (discussing 1972 amendments, extending Title VII to public employers).

[163] See *City of Canton v Harris*, 489 US 378 (1989).

mative measures to comply with federal civil rights mandates. The Court in *Yeskey* virtually invited a properly raised challenge to the provisions of the Americans with Disabilities Act that require state accommodation of the needs of handicapped individuals, but such a challenge could not be sustained without overturning large elements of the federal civil rights regime.[164]

B. JUSTIFICATION

The question remains whether a distinction between Congress's powers under the Reconstruction Amendments and Congress's powers under Article I can be justified. The proposition that Congress must have the authority to override putative state-sovereignty constraints, pursuant to its powers under the Reconstruction Amendments, is perfectly consistent with the proposition that Congress should also have such authority pursuant to its powers under the Commerce Clause and the other power-conferring provisions of Article I. After all, although the provisions of the Fourteenth Amendment "by their own terms embody limitations on state authority,"[165] the Commerce Clause has also been understood since *Gibbons v Ogden*[166] to limit state authority, and the Supremacy Clause explicitly mentions the states. Nonetheless, we believe that a distinction between the Reconstruction Amendments and Article I, for purposes of federalism constraints on the national government, is indeed justified by federalism values.

Innovation and diversity. A capacity of state government to experiment with the rights protected by the Fourteenth Amendment[167]

---

[164] To the extent one can read tea leaves, the ADA might well be sustained against such a challenge. The Court denied certiorari after *Yeskey* in *Armstrong v Wilson*, a prison case where the Ninth Circuit rejected a plain-statement challenge to the entry of a structural injunction under the ADA, and *Clark v California*, which held that the ADA was a legitimate exercise of congressional power under Section 5 of the Fourteenth Amendment and thus properly abrogated the states' Eleventh Amendment immunity. See *Armstrong v Wilson*, 124 F3d 1019 (9th Cir 1997), cert denied, 118 S Ct 2340 (1998); *Clark v California*, 123 F3d 1267 (9th Cir 1997), cert denied, 118 S Ct 2340 (1998). While this article was in press, the Court specifically amended an order granting certiorari to exclude the question of whether the ADA exceeds congressional powers under Section 5 of the Fourteenth Amendment. *Olmstead v L.C.*, 119 S Ct 633 (1998).

[165] *Fitzpatrick v Bitzer*, 427 US at 456.

[166] 22 US 1 (1824).

[167] For the sake of analytic clarity and simplicity, the following discussion focuses on the distinction between Section 5 of the Fourteenth Amendment and the Commerce Clause; but we believe that our arguments can be generalized to support a distinction between all of the enforcement provisions of the Reconstruction Amendments and all of Congress's Article I powers.

cannot rest on the usual federalist arguments about state innovation and responsiveness. The case for interstate variation is usually framed in terms of the maximization of preference satisfaction (or, more generally, the maximization of good consequences).[168] A system in which constituent preferences are better satisfied is, ceteris paribus, taken to be a superior one; and, at this level, all preferences are taken to be pretty much equal. In short, the normative presuppositions underlying the innovation and diversity arguments for federalism, as these arguments are usually framed, are straightforwardly consequentialist. And the political economy of Commerce Clause legislation fits nicely with these consequentialist presuppositions. Such legislation is, for the most part, the product of "low" or "ordinary" politics.

By contrast, a Section 5 determination is (usually) a matter of "high politics." It purports to implement basic rights that trump (ordinary) measures of good or bad consequences. Indeed, after *Boerne*, legislation grounded upon Section 5 must be commensurate with a threatened or past violation of the Constitution recognized by the Court itself.[169] Whereas Commerce Clause statutes may serve any plausible account of the national interest, statutes under the Fourteenth Amendment must be keyed to preserving the rights of individuals under the Due Process or Equal Protection Clauses.

The degree to which citizen preferences are satisfied by such statutes, or to which they maximize good consequences, is not the relevant criterion. Our system of constitutional federalism does not contemplate that Americans should lose human rights embedded in our national Constitution when they travel from state to state,[170] and states may not in general legitimately act on the proposition that they would prefer not to enforce national norms of equality and liberty. The "privileges" and "immunities" of citizenship are national, not local.

To be sure, one might argue that a decision by state officials to decline compliance with national mandates is a potentially important judgment that should be grappled with by the national polity

---

[168] For a clear example, see McConnell, 54 U Chi L Rev at 1493–94 (cited in note 24).

[169] See Part IV.C.

[170] States may, pursuant to their own constitutions, statutes, or case law, protect these interests to a greater degree than the national norms require, but they may not fall below the national baseline.

in making appropriate decisions about how best to realize constitutional aspirations.[171] This argument is not without force, but we find it ultimately unpersuasive.

First, it is worth considering exactly who the participants in the dialogue are likely to be. To the extent that the anticommandeering doctrine protects only against requiring state or local legislatures to adopt statutes according to federal design, the argument seems plausible. Legislatures are potential coauthors of an ongoing constitutional specification, and the doctrine parallels the Court's reluctance to allow state and local legislators to be sued for adopting unconstitutional laws.[172] Just as legislative immunity can be defended as a means of allowing state and local challenges and constitutional dialogue regarding controversial decisions of the Court, the ability of state and local legislatures to refuse to participate in congressional interpretations of the Constitution may be salutary. But, as currently framed, the anticommandeering principle is hardly so limited. After *Printz*, it includes every state nonjudicial official who exercises governmental power, and there is reason to doubt whether the constitutional understanding of the sheriff's deputy in Boise, Idaho, the welfare caseworker in New York, and the librarian in Huntsville, Alabama, carries the same normative force as the Kentucky and Virginia Resolutions.[173] Just as the Court declines to extend immunity to such executive officials for defiance of constitutional norms under Section 1983, there is good reason to refuse them the immunity of the anticommandeering doctrine.[174]

Second, since every state nonjudicial official has license to participate in the dialogue in question, the "discussion" is likely to be less than a focused interaction on matters of constitutional prin-

---

[171] See, for example, Barry Friedman, *Dialogue and Judicial Review*, 91 Mich L Rev 577 (1993); Robert A. Burt, *The Constitution in Conflict* (Belknap, 1992); Louis Fisher, *Constitutional Dialogues: Interpretation as Political Process* (Princeton U Press, 1988); Robert M. Cover, *The Supreme Court, 1982 Term—Foreword: Nomos and Narrative*, 97 Harv L Rev 4 (1983).

[172] See cases cited in note 65.

[173] See David Yassky, *Eras of the First Amendment*, 91 Colum L Rev 1699, 1712 (1991) (describing Kentucky and Virginia Resolutions).

[174] See Adler, 145 U Pa L Rev at 813–44 (cited in note 45) (arguing that judicial review of agency decisions may not be countermajoritarian even if judicial review of statutes is); Seth F. Kreimer, *Exploring the Dark Matter of Judicial Review: A Constitutional Census of the 1990s*, 5 Wm & Mary Bill of Rts J 427, 506–08 (1997) (arguing that street-level bureaucrats are not likely to be good constitutional decision makers).

ciple. When every such official may demand her reservation price as the condition of participating in a federal program, what emerges is a market that measures the desire of state officials to resist national norms. Since these norms represent judgments by the national polity that the states are inadequately protecting the rights of their minorities in the first place, it is no surprise that state officials disagree. The strength of their disagreement is less than a persuasive ground for rethinking national priorities.

Finally, the variation that will emerge from normative dialogue by states has costs. One of the boasts of America in the aftermath of the Civil War is that all have identical rights of national citizenship. The Fourteenth Amendment rejected the proposition in *Dred Scott*[175] that national rights are derived from state citizenship. Section 5 legislation purports to provide the benefits of the Fourteenth Amendment to all the citizenry; the interstate equality of constitutional rights, and of statutory rights that enforce them, is, we suggest, in part what constitutes the United States as a *national* political community.

Tyranny prevention. In the area of Commerce Clause legislation, the outcome of a legitimate state political process may provide a locus of justifiable resistance to national tyranny. A tyrannical national initiative would, on this theory, be met not with armed resistance, but with the increased costs, both political and practical, that come from determined noncooperation by state governments.[176] But the theory rests on the premise that the state decision of noncooperation is the outcome of a legitimate process—specifically, in this context, a process that is less likely to be unjustifiably responsive to the interests of particular groups, that is, "tyrannical." The theory does not plausibly extend, for example, to trash haulers who wish passively to resist the Resource Conservation and Recovery Act. The "double security" claim is not a brief for anarchy, but for countervailing legitimate public power.

Unlike Commerce Clause legislation, the mandates of the Fourteenth Amendment set the parameters of what constitutes a legitimate polity. To the extent that constitutional provisions can be

---

[175] *Scott v Sandford,* 60 US 393 (1857).

[176] Consider the unsuccessful efforts by New York City to invoke *Printz* in refusing to cooperate with federal anti-immigrant initiatives. *City of New York v United States,* 971 F Supp 789 (SDNY 1997).

clearly characterized as protecting the elements of a functioning democracy, the point is obvious. A decision made by a state entity that fails to abide by baseline notions of equality and political participation cannot be credited with resisting national tyranny. Where it undercuts the very norms that block the capture of state governments by powerful factions, state resistance to national mandates abets tyranny rather than reducing it.

The harder case arises where the constitutional rights Congress seeks to enforce are not quite so directly connected with political participation.[177] Consider, for example, the obligation imposed by the Americans with Disabilities Act to affirmatively accommodate citizens with disabilities who seek services from state authorities.[178]

The legitimacy of such interventions arises from the nature of legislation under the Fourteenth Amendment. As we noted earlier, in federal-state conflicts there are cross-cutting risks of tyranny: a failure of federal intervention may permit state tyranny, but imposition of federal determinations risks national tyranny. In the case of Commerce Clause legislation, nothing in the nature of the Commerce Clause doctrine suggests that such legislation will systematically represent anything more than the desires of a national majority. By contrast, after *Boerne*, proponents of legislation enacted under Section 5 of the Fourteenth Amendment must persuade a court that the legislation is commensurate with the requirements of the Fourteenth Amendment.

At a minimum, then, where the federal courts conclude that federal intervention is justified under *Boerne*, the probability of national tyranny is substantially diluted. Further, to the extent that constitutional rights, albeit not protective of the democratic process itself, are nonetheless targeted against tyranny in the sense that they prohibit outcomes likely to be the result of unjustified responsiveness to particular groups or persons—the Takings Clause is an example—then a Section 5 statute will be doubly different from the ordinary Commerce Clause statute. In such a case, the risk of national tyranny will be lower, and the risk of state

---

[177] Of course, some commentators claim that large elements of the Bill of Rights are in fact crucially linked to the preservation of a legitimate political process. See, for example, John Hart Ely, *Democracy and Distrust: A Theory of Judicial Review* (Harv U Press, 1980); Akhil Reed Amar, *The Bill of Rights as a Constitution*, 100 Yale L J 1131 (1991).

[178] See 42 USC §§ 12131 et seq (1994).

tyranny will be higher, as compared to the case where Congress is simply operating under the Commerce Clause.

Political community. The final federalist value we have highlighted prizes state decision making because of the intrinsic value of democratic politics. But the point we made above about the role of the Reconstruction Amendments in defining political legitimacy can be repeated here. To the extent that congressional determinations under Section 5 implement constitutional norms that define political legitimacy, countervailing determinations by states do not promote the value of political community. There is nothing intrinsically valuable or important about citizen "participation" in state institutions that fail to abide by baseline, legitimacy-defining norms of equality and due process. And although, with respect to other kinds of constitutional rights, there may in fact be intrinsic, democratic values realized by the process of state dissent from federal statutes enforcing such rights under the Fourteenth Amendment, we hope to have shown here how such statutes are sufficiently different from straight Commerce Clause statutes—with respect to the remaining federalism values of innovation, diversity, and tyranny prevention—to warrant a general exception from the anticommandeering doctrine.

C. LIMITS

The Fourteenth Amendment is capacious. The Due Process Clause protects all "liberty" and "property" against arbitrary deprivation; the Equal Protection Clause potentially implicates every government decision that classifies its subjects. In the absence of some limiting principle, therefore, a Section 5 exception from the anticommandeering doctrine might reach so widely as to eviscerate the practical import of *Printz* and *New York*. Almost any federal intervention might be, with one degree of persuasiveness or another, justified as an effort to prevent the oppression of some in-state minority.[179] Similarly, any government action that threatens

---

[179] For examples of some far-reaching claims, see *Wheeling & Lake Erie Railway Co. v PUC*, 141 F3d 88 (3d Cir 1998) (holding that the Railroad Revitalization and Regulatory Reform Act is Section 5 legislation protecting railroads from discriminatory taxation); *Oregon Short Line Railroad Co. v Dept. of Revenue*, 139 F3d 1259 (9th Cir 1998) (same); *CSX Transportation, Inc. v Bd. of Public Works*, 138 F3d 537 (4th Cir 1998) (leaving issue open); *Abril v Virginia*, 145 F3d 182 (4th Cir 1998) (rejecting the claim that the Fair Labor Standards Act is Section 5 legislation); id at 185–86 (citing decisions from four other circuits rejecting this claim); *Biddlecome v University of Texas*, 1997 WL 124220 (SD Tex 1997)

the liberty or property of any citizen might conceivably be subject to federal regulation as a prophylactic protection against arbitrary deprivation.[180]

The *Boerne* Court adopted a tailoring doctrine to limit the scope of congressional power under the Fourteenth Amendment. The Court's standard requires a "congruence between the means used and the ends to be achieved. The appropriateness of remedial measures must be considered in light of the evil presented. Strong measures appropriate to address one harm may be an unwarranted response to another, lesser one."[181] The principle appears to have two dimensions. First, before it may be accepted as a legitimate exercise of enforcement power under Section 5, a statute must be shown to be directed toward the remedy or prevention of a harm that would be regarded as a constitutional violation under the principles enunciated by the Court. Second, the degree of intrusion into state prerogatives must be "proportional[]" to the degree or likelihood of a constitutional violation.[182]

The *Boerne* limitations serve to cabin what would otherwise be a potentially all-engulfing exception from the anticommandeering doctrines, and to bolster the normative case (in light of federalism values) for the existence of that exception. Our normative arguments, above, for such a distinction generally assumed that Section 5 legislation would be fairly closely tied to the underlying constitutional norms. But it bears emphasis that *Boerne*'s tailoring doctrine itself is fuzzy, not clear. How well settled a constitutional proposition must be to support a Section 5 statute, how analogous the evil aimed at must be to what the Court would recognize as a constitutional violation, how likely the evil at issue must be, and how narrowly tailored an intrusion must be to survive scrutiny un-

---

(holding that Family and Medical Leave Act is Section 5 legislation); *Thomson v Ohio State Univ. Hosp.*, 5 F Supp 2d 574 (SD Ohio 1998) (holding that FMLA is not).

[180] Compare *College Savings Bank v Fla. Prepaid Postsecondary Education Expense Bd.*, 148 F3d 1343 (Fed Cir 1998) (holding that protection of patent rights against deprivation without due process constitutes a Section 5 basis for statute that permits suit against state for patent infringement), cert granted 1999 WL 5331 (US), with *College Savings Bank v Fla. Prepaid Postsecondary Education Expense Bd.*, 131 F3d 353 (3d Cir 1997) (rejecting comparable claim under Lanham Act), cert granted 1999 WL 5330 (US), and *Chavez v Arte Publico Press*, 157 F3d 282 (5th Cir 1998) (same). See also *In re Sacred Heart Hosp.*, 133 F3d 237 (3d Cir 1998) (rejecting "privilege or immunity" clause as basis for abrogation of Eleventh Amendment immunity by Bankruptcy Code).

[181] *Boerne*, 117 S Ct at 2169 (citation omitted).

[182] Id at 2164.

der *Boerne* are all matters of degree. Any one of these variables offers room for extensive debate. Since the ultimate judgment under *Boerne* will be a function of all the variables taken together, we have serious doubts whether the tailoring doctrine will prove workable. And since the Section 5 demarcation within anticommandeering jurisprudence is tied to *Boerne*, we similarly doubt the clarity and workability of that line, as now drawn by the Court.[183]

V. An Expressive Defense?

We have argued above that the bases for most of the distinctions the Court has used to cabin the disruptive potential of the anticommandeering principle are at best obscure. On many of these fronts, the best explanation one can muster for the lines the Court has drawn seems to be that permitted actions "look" or "feel" different. So, too, the actual placement of the line between permissible and impermissible federal programs is difficult to discern. The important fact seems to be that some line has been drawn, not exactly where the line falls.

The absence of a (nonexpressive) justification for the lines of demarcation combined with the lack of definition of the lines themselves suggests that the Court is not so much implementing an effort to achieve particular policy goals or to embody particular historical understandings as to express what it regards as the core of American federalism. In line with the suggestion advanced by a number of recent commentators that the law's "expressive function" may justify rules that are inexplicable apart from what the rules "say" or "mean,"[184] the prohibition on commandeering as defined by the Court could be justified as expressive of our regime of constitutional federalism.

---

[183] The opinion in *Boerne* is focused on Section 5 of the Fourteenth Amendment. But if, as we assume, its tailoring doctrine is also applicable to the parallel enforcement provisions of the Thirteenth and Fifteenth Amendments, our critique can be generalized: the line between a permissible commandeering grounded in one of the Reconstruction Amendments, and an impermissible commandeering merely grounded in Article I, will prove unclear and perhaps unworkable.

[184] See, for example, Cass R. Sunstein, *On the Expressive Function of Law*, 144 U Pa Rev 2021 (1996); Lawrence Lessig, *The Regulation of Social Meaning*, 62 U Chi L Rev 943 (1995); Richard H. Pildes and Richard G. Niemi, *Expressive Harms, "Bizarre Districts," and Voting Rights: Evaluating Election-District Appearances after Shaw v Reno*, 92 Mich L Rev 483 (1993).

The expressive story proceeds at two levels.[185] First, just as it is argued that some laws may be valuable as a means of altering the norms that are ultimately internalized and implemented by private actors, the prohibition of commandeering could be a mechanism for strengthening the norm of regard for state interests in the federal political process. Second, the Court's decisions may be *intrinsically* important for the statements they make. *Printz* and *New York* may in and of themselves express the nation's constitutive commitment to state autonomy in a way that defines us as a nation.

A. INSTRUMENTAL EFFECTS ON POLITICAL NORMS

1. *The mechanisms.* An instrumental expressive account could be fleshed out in several ways. First, the prohibition of commandeering could alter the structure of political decision making: by forcing federal legislators (or at least legislative assistants) to think about where proposed legislation falls on a series of vaguely defined boundaries, the doctrine will, at the very least, temporarily put issues of federalism on the legislative agenda. In framing any legislation that affects states, a federal legislator must contemplate whether the legislation constitutes commandeering or preemption, and—if the former—whether it falls within the exceptions the Court has recognized to the anticommandeering principle. None of these evaluations will necessarily prevent enactment of the legislation, but like rules of etiquette in the private sector, they may tend to guard against unthinking violation of relevant values (in this case, the values of federalism).[186]

A second, complementary, line of analysis rests on the proposi-

---

[185] These two levels track Professor Sunstein's account of two types of expressive theories of law. See 144 U Pa L Rev at 2025–27 (cited in note 184).

[186] The following excerpt from oral argument in *New York v United States*, see 1992 US TRANS LEXIS 197, *10–*11, suggests that the Court understands an anticommandeering principle will be indicative rather than determinative:

MR. SCHIFF: No. We think *FERC* is quite distinguishable. The majority of this Court in *FERC* made it quite clear that the state had a choice. It didn't really have to do what that act of Congress required it to do because it didn't have to regulate public utilities, while—

QUESTION: Well, you know that it, you know that's a, just a dream world. . . . What are the underlying values that you're trying to further by the Tenth Amendment argument that you urge upon us? Is it, is this simply just a matter of etiquette and form, the etiquette of federalism, or is there something more substantial?

tion that the Supreme Court's decisions have independent norm-generating force beyond the specific threat of judicial invalidation. When the Supreme Court invalidates commandeering legislation as inconsistent with the values of federalism, even if the precise reasoning behind the determination is obscure, the Court lends support to those who argue against federal legislation on grounds of state autonomy. Recognition that the Supreme Court views the limitation of federal interference with state decision making as constitutionally enforceable could galvanize these proponents of autonomy.[187] Within Congress itself, legislators who regard the Court as a source of normative guidance will view infringements on state sovereignty with a more skeptical eye. To be sure, Congress has not infrequently asserted a willingness to take issue with the Court, but the norm-reinforcing effect of the Court's decisions need only change the vote of the marginal legislator to be significant. At the very least, pro-federalism decisions by the Supreme Court make claims of constitutionally based state autonomy a legitimate part of political discourse.

Third, the anticommandeering doctrine may be a part of a strategy of normative change directed at the federal judiciary itself. A requirement that lower court judges engage in the exercise of distinguishing commandeering from noncommandeering statutes might make them sensitive to federalism concerns in other areas. This doctrine may constitute one part of a broader revival of state autonomy that, along with *Lopez, Boerne,* and *Seminole Tribe,* could unleash the common-law evolution of federalism jurisprudence in the lower federal courts. And allowing state attorneys general to invoke *Printz* in adjudication might embolden them to press federalist claims in other areas. Arguably this has in fact occurred, although it is not often that such "law reform" arguments (justifying legal change in one area of law, by reference to what is needed in another) carry the day.

2. *The virtues of ambiguity.* In each of these scenarios, the formidable obscurity of the anticommandeering doctrine is arguably a benefit rather than a cost. Justice Scalia commented in *Printz* that

---

[187] Just as *Brown v Board of Education* and subsequent cases gave social force to claims of proponents of African-American rights, the Court's recent series of statutory invalidations may provide an impetus to proponents of state autonomy.

"an imprecise barrier against federal intrusion upon state authority is not likely to be an effective one."[188] We have argued that, despite this disclaimer, anticommandeering doctrine, as set forth by the Court, is in fact made up of a series of "imprecise barriers." For purposes of changing political norms, however, unclear boundaries may sometimes be better than clear ones.

Insofar as the point of *New York* and *Printz* is to establish rules of etiquette that highlight the importance of state autonomy within Congress, the enemy of meaningful ritual is rote. In the normal course of events, we might expect the following cycle over time. At the first stage, Congress begins to pass legislation without a backward glance at state autonomy. At the second, the Court imposes boundaries that put federalism back on the agenda because they require Congress to affix some sort of formal "seal" indicating it has considered federalism. The seal may take the form of a clear statement; the inclusion of a background threat of preemption (to bring the statute within the permissible category of conditional preemption) or a provision applying it to private parties (to make it generally applicable); or a statement of findings in the legislative history articulating a connection to interstate commerce or constitutional violations. But, whatever the formal prerequisites, in order to affix the seal, someone in the legislative process has to think about federalism.

The difficulty, from the point of view of the Court, is that such a level of attention will not be stable. If doctrine is predictable, a third stage is likely to evolve in which congressional aides discover a repertoire of standard techniques that meet the formal requirements imposed by the Court, and begin to employ those techniques as a matter of course. Once the forms are safely in the word processor, federalism becomes a matter of an aide calling up the appropriate language, and Congress returns to its first mode of proceeding in routine disregard of state autonomy where politics so dictates.[189]

---

[188] 117 S Ct at 2381 (rejecting proposed distinction between policy-making and non-policy-making functions).

[189] This is the equilibrium in the Eleventh Amendment area that emerged in response to the clear statement rule of *Atascadero State Hosp. v Scanlon*, 473 US 234, 238–39 (1985). Congress pretty quickly learned the drill. See, for example, *Seminole Tribes of Fla. v Florida*, 517 US 44 (1996) (clear statement in Indian Gaming Regulatory Act; abrogation of Eleventh Amendment immunity held ineffective on other grounds); *Dellmuth v Muth*, 491 US 223, 229–30 (1989) (noting apparent clear statement in amendments to Rehabilitation Act).

One virtue of an opaque doctrine lies in its ability to delay the emergence of the third stage of the process. As long as the Court's doctrine lacks clarity, congressional drafters can never be sure that any particular rote mechanism will avoid invalidation, and so must proceed mindful of the brooding presence of the value of state autonomy. Clear boundaries would allow proponents of federal legislation to defend appropriately structured interventions on the ground that the statutes do not violate norms of federalism. By contrast, a doctrine precluding commandeering whose exact parameters are indeterminate casts a normative pall over every piece of legislation that interferes with state activities. Further, as a matter of judicial realpolitik, an opaque doctrine may be superior, for it allows the Court to threaten invalidation of a wide array of legislation, without binding itself to invalidate any particular (and popular) mandate. In this way, the Court puts federalism on the political agenda without depleting its own political capital.

Finally, if the Court is seeking to inculcate a sensitivity among lower courts and governmental officials to the importance of values of federalism, clarity is not as much of a virtue as generativity. The Court has embarked on a common-law effort to elaborate a series of limitations on federal authority. Although it cannot specify exactly what federalism requires, the Court can identify certain cases that clearly overstep the bounds, and over time the nature of the requirements will be fleshed out by the particular choices it makes and the distinctions it draws. To facilitate this process, an initial doctrine that throws up a large number of controverted examples in the lower courts is preferable to one that allows courts and litigants to resolve issues without reflection.

3. *The dark side of norm manipulation.* Although the instrumental, expressive argument just sketched out has some plausibility—the anticommandeering doctrines might be explained as an attempt, by the Court, to express regard for federalism and thereby to shape norms governing political actors—we are ultimately unpersuaded.

First, we doubt the empirical presuppositions of the argument.

So, too, in the area of Commerce Clause regulation. The practice of deference to congressional fact finding, see, for example, *Perez v United States*, 402 US 146, 155–57 (1971); *Katzenbach v McClung*, 379 US 294, 299–301 (1964), resolved into a ritual announcement of an effect on interstate commerce as the predicate for the exertion of national power. One function of the lack of clarity of the Court's opinion in *United States v Lopez*, 514 US 549 (1995), is to allow the Court to announce the existence of new limits that Congress must worry about, without providing easily evaded boundaries.

For the anticommandeering doctrines to exert normative force on members of Congress and other political actors, the doctrines should at least be a subject of discussion. But a LEXIS survey of the Congressional Record disclosed only six mentions of *Printz*.[190] *New York* was referred to marginally more often (21 times in six years).[191] The cases appear somewhat more often in congressional testimony,[192] and perhaps this could support a claim that their expressive effect is the mobilization of interest groups that will raise the flag of federalism. But it is equally consistent with the hypothesis that—encased in a doctrine too opaque for most observers to justify or fathom—the message has had little serious impact on dialogue or decisions by Congress.[193]

---

[190] The references in 1998 were contained in one article on the inscrutability of Supreme Court decisions, authored by a Judge Jerome Ferris, inserted into the Congressional Record by Senator Leahy, see 144 Cong Rec S 11872, 11880 (Oct 8, 1998); two claims that preemption of state products liability laws would be unconstitutional, authored by the National Conference of State Legislatures and inserted into the Congressional Record, see 144 Cong Rec 7707 (July 9, 1998); 144 Cong Rec S 7526 (July 7, 1998); and a claim by Senator Hatch that limitations on attorneys fees in tobacco settlements violate *Printz*, see 144 Cong Rec S 6149, 6168 (June 11, 1998). The 1997 references were contained in an article inserted into the record by Senator Leahy which criticized conservative judicial activism, see 143 Cong Rec S 11938, 11939 (Nov 7, 1997); and a list of recent Supreme Court cases, see 143 Cong Rec S 12023, 12026 (Nov 7, 1997).

[191] A LEXIS search on November 29, 1998, of the Congressional Record in the Genfed; Record library for "New York v. United States and Date > 1991" yielded 21 citations. Nor do the cases appear frequently in legislative history. A November 29, 1998, LEXIS search for "Printz v. United States or New York v. United States and Date > 1991" in the Legis;Cmtrpt library identified only three committee reports. Two involved legislation that was crafted to avoid the anticommandeering limitation by attaching requirements to spending programs. See Committee on Commerce, *National Salvage Motor Vehicle Consumer Protection Act of 1997*, HR Rep No 105-285 pt 1, 105th Cong, 1st Sess (Sept 30, 1997); Committee on Commerce, Science, and Transportation, *Internet Filtering Systems*, S Rep No 105-226, 105th Cong, 2d Sess (June 25, 1998). One involved an assertion that *Printz* had little impact because it only struck down an interim provision and "the vast majority of local law enforcement officials" complied voluntarily. Committee on Judiciary, *Violent and Repeat Juvenile Offender Act of 1997*, S Rep No 105-108, 105th Cong, 1st Sess 203 (Oct 9, 1997) (views of Senators Kennedy, Biden, Kohl, Feinstein, Durbin, and Torricelli).

[192] A Nov 29, 1998, LEXIS search for "Printz v. United States" in the Legis;Cngtst library of testimony before congressional committees yielded 21 citations; a LEXIS search for "New York v. United States and Date > 1991" yielded 47 citations.

[193] It might be argued that the Court's overall activism in the area of federalism has raised the profile of Tenth Amendment constraints on federal authority, even though no particular case is mentioned in congressional debate. The evidence here might initially suggest such an effect. Our LEXIS research revealed that, in the six years between June 1986 and July 1992, the Tenth Amendment was mentioned in 88 documents in the Congressional Record; the period between June 1992 (following *New York*) and July 1998 contains 287 documents mentioning the Tenth Amendment. But the profile of these mentions makes another explanation more likely. The period 1992–93 contains 17 documents mentioning the Tenth Amendment; 1993–94 contains 21. In 1994–95 the documents surge to 108, but 1995–96 contains 63 documents, 1996–97 contains 34, and 1997–98 contains 44. The fact that the

The second difficulty with an expressive justification is that, whatever the impact on norms of political discourse and decision making, the Court's message is conveyed by invalidating duly enacted federal statutes. Invalidation may impose substantial collateral damage on real people and entities who seek the benefits of the statutes. In both *New York* and *Printz*, the Court was in a position to deliver its message essentially cost-free. In *New York*, the Court upheld two of three mechanisms for implementing the low-level nuclear waste statute, and these two were likely to be adequate to the task. In *Printz*, the Court struck down an enforcement mechanism for the Brady Act that was due to be superseded in short order[194] and that, in any event, most states voluntarily followed.[195] But the reach of the anticommandeering principle is hardly limited to issues of peripheral practical importance. The doctrine's lack of clarity and potential expansiveness are likely to invite activist members of the lower federal judiciary to constitute themselves as censors of the federal government in more important cases. In these subsequent cases, the opportunity to exhort Congress may not come so cheaply.

The imperative not to overrule large bodies of existing case law has already led the Court to install a series of escape hatches in the anticommandeering doctrine. In circumstances where significant federal statutes are at stake, we expect the Court to make use of those exceptions to allow Congress to work its will, or to find new exceptions to permit the statute at hand. With the emergence of a patchwork of ad hoc exceptions, the doctrine will lose whatever normative force it had initially.

Indeed, the nature of the federal judicial system itself will impose a continued pressure to abandon the field. The Supreme

---

surge in 1994–95 preceded the Court's exertions in *Lopez* and *Seminole Tribe* (70 of the 108 mentions in 1994–95 preceded *Lopez*, the earlier decision) and subsided at the end of the congressional term despite the Court's continued activism persuades us that the increase is better accounted for by the election of 1994 and the Contract with America. For discussion of the political climate of the period and congressional maneuvering on the issue of unfunded mandates, see Timothy J. Conlan et al, *Deregulating Federalism? The Politics of Mandate Reform in the 104th Congress*, PUBLIUS 23 (Summer 1995).

[194] Specifically, the provisions struck down in *Printz* were interim provisions, to be superseded by the Attorney General's establishment of a national instant background check system, which the Act required him to do by Nov 30, 1998. See 117 S Ct at 2368–69.

[195] See Committee on Judiciary, *Violent and Repeat Juvenile Offender Act of 1997*, S Rep No 105–108, 105th Cong, 1st Sess 203 (Oct 9, 1997) (views of Senators Kennedy, Biden, Kohl, Feinstein, Durbin, and Torricelli).

Court cannot review every case decided by the lower federal judiciary; its doctrine will be applied by a series of lower court judges around the country. In the absence of some doctrinal regularity, the total work product of the judiciary will collapse into an unworkable hodgepodge. One of the potential virtues of the kind of common-law approach followed by the Court in the anticommandeering area is the treatment of similarly situated individuals and institutions in a similar fashion. But, absent some degree of doctrinal predictability, congressional authority will vary from circuit to circuit, and neither state nor federal officials will be able to foresee the scope of their legal authority. The easiest way for the Court to avoid a flood of federalism litigation, and to achieve predictability and uniformity, will be to abandon the field. This was the fate of *National League of Cities*, and the decision to dodge the constitutional issue in *Yeskey*, combined with the denial of certiorari in the parallel case raising the question whether the ADA is Section 5 legislation,[196] suggests that the Supreme Court has started down the same road.

To the extent the Court does in fact sustain some commandeering challenges, the instrumental difficulty takes on another cast. Since, as we have argued, the doctrinal lines between permissible and impermissible exercises of national power are unjustified in light of federalism values, the damage to the interests of the citizenry will be arbitrarily distributed. A doctrine that reinforces pro-federalism norms in the political process, at the expense of the interests of an arbitrarily selected segment of the citizenry, is not one which does the Court much credit, or which is likely to strengthen respect for federalism over the long run.

B. EXPRESSING OUR FEDERALISM

Some recent proponents of the expressive function of law maintain that the message contained in a law can play not just the instrumental role of changing norms, but the intrinsic role of consti-

---

[196] See *Clark v California*, 123 F3d 1267 (9th Cir 1997), cert denied, 118 S Ct 2340 (1998). While this article was in press, the Court followed the pattern of *Yeskey* and *Clark* by specifically amending an order granting certiorari to exclude the question of whether the ADA exceeds congressional powers under Section 5 of the Fourteenth Amendment. *Olmstead v L.C.*, 119 S Ct 633 (1998).

tuting "the political identity of a state."[197] By parity of reasoning, the anticommandeering principle of *Printz* might express the fact and importance of our regime of constitutional federalism—and thereby be partly constitutive of that regime—quite apart from any effect on the political process. Conversely, one might argue that a law that commandeers state officials expresses an understanding of the political structure at odds with the core federalist commitments of America.

At one level it is hard to disagree with these kinds of claims, since what is expressed to some extent lies in the eye of the beholder. If a majority of the Court says that commandeering expresses values at odds with Our Federalism, who can argue? Such legislation apparently expresses those values to a majority of the Court.

Still, this is an awfully loose concept with which to make legal decisions. As we argued above, it is likely to be unstable. Moreover, as it stands, the doctrine is both substantially overinclusive and substantially underinclusive relative to federalism values and, relatedly, to the subjective reactions of most of the polity. Despite some overheated rhetoric surrounding the issue, it is difficult to believe that the provisions of the Brady Act at issue in *Printz*—requiring state law enforcement officers to expend reasonable efforts to determine the legality of gun purchases—express disrespect for federalism sufficient to make them unconstitutional. Does anyone think that the Brady Act was really read by a substantial segment of the public as the precursor to the elimination of state sovereignty? *New York* might have been a stronger case for the expressivist, but the Court has specifically declined to limit the anticommandeering principle to areas which involve political choices and to policy-making.[198]

Reciprocally, given the demarcations that surround it, the anticommandeering doctrine appears to strain at gnats while swallowing camels. On any sensible definition of federalism, it is hard to distinguish—in terms of regard for state autonomy—the message expressed by a federal requirement whose sanctions are that a state "take title" to nuclear wastes (the requirement invalidated by *New*

---

[197] Jean Hampton, *Punishment, Feminism and Political Identity: A Case Study in the Expressive Meaning of the Law*, 11 Can J L & Juris 23, 23 (1998).

[198] See *Printz*, 117 S Ct at 2380–81.

York) from the message expressed by federal requirements backed by the threat of preempting state law or of eliminating state access to federal resources (the requirements upheld in *New York*). And does anyone believe that a total preemption of state gun laws would express less intrusion on state sovereignty than the Brady Act?[199]

To put the point more generally: an intrinsic, expressive theory of federalism doctrine, to be plausible, must presuppose some objective semantic rules for attaching "meanings" to acts of federal legislation. But we know of no such rules independent of the federalism values at stake in this area. A federal statute seems to (objectively) say the right thing about federalism just insofar as it is otherwise justified on federalism grounds. Because the anticommandeering doctrines cannot, we have argued, be otherwise justified on federalism grounds, the expressive story fails as well.

VI. Conclusion

This article has presented an internal critique of the anticommandeering doctrines emerging in *New York*, *Printz*, and *Yeskey*. Someone who denies that a federal structure serves important values, or that those values take constitutional status, or that the thus-constitutionalized values ought to be judicially enforced, will need little persuading that the anticommandeering doctrines are misconceived. So we have assumed (without endorsement) the view that *some* federal statutes should be invalidated by constitutional reviewing courts on federalism grounds, and have argued that the emerging doctrines fail to sort between permissible and impermissible statutes in a coherent and attractive way.

The proponent of the doctrines might respond that they have a textual or originalist warrant. But in fact they have no such warrant, as other scholars have shown.[200] We have therefore directed

---

[199] While this article was in press, the Court upheld the jurisdiction of the Federal Communications Commission, under the Telecommunications Act of 1996, to promulgate rules concerning local telephone pricing and other aspects of local telephone markets, to be implemented by state commissions. This led Justice Breyer, in dissent, to object that "[t]oday's decision does deprive the States of practically significant power, a camel compared with *Printz*'s gnat." *AT&T Corp. v Iowa Utilities Board*, 1999 WL 24568, * 32 (US) (Breyer concurring in part and dissenting in part).

[200] See Jackson, 111 Harv L Rev at 2199–2200; Caminker, 1997 Supreme Court Review at 209–17; Caminker, 95 Colum L Rev at 1030–50 (all cited in note 1); Erik M. Jensen and Jonathan L. Entin, *Commandeering, the Tenth Amendment, and the Federal Requisition*

our attention, instead, to the question whether the lines of demarcation constitutive of the anticommandeering doctrines can be justified in light of standard federalism values, and we have answered that question in the negative. It is no response, either, that any rule-like doctrines will be underinclusive or overinclusive relative to supporting values. For what we have shown—if we have been successful—is that the *Printz*, *New York*, and *Yeskey* demarcations do not even track federalism values in a probabilistic way, let alone perfectly. There is simply no difference, even in general, between permissible preemption and impermissible commandeering with respect to the values of innovation, diversity, tyranny prevention, and political community—and the same is true of all the other demarcations except for the Reconstruction Amendment demarcations. Further, the sacrifice in accuracy associated with rule-like doctrines ought to be made up by a gain in clarity; and yet the doctrines at issue here are generally quite unclear. These normative failures in the doctrines have, in turn, emboldened us to make the positive prediction that the doctrines will soon be abandoned, as was *National League of Cities* a generation ago. A jurisprudence that consists of nothing more than some arbitrary rules of "etiquette" ought to be, and we hope soon will be, outgrown.

Power: New York v. United States Revisited, 15 Const Comm 355 (1998). See also Saikrishna Bangalore Prakash, *Field Office Federalism*, 79 Va L Rev 1957 (1993) (arguing that original understanding supports anticommandeering rule for state legislatures but not executives).

EVAN TSEN LEE
AND ASHUTOSH BHAGWAT

THE McCLESKEY PUZZLE: REMEDYING PROSECUTORIAL DISCRIMINATION AGAINST BLACK VICTIMS IN CAPITAL SENTENCING

In this article we analyze possible legislative and judicial alternatives for redressing prosecutorial race discrimination against murder victims. There are both substantive and procedural obstacles to such remedies. The substantive obstacle is the doctrine that requires proof of intentional discrimination to make out a violation of the Equal Protection Clause. The procedural obstacles arise out of the standing doctrine and the law of official immunity. We conclude that the most promising remedies are to commute the death sentences of defendants whose victims' lives have been overvalued on the basis of race and to award damages to the families of murder victims whose lives have been undervalued on the basis of race.

Evan Tsen Lee is Professor of Law, University of California, Hastings College of Law. Ashutosh Bhagwat is Associate Professor of Law, University of California, Hastings College of Law.

AUTHORS' NOTE: We would like to thank Vik Amar, David Faigman, and Rory Little for their helpful comments and Alyson Lewis and Matt Borden for excellent research assistance.

I. McCleskey v Kemp and Discrimination in Capital Sentencing

We begin with *McCleskey v Kemp*[1] because, although the scope of our inquiry considerably exceeds the factual radius of *McCleskey*, the topic of prosecutorial race discrimination among murder victims simply cannot be comprehended without reference to that decision. In 1978, Warren McCleskey was sentenced to death by a Georgia jury for the murder of a white police officer. The killing occurred during the course of an armed robbery committed by McCleskey and three accomplices.[2] McCleskey was "eligible" for the death penalty because of two aggravating factors found by the jury: the murder was committed during the course of an armed robbery, and it was committed on a peace officer engaged in the performance of his duties.[3] McCleskey eventually brought a petition for a writ of habeas corpus in federal district court, arguing that "the Georgia capital sentencing process is administered in a racially discriminatory manner in violation of the Eighth and Fourteenth Amendments to the United States Constitution."[4]

McCleskey's primary evidence in support of this claim was the so-called Baldus study, a sophisticated statistical analysis performed by Professors David C. Baldus, Charles Pulaski, and George Woodworth of the role played by race in capital sentencing proceedings in Georgia in the 1970s. The Baldus study was based on data from more than 2,000 Georgia murder cases during the relevant period. It considered 230 potentially relevant, nonracial variables that might explain disparities in capital sentencing. The

---

[1] 481 US 279 (1987).

[2] Warren McCleskey was executed by the State of Georgia in 1991. See Peter Applebome, *Georgia Inmate Is Executed After "Chaotic" Legal Move*, New York Times A18 (September 26, 1991). He had the dubious distinction of producing in the course of his appeals not one but two Supreme Court decisions that were highly unfavorable to capital defendants. See *McCleskey v Kemp*, 481 US 279 (1987); *McCleskey v Zant*, 499 US 467 (1991) (establishing "abuse of writ" rule prohibiting defendants from filing successive federal writs of habeas corpus, absent a showing of "cause and prejudice").

[3] *McCleskey*, 481 US at 283–85.

[4] Id at 286. This article will not discuss McCleskey's claim that racial discrimination in capital sentencing violates the Eighth Amendment's prohibition on "Cruel and Unusual Punishment," primarily to keep our inquiry within manageable proportions, but also because we believe that both historically and doctrinally, the Equal Protection Clause offers the best fit for addressing discrimination against black murder victims.

Baldus study is generally accepted within the social scientific community as a thorough, carefully conducted analysis, and its results as almost certainly statistically valid.[5]

The results of the Baldus study are striking. The race of the victim was an overwhelmingly important indicator of the likelihood that a capital sentence would be imposed. After controlling for the thirty-nine most relevant nonracial variables, murderers of whites were 4.3 times as likely to receive a death sentence as murderers of blacks.[6] The race of the defendant was hardly influential at all: black defendants were only 1.1 times (i.e., 10%) more likely to receive a death sentence than white defendants, and later writings by the authors of the Baldus study suggest that this result is not statistically significant.[7] Furthermore, the Baldus study's findings regarding the prevalence of race-of-victim discrimination in capital sentencing (and indeed its findings regarding the *lack* of race-of-defendant discrimination) are fully supported by other social scientific research.[8]

In addition to its findings regarding end-result discrimination, the Baldus study also sheds light on the loci of discrimination

---

[5] See Randall L Kennedy, *McCleskey v Kemp: Race, Capital Punishment, and the Supreme Court,* 101 Harv L Rev 1388, 1398–1400 and nn 40–47. It should be noted that while the District Court in the *McCleskey* case questioned the validity of the study, both the Court of Appeals and the Supreme Court assumed its validity. *McCleskey,* 481 US at 291 n 7. Moreover, the grounds upon which the District Court questioned the study appear to have been ill-informed, and almost certainly incorrect as a matter of statistical methodology. For a discussion, see Kennedy, 101 Harv L Rev at 1400 and nn 44–45.

[6] *McCleskey,* 481 US at 287.

[7] See Kennedy (cited in note 5), 101 Harv L Rev at 1390–91 n 13 (citing David C. Baldus, George Woodworth, and Charles Pulaski, *Arbitrariness and Discrimination in the Administration of the Death Penalty: A Challenge to State Supreme Courts,* 15 Stetson L Rev 133, 158 (1986); Baldus, Woodworth, and Pulaski, *Monitoring and Evaluating Contemporary Death Sentencing Systems: Lessons from Georgia,* 18 UC Davis L Rev 1375, 1404 (1985)); Baldus, Woodworth, and Pulaski, *Equal Justice and the Death Penalty* 185 (1990) ("Statewide, we see no evidence of race-of-defendant discrimination").

[8] In 1990, the General Accounting Office issued a report summarizing and analyzing existing studies regarding the role played by racial factors in capital sentencing. U.S. General Accounting Office, *Death Penalty Sentencing: Research Indicates Pattern of Racial Disparities* (1990) ("GAO Report"), cited in Note, *Easing the Fear of Too Much Justice: A Compromise Proposal to Revise the Racial Justice Act,* 30 Harv CR-CL L Rev 543, 543 and n 4 (1995). After reviewing a large number of studies that themselves examined a variety of state systems and spanned a time period from 1979 to 1990, the Report concluded unambiguously that the findings of race-of-victim discrimination were "remarkably consistent." As with the Baldus study, however, the studies were less likely to find race-of-defendant discrimination, and if found, such discrimination was likely to be less serious. GAO Report at 5–6 (quoted in Note, 30 Harv CR-CL L Rev at 544–45).

within the capital sentencing system. While the study found discrimination in every stage of the process,[9] it found race to be particularly important in the *charging decision* made by prosecutors following a jury conviction for murder. Prosecutors were many times more likely to seek the death penalty in a case involving a white victim than in a case involving a black victim. Once again, these results were statistically significant after being subjected to a multivariate regression analysis;[10] and, once again, other research fully confirms these findings.[11]

Despite these results, the Supreme Court, as well as every other court to hear the case, rejected McCleskey's claim of a constitutional violation.[12] The basis for the Court's holding was that to prove an equal protection violation, McCleskey was required to "prove that the decisionmakers in his case acted with discriminatory purpose." According to the Court, the statistical findings of the Baldus study, without more, were inadequate to establish purposeful discrimination.[13] The Court's primary objection to McCleskey's claim appeared to be that he was unable to prove that any of the specific actors in his case, whether it be the prosecutor, judge, or jurors, had acted with discriminatory intent. According to the Court, statistical evidence alone could not make out such proof because, given the large number of factors that are potentially relevant to the charging and sentencing decisions, there

---

[9] *McCleskey*, 481 US at 350–51 (Blackmun, J, dissenting); id at 356 n 11 (Blackmun, J, dissenting).

[10] Id at 350–51, 356–57 (Blackmun, J, dissenting); Baldus, Woodworth, and Pulaski, *Equal Justice and the Death Penalty* 162 (1990); Note, *Easing the Fear of Too Much Justice: A Compromise Proposal to Revise the Racial Justice Act*, 30 Harv CR-CL L Rev 543, 549 n 22 (1995).

[11] See Kennedy, 101 Harv L Rev at 1435 n 213 (citing Joseph E. Jacoby and Raymond Paternoster, *Sentencing Disparity and Jury Packing: Further Challenges to the Death Penalty*, 73 J Crim L & Criminol 379 (1982); Raymond Pasternoster, *Race of Victim and Location of Crime: The Decision to Seek the Death Penalty in South Carolina*, 74 J Crim L & Criminol 754 (1983); Michael L. Radelet and Glenn L. Pierce, *Race and Prosecutorial Discretion in Homicide Cases*, 19 L & Society Rev 587 (1985)); Baldus, Woodworth, and Pulaski, *Equal Justice and the Death Penalty* 257 (1990) (citing Raymond Pasternoster, *Prosecutorial Discretion in Requesting the Death Penalty: A Case of Victim-Based Racial Discrimination*, 18 L & Society Rev 437 (1984); Elizabeth Lynch Murphy, *Application of the Death Penalty in Cook County*, 73 Ill Bar J 90 (1984)); Thomas J. Keil and Gennaro F. Vito, *Race and the Death Penalty in Kentucky Murder Trials: 1976–1991: A Study of Racial Bias as a Factor in Capital Sentencing*, http://dpa.state.ky.us/~rwheeler/archives/race/vito.txt, p. 8 (1995).

[12] *McCleskey*, 481 US at 289–91.

[13] Id at 292–94.

could be no confidence that race played a role in any particular case.[14] In the Court's words, "[A]t most, the Baldus study indicates a discrepancy that appears to correlate with race."[15] The Court asserted that the statistical evidence of the Baldus study did not make out even a prima facie case that McCleskey himself was subjected to racial discrimination "because a legitimate and unchallenged explanation for the decision [to sentence McCleskey to death] is apparent from the record: McCleskey committed an act for which the United States Constitution and Georgia laws permit imposition of the death penalty."[16]

Some implications quite plainly follow from the extensive race-of-victim discrimination that exists in capital sentencing. First, if the death penalty in fact has any deterrent value, then the disinclination to impose the penalty in black-victim cases would tend to increase the murder rate against blacks, and thus systematically provide blacks less protection.[17] Second, even if the death penalty does not deter, the disinclination to impose the penalty in black-victim cases imposes intangible but important harms on black victims' families because it denies them the sense of closure and "justice" that the death penalty affords, and also stigmatizes them as inferior in the eyes of the law.[18]

---

[14] Id at 295 and n 15.

[15] Id at 312. The Court's description of the study is inaccurate because a multivariate regression shows more than a mere correlation; if the underlying model is properly specified and relevant independent variables are properly included, as was apparently the case with the Baldus study, such an analysis tends to show causation, since other possible explanations have been accounted for and rejected by the model. For a more detailed discussion, see Part II.

[16] Id at 297.

[17] For similar arguments, see Kennedy, 101 Harv L Rev at 1425 (cited in note 5); Stephen L. Carter, *When the Victims Happen to Be Black*, 97 Yale L J 444 (1998). Of course, the deterrent effects of the death penalty remain highly controversial, with many studies concluding that such effects are small or nonexistent. See Note (cited in note 8), 30 Harv CR-CL L Rev at 547 and n 14 (citing Hugo Adam Bedau, *The Death Penalty in America* 95–185 (3d ed 1982); Walter Berns, *For Capital Punishment: Crime and the Morality of the Death Penalty* 83–127 (1979); Mark Tushnet, *The Death Penalty* 5–10, 134 nn 5–8 (1994)); Kennedy, 101 Harv L Rev at 1425 and n 171 (cited in note 5).

[18] A primary, if not the only, function performed by the death penalty in our society is retributive—the death penalty serves to satisfy society's, and a victim's friends' and family's, need for retribution and justice. Viewed in this light, the death penalty is a benefit that the law dispenses to the survivors of murder victims, apparently in a highly discriminatory manner.

II. Equal Protection as Protecting Equally:
The Problem of Intent

The systematic race-of-victim discrimination that infects the administration of the death penalty would seem to seriously implicate the equal protection rights of blacks who are potential or actual victims of crime. Indeed, such discrimination conflicts with one of the core, historical objectives of the Equal Protection Clause, which was to require southern states to protect newly freed slaves from private violence by southern whites, and to prosecute those who engaged in violence against blacks in the same manner that they prosecuted those who attacked whites.[19] But to establish an actual violation of these rights, such black victims must satisfy the "purposeful discrimination" requirement of *McCleskey* and the Supreme Court's modern equal protection doctrine.

McCleskey rested on the "intent" requirement of modern equal protection doctrine. Since its landmark decision in *Washington v Davis* in 1976,[20] the Supreme Court has consistently held that in order to establish a violation of the Equal Protection Clause based on racial discrimination, a litigant must show that the state has engaged in purposeful, or intentional, discrimination. Mere statistical disparity, or unequal effect, will not suffice. Thus, in *Arlington Heights v Metropolitan Housing Dev. Corp.*,[21] the Court rejected an equal protection challenge to a city's zoning ordinance even though it excluded low-income housing residents, a large percentage of whom were minorities (primarily blacks). More recently, in

---

[19] As Justice Blackmun pointed out in his dissent in *McCleskey*, southern violence against blacks was very much in the minds of the drafters of the Equal Protection Clause. See *McCleskey*, 481 US at 346–47 and n 2 (Blackmun, J, dissenting) (quoting extensive testimony before the Joint Committee on Reconstruction of violence against blacks, and inaction by state officials). Furthermore, just three years after the ratification of the Fourteenth Amendment, Congress enacted legislation enforcing the Amendment, the Ku Klux Klan Act of 1871, which specifically targeted private southern violence against blacks. See Act of April 20, 1871, ch 22, 17 Stat 13; *Briscoe v LaHue*, 460 US 325, 337–38 (1983); Robert J. Kaczorowski, *The Nationalization of Civil Rights* 166 and n 10 (1987); John Harrison, *Reconstructing the Privileges and Immunities Clause*, 101 Yale L J 1385, 1427 and nn 213–15 (1992); Earl A. Maltz, *The Concept of Equal Protection of the Laws—a Historical Inquiry*, 22 San Diego L Rev 499, 521–22 (1985).

[20] 426 US 229 (1976). The *Davis* Court held that the Equal Protection Clause was not violated by the Washington, D.C., Police Department's use of a written examination to screen applicants, even though the test disqualified black applicants at a much higher rate than whites.

[21] 429 US 252 (1977).

Personnel Administrator v Feeney,[22] the Court held that a Massachusetts law granting a preference in state hiring to veterans did not
violate the Equal Protection Clause even though the law sharply
reduced the public employment opportunities available to women
(because the vast majority of eligible veterans are men). Crucially,
in *Feeney* the Court noted that it would not matter for equal protection purposes that the legislators knew at the time they adopted
the preference that the law would disadvantage women, so long
as it was not the reason for their decision. The Court explained
that the Equal Protection Clause would not be violated unless the
government acted "at least in part 'because of,' not merely 'in spite
of,' its adverse effect upon an identified group."[23]

The zenith of the "intent" standard—some would say the nadir[24]—was *McCleskey*. Justice Powell's majority opinion rejected
McCleskey's challenge to the Georgia death penalty system because he had failed to prove that he was the victim of intentional
discrimination,[25] invoking the language in *Feeney* that intentional
discrimination must occur "because of," not merely "in spite of,"
race.[26] In particular, the Court held that the purely statistical evidence presented by McCleskey (i.e., the Baldus study) did not
demonstrate that any state actor had purposefully discriminated
in McCleskey's own case. Nor, in the Court's estimation, did it
demonstrate that Georgia had adopted or maintained its death
penalty system as a whole "because of" its racially skewed impact.
The Court therefore concluded that McCleskey had not proven a
violation of the Equal Protection Clause.

What does "intent" mean in the equal protection context? Some
have equated discriminatory intent with "malice," or a desire to
harm a subjugated group.[27] Others have equated intent with con-

---

[22] 442 US 256 (1979).

[23] Id at 279. See also *City of Memphis v Greene*, 451 US 100, reh'g den 452 US 955 (1981)
(rejecting claim that a city's decision to close a street within a white neighborhood used
primarily by black motorists constituted "intentional" discrimination).

[24] *McCleskey* has been variously described as the "most troubling," and "most controversial
and, to some, notorious" of the cases applying the intent rule. See Theodore Eisenberg
and Sheri Lynn Johnson, *The Effects of Intent: Do We Know How Legal Standards Work?* 76
Cornell L Rev 1151, 1159–60 (1991) ("most troubling"); Daniel Ortiz, *The Myth of Intent
in Equal Protection*, 41 Stan L Rev 1105, 1142 (1989) ("most controversial").

[25] *McCleskey v Kemp*, 481 US 279, 292–93, 298–99 (1987).

[26] Id at 298.

[27] See, e.g., Reva Siegel, *Why Equal Protection No Longer Protects: The Evolving Forms of
Status-Enforcing State Action*, 49 Stan L Rev 1111, 1134–35 (1997); Linda Hamilton Krieger,

scious awareness or deliberate behavior.[28] However, these understandings are inadequate and inconsistent with the Court's own
case law.[29] The notion that intent equates to malice is peculiar.[30]
Imagine a state official who refused to hire racial minorities into
government jobs not because he disliked minorities, but only because he wished to benefit his own ethnic group by hiring them.
Surely such actions would constitute "intentional" discrimination.
Consider also *Palmore v Sidoti*, where the Court unanimously held
that a state's denial of child custody to a divorced mother because
she was part of a interracial couple violated the Equal Protection
Clause, even though the denial of custody was motivated by "the
best interests of the child" in that the state's purpose was to protect
the child from the discrimination that such couples are likely to
face.[31] *Palmore* seems to establish quite clearly that intent may exist
without malice.

The reasons why "intent" cannot be equated with conscious
awareness are more complex, but ultimately also powerful. *Feeney*
establishes that conscious awareness of harm, standing alone, does
not constitute discrimination, and that intent is not the same thing
as consciousness. But *Feeney* does not exclude the possibility that
conscious awareness may be a necessary element of intent. In considering this issue it is necessary to first ask what else "intent"

---

*The Content of Our Categories: A Cognitive Bias Approach to Discrimination in Equal Employment
Opportunity*, 47 Stan L Rev 1161, 1177 (1995); Kennedy, 101 Harv L Rev at 1404–05 (cited
in note 5).

[28] See, e.g., Barbara J. Flagg, *"Was Blind, But Now I See": White Race Consciousness and
the Requirement of Discriminatory Intent*, 91 Mich L Rev 953, 980 (1993); see generally Michael Selmi, *Proving Intentional Discrimination: The Reality of Supreme Court Rhetoric*, 86
Georgetown L J 279, 288–89 and n 5 (1997).

[29] Id at 288–89.

[30] Recent cases establish quite clearly that proof of malice is *not* required to challenge
government action that is explicitly race-based. The Court in recent years has invalidated
on equal protection grounds many state and federal affirmative action programs designed
to benefit racial minorities. See, e.g., *Adarand Constructors, Inc. v Pena*, 515 US 200 (1995);
City of Richmond v JA Croson Co., 488 US 469 (1989); see also *Hopwood v Texas*, 78 F3d
932 (5th Cir 1996), cert den 116 S Ct 2580 (1996). No one would seriously suggest that
such programs are motivated by malice against their white "victims." Nonetheless, such
programs are regularly struck down. In another line of recent cases, involving racially based
resdistricting, the Court has invalidated "majority-minority" legislative districts drawn in
unusual shapes for the apparent purpose of enhancing the voting power of racial minorities.
See, e.g., *Bush v Vera*, 116 S Ct 1941 (1996); *Miller v Johnson*, 515 US 900 (1995); *Shaw
v Reno*, 509 US 630 (1993). Once again, the creation of such districts cannot seriously be
ascribed to "malice" toward whites, but they have been nonetheless held to "intentionally
discriminate."

[31] 466 US 429 (1984).

could possibly be. If neither malice nor conscious awareness is intent, then what is it? In a recent paper, Michael Selmi points out that when one examines the Court's "intent" decisions closely, especially *Feeney* and *McCleskey*, what the Court really seems to mean by intent is causation—whether, in fact, particular government conduct was caused by the race of the adversely affected parties. Such an explanation is consistent with the "because of" language of *Feeney* and *McCleskey*, and with the reasoning and results in the vast majority of the Court's decisions, in a way that no other theory can match.[32] The term "causation," as used here, is essentially equivalent to the concept of "but for" causation as used in tort and criminal law, rather than "legal" or "proximate" cause. There are some practical differences between causation in this context and criminal or tort causation, particularly in terms of ease of proof, but the fundamental inquiry is the same. In the tort and criminal contexts, but-for causation generally turns on whether as a matter of objective, physical fact a particular outcome resulted from the particular conduct by an individual. Causation in the equal protection context requires an examination of the decision-making process engaged in by a government actor to determine if race was a determinative input into that process (for this reason, it is not incongruous to use the term "intent" to describe this analysis). Note that even the equal protection causation test is not primarily an inquiry into the subjective state of mind of the decision maker. Instead, it seeks to determine whether the ultimate result would have been the same if the races of the affected individuals were different with all other factors left unchanged.[33]

Assuming that the best reading of the Court's cases is that "intent" in the equal protection context refers to causation, the question left open in *Feeney* remains: whether the intent standard requires that the relevant government actors be conscious that race

---

[32] See Selmi, 86 Georgetown L J at 289–94 (cited in note 28); see also George Rutherglen, *Discrimination and Its Discontents*, 81 Va L Rev 117, 127 (1995); Paul J. Gudel, *Beyond Causation: The Interpretation of Action and the Mixed Motives Problem in Employment Discrimination Law*, 70 Tex L Rev 17, 93 (1991).

[33] This understanding of "intent," as essentially an inquiry into causation, is probably best expressed by David Strauss's proposed "reversing the groups" test: to determine if intentional discrimination exists, one must ask whether if the race (or gender) of the affected individuals had been reversed, the same action would have been taken. Selmi, 86 Georgetown L J at 291–94 (cited in note 28) (citing David Strauss, *Discriminatory Intent and the Taming of Brown*, 56 U Chi L Rev 935, 958 (1989)).

has affected their decision making. Of course, this issue arises only if one believes that certain kinds of mental processes can be influenced, even decisively influenced, by factors of which the person is unaware. In the late twentieth century, however, few people would seriously deny that some mental processes occur below the conscious level. As Charles Lawrence has demonstrated, overwhelming psychological evidence supports the proposition that racism, meaning decision making influenced by racial factors, is one of those processes that often occurs within the unconscious.[34] What, then, is the constitutional status of governmental action *caused* by racial factors—meaning that if race alone had been different, the state would have acted differently—but where the government actor was not consciously aware of those racial factors?

The Court has never squarely considered the possibility. There are, however, strong reasons why the government actor's conscious mental state should be irrelevant to the constitutional analysis. If a plaintiff is able to prove that government action was taken *because of* race, to ask the plaintiff to further prove that the state actor was consciously aware of this fact imposes an almost insurmountable burden of proof (except in the rare instance where the decision maker admits the awareness). It is also not clear what policies would be advanced by such a requirement.[35] Moreover, the argument in favor of a purely causation-based approach to intent, powerful as it is when applied to individual governmental decision makers, becomes overwhelming when the government conduct at issue is the product of collective decision making, as many discriminatory state policies are. In the collective context, the concept of conscious intent is not merely difficult to prove, it is meaningless. Groups do not have mental states, and while individual members of groups might be shown to possess particular mental states, there is no evident reason to attribute the motive of any particular indi-

---

[34] Charles R. Lawrence III, *The Id, the Ego, and Equal Protection: Reckoning with Unconscious Racism*, 39 Stan L Rev 317, 328–44 (1987). We concede that it may be controversial to use the word "racism" to describe such unconscious racially influenced behavior. Terminology, however, is beside the point—the issue is whether such behavior is proscribed by the Equal Protection Clause.

[35] See Selmi, 86 Georgetown L J at 294 (cited in note 28); Charles R. Lawrence III, 39 Stan L Rev 317 (cited in note 28); Paul Brest, *Foreword: In Defense of the Antidiscrimination Principle*, 90 Harv L Rev 1, 14–15 (1976).

vidual to the group as a whole. Causation, on the other hand, remains a coherent (though complex) inquiry in the group context. As a consequence, when assessing the constitutionality of collective decision making, a causation analysis is not only a possible mode of inquiry in defining intent, it is the most coherent mode of inquiry.

The above discussion of the meaning of the intent standard and its proper application in the context of unconscious racism and collective decision making is crucial to a proper assessment of *McCleskey*. The racial disparities observed in modern death penalty schemes, especially the differing treatment of *victims* of different races, are almost certainly not a product of racial animus, and indeed probably not even of conscious racism.[36] Instead, the results are probably best explained as a result of a selective indifference on the part of prosecutors (and jurors) toward the plight of black victims. In short, decision makers, whether consciously or not, do not value the lives of black victims at the same level as they value the lives of white victims, leaving aside for now the question of which valuation is "correct."[37] Race is thus a *causal* factor with respect to government decision making in this context, in the sense that it is a but-for cause, even if it is not the motive for the decision or even in the conscious awareness of the various actors. That should be sufficient to establish a violation of the Equal Protection Clause.

One further matter merits discussion. It is possible that prosecutors (many of whom are elected) are choosing not to punish murderers of blacks in the same way as murderers of whites not because the prosecutors value the lives of black victims less, but because they perceive that the public does so. These prosecutors may wish to maximize their political gain from death penalty prosecutions, or to maximize their probability of obtaining a verdict of death from juries who are infected by the same biases as the general public.[38] The Court's decision in *Palmore v Sidoti* makes

---

[36] See Randall L. Kennedy, *McCleskey v Kemp: Race, Capital Punishment, and the Supreme Court*, 101 Harv L Rev 1388, 1419–21 (1988); Carter, 97 Yale L J at 420, 444 (cited in note 17).

[37] See Part III.B. for a discussion of the "baseline" problem raised by such discriminatory evaluation.

[38] Compare Samuel R. Gross and Robert Mauro, *Patterns of Death: An Analysis of Racial Disparities in Capital Sentencing and Homicide Victimization*, 37 Stan L Rev 27, 106–09 (1984).

clear, however, that a decision by a governmental actor effectuating or catering to private discrimination itself violates the Equal Protection Clause.[39]

Finally, we reach that most perplexing facet of *McCleskey*—the relationship between the "intent" requirement and the use of statistical evidence. At bottom, *McCleskey* rests on the conclusion that even the sophisticated, multivariate regression analysis of the Baldus study is inadequate *as a matter of law* in this context to "prove" intentional discrimination in a particular case. *McCleskey* did not hold that statistical evidence is always insufficient to prove intent. Indeed, the Court acknowledged that in jury selection and employment discrimination cases, statistical evidence is regularly accepted as evidence of intent. But the Court distinguished the death penalty context primarily on the ground that the presence of substantial discretion in capital sentencing made reliance on statistical evidence inappropriate.[40]

The Court's reasoning reflects a profound misunderstanding of the nature of statistical evidence and of discretion. The existence of discretion does not mean that decisions are random or that they are not produced by guiding factors. If that is what discretion meant, then the death penalty would be generally unconstitutional under the Eighth Amendment.[41] Discretion means that a decision is properly influenced by numerous, often incommensurate factors. Without a doubt, the presence of substantial discretion often makes it difficult to determine with precision the true causes of a decision. But isolating such causes is exactly what multivariate regression analysis does. The purpose of such analysis is to ferret out causation when direct evidence is lacking. Multivariate regression analysis seeks to determine the causal influence of a variety of factors, all of which are understood to have an impact on a final result. It achieves this by holding other variables constant, thus

---

[39] 466 US 429, 433 (1984) ("[t]he Constitution cannot control [private] prejudices but neither can it tolerate them. Private biases may be outside the reach of the law, but the law cannot, directly or indirectly, give them effect. 'Public officials sworn to uphold the Constitution may not avoid a constitutional duty by bowing to the hypothetical effects of private racial prejudice that they assume to be both widely and deeply held.'" (quoting *Palmer v Thompson*, 403 US 217, 260–261 (1971) (White, J, dissenting))); see note 31 and accompanying text.

[40] See *McCleskey*, 481 US at 292–97.

[41] See *Furman v Georgia*, 408 US 238 (1972).

isolating the effects of the suspected variable. Of course, statistical evidence can never provide *direct* evidence of intent (or causation) in any particular case. And there is always the danger that any particular statistical analysis has left out an important causal variable, thereby undermining the validity of its results. No scientific study is any better than the methodology that produces it. But a careful analysis based on a well-formulated model can provide valid circumstantial evidence of causation.[42]

The statistical evidence of race-of-the-victim discrimination in the capital sentencing system is more than sufficient to establish causation. The Baldus study controlled for every relevant variable other than race, which is why the study is regarded as an exemplary piece of social science research.[43] Furthermore, as noted above, the results of the Baldus study have been replicated in a number of other sophisticated studies. Such consistency of results, across different data sets, different models, and different time periods, is more than sufficient to establish that race is a causal factor in the capital sentencing system.

Why, then, did the Court reject McCleskey's statistical challenge to the Georgia death penalty system? Though the majority opinion is somewhat opaque on this point,[44] it seems to suggest that statistical evidence, no matter how powerful, cannot prove causation in a particular case; and the primary basis for this conclusion appears to have been concerns about the practical consequences of permitting statistical evidence to make out even a prima facie case of intentional discrimination:

> [T]o prevail under the Equal Protection Clause, McCleskey must prove that the decisionmakers in *his* case acted with dis-

---

[42] For an example of the relationship between causation and statistical evidence, consider the example of tobacco and lung cancer. Until recently, medical science had been unable to determine the direct chain of events between smoking cigarettes and developing lung cancer. See David Stout, *Direct Link Found Between Smoking and Lung Cancer*, New York Times A1 (Oct. 18, 1996) (reporting recent scientific study claiming to find first direct, causal link between smoking and lung cancer). In other words, scientists were unable to find direct evidence of causation. Nonetheless, there was overwhelming statistical evidence of the link between smoking and lung cancer, see *The Health Consequences of Smoking: A Report of the Surgeon General, 1982* 6–42 (1982), and few respectable scientists (other than those working for tobacco companies) doubted that a causal link existed between the two.

[43] See note 5.

[44] The Court stated, "The unique nature of the decisions at issue in this case also counsels against adopting [an inference of discrimination] from the disparities indicated by the Baldus study." 481 US at 297. The Court declined to specify what that "unique nature" was.

criminatory purpose. He offers no evidence specific to his own case that would support an inference that racial considerations played a part in his sentence. Instead, he relies solely on the Baldus study. McCleskey argues that the Baldus study compels an inference that his sentence rests on purposeful discrimination. McCleskey's claim that these statistics are sufficient proof of discrimination, without regard to the facts of a particular case, would extend to all capital cases in Georgia, at least where the victim was white and the defendant is black.[45]

There are several responses to the last sentence in this passage. First, the Court is simply wrong when it asserts that acceptance of the Baldus study would invalidate all capital sentences in Georgia "where the victim was white and the defendant is black." The Baldus study found that the race of the defendant was not an important variable in capital sentencing decisions. Not all black defendants convicted of killing white victims would be entitled to relief, and it is conceivable that some white defendants convicting of killing white victims might be entitled to relief. Second, McCleskey's claim works only in cases involving comparable levels of heinousness. The Baldus study found little divergence between white-victim cases and black-victim cases where the killings were especially aggravated or relatively unaggravated. Third, acceptance of the Baldus study does not require *invalidation* of all suspect sentences, it only creates a prima facie case against them. Prosecutors would remain able to rebut any inference of discrimination raised by statistical evidence, and so to save death sentences from invalidation. Finally, it is quite possible that under the Supreme Court's holding in *Teague v Lane*,[46] which postdated *McCleskey* by two years, a decision recognizing claims such as McCleskey's would not be applied retroactively on federal habeas review, so that only death sentences still on direct review, and of course future trials, would be affected.

The Court's response to its concerns over the effects of ruling for McCleskey was to paper over the issue of the requisite quantum of proof for McCleskey's equal protection claim. The Baldus study did not prove to a moral certainty or beyond a reasonable

---

[45] 481 US at 292–93 (footnote omitted).

[46] 489 US 288 (1989).

doubt that race caused McCleskey's capital sentence. But constitutional claims ordinarily need be proven only by a preponderance of the evidence. Viewing the evidence in the light most favorable to McCleskey, which the Court was required to do, a reasonable finder of fact certainly could have concluded that racial factors more likely than not caused the prosecutor to seek the death penalty against McCleskey. The Court, however, apparently held McCleskey to a higher standard of proof than preponderance of the evidence. "Because discretion is essential to the criminal justice process, we would demand exceptionally clear proof before we would infer that the discretion has been abused," Justice Powell wrote.[47] When the Court says that it will disturb prosecutorial decisions about the death penalty only upon "exceptionally clear proof" of discrimination, it is saying that prosecutors are free to discriminate against victims on the basis of their race as long as they do not advertise it by admitting to the discrimination or uttering racial epithets in public. This is a stunning message. Moreover, the Court has not accorded prosecutors that level of discretion in exercising peremptory challenges in criminal cases. A *Batson* claimant must prove intent to discriminate, but the Court has never suggested that such intent must be proved by "exceptionally clear" evidence.

Ultimately, *McCleskey* appears to rest on a misunderstanding of the statistical evidence provided by the Baldus study. The Court in *McCleskey* equated the regression analysis in that case with the simple racial correlations at issue in *Davis, Arlington Heights,* and *Feeney.*[48] But there is a critical difference between the statistical evidence in *McCleskey* and the evidence in the earlier cases. By relying only on simple correlations to assert an equal protection challenge, none of the plaintiffs in the earlier cases had proved that race or gender was a cause of the challenged conduct, rather than some other causal factor which correlated with race or gender. In *McCleskey,* on the other hand, the Baldus study established that in a substantial number of capital cases, the same result would *not* have occurred but for the race of the victim, and that there was therefore a substantial probability that McCleskey's sentence

---

[47] 481 US at 297.

[48] See notes 20–23 and accompanying text.

would not have been the same had the race of his victim been different.[49]

An account of the Court's misadventures with statistical evidence, however, tells only one story about *McCleskey*. In fact, there was more at work in *McCleskey* than a dispute over statistics, or a technical error by the Court. As almost every commentator has noted, *McCleskey* was clearly influenced by the Court's concerns about the practical and societal consequences of granting *McCleskey* relief.[50] In particular, the Court was concerned that granting relief might undermine the criminal justice system by allowing great numbers of defendants to challenge their sentences.[51] Moreover, one of the most intractible issues in *McCleskey* involved the precise nature of the equal protection claim. Relatively early in its opinion, the Court stated that McCleskey was not seeking to litigate the rights of victims who may have been discriminated against by the Georgia capital sentencing system.[52] As noted above, however, victim-based discrimination is the *only* form of discrimination in capital sentencing for which statistical analyses have presented strong evidence. This raises the question of the precise nature of the claim that McCleskey sought to raise and that the Court rejected. As Randall Kennedy notes, it became clear during oral argument in *McCleskey* that the justices were quite concerned about the justiciability issues raised by the interaction between a victim-based claim and a defendant claimant. But as he also notes, the

---

[49] There is a telling passage in Justice Powell's majority opinion. Toward the end of the discussion rejecting McCleskey's statistical evidence, the Court states that there is no reason to infer discriminatory intent from the Baldus study "because a legitimate and unchallenged explanation for the decision [to sentence McCleskey to death] is apparent from the record: McCleskey committed an act for which the United States Constitution and Georgia laws permit imposition of the death penalty." 481 US at 297. This statement suggests that the Court did not fully understand McCleskey's argument. The Baldus study proved that a large number of people in McCleskey's situation would not have been sentenced to death if their victims had been black. Every single one of these people had "committed an act for which the United States Constitution and Georgia laws permit imposition of the death penalty." That McCleskey was eligible for the death penalty did nothing to distinguish him from them, and therefore did nothing to negate the substantial probability that he would not have gotten the death penalty had his victim been black. To support its conclusion, the Court had to distinguish McCleskey from other "midrange" killers of black victims who did not receive the death penalty. It did not.

[50] See, e.g., Ortiz, 41 Stan L Rev at 1142–49 (cited in note 24); Kennedy, 101 Harv L Rev at 1413–15 (cited in note 5); Carter, 97 Yale LJ at 440–41 (cited in note 17); Selmi, 86 Georgetown L J at 320–23, 347 (cited in note 28).

[51] *McCleskey*, 481 US at 314–19.

[52] Id at 292 n 8.

opinions in the case failed to examine this issue.[53] In the remainder of this article, we will explicate the complex relationships between race-of-victim discrimination and modern justiciability law, with a particular focus on the remedial alternatives open to legislatures and courts in responding to unconstitutional prosecutorial discrimination against black murder victims.

III. ASCERTAINING THE NATURE OF EQUAL PROTECTION VIOLATIONS

In the previous section, we have tried to demonstrate that a prosecutor violates the Equal Protection Clause when he even unconsciously elects not to seek the death penalty because the victim is black or elects to seek the death penalty because the victim is white. But there remains the rather puzzling matter of crafting an appropriate remedy.

A. OVERVALUATION AND UNDERVALUATION OF VICTIMS' LIVES

The soundest approach to analyzing possible remedies for prosecutorial discrimination against victims on the basis of race is to divide such discrimination into two categories: (1) cases where the prosecutor seeks the death penalty because the prosecutor "overvalues" a white victim because of race, and (2) cases where the prosecutor chooses not to seek the death penalty because the prosecutor "undervalues" a black victim because of race. The following matrix illustrates the relationship between the nature of the constitutional violation and the party structure of the litigation.

	Overvaluation	Undervaluation
Defendants	Cell 1	Cell 3
Victims' Families	Cell 2	Cell 4

This approach links the remedy with the nature of the equal protection violation. In theory, every equal protection case poses the problem of whether to "level up" or "level down."[54] If Group A

---

[53] Kennedy, 101 Harv L Rev at 1392 n 15 (cited in note 5).

[54] See *Welsh v United States*, 398 US 333, 361 (1970) (Harlan, J, concurring in result).

is being treated worse than Group B for no constitutionally permissible reason, the court must decide whether to raise Group A to Group B's level or whether to lower Group B to Group A's level. (If the subject matter is amenable, the court might have the groups meet halfway.) But without some normative baseline, the choice between these remedies is arbitrary. As we explain later, in choosing a remedy, the Equal Protection Clause requires the court to ascertain how the governmental actor would have behaved had it not used the impermissible classification.[55] On rare occasions, the governmental actor has already expressed its view of whether to level up or down if a court should find that the act violates equal protection. The court must respect this intent. Usually, however, the governmental actor has not considered what should happen if its act is held unconstitutional. In that case, the court must do its best to ascertain what the actor would have done had it not taken any impermissible consideration into account.

In the preceding matrix, the horizontal axis depicts the dichotomy between equal protection violations consisting of the overvaluation of white victims' lives versus those consisting of the undervaluation of black victims' lives. The vertical axis represents the two groups of litigants who might seek to challenge discrimination on the basis of the victim's race—first, defendants facing capital punishment for killing white victims; second, the families of black murder victims. In this matrix, we assume that all defendants facing capital punishment who challenge discrimination in favor of white victims seek to have their sentences commuted to life imprisonment—that is, to be treated in the same way as defendants who murder black victims. Presumably, they are uninterested in winning damages.

We conclude that the viable remedies for prosecutorial race discrimination against murder victims lie in Cells 1 and 4. A capital defendant should be able to seek commutation of his death sen-

---

[55] See notes 106–10 and accompanying text; *Heckler v Mathews*, 465 US 728, 738–39 and n 5 (1984) (suggesting that if the legislature has indicated a preference regarding the proper remedy, courts should generally abide by that preference). See also *People v Liberta*, 474 NE 2d 567 (NY 1984), in which the New York Court of Appeals held that unmarried men were denied equal protection because, unlike married men, they could not rape their significant others with impunity. The court had two choices: extend rape law to married men or abolish it for unmarried men. The court stated that it was required to "discern what course the Legislature would have chosen to follow if it had foreseen our conclusions. . . . "

tence when he proves that the prosecutor's overvaluation of his white victim's life constituted a "but-for" cause of the death sentence. The relatives of a black victim should be able to recover damages if they prove that the prosecutor's undervaluation of the victim's life was a "but-for" cause of the decision not to seek the death penalty. In the balance of this article we explain further our analytic framework and conclusions.

B. PROVING OVERVALUATION AND UNDERVALUATION

How can one tell whether a prosecutor has overvalued, undervalued, or properly valued a victim's life? How can one possibly know what a "correct" nonracial valuation would be in any particular case? We do not claim that there is an objectively correct valuation. Rather, the correct valuation is whatever the prosecutor would have decided had he been blind to the victim's race. If a prosecutor would have pursued the death penalty without knowing the victim's race, but declined to seek the death penalty knowing the victim was black, then he has undervalued the victim's life on the basis of race. If the prosecutor would have forgone the death penalty not knowing the victim's race, but sought it knowing the victim was white, then he has overvalued the victim's life. The "correct" valuation is a purely subjective matter.

How would a claimant prove an equal protection violation on either an overvaluation or undervaluation theory? The first step would be to ascertain a baseline. To do this, we must know two things: (1) the relevant aggravating and mitigating factors, and (2) the rate at which prosecutors seek the death penalty in cases with similar factors. We will refer to the first consideration as the "aggravation level" and the second as the "seek rate." The aggravation level for a particular case is determined by the application of an "aggravation index." The index consists of a list of factors correlating strongly with prosecutorial decisions to seek the death penalty. Each factor is assigned a value based on the strength of its correlation with decisions to seek capital punishment. The cumulation of these values produces an "aggravation level" for the case.

For illustrative purposes, we have reprinted a table from the Baldus study that could be used as a model aggravation index (see

Table 1).[56] Baldus explains that the "key measures of the impact of a given variable are the logistic-regression coefficient . . . and the odds multiplier, which is the antilog of the logistic-regression coefficient."[57] The higher the odds multiplier or logistic-regression coefficient, the greater the influence on the capital sentencing decision. The variables present in any particular case are combined to produce an overall aggravation level. Next, cases are grouped according to aggravation levels and it is determined how often prosecutors seek the death penalty for that particular aggravation range. We have also reprinted a graph from the Baldus study showing the relationship between aggravation levels and the corresponding death sentencing rates (see Fig. 1). Because our proposal covers prosecutorial discrimination only, we would substitute seek rates for actual death sentencing rates.

Consider the following hypothetical. The prosecutor seeks the death penalty in a case in which the defendant murdered a white person under factual circumstances that place the case at 0.48 on the aggravation index. The seek rate for cases in this range is 26 percent. This means that in 74 percent of aggravation-comparable cases cutting across race, prosecutors do not seek the death penalty.

We already have enough information to question the prosecutor's decision. The aggravation index is drawn from the Baldus study's thirty-nine-variable model,[58] which already has taken into account the most significant reasons why a prosecutor would or

---

[56] The Baldus study covered only Georgia. Because of peculiarities in the capital sentencing systems of individual states, challenges to capital sentencing would have to be based on statistical studies specific to those states. Several such studies have already been conducted. See, e.g., Michael L. Radelet and Glenn L Pierce, *Choosing Those Who Will Die: Race and the Death Penalty in Florida*, 43 Fla L Rev 1 (1991); Thomas J. Keil and Gennaro F. Vito, *Race and the Death Penalty in Kentucky Murder Trials: 1976–1991: A Study of Racial Bias as a Factor in Capital Sentencing*, http://dpa.state.ky.us/~rwheeler/archives/race/vito.txt (1995); but see Stephen P. Klein and John E. Rolph, *Relationship of Offender and Victim Race to Death Penalty Sentences in California*, 32 Jurimet J 33 (1991) (finding no statistically significant racial discrimination in the imposition of the death penalty in California).

[57] Baldus, Woodworth, and Pulaski, supra, *Equal Justice and the Death Penalty* at 71 n 34 (cited in note 7).

[58] The model contains thirty-nine nonracial variables plus the race of the defendant and the race of the victim. The race of the defendant was found not to exert much influence on the capital sentencing process; the race of the victim was found to exert great influence. Baldus, Woodworth, and Pulaski, *Equal Justice and the Death Penalty* at 319 (Table 52) (cited in note 7).

TABLE 1

Logistic-Regression Coefficients, Estimated for Selected Aggravating and Mitigating Factors and the Race of Victim and Defendant in an Analysis of Death-Sentencing Outcomes, CSS

Variable Label and Name	Death-Odds Multiplier	Adjusted Logistic Regression Coefficient (with Level of Statistical Significance)
1. Defendant was not the triggerman (NOKILL)	.06	−2.75 (.0001)
2. Defendant admitted guilt and no defense asserted (DEFADMIT)	.28	−1.27 (.12)
3. Defendant had a history of drug or alcohol abuse (DRGHIS)	.36	−1.01 (.007)
4. Defendant was under 17 years of age (SMYOUTH)	.41	−.88 (.23)
5. Jealousy motive (JEALOUS)	.47	−.74 (.53)
6. Family, lover, liquor, or barroom quarrel (BLVICMOD)	.54	−.61 (.15)
7. Defendant was retired, student, juvenile, housewife (MITDEFN)	.54	−.61 (.64)
8. Hate motive (HATE)	.71	−.34 (.69)
9. Pecuniary gain motive for self/other (LDFB4)*	.80	−.22 (.70)
10. *Defendant was black* (BLACKD)	.94	−.06 (.88)
11. Number of prior defendant felony prison terms (PRISONX)	1.1	.08 (.67)
12. Defendant caused death risk in public place to 2 or more people (LDFB3)	1.1	.14 (.74)
13. One or more coperpetrators involved (COPERP)	1.3	.24 (.56)
14. Defendant was a female (FEMDEF)	1.3	.28 (.70)
15. One or more convictions for a violent personal crime, burglary, or arson (VPCARBR)	1.35	.30 (.53)
16. Nonproperty-related contemporaneous crime (NONPROPC)	1.4	.35 (.64)
17. Killing to avoid, stop arrest of self, other (LDFB10)	1.5	.41 (.32)
18. Victim was a police or corrections officer on duty (LDFB8)	1.7	.52 (.58)
19. Defendant primary mover in planning homicide or contemporaneous offense (DLEADER)	1.7	.55 (.33)
20. Rape/armed robbery/kidnapping plus silence witness, execution, or victim pleaded for life (LDFB7D)	1.8	.60 (.16)
21. Coperpetrator received a lesser sentence (CPLESSEN)	2.2	.78 (.09)
22. Multiple shots (MULSH)	2.2	.79 (.04)
23. Victim was drowned (DROWN)	2.6	.96 (.24)
24. Victim was a stranger (STRANGER)	2.8	1.03 (.01)
25. Victim bedridden/handicapped (VBED)	2.8	1.04 (.33)
26. Kidnapping involved (KIDNAP)	2.9	1.06 (.17)

TABLE 1   (*Continued*)

Variable Label and Name	Death-Odds Multiplier	Adjusted Logistic Regression Coefficient (with Level of Statistical Significance)
27. Victim weak or frail (VWEAK)	3.1	1.13 (.19)
28. Defendant had a prior record for murder, armed robbery, rape, or kidnapping with bodily injury (LDFB1)	4.1	1.40 (.009)
29. Armed robbery involved (ARMROB)	4.2	1.43 (.02)
30. *One or more white victims* (WHVICRC)	4.3	1.45 (.003)
31. Multiple stabbing (MULTSTAB)	4.7	1.54 (.002)
32. Victim was 12 or younger (VICCHILD)	4.8	1.56 (.03)
33. Number of defendant prior murder convictions (MURPRIOR)	5.2	1.66 (.27)
34. Murder for hire (LDFB6)	5.9	1.77 (.08)
35. Defendant was a prisoner or escapee (LDFB9)	7.7	2.04 (.002)
36. Defendant killed two or more people (TWOVIC)	7.9	2.07 (.005)
37. Mental torture involved (MENTORT)	9.7	2.27 (.009)
38. Rape involved (RAPE)	12.8	2.55 (.001)
39. Defendant's motive was to collect insurance (INSMOT)	20.1	3.01 (.01)
40. Victim was tortured physically (TORTURE)	27.4	3.31 (.003)
41. Motive was to avenge role by judicial officer, D.A., lawyer (AVENGE)	28.9	3.36 (.25)
Constant		−6.15 (.0001)

SOURCE.—From David C. Baldus, George Woodworth, and Charles A. Pulaski, Jr., *Equal Justice and the Death Penalty: A Legal and Empirical Analysis* 321 (fig. 32) (1990).

NOTE.—The table reports the odds multiplier and coefficients for the race-of-defendant and the race-of-victim variables in the thirty-nine-variable core model. The outcome variable was DSENTALL, coded: 1 = Death Sentence, 0 = Other Sentence.

* The negative sign of the coefficient for LDFB4 (pecuniary gain motive) is perverse. We attribute the sign of LDFB4 to its correlation with the variable for armed robbery (ARMROB).

would not seek the death penalty. Knowing the aggravation level, but without knowing the race of his victim, we would predict that the prosecutor would not seek the death penalty. When it is revealed that the prosecutor sought capital punishment, and that the victim was white, we have good reason to suspect that race played a proximate role in the decision.

Why do our suspicions gravitate toward race? We look first to race because the Baldus study strongly indicates that the race of the victim exerts a high degree of influence on the capital sentencing process in the midrange-aggravation cases. When the case involves one or more white victims, the odds of receiving a death

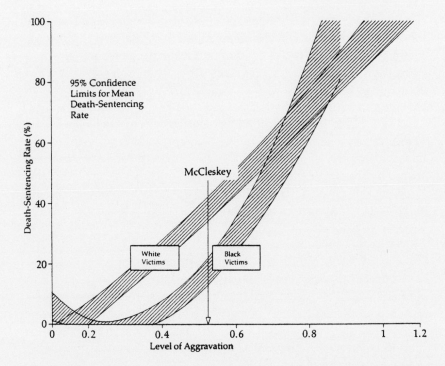

Fig. 1.—Black defendant model, Georgia Charging and Sentencing Study, 1973–1979. (From David C. Baldus, George Woodworth, and Charles A. Pulaski, Jr., *Equal Justice and the Death Penalty: A Legal and Empirical Analysis* 321 (Fig. 32) (1990).)

sentence are multiplied on average by a magnitude of 4.3.[59] As Justice Brennan pointed out in his *McCleskey* dissent, this puts the influence of the victim's race virtually on a par with the influence of multiple stabbing, a serious prior criminal record, or involvement in an armed robbery.[60] Because the race of the victim is so influential, and because it is not taken into account in the aggravation index, while all other, properly relevant factors are, our suspicions naturally turn to that factor.

This reason for suspecting race can be illustrated in another way. Consider the differential between seek rates for cases involving white and black victims. The average seek rate for white-victim

---

[59] This odds multiplier cuts across all aggravation levels. The odds multiplier at McCleskey's specific aggravation level is closer to 2.2 (37 percent divided by 17 percent). See note 62 and accompanying text.

[60] 481 US at 326 (Brennan, J, dissenting).

cases in the 0.4 to 0.6 range is 37 percent. The average seek rate for black-victim cases in the same range is 17 percent.[61] Prosecutors are more than twice as likely to seek the death penalty in a white-victim case in this range as in a black-victim case, even after controlling for the aggravation of the offense. Something has to explain a discrepancy that large, and race is the leading candidate.

At this point it is critical to emphasize what we have *not* said. We have not claimed that the statistics prove race discrimination in this particular case. Rather, we claim that the statistics create a strong suspicion of race discrimination—specifically, an overvaluation of the white victim's life.[62] This statistical showing should make out a prima facie case under the Equal Protection Clause. Because the defendant has shown that prosecutors in most aggravation-comparable cases do not seek the death penalty, he has shown that, more likely than not, race discrimination "caused" the decision to seek the death penalty. The burden should now shift to the prosecutor to offer a legitimate, persuasive nonracial rationale for seeking the death penalty.[63] This burden-shifting scheme is virtually identical to what the Court has adopted in jury discrimination challenges under *Batson v Kentucky*[64] and in disparate treatment cases under Title VII.[65]

Once the judge has decided that the claimant has established a prima facie case, the prosecutor may discharge his burden by giv-

---

[61] Recall that we have fictitiously substituted seek rate for death-sentencing rate in the Baldus graph.

[62] Similarly, to prove undervaluation of a black victim's life a claimant must show that in similar-aggravation cases, most prosecutors would seek the death penalty if the victim were white.

[63] Before considering how the prosecutor might rebut such a prima facie case, we pause to consider how large a differential must exist between seek rates for murderers of whites and murderers of blacks. In our hypothetical case, the difference was dramatic—more than 2 to 1. In such circumstances, the claimant has clearly made out a prima facie case. Suppose, however, that the differential was much smaller. Suppose it was 19 percent to 17 percent. Has the claimant still made out a prima facie case? The answer depends on two factors. One is the size of the relevant statistical universe; the other is the quality of the research methodology. If the number of death-eligible defendants in the jurisdiction is extremely large, and if the research methodology is impeccable, a difference of 19 percent to 17 percent could establish a prima facie case. The issue is no different than in other cases involving statistical proof.

[64] 476 US 79 (1986). See also *Purkett v Elem*, 514 US 765 (1995) (in order to rebut prima facie case, prosecutor need not articulate plausible nonracial explanation for using strike, but only facially nonracial explanation).

[65] See *McDonnell Douglas Corp. v Green*, 411 US 792 (1973); *Texas Dept. of Community Affairs v Burdine*, 450 US 248 (1981).

ing any number of explanations. Perhaps the prosecutor had a
close relative who died under similar circumstances. Perhaps the
defendant was a member of a particularly vicious gang. Perhaps
the prosecutor needed to seek the death penalty in this case to get
re-elected. All of these rationales go beyond the factors examined
in the Baldus study and might satisfactorily explain why the prosecutor sought the death penalty in this particular case, without regard to race.

In many (if not most) cases, however, the prosecutor will be
unwilling or unable to point to a specific factor outside the Baldus
study. A prosecutor may simply say that he sought the death penalty because the defendant had committed a heinous murder.
Other prosecutors might not find it heinous, but that is not the
issue. The prosecutor in this case found it heinous, and that is not
a racial reason for seeking the death penalty.

If it is so easy for a prosecutor to articulate a nonracial rationale
for seeking the death penalty, then what good is it to afford the
claimant a cause of action? The answer is that the prosecutor's
proffer must be *credible*. The judge must be persuaded that the
prosecutor has not simply conjured up an after-the-fact rational-
ization for the decision. The multivariate analysis may not prove
what this particular prosecutor thinks about the heinousness of the
facts of this particular case, but it does tell us what most prosecutors think about it. And, unless there is a special reason to think
that this prosecutor regards heinousness quite differently than
other prosecutors, the judge is entitled to find that the proffered
rationale lacks credibility.

Moreover, once the prosecutor has articulated a nonracial rationale for seeking (or forgoing) the death penalty, the claimant now
has the opportunity to show that the proffered rationale is a pretext
for discrimination. Notice that in this context, a "pretext" may be
one that the prosecutor has offered in good faith, unaware of his
own unconscious racism. The claimant's burden of demonstrating
pretext now "merges" with his or her ultimate burden of persuading the trier of fact that, more likely than not, the prosecutor discriminated on the basis of race.[66] The claimant is entitled to discovery of the prosecutor's prior record in cases where the facts
would have supported the death penalty. The claimant may intro-

---

[66] Compare *Texas Department of Community Affairs v Burdine*, 450 US 248 (1981).

duce evidence that the prosecutor has a pattern and practice of seeking the death penalty in cases where the victim is white, but not where the victim is black.[67] Even if a particular prosecutor has no record at all in capital cases, the judge is entitled to find the prosecutor's proffer noncredible.[68]

In the real world, judges may tend to accept prosecutors' stated rationales. This appears to have happened with *Batson*.[69] But even if this happens, there is considerable value in requiring prosecutors to articulate their reasons. As noted earlier, many prosecutorial decisions about capital sentencing appear to be influenced by unconscious racial thinking. The very existence of a capital sentencing remedy may lead prosecutors to think more carefully about why they do and do not seek the death penalty in particular cases.

IV. Remedies and Justiciability

In this section, we will individually analyze the possibility of a successful claim, and the remedial possibilities, in each of the four cells of our proposed "matrix."[70]

A. OVERVALUATION OF WHITE VICTIMS—DEFENDANT SEEKS COMMUTATION

In Cell 1, the defendant argues that he was sentenced to death because his victim was white. He argues that he would not have been sentenced to death if the prosecutor had valued the victim's

---

[67] Although most prosecutors have not actually sought the death penalty in a large number of cases, that is not the relevant comparison pool. The relevant pool consists of all cases in which the defendant was *indicted* for (or perhaps merely *committed*) a crime that would have supported the death penalty. This includes cases where the prosecutor ultimately reduced the charges to voluntary manslaughter or decided to settle for life imprisonment on a murder conviction. This is a much larger pool of cases, and will often stand ready to contradict a prosecutor's fabricated rationale for seeking the death penalty.

[68] Unless the prosecutor has utterly failed to articulate a nonracial rationale, the ultimate burden of persuasion always rests on the claimant. Cf. *St. Mary's Honor Center v Hicks*, 509 US 502 (1993) (claimant retained burden of persuasion even where trial judge found defendant's proffer of legitimate reasons implausible). We do not necessarily endorse *Hicks*. We simply think there is no reason to treat this issue any differently in the capital sentencing context than in the disparate treatment context of Title VII.

[69] See Susan H. Herman, *Why the Court Loves Batson: Representation-Reinforcement, Color-blindness, and the Jury*, 67 Tulane L Rev 1807, 1830 n 93 (1993) ("overcoming the race-neutral explanation hurdle has not been that difficult") (citing examples).

[70] See text display (page 127).

life "properly." Assuming the defendant can prove this claim, he still faces two doctrinal obstacles—first, that he may lack standing; second, even if the prosecutor did consider the victim's race, this may not make out a constitutional claim in favor of a defendant.

1. *Standing.* The Supreme Court has held that the "case or controversy" requirement of Article III imposes three requirements on any litigant who wishes to assert rights in federal court. First, the litigant must have suffered particularized "injury-in-fact."[71] That is, the litigant must have suffered a tangible harm not common to all of society.[72] Second, the defendant's conduct must have actually caused the injury.[73] Third, the litigant must seek relief that would redress the injury.[74] In addition to these constitutional requisites of standing, the Court has held that the litigant generally must assert his own rights and that he is generally prohibited from asserting the rights of third parties.[75]

The defendant who claims that his victim's life has been overvalued has no difficulty with the injury-in-fact requirement. His injury is the sentence of death. He also satisfies the causation requirement because the overvaluation of the white victim's life is a but-for cause of the death sentence. And redressability poses no problem because the injury (the death sentence) would be fully redressed by the requested relief (commutation).

The tricky question concerns the prohibition against third-party standing. If we focus on the inequality between white and black victims, the rule against third-party standing would apply. The prosecutor has overvalued the lives of white victims, which violates the right of black victims to equal protection of the laws. Yet this violates no right of the defendant. On the other hand, if we focus on the inequality between the killers of white people and the killers of black people, the rule against third-party standing does not

---

[71] See *Sierra Club v Morton*, 405 US 727 (1972).

[72] See *Frothingham v Mellon*, 262 US 447 (1923); *Schlesinger v Reservists Comm. to Stop the War*, 418 US 208 (1974).

[73] See *Linda R.S. v Richard D.*, 410 US 614 (1973); *Warth v Seldin*, 422 US 490 (1975); *Simon v Eastern Kentucky Welfare Rights Org.*, 426 US 26 (1976).

[74] Id.

[75] *Tileston v Ullman*, 318 US 44 (1943) (per curiam); *McGowan v Maryland*, 366 US 420 (1961). The Supreme Court has created one other standing requirement not relevant here. In cases brought under the Administrative Procedure Act, the litigant must fall within the "zone of interests" that Congress sought to protect when it enacted the statute in question. See *Assn of Data Processing Service Organizations, Inc. v Camp*, 397 US 150 (1970).

apply. By overvaluing the lives of white victims, the government treats killers of whites differently than the killers of blacks. This denies killers of whites equal protection of the laws.

In *McCleskey*, the Court assumed that the murderer of a white person has first-party standing to seek commutation of his death sentence, but its treatment of this issue was relegated to a footnote:

> Although McCleskey has standing to claim that he suffers discrimination because of his own race, the State argues that he has no standing to contend that he was discriminated against on the basis of his victim's race. While it is true that we are reluctant to recognize "standing to assert the rights of third persons," . . . this does not appear to be the nature of McCleskey's claim. He does not seek to assert some right of his victim, or the rights of black murder victims in general. Rather, McCleskey argues that application of the State's statute has created a classification that is "an irrational exercise of governmental power," . . . because it is not "necessary to the accomplishment of some permissible state objective." . . . It would violate the Equal Protection Clause for a State to base enforcement of its criminal laws on "an unjustifiable standard such as race, religion, or other arbitrary classification." . . . Because McCleskey raises such a claim, he has standing.[76]

It is worth pausing a moment to digest what the Court has said here. It distinguishes between two types of equal protection claims: race-based classifications in particular, and arbitrary classifications in general. If McCleskey had tried to assert the rights of victims not to be discriminated against because of their race, he would confront the Court's prohibition against third-party standing. But (according to the Court) he made no such claim; he instead claimed that race discrimination against victims constituted an arbitrary classification in the enforcement of the criminal law. Thus, McCleskey did not seek to assert the right of victims not to be discriminated against on the basis of race, but his own right not to have the criminal law enforced against him on the basis of an arbitrary classification.[77] But could he have raised the rights of black victims?

---

[76] *McCleskey v Kemp*, 481 US at 291–92 n 8.

[77] Compare Henry P. Monaghan, *Overbreadth*, 1981 Supreme Court Review 1 (litigants are always permitted to challenge the validity of rules pursuant to which they are sanctioned).

If the prohibition against third-party standing were absolute, one in McCleskey's position clearly would be unable to assert the rights of victims. But the Court has recognized three exceptions to the general prohibition. First, if a statute is "substantially overbroad," defendants whose conduct is unprotected may nonetheless assert the First Amendment rights of third persons whose protected conduct would fall within the challenged statute.[78] Second, a claimant may assert the rights of third parties who are unable to assert their own rights if the claimant would represent the holders of the rights adequately. For example, in *Barrows v Jackson*,[79] a white vendor sold land to a black family in violation of a racially restrictive covenant. Other parties to the covenant sued the vendor for damages. The vendor was permitted to defend on the ground that enforcement would violate the black family's right to equal protection. The buyers, not being parties to the covenant, had no procedural vehicle to assert their rights. Third, the Court on occasion has permitted claimants to assert the rights of those with whom they have some sort of a relationship. For example, in *Craig v Boren*,[80] Oklahoma had prohibited sales of 3.2 percent beer to males under twenty-one and females under eighteen. A beer vendor challenged the law on the ground that it violated the equal protection rights of males between the ages of eighteen and twenty-one. The Supreme Court recognized the vendor's standing to assert "those concomitant rights of third parties that would be 'diluted or adversely affected' should [the] constitutional challenge fail and the statutes remain in force."[81] Similarly, in *Powers v Ohio*,[82] a white criminal defendant challenged a prosecutor's use of peremptory challeges against black prospective jurors. The Court found that he had standing to assert the equal protection rights of these prospective jurors because such discrimination "places the fairness of a criminal proceeding in doubt" and because the rela-

---

[78] See *Broadrick v Oklahoma*, 413 US 601 (1973) (overbreadth must be "substantial"); *Thornhill v Alabama*, 310 US 88 (1940 (creating overbreadth exception).

[79] 346 US 249 (1953). See also *NAACP v Alabama*, 357 US 449 (1958) (permitting NAACP to assert its members' rights not to disclose their identities).

[80] 429 US 190 (1976).

[81] Id at 194.

[82] 499 US 400 (1991).

tionship between the defendant and the jurors "continues throughout the entire trial."[83] Moreover, the prospective jurors had no ready means to challenge their own exclusion.

Does *McCleskey* fit any of these exceptions? In part, the answer depends on whether the families of black victims may sue prosecutors or their employers and vindicate their rights. If so, they need not rely on condemned murderers to assert the equal protection rights of black victims. Under present doctrine, however, it is not clear whether they would succeed in such actions.[84] Assuming that such lawsuits are barred, a person in McCleskey's situation should have standing to assert the rights of black victims. There can be no doubt that the condemned "will be a motivated, effective advocate" for the black victim's equal protection rights.[85] His life depends on it. And, as in *Powers*, the overvaluation of the lives of white victims "places the fairness of a criminal proceeding in doubt."[86] Although the relationship between a condemned killer of a white person and the family of a black victim may not go any deeper than their common interest in vindicating equal protection rights, the Court has several times permitted third-party standing on the basis of less than profound relationships. In *Craig*, the beer vendor presumably had no personal relationship with males between eighteen and twenty-one, since they could not legally purchase beer. In *Powers*, the criminal defendant and the excluded venireperson had never before met, and their common interest was limited to eradicating race discrimination from that single judicial proceeding. In *Buchanan v Warley*, the Court even permitted a litigant to assert the rights of someone with whom he had an antagonistic relationship.[87] A white seller of land sued the black purchaser for specific performance. The purchaser defended on the ground that a racially restrictive ordinance prohibited him from living in the house. The Supreme Court permitted the white plaintiff to assert the defendant's right not to be discriminated against on the basis of race, even though the defendant obviously wished not to

---

[83] Id at 411, 413.

[84] See Part IV.D.

[85] *Powers*, 499 US at 414.

[86] Id at 411.

[87] 245 US 60 (1917).

assert the right. McCleskey's basis for third-party standing was at least as strong as in these cases.

2. *The appropriate standard of review.* We thus conclude that a killer of a white, such as McCleskey, who is able to prove that the prosecutor overvalued the life of his white victim and that if his victim had been black he would not have received the death penalty, clearly has first-party standing to challenge his capital sentence directly; and probably he also has third-party standing to raise the rights of black victims who have been discriminated against by his prosecutor's actions. At this point, the constitutional standard of review becomes critical. What standard should govern overvaluation claims brought by defendants—strict scrutiny or simple rationality? The answer is intertwined with the standing analysis discussed above. If a defendant such as McCleskey were granted third-party standing to raise the claims of black victims, then the standard of review would of course be strict scrutiny—and the defendant would almost certainly succeed in obtaining commutation, since the Court has not upheld a racial classification under strict scrutiny analysis since its infamous *Korematsu* decision.[88] We have concluded that someone in McCleskey's position may assert such third-party standing.

Assuming for the sake of analysis that we are wrong in this conclusion, and that McCleskey had standing to assert only his own Fourteenth Amendment right not to be convicted on the basis of an arbitrary classification (which was the only claim, remember, that McCleskey himself raised), a difficult question arises. The defendant's death sentence is the product of an arbitrary, racial classification, but based on his *victim's* race, not his own. What is the appropriate constitutional standard of review for such a claim?

The question of what standard of review should apply to an equal protection claim in which the claimant is disadvantaged because of a classification based on the race of another person appears to remain open in the Supreme Court. The issue arose in the Court's recent decision in *Miller v Albright*,[89] but remained unresolved by the Court as a whole. *Miller* involved an equal protec-

---

[88] *Korematsu v United States*, 323 US 214 (1944) (upholding internment of Japanese-Americans during World War II); see also *Hirabayashi v United States*, 320 US 81 (1943).

[89] 118 S Ct 1428 (1998).

tion challenge brought by the illegitimate, foreign-born daughter of a U.S. citizen father against a federal statute that made it easier for the illegitimate, foreign-born children of American women to claim U.S. citizenship than the foreign-born children of American men. The plaintiff thus challenged a gender-based statute that disadvantaged her because of the gender of a third person, her father, rather than on her own gender.[90] A highly fractured Court rejected her claim on a variety of grounds, several of which were unrelated to the issue at hand.[91] In a concurring opinion, however, Justice O'Connor, joined by Justice Kennedy, found that the plaintiff lacked third-party standing to raise her father's equal protection rights, and that *her* claim was therefore subject only to rational basis review.[92] If O'Connor's analysis is correct, then an equal protection challenge by a capital defendant to victim-based discrimination would also be subject only to rational basis review, absent third-party standing. In a dissenting opinion, Justice Breyer, joined by Justices Souter and Ginsburg, questioned this aspect of Justice O'Connor's reasoning,[93] but neither Justice O'Connor nor Justice Breyer cited any pertinent authority for their position, and the Court as a whole found it unnecessary to resolve the issue.

Lower court authority on this question is sparse. In a few early cases, courts granted first-party standing to developers suing municipalities alleged to have intentionally excluded minority tenants. The courts in these cases applied heightened scrutiny, suggesting

---

[90] Gender is considered a "semi-suspect" classification under the Equal Protection Clause, and therefore gender-based classifications are subject to "heightened" scrutiny (though not quite as heightened as the "strict" scrutiny to which race-based classifications are subject). See, e.g., *United States v Virginia*, 518 US 515 (1996).

[91] In particular, the plurality opinion by Justice Stevens (joined by Chief Justice Rehnquist) granted Miller third-party standing to raise her father's claims, but found that the statute survived heightened scrutiny, 118 S Ct at 1436–42; while a concurring opinion by Justice Scalia, joined by Justice Thomas, reasoned that, for reasons relating to the separation of powers, the Court lacked authority to grant Miller the relief that she requested, which was U.S. citizenship, id at 1446–49.

[92] Id at 1445 (O'Connor, J, concurring in the judgment). Justices O'Connor and Kennedy provided the fifth and sixth votes for the result.

[93] Justice Breyer did not provide any support for his suggestion that Miller's claim should be subject to heightened scrutiny other than a rather weak analogy to laws that discriminate based on racial or religious ancestry. The analogy is poor because racial identity is of course almost by definition transmitted to descendants, and even "religious ancestry" is often transmitted in the sense that children often adopt the faiths of their parents. "Gender ancestry," however, is a meaningless concept, since we all have the same "gender ancestry"—one man, one woman (at least for now).

that the challenged classification does not have to be based on a claimant's own race.[94] More recently, courts in analogous situations (primarily challenges brought by employers and general contractors to government-imposed affirmative action requirements) have tended to find third-party standing on the part of claimants seeking to raise the rights of others, and therefore have not considered the applicable standard of review absent such standing.[95] Finally, in a handful of recent decisions, some courts have suggested, without explanation, that the identity of the discrimination victim alleged *does* affect the standard of review (i.e., the O'Connor position) by denying third-party standing and then applying deferential review to equal protection claims; but again, courts have failed to directly address the difficult standard-of-review question.[96]

The proper standard of scrutiny for a defendant's challenge to victim-based discrimination thus remains unresolved. But it is our view that Justice O'Connor's conclusion in *Miller* is probably "correct," in the sense that it is more consistent with the modern Court's approaches to standing and equal protection issues, and so better predicts the Court's likely resolution of this question (leaving aside the question of whether we agree with those approaches; we do not). In particular, it is clear that in recent years the Court's understanding of the *nature* of the equal protection right has shifted dramatically from a group-based vision to an extremely individualized approach. That understanding is plainly more consistent with a regime where strict scrutiny may be invoked only by claimants who can show that they were treated differently because of *their* race (or other suspect characteristic).[97]

---

[94] See *G.T. Scott v Greenville County*, 716 F2d 1409 (4th Cir 1983); *Des Vergnes v Seekonk Water District*, 601 F2d 9, 17 (1st Cir 1979); *Park View Heights Corp. v City of Black Jack*, 467 F2d 1208 (8th Cir 1972).

[95] See, e.g., *Lutheran Church–Missouri Synod v FCC*, 141 F3d 344 (DC Cir 1998) (FCC-licensed radio station may challenge FCC rule requiring licensees to engage in affirmative action hiring, by raising the rights of potential applicants); compare *Monterey Mechanical Co. v Wilson*, 125 F3d 702, 707–08 (9th Cir 1997) (finding first-party standing for a general contractor to challenge a requirement of hiring minority subcontractors, but imposing heightened scrutiny only because the plaintiff was disadvantaged vis-à-vis other *general contractors* who were woman- or minority-owned).

[96] See, e.g., *Ablang v Reno*, 52 F3d 801, 804–05 and n 4 (9th Cir 1995); *Alexander v Whitman*, 114 F3d 1392, 1400–02, 1407–08 (3rd Cir 1997).

[97] To explain briefly, if the equal protection right is understood as a group-based right, then any member of a group may properly raise an equal protection claim and invoke heightened scrutiny so long as there is injury-in-fact (which of course is not a concern when a defendant seeks to commute a death sentence). Under this view, any black defendant

The counterargument would be that *any* official use of race should trigger strict scrutiny, even if the claimant herself has not been discriminated against; but this position does not accord well with the modern Court's view that the Equal Protection Clause's primary effect is to protect individuals against being treated differently because of their race,[98] and finds little support in recent case law. Therefore, it is probably true that under current equal protection jurisprudence, challenges to classifications based on the suspect characteristics of *others* are only subject to rational basis review.

Of course, concluding that more deferential scrutiny should apply does not necessarily resolve the question of whether a claim such as McCleskey's should prevail. Indeed, one can imagine an argument that *any* use of a racial classification within the criminal justice system, no matter how indirect, is so irrational and unacceptable that it should be struck down under any standard of scrutiny. But it is quite unlikely that such an argument would prevail under current standards, and indeed *McCleskey* might be fairly read to reject it. The reasons for this are somewhat counterintuitive, but follow from the nature of a standard of review. The crucial consequence of subjecting a governmental classification to "strict scrutiny" is that the classification then becomes presumptively un-

---

should be able to invoke strict scrutiny to challenge a racially biased capital sentencing system, even one tainted only by *victim* discrimination, but white defendants would not. If, however, the right is an individual one, then it would seem that only a person who is discriminated against because of *his own* suspect characteristic may invoke heightened equal protection scrutiny. At the time *McCleskey* was decided, the Court had not given much attention to this dichotomy—which perhaps explains the ambiguity of the Court's standing discussion in *McCleskey*. The same ambiguity is demonstrated in the Court's decision just one term earlier in *Batson v Kentucky*, 476 US 79 (1986), where the Court permitted a criminal defendant to challenge race-based peremptory challenges employed by prosecutors against jurors, without any discussion of standing. Later cases in the *Batson* line, however, clearly understand the *Batson* right as belonging to the juror who has been discriminated against on the basis of her race, which litigants are awarded third-party standing to invoke. See, e.g., *Powers v Ohio*, 490 US 400 (1991) (white defendant has third-party standing to raise equal-protection rights of dismissed black jurors); *Campbell v Louisiana*, 118 S Ct 1419 (1998) (*Batson* and *Powers* apply to grand juror selection). Thus since the *McCleskey* era, the Court appears to have moved toward an individualized understanding of the equal protection right, which in turn would suggest that only rational basis scrutiny would apply to a defendant's equal-protection challenge to victim-based discrimination in capital sentencing, unless the defendant were granted third-party standing to raise the rights of black victims. Note also that a defendant might be able to raise a due process challenge to victim-based racial discrimination in capital sentencing. See *Peters v Kiff*, 407 US 493 (1972); *Campbell*, 118 S Ct at 1424–25.

[98] See, e.g., *United States v Hays*, 515 US 737, 745 (1995).

constitutional, and the burden falls on the government to establish an extremely persuasive justification for use of that classification (a burden which is essentially never met). When a classification is subject only to rational basis review, however, the presumption is in favor of constitutionality, and the claimant has the burden of excluding all possible, legitimate justifications for the classification. Notice the consequence of this: if, as the above discussion suggests, the Court will sometimes subject an official racial classification to only rational basis scrutiny, then the use of race is not always, or even presumptively, unconstitutional.[99] Therefore, in rational basis cases, simply proving that a racial classification was employed—in this context, that race was a *cause* of the decision to seek the death penalty—is insufficient to make out a valid claim.[100] Something more is needed, and the Court's opinion in *McCleskey* might fairly be read to require that when a classification is subject only to rational basis review, a claimant may be required to introduce particularized evidence of "animus" on the part of the decision maker, because such a showing would tend to exclude the possibility of other legitimate justifications for the use of race.[101] Under this view, the statistical evidence presented in the Baldus study, while perhaps sufficient to make out a prima facie case for unconstitutionality under the strict scrutiny standard, is almost surely insufficient under the rational basis standard because one can easily envision rational reasons why a prosecutor may take into account the race of a victim in determining whether to seek a death sentence, other than simple animus toward blacks. These might include concerns about the prosecutor's ability to prevail before a jury, combined with problems of limited resources. As noted above, such justifications cannot, under the Court's jurisprudence, survive strict scrutiny; but the same might not be true about rational basis review, with its strong presumption of constitutionality.

---

[99] Oddly, whether or not the classification is presumptively invalid will depend not on the nature of the classification, but on the identity of the plaintiff, since it is in cases where the classification turns on the race of a third party, rather than the plaintiff, that rational basis review is applied. If the third party challenged the classification, strict scrutiny would apply.

[100] This is the strong implication of Justice O'Connor's opinion in *Miller*, which as explained above is consistent with the general tenor of the Court's current jurisprudence.

[101] Further support for this position can be found in the Court's recent decision in *Romer v Evans*, 116 S Ct 1620 (1996), where a provision was struck down because it was found to be motivated by animus toward homosexuals. See generally Ashutosh Bhagwat, *Purpose Scrutiny in Constitutional Analysis*, 85 Cal L Rev 297, 327, 330 (1997).

B. OVERVALUATION OF WHITE LIVES—BLACK VICTIM'S FAMILY SEEKS
REMEDY

In Cell 2, the family of a black victim seeks the death penalty
on the ground that there exists a difference in the treatment between killers of whites and blacks attributable to the overvaluation
of white lives.[102]

Standing is an issue. What injury has the family suffered? The
inclination would be to say they have suffered insufficient punishment of their relative's killer. But the overvaluation scenario posits
that the killers of blacks receive an appropriate level of punishment. It is the killers of whites who are punished too severely.

The family might claim, however, that they have been stigma-
tized by the difference in treatment between killers of whites and
the killer of their relative.[103] Such a claim would raise an intriguing
standing problem. In *Allen v Wright*,[104] the Court rejected the
plaintiffs' claim of stigmatic injury resulting from race discrimina-

---

[102] One potential doctrinal barrier to judicial relief for black victims or their families can
be quickly dismissed. Recent case law interprets the Due Process Clause of the Fourteenth
Amendment as not requiring states to take positive action to protect their citizens. But
these cases are not inconsistent with the view that the Equal Protection Clause sometimes
might impose just such an obligation. In the leading case, *DeShaney v Winnebago County
Department of Social Services*, 489 US 189 (1989), the Court held that "nothing in the Due
Process Clause itself requires the State to protect the life, liberty, and property of its citizens
against invasion by private actors. The clause is phrased as a limitation on the State's power
to act, not as a guarantee of certain minimum levels of safety and security." Id at 195. The
Court also noted in its opinion, however, that its holding was limited to the question of
whether the Due Process Clause imposed a *general* obligation to protect citizens; and, in
particular, that the decision did not preclude an equal protection challenge to a state's
failure to act, since "[t]he State may not, of course, selectively deny its protective services
to certain disfavored minorities without violating the Equal Protection Clause." Id at 1973.
Moreover, in *Briscoe v LaHue*, 460 US 325, 338 and n 19 (1983), the Court has specifically
pointed to the historical context of the Equal Protection Clause, recognizing that a state's
failure to equally protect citizens and punish those who commit violence against them violates the Fourteenth Amendment.

[103] Characterizing the injury as stigma eludes any problem that might otherwise be posed
by *Linda R.S. v Richard D.*, 410 US 614 (1973). There, a woman sued for an injunction
that would have required prosecutors to enforce the criminal child support law against the
father of her illegitimate child. The Supreme Court held that she lacked standing. The
Court ruled that nonenforcement of criminal laws does not constitute cognizable injury-
in-fact. Id at 619. The plaintiff did suffer a different sort of injury—failure to receive support payments. However, it was not clear that the failure to enforce the child support law
caused the husband to withhold support payments. Nor was it clear that enforcement of
the law would actually produce such payments. Once the injury is recast as stigma, however,
these problems disappear. Stigma from race discrimination is judicially cognizable. It is
clearly caused by prosecutors' race-based actions, and it clearly would be redressed by an
injunction against future race-based actions.

[104] 468 US 747 (1984).

tion on the ground that the stigma was too abstract. Parents of black public schoolchildren sued the Internal Revenue Service, alleging that it had failed to crack down on tax-exempt private schools that discriminated against blacks. The Court held that this claim of stigma failed to satisfy the "injury-in-fact" requirement:

> [Plaintiffs do not] have standing to litigate their claims based on the stigmatizing injury often caused by racial discrimination. There can be no doubt that this sort of noneconomic injury is one of the most serious consequences of discriminatory government action and is sufficient in some circumstances to support standing. See *Heckler v Mathews*, 465 U.S. 728, 739-740 (1984). Our cases make clear, however, that such injury accords a basis for standing only to "those persons who are personally denied equal treatment" by the challenged discriminatory conduct, *ibid.*
>
> * * *
>
> The consequences of recognizing respondents' standing on the basis of their first claim of injury illustrate why our cases plainly hold that such injury is not judicially cognizable. If the abstract stigmatic injury were cognizable, standing would extend nationwide to all members of the particular racial groups against which the Govenrment was alleged to be discriminating by its grant of a tax exemption to a racially discriminatory school, regardless of the location of the school. . . . A black person in Hawaii could challenge the grant of a tax exemption to a racially discriminatory school in Maine. Recognition of standing in such circumstances would transform the federal courts into "no more than a vehicle for the vindication of the value interests of concerned bystanders."[105]

In this passage, the Court says two things. First, it confirms that stigma from race discrimination constitutes injury-in-fact. Second, it states that the stigma must be peculiar to the claimants. In Cell 2, the stigma meets this requirement. The claimants are the immediate relatives, and the stigma therefore affects them in a way that it does not affect anyone else. Even if the family's stigma is too attenuated, it can sue on behalf of the victim, who was "personally denied equal treatment." Thus, the stigma from differential prosecutorial treatment constitutes particularized injury-in-fact.

The next question is whether there exists a sufficient causal relationship between the stigma and the challenged conduct. One

---

[105] Id at 755–56 (citation omitted).

might argue that there is no causal relationship because in Cell 2—where we assume overvaluation of white lives—the harm is caused by the improper decisions to pursue the death penalty against killers of white victims in other cases, not by the decision to forgo the death penalty in the case at bar. But such an analysis is flawed. There is no reason to characterize the "challenged conduct" as the decision to forgo the death penalty in the present case rather than as the improper decisions to seek the death penalty in other cases. The fact that the plaintiff seeks to have the former decision reversed is irrelevant to causation. The issue of relief is not relevant in a standing analysis until the third stage—redressability. The challenged conduct in this case consists of the improper decisions to seek the death penalty in other cases, and those decisions clearly "cause" the plaintiffs' stigmatic injury.

The redressability inquiry asks whether the relief sought will redress the plaintiff's injury-in-fact. In Cell 2, the plaintiffs seek to have the prosecutor pursue the death penalty against the killer of their relative. Presumably, this would eliminate (or at least ameliorate) the stigma caused by differential prosecutorial treatment based on race.

Standing, then, is not a problem where the black victim's family seeks the death penalty. There is, however, a substantive barrier to the family's claim, tied to the remedy that they seek. Where the violation consists of the overvaluation of other lives, the Equal Protection Clause does not authorize an order requiring the prosecutor to seek the death penalty. Rather, the only proper remedy is to commute the death sentences of killers whose victims' lives were overvalued. It is true that either remedy would achieve equality. But where overvaluation of victims' lives is the problem, the Equal Protection Clause authorizes only a "leveling down"—here, commutation of death sentences. By the same token, when undervaluation is the problem, the clause authorizes only "leveling up"—imposition of the death penalty or damages.

This requires explanation. In every equal protection case where a governmental benefit has been denied a disfavored class, the court faces the choice in designing a remedy of extending the benefit to that class, or denying the benefit to all.[106] It is sometimes

---

[106] See *Welsh v United States*, 398 US 333, 361 (1970) (Harlan, J, concurring in result).

said that courts finding equal protection violations have discretion
to choose their preferred remedy, and that the presumptive remedy is to extend the benefit to all.[107] The Supreme Court's decisions clearly indicate, however, that this is incorrect. Instead, the
proper remedy is determined by the ex ante intent of the legislature, or other government actor, that established or dispensed the
benefit in the first place. The court is required to ascertain whether
the governmental actor, blinded to the impermissible consideration, would have treated everybody at the favored group's level
or the disfavored group's level. If the actor would have treated
everybody at the favored group's level, then the disfavored group
must be brought up to that level. If the actor would have treated
everyone at the disfavored group's level, then the favored group
must be brought down.[108] Furthermore, this intent must be determined at the time the benefit was dispensed or the program established, not after litigation.[109] This limitation is especially important
when the relevant government actor is an individual rather than
a legislature, because while a legislature may of course eliminate
a benefits program at any time, even after litigation, and so ultimately impose a "leveling down" solution on all,[110] permitting individuals to "choose a remedy" after litigation would in effect permit defendants to nullify constitutional rights based on nothing
more than a promise to cease discriminating in the future.

In the context of discrimination in capital sentencing, the gov-

---

[107] The source of this confusion might be, at least in part, some language in the Supreme
Court's opinion in *Califano v Westcott*, 443 US 76, 89–90 (1979), indicating that ordinarily
courts have treated the extension of benefits as the proper remedy.

[108] See *Heckler v Mathews*, 465 US 728, 738–39 and n 5 (1984); *Califano*, 443 US at 90;
id at 94 (Powell, J, concurring in part and dissenting in part); *Miller v Albright*, 118 S Ct
1428, 1448–49 (1998) (Scalia, J, concurring in the judgment); Note, Evan Caminker, *A
Norm-Based Remedial Model for Underinclusive Statutes*, 95 Yale L J 1185, 1187–88 (1986)
("[t]he current remedial model requires courts to defer to the legislative branch and choose
the option that they believe the enacting legislature would have preferred had it known
that its intended discrimination was unlawful"). For example, if the legislature gave each
white person $100 and each non-white person nothing, the grant would violate equal pro-
tection. The relevant remedial question is how much the legislature—blinded to race—
would have given each citizen. The answer may be $100, nothing, or something in between.
If the answer is $100, then the court must award all non-white persons $100. If the answer
is nothing, then the court must prohibit the grant to white persons. If the answer is $50,
then the court must prohibit the state from giving white persons anything more than $50,
and it must award all non-white persons $50.

[109] Id at 1188 n 9.

[110] Compare *Palmer v Thompson*, 403 US 217 (1971).

ernmental actor is the prosecutor. If, blinded to the victim's race, he would not have sought the death penalty against a particular defendant, then the proper remedy is to "level down"—that is, commute the defendant's sentence to life. If, blinded to the victim's race, he would have sought the death penalty against a defendant, then the proper remedy is to "level up." Ideally, this would consist of requiring the prosecutor to seek the death penalty, but because of practical problems, it may only consist of damages to the victim's family.[111]

In Cell 2, the violation is one of overvaluing white victims' lives. By definition, the prosecutors in those cases would not have sought the death penalty if they had ignored race. The correct remedy would be to commute any death sentences that were imposed in those cases. Thus the families in Cell 2 are not entitled to the remedy they seek, which is for the prosecutor to seek the death penalty against the killer of their loved one. This raises an interesting further question: Would an altruistic black family have standing to seek the commutation of the death sentences of killers whose white victims' lives were overvalued? The answer is no. There is nothing to differentiate one black victim's family from any other. In each of their cases, the prosecutor properly decided not to seek the death penalty. Their identical stigmatic injuries are caused by prosecutors elsewhere improperly deciding to seek the death penalty where the victims are white. The claim presents a "generalized grievance" falling outside the scope of Article III. Here, *Allen v Wright* is directly on point.[112] Clearly, the proper persons to seek commutation are the condemned defendants.

C. UNDERVALUATION OF THE LIVES OF BLACK VICTIMS— DEFENDANT SEEKS COMMUTATION

In Cell 3, the killer of a white person seeks to have his death sentence commuted on the ground that similarly situated killers of blacks receive life sentences. Cell 3 assumes that the life of the white victim has been properly valued, whereas the lives of similarly situated black victims have been undervalued.

We conclude that a defendant lacks standing to pursue such a

---

[111] See Part IV.D.

[112] See notes 104–05 and accompanying text.

claim because of the second element of the standing inquiry—causation. The defendant's injury is the death sentence, yet it was not caused by the undervaluation of the lives of black victims. Therefore, the defendant has no standing to seek commutation on the basis of the undervaluation of black lives. The defendant might portray his injury differently in an effort to create standing, but changing the injury also changes the remedy. The defendant might claim that his injury is not the death sentence itself, but rather being sentenced to death under a system that employs an arbitrary classification—race. Assuming that the courts would recognize such an injury,[113] he would now have standing. However, he would not have standing to seek commutation. He would have standing only to seek resentencing under a nonarbitrary process. The proper remedy in this scenario is for him to be resentenced to death as part of a process that sentences all similarly situated killers of black victims to death. In theory, at least, this would be a hollow victory.[114]

Finally, even if the killer of a white did have standing to seek commutation of his death sentence based on the undervaluation of black victims' lives, he would run into the same remedial difficulties discussed in Cell 2.[115] Since the constitutional violation identified by the defendant is undervaluation, the proper remedy is "leveling up," which is to say, sentencing killers of blacks to death, because by definition that is what prosecutors would have done if blinded to race. However, this remedy is not what the defendant is seeking, and helps him not at all.

D. UNDERVALUATION OF BLACK VICTIMS' LIVES— POSSIBLE REMEDIES FOR FAMILY

In Cell 4, the prosecutor undervalues the life of a black victim, and the victim's family seeks redress. Standing is not a barrier, for

---

[113] The extremely brief discussion of standing in *McCleskey* suggests that such an injury is cognizable, 481 US at 291–92 n 8, but serious questions might be raised about whether the current Court would consider such an injury sufficiently "concrete." See, e.g., *Lujan v Defenders of Wildlife*, 504 US 555, 572–73 (1992).

[114] In practice, this remedy might be of some value to the defendant because of delays inherent in litigation.

[115] See Part IV.B.

the reasons discussed in Cell 2.[116] It is possible to imagine at least four different remedies in this situation, all problemmatic: an injunction to prevent future discrimination against black victims; allowing the victim's family to intervene in the penalty phase of the murder trial to seek the death penalty; damages against the prosecutor; and damages against the governmental unit employing the prosecutor.

1. *Injunction.* The victim's family could seek an injunction prohibiting discrimination against future black murder victims. The family could proceed individually or on behalf of the class of future black murder victims. Of course, any injunction would come too late to help the family's murdered relative. But, if the death penalty deters, it could help prevent future murders.

Such an attempt to secure injunctive relief would face daunting justiciability problems. The injunction would require prosecutors to pursue the death penalty in cases where they would otherwise be disinclined to seek it. Moreover, the lawsuit would be moot as to the victim. The "capable of repetition, yet evading review" doctrine would not apply because the same victim can never be murdered again.[117] Although the family members are themselves potential murder victims, this is equally true of every black person in the jurisdiction. The family members can demonstrate no particularized injury in terms of future harm, and the Court has stated unequivocally that generalized grievances fall outside the scope of judicial power under Article III.[118]

---

[116] See Part IV.B. Remember that to state a cognizable claim, the family's alleged injury cannot be failure to punish its relative's killer, simipliciter, but rather it must be the stigma created by unequal treatment of their relative.

[117] See *DeFunis v Odegaard*, 416 US 312 (1974), in which a rejected law school applicant sued to gain admission on the ground that the school's affirmative action policy discriminated against him on the basis of race. The trial court ordered him admitted, and he matriculated during appeals. During oral argument to the Supreme Court, counsel for the school admitted that the plaintiff would receive his degree no matter how the Court ultimately ruled. The Court held that the case was moot and did not fall within the "capable of repetition, yet evading review" exception because the plaintiff himself "will never again be required to run the gantlet of the Law School's admission process, and so the question is certainly not 'capable of repetition' so far as he is concerned." Id at 319. The Court has since reaffirmed that the relevant question concerns the possibility of recurrence with respect to the complaining party, not others similarly situated. See *Weinstein v Bradford*, 423 US 147, 149 (1975); *Murphy v Hunt*, 455 US 478, 482 (1982).

[118] See *Lujan v Defenders of Wildlife*, 504 US 555 (1992). The Court recently held that the prohibition against generalized grievances extends only to abstract injuries, not concrete ones. See *Federal Election Comm'n v Akins*, 118 S Ct 1777 (1998). It seems likely that the Court would find stigma more abstract than concrete.

2. *Intervention*. Can the victim's family intervene in the penalty phase of the murder trial to compel the prosecution to seek the death penalty? We begin with a sketch of what such an intervention procedure might entail. The prosecutor would be required to announce a certain amount of time before trial whether he intends to seek the death penalty. The announcement of a decision not to seek the death penalty would trigger a brief period during which the black victim's next of kin would request a court order requiring the prosecutor to seek the death penalty. The trial court would then review the relevant statistical and other evidence to decide whether, if the victim had been white, the prosecutor would have sought the death penalty. If the court decides in the affirmative, then it would order the prosecutor to seek the death penalty.

The advantage of this procedure is obvious. The intervention is on behalf of a specific murder victim, not "all black victims," or "all potential black victims," and it cannot be denied that there exists a genuine, sharply defined "case or controversy" between the victim's family and the prosecutor.[119] But intervention would cause intolerable delays. In order to decide whether the prosecutor had discriminated against the victim on the basis of race, the trial court would need to know the precise circumstances surrounding the killing. This would entail a mini-trial. Moreover, the court would have to consider the relevant statistical evidence and entertain argument regarding the charge of discrimination. Capital litigation is lengthy enough as it is. An intervention procedure is simply impracticable.[120]

3. *Damages*. Another possible remedy would be to allow the victim's family or the victim's estate damages from the prosecutor.

---

[119] The prosecutor's failure to seek the death penalty creates a race-based difference in treatment that directly stigmatizes the family as well as the victim. See Part IV.B.

[120] Intervention proceedings could also hamper the prosecution's ultimate effort to obtain a conviction. Presumably the victim's family would want to call the prosecutor as an adverse witness during the intervention proceedings, or at least to cross-examine the prosecutor on his or her assertions. Not only would this distract the prosecutor from his or her trial preparation, it might also provide ammunition for the murder defendant. If the prosecutor testifies, the victim's family would offer all available impeachment evidence. Some of this evidence might prove embarrassing or outright damaging in the murder trial, or in any penalty phase that might ensue. On the other hand, if the intervention statute prohibits the victim's family from calling the prosecutor as an adverse witness, or prohibits them from cross-examination, it unfairly hamstrings the intervention effort. Still another problem with intervention is psychological. Formal and protracted adversary proceedings pitting the victim's family against the prosecutor are bound to dampen the prosecutor's zeal in obtaining "justice" for the victim.

But the Supreme Court has held that prosecutors acting in their official capacity are absolutely immune from damages actions under Section 1983, so this remedy is currently unavailable.[121]

Could the victim's family or the victim's estate seek damages from the governmental unit employing the prosecutor? In *Monell v Department of Social Services*,[122] the Court ruled that a municipality is liable for damages under Section 1983 if the plaintiff demonstrates that a municipal custom or policy caused the violation. The municipality may not be held liable under a respondeat superior theory. Would a prosecutor's decision not to seek the death penalty on the basis of the victim's race constitute a "custom or policy" within the meaning of *Monell*?

The leading case in favor of characterizing such a decision as a "custom or policy" is *Pembaur v City of Cincinnati*.[123] A county prosecutor had instructed police to make an unconstitutional entry into a physician's clinic. The physician sued for damages under Section 1983. The Court held that the single decision of the prosecutor—who had authority under state law to decide whether the officers should enter—"may fairly be said to represent official policy."[124] By analogy, the family of a black murder victim would argue that the prosecutor, having authority to decide what criteria should be employed in deciding whether to seek the death penalty, makes discriminatory policy every time he elects not to seek the death penalty because of the victim's race.

Since *Pembaur*, however, the Court has cut back on the situations in which the action of a municipal employee constitutes "custom or policy."[125] As one commentator has noted, "In all of the decisions following *Monell*, the Justices seem to be trying to limit local government liability to those situations in which fault can be attributed not simply to an individual officer but to the governmental entity itself."[126] In *Bd. of County Commissioners of Bryan*

---

[121] *Butz v Economou*, 438 US 478 (1978). Congress could, of course, eliminate prosecutors' immunity from damages, but it seems unlikely to do so.

[122] 436 US 658 (1978).

[123] 475 US 469 (1986).

[124] *Pembaur*, 475 US at 480.

[125] See, e.g., *City of St. Louis v Praprotnik*, 485 US 112 (1988) (state law determines who is a policymaking official); *City of Canton v Harris*, 489 US 378 (1989) (municipal liability for "failure to train" only where officials harbored "deliberate indifference" to citizens).

[126] Richard H. Fallon et al, *Hart and Wechsler's The Federal Courts and the Federal System* 1131 (4th ed 1996).

County v Brown,[127] for example, the plaintiff was a passenger in a car that had been chased by police. When a deputy sheriff ordered her out of the vehicle, she refused. He then pulled her out so violently that she suffered severe and permanent damage to both knees. She sued the county on the theory that the sheriff had failed adequately to review the deputy's background before hiring him. As it turned out, the deputy—who was the sheriff's nephew's son—had previously pleaded guilty to several offenses, including assault and battery, resisting arrest, and public drunkenness. The Court nonetheless rejected municipal liability. Specifically, a review of the deputy's criminal record would not have provided sufficient reason for the sheriff to conclude that the deputy's use of excessive force would be a "plainly obvious consequence of the hiring decision."[128] More generally, the Court emphasized the need to find aggravated mental culpability before imposing municipal liability:

> As our Section 1983 municipal liability jurisprudence illustrates . . . it is not enough for a Section 1983 plaintiff merely to identify conduct properly attributable to the municipality. The plaintiff must also demonstrate that, through its *deliberate* conduct, the municipality was the "moving force" behind the injury alleged. That is, a plaintiff must show that the municipal action was taken with the requisite degree of culpability and must demonstrate a direct causal link between the municipal action and the deprivation of federal rights.[129]
>
> * * *
>
> As we recognized in *Monell* and have repeatedly reaffirmed, Congress did not intend municipalities to be held liable unless *deliberate* action attributable to the municipality directly caused a deprivation of federal rights.[130]

Most prosecutorial discrimination against victims is probably unconscious. If *Brown* means that no municipal liability shall be imposed for anything less than "deliberate" or "intentional" wrongdoing, then municipal liability would ordinarily be unavailable to families of victims. *Brown* may not, however, stand for that

---

[127] 117 S Ct 1382 (1997).

[128] Id at 1392 (footnote omitted).

[129] Id at 1388.

[130] Id at 1394.

proposition. In *City of Canton v Harris,*[131] the Court seemed to attribute great significance to the difference between active malfeasance and nonfeasance. The plaintiff in *Harris* had alleged that the city's failure to train its personnel properly caused her injury. The Court stated that a "failure to train" theory would withstand challenge only "where the failure . . . amounts to *deliberate indifference* to the rights of persons with whom the police come into contact."[132] Like *Harris, Brown* was a case of nonfeasance—failure to screen.[133] It may be that culpability must rise to the level of "deliberate" or "intentional" only in these nonfeasance cases, and that the fault standard in cases of malfeasance is lower.[134] Therefore, it is unclear under existing law whether a victim's family could obtain damages. For these reasons, it is our view that Congress should expressly amend Section 1983 to authorize such relief.

Where the governmental unit employing the prosecutor is a state rather than a municipality, there are additional procedural hurdles. The Court has held that states are not "persons" within the meaning of Section 1983 when being sued for retrospective relief such as damages.[135] Moreover, the Eleventh Amendment generally bars federal courts from awarding damages against states in federal court.[136] Congress should amend Section 1983 to make states "persons" for the limited purpose of damages in prosecutorial discrimination cases. It should also use its authority under Section 5 of the Fourteenth Amendment to abrogate states' Eleventh Amendment sovereign immunity in prosecutorial discrim-

---

[131] 489 US 378 (1989).

[132] Id at 388 (emphasis added).

[133] For purposes of this article, we assume that it is both possible and sensible to distinguish between cases of malfeasance and cases of nonfeasance. This assumption may be improvident. *Harris* might well be characterized as a case of actively culpable administration, just as *Brown* could be viewed as a case of reckless hiring. Justice Frankfurter once admonished the Court for insisting upon "Year-Book distinctions between feasance and nonfeasance—a distinction that may have significance in the evolution of common-law notions of liability, but is inadmissible as a line between constitutionality and unconstitutionality." *Lambert v California,* 355 US 225, 231 (1957) (Frankfurter, J, dissenting). Discussion of this problem, however, would divert us from our more immediate objective of exploring possible remedies for prosecutorial discrimination against victims.

[134] Although the Court has squarely held that mere negligence does not rise to the level of a Due Process violation. See *Daniels v Williams,* 474 US 327 (1986); *Davidson v Cannon,* 474 US 344 (1986).

[135] See *Will v Michigan Dept of State Police,* 491 US 58 (1989).

[136] See *Edelman v Jordan,* 415 US 651 (1974).

ination cases.[137] Finally, Congress should waive federal sovereign immunity in cases alleging prosecutorial discrimination against victims on the basis of race in federal capital cases.

What are the final results of our matrix analysis? In Cell 1, we found that a defendant whose white victim's life was overvalued has both first- and (probably) third-party standing to seek commutation of his death sentence. He is better off asserting the equal protection rights of undervalued black murder victims because such a claim would trigger strict scrutiny; the claim based on his own equal protection rights would be reviewed for a rational basis only. In Cell 2, we found that the family of a black victim has standing to seek the death penalty based on the overvaluation of white lives, but that imposition of the death penalty is the wrong remedy. The proper remedy for overvaluation of white lives is to commute the death sentences of the murderers of white victims— a remedy that the family of a black victim has neither standing nor incentive to seek. In Cell 3, we found that the condemned murderer of a white person does not have standing to seek commutation of his death sentence based on the undervaluation of black lives in other cases, and in any event, commutation is not the proper remedy for such a violation. He may have standing to insist upon being resentenced to death by a process that sentences similarly situated killers of blacks to death, but such a remedy does him little good. In Cell 4, we concluded that the family of a black victim should be able to sue the relevant governmental unit for undervaluation of its relative's life. We argued that Congress should amend Section 1983 to allow damages against municipalities and states in cases of prosecutorial discrimination against victims, and that Congress should waive federal sovereign immunity in such cases.

V. CONCLUSION

Devising a remedial scheme for race-of-the-victim discrimination in capital sentencing is difficult, but not impossible. The

---

[137] See *Fitzpatrick v Bitzer*, 427 US 445 (1976) (Section 5 of Fourteenth Amendment authorized Congress to abrogate states' Eleventh Amendment sovereign immunity with respect to Title VII actions). Congress's abrogation powers pursuant to the Civil War amendments survived the decision holding that Congress has no authority to abrogate pursuant to Article I. See *Seminole Tribe v Florida*, 517 US 44 (1996).

most promising solutions would be to allow defendants who murder whites to seek commutation of their sentences, and families of black victims to seek damages against the governmental units that employ prosecutors who discriminate. Each of these claimants could rely entirely on statistical evidence to make out a prima facie case of discrimination. Once the claimant has carried this burden, the burden should shift to the prosecutor to articulate a legitimate, nonracial rationale for seeking the death penalty in that particular case. If the prosecutor offers such a reason, the claimant should bear the ultimate burden of persuasion. To make these solutions work, several reforms are required. The Supreme Court should reinterpret the "intent" requirement of *Washington v Davis* and *Arlington Heights* to mean that the result would have been different if the race of the affected party had been different, and should permit the use of statistical evidence to establish this "causation" requirement. Moreover, Congress should amend Section 1983 to permit damages actions against governmental entities whose prosecutors discriminate on the basis of the victim's race.

This proposal would improve the law. The Baldus and similar studies prove that prosecutors discriminate based on the race of murder victims. For courts and legislatures simply to shrug their shoulders and say nothing can be done fosters cynicism and disrespect for the criminal justice system.

JESSE H. CHOPER AND TUNG YIN

STATE TAXATION AND THE DORMANT COMMERCE CLAUSE: THE OBJECT-MEASURE APPROACH

It has been well settled for more than a century that the federal courts may invoke the Commerce Clause, which states that "Congress shall have Power . . . To regulate Commerce . . . among the several States,"[1] even in the absence of relevant Congressional legislation, to invalidate various forms of state regulations that discriminate against interstate commerce or subject it to undue burdens. Over the past twenty years, the Court has resolved challenges to the validity of state taxes that affect interstate commerce by applying a four-part test first announced in *Complete Auto Transit, Inc. v Brady*.[2] Our thesis is that the *Complete Auto* test embodies the basic values underlying the Dormant Commerce Clause, but that it is more complicated than it needs to be, primarily because several of its parts are functionally redundant. This article proposes a new, simplified approach: a nondiscriminatory tax on an activity that can be reached by only one state should generally be upheld without the need for apportionment; but a nondiscriminatory tax on an activity that can be reached by more than one state must be apportioned to be valid. Our primary goal is not to reexamine

Jesse H. Choper is Earl Warren Professor of Public Law, University of California, Berkeley (Boalt Hall). Tung Yin is an Associate, Munger, Tolles & Olson.

AUTHORS' NOTE: We wish to thank Richard H. Fallon, Jr., Robert C. Post, Howard A. Shelanski, Michael E. Smith, and John C. Yoo for very helpful comments.

[1] US Const, Art I, § 8, cl 3.

[2] 430 US 274 (1977); see Part I.B.

the generally accepted purposes of judicial review under the Dormant Commerce Clause, but rather to develop a more workable approach for their fulfillment. Because of its greater clarity, simplicity, and ease of application, the object-measure standard should allow litigants, legislators, and lower courts, which must currently struggle with understanding and applying *Complete Auto*, to predict the outcomes of Dormant Commerce Clause challenges more reliably.

Part I of this article briefly traces the history of the Supreme Court's review of state taxation that affects interstate commerce. The Court initially developed a formalistic approach: interstate commerce itself was immune from state taxation. After several decades of gradual modifications, the Court, in 1977, explicitly discarded the old formalism in *Complete Auto*. Since then, *Complete Auto* has been applied in every case involving a Commerce Clause challenge to a state tax. Part II analyzes the problems of the *Complete Auto* test. Part III explains the suggested new approach, shows that it comprehends the values of the *Complete Auto* test, and defends it from potential criticisms from the rationales of other commentators. Finally, Part IV applies this approach to a variety of state taxes. Since this approach embodies the essential values of both the Dormant Commerce Clause and the *Complete Auto* test, it is not surprising that it yields the same results as most Supreme Court decisions dealing with state taxation of interstate commerce.

I. DEVELOPMENT OF THE COURT'S APPROACH

An extended discussion of the development of the Court's "historically unstable analysis of state taxes under the dormant Commerce Clause" is not necessary and is well told elsewhere.[3] Nevertheless, a brief review will provide context by which to judge the *Complete Auto* test and our alternative for analyzing Commerce Clause challenges to state taxes.

---

[3] Walter Hellerstein et al., *Commerce Clause Restraints on State Taxation After Jefferson Lines*, 51 Tax L Rev 47, 50 (1995); see generally Paul J. Hartman, *Federal Limitations on State and Local Taxation* § 2:9 to § 2:17 (1981); 1 Jerome R. Hellerstein and Walter Hellerstein, *State Taxation* (2d ed 1993); John E. Nowak and Ronald D. Rotunda, *Constitutional Law* § 8.11 (4th ed 1991); Laurence H. Tribe, *American Constitutional Law* § 6-15 to § 6-20 (2d ed 1988); Walter Hellerstein, *State Taxation of Interstate Commerce: Perspective on Two Centuries of Constitutional Adjudication*, 41 Tax Law 37, 38–50, 53–61 (1987).

A. THE RISE AND FALL OF FORMALISM

Prior to 1977, the Court often struck down state taxes on interstate commerce on the formalistic ground that they were invalid attempts to regulate interstate commerce itself.[4] For example, in *Freeman v Hewitt*,[5] the Court invalidated a gross receipts tax assessed on interstate sales made within the state, not because it created the risk of multiple taxation, but simply because the Dormant Commerce Clause "created an area of trade free from interference by the States."[6] The Court reasoned that a gross receipts tax on interstate sales was a direct tax on interstate commerce and thus would not be allowed, even though taxes that reached interstate commerce indirectly were acceptable.[7] Similarly, in *Spector Motor Service, Inc. v O'Connor*,[8] the Court invalidated a Connecticut tax "imposed upon the franchise of a foreign corporation for the privilege of doing business within the State." The Court concluded that Spector Motor Service, which engaged solely in interstate trucking, in that all freight that it picked up in Connecticut was delivered outside the state, could not be required to pay a tax for the privilege of engaging in interstate commerce, as only Congress could grant such a right or privilege.[9]

B. COMPLETE AUTO

In 1977, the Court issued its landmark ruling in *Complete Auto*,[10] which overruled the formalistic approach of *Spector* and *Freeman*,

---

[4] See, e.g., *Spector Motor Service, Inc. v O'Connor*, 340 US 602 (1951); *Joseph v Carter & Weekes Stevedoring Co.*, 330 US 422 (1947); *Freeman v Hewit*, 329 US 249 (1946); *McLeod v J. E. Dilworth Co.*, 322 US 327 (1944); *Philadelphia Steamship Co. v Pennsylvania*, 122 US 326 (1887); *Case of the State Freight Tax*, 82 US (15 Wall) 232 (1872).

[5] 329 US 249 (1946).

[6] Id at 252.

[7] Id at 256–57. This distinction between "direct" and "indirect" burdens on interstate commerce developed in the late nineteenth century in cases such as *Sanford v Poe*, 69 F 546 (6th Cir 1895), aff'd as *Adams Express Co. v Ohio State Auditor*, 165 US 194, 220 (1897). After fuller recognition in *Southern Ry. v King*, 217 US 524 (1910), it faded in *Western Live Stock v Bureau of Revenue*, 303 US 250, 256–58 (1938), and then resurfaced in *Freeman*. The most prominent judicial attack on the distinction came in *Di Santo v Pennsylvania*, 273 US 34, 44 (1927) (Stone dissenting). For influential scholarly criticism, see Noel T. Dowling, *Interstate Commerce and State Power*, 27 Va L Rev 1 (1940).

[8] 340 US 602, 603 (1951).

[9] Id at 608–09.

[10] 430 US 274 (1977).

and instead considered the practical effects of state taxes on interstate commerce. Complete Auto Transit transported automobiles into Mississippi for sale within the state. Mississippi imposed a privilege tax for doing business within the state, based on the gross income derived therefrom. The Court upheld this tax against the sole challenge that the state was forbidden from taxing the privilege of engaging in interstate commerce.[11] Synthesizing previous decisions, the Court held that a tax would be upheld against a Commerce Clause challenge "when the tax is applied to an activity with a substantial nexus with the taxing State, is fairly apportioned, does not discriminate against interstate commerce, and is fairly related to the services provided by the State."[12] The basis for Complete Auto Transit's claim was that interstate commerce was exempt from state taxation, but while *Spector* and *Freeman* had not yet been overruled, the Court noted that they had "been stripped of any practical significance."[13]

Reaction to *Complete Auto* was generally positive. Commentators hailed it as a complete repudiation of the old formalism that had initially gripped and later greatly influenced the Court for about three decades.[14]

C. POST–COMPLETE AUTO

Since *Complete Auto*, the Court has reviewed a number of different state taxes, rejecting most Commerce Clause challenges,[15]

---

[11] The Court "considered not the formal language of the tax statute, but rather its practical effect." Id at 279.

[12] Id.

[13] Id at 288.

[14] Tribe, *American Constitutional Law* § 6-15 at 442 (cited in note 3); William B. Lockhart, *A Revolution in State Taxation of Commerce*, 65 Minn L Rev 1025, 1026–27 (1981).

[15] *Oklahoma Tax Comm'n v Jefferson Lines*, 115 S Ct 1331 (1995) (gross receipts tax on sales of interstate transportation tickets); *Barclays Bank PLC v Franchise Tax Board*, 114 S Ct 2268 (1994) (corporate franchise tax); *Itel Containers Int'l Corp. v Huddleston*, 507 US 60 (1993) (sales tax on lease of cargo containers); *Trivonia Corp. v Michigan Dept. of Treasury*, 498 US 358 (1991) (single business tax); *Amerada Hess Corp. v Director*, 490 US 66 (1989) (windfall profit tax); *Goldberg v Sweet*, 488 US 252 (1989) (tax on telephone calls); *D. H. Holmes Co. v McNamara*, 486 US 24 (1988) (use tax); *Container Corp. v Franchise Tax Board*, 463 US 159 (1983) (franchise tax); *Commonwealth Edison Co. v Montana*, 453 US 609 (1981) (severance tax on coal); *Department of Revenue v Association of Washington Stevedoring Cos.*, 435 US 734 (1978) (business and occupation tax).

though sustaining a few.[16] Several cases have made important refinements of aspects of the *Complete Auto* test.

In *Container Corp. v Franchise Tax Board*,[17] the Court upheld California's unitary "doing business" tax as applied to domestic-based multinational corporations. The tax is calculated by considering the company's entire integrated business, including subsidiaries, and then using a formula to determine the fraction of corporate income attributable to business activity within the state.[18] The Court supplemented its definition of *Complete Auto*'s fair apportionment prong, explaining that it encompassed an internal consistency test and an external consistency test.[19] An internally consistent tax is one that, "if every State were to impose an identical tax, no multiple taxation would result."[20] To test for internal consistency, the Court does not compare actual state taxes; it merely "hypothesizes a situation where other States have passed an identical statute."[21] The Court's definition of "external" is more difficult to pin down. It has described an externally consistent tax as one that taxes "only that portion of the revenues from the interstate activity which reasonably reflects the in-state component of the activity being taxed,"[22] emphasizing that external consistency is aimed at determining the "practical or economic effect of the tax."[23] Putting it yet another way, the Court explained that external consistency is aimed at ensuring that "the factor or factors used in the apportionment formula . . . actually reflect a reasonable sense of how income is generated."[24] Having created these two tests, the Court did not appear clearly to apply them to the tax in question, but its decision can probably be read as intending

---

[16] *Fulton Corp. v Faulkner*, 116 S Ct 848 (1996) (intangibles tax); *Associated Industries of Missouri v Lohman*, 114 S Ct 1815 (1994) (use tax); *Quill Corp. v North Dakota*, 504 US 298 (1992) (use tax on out-of-state mail-order house); *American Trucking Assns. v Scheiner*, 483 US 266 (1987) (flat axle tax); *Tyler Pipe Industries v Department of Revenue*, 483 US 232 (1987) (doing business tax); *Armco v Hardesty*, 467 US 638 (1984) (gross receipts tax).

[17] 463 US 159 (1983).

[18] Id at 164–65.

[19] Id at 169. *Complete Auto* made no mention of internal or external consistency.

[20] *Goldberg v Sweet*, 488 US 252, 261 (1989) (citing *Container Corp.*, 463 US at 169).

[21] Id.

[22] Id at 262 (citing *Container Corp.*, 463 US at 169–70).

[23] Id.

[24] *Container Corp.*, 463 US at 170.

to hold that the California tax's apportionment scheme was reasonable.[25]

Goldberg v Sweet[26] further illustrates the operation of the internal and external consistency tests. Illinois imposed a 5 percent tax "on the gross charge of interstate telecommunications (1) originated or terminated in Illinois . . . and (2) charged to an Illinois service address, regardless of where the telephone call is billed or paid."[27] It was not difficult to conclude that this tax was internally consistent, because if every state taxed only interstate calls billed to addresses within it, each such interstate call would be taxed only once.[28] But the Court further blurred the nature of external consistency by finding it met here because the tax "reasonably reflect[ed] the way that consumers purchase[d] interstate telephone calls."[29] Since external consistency "is essentially a practical inquiry," the Court found it satisfied because it would be infeasible to apportion interstate telephone calls by mileage or other geographic units.[30]

In *Commonwealth Edison Co. v Montana*,[31] the Court provided insight into other prongs of the *Complete Auto* test. It explained that the fourth prong (that the tax be "fairly related to the services provided by the State") was closely connected to the first prong ("substantial nexus"), and merely added the "limitation that the measure of the tax must be reasonably related to the extent of the contact."[32] The "fairly related" prong was said to be satisfied by the "general services" provided by the state to the taxpayer.[33]

The Court's recent Dormant Commerce Clause decision, *Oklahoma Tax Commission v Jefferson Lines, Inc.*,[34] did little to clarify the unsettled aspects of the doctrine. *Jefferson Lines* involved a tax

---

[25] Id at 180–83.

[26] 488 US 252 (1989).

[27] Id at 256.

[28] Id at 261.

[29] Id at 262.

[30] Id at 264–65. For further confusion surrounding the external consistency test, see note 52 and accompanying text.

[31] 453 US 609 (1981).

[32] Id at 626.

[33] *Goldberg*, 488 US at 267.

[34] 115 S Ct 1331 (1995).

imposed on the sale of certain goods and services in the state. The primary dispute in the case was largely over whether such a tax, as applied to the sale of tickets for interstate bus transportation, was externally consistent. Although the Court acknowledged the superficial similarity of the case to *Central Greyhound Lines, Inc. v Mealey*,[35] it ultimately concluded that the Oklahoma tax was externally consistent because it fell on the buyer and not the seller, unlike the tax in *Central Greyhound*. The buyer of the bus ticket could not be subjected to double taxation, just as a buyer of a good could not be.[36] This understanding of external consistency, however, looks exactly like internal consistency, thereby blurring the distinction between the two.

Since *Complete Auto*, then, although the Court has tinkered with and refined its test, each iteration, rather than clarifying the meaning of internal and external consistency (and the purpose of the fair relation requirement), has only served to muddle the *Complete Auto* approach, specifically raising the question whether there is now any distinction between internal and external consistency.

II. THE PROBLEM WITH COMPLETE AUTO

The central problem with *Complete Auto* is that its four prongs are functionally overlapping and redundant in attempting to fulfill the bedrock constitutional value served by judicial review of state taxation of interstate commerce: nondiscrimination against interstate commerce.[37] Although the question of what constitutes discrimination is complex and multifaceted, the evil, generally stated, is a state policy whose purpose *or* effect is to confer advantages on local interests at the expense of out-of-staters. The Court did not fully discuss the theoretical underpinnings of the test announced in *Complete Auto*, but it can be seen as securing two precepts that further the Dormant Commerce Clause's core prohibi-

---

[35] 344 US 653 (1948) (discussed in note 143). See 115 S Ct at 1340.

[36] Id at 1341.

[37] Hellerstein, *State Taxation of Interstate Commerce*, 41 Tax Law at 46, 60 (cited in note 3) ("The rule prohibiting state taxes that discriminate against interstate commerce has been . . . more firmly entrenched and consistently applied than any other . . . enunciated in this field.").

tion of discrimination against interstate commerce: avoidance of
(*a*) multiple taxation on interstate commerce,[38] and (*b*) direct
commercial advantage to local businesses at the expense of
multistate enterprises.[39] This principle—that "the commerce
clause prohibits taxes that bear more heavily on the interstate than
the intrastate enterprise merely because the former does business
across state lines"[40]—articulated a specially directed, yet expan-
sive conception of nondiscrimination, one that seemingly differs
somewhat in both purpose and effect from that concerning judicial
review of state *regulation* of interstate commerce. Thus, when a
state rule "regulates evenhandedly to effectuate a legitimate local
public interest,"[41] it may still be rejected by the Court if "the burden imposed on commerce is clearly excessive in relation to the
local benefits,"[42] even though neither its purpose nor effect is to
treat interstate business any more onerously than local enterprises.[43] This is not the Court's focus, however, when it reviews
state taxes. Even though a particular state's system or rates of taxation may impose exceedingly heavy burdens on business enterprises, thus significantly deterring entry of interstate commerce,
the decisions show that the Court will not ordinarily invalidate the

---

[38] *Complete Auto* quoted generously from *Western Live Stock v Bureau of Revenue*, 303 US
250, 254 (1938), for the proposition that "[i]t was not the purpose of the commerce clause
to relieve those engaged in interstate commerce from their just share of state tax burden
even though it increases the cost of doing business." 430 US at 288. This principle of not
burdening interstate commerce with additional taxes dates to the drafting of the Constitution. See Federalist 42 (Madison) in Clinton Rossitor, ed, *The Federalist Papers* 264, 267–
68 (Mentor, 1961); see also *Northwestern States Portland Cement Co. v Minnesota*, 358 US
450, 458 (1959); *Michigan-Wisconsin Pipe Line Co. v Calvert*, 347 US 157, 166 (1954); *J. D.
Adams Manufacturing Co. v Storen*, 304 US 307, 311 (1938).

[39] *Associated Industries of Missouri v Lohman*, 114 S Ct 1815, 1820 (1994) ("The [Com-
merce] Clause prohibits economic protectionism—that is, 'regulatory measures designed
to benefit in-state economic interests by burdening out-of-state competitors.' "); *Boston Stock
Exchange v State Tax Commission*, 429 US 319, 329 (1977); *Northwestern States*, 358 US at
458; *Memphis Steam Laundry Cleaner v Stone*, 342 US 389, 395 (1952); *Nippert v City of
Richmond*, 327 US 416, 425 (1946); Donald H. Regan, *The Supreme Court and State Protectionism: Making Sense of the Dormant Commerce Clause*, 84 Mich L Rev 1091, 1094–95 (1986)
(observing that the Court's essential responsibility in this area is preventing purposeful
economic protectionism and cumulative tax burdens).

[40] Walter Hellerstein, *Is "Internal Consistency" Foolish? Reflections on an Emerging Commerce
Clause Restraint on State Taxation*, 87 Mich L Rev 138, 164 (1988).

[41] *Pike v Bruce Church, Inc.*, 397 US 137, 142 (1970).

[42] Id.

[43] See, e.g., *Southern Pacific Co. v Arizona*, 325 US 761 (1945).

tax as long as in-state businesses are subject to the same financial disadvantage.[44]

The bar of discrimination against interstate commerce contributes important clarification of the concept of "multiple taxation." The mere fact that a taxpayer is subjected to a number of different taxes does not violate the prohibition against multiple taxation if those taxes are imposed on unrelated activities, such as a sales tax, a property tax, an income tax, and a gasoline tax.[45] On the other hand, if two states both imposed their respective income taxes on all the earnings of a taxpayer who produced income in both states, that taxpayer *would* be subjected to multiple taxation. A business earning $50,000 all in one state would pay income tax to one state on that amount, but a multistate enterprise earning $50,000, half in one state and half in another, would pay income tax on the full amount twice. The obvious effect is discrimination against interstate commerce.

The problematic nature of the *Complete Auto* test may be sharply illustrated by considering each prong and the role it purportedly plays in protecting interstate commerce from either intentional or effective discrimination.

---

[44] Although our focus is primarily on discrimination against interstate firms, discrimination against goods moving in interstate commerce is no less objectionable. Such discrimination, however, typically occurs through regulation, as compared to taxation.

Various reasons have been offered as to why discrimination against interstate firms is problematic, including "concept of union," "resentment/retaliation," and "efficiency." Regan, *The Supreme Court and State Protectionism*, at 1112–13 (cited in note 39). Although the subject is beyond the scope of this article, these three reasons, not all of which Regan accepts, tend to revolve around the concept of "protectionist" legislation as the "economic equivalent of war." Id at 1113. Thus, if Nevada enacts legislation that adversely affects California firms doing business in Nevada, California may retaliate with similar legislation, perhaps setting off escalating taxation.

An additional possible objection to discrimination against interstate firms due to their interstate character is that these firms typically do not have adequate representation in the taxing jurisdiction. See *South Carolina State Highway Dep't v Barnwell Bros.*, 303 US 177, 184 n 2 (1938); compare Herbert Wechsler, *The Political Safeguards of Federalism: The Role of the States in the Composition and Selection of the National Government*, 54 Colum L Rev 543 (1954); Jesse H. Choper, *Judicial Review and the National Political Process* 176–80, 206–07 (1980) (contrasting the adequate representation of states in the national government structure with the insufficient reflection of the national interest in the state legislative scheme). Thus, the only recourse available to interstate firms facing excessively high taxes is to refrain from doing business in that taxing jurisdiction, clearly an undesirable result.

[45] See *Jefferson Lines*, 115 S Ct at 1331 ("[T]he Commerce Clause does not forbid the actual assessment of a succession of taxes by different States on distinct events as the same tangible object flows along").

The first proviso—that the tax be applied to an activity with a substantial nexus to the taxing state—ensures that there is a sufficient basis for applying the tax to the conduct within the state that triggers it. There is an obvious parallel between this prong and the Due Process requirement of "minimum contacts" with the forum state in order to justify personal jurisdiction over a defendant.[46] The Court has ruled, however, that the "substantial nexus" requirement is more stringent in that it might not be satisfied by some taxes that nevertheless meet the minimum contacts demand.[47]

In *Quill Corp. v North Dakota*, the Court reasoned that due process is concerned with "the fundamental fairness of government activity," whereas the Commerce Clause focuses on "structural concerns about the effects of state regulation on the national economy."[48] But the fact that the two clauses address different policies does not explain why the substantial nexus requisite is more stringent than minimum contacts. In fact, the Court's analysis centered on whether a state tax on vendors whose only contact with the state was by mail or common carrier violated the Dormant Commerce Clause.[49] *Quill* provided no guidance as to when substantial nexus would be more stringent than minimum contacts. This prong is thus something of an enigma.

The second prong—that the tax be fairly apportioned—is designed to protect interstate commerce both structurally (through the internal consistency requirement) and practically (through the external consistency requirement). Although these two conditions plainly further the goals of the Dormant Commerce Clause, an apparent redundancy has developed in the application of the test.

Until recently, external consistency, while rather opaque, seemed to retain a separate identity from internal consistency. Although apportionment was not required merely because it was feasible, the description of external consistency as a practical inquiry suggested that apportionment would usually be required where interstate commerce was involved.[50] However, in *Oklahoma Tax*

---

[46] *International Shoe Co. v Washington*, 326 US 310 (1945).

[47] *Quill Corp. v North Dakota*, 504 US 298, 313 (1992) (discussed in notes 79 and 80).

[48] Id at 312.

[49] Id at 313–15.

[50] See, e.g., *Goldberg v Sweet*, 488 US 252, 264–65 (1989) (not requiring apportionment because it would be "infeasible").

Commission v Jefferson Lines, Inc.,[51] the Court indicated otherwise. Oklahoma's tax was externally consistent largely because "no other State can claim to be the site of [agreement, payment, and delivery of services]."[52] Yet, this same feature ensured that the tax would be internally consistent; Jefferson Lines would be taxed only once even if every state imposed the same tax. External consistency thus becomes irrelevant because an internally consistent tax will be externally consistent as well.

The third prong, which fulfills the Court's long established mandate that a state tax that is facially discriminatory against interstate commerce must be invalid,[53] has been held merely to prohibit states from setting differential tax rates for in-state and out-of-state taxpayers.[54] While this establishes a significant threshold for state taxes to pass in order to satisfy the values of the Dormant Commerce Clause, it is also easily met. Since the core goals of the Dormant Commerce Clause are to prevent the conferral of benefits to in-staters at the expense of out-of-staters, particularly in the forms of multiple taxation on interstate commerce and direct commercial advantages to local businesses to the prejudice of interstate

---

[51] 115 S Ct 1331 (1995).

[52] Id at 1341.

[53] See *Boston Stock Exchange v State Tax Commission*, 429 US 318, 329 (1977) (noting the "fundamental principle that . . . no state, consistent with the commerce clause, may 'impose a tax which discriminates against interstate commerce . . . by providing a direct commercial advantage to local business' "); Hellerstein, 87 Mich L Rev at 164 (cited in note 40) ("Aside from Justice Scalia's skepticism [regarding the Dormant Commerce Clause], no sitting Supreme Court Justice would dissent from the view that the commerce clause prohibits taxes that bear more heavily on the interstate than the intrastate enterprise merely because the former does business across state lines."). For a more subtle example, in *Armco v Hardesty*, 467 US 638, 640 (1984), West Virginia imposed a gross receipts tax "on persons engaged in the business of selling tangible property at wholesale." The state, however, exempted local manufacturers from the tax, on the grounds that they were already subject to a higher manufacturing tax. In invalidating the tax, the Court concluded that the higher manufacturing tax did not save it, since wholesaling and manufacturing were not substantially equivalent events. Thus, the compensatory tax doctrine, see Part III.C.3, did not apply. Id at 643. The Court noted that an out-of-state manufacturer would be subject to the West Virginia gross receipts tax, as well as the other state's manufacturing tax, while an in-state manufacturer would only be subject to West Virginia's manufacturing tax. Id at 644. See also *National Meat Assn. v Deukmejian*, 743 F2d 656, 660–61 (9th Cir 1984) (striking down as facially discriminatory a California tax of $1 per head of cattle for in-state beef processors, but a variable tax according to quantity on out-of-state processors). See generally Michael E. Smith, *State Discriminations Against Interstate Commerce*, 74 Cal L Rev 1203 (1986).

[54] *Commonwealth Edison Co. v Montana*, 453 US 609, 618–19 (1981) (holding that because the rate of the tax in question did not treat in-staters and out-of-staters differently, it satisfied the third prong).

firms, the more challenging inquiry is whether a facially neutral tax nevertheless discriminates against or otherwise impermissibly burdens interstate commerce.

More importantly, this prong is superfluous, because any tax that sets different rates for in-staters as compared to out-of-staters will necessarily be internally inconsistent. If every state taxed out-of-staters at a higher rate than in-staters, then enterprises engaging in interstate business would face higher tax burdens than their intrastate counterparts.

Finally, there is the fourth requirement—that the tax be fairly related to the services provided by the state. In *Commonwealth Edison Co. v Montana*, the Court explained that the fourth prong "is closely connected to the first prong" while "impos[ing] . . . [an] additional limitation."[55] If the fourth prong really does impose a substantive limitation beyond that of the first prong, then a state theoretically could apply a tax on an activity with a substantial nexus to the state but which lacks a sufficient relationship to the state. That is, a tax could satisfy the first prong but still fail the fourth.

In practice, however, the fourth part of the *Complete Auto* test has failed to impose any additional hurdle. The Court has yet to invalidate a tax under it, as "services" has been defined so broadly—"receipt of police and fire protection, the use of public roads and mass transit, and other advantages of civilized society"[56]—that this condition is virtually meaningless. None of the five cases in which the Court has struck down state taxes under *Complete Auto* even discusses the fairly related prong,[57] and in other cases, taxpayers have not even bothered to contest the issue.[58]

---

[55] 453 US 609, 626 (1981) (quoting *Western Live Stock v Bureau of Revenue*, 303 US 250, 254 (1938)).

[56] Id; see also *Amerada Hess Corp. v Director*, 490 US 66, 79 (1989); *D. H. Holmes Co. v McNamara*, 486 US 24, 32 (1988); *Japan Line, Ltd. v County of Los Angeles*, 441 US 434, 445 (1979); *Itel Containers Int'l Corp. v Cardwell*, 814 SW2d 29, 35 (Tenn), aff'd as *Itel Containers Int'l Corp. v Huddleston*, 507 US 60, 73 (1991).

[57] See note 16. This neglect is especially telling, since each of the other three prongs has been the basis for invalidating at least one state tax. See *Fulton Corp. v Faulkner*, 116 S Ct 848 (1996) (facially discriminatory against interstate commerce); *Quill Corp. v North Dakota*, 504 US 298 (1992) (no substantial nexus); *American Trucking Assns. v Scheiner*, 483 US 266 (1987) (internally inconsistent); *Tyler Pipe Industries v Department of Revenue*, 483 US 232 (1987) (facially discriminatory); *Armco v Hardesty*, 467 US 638 (1984) (not fairly apportioned and also facially discriminatory).

[58] *Trivonia Corp. v Michigan Dept. of Treasury*, 498 US 358, 373 (1991); see also *Barringer v Griffes*, 1 F3d 1331, 1335 (2d Cir 1993) (not challenging first and fourth prongs); *Merrion*

It is not difficult to see why the fourth prong has become so insignificant. Any taxpayer with a substantial nexus to the taxing state (the first prong) would appear necessarily to benefit from police and fire protection, as well as the amorphous "other advantages of civilization." The fourth prong, as defined by the Court, has become wholly subordinated to the first.

III. A Simpler Approach

A. BASIC PREMISE

From its seemingly straightforward beginnings, the *Complete Auto* test has evolved into a collection of disparate requirements, some redundant, some toothless, others rather opaque.[59] This is especially true in respect to facially neutral revenue rules. When imposing its four criteria, the Court usually reaches the correct result, but sometimes despite, rather than because of, the reasoning used to explain their application. We propose a more straightforward and more easily applicable approach to nondiscriminatory taxes[60] that emphasizes the distinction, never sharply identified by the Court, between the *object* of the tax and its *measure*.

The "object" of a tax is the activity or tangible thing that the state is taxing. For example, the object of a sales tax is the activity of the sale. The object of a property tax is the property present in the state. The object of a "doing business" tax (often referred to as a "privilege" tax or a tax for the "privilege of doing business") is business activity—such as manufacturing, sales, or any other commercial operations—being conducted within the state.

---

v Jicarilla Apache Tribe, 617 F2d 537, 546 n 4 (10th Cir 1980) (declining to address the issue of fair relation because the appellant failed to build a factual foundation).

[59] Other commentators have characterized the Court's current doctrine as "confusing" and "elusive." See Julian N. Eule, *Laying the Dormant Commerce Clause to Rest*, 91 Yale L J 425, 426 n 2 (1982); Ferdinand P. Schoettle, *Commerce Clause Challenges to State Taxes*, 75 Minn L Rev 907, 919 (1991); David F. Shores, *State Taxation of Interstate Commerce: Quill, Allied Signal and a Proposal*, 72 Neb L Rev 682, 683–84 (1993); Winkfield F. Twyman, Jr., *Beyond Purpose: Addressing State Discrimination in Interstate Commerce*, 46 SC L Rev 381, 383 (1995); see also Daniel Shaviro, *An Economic and Political Look at Federalism in Taxation*, 90 Mich L Rev 895, 937–41 (1992) (discussing ten pairs of inconsistent Dormant Commerce Clause cases).

[60] For an explanation of how our approach remains faithful to the *Complete Auto* values, see Part III.C.1.

The "measure" of a tax is the price or value of the activity or tangible thing by which the tax is calculated.[61] For example, the measure of a sales tax is the price of the product being sold; the measure of a property tax is the assessed value of the property.

Sometimes the object and the measure of the tax will be the same, such as with a business income tax. The object of such a tax is the activity of generating business income, and the measure of the tax is that same income.

Under our proposal, if the object of the tax is something that only one state has the ability to tax, such as (a) an intrastate sale or (b) real property located in the state, then an unapportioned tax should usually be held valid.[62] This should be true even if part or all of the measure might be used by another state as the measure of a different tax.[63]

On the other hand, if the object of the tax can be reached by more than one state, such as (a) the income of a multistate corporation or (b) property that moves from one state to another, then each state's tax must be fairly apportioned in order to avoid undermining Dormant Commerce Clause doctrine.[64] Note that for

---

[61] It is admittedly difficult to define this term with any more precision without resorting to circularity, such as "the way of measuring the tax."

[62] The presumption of validity can be overcome in two instances: (1) if the tax was adopted with the intent to burden interstate commerce, as in the case of a state that tries to exploit a natural advantage; and (2) if the nation's federal structure inherently disadvantages multistate enterprises. These issues of (1) "state pretext" and (2) "federal prejudice" are discussed at Part III.D.4.

[63] Although neither the Court nor commentators have advocated this specific approach, there have been hints of it. For example, *Western Live Stock v Bureau of Revenue*, 303 US 250 (1938), involved a privilege tax on the business of publishing newspapers and magazines, measured by the gross receipts from the sale of advertising space. The Court upheld the tax as applied to a locally published, but nationally circulated magazine. Even though the gross receipts from the sale of advertising space might also be used as the measure of, say, another state's tax on the sale of advertising, Justice Stone noted that "[t]he tax is not one which in form or substance can be repeated by other states in such manner as to lay an added burden on the interstate distribution of the magazine." Id at 260.

[64] A fair apportionment scheme is a central part of the object-measure approach's framework and is often critically important in avoiding the burden of deliberate *or* operational multiple taxation.

The question of a proper method of apportionment has reached the Supreme Court periodically. Under current doctrine, states may apportion various income taxes under a three-factor formula, or even a one-factor formula. If three factors are used, they are usually the ratios of property, payroll, and sales within the state to the total property, payroll, and sales. *Container Corp. v Franchise Tax Board*, 463 US 159, 170 (1983) (three factors); *Moorman Manufacturing Co. v Bair*, 437 US 267, 272 (1978) (one factor: gross sales).

In *Moorman*, the Court found Iowa's single-factor apportionment formula to be presump-

this second category of taxes, the possibility that more than one state can reach the object is sufficient to require apportionment; the taxpayer need not show that it is actually burdened by multiple taxes. "First, as the Court pointed out in *Armco* [*v Hardesty*], '[a]ny other rule would mean that the constitutionality of West Virginia's tax laws would depend on the shifting complexities of the tax codes of 49 other States, and that the validity of the taxes imposed on each taxpayer would depend on the particular other States in which it operated.' . . . Second, even if acceptable as a matter of principle, it is undesirable as a matter of practice. Taxpayers would face uncertainties in determining their state tax liabilities, states would face uncertainties in predicting state tax collections, and compliance and administration difficulties would be exacerbated. Finally, even if otherwise acceptable, there is something unseemly about determining state tax liabilities 'on a first-come-first-tax basis.' Given the fundamental concerns underlying the commerce clause, it would be perverse indeed to constitutionalize a rule rewarding beggar-thy-neighbor state tax policies with state tax collections depending on who won the race to the taxpayer's door."[65]

To illustrate: suppose that Acme manufactures in California and Nevada, but sells only in California. Acme's annual gross sales from its operations are $1 million; $750,000 of the value of the products sold is manufactured in California and the other $250,000 is manufactured in Nevada. Suppose that California and Nevada both have a manufacturing tax and a sales tax. Under our ap-

---

tively valid and upheld it because the challenging taxpayer had failed to show by "clear and cogent evidence" that the formula led to results "out of all appropriate proportion." 437 US at 273–74. However, the Court has also implied that the three-factor apportionment formula—utilized by "forty-four of the forty-five States (including the District of Columbia) other than Iowa that impose a corporate income tax," id at 296 (Powell, J, dissenting)—is the preferred approach: Although the one-third weight given to each of the three factors—payroll, property, and sales—is not a precise apportionment for every case, the formula "has gained wide approval precisely because payroll, property, and sales appear in combination to reflect a very large share of the activities by which value is generated." *Container Corp.*, 463 US at 183. It has become "something of a benchmark against which other apportionment formulas are judged." Id.

Although the Court's treatment of the issue of what constitutes a fair apportionment could be improved, a full-scale discussion is not necessary to implement the object-measure approach and is thus beyond the scope of this article. It should be noted, however, that while a single-factor apportionment scheme may be valid, it would be subject to the pretext analysis mentioned in note 62. See notes 171 and 172 and accompanying text.

[65] Hellerstein, 87 Mich L Rev at 169–70 (cited in note 40).

proach, California would be able to apply its sales tax on the full $1 million, since the sales take place exclusively in California. The object of this tax is sales within the state, and since no other state can reach that object, the sales tax does not need to be apportioned.

The matter is more complicated, however, with respect to the manufacturing tax. The object is manufacturing. Acme conducts such activity within both states, and thus a manufacturing tax would have to be apportioned fairly in order to avoid the imposition of multiple tax burdens on interstate commerce.[66]

Note that the object-measure approach does not require a nexus between the taxing state and the object of the tax beyond that mandated by the Due Process Clause.[67] The approach thus differs in this regard from the *Complete Auto* test, which contains a "substantial nexus" requirement more stringent than that imposed by the Due Process Clause.[68] Of course, a tax whose object can be reached by only one state will necessarily involve sufficient contacts for that state to impose the tax. In the case of a tax whose object can be reached by multiple states, however, it may be that one or more states lack the necessary minimum contacts to apply their taxes on the interstate transaction.[69] Under the object-measure approach, these states would be prohibited by the Due Process Clause, not the Commerce Clause, from applying their taxes.

B. A LEGISLATIVE ROLE FOR THE COURT

In reviewing Dormant Commerce Clause challenges to state taxes, it is important to note that the Court is *not* engaging in true judicial review, but rather is subject to revision by ordinary federal statutes.[70] The essence of Dormant Commerce Clause adjudication is that the Court is acting in the absence of Congressional legisla-

---

[66] Under a one-factor (gross sales) apportionment scheme, see note 64, California would apply its manufacturing tax to $750,000. Nevada would apply its manufacturing tax to $250,000. It cannot apply its sales tax, because none of Acme's sales take place in Nevada.

[67] See generally *International Shoe Co. v Washington*, 326 US 310 (1945) (requiring "minimum contacts" for the exercise of personal jurisdiction), discussed at note 46.

[68] See *Quill Corp. v North Dakota*, 504 US 298, 313 (1992), discussed in notes 72 and 80.

[69] For recent discussion of the due process requirements for tax jurisdiction, see Christina R. Edson, *Quill's Constitutional Jurisprudence and Tax Nexus Standards in an Age of Electronic Commerce*, 49 Tax L Rev 893 (1996).

[70] Choper, *Judicial Review and the National Political Process* at 207–08 (cited in note 44).

tion.[71] If Congress disagrees with the Court's rulings, it can enact laws to undo the judicial decision.[72]

The most commonly discussed example of this special judicial role in respect to state taxation of interstate commerce is the Court's decision in *Northwestern States Portland Cement Co. v Minnesota.*[73] In *Northwestern States,* the Court upheld state taxation of the income of a multistate business, based solely on the fact that the business had a sales office in the taxing state. Seven months later, Congress reversed the result by statute.[74] Similarly, after the Court upheld a head charge on airline passengers in *Evansville-Vanderburgh Airport Authority District v Delta Airlines, Inc.,*[75] Congress enacted Section 7(a) of the Airport Development Acceleration Act of 1973.[76] Concluding that airport taxes of the sort permitted by *Evansville-Vanderburgh* were exposing interstate travelers to double taxation, Congress prohibited the imposition of such taxes.[77]

---

[71] Id at 208; Martin H. Redish and Shane V. Nugent, *The Dormant Commerce Clause and the Constitutional Balance of Federalism,* 1987 Duke L J 569, 570.

[72] See, e.g., *Quill Corp. v North Dakota,* 504 US 298, 318 (1992) ("No matter how we evaluate the burdens that use taxes impose on interstate commerce, Congress remains free to disagree with our conclusions."). Moreover, Congressional overruling in this area should not engender the friction that it might in other circumstances, since under the Dormant Commerce Clause, Congress's authority is unquestionably superior to that of the Court. See generally Abner J. Mikva and Jeff Bleich, *When Congress Overrules the Court,* 79 Cal L Rev 729, 732–33 (1991).

Finally, while the fragmentary nature of Congress makes it unlikely that a Supreme Court decision affecting the taxation scheme of only one or a few states will adequately attract Congress's attention, the ordinary broad applicability of a Supreme Court decision on state taxation, such as one implementing the object-measure approach, makes it more likely that Congress would respond if it finds the results inadequately subtle or economically undesirable. Those adversely affected by tax decisions, such as large businesses and state governments, may well successfully mobilize against it.

[73] 358 US 450 (1959).

[74] 73 Stat 555, 15 USC §§ 381–84. This Act prohibits states from taxing interstate business based only on "solicitation of orders . . . in such State for sales of tangible personal property, which orders are sent outside the State for approval or rejection, and, if approved, are filled by shipment or delivery from a point outside the State." Id at § 381.

[75] 405 US 707 (1972).

[76] 49 USC § 1513.

[77] Section 7(a) is discussed in *Aloha Airlines, Inc. v Director of Taxation of Hawaii,* 464 US 7 (1983). As an example of a Court decision regarding regulation as opposed to taxation of interstate commerce that was changed by Congress, see *United States v South-Eastern Underwriters Association,* 322 US 533 (1944), where the Court held that the business of insurance was within the federal regulatory power under the Commerce Clause. In response, Congress enacted the Ferguson-McCarran Act of 1945, 59 Stat 33, codified at 15

In other instances, Congress has contemplated, but ultimately rejected, legislation that would undo Supreme Court decisions in this area. For example, in *National Bellas Hess, Inc. v Department of Revenue*,[78] the Court held that, under the Due Process Clause, a "seller whose only connection with customers in the State is by common carrier or the United States mail" did not have sufficient contacts with the state to justify requiring the seller to collect a use tax.[79] There have been eight bills introduced in the House and Senate aimed at reversing the *Bellas Hess* rule.[80]

One result of the special judicial role in this area, as compared to cases involving "true" judicial review, is that the Court is more justified in taking a quasi-legislative approach, one that is particularly appropriate for challenges to state taxes, where the Court, as Justice Scalia disapprovingly contends, must engage in "balancing the importance of the State's interest in this or that . . . against the degree of impairment of commerce."[81] This role, akin to statutory

---

USC § 1011, which delegated the authority to regulate insurance companies to the states. The statute was upheld in *Prudential Ins. Co. v Benjamin*, 328 US 408 (1946).

In some instances, Congress has exercised its authority to undo the decisions of state courts. For example, in *Alaska Airlines v Dept. of Revenue*, 769 P2d 193, 198 (Or 1989), the state supreme court held that Oregon could tax overflight mileage of airplanes. Congress promptly passed a law to forbid this practice. See Pub L No 101-508, § 9125, 104 Stat 1388, codified at 49 USC § 1513(f).

[78] 386 US 753 (1967).

[79] Id at 758. This Due Process rationale of the *Bellas Hess* decision was overruled by *Quill Corp. v North Dakota*, 504 US 298, 308 (1992). See note 80. *Quill*, however, nevertheless struck down the use tax in question under the Commerce Clause on the grounds that it failed the first prong of the *Complete Auto* test. The Court held that an out-of-state mail vendor lacked a substantial nexus with the taxing state. *Quill*, 504 US at 311–12.

[80] *Quill*, 504 US at 318 n 11 (citing HR 2230, 101st Cong, 1st Sess (1989); S 2368, 100th Cong, 2d Sess (1988); HR 3521, 100th Cong, 1st Sess (1987); HR 3549, 99th Cong, 1st Sess (1985); S 983, 96th Cong, 1st Sess (1979); S 282, 93d Cong, 1st Sess (1973)).

It is worth noting that these bills present special constitutional problems. As pointed out above, the holding in *Bellas Hess* was based on the Court's then understanding of the requirements of the Due Process Clause, not the Commerce Clause. Since the Court acts as a final arbiter of constitutionality under the Due Process Clause, rather than in a quasi-legislative role as under the Dormant Commerce Clause, there is a serious question as to whether Congress could "undo" the due process requirement through ordinary federal legislation.

Quill overruled *Bellas Hess* on the ground that intervening cases had redefined the requirements of the Due Process Clause in such a way that physical contact was no longer necessary. See, e.g., *Shaffer v Heitner*, 433 US 186, 212 (1977) (applying the minimum contact analysis of *International Shoe Co. v Washington*, 326 US 310 (1945)). Thus, the Court suggested that Congress could in fact change the result legislatively without fear that the Due Process Clause would prohibit such a result. See Edson, 49 Tax L Rev at 924 n 185 (cited in note 69).

[81] *American Trucking Assns. v Smith*, 496 US 167, 203 (1990) (Scalia concurring).

interpretation rather than to judicial review because of Congress's ability to overturn the Court's ruling by ordinary legislation, would be the same as if Congress had enacted a broadly worded statute, pursuant to the Commerce Clause, prohibiting state taxes that placed an undue burden or discriminated against interstate commerce.[82] Indeed, it is wholly fair to infer such an implicit authorization from Congress based on the long-standing practice.[83]

Despite this unusually spacious discretion that results from the operation of the judiciary's adoption of Dormant Commerce Clause review, we believe that the special complexities of permissible state taxation of interstate commerce call for the Court's developing rules that are relatively simple for legislators, litigants, and judges to understand and apply, even though in some instances they may be less than optimal under principles of economics and public finance. The primary justification for this may be seen by comparing the much greater judicial effort required to assess the claim of multiple taxation in the typical state tax case than to adjudicate the issue of undue burden in the conventional state regulation case.[84] It is a fairly commonplace task for a trial court to determine (and for an appellate court to review) factual matters such as whether contour-shaped mudflaps are better than straight ones in keeping highway debris off the windshields of following vehicles,[85] or whether double trailer trucks cause more traffic accidents than singles.[86] There is no comparable decision grounded in adjudicative facts or physical experience, however, in an ordinary state tax dispute. Rather, the only real issues for judgment to which the court must immediately proceed—for example, whether, under the *Complete Auto* criteria, a single factor apportionment formula for a net income tax is "fair,"[87] or whether a coal severance tax is "fairly related to the services provided by the State"[88]—are wholly dependent on non-fact-finding policies and values. In some ways, these are similar to the "undue burden" conclusion in state regula-

---

[82] Shaviro, *An Economic and Political Look at Federalism in Taxation*, 90 Mich L Rev at 949 n 214 (cited in note 59).

[83] Dowling, *Interstate Commerce and State Power* (cited in note 7).

[84] *Pike v Bruce Church, Inc.*, 397 US 137 (1970).

[85] *Bibb v Navajo Freight Lines*, 359 US 520 (1959).

[86] *Kassell v Consolidated Freightways Corp.*, 450 US 662 (1981).

[87] *Moorman Manufacturing Co. v Bair*, 437 US 267 (1978).

[88] *Container Corp.*, 463 US at 170.

tion challenges, but they are also significantly different. In the end, the state regulation issue turns almost entirely on balancing two incommensurable values: the strength of the state's interest in the regulation versus the weight of the burden it imposes on interstate commerce. Final resolution of the state tax issue, on the other hand, requires application of sophisticated principles of economics and public finance, such as the incidence and impact of various taxes, matters on which the experience and expertise of courts are especially limited.[89]

Admittedly, a bright-line rule such as the object-measure approach may not take into account subtle effects of state taxes, nor match more economically sophisticated efforts to resolve the problem. Rather, its utility is a sensible and workable standard that does not incur the fairly complicated inquiries and attendant steep fact-finding costs associated with these more elegant or discriminating approaches.[90]

C. THE OBJECT-MEASURE APPROACH IN OPERATION

1. *Preserving the values of Complete Auto.* Despite its problems of opacity, redundancy, and unnecessary complexity, *Complete Auto*

---

[89] See *United States v Topco Associates, Inc.*, 405 US 596, 609 (1972); Frank H. Easterbrook, *Foreword: The Court and the Economic System*, 98 Harv L Rev 4 (1984).

Whether balancing in state regulation cases is desirable, see *American Trucking Assns. v Smith*, 496 US 167, 203 (1990) (Scalia concurring) (balancing leads to "inherently unpredictable" results because courts are forced to act as legislatures), and whether the Court actually engages in that process, see Regan, 84 Mich L Rev at 1092 (cited in note 39), is beyond the scope of our discussion. But to the extent that the Court is serious about balancing in the state regulation cases, we believe that this exercise is less appropriate in state taxation cases. And to the extent that balancing is improper, our approach avoids a court having "to accommodate, like a legislature, the inevitably shifting variables of a national economy." *Smith*, 496 US at 203. Thus, while we suggest that the Court take a quasi-legislative approach, it should do so more in terms of formulating the rule to be applied in future cases, rather than to legislating on an ad hoc case-by-case basis.

[90] For example, one commentator suggests that a Dormant Commerce Clause inquiry should consider whether the entity being taxed has a "substantial economic presence" above and beyond that required to satisfy due process, with this additional analysis concentrating on "the percentage of the taxpayer's business conducted to insure that a business is not economically discouraged from doing business in that state." Edson, 49 Tax L Rev at 946 (cited in note 69). This is a fair argument, as it seems to be economically undesirable to require a taxpayer to incur a large tax preparation fee for a minuscule portion of its business. See id at 946 n 272. However, approaches that attempt to take into account these subtle effects quickly become extremely complex. Ferdinand Schoettle advocates evaluating the constitutionality of state taxes by examining whether they impose different marginal costs on in-state versus out-of-state taxpayers. Schoettle, 75 Minn L Rev at 911 (cited in note 59). Although Schoettle's approach is conceptually defensible, it would require fairly detailed fact-finding by district courts regarding marginal costs in multiple jurisdictions, pre-

does advance the essential values for judicial review under the Dormant Commerce Clause—that is, no advantage for in-staters at the expense of out-of-staters. We have already seen that the object-measure approach is easier to apply than *Complete Auto*. That simplicity does not come, however, at the expense of failing to achieve the goals of all four of *Complete Auto*'s prongs.

The first prong of *Complete Auto* is that the tax be "applied to an activity with a substantial nexus with the taxing State."[91] An unapportioned tax whose object is one that only the taxing state can reach—which is permitted by the proposed object-measure approach—must necessarily satisfy the first prong of *Complete Auto:* that only this state can reach the object mandates that the object be one that has a substantial nexus with the taxing state. On the other hand, if the object of the tax can be reached by more than one state—in which case the proposed approach requires apportionment—the Due Process Clause's requirement of minimum contacts will ensure a constitutional nexus. Note that our approach differs slightly here from *Complete Auto*. We do not interpret the Commerce Clause to require a separate nexus more stringent than that imposed by the Due Process Clause because that is not required to further protect interstate commerce against state taxes that accord a preference to local enterprises.

The second prong of *Complete Auto* is that the tax be fairly apportioned, meaning that it satisfies internal and external consistency. A tax whose object is one that only the taxing state can reach—which requires no apportionment under the object measure approach—will always be internally consistent, since only the taxing state can apply this tax. If every state imposed a similar tax, there would be no extra burden on interstate commerce, since it would be taxed in only one state. On the other hand, under the object-measure approach, a tax whose object is one that more than one state can reach must be apportioned and, consequently, will be internally consistent: if every state imposed a fairly apportioned tax, there would be no multiple tax burden.

Demonstrating that the object-measure approach satisfies exter-

---

sumably based on testimony from economists. See id at 932 & n 109. For discussion of "the court's institutional competence to detect . . . [the wide range of] problems and design workable solutions," see Shaviro, 90 Mich L Rev at 988–89 (cited in note 59).

[91] *Complete Auto Transit, Inc. v Brady*, 430 US 274, 279 (1977).

nal consistency is somewhat difficult to do because of the fluctuating definition of the term. Nevertheless, to the extent that external consistency retains any independent meaning from internal consistency, it is satisfied by the object-measure approach. Thus, a tax whose object can be reached by only one state will be externally consistent for the same reason that the taxes in *Jefferson Lines* and *Goldberg v Sweet* were externally consistent: no other state can reach the object, and therefore the taxing state is not seeking to claim more than its fair share of taxable proceeds. On the other hand, if the object is one that more than one state can reach, the object-measure approach requires that the tax be properly apportioned, which indicates that the taxing state is not seeking to claim more than its fair share, that is, a share that would result in interstate commerce bearing a greater tax burden simply because of its interstate activities.[92]

The third prong of *Complete Auto* requires that the tax not discriminate against interstate commerce.[93] Under current doctrine, this requirement appears to be satisfied if the tax is applied at the same rate to intrastate and interstate business. In *Jefferson Lines*, the Court held that the sales tax did not discriminate against interstate commerce because "all buyers pay tax at the same rate on the value of their purchases."[94] In *Commonwealth Edison*, the Court held that Montana's severance tax did not discriminate against out-of-staters, even though the majority of the tax was paid by them. The Court focused instead on the fact that "the tax burden is borne according to the amount of coal consumed and not according to any distinction between in-state and out-of-state consumers."[95] Since the object-measure approach only comes into play if the discrimination prohibition is already satisfied, it obviously comports with *Complete Auto*'s third prong.

---

[92] Admittedly, there is a certain amount of circularity here due to the fact that "fairly apportioned" has been defined in part by reference to external consistency. *See Jefferson Lines*, 115 S Ct at 1338. However, external consistency seems to be defined by reference back to fair apportionment. Id at 1339.

[93] Defining "discrimination" in this context is a daunting task, as Daniel Shaviro discusses. See Shaviro, 90 Mich L Rev at 935 (cited in note 59). For a recent illustration of the difficulty, see the opinions in *Camps Newfound/Owatonna v Town of Harrison*, 117 S Ct 1590 (1997). We note merely that discrimination is forbidden by the Dormant Commerce Clause. The object-measure approach concerns taxes that survive this initial bar.

[94] Id at 1345.

[95] *Commonwealth Edison Co. v Montana*, 453 US 609, 619 (1981).

Finally, the last prong is that the tax be "fairly related to the services provided by the State."[96] As mentioned earlier, this prong appears redundant considering the first prong, particularly in light of the Court's holding that the tax revenue need not be limited to the cost of the activity being taxed or the benefits actually conferred on the taxpayer.[97] The object-measure approach, as we have pointed out, at minimum requires a nexus that satisfies due process. That nexus means that the entity being taxed derives some benefits and conveniences from the taxing state's maintenance of civilization. Under the current doctrine, this connection is sufficient to satisfy the last prong of *Complete Auto*.[98]

2. *Layers of taxes.* An important postulate of the object-measure approach is that each state has the ability to levy a variety of complementary and overlapping taxes on different objects. For example, a state could theoretically impose a tax on the same company for sales, doing business, and gross receipts, even though the measure of these taxes is essentially the same.[99] In addition, the same company could be subject to state taxes for use of the roads, the presence of real property, and the severance of natural resources— to name but a few additional state revenue raising programs.

Of course, in practice, states will never levy every possible type of tax. For one thing, these taxes can be redundant. A doing business tax of 10 percent of sales, as applied to a retailer, is the equivalent of applying a 5 percent sales tax and a 5 percent doing business tax. Moreover, states that are poor in natural resources might not impose a severance tax, choosing to rely on other more productive taxes instead. Nevertheless, a meaningful qualification for any approach to state taxation of interstate commerce is to determine its ability to ensure that if every state were to impose every possible tax, interstate commerce would be at no disadvantage compared to intrastate commerce.

The object-measure approach satisfies this qualification. Only two types of taxes will pass the object-measure approach: (1) those

---

[96] Id.

[97] *Oklahoma Tax Commission v Jefferson Lines, Inc.*, 115 S Ct 1331, 1345 (1995).

[98] After *Consolidated Edison*, the Court has virtually stripped this prong of any significance.

[99] "In fact, states with gross receipts taxes almost always impose retail taxes as well." Walter Hellerstein, Michael J. McIntyre, and Richard D. Pomp, *Commerce Clause Restraints on State Taxation After Jefferson Lines*, 51 Tax L Rev 47, 78 (1995).

whose objects can be reached only by the taxing state, or (2) those that are fairly apportioned. First, if every state imposed a tax of the initial type, interstate commerce would not be disadvantaged relative to intrastate commerce. A business would pay a given tax only once per taxable event, regardless of the number of states in which it does business. For example, if every state imposed the Oklahoma tax at issue in *Jefferson Lines*, a company selling 50,000 bus tickets would pay the gross receipts tax once on each ticket, regardless of whether these tickets were sold entirely in one state or 1,000 in each of all fifty states. Similarly, if every state imposed the telephone tax at issue in *Goldberg v Sweet*, a taxpayer would pay the telephone tax only once per call, regardless of whether it made calls to people in one state or in multiple states.

Second, if every state imposed the same fairly apportioned tax, interstate commerce would again not suffer relative to intrastate commerce because fair apportionment ensures that there is no multiple taxation. For example, if every state imposed the unitary tax at issue in *Container Corp.*, a business located entirely in California with income of $1 million would be taxed on the full amount in California, while a business with income of $1 million, half from operations in California and half from operations in Nevada, would be taxed by each state, but only on half its income.

3. *Avoidance of tax comparisons.* An important practical benefit of the object-measure approach is that it ordinarily avoids the problem of having to compare disparate state taxes to determine whether a given tax discriminates against or improperly burdens interstate commerce.[100] The problems with comparisons of taxes arise in two ways. First, the Court must determine which taxes are actually comparable. Yet the Court has indicated that comparing different taxes is a task for which it is not well suited.[101] The major exception to this rule is the Court's "compensatory tax" doctrine, under which a tax that imposes on interstate commerce the equivalent of an "identifiable and substantially similar tax on intrastate commerce does not offend the negative Commerce Clause."[102] To

---

[100] There is a "pretext" exception. See Part III.D.4.

[101] *Nippert v City of Richmond*, 327 US 416, 430–31 (1946). But see *Alaska v Arctic Maid*, 366 US 199, 204 (1961) (comparing Alaska's doing business tax levied on freezing ships to the state's cannery tax).

[102] *Oregon Waste Systems, Inc. v Dept. of Environmental Quality of Oregon*, 114 S Ct 1345, 1352 (1994).

satisfy this doctrine, the interstate commerce tax must be levied on a "substantially equivalent event" as that on which the intrastate tax is levied.[103]

The paradigm of a "compensatory tax" is a use tax, which is imposed on the use of certain goods within the state, to complement a sales tax, which is imposed on the sale of goods within the state. A use tax appears on its face to discriminate against interstate commerce, since it is applied only on goods that are purchased outside the taxing state. However, the use tax does not conflict with the values of the Commerce Clause; rather, it simply assures that interstate commerce will not be *benefited* at the expense of intrastate commerce. For example, assuming that all prices are equal, if California imposes a sales tax of 8.5 percent, and Nevada imposes one of 6 percent, a consumer living on the California side of Lake Tahoe would have an incentive to purchase everything on the Nevada side of Lake Tahoe, thereby saving 2.5 cents in sales taxes on every dollar spent. California's use tax seeks to ensure that goods on the Nevada side of the lake—at least high cost goods—are no more attractive than those on the California side.[104] Thus, as the Court has noted, despite the facially discriminatory use tax, "the stranger from afar is subject to no greater burdens as a consequence of ownership than the dweller within the gates. The one pays upon one activity or incident, and the other upon another, but the sum is the same when the reckoning is closed."[105]

Otherwise, however, the Court has been reluctant to make such comparisons for other pairs of taxes. For example, in *Fulton Corp. v Faulkner*,[106] the Court refused to compare North Carolina's intangibles tax on stock having a business situs within the state to its corporate income tax because these taxes were not substantially similar.[107] The Court has also indicated that manufacturing and wholesaling are not substantially equivalent events,[108] nor are sev-

---

[103] *Maryland v Louisiana*, 451 US 725, 759 (1981).

[104] As a practical matter, the use tax catches only sales of big ticket items that can be administratively tracked, e.g., automobiles that must be registered in the user state.

[105] *Henneford v Silas Mason Co.*, 300 US 577, 584 (1937).

[106] 116 S Ct 848 (1996).

[107] Id at 857.

[108] *Tyler Pipe Industries, Inc. v Washington State Dept. of Revenue*, 483 US 232, 242–43 (1987) (discussed in Part III.D.3); *Armco v Hardesty*, 467 US 638, 642–43 (1984).

erance and first use.[109] Given the Court's hesitance to make such difficult comparisons, any approach to Commerce Clause challenges should avoid requiring the Court to do so.

The second problem is that, even if the taxes apply to substantially equivalent activities, it is extremely difficult to make an accurate comparison of the burdens they impose. A proper analysis would be based on a number of factors: tax rate, economic effect of the tax on business, and so on.[110] Compounding the number of factors to consider is the fact that the effects of taxes in the real world "depend on elasticities of supply and demand, the ability of producers and consumers to substitute one product for another, the structure of the relevant market, the time frame over which the tax is imposed and evaluated, and so on."[111]

Under the object-measure approach, the Court does not make comparisons between different state taxes. The first part of the approach merely considers whether the object of the tax is one that more than one state can reach, and the second part merely considers whether the tax is fairly apportioned. Note that determining whether the object of the tax can be reached by more than one state does not require comparison of different taxes. Instead, the Court need only consider the nature of the activity being taxed, without reference to the taxes of other states or to other taxes of this state.

4. *The role of credits.* Under the object-measure approach, a state need not ordinarily give a credit for taxes paid to other states.[112]

---

[109] *Maryland v Louisiana*, 451 US at 758–59.

[110] *Commonwealth Edison Co. v Montana*, 453 US 609, 628 (1981).

[111] *Fulton*, 116 S Ct at 859. Elasticity is a measure of "the *responsiveness* of the quantity demanded (or supplied) to a change in a given variable (such as own price, price of another good, or income)." James P. Quirk, *Intermediate Microeconomics* 36 (2d ed 1982). Because elasticity varies from product to product, a tax of general applicability, such as a sales tax, will alter the demand from products in significantly different ways, even though the price for each is being raised by the same proportional amount. Id at 38. Thus, an attempt to compare taxes would, to be accurate, require the Court to calculate the elasticities of a multitude of products and services, a task requiring the use of differential calculus. See Hal R. Varian, *Microeconomic Analysis* 80 (2d ed 1984).

The substitutability of one product for another will affect the elasticity. For example, if Kansas imposed a tax on, among other things, wheat, wheat buyers might turn to farmers in other Midwest states, because Iowa wheat is a close (or perfect) substitute for Kansas wheat, and, other costs being roughly equal, would be cheaper without the Kansas tax. See Quirk, *Intermediate Microeconomics* at 38.

[112] The Court has not yet made such reciprocity a constitutional requirement, although it has hinted it may do so in the future. See *Oklahoma Tax Commission v Jefferson Lines, Inc.*, 115 S Ct 1331, 1342 n 6 (1995).

If the object of the tax is one that only the taxing state can reach, taxes paid to other states would not be applicable to this tax. If the object of the tax is one that other states can reach, then our approach requires that the tax be properly apportioned, and therefore, the fact that taxes have been paid to other states is already accounted for.

However, if a taxing state explicitly grants a credit for other taxes paid, then the Court's universally accepted prohibition of facial discrimination against interstate commerce, which must be satisfied before the object-measure approach comes into play, would require that the credit be given equally to out-of-staters and in-staters. For example, if a state imposes a doing business tax measured by total receipts within the state, and also a sales tax measured by sales within the state, and gives a credit on the doing business tax for sales tax paid to the state, it would have to offer *that* credit to *all* businesses that pay a sales tax, including those that conduct their business and pay a sales tax outside the state.[113]

Note, however, that whether a state grants a credit to out-of-staters as well as in-staters is relevant only to the issue of whether the state is engaging in facial discrimination against interstate commerce. It has no bearing on the issue of apportionment, and is certainly not an alternative to apportionment.[114] Allowing credits to satisfy the apportionment requirement would, in effect, say that unapportioned taxes are invalid only when the challenging taxpayer shows *actual* multiple taxation. As we observed earlier, requiring the taxpayer to show actual burden is undesirable.[115]

D. RESPONSES TO POTENTIAL CRITICISMS

The writings of several prominent commentators suggest that they may find the object-measure approach overly formalistic, or nothing more than a reduction of *Complete Auto* to the internal consistency requirement. Others might view it as unfair, in that it

---

[113] See *Williams v Vermont*, 472 US 14, 23–24 (1985) (invalidating on Equal Protection grounds a credit on sales taxes paid only to residents). See also *Tyler Pipe Industries* and *Armco*, discussed in note 16; *Barringer v Griffes*, 1 F3d 1331, 1336–37 (2d Cir 1993) (striking down a use tax that provided a credit for in-state sales tax paid but not for out-of-state sales taxes).

[114] See Hellerstein, 87 Mich L Rev at 185–86 (cited in note 40).

[115] See note 65 and accompanying text.

would allow an interstate business that manufactures in one state and sells in another state to be taxed by both states if the first imposes a tax on in-state manufacturing and the second a tax on in-state sales. Finally, the object-measure approach may not appear to respond to the ability of states to exploit special advantages and thereby "export" their tax liabilities to out-of-staters.

1. *Reincarnation of the Formal Rule.* Shortly after the decision in *Complete Auto*, William B. Lockhart praised the apparent demise of what he termed the "Formal Rule,"[116] referring to the Court's early Commerce Clause doctrine that "a state tax on any activity or process of interstate commerce was an invalid 'regulation of commerce.' "[117] The major shortcoming of the Formal Rule was that it failed to take into account the practical realities of taxes, concentrating instead on the formal language used to describe the tax.[118] As the Court itself noted in *Complete Auto*, legal formalities tended to create a "trap for the unwary draftsman."[119]

The object-measure approach may appear to embody a certain amount of formalism, primarily because the label affixed to the object may determine whether the state must apportion the tax.[120] For example, if California applies a tax to sales within the state, the tax need not be apportioned even if the goods sold originally came from or will eventually go into interstate commerce. But if California applies a tax on doing business to an interstate company, then the tax would have to be apportioned in respect to that part of the business fairly attributable to California. Although the ap-

---

[116] Lockhart, 65 Minn L Rev at 1027 (cited in note 14).

[117] Id.

[118] Id at 1034. Lockhart lists three explanations for the Formal Rule's persistence. First, it represented a judgment by the federal judiciary that allowing taxation of interstate commerce would create unmanageable burdens on commerce. Id at 1031. Second, such taxation interfered with free trade among the states. Id at 1032. Finally, "[t]he justices were saying that because the state cannot forbid engaging in interstate business, a premise no one questions, it cannot tax engaging in such a business—a sheer non-sequitur." Id at 1033.

[119] 430 US at 279.

[120] Thus, Walter Hellerstein criticizes the Court's reasoning in *Tyler Pipe*, which agrees with the object-measure approach, as "a retreat into the very formalism that the Court had purportedly abandoned in *Complete Auto*. . . ." See Hellerstein, 87 Mich L Rev at 172 (cited in note 40). The Court viewed wholesaling and manufacturing as separate activities which could each be subject to a tax (in the state in which each occurred). 483 US at 251. As a consequence, a business that manufactured in one state and wholesaled in another could be subject to a tax in both states, each measured by the unapportioned value of the same goods. But, as discussed in Part III.D.3., this is not inconsistent with the basic values of the Dormant Commerce Clause.

proach may appear to allow the state to dictate whether the tax needs to be apportioned depending on how it labels the object, thus amounting to nothing more than an exercise in semantics,[121] further analysis demonstrates that this is not so.

Although the object-measure proposal ordinarily permits the state to affix any label to the object of the tax that it designates, the labeling will be disregarded if it is a misdescription or subterfuge. Adjudication of Dormant Commerce Clause challenges to state taxes indicates that the issue should arise only infrequently. Most state and local taxes fall into familiar categories. When they do not,[122] the Court should examine the structure of the tax and determine as its true object that which has a proper (or reasonable)[123] nexus between the object of the tax and its measure. The absence of such a nexus indicates that the state is seeking to tax something beyond its reach, thus threatening imposition of multiple burdens on interstate commerce.

Consider the sales tax/doing business tax example mentioned above. If California wants to tax sales within the state, it can tax the full amount of that sale, even if the sale involves interstate commerce. As discussed earlier, California may do so because no other state can tax the sale. It should be clear, however, that the measure of this sales tax must be sales that take place *within* the state. If California were to include in its measure receipts from out-of-state sales, there would be no reasonable (or proper) nexus between the designated object of the tax (sales within the state) and the measure. The out-of-state sales do not conform to the object as defined by the state, and thus the Court cannot be bound by the state's definition. Similarly, if California wishes to impose a tax for doing business within the state, it can measure it by all revenue generated within the state, even if the taxpayer operates

---

[121] Similarly, recall the telecommunications tax upheld in *Goldberg v Sweet* discussed in Part I.C. Walter Hellerstein contends that "[i]nsofar as the Illinois Supreme Court sought to justify the levy on the ground that it was imposed on a local 'taxable event,' it smacks of the formalism that the Court has discarded and replaced with a commerce clause jurisprudence rooted in practical economic reality." Hellerstein, 87 Mich L Rev at 187 (cited in note 40); but see Part IV.E.2.a.

[122] See, e.g., *Goldberg v Sweet*, discussed in Part I.C.; *Central Greyhound Lines, Inc. v Mealey*, discussed in note 143.

[123] "Proper" or "reasonable," unfortunately, are nebulous modifiers, as is "fairly related." None of these terms probably conveys the concept any better than the others. Consequently, the concept is best explained by examples.

in interstate commerce. Once again, California may do so because no other state can reach the object of doing business within California. But if California were to measure this tax by income produced in other states, it would belie its characterizing the object as doing business within the state. Thus, unlike some applications of the Formal Rule, results under the object-measure approach do not turn on mere semantics.

2. *"Super internal consistency."* Does the object-measure approach do nothing more than reduce the *Complete Auto* test to internal consistency, which is the requirement that there be no multiple taxation even if every state adopted an identical tax? Walter Hellerstein has concluded that internal consistency, despite its preserving the values of the Commerce Clause, creates more confusion in practice than it resolves.[124] Hellerstein's criticism is not so much an indictment of internal consistency as questioning why the Court chose not to give stronger bite to the fair apportionment requirement instead.[125] He sees internal consistency as problematic in that it has far-reaching and probably unintended consequences, and that it has supplanted the role of fair apportionment. According to Hellerstein, the doctrine of internal consistency "undermines the authority of a number of Supreme Court precedents and places many existing state taxes in constitutional jeopardy."[126] While he acknowledges the possibility that those taxes are not worth saving, he questions whether the Court needed to use such a novel concept.[127]

The object-measure approach differs from "super internal consistency" in a significant way. Under *Complete Auto*, a tax that fails the internal consistency prong is automatically invalid, regardless

---

[124] Hellerstein, 87 Mich L Rev at 188 (cited in note 40).

[125] Id at 176–77.

[126] Id at 164.

[127] Id at 165 ("[I]t is worthwhile inquiring whether the Court could have faithfully effectuated its commerce clause policy by more familiar means").

However, the treatise that Hellerstein co-authored explains that internal consistency is not a new concept, but rather falls out of the multiple taxation doctrine:

Unlike Minerva, who sprang in full armor from Jupiter's brow, the internal consistency test did not spring unprecedented from Justice Brennan's brain as a fresh, new approach to state taxation of interstate commerce. Instead, Justice Brennan articulated what he regarded as merely an "obvious" corollary of existing doctrine.

2 Hellerstein and Hellerstein, *State Taxation* § 4.08 at 4–42 (cited in note 3).

of whether it passes the other prongs of the test.[128] This result occurs because "[a] failure of internal consistency shows as a matter of law that a State is attempting to take more than its fair share of taxes from the interstate transaction."[129] In addition, a tax that is internally consistent may nevertheless be struck down if it fails a different prong of the *Complete Auto* test.[130] Thus, the requirement of internal consistency is a necessary but not sufficient condition of constitutionality.

The object-measure approach, on the other hand, is less complicated. Whereas internal consistency is one of four prongs that must all be satisfied for a tax to pass the *Complete Auto* test, the two parts of the object-measure approach are complementary. A tax will be presumed valid either if it is one whose object can be reached by only one state or if it is fairly apportioned.[131] The latter part of the object-measure approach encompasses Hellerstein's emphasis on the fair apportionment requirement to vindicate the central value of the Dormant Commerce Clause. The principal difference between the object-measure proposal and both the *Complete Auto* test and Hellerstein's approach is that our proposal excuses certain taxes from the fair apportionment requirement—namely, those whose objects can be reached by only one state. Without such an exception, requiring an apportionment of taxes such as that upheld in *Goldberg v Sweet*,[132] a tax on telephone calls billed to in-state addresses, would present exceedingly difficult administrative problems that are unnecessary in order to avoid multiple taxation.[133]

---

[128] See, e.g., *American Trucking Assns. v Scheiner*, 483 US 266 (1987). *Scheiner* is discussed at Part IV.E.1.b.

[129] *Oklahoma Tax Commission v Jefferson Lines, Inc.*, 115 S Ct 1331, 1338 (1995).

[130] The use tax struck down because of inadequate nexus in *Quill Corp. v North Dakota*, 504 US 298 (1992), appeared to be internally consistent, though the Court did not address this issue. The tax required out-of-state mail-order businesses to collect and remit use taxes on goods purchased for use in the taxing state. Id at 301. If every state imposed such a tax, interstate commerce would not face multiple taxation, since only one state can apply a use tax per transaction.

[131] The presumption of validity can be overcome if the person challenging the tax can show that the state adopted the tax intending to discriminate against interstate commerce, or that the state had some "special advantage." See Part III.D.4.

[132] 488 US 252 (1989). For an argument against the validity of the tax in *Goldberg* because of unfair apportionment, see Hellerstein, 87 Mich L Rev at 187 (cited in note 40) (discussed in note 121).

[133] Id at 264–65.

3. *Apparent unfairness.* By allowing states to apply unapportioned taxes to activities that involve interstate commerce, does the object-measure approach permit multiple taxation of interstate activity? For example, suppose that California imposes a tax on sales occurring within the state (measured by the sales price of the goods sold), and that Nevada imposes a tax on manufacturing conducted within the state (measured by the sales price of the goods manufactured). If Acme manufactures widgets in Nevada, but sells them only in California, Acme will have to pay two taxes on each widget (each measured by the full sales price). This apparent multiple burden disappears, however, when we hypothesize a second company. If Failsafe also produces and sells widgets, but manufactures widgets in California and sells them only in Nevada, it pays no sales tax to California, and no manufacturing tax in Nevada.

The fact that Acme pays two taxes and Failsafe pays none reflects an unfortunate business setup for Acme and a clever (or fortunate) one for Failsafe. "This type of discrepancy is simply the price the United States pays for federalism,"[134] and is analogous to the disparity in taxes paid by companies that do business in high-tax states versus those that do business in low-tax states.[135] While certain individual companies may pay more (or higher) taxes because they undertake particular business activities in one state rather than another, and although there may be economic problems that stem from such incentives,[136] they are not the *systemic* evils that the Dormant Commerce Clause was designed to address because they are neither protectionist in nature[137] nor do they im-

[134] Hellerstein et al., 51 Tax L Rev at 65 (cited in note 3).

[135] See, e.g., Hellerstein, 87 Mich L Rev at 180 n 221 (cited in note 40) (noting that "the Court has found such adventitious burdens resulting from states' different taxing schemes constitutionally tolerable").

[136] This "locational disparity" is the subject of Shaviro's economic analysis of federalism. See Shaviro, 90 Mich L Rev at 900–02 (cited in note 59). The principle of location neutrality is that "it is optimal that the tax levied on a given amount of profit or a given taxpayer be invariant with regard to where property or persons are located." Id at 900. The optimality stems from the fact that taxes distort the prices of the goods on which they are imposed. Thus, if different states have different tax rates, economically rational actors will take those differences into account and adjust their consumption patterns accordingly. Id at 900, 902.

[137] The concept of "protectionism" is the centerpiece of an influential article by Donald Regan. Regan would consider a tax to be protectionist if it "was adopted for the purpose of improving the competitive position of local (in-state) economic actors . . . vis-à-vis their foreign (by which I mean simply out-of-state) competitors" and it is analogous to a tariff,

pose multiple taxes on interstate businesses simply because they engage in interstate commerce.[138]

Adopting this analysis in *Tyler Pipe Industries v Department of Revenue*,[139] the Court, though holding that the Washington taxes in question violated the Dormant Commerce Clause on other grounds, observed that Washington could tax the full value of both in-state wholesaling and manufacturing, and have both measured by the gross receipts of the activity: "[T]he activity of wholesaling—whether by an in-state or an out-of-state manufacturer—must be viewed as a separate activity conducted wholly within Washington that no other State has jurisdiction to tax."[140] It follows that Washington could choose to tax only one of these activities—say, manufacturing—while Oregon could choose to tax wholesaling, and both states could measure their respective taxes by gross receipts (i.e., the value of the goods manufactured and wholesaled). This could, of course, result in Taxpayer *A*, who manufactures in Washington and wholesales in Oregon, paying both taxes, each measured by the same value.

Hellerstein strongly criticizes this consequence of the Court's reasoning in *Tyler Pipe* and, by implication, the object-measure approach. He believes that "part of [Taxpayer *A*'s] gross receipts that [Oregon] was taxing as attributable to wholesaling in the state was actually attributable to the value of the goods before they entered [Oregon]."[141] He contends that only "apportionment of the tax measure—gross receipts—would ensure . . . that the same tax measure was not taxed twice to the same taxpayer merely because the legislature had included it in the tax base under two taxable subjects—manufacturing and wholesaling. . . . Otherwise the state, under the guise of taxing some 'local incident' of that interstate activity, would be able to sweep into its tax base gross receipts, net income, or other values that other states could include in their

---

quota, or embargo. Regan, 84 Mich L Rev at 1094–95 (cited in note 39). These facts would trigger the object-measure "pretext" analysis, discussed in Part III.D.4.

[138] For discussion of why neither "duplicative" taxation by different states nor different state taxes that "overlap" necessarily present risks that "rise to constitutional proportions," see *Moorman Manufacturing Co. v Bair*, 437 US 267, 278–79 (1978).

[139] 483 US 232 (1987), discussed in note 120.

[140] Id at 251.

[141] Hellerstein et al., 51 Tax L Rev at 99 (cited in note 99).

tax bases with equal justification by identifying some other 'local incident' of that interstate activity. The risk of multiple taxation to which such a regime would expose interstate commerce is plain."[142]

We disagree. Just as Taxpayer A would be taxed on 100 percent of its gross receipts for Washington's manufacturing tax, and 100 percent for Oregon's wholesaling tax, Taxpayer B, who manufactures in Oregon and wholesales in Washington, would not be subject to any manufacturing tax or any wholesaling tax. And no taxpayer would be taxed more than 100 percent on either wholesaling or manufacturing.[143] Although Congress may legislate against this form of "multiple taxation" if it shares Hellerstein's concern, this is not the kind of systemic disadvantaging of interstate businesses

---

[142] Hellerstein, 87 Mich L Rev at 173, 177 (cited in note 40).

[143] This distinction suggests that, under the object-measure approach, the tax at issue in *Central Greyhound Lines, Inc. v Mealey*, 334 US 653 (1948), should probably have been upheld. The case involved an "emergency tax on the furnishing of utility services," as applied to bus travel originating within and ending in New York. It was measured by gross receipts "derived from continuous transportation of passengers between New York points," id at 665, even though some of the routes traversed Pennsylvania or New Jersey. The Court held that the unapportioned tax violated the Commerce Clause, because New Jersey and Pennsylvania could also tax some portion of Central Greyhound's gross receipts. Id at 662.

The statutory scheme made clear that New York sought to tax transportation between cities in the state, measured by the gross receipts from that activity. Since this "emergency tax" does not fit tightly into a standard tax mold, it presents a difficulty in applying the object-measure approach. The problem is whether the object of the tax should be characterized as being for the *sale* or the *service* of the transportation. Under the object-measure proposal, Central Greyhound could be taxed 100 percent on its sales (assuming that all of its sales take place within New York), but only on an apportioned amount of its providing services, which in this case was 57.47 percent within New York. Id. Pennsylvania and New Jersey could similarly tax apportioned amounts of Central Greyhound's services, but not on its sales (assuming that they all took place in New York). Since the New York tax did not apply at all to transportation between points in New York and out-of-state points, id, despite the fact that service would take place within New York, it would seem most sensible to conclude that the object of the tax was the sale.

Would interstate commerce be disadvantaged if the tax, as so characterized, were upheld? In that situation, Central Greyhound would pay New York's tax for sales on 100 percent of its gross receipts, and Pennsylvania's and New Jersey's apportioned doing business tax for services on 43.53 percent of its gross receipts. A wholly intrastate company in New York would pay the tax on 100 percent of its gross receipts as well, but it would not be subject to any doing business taxes from other states. So Central Greyhound appears disadvantaged relative to intrastate commerce. But if New York imposed doing business taxes on sales *and* services, an intrastate business would pay two taxes, both measured by 100 percent of gross receipts. This wholly intrastate company appears disadvantaged relative to Central Greyhound.

On the other hand, suppose Pennsylvania imposed only a doing business tax on services. The wholly intrastate New York company pays 100 percent again, but a bus company that sells only in New York but operates in Pennsylvania and New York would pay only an apportioned tax in New York (less than 100 percent of its gross receipts) and no tax in Pennsylvania, since it has no sales there. The intrastate bus company would simply be another business with an unfortunate setup.

that should trigger judicial invalidation under the Dormant Commerce Clause.

4. *Special advantages and impure motives.* How does the object-measure approach address the matter of states that seek to exploit special advantages to the detriment of other states by "exporting" their tax liabilities to out-of-staters, thus benefiting in-staters at the expense of interstate commerce? An example of this phenomenon is a hotel tax. This tax is applied at the same tax rate to in-staters as out-of-staters. But because the renting of hotel rooms is an activity that those outside the taxing authority (whether inside or outside the state) are more likely to engage in than insiders, this tax falls more heavily on outsiders. Thus, a state whose economy is tourism-driven (say, Nevada) can apply a relatively high hotel (and sales) tax, knowing that the bulk of these taxes is borne by out-of-staters.[144]

A state that is rich in natural resources presents an even plainer example of a "special" advantage. By enacting a high severance tax and comparatively low income and property taxes, a legislature can structure a tax system in which state residents bear a comparatively small proportion of the state's tax liability. While it must be recognized that identifying a special or natural advantage is a matter of degree, another example may be found in the geographic advantage of port states, since they can tax activities connected with the onloading and offloading of cargo and pass that tax along to out-of-staters who are shippers or receivers of the cargo.

States can also exploit natural advantages through regulations that impose economic burdens on interstate commerce, thereby effectively acting as taxes. Two examples are *Cities Service Gas Co. v Peerless Oil & Gas Co.*[145] and *Parker v Brown.*[146] In *Parker*, California regulated the supply of raisins, even though 95 percent of those

---

[144] See, e.g., John F. Due and John L. Mikesell, *Sales Taxation: State and Local Structure and Administration* 12 (1983); Betsy Wade, *Tax Collectors Lean on the Out-of-Towners*, NY Times § 5 at 3 (Aug. 25, 1991).

See also Carol L. Powers, *State Taxation of Energy Resources: Affirmation of Commonwealth Edison Co. v Montana*, 10 BC Envir Aff L Rev 503, 512 (1982): "Nevada exports a substantial portion of its taxes in the form of gambling taxes; Delaware does the same with its corporate franchise tax; as does Michigan with a production tax on automobiles; Florida with a sales tax geared to raise revenue from tourists; North Carolina from Tobacco; California from produce and vineyards; and New York from its stock exchange transactions."

[145] 340 US 179 (1950).

[146] 317 US 341 (1943).

raisins were destined for shipment in interstate commerce and even though California could dictate the national price of raisins by controlling its supply of raisins.[147] In *Cities Service*, Oklahoma regulated the price at the wellhead on natural gas, 90 percent of which was sold to out-of-staters.[148] Since both cases involved state regulatory systems that raised prices, the burden of which was borne vastly by interstate commerce, they are functionally similar to the severance tax at issue in *Commonwealth Edison Co. v Montana*,[149] discussed below.

The exploitative possibilities for states with natural advantages are not eliminated by the simple observation that if the rest of the country does not want to pay Montana's severance tax on coal, it need not buy the coal. For one thing, that argument would apply equally to an improperly unapportioned doing business tax—an interstate business that does not wish to pay such a tax (or any other tax that multiplies burdens or discriminates against interstate commerce) need not conduct business within the state. Yet, such taxes are plainly invalid under the Dormant Commerce Clause. For another thing, it may not always be practicable "not to buy the coal."[150] Suppose that California, Oregon, and Washington collectively decided to impose large port handling taxes. The opportunity to buy elsewhere, noted above, relies on a free and competitive market; yet, in this example, there may not be a commercially practicable substitute for shipping goods through the western coastal states.[151]

---

[147] Id at 359.

[148] 340 US at 180.

[149] 453 US 609 (1981).

[150] Montana has 25 percent of the known coal reserves in the country, and over half of the low-sulphur coal reserves. *Commonwealth Edison Co. v Montana*, 453 US 609, 638 (1981) (Blackmun dissenting). Special advantages are most successfully exploited where they stem from monopolies. Thus, tourism-driven San Francisco cannot enact an excessively high hotel tax, since doing so would drive tourists away to vacation in other cities. But New Jersey could probably enact a high gasoline tax or highway toll to take advantage of the traffic between New York to its north and Pennsylvania, Delaware, Maryland, and Washington, D.C., to its south. Although such a tax would fall heavily on New Jersey residents, it would presumably generate enough revenue that New Jersey would be able to lower (or even eliminate) its income tax, and thereby export some portion of its tax liability to out-of-state taxpayers. These are, of course, all matters of degree, depending on the elasticity of demand and the cost and attractiveness of substitutes. For a theoretical discussion of elasticity, see Varian, *Microeconomic Analysis* at 70–72, 80 (cited in note 111).

[151] Again, the natural advantage is one of degree. See note 150. Of course, Congress is free to pursue a systematic and sophisticated economic analysis in enacting statutes in this area.

The *Complete Auto* test fails to take account of facially neutral taxes that exploit special (or natural) advantages.[152] In upholding a severance tax, even though the bulk of the cost is paid by out-of-staters, the Court reasoned that because states can constitutionally impose a severance tax of *some* rate, the rate itself is a question better left to the political process.[153]

The object-measure approach deals with the problem of special advantages by treating a tax whose object can be reached by only one state as *presumptively* valid. This presumption can be overcome if the entity challenging the tax can show that the state adopted the tax intending to discriminate against interstate commerce.[154] This showing will be difficult to make, as it is meant to be.[155] Our effort to achieve simplicity and workability will inevitably come up short in rooting out *all* discrimination against interstate commerce. But any requirement other than clear intent to discriminate would embroil federal courts in the task of comparing a number of different types of taxes in order to determine whether the state is exporting its tax liabilities.[156] For example, if Nevada, as a state with a tourism-driven economy, imposes a sales tax that is much higher than the average sales tax, is it exporting its tax liabilities to out-of-state tourists, or is it simply adopting a tax structure that is, in the view of its legislators, most efficient? The Court has expressed a reluctance to answer such questions as requiring arduous fact-finding beyond the scope of its abilities, and as a determination more properly made by state legislatures and by Congress.[157]

---

[152] Indeed, the Court appears to be satisfied that it is for Congress to address the situation. *Commonwealth Edison*, 453 US at 637–38 (White concurring); see also *Quill Corp. v North Dakota*, 504 US 298, 318–19 (1992) (citing *Commonwealth Edison* for the same proposition).

[153] *Commonwealth Edison*, 453 US at 628.

[154] By intent to discriminate, we mean "things a legislator hopes to accomplish *by the operation of the statute.*" Jesse H. Choper, *Securing Religious Liberty: Principles for Judicial Interpretation of the Religion Clauses* 45 (1995) (quoting John Hart Ely, *Legislative and Administrative Motivation in Constitutional Law*, 79 Yale L J 1205, 1218 (1970)) (emphasis in original).

[155] Difficult, but not impossible. The Court has, in other contexts, been able to ascertain legislators' intent in discriminating against racial and religious minorities, and there is no reason to believe that the Court would not be able to ascertain the intentions of state legislators in particularly egregious cases with respect to discriminating against interstate commerce. See id at 48–52.

[156] See Part III.C.3.

[157] The Court has noted that:

> [I]t is doubtful whether any legal test could adequately reflect the numerous and competing economic, geographic, demographic, social, and political considerations that must inform a decision about an acceptable rate or level of state taxation.

The facts in *Commonwealth Edison Co. v Montana*[158] illustrate how a showing of intent to discriminate might be made. Montana applied a severance tax of up to 30 percent of the contract sales price on the output of the state's coal mines. At least 50 percent of the revenue generated by this tax was required to be paid into a permanent trust fund that could be appropriated only by agreement of three-fourths of the state legislators.[159] Moreover, 90 percent of the coal mined within the state ultimately was exported to the other forty-nine states.[160] Montana legislators clearly understood the consequences of raising the severance tax when they looked to the effect of Alberta, Canada's raising of its natural gas royalty tax while financing "universities, hospitals, reduction of other taxes, etc."[161] Due to the revenue generated by this tax, Montana was able to lower its property and income taxes and thereby keep its overall tax revenue constant while providing tax relief for state residents.[162] The juxtaposition of the increase in the severance tax rate along with a decrease in local taxes is strong circumstantial evidence of intent to discriminate against or improperly burden interstate commerce.[163]

Similarly, in *Hunt v Washington State Apple Advertising Commission*,[164] North Carolina enacted a statute prohibiting the labeling of apples as being of any grade other than the "applicable U.S. grade or standard." Washington, through a stringent inspection program, had implemented a grading system that was "the equivalent of, or superior to, the comparable grades and standards

---

Commonwealth Edison Co. v Montana, 453 US 609, 628 (1981). As Justice Blackmun noted in dissent, however, it was extremely improbable that Montana legislators would ever lower the severance tax, since it accounted for 20 percent of the state's total revenue in 1981. Id at 642 (Blackmun dissenting).

[158] 453 US 609 (1981).

[159] Id at 612–13.

[160] Id at 639 (Blackmun dissenting).

[161] Id at 640 (Blackmun dissenting) (citing Statement to Accompany the Report of the Free Joint Conference Committees on Coal Taxation 1 (1975)).

[162] Id at 642 (Blackmun dissenting). In fact, the changes in severance, property, and income tax rates occurred simultaneously. See Shaviro, 90 Mich L Rev at 957 (cited in note 59).

[163] It is possible, of course, that despite an improper legislative intent, the tax, in fact, might still not improperly burden interstate commerce. For consideration of why "in-state producers or landowners might bear most or all of the real tax burden" of Montana's scheme, see Shaviro, 90 Mich L Rev at 956–57 (cited in note 59).

[164] 432 US 333, 335 (1977).

adopted by the United States Department of Agriculture."[165] Thus, the statute—"unique in the 50 states"[166]—disadvantaged Washington by raising the cost of selling apples in North Carolina and by erasing Washington's comparative advantage earned through its grading system.[167] In invalidating the statute, the Court also noted indications that North Carolina had adopted the statute with the specific intent of discriminating against Washington.[168]

Intent to discriminate against interstate commerce could also be demonstrated more dramatically by the existence of a "smoking gun," such as a state-sponsored study of ways of exporting tax liability,[169] or other circumstantial or direct evidence.[170] Thus, it has been contended that Iowa's enactment of a single-factor sales formula for apportioning business income[171] was deliberately intended "to improve the economic position of the Iowa-based businesses over its competitors," the evidence being "that Iowa is a market state," and "insofar as out-of-state businesses are engaged in economic activity in Iowa it is likely to be through sales to Iowa customers."[172]

This pretext analysis seeks to prevent states from engaging in opportunistic taxation by choosing tax bases that favor themselves.[173] While no realistic approach can assure that every tax base is taxed exactly once, *no* tax base should be used to subject interstate commerce to multiple taxation under the object-measure approach.

A final kind of "special advantage" remains to be considered.

---

[165] Id at 336.

[166] Id at 337.

[167] Id at 351–52.

[168] Id at 352.

[169] Compare *Amadeo v Zant*, 486 US 214, 217–18 (1988) (discussing the existence of a handwritten memorandum as evidence of a scheme to underrepresent women and blacks on juries).

[170] Choper, *Securing Religious Liberty* at 46 (cited in note 154). For example, Daniel Shaviro notes as evidence of tax exportation: "(i) use of a tax base that disproportionately reaches outsiders, at least as to direct incidence or in the short run; and (ii) the application to that base of a tax rate that is higher than the rate applied within the jurisdiction to other fiscally significant tax bases." Shapiro, 90 Mich L Rev at 916 (cited in note 59).

[171] *Moorman Manufacturing Co. v Bair*, 437 US 267, 272 (1978), discussed in note 64.

[172] Walter Hellerstein, 85 Mich L Rev at 765 (cited in note 3). See also Shaviro, 90 Mich L Rev at 955 (cited in note 59): "[O]nly Iowa fails to use a three-factor allocation formula for business income—although other states opportunistically vary the formula, for example, by giving greater weight to the sales factor in what are predominantly market states."

[173] See Shaviro, 90 Mich L Rev at 916 (cited in note 59).

Like several of the taxes just reviewed, certain types of flat taxes, though facially neutral, can be used to export tax liability to outsiders. For example, in *American Trucking Associations v Scheiner*,[174] Pennsylvania imposed a flat tax of $36 per vehicle axle per year for the privilege of using the state's highways, and applied the tax to trucks used in many states as well as those that traveled exclusively in Pennsylvania. As a consequence, a truck that traveled 100,000 miles annually in Pennsylvania would pay $36 per axle, but a truck that was driven the same distance over a five-state area might pay five times that amount if each state imposed a similar flat axle tax. Flat taxes of this kind effectively discriminate against interstate commerce in that they "bear more heavily on the interstate than the intrastate enterprise merely because the former does business across state lines."[175]

Similar to the situation of natural advantages, flat taxes such as those in *Scheiner* present exploitative possibilities despite the fact that they are assessed against an object that only the taxing state can reach.[176] Instead of an advantage such as an abundance of a rare natural resource or geographic location along a coastline, flat taxes capitalize on the benefit in this context that the nation's federal structure confers, especially on smaller states that are strategically located. Since every state is able to assess taxes, the number of states in the union plainly affects the amount of taxation that a national corporation must endure. For example, a corporation doing business in New England could conceivably have to pay six flat highway taxes—totaling $216 per axle under the rate assessed in *Scheiner*—whereas that same corporation would only have to pay $36 per axle in California, even though California is much larger geographically than the six New England states. Similarly, if California were to split into three states, the western corporation would suddenly have to pay three times as many flat highway taxes as before. Because of this inherent structural prejudice for multistate enterprises, these types of flat taxes should be invalidated regardless of the state's intention in imposing them.

It should be noted that not all flat taxes present a similar prob-

---

[174] 483 US 266 (1987).

[175] See note 40.

[176] For example, the object of the axle tax in *Scheiner* was the use of highways within Pennsylvania, an object that only Pennsylvania could reach.

lem. For example, a state could assess an airport use tax as a flat dollar amount per ticket, rather than as a percentage of the price of the ticket. This type of "proportionate" flat tax presents little problem of multiple taxation, since an intrastate airline carrying one million passengers a year would have to collect and remit the same amount of tax as an interstate airline transporting the same number of passengers. On the other hand, under Pennsylvania's flat highway tax, an intrastate company pays only one such flat tax, while an interstate company with the same total volume of business or amount of highway use must pay one such flat tax for each state in which it conducts business. Thus, if instead of assessing a flat dollar tax per ticket, as was done in *Evansville-Vanderburgh Airport Authority District v Delta Airlines*,[177] a state imposed a flat airport use tax of $10,000 per year on every airline using airports in the state, an airline operating ten intrastate flights a day pays a total of $10,000 in airport use taxes, while an airline operating ten interstate flights a day must pay at least two such taxes—and theoretically up to twenty.[178] In that instance, the hypothetical tax would resemble the one struck down in *Scheiner* and would be invalidated under our approach.

IV. APPLICATION OF THE PROPOSED APPROACH

Because the object-measure approach and the *Complete Auto* test further the same underlying Dormant Commerce Clause prin-

---

[177] 405 US 707 (1972).

[178] For other types of flat taxes that are probably invalid under *Scheiner* and that would be invalid under the object-measure approach, see *City of Chicago v Willett Co.*, 344 US 574 (1953) (flat license taxes on "carters"); *Wagner v City of Covington*, 251 US 95 (1919) (flat license tax applied on vendor of soft drinks); *Browning v City of Waycross*, 233 US 16 (1914) (flat occupation tax applied on vendor of lightning rods); *Center for Auto Safety, Inc. v Athey*, 37 F3d 139, 142 (4th Cir 1994); *New Hampshire Motor Transport Assn. v Flynn*, 751 F2d 43, 48 (1st Cir 1984); see generally Hellerstein, 87 Mich L Rev at 154 (cited in note 40). However, with regard to regulatory licensing fees, such as state bar dues or driver's license fees, a state that can justify the fee as an actual cost would not run afoul of the object-measure approach. These are regulations, not taxes, and would be judged accordingly under the Dormant Commerce Clause. See Hellerstein, 87 Mich L Rev at 156–57 (cited in note 40). It may be that a "licensee carrying on his trade in more than one jurisdiction bears a greater financial burden than his intrastate competitor." Id at 157. If the fee "is not designed as a revenue-raising measure," however, but rather as "a reasonable charge to cover administrative costs," *Ferndale Laboratories, Inc. v Cavendish*, 79 F3d 488 (6th Cir 1996) (upholding registration of pharmaceutical wholesalers), it may be justified under the Dormant Commerce Clause on the ground that a licensee who benefits from regulatory schemes in several states should pay for the costs of doing so.

ciples, it is not surprising that the object-measure approach would usually produce results quite similar to *Complete Auto*. Consequently, its virtues of clarity, simplicity, and ease of application may be achieved without any radical modification of Supreme Court doctrine.

A. AD VALOREM PROPERTY TAXES

An ad valorem property tax is one based upon the value of the property being taxed. The cases have primarily involved real property, instrumentalities of interstate commerce, or cargo in transit between states.

1. *Real property.* Under the object-measure approach, a tax on real property that is located within the state need not be apportioned, since the object of the tax—real property—is one that only the state in which it is located can reach.[179] This result is in accord with current doctrine.

2. *Property being used to transport goods interstate.* States may also apply a property tax on "instrumentalities of interstate commerce," such as airplanes, railroad cars, and trucks being used to transport goods through the state. Since the object of this tax, an instrumentality that moves in interstate commerce, is one that more than one state can reach, the property tax would have to be fairly apportioned under the object-measure approach.

The Court's current doctrine, which allows such ad valorem property taxes if there is a taxable "situs" (or nexus) between the property and the state[180] and if the tax is fairly apportioned,[181] is again in accord with the object-measure approach.

3. *Cargo in transit.* The object of a tax imposed on the value of personal property that is being transported through the state is personal property. Unlike real property or personal property permanently located within the taxing state, this property is traveling between states, and more than one state can tax it. Thus, under the object-measure approach, the tax must be properly apportioned.

---

[179] Of course, if the real property spanned more than one state, each state could only tax that part located within it.

[180] See *Braniff Airways v Nebraska Board of Equalization*, 347 US 590, 601 (1954) (holding that an airplane has a taxable situs in a state where the airline company owned no property but made eighteen regularly scheduled flights a day from rented depot space).

[181] See *Union Tank Line Co. v Wright*, 249 US 275 (1919).

A tax on cargo in transit can be apportioned to eliminate the problem of multiple taxation by assessing the tax on a given "lien date" to reflect the proportion of time that mobile goods spend in the state.[182] This method avoids the problem of multiple taxation, even if different states use different lien dates. For example, if California, Oregon, and Washington select the first Monday, Tuesday, and Wednesday in January, respectively, as their lien dates, cargo shipped through California on Monday, Oregon on Tuesday, and Washington on Wednesday pays three taxes. Nonetheless, this is not impermissible multiple taxation on interstate commerce because a shipment beginning one day later would pay no taxes. The lien date is simply used to extrapolate the total value of cargo present in the state over the year without the need for assessing such values every day.

B. DOING BUSINESS TAXES

Taxes imposed for engaging in business—often referred to as doing business taxes, gross receipts taxes, license taxes, occupation taxes, or franchise taxes—are ordinarily apportioned through a measure that seeks to approximate the percentage of revenue derived within the state. Thus, under the *Complete Auto* test, a privilege tax for doing business may be applied to a trucking company that delivers goods from outside the state, measured by the gross income derived from transporting goods within the state.[183] A state may also apply an occupation tax on all businesses, based on gross income derived within the state, to a stevedoring company operating within the state that loads and unloads ships carrying cargo destined for interstate commerce.[184]

The object-measure approach works similarly. Since every state in which a multistate corporation conducts business can apply a doing business tax, the object-measure approach demands that such a tax be fairly apportioned.

---

[182] In *Japan Line, Ltd. v County of Los Angeles*, 441 US 434, 445 n 8 (1979), the Court noted that "if each of appellants' containers is in California for three weeks a year, the number present on any arbitrarily selected date would be roughly 3/52 of the total entering the State that year. Taxing 3/52 of the containers at full value, however, is the same as taxing all the containers at 3/52 value."

[183] *Complete Auto*, 430 US at 287.

[184] *Washington Revenue Dept. v Association of Washington Stevedoring Cos.*, 435 US 734 (1978).

Finally, as discussed above,[185] there may be circumstances in which a doing business tax applied to a solely intrastate object will be invalid under our approach. In certain instances, a state (or other taxing jurisdiction) might be exploiting a special or natural advantage through a facially neutral doing business tax, such as one applied, for example, to stevedoring. Stevedoring is an activity that only the taxing state can reach, and yet, like severance of natural resources, is one whose cost may be disproportionately borne by interstate commerce. Thus, a high doing business tax applied to stevedoring could result in the "exporting" of tax liability. Now, if the taxing jurisdiction is a large commercial state, say, California, there is little danger that a general doing business tax applied to stevedoring as well will be exploitative; since the tax is applied to so many other types of businesses, it is very unlikely that its high rate was meant to discriminate against interstate commerce. Similarly, the fact that a tax with a burdensome rate happens to affect a large percentage of interstate business should not make it vulnerable unless an intent to prejudice them can be shown. On the other hand, if the taxing jurisdiction is, say, a port city without a broad base of general businesses, there may be a danger of exploitation of a natural advantage. In such a situation, the pretext element of the object-measure approach would potentially invalidate such a tax.

C. SALES AND USE TAXES

A sales tax is a tax levied upon sales consummated within the taxing jurisdiction. A use tax is imposed on a person who uses within the state goods purchased outside the taxing state which are thus not subject to the consumer state's sales tax. As discussed above,[186] the purpose of use taxes is to prevent residents from purchasing goods outside the state in order to avoid their state's sales tax.

1. *Sales tax by "seller" state.* A sales tax imposed by the state in which the seller sells and delivers goods to an in-state buyer would be permissible under the object-measure approach, because no other state can tax that sales transaction fully consummated within

---

[185] See Part III.D.4.
[186] See Part III.C.3.

the taxing state. But suppose a state taxes sales by sellers in the taxing state to buyers who are not in the taxing state, such as a state that taxes all mail-order sales of an in-state seller, including those to out-of-state buyers.

In order to resolve this problem under the object-measure approach, one must determine (or define) where the event of the sale occurs. There are three possibilities: sales can be treated as occurring (1) in the state in which the seller resides,[187] (2) in the state in which the buyer takes possession of the good,[188] or (3) in both states, thus requiring apportionment. As long as one of these three possibilities is used consistently, there will not be a threat of multiple taxation on interstate commerce. Under the "seller state" or "buyer state" definitions, the object of the sales tax is one that only one state can reach: the seller state or buyer state, respectively. Under the "both states" approach, the tax must be apportioned, again avoiding the burden of multiple taxation.

The object-measure approach opts for the "seller state" definition: a seller state would be able to impose an unapportioned sales tax regardless of where the buyer takes possession of the item sold. The object of the sales tax is the sale itself, and regardless of how many states the good travels through before it is delivered to the buyer, the sale is defined as occurring in only one state. Since the object of the tax can be reached by only one state, the tax need not be apportioned.

Admittedly, this choice is somewhat arbitrary.[189] The "both states" definition is theoretically appealing in that apportionment would allocate tax revenue to the various states that had "connections" to the sales transaction. But it is highly impractical. First, it is unclear how an interstate sale would be apportioned. For example, if the seller resides in California and the buyer in Washington, would each state be entitled to apply its sales tax to half of the value of all such sales? How would the apportionment be affected if the California seller and Washington buyer signed the sales contract in Oregon? Second, requiring the seller to collect,

---

[187] Thus, if a seller in California sells a good and ships it to Nevada, the sale would be viewed as occurring in California.

[188] Thus, in the California-Nevada example above, the sale would be viewed as occurring in Nevada.

[189] See, e.g., Shaviro, 90 Mich L Rev at 914 (cited in note 59) ("There may be no right answer as to where the sale occurred.").

apportion, and remit sales taxes to both the seller state and the buyer state on all interstate sales would increase the administrative burden on sellers by up to fifty times of either of the other approaches.[190]

The "buyer state" also has a plausible claim to justify application of a sales tax.[191] As William Lockhart noted, in respect to many types of interstate sales, it is in the buyer state that "the buyer acts to form the contract of sale . . . accepts the offer to sell or makes a counter-offer . . . makes payment for the goods . . . receives final delivery of the goods . . . and . . . finally uses or disposes of them."[192] The buyer state also has a reasonable claim because it is the state in which the object of the sale will presumably be used. On the other hand, many parallel acts of the sale occur in the seller state. To the extent that the buyer state has a claim because it provides the market for the sale, a similar claim may be made by the seller state: one regulates and protects demand for goods, the other supply. Perhaps the principal reason for preferring the "seller state" approach is efficiency and the reduction of administrative burden, since the seller need only deal with the sales tax of its own state. Under the "buyer state" approach, the seller assumes the same burden required for apportionment by the "both states" approach, in that sellers must keep track of the sales taxes of fifty or more jurisdictions.

The current doctrine on sales taxes is that a seller state may apply its full sales tax to a sale as long as the sale is consummated within the state, meaning that the buyer takes possession within the state, even though the good is used in other states.[193] However, in *J. D. Adams Manufacturing Co. v Storen*,[194] the Court held that the Commerce Clause prohibits a seller state from imposing an "unapportioned" sales tax on sales to buyers outside the state.[195]

---

[190] In fact, the burden on sellers could increase by more than fifty times if a formula more complex than a straight 50–50 split were used to apportion the sale. And the multiplier would be much greater if local sales taxes were taken account of.

[191] The Multistate Tax Compact suggests this approach, with a requirement that credits be given for any sales or use taxes paid in other states. See Shaviro, 90 Mich L Rev at 977 (cited in note 59).

[192] Lockhart, 65 Minn L Rev at 1049 (cited in note 14).

[193] *International Harvester Co. v Department of Treasury*, 322 US 340, 345 (1944).

[194] 304 US 307 (1938).

[195] Id at 310.

The Court has never passed on a seller state's attempt to apply an "apportioned" sales tax in this context, and it appears that such taxes do not exist. As discussed above, the object-measure approach yields a different result in this instance because we have defined the state in which an interstate sale occurs differently than the Court has (as will be further explained in the next subsection).

2. *Sales tax by "consumer" state.* An unapportioned tax on interstate sales by sellers outside the taxing state to buyers within the taxing state—as illustrated by a state that required an out-of-state mail order company to collect and remit that state's sales tax on sales made to its residents—would be invalid under the object-measure approach. The object of the tax—the sale—is something that is beyond the reach of the consumer state, because it has been defined as taking place in the selling state.[196]

Under existing doctrine, a consumer state may not generally impose a sales tax on goods shipped by common carrier from a seller outside the state.[197] The Court will allow a consumer state to impose a sales tax under such circumstances only if the interstate seller has substantial contacts in the state.[198] Substantial contacts generally means an office, salesroom, or other property. However, if the only presence of the seller consists of "drummers,"[199] the consumer state may not impose a sales tax.[200]

The object-measure approach may produce results that differ from those reached under the Court's current doctrine, stemming from the object-measure approach's definition of where the sale occurs. Consider, for example, the result if the object-measure approach defined the sale as taking place in the consumer state. Since the object of a sales tax is the sale within the state, only the consumer state would be able to reach that object, and therefore the consumer state would be able to impose an unapportioned sales tax. With the site of the sale defined in this way, the object-

---

[196] Of course, as discussed earlier, this result stems from the object-measure approach's arbitrary definition of a sale as occurring within the seller state. For discussion of the additional complexities involved in defining where a sale of services (rather than goods) has occurred, see Hellerstein et al., 51 Tax L Rev at 104–06 (cited in note 99).

[197] *McLeod v J. E. Dilworth*, 322 US 327 (1944).

[198] *McGoldrick v Berwind-White Coal Mining Co.*, 309 US 33, 48–49 (1940).

[199] A drummer (or "traveling salesperson") solicits orders in the consumer state, with the orders subject to approval at the seller's out-of-state office.

[200] *McLeod v J. E. Dilworth Co.*, 322 US 327, 330 (1944).

measure approach would yield a result closer to current doctrine which, as has just been discussed, permits a consumer state to apply a sales tax to some sales of goods coming from outside the state, but which has operated to deprive a seller state from imposing its sales tax on sales to buyers outside the selling state.

3. *Use taxes.* As discussed earlier, use taxes are constitutionally valid under the compensatory tax doctrine, despite the fact that they appear facially discriminatory.[201] A use tax matches a sales tax to make up for the state's lost tax revenue "occasioned by in-state persons travelling to other states to make purchases of products that they will then use in the use tax state."[202]

The object of a use tax—the enjoyment of a good within the taxing state[203]—is one that only the taxing state can reach. Thus, under the object-measure approach, use taxes are presumptively valid.

D. SEVERANCE TAXES

The object of a severance tax is the extraction of natural resources from the state, and the usual measure is the value of such resources. Necessarily, the only state that can apply a severance tax to this object is the one that possesses the natural resource. Since the object can be reached by only one state, the tax is presumptively valid and need not be apportioned under the object-measure approach.[204]

The Court presently allows unapportioned severance taxes, on

---

[201] See Part III.C.3.

[202] John E. Nowak and Ronald D. Rotunda, *Sales and Use Tax Credits, Discrimination Against Interstate Commerce, and the Useless Multiple Tax Concept*, 20 UC Davis L Rev 273, 278 (1987).

[203] As has been made clear, see Part III.C.3, use taxes are fully consistent with the values of the Dormant Commerce Clause. Still, one might reasonably quarrel with the above description of the object of a use tax (see Part III.D.1) on the ground that its acknowledged "object" is to capture lost sales tax revenue. We believe, however, that the description should be sustained.

It is true that, as an operational matter, very few persons who make "use of good within the taxing state" actually pay the use tax. They are excused from paying it because they effectively receive a credit for paying a sales tax. But this neither refutes the accuracy of the description of the object for purposes of the object-measure approach, nor undermines the goal of nondiscriminatory treatment for interstate commerce (assuming that the sales tax credit applies to payments both inside and outside the state; see Part III.C.4).

[204] But see Part III.D.4 (discussing pretext).

the ground that such taxes satisfy the *Complete Auto* test.[205] Since
the minerals are taken from the taxing state, there is a "substantial
nexus" between the tax and the state. Since extraction cannot occur
in any other state, severance taxes are necessarily internally and
externally consistent. Since the tax rate is the same for in-state
and out-of-state consumers, these taxes do not discriminate against
interstate commerce.[206] Finally, as long as the tax is imposed on
activity within the state, the Court will not inquire into the amount
of the tax or the value of the benefit conferred upon the taxpayer.[207]

E. POST–COMPLETE AUTO CASES

This section compares the results under the object-measure approach with those reached by the Court using the *Complete Auto*
test in a number of cases decided after 1978. Although the object-
measure approach is generally consistent with the Court's rulings,
the analysis is different, particularly in those cases where the Court
invalidated the taxes in question. In those cases where the Court
upheld the challenged taxes, the object-measure approach provides
a clearer and simpler analysis.

1. *Taxes struck down.* There are two significant cases in which
state taxes on interstate commerce were held to be in conflict with
the Dormant Commerce Clause: *Quill Corp. v North Dakota*[208] and
American Trucking Associations v Scheiner.[209]

a) Quill. In *Quill,* North Dakota required out-of-state mail vendors to collect and remit a use tax on goods purchased for use
within the state, even if the vendors had no in-state outlets or sales
representatives.[210] The Court concluded that such vendors had the
requisite minimum contacts with North Dakota so as to satisfy the
requirements of the Due Process Clause.[211] However, the Court

---

[205] *Commonwealth Edison Co. v Montana,* 453 US 609, 629 (1981).

[206] Id at 618.

[207] Id at 620–21; see also *Oklahoma Tax Commission v Jefferson Lines, Inc.,* 115 S Ct 1331,
1345 (1995) ("The fair relation prong of *Complete Auto* requires no detailed accounting of
the services provided to the taxpayer on account of the activity being taxed, nor, indeed,
is a State limited to offsetting the public costs created by the taxed activity.").

[208] 504 US 298 (1992).

[209] 483 US 266 (1987).

[210] 504 US at 301.

[211] Id at 306–08.

held that the tax failed the first prong of the *Complete Auto* test, as it did not apply to an activity bearing a substantial nexus with the taxing jurisdiction. The difference between the Due Process and Commerce Clauses was that the former concerned "the fundamental fairness of governmental activity," while the latter concerned "the effects of state regulation on the national economy."[212] Thus, with respect to the Commerce Clause, *Quill* focused on the administrative burdens that such use taxes would impose on interstate taxpayers, particularly if "the Nation's 6,000-plus taxing jurisdictions" imposed similar taxes.[213]

Under the object-measure approach, a use tax on goods purchased for use within the state would be presumptively valid because the object of the tax—use of goods within the state—is one that only the taxing state can reach. Interstate businesses that pay a sales tax in the seller state under the object-measure approach would not suffer discrimination because "[v]irtually all states with use taxes grant, as a credit against the use tax, the amount of sales taxes paid to other states."[214] Therefore, the Due Process Clause rather than Dormant Commerce Clause values should determine whether an out-of-stater who maintains no outlets or sales representatives in the state may be required to collect and remit the tax.[215]

b) Scheiner. In *Scheiner*, Pennsylvania imposed a flat tax of $36 per vehicle axle per year for the privilege of using the state's highways.[216] The Court struck down this tax as not being internally

---

[212] Id at 312.

[213] Id at 313 n 6.

[214] Nowak and Rotunda, 20 UC Davis L Rev at 274 (cited in note 202).

[215] Thus, the only true burden on interstate commerce is the burden of record-keeping mentioned by the Court. However, as noted by Justice White in his dissent, this justification is illogical, in that "an out-of-state seller with one salesperson in a State would be subject to use tax collection burdens on its entire mail order sales" while "an out-of-state seller in a neighboring State could be the dominant business in the putative taxing State . . . yet not have to collect such taxes if it lacks a physical presence in the taxing State." *Quill*, 504 US at 329–30 (White concurring in part and dissenting in part). If the mere burden of having to keep track of the additional taxes to which an interstate business is subject is enough to constitute a significant effect on interstate commerce, then many apportioned taxes would be in jeopardy. For example, the standard doing business tax imposes a greater administrative burden on interstate businesses, which must determine the apportioned taxable income for each taxing jurisdiction, than on a purely intrastate business, which need only pay one tax. Of course, Congress can always change the rule based on a more careful appraisal of various administrative costs.

[216] 483 US 266, 274 (1987).

consistent, since if every state imposed flat highway taxes, interstate commerce would suffer a disadvantage relative to intrastate
commerce.[217]

Under the object-measure approach, this tax would be invalid
because of the peculiar problems for interstate businesses posed
by flat taxes within the nation's federal structure.[218]

2. *Taxes upheld.* The taxes that have been upheld under *Complete
Auto* require briefer discussion than those that were struck down.

a) Goldberg. In *Goldberg*, the Court upheld Illinois' telecommunications tax, "a 5% tax on the gross charge of interstate telecommunications (1) originated or terminated in Illinois . . . and
charged to an Illinois service address, regardless of where the telephone call is billed or paid."[219]

Under the object-measure approach, this tax would be presumptively valid, since the object of the tax—telephone calls charged
within the state—is one that only Illinois could reach. Moreover,
since the tax is applied as a percentage of the price of each individual call, it does not burden interstate commerce more heavily than
intrastate commerce.

b) D. H. Holmes. In *D. H. Holmes*, petitioner challenged imposition of Louisiana's use tax on the cost of catalogs printed out-of-
state but distributed by Holmes within state to its customers via
U.S. mail.[220] The Court concluded that it satisfied all four prongs
of the *Complete Auto* test. The tax was fairly apportioned, since it
offered a credit for sales taxes paid in other states, and since it
was applied only to catalogs distributed for use within the state.[221]
Because the catalog was intended to bolster the name recognition
of D. H. Holmes within the state, the use of the catalogs had a
substantial nexus with Louisiana.[222]

Under the object-measure approach, Louisiana would be able

---

[217] Consider, for example, two businesses whose two-axle trucks travel 10,000 miles a
year. The first business operates entirely within Pennsylvania, and thus must pay $72 a
year. The second business' truck travels 5,000 miles a year in Pennsylvania and 5,000 miles
a year in New York (which, for the sake of this example, also imposes a flat highway tax)
resulting in $144 a year in flat taxes.

[218] See Part III.D.4.

[219] 488 US 252, 256 (1989) (citations omitted). See Part I.C.

[220] *D. H. Holmes Co. v McNamara*, 486 US 24, 26 (1988).

[221] Id.

[222] Id.

to apply its use tax on the catalogs. The object of a use tax is the use of goods within the taxing state. As long as the use tax is imposed only on catalogs distributed within the state,[223] only Louisiana can reach that object. Thus, the use tax need not be apportioned, despite the fact that the catalogs originated in interstate commerce. However, because Louisiana offers a credit against the use tax for payments of its own sales tax, the basic prohibition against discrimination requires that it offer that same credit for payments of out-of-state sales taxes. Since it does so,[224] the tax would be valid under the object-measure approach.

  c) Container Corp. In *Container Corp.*, the Court upheld California's unitary business tax, as applied to domestic-based multinational businesses. As noted earlier, this is a doing business tax measured by corporate income attributable to business conducted within the state.

The object of the California tax is doing business, an object that can be reached by more than one state. Therefore, under the object-measure approach, the tax would have to be fairly apportioned. Since the California tax is apportioned, it would be valid under the object-measure approach.

  d) Commonwealth Edison. In *Commonwealth Edison*, the Court upheld Montana's tax imposed on the activity of coal severance. The object-measure approach might (well) have concluded that the severance tax was invalid, even though only Montana could reach the object. While presumptively valid, the Montana severance seems vulnerable to the charge that it was established with the intent of exporting tax liability to the other states that purchased Montana's coal.[225] If so, the severance tax would be invalidated.

  e) Jefferson Lines. Applied to the Oklahoma tax in *Jefferson Lines*, the object-measure approach reaches the same result that the Court did: despite its lack of apportionment, the tax does not violate the Dormant Commerce Clause. The object of the Oklahoma tax is the intrastate sale of particular goods and services—bus tickets in the specific case of Jefferson Lines. No other state could reach the object of the Oklahoma tax because no other state could apply a sales tax on ticket sales occurring within Oklahoma regard-

---

[223] Only 18 percent of the catalogs were distributed out-of-state. Id at 26.

[224] Id at 31.

[225] See Part III.D.4.

less of whether the ticket was for intrastate or interstate transportation.[226] If Jefferson Lines also sold bus tickets in Kansas for intrastate or interstate travel, Oklahoma could not apply its sales tax on those sales, but Kansas could. Nor is Jefferson Lines subject to a disproportionate amount of sales tax as compared to wholly intrastate businesses. Suppose, as above, that Jefferson Lines sells bus tickets in both Oklahoma and Kansas for interstate travel, and that a competitor, having the same total volume of sales, sells bus tickets for intrastate travel only in Oklahoma. Both companies are taxed on the same overall volume of ticket sales, although Jefferson Lines' sales are taxed in either (but not both) Oklahoma or Kansas, while the intrastate competitor's sales are taxed entirely in Oklahoma.

* * *

The central goal of the object-measure approach is similar to, but slightly broader than, the *Complete Auto* test in attempting to satisfy the tenets of the Dormant Commerce Clause: to guard against conferring advantages on in-staters at the expense of interstate commerce. *Complete Auto* requires the application of four different subtests, some (such as the fair relation prong) that are functionally irrelevant, and others (such as internal and external consistency) that are not easily susceptible to application. We have proposed a more straightforward method for determining whether state taxes violate the Dormant Commerce Clause. Although simplicity may not be a sufficient reason by itself to adopt a new doctrine, the object-measure approach is more readily administered on a practical basis, which should result in more efficient litigation and legislation. By being able to predict the outcome of Dormant Commerce Clause challenges more reliably, parties should have more accurate assessments of their bargaining positions. Similarly, lawmakers should be able better to determine whether a proposed tax on interstate commerce will survive a Dormant Commerce Clause challenge.

---

[226] A different problem would be presented if the sale involved interstate delivery of the ticket, such as if the ticket had been issued in Oklahoma but mailed to the buyer in California. In *J. D. Adams Manufacturing Co. v Storer*, 304 US 307 (1938), the Court ruled that an unapportioned sales tax imposed by the selling state on a good delivered to an out-of-state buyer violated the Dormant Commerce Clause. For a detailed discussion of *Adams Manufacturing* and the different result reached by our analysis, see Part IV.C.1.

ARTHUR D. HELLMAN

LIGHT ON A DARKLING PLAIN: INTERCIRCUIT CONFLICTS IN THE PERSPECTIVE OF TIME AND EXPERIENCE

One of the lesser-known rituals of the Supreme Court of the United States is the annual appearance by two of the Justices at hearings of the appropriations committees of the House and the Senate. The legislators generally do not have much to say about the Court's budget, so the discussion often turns to other aspects of the Court's operations. A few years ago, a member of the House subcommittee asked about the dramatic decrease in the number of cases heard and decided by the Court. Justice Anthony M. Kennedy acknowledged the phenomenon and made clear that he viewed it as a healthy development. He told the subcommittee, "We are a Court that is constituted and committed to give doctrinal guidance to the judicial system as a whole. To the extent that we can do that in 100 cases rather than 140 cases we are fulfilling that function."[1] Justice David Souter agreed with Justice Kennedy's assessment.[2]

Arthur D. Hellman is Professor of Law, University of Pittsburgh School of Law. The studies reported in this article were carried out, in large part, under a contract with the Federal Judicial Center. However, the views expressed are those of the author; the Center speaks only through its Board. Throughout the project, Judith McKenna of the Center's Research Division provided invaluable counsel. Three graduates of the University of Pittsburgh School of Law—David Gray, Benjamin Hinerfeld, and Michael Wagner—helped in important ways with the field research reported in Part III.

[1] Departments of Commerce, Justice, and State, the Judiciary, and Related Agencies Appropriations for 1997: Hearings Before a Subcommittee of the House Committee on Appropriations, 104th Cong, 2d Sess, Pt 6 at 23 (1996).

[2] Id at 24.

The Justices' comments stand in stark contrast to the picture painted by two Congressionally created study groups. In the mid-1970s, the Commission on Revision of the Federal Court Appellate System (Hruska Commission) identified what it believed to be a serious problem, the "failure of the federal judicial system to provide adequate capacity for the declaration of national law."[3] The Commission placed particular emphasis on one consequence of this failure: the existence of conflicts between federal judicial circuits that the Supreme Court did not resolve. In 1990, another blue-ribbon group, the Federal Courts Study Committee, expressed similar concerns about the capacity of the federal judicial system to provide a uniform construction of federal law where uniformity is needed.[4] The Study Committee urged Congress to authorize a pilot project under which the Supreme Court could refer selected conflict cases to a randomly chosen court of appeals for resolution.

What happened to the problem of unresolved intercircuit conflicts? Certainly there has been no amelioration in the conditions that led the Hruska Commission and the Federal Courts Study Committee to their conclusions. With one minor exception, Congress has taken no steps to expand the capacity of the system to resolve issues at the national level.[5] It did not establish a National Court of Appeals as the Hruska Commission recommended, nor did it authorize the pilot project suggested by the Study Committee. The Supreme Court, as already noted, has actually reduced the number of cases that it hears and decides on the merits.[6] Meanwhile, the volume of adjudications in the courts of appeals has continued to burgeon.[7]

The explanation, I suggest, is that the Hruska Commission and

---

[3] Commission on Revision of the Federal Court Appellate System, *Structure and Internal Procedures: Recommendations for Change*, 67 FRD 195, 217 (1975) (hereafter *Hruska Commission Report*). I served as Deputy Director of the Commission and helped to write its report.

[4] Federal Courts Study Committee, *Report of the Federal Courts Study Committee* 125 (1990) (hereafter Study Committee Report).

[5] In 1982, Congress established the Court of Appeals for the Federal Circuit and gave it exclusive jurisdiction over appeals in certain classes of cases, notably those involving patents. See generally Rochelle Dreyfuss, *The Federal Circuit: A Case Study in Specialized Courts*, 64 NYU L Rev 1 (1989).

[6] See Arthur D. Hellman, *The Shrunken Docket of the Rehnquist Court*, 1996 Supreme Court Review 403 (1997).

[7] See Richard A. Posner, *The Federal Courts: Challenge and Reform* 53–64 (Harvard, 1996).

the Study Committee, like others who have viewed unresolved conflicts as a major problem, have looked at the legal landscape from an unduly narrow perspective. They have counted the number of conflicts in existence at a particular moment in time without asking what happens to those conflicts over a span of years and without considering the significance of the conflicts—in particular, their effect on outcomes. In an article published in 1995, I took the first step toward providing that broader perspective. I presented the results of an empirical study of conflicts that the Supreme Court did not resolve.[8] The study paid particular attention to the tolerability and persistence of the conflicts. It concluded that unresolved intercircuit conflicts do not constitute a problem of serious magnitude in the federal judicial system.

Of course, no single study can be definitive, especially when the subject involves the operation of precedent in a common-law system. Moreover, not everyone agrees with the conclusion. The chairman of the Federal Courts Study Committee has lamented that "only a small number of the ever increasing disparate decisions by the courts of appeals can be reconciled by the Supreme Court. Practically speaking, this means that litigants in various parts of the country are governed by federal case law that differs from circuit to circuit."[9] Professor Thomas Baker insists that "some conflicts are going unresolved and that they are accumulating faster than the system is correcting [them]."[10]

To supplement the research reported in the 1995 article, I have pursued two additional lines of empirical inquiry. First, I have investigated the later history of a group of unresolved conflicts identified in the earlier study. Second, I have carried out a program of field research to determine the actual effect of unresolved conflicts on the practice of law. The results of the new studies are reported in this article. Before turning to the new data, I provide some background, including a brief summary of the initial study.

---

[8] Arthur D. Hellman, *By Precedent Unbound: The Nature and Extent of Unresolved Intercircuit Conflicts*, 56 U Pitt L Rev 693 (1995) (hereafter Hellman, *By Precedent Unbound*).

[9] Statement of Joseph F. Weis, Jr., before the Commission on Structural Alternatives for the Federal Courts of Appeals, New York, April 24, 1998. At the time this article was prepared, Judge Weis's statement was available on-line at the Commission's website, http://app.comm.uscourts.gov.

[10] Thomas E. Baker, *The U.S. Courts of Appeals: Problems and Solutions*, Federal Lawyer (August 1998) at 31, 32.

I. Background

Concern about the adequacy of the "national appellate capacity"[11] can be traced at least as far back as 1968, when a committee of the American Bar Foundation warned that "the function of the Supreme Court as an agency for harmonizing and unifying federal law is spread ever more thinly."[12] Over the next two decades, similar themes were sounded by prominent scholars and jurists as well as by the Hruska Commission.[13] In 1990, the Federal Courts Study Committee recommended a more focused study to complement its proposed "pilot project."[14] Congress acted on that recommendation in Section 302 of the Judicial Improvements Act of 1990. In Section 302, Congress asked the Federal Judicial Center, the research arm of the federal judiciary, to conduct a study to ascertain "the number and frequency of conflicts among the judicial circuits . . . that remain unresolved because they are not heard by the Supreme Court."[15] Congress further requested that the Center determine the extent to which the unresolved conflicts are "intolerable." The Center asked me to design and conduct the study.

A. IDENTIFYING CONFLICTS

Scholars, judges, and lawyers have disagreed for more than half a century over what constitutes an intercircuit conflict.[16] In Section 302, Congress framed the inquiry in a way that made it largely unnecessary to rely on any abstract definition. The statutory language suggested that the task of assessing the consequences of conflicts—and thus their tolerability—should be separated from the determination whether a conflict exists. The legislative history called for a study that would provide, to the extent possible, objec-

---

[11] See *Hruska Commission Report* at 246 (cited in note 3).

[12] American Bar Foundation, *Accommodating the Workload of the United States Courts of Appeals* 6 (1968).

[13] See, for example, Paul M. Bator, *What Is Wrong With the Supreme Court?* 51 U Pitt L Rev 673 (1990) (lecture delivered in 1987).

[14] Study Committee Report at 125 (cited in note 4).

[15] Pub L No 101-650, § 302, 104 Stat 5089, 5104 (1990).

[16] See, for example, Felix Frankfurter and Henry M. Hart, Jr., *The Business of the Supreme Court at October Term, 1933,* 48 Harv L Rev 238, 268 (1934).

tive data. These themes shaped the methods I adopted and the criteria I used.

The study was carried out in two phases. In the first phase, I analyzed two sets of cases that the Supreme Court declined to hear. The first group included all cases in the 1988, 1989, and 1990 Terms in which Justice Byron White dissented from the denial of certiorari. This set of cases was chosen as the starting point because, over the years, Justice White repeatedly called attention to the Court's failure to resolve intercircuit disagreements.[17] The "Dissent Group," as I called it, included 237 cases. The second group was a random sample drawn from the 1989 Term. The sample encompassed one of every five paid cases denied review in that Term after the filing of a brief in opposition. The "Random Group" consisted of 253 cases.

To determine whether a Study Group case involved a conflict between circuits, I followed an approach that was essentially reportorial. I began by asking whether a claim of conflict was presented in the certiorari petition and other materials submitted by the parties. If it was, I examined the allegedly conflicting decisions to ascertain if the disagreement was acknowledged by one or more of the courts of appeals that had decided the issue. Acknowledged conflicts were included in the tally without any attempt to determine whether the conflict was "genuine." If the conflict was not acknowledged, I proceeded with research to discover whether the assertion of conflict was supported by writings of judges, commentators, or other participants in the legal system. Recognized conflicts were also included in the tally without independent analysis. Only when all of these sources proved unavailing did I undertake my own assessment of whether the decisions were truly in conflict.

Using these techniques, I found 166 substantiated claims of conflict among Justice White's dissents: 38 in the 1988 Term, 59 in 1989, and 69 in 1990. All but 11 of the 166 were either acknowledged by a court of appeals or recognized by other participants in the system. Applying the same criteria to the paid cases in the Random Group, I found 44 conflicts, all but two of which were acknowledged or recognized.

---

[17] Justice White retired at the end of the 1992 Term, and no Justice has taken his place in publicly calling attention to conflict cases. Thus the method of the study could not be replicated today.

These data answered the first of the questions posed by Congress. The number of intercircuit conflicts that are not heard by the Supreme Court is large enough that the existence of a problem of "inadequate national capacity" could not be ruled out on the basis of raw numbers alone. But that finding only set the stage for the next level of inquiry: investigating the "tolerability" of the unresolved conflicts.

B. ASSESSING TOLERABILITY

"Tolerability" is a shorthand for the effect of conflicts on litigation, counseling, and primary activity. The Federal Courts Study Committee identified four consequences that would tend to make a conflict intolerable: nonacquiescence by federal government agencies, harm to multicircuit actors, forum shopping among circuits, and unfairness to litigants in different regions of the country.[18] To assess the tolerability of the Phase I conflicts, I began by identifying objectively defined characteristics that are likely to correlate with one or more of these consequences. I then built upon that framework to analyze the conflicts in the Study Group. The findings were quite striking.

The first of the consequences identified by the Study Committee—nonacquiescence—can virtually be ruled out as an element of intolerability. The essence of the evil, as the Study Committee viewed it, is that federal administrative agencies are forced to choose "between the uniform administration of statutory schemes and obedience to the different holdings of courts in different regions."[19] But examination of the Study Group cases reveals that there is almost no overlap between nonacquiescence and unresolved intercircuit conflicts.[20] Nonacquiescence may be a problem in the legal system, but it is not a problem that results from the Supreme Court's failure to resolve the conflicts that are brought to it.

A second of the Study Committee's factors—forum shopping among circuits—can be put to one side for a different reason. Upon analysis, forum shopping between circuits proves to be an

---

[18] See Study Committee Report at 125 (cited in note 4).

[19] Id.

[20] See Hellman, *By Precedent Unbound* at 742–48 (cited in note 8).

evil only to the extent that it threatens harm to multicircuit actors or causes unfairness to litigants in different regions.[21] Intolerability thus depends entirely on the latter two factors.

The possibility of inflicting harm on multicircuit actors, I concluded, depends in the first instance on the subject matter of the conflict and the nature of the issues. On the basis of those variables alone, the research tells us that a substantial majority of the unresolved conflicts would have no impact on the legal position of entities whose activities cross circuit lines.[22] Included here are almost all conflicts in several important categories of federal law: the constitutional rights of criminal defendants, the elements of typical federal crimes, the interpretation of 42 USC § 1983, and the availability of federal habeas corpus for state prisoners. Thus, under the approach suggested by the Study Committee, these conflicts would be deemed intolerable only to the extent that they give rise to unfairness to litigants in different circuits.

In giving content to the concept of "unfairness," I drew upon the insights of scholars and judges in two analogous contexts: the *Erie* doctrine[23] and retroactivity.[24] I concluded that unfairness to litigants in different circuits, like the other consequences that concerned the Study Committee, depends primarily on the extent to which the difference in circuit law produces divergent outcomes in similar cases. From this perspective, the conflicts could be divided into three broad groupings: those that are outcome-determinative, those that produce systematic bias, and those that do not generate either of those consequences.

A conflict is classified as outcome-determinative if the choice of rule can be expected to control the resolution of a claim or defense in all cases in which the issue arises, or in any class of cases that can be identified ex ante. Because most legal rules contain elements of indeterminacy or are tempered in their operation by other rules, only a small proportion of the conflicts fit this pattern. More commonly, conflicts fall into the intermediate grouping: the choice of

---

[21] Id at 754–56.

[22] Id at 748–51.

[23] See generally John Hart Ely, *The Irrepressible Myth of Erie*, 87 Harv L Rev 693, 712–17 (1974).

[24] Particularly helpful was the opinion of Judge Posner in *Luddington v Indiana Bell Tel. Co.*, 966 F2d 225, 228 (7th Cir 1992).

rule will not lead to divergent outcomes in an identifiable class of cases, but it can be expected to bias decision systematically in favor of one side in a recurring class of disputes.[25]

A strong argument can be made that systematic bias differs in degree but not in kind from the indeterminacy that is inherent in common law adjudication. If one accepts this view, analysis of the Phase I cases establishes that a majority of unresolved conflicts— indeed, probably a substantial majority—will not generate any of the consequences that would put them in the realm of the "intolerable."

C. INVESTIGATING PERSISTENCE

At this point I had taken objective analysis based on the Study Committee factors as far as it could go. But that did not mean that I had to abandon efforts to evaluate the significance of unresolved conflicts. Although the Study Committee did not develop the point, it implicitly recognized that conflicts have a temporal dimension.[26] Further, my own prior research provided numerous instances of conflicts that were denied review in one Supreme Court Term but resolved in a subsequent Term when brought to the Court by another petitioner. I therefore undertook an investigation of the persistence of unresolved conflicts.

Persistence in the broad sense can be viewed as an element of tolerability; the difference lies in the temporal perspective. In analyzing the tolerability of the Phase I conflicts, I took as a given the landscape of the law at the time the Supreme Court denied review. A study of persistence, on the other hand, concentrates on what happens to the conflicts that the Court does not hear. Do they "remain unresolved" for long periods of time? Does the Court step in when the same issue is presented in another case? Or do the conflicts disappear or become irrelevant without a Supreme Court decision?

The cases studied in Phase I could provide only limited insights into the persistence of unresolved conflicts because the denials of

---

[25] For elaboration and examples, see Hellman, *By Precedent Unbound* at 765–69 (cited in note 8).

[26] See Study Committee Report at 125 (cited in note 4) (emphasizing importance of providing a "nationally binding construction" of statutes "within a reasonable time").

certiorari were so recent. Thus, to pursue this line of inquiry, it was necessary to investigate the fate of conflicts denied review in earlier years. To that end, in Phase II of the study I went back to the 1984 and 1985 Terms of the Supreme Court and traced the subsequent history of 142 conflicts that were "not heard" by the Court during that period. I selected that period because a compilation of conflicts was available as part of an unpublished study conducted at the request of Chief Justice Burger.

After analyzing court rulings and secondary sources, I found fewer than 40 conflicts out of the 142 that (a) had not been put to rest by a Supreme Court decision or otherwise, (b) continued to generate litigation, and (c) controlled outcomes in one or more reported cases. Of these, perhaps a dozen had some potential for encouraging nonacquiescence or causing harm to multicircuit actors; the remainder implicated only the "unfairness" factor. In short, the research indicated that most of the conflicts the Supreme Court does not hear either do not generate the consequences that concerned the Study Committee or do so only for a short period of time.

In reliance on the research conducted in Phase I and Phase II, the long-range planning committee of the Judicial Conference of the United States recommended that "[t]he United States Supreme Court should continue to be the sole arbiter of conflicting precedents among the courts of appeals."[27] That recommendation was endorsed by the Conference itself.[28] But not everyone agrees that unresolved conflicts are not a cause for worry. I have already quoted observations by Judge Weis and Professor Baker;[29] former Solicitor General Kenneth W. Starr has spoken in a similar vein.[30] Thus it is appropriate to pursue new lines of inquiry to determine whether the complacency of Justice Kennedy and Justice Souter is warranted.

---

[27] Committee on Long Range Planning [of the] Judicial Conference of the United States, Proposed Long Range Plan for the Federal Courts 43 (Recommendation 20) (1995).

[28] Judicial Conference of the United States, Long Range Plan for the Federal Courts 46 (Recommendation 19) (1995). The Judicial Conference and its committee based their conclusion on the Draft Final Report on the research. See id at n 10.

[29] See notes 9–10 and accompanying text.

[30] Kenneth W. Starr, *The Supreme Court and the Federal Judicial System*, 42 Case Western L Rev 1209, 1212 (1992).

II. The Later History of the Phase I Conflicts

In the study cited by the Judicial Conference and its long-range planning committee, I analyzed the tolerability of the substantiated conflicts in the Phase I Study Group and the persistence of the substantiated conflicts in the Phase II Study Group. Because the denial of certiorari in the Phase I cases was still recent, I had only fragmentary information about the later history of those issues. With the passage of time, however, it became possible to investigate the persistence of the Phase I conflicts. Although resources did not permit research on the comprehensive scale of the initial enterprise, I was able to trace and analyze later developments in sufficient depth to answer the basic questions: How many of the conflicts remain alive? To what extent are they likely to give rise to the consequences that make for intolerability?

As explained in the preceding section, the Phase I Study Group encompassed two sets of cases that the Supreme Court declined to hear. The first group included all cases in the 1988, 1989, and 1990 Terms in which Justice White dissented from denial of certiorari. That group gave us a total of 166 substantiated conflicts. The second group was a random sample drawn from the 1989 Term. That sample ultimately yielded a total of 44 substantiated conflicts. Nine conflicts appeared twice in the Study Group: five cases in the Dissent Group also turned up in the random sample, and four conflicts from the random sample prompted a dissent by Justice White in a different case. Thus, for the follow-up study, I investigated the later history of 201 conflicts that were denied review in the Supreme Court's 1988, 1989, and 1990 Terms.[31] The bulk of the work was carried out in late 1997 and early 1998, with some additional research in early fall of 1998. The analysis reflects all Supreme Court action through the end of the 1997–98 Term.[32]

The new research strongly reinforces the conclusion set forth in the earlier article. Of the 201 conflicts, 62 have been put to rest by legislative or judicial action. Another 63 conflicts have died a natural death; either the underlying issue has disappeared or there

---

[31] In reporting the findings, I shall use "case" and "conflict" interchangeably.

[32] Detailed write-ups on the individual cases are on file with the author and with the Federal Judicial Center. Cases discussed in this article are identified by record number ("RN").

is no longer any evidence of intercircuit disagreement. Among the conflicts that have not been put to rest, there are no more than 50 that manifest characteristics that contribute to intolerability.

In addition to the findings, the new research further refines the analytical framework. It is now clear that a conflict can "evaporate" even though the issue remains alive at a some higher level of generality. For conflicts that cannot be said to have evaporated, a critical question is whether any later court has found it necessary to reject a precedent from another circuit.

A. CONFLICTS PUT TO REST

Shortly after Justice White retired from the Supreme Court, Justice Antonin Scalia offered an explanation of why the Court so often rejects a certiorari petition notwithstanding the presence of an intercircuit conflict. In remarks to a group of judges and lawyers, Justice Scalia suggested that "in many . . . , perhaps most of the cases that Justice White used to write about," the Court did not deny certiorari because "the rest of us didn't think the conflict was significant enough"; rather, the Court denied certiorari because "there was the problem of a threshold question that you would have to overcome in order to reach the question that you're interested in."[33] Justice Scalia added pointedly: "If it's really an important issue, it's going to be back next term; it may be back later this term."[34]

The findings of this study provide some support for Justice Scalia's assessment. Of the 201 conflicts in the Study Group, 45 were resolved when the Supreme Court granted review in a later case. Thirty-two decisions explicitly addressed the issue on which courts of appeals disagreed. Generally the Court's opinion specified the conflict as the reason for granting review and cited one or more of the appellate rulings that were brought to the Court's attention in the earlier petition. Another 13 conflicts were implic-

---

[33] Proceedings of the Fifty-Fifth Judicial Conference of the District of Columbia Circuit, 160 FRD 169, 215 (1994) (remarks of Justice Scalia).

[34] Id. Chief Justice Rehnquist pointed to another reason why the Court denied review in some of the conflict cases flagged by Justice White: the rule rejected by the court below was less favorable to the petitioner than the competing rule, so that the petitioner "would lose whichever of these rules is adopted." Id at 216 (remarks of Chief Justice Rehnquist). That too would lead the Court to wait for another case "next term [or] later this term."

itly resolved when the Supreme Court decided a case involving a closely related question.[35]

Although Justice Scalia did not mention it, the Supreme Court is not the only institution that has the power to end litigation over a conflict issue. Legislative bodies can change the law, and courts of appeals can change their minds. Among the Study Group conflicts, 10 have been mooted through some kind of legislative action—Acts of Congress, amendments to the Sentencing Guidelines, or revisions to procedural rules. Seven conflicts were eliminated when the minority circuit overruled the nonconforming decision. In all, 62 conflicts had been put to rest by judicial or legislative action when the Court's 1997 Term ended in June 1998.

If no judicial or legislative body has taken action to put a conflict to rest, does that mean that the conflict remains alive? Not necessarily. On the contrary, one of the major findings of this research is that conflicts can die without any directed or self-conscious intervention by a judicial or legislative body. There are two distinct ways in which this can happen. One is quite straightforward; the other is somewhat more subtle.

In 35 cases, the conflict died a natural death through what can be described as "burial" of the underlying issue.[36] Some of the issues never generated a reported decision after the denial of certiorari. Half a dozen hung on until early 1994 (or in one instance late 1994). The remaining issues disappeared from sight sometime during the early 1990s.

I recognize, of course, that reported decisions do not necessarily reflect the universe of lawsuits or the realities of legal practice. However, with one or two exceptions, I am confident that the issues I have classified as "buried" have little prospect for revival. Further, many of the now-dead conflicts were quite attenuated to begin with. Even if the issues were to reappear in some form, the likelihood is small that they would entail any of the consequences that make for intolerability.

In 28 cases, the issue remained alive to a greater or lesser degree;

---

[35] An example is the conflict over the availability of punitive damages for injuries suffered by seamen. For discussion, see Part IV.

[36] See *Darr v Burford*, 339 US 200, 227 (Frankfurter, J, concurring) (noting that the passage of time may "bury [a] question.").

however, the conflict presented to the Supreme Court has evaporated. This is a phenomenon that I have not previously identified. "Evaporation" refers to the situation in which courts continue to cite precedents on one or both sides of a once-live conflict, but there is no recent evidence that any court has seen a need to choose between precedents or that the law differs from one circuit to another.

The phenomenon is illustrated, rather surprisingly, by a case in the Random Group. In *Berda v CBS Inc.*,[37] the Third Circuit confronted what the court described as "a circuit-splitting question: whether state contract and tort claims for monetary relief brought by a bargaining unit employee against his employer based upon alleged misrepresentations of job security, made before the employee became a member of the bargaining unit, . . . are preempted by § 301 of the LMRA [Labor-Management Relations Act]."[38] The court held that the plaintiff's claims were not preempted; it noted that the Ninth Circuit had reached a different result on "similar facts" in *Bale v General Telephone Co.*[39] Notwithstanding the acknowledged disagreement, the Supreme Court denied certiorari. Litigation continued, and in the early 1990s the conflict appeared to be one of the most acute in the Random Group.[40]

Today the picture looks very different. A recent commentator, surveying decisions in all circuits over a period of nearly 10 years, found that "virtually every lower federal court considering the issue has held that pre-collective bargaining agreement assurances of job security are not preempted by section 301."[41] The Ninth Circuit, which might have been viewed as an outlier, has distinguished *Bale* and held that a claim for negligent misrepresentation was not preempted.[42] To be sure, there remains more than a little uncertainty about the scope of Section 301 preemption in other

---

[37] 881 F2d 20 (3d Cir 1989), cert denied, 493 US 1062 (1990) (RN 335).

[38] Id at 20.

[39] 795 F2d 775 (1986).

[40] The issue was again presented to the Court in the 1991 Term. See *White v National Steel Corp.*, 938 F2d 474 (4th Cir), cert denied, 502 US 974 (1991). This time Justice White dissented from the denial of certiorari.

[41] Richard A. Bales, *The Discord Between Collective Bargaining and Individual Employment Rights: Theoretical Origins and a Proposed Reconciliation*, 77 BU L Rev 687, 760 n 147 (1997).

[42] See *Beals v Kiewit Pacific Co.*, 114 F3d 892, 895 (9th Cir 1997).

contexts.[43] But no court in several years has had to choose between circuit positions on the issue presented in *Berda*—preemption of claims involving pre-hire misrepresentations of job security—and no court has acknowledged or recognized any intercircuit disagreement. The conflict is no more.

I have recounted this history to show how a conflict that once loomed large can lose all potency, not to suggest that *Berda* is typical of the conflicts that have evaporated. It is not. Few of the conflicts in this category are associated with a broader issue that remains unsettled. Many had little substance even at the time certiorari was denied in the Study Group case. Some of the underlying issues are all but buried. The details vary; what is clear in each of the cases is that there is no longer a disgreement that leads to divergent outcomes depending on the circuit where a dispute is litigated.

B. CONFLICTS NOT PUT TO REST

The analysis thus far accounts for all but 76 of the conflicts in the Phase I Study Group. These are the conflicts that cannot be deemed to have been put to rest. But the fact that a conflict remains alive is not necessarily cause for concern. Rather, we must ask whether the continued existence of the conflict has generated one or more of the consequences that the Federal Courts Study Committee identified as contributing to intolerability.

In my earlier analysis, I suggested that the key to intolerability is effect on outcomes. As explained in the account of the Phase II Study Group, "Unless the choice between the competing rules leads courts to reach divergent results in similar cases, none of the consequences that concerned the Study Committee are likely to materialize."[44] I adhere to that view, but, in light of the limited resources available for research in this phase, I looked for another benchmark that would more readily identify those conflicts that have truly made a difference. I found it in the course of working on a related project.[45] A strong signal that a conflict leads to divergent

---

[43] The Supreme Court itself has said that "the Courts of Appeals have not been entirely uniform in their understanding and application of the principles set down in [two Supreme Court decisions]." *Livadas v Bradshaw*, 512 US 107, 124 n 18 (1994).

[44] Hellman, *By Precedent Unbound* at 785 (cited in note 8).

[45] See Arthur D. Hellman, *Precedent, Predictability, and Federal Appellate Structure*, 60 U Pitt L Rev (forthcoming 1999).

outcomes is the rejection by a court in one circuit of another circuit's precedent.[46] Applying this new framework and examining decisions over the last four years,[47] I found that the conflicts fell into four groups: the vestigial, the dynamic, the static, and the receding.

Vestigial conflicts. At one end of the spectrum are eight conflicts that remain alive, if at all, only in some vestigial form. On some of the issues there is evidence of confusion or uncertainty and perhaps some lingering disagreement; what we do not find is a recent decision that rejects another circuit's precedent. By the same token, there is at most a bare minimum of evidence to suggest that the outcome of any of the cases might have been different in another circuit. Thus, although I am not quite prepared to say that these conflicts have been put to rest, I am confident that they have not given rise to any of the consequences specified by the Federal Courts Study Committee.

Illustrative of this category is *Zamboni v Stamler*,[48] a case growing out of the Supreme Court's holding in *Connick v Myers*[49] that the First Amendment protects public employees against adverse personnel action only when their speech involves matters of public concern. The petitioner in *Zamboni* pointed to an apparent conflict on whether the categorization of speech depends on the employee's primary motive in speaking. Justice White, the author of *Connick*, voted to grant certiorari in the 1988 Term, but he dissented alone. Since then, the lower courts have continued to struggle with the role of motive and intent in public employee speech cases. But the decisions are intensely factual. Although some courts and commentators have identified distinct "approaches," the writers put cases from the same circuit on both sides of the supposed divide.[50]

In these circumstances, the indicia of intolerability are virtually nonexistent. As with most constitutional issues, only one of the Study Committee's factors comes into play: unfairness to litigants

---

[46] In the predictability study, I considered only rejection by another court of appeals. However, for this research I also included rejection by courts of first instance.

[47] I also looked at earlier decisions, but the classifications are based primarily on developments since January 1, 1994.

[48] 847 F2d 73 (3d Cir), cert denied, 488 US 899 (1988) (RN 15).

[49] 461 US 138 (1983).

[50] See, for example, *O'Connor v Steeves*, 994 F2d 905, 913 (1st Cir 1993); Rosalie Berger Levinson, *Silencing Government Employee Whistleblowers in the Name of "Efficiency,"* 23 Ohio N U L Rev 17, 36–37 n 95 (1996).

in different circuits. Unfairness would exist if, as a result of differences in circuit law, courts were recognizing federal rights in one circuit that were being denied elsewhere.[51] But that is precisely what the evidence does not show.

Dynamic conflicts. At the other end of the spectrum are 25 conflicts that remain very much alive. These are the "dynamic" conflicts, and the likelihood is high that the choice of rule has affected outcomes in at least some cases. Within this group, I have identified three patterns, rank-ordered as follows (starting with the conflicts manifesting the strongest indicia of intolerability):

- On 10 conflicts, there have been recent decisions that have followed precedents on both sides of the issue, and at least one case on each side has rejected a precedent on the other side. This combination of circumstances provides the strongest evidence that the conflict perpetuates uncertainty and leads to divergent outcomes.
- On 11 conflicts, there have been recent decisions on both sides, and at least one decision from a court not bound by precedent has rejected another circuit's decision or has chosen between competing precedents.
- On four conflicts, although there have not been recent decisions on both sides, at least one court not bound by precedent has rejected another circuit's decision or has chosen between competing precedents.

Even among the conflicts that I have classified as dynamic, there were some that did not affect outcomes, at least on the evidence of reported cases. For example, on the issue of recovery for emotional distress under the Labor Management Reporting and Disclosure Act,[52] there was only one decision, by a district court in a circuit that had not decided the issue.[53] The court endorsed the reasoning

---

[51] See Study Committee Report at 125 (cited in note 4) (citing, as illustration of unfairness, conflicts that "allow[ ] federal benefits in one circuit that are denied elsewhere").

[52] See *Guidry v International Union of Operating Engineers*, 882 F2d 929 (5th Cir 1989). The issue was presented to the Supreme Court in a later phase of the long-drawn-out litigation. *Guidry v International Union of Operating Engineers*, 907 F2d 1491 (5th Cir 1990), cert denied, 498 US 1016 (1990) (RN 640). See discussion in Hellman, *By Precedent Unbound* at 771 (cited in note 8).

[53] *Glover v Ossey*, 1995 WL 374029 (ND Ill 1995).

of the Fifth Circuit in the Study Group case, noting that the Fifth Circuit had rejected the approach taken by the Second Circuit. But the judge explicitly indicated that adoption of "the Second Circuit's more restrictive interpretation of actual injury" would not have led to a different outcome.[54] That, however, is not typical of the conflicts in this group.

Static conflicts. One step removed from the dynamic conflicts are 20 conflicts that can be characterized as "static." The common thread is that precedents on both sides are still good law in their respective circuits, but no court not bound by precedent has chosen between the competing lines of authority. The cases fall into two subgroups.

For nine of the conflicts, there is at least one recent decision in which a court has rejected an out-of-circuit precedent as inconsistent with binding circuit law. However, no court not bound by precedent has rejected another circuit's ruling, nor has any new court chosen between competing precedents. Thus, the conflict has not widened, but the recent reiteration of disagreement gives reason to believe that it will persist. Further, there are at least some cases in which the choice of rule appears to have affected the outcome.

For 11 other conflicts, there have been recent decisions that have followed precedents on both sides,[55] but no recent decision has rejected any out-of-circuit precedent or chosen between precedents. Generally, these are situations in which the competing circuit positions are well established; thus, it is reasonably clear that the law differs from one circuit to another. What is less clear is that the difference in circuit rules has affected outcomes. Indeed, in some cases there is affirmative evidence that the choice of rule did not control the result.

A good example is the conflict on the standard to be applied to claims by a criminal defendant that jury exposure to extrinsic material requires a new trial.[56] Under the law of the Tenth Circuit, a new trial is warranted as long as there is the "slightest possibility"

---

[54] Id at *10.

[55] In one instance there has been a decision applying one of the competing precedents but none applying the other.

[56] The issue was presented to the Supreme Court in *Sherman v Maryland*, 498 US 950 (1990) (RN 627; unpublished decision below).

that the jury's view of the unadmitted evidence affected the verdict.[57] In contrast, the Seventh Circuit holds that a defendant is entitled to a new trial only if the extraneous material had a "reasonable possibility of prejudicing the jury."[58] As the Tenth Circuit has recognized, the "slightest possibility" standard is the "less exacting" of the two.[59] But in August 1996, the Seventh Circuit, applying the "reasonable possibility" standard, affirmed a district court ruling granting a new trial.[60] Almost simultaneously, the Tenth Circuit applied its more demanding test and denied relief.[61] Thus, the conflict persists (albeit without recent acknowledgment),[62] but the verbal standard does not appear to be the dispositive factor in determining case outcomes.

Receding conflicts. Finally, there are what might be called the receding conflicts. A conflict is "receding" when recent decisions have pointed so overwhelmingly in one direction that the precedents on the other side, although not overruled, will carry little weight with lawyers or judges. Under these circumstances, the continuing existence of the conflict is unlikely to make much difference in the outcome of new decisions.

Again, there are two subgroups. In 10 cases, although all recent decisions take one side of the conflict, the authority on the other side still retains some vitality: it has been cited with apparent approval by the court of appeals or applied by a lower court in the minority circuit. But it has not been the basis for a court of appeals decision, so that there has been no opportunity for the minority circuit to reconsider the precedent. Overall, there is substantial evidence that the minority precedent is destined for oblivion, but the obsequies cannot yet be pronounced.

In the remaining 13 cases, courts continue to choose between competing precedents or positions, but recent decisions are all on one side, and the authority on the other side has not been reaffirmed or cited with approval in any recent case. The most one

---

[57] *United States v Wood*, 958 F2d 963, 966 (10th Cir 1992).

[58] *United States v Bruscino*, 687 F2d 938, 940 (7th Cir 1982) (en banc).

[59] *Wood*, 958 F2d at 966.

[60] *United States v Berry*, 92 F3d 597 (7th Cir 1996).

[61] *United States v Jaramillo*, 98 F3d 521 (10th Cir 1996).

[62] The 1992 decision in *Wood* is the only case after 1990 that cites the competing rules on jury exposure to extrinsic evidence.

can say is that the minority precedent may still be good law in its own circuit—and sometimes even that is questionable. For example, the Second Circuit has never overruled its *Toscanino*[63] decision, which held that a federal criminal defendant can defeat personal jurisdiction by showing gross illegality in the government's conduct in seizing him overseas.[64] But no court in the Second Circuit has ever applied *Toscanino* to dismiss an indictment.[65]

When the precedents on one side have been rejected by every court to consider the issue over a substantial period of time, it is highly doubtful that any of the consequences specified by the Federal Courts Study Committee will ensue. Whether we look at the treatment of litigants in reported cases or at the predictability of future outcomes, the fact that the minority precedent remains on the books is almost an irrelevance. Indeed, if the minority precedent has been sufficiently discredited, the continued existence of the conflict may be regarded as more theoretical than real.

C. CONCLUSION

In the 1995 article I presented the results of analyzing the later history of 142 conflicts that were denied review in the 1984 and 1985 Terms. I found fewer than 40 conflicts that (*a*) were not put to rest by a Supreme Court decision or otherwise, (*b*) continued to generate litigation, and (*c*) controlled outcomes in one or more reported cases. How do the results of the new research compare with these findings?

As already noted, complete comparison is not possible because of limited resources for this follow-up study. Nevertheless, the broad patterns are clear enough. Of the 201 conflicts that were denied review in the 1988, 1989, and 1990 Terms, 97 have been put to rest or have otherwise ceased to generate litigation.[66] Another 36 conflicts plainly have not controlled outcomes in any re-

---

[63] *United States v Toscanino*, 500 F2d 267 (2d Cir 1974).

[64] The Phase I Study Group case is *Matta-Ballesteros v Henman*, 896 F2d 255, 261 (7th Cir), cert denied, 498 US 878 (1990) (RN 604). The issue also appeared in the Phase II Study Group. See Hellman, *By Precedent Unbound* at 786 n 358 (cited in note 8).

[65] See *United States v Yousef*, 927 F Supp 673, 676 (SD NY 1996).

[66] This figure includes the 62 conflicts that have been mooted, eliminated, or resolved, along with the 35 conflicts that have been "buried."

cent reported cases.[67] That leaves only 68 conflicts that have any potential for affecting outcomes. I am confident that if I applied the criteria used in the study of the 1984 and 1985 Terms, at least 20 of the 68 conflicts would be found not to have produced divergent outcomes in any pair of reported cases for five years or more.[68]

I conclude, therefore, that among the conflicts that have not been put to rest, there are no more than 50 that continue to produce any of the effects that contribute to intolerability. That figure accords closely with the findings reported in the earlier study. And it supports the conclusions previously reached:

1. Simply counting the conflicts that the Supreme Court declines to hear in a particular Term gives a distorted view of the extent to which unresolved intercircuit conflicts pose a problem in the legal system.

2. When one considers both the tolerability of the unresolved conflicts and their persistence, the evidence points strongly to the conclusion that unresolved intercircuit conflicts do not constitute a problem of serious magnitude in the federal judicial system today.

III. INTERCIRCUIT CONFLICTS AND THE PRACTICE OF LAW:
    FIELD RESEARCH

As the preceding section demonstrates, the analytical approach can take us a long way toward determining the extent to which unresolved intercircuit conflicts present a problem in the legal system. Nevertheless, reliance on the analytical approach alone is not entirely satisfactory. The premise of the Federal Courts Study Committee is that unresolved conflicts become intolerable when they affect behavior in ways that cause harm.[69] But the analytical approach can give us only indirect information about how conflicts actually influence behavior. To secure more direct evidence, I undertook a program of field research. The methods I used ultimately included individual and group interviews of attor-

---

[67] This figure includes the 28 conflicts that have evaporated and the eight that I have classified as "vestigial."

[68] I put most of the receding conflicts into this category. Some of the static conflicts can be included as well.

[69] See Hellman, *By Precedent Unbound* at 708 (cited in note 8).

neys, examination of continuing legal education materials, and an in-depth survey of members of two specialty bars. The work was carried out with the help and support of the Federal Judicial Center;[70] however, I take sole responsibility for the conclusions.

The field research began where the analytical approach left off. Its purpose was not to secure an independent estimate of the "number and frequency" of unresolved conflicts.[71] Even if it were possible to obtain quantitative data of that kind through interviews and surveys, the effort would have been difficult and expensive, and it would have made poor use of limited resources. Rather, the purpose was twofold. First, I wanted to pursue questions about the Study Group conflicts that case analysis alone could not answer. Second, I believed that the experiences of practicing lawyers could provide a real-world perspective against which to test conclusions based on the analytical approach. Thus, the field research would address questions such as these: To what extent do conflicts that have the potential for inflicting harm on multicircuit actors actually affect conduct at the primary level? What is the effect of the conflicts on the litigation of federal questions in the lower courts? Where do intercircuit conflicts fit into the totality of factors that influence lawyers' behavior?

The account begins by elaborating on the particular aspects of conflicts that were chosen as the focus for investigation. The remainder of the section describes the methods used, summarizes the results of the research, and explores the implications of the findings.

A. REFINING THE QUESTIONS

In assessing intolerability through analysis of court decisions and other library materials, I concentrated on looking for characteristics that would correlate with the four nonexclusive factors set forth in the Federal Courts Study Committee report and repeated in Section 302 of the Judicial Improvements Act. For purposes of the field research, however, I did not want to assume that the four factors exhaust the ways in which intercircuit conflicts might affect lawyers' behavior. Rethinking was in order, and that rethinking led

---

[70] For that reason, I sometimes use "we" in describing the method of the study.

[71] See text accompanying note 15 (quoting the Judicial Improvements Act).

to some modification of the Study Committee framework. One threshold question and one new factor came to the fore, and the considerations listed by the Study Committee took on a somewhat different cast.

Awareness of circuit law. The Study Committee seemed to assume that, as a general matter, lawyers are aware of "the law of the circuit"[72] and take account of circuit differences in planning litigation and advising clients. But the idea of a "law of the circuit" stands on shaky ground, both in theory and in practice. In theory, "[t]he federal courts comprise a single system applying a single body of law."[73] More broadly, in a common law system the assumption is that "all the cases everywhere can stand together."[74] While no one would accept either of these propositions as a description of reality in the federal courts, they do reflect a tradition, and that tradition may be strong enough to affect the way lawyers think about the law, at least in the absence of an acknowledged intercircuit conflict. Moreover, it remains the exception rather than the rule for treatises and practice manuals to focus on individual circuits as espousing particular rules or doctrines.[75]

None of these considerations necessarily negate the premise that lawyers take account of the law of the circuit. Indeed, when a conflict is acknowledged by one or more of the courts or recognized by other authorities, there is every reason to think that the premise is correct. Nevertheless, from an empirical perspective it is necessary to investigate, rather than to take as a given, lawyers' attitudes toward intercircuit differences. This inquiry would embrace questions such as: In the absence of contrary evidence, do lawyers generally treat federal decisional law as a single body of rules, or do they focus on the law of a particular forum, as a lawyer would do

---

[72] This phrase came into general currency after Judge Friendly used it in the title of a widely cited article. See Henry J. Friendly, *The "Law of the Circuit" and All That*, 46 St John's L Rev 406 (1972).

[73] *H. L. Green Co. v MacMahon*, 312 F2d 650, 652 (2d Cir 1962); see also *Critical Mass Energy Project v Nuclear Regulatory Comm'n*, 975 F2d 871, 881 (DC Cir 1992) (en banc) (Randolph, J, concurring) (although the number of different panels in the 13 circuits may exceed 6,000, the federal courts, "in theory at least, . . . constitute one judicial system.").

[74] Karl Llewellyn, *The Bramble Bush* 50 (Oceana Publications, 1981; work originally published 1930).

[75] This was the impression I had when I began the field research; it was confirmed during the course of the work. For discussion of one exception, see note 125 and accompanying text.

today for matters controlled by state law? How much evidence of
conflict does it take to arouse suspicion that the choice of circuit
may be outcome-determinative? How much weight is given to differences in articulated rules, and how much to patterns in the reported decisions? Does the approach vary depending on the nature
of the issue? Are procedural questions treated differently from substantive questions, constitutional issues differently from those governed by statutes? What other variables are taken into account?

Factors not warranting inclusion in field research. For very different
reasons, I concluded that two of the factors listed in Section 302
should be omitted from survey instruments for field research.
These were nonacquiescence and unfairness.

As shown in the 1995 study, no more than a handful of the
conflicts in the Phase I Study Groups even had the potential for
"encourag[ing] nonacquiescence by Federal agencies in the holdings of the courts of appeals for different circuits."[76] With instances so few and so scattered, it did not seem worthwhile to for-
mulate questions for the survey instruments to shed further light
on their significance. Nor would it have been desirable to impose
upon the lawyer respondents the burden of answering inquiries
that at best would add only marginally to what we know about the
tolerability of unresolved conflicts.

In contrast, the factor of "unfairness to litigants in different circuits" remains very much in the picture. But it is not a factor that
lends itself to investigation through surveys and interviews or other
field research. "Unfairness" is defined as differential treatment that
raises "the sort of equal protection problems which troubled the
[Supreme] Court in *Erie*."[77] The concept thus includes an evalua-
tive component. While, in theory, it might be useful to ascertain
the opinions of a representative sample of lawyers as to the unfairness of particular conflicts, the results would be misleading unless the respondents were given full information about the conflict
issues and their context. I do not think that it would be possible
to provide that information without making the survey instruments
hopelessly lengthy and cumbersome.

This does not mean that we must give up on the possibility of

---

[76] Pub L No 101-650, § 302, 104 Stat 5089, 5104 (1990); see Hellman, *By Precedent
Unbound* at 742–48 (cited in note 8).

[77] Id at 757 (quoting *Hanna v Plumer*, 380 US 460, 468 (1965)).

using field research to add to our understanding of unfairness. If an intercircuit disagreement is important enough to lead lawyers to litigate in one circuit rather than another, we would probably conclude that the conflict does result in differential treatment of a kind that would be deemed unfair. Thus the inquiry into unfairness could be pursued by asking lawyers about forum shopping. That aspect of the research is discussed below.

Harm to multicircuit actors. Intercourt conflicts arouse greatest concern when they impose inconsistent directives to govern the same primary conduct.[78] Almost as troublesome, in a system that accords nationwide precedential effect only to decisions of the United States Supreme Court,[79] are conflicts that force multicircuit entities to choose between disuniformity in their operations and obedience to the unfavorable rule of a single circuit. These are the consequences that the Federal Courts Study Committee referred to when it spoke of conflicts that "impose economic costs or other harm to multi-circuit actors."[80]

Of the conflicts identified in Phase I, about one-quarter—just over 50—had some potential for inflicting injury of this kind. For the most part, though, that classification meant only that, on the basis of subject matter and the nature of the issues, the possibility of harm to multicircuit actors could not be ruled out. Whether harm in fact occurred would depend on factors that would not necessarily be reflected in library materials. One purpose of field research is to ascertain the extent to which the scenarios hypothesized by the Federal Courts Study Committee have actually been played out in law offices and boardrooms.

That is not an easy task. The most formidable challenge is to isolate the harms caused by intercircuit conflict from those attributable to uncertainty stemming from other aspects of the legal system. For example, the *Guide to Antitrust Compliance* prepared by a food company observes that "there is no consensus among courts as to what constitutes unlawful predatory pricing."[81] That sounds

---

[78] See Arthur D. Hellman, *Breaking the Banc: The Common-Law Process in the Large Appellate Court*, 23 Ariz St L J 915, 922–23 (1991).

[79] See Hellman, *By Precedent Unbound* at 743 (cited in note 8).

[80] Study Committee Report at 125 (cited in note 4).

[81] American Bar Ass'n Section of Antitrust Law, *Compliance Manuals for the New Antitrust Era* 201 (1990). Another company's guide says only, "This is a complex area of the law." Id at 336.

like a reference to intercircuit conflict. But the writer might also be using "courts" in a less technical sense that encompasses different panels of the same court. After all, perceptions of conflict within circuits on that particular issue are not unknown.[82]

This ambiguity probably will not arise when the conflict issue is binary and discrete. That is not the norm, however, and in other situations the consequences of the unresolved intercircuit conflict will be more difficult to disentangle. I have in mind a recurring pattern in the cases in the Random Group: the conflict is acknowledged or recognized, but the issue is not binary, and within at least some of the circuits there are multiple precedents that point in different directions. In this setting, multicircuit actors might well experience difficulty in ordering their affairs in a way that would yield predictable outcomes if disputes were to go to court. But these circumstances also make it unlikely that outcomes will be determined by the choice of one circuit's law over another's. Thus, from the perspective of the Section 302 factors, it cannot be said that the *conflict* has imposed economic costs. Careful formulation of the questions is required in order to secure responses that shed light on the single aspect of precedent that is the subject of this research.[83]

Forum shopping. In the course of analyzing the conflicts in the Phase I Study Group, I concluded that forum shopping among circuits becomes an evil only when it causes harm to multicircuit actors or results in unfairness to litigants in different circuits.[84] Thus, the possibility of "encourag[ing] forum shopping" should be given no independent weight in evaluating the consequences of an unresolved conflict. By the same token, however, when conflicts do affect the selection of a forum, we have strong evidence that

---

[82] See, for example, *William Inglis & Sons Baking Co. v ITT Continental Baking Co.*, 668 F2d 1014, 1060 (9th Cir 1981) (Wallace, J, dissenting from denial of rehearing en banc). The writer might also have been referring to disharmonies between federal and state courts. See generally William J. Haynes, Jr., *Will the Answers Be Different Under State Antitrust Laws?* in *34th Annual Advanced Antitrust Seminar: Distribution and Marketing* at 519 (Practicing Law Institute, 1995).

[83] Implicit in this discussion is the view that conflict between circuits is only one of the ways in which the operation of the system of precedent may fail to satisfy the desires of lawyers and citizens for predictability and uniformity in the law. Implicit, too, is the suggestion that the effect of intercircuit conflict cannot be fully assessed without consideration of other sources of uncertainty.

[84] See Hellman, *By Precedent Unbound* at 754–56 (cited in note 8).

the choice of rules is important to a degree that will implicate the other two factors. In the context of field research, this means that forum shopping can serve to some extent as a proxy for unfairness and the possibility of harm to multicircuit actors.

Forum shopping also appears to be a phenomenon that is relatively straightforward to investigate. Choosing a forum after the decision has been made to pursue litigation will generally be a discrete, one-time event that lawyers will be able to describe with relative ease. Thus, focusing on specific conflicts identified in Phase I, we planned to ask such questions as: Had the lawyer encountered the conflict in his or her practice? Under what circumstances, if any, would the different rules lead the lawyer to file suit in one circuit rather than another? In disputes growing out of continuing relationships, would the lawyer initiate a "preemptive strike" to assure litigation in a circuit with a favorable rule? How much weight would the lawyer give to the presence of an intercircuit conflict in comparison with other factors that bear upon the choice of forum?

Effect on litigation in other circuits. Choice of forum is not the only aspect of litigation that may be affected by the existence of an intercircuit conflict. Review of the literature suggested one additional consequence not mentioned in the statute or the Federal Courts Study Committee report (though it has been discussed by the chairman of the Study Committee)[85] that appeared to warrant investigation through field research. The area of inquiry involves the effect on litigation and motions practice in circuits where the court of appeals has not ruled on the issue. For example: other things being equal, would a lawyer be more apt to litigate rather than settle when there are court of appeals decisions on both sides than when the only circuit precedent was against him? Once litigation is in progress, would the conflict influence the lawyer to pursue a point (or pursue it with more vigor)? How does the conflict situation compare with the situation where no circuit has ruled on the issue? In short, does the existence of a conflict encourage *relitigation* of issues that might otherwise be regarded as not worth litigating?

---

[85] Statement of Judge Joseph F. Weis, Jr., Before the Subcommittee on Courts and Administrative Practice of the Senate Judiciary Committee at 14–15 (Oct 3, 1991).

B. METHODS FOR ASCERTAINING IMPACT

To ascertain the actual impact of unresolved conflicts on counseling and litigation, I expected to use conventional techniques of field research such as mail surveys, in-person interviews, telephone interviews, and group discussions or focus sessions. The survey instruments would describe a group of conflicts selected from among those identified as having some potential for encouraging forum shopping or inflicting harm on multicircuit actors.[86] With respect to each conflict, the lawyer respondents would be asked such questions as: Were they aware of the conflict before we called it to their attention? Did it offer any opportunity for forum shopping? If so, would the lawyers take advantage of the opportunity? What economic costs, if any, would the inconsistent rules impose on clients operating in more than one circuit?

The first step was to define the population from which the interviewees and survey respondents would be selected. Plainly, it would not have served the purpose to draw from a random group of lawyers, or even from a random group of lawyers practicing in the federal courts. The consequences that I was investigating would generally be experienced only by two classes of attorneys: those who represent national corporations, pension funds, and other entities whose activities cross state lines; and those who regularly represent individuals with claims against such entities. In addition, I wanted to maximize the likelihood that the respondents would have encountered more than one or two of the conflict issues.

With these considerations in mind, I decided to limit the field research to areas of law that gave rise to half a dozen or more conflicts in the Phase I Study Group. Four areas of federal practice fit that description: antitrust, ERISA, labor and employment, and maritime law.[87] For each of those areas I compiled an annotated

---

[86] This approach meant that I excluded conflicts whose existence might encourage relitigation, but which were unlikely to influence the choice of forum or affect the primary conduct of multicircuit actors. I did not think this category was large, and in any event there were other reasons for limiting the scope of the research.

[87] Maritime law barely qualified, but I included it anyway because the preliminary report of the Federal Courts Study Committee made explicit mention of conflicts on maritime issues. Federal Courts Study Committee, *Tentative Recommendations for Public Comment* 119 (Dec 22, 1989). The reference was not included in the Study Committee's final report.

list of the conflict issues for inclusion in the survey instruments. The lists included not only the Phase I conflicts, but also the conflicts in that particular area from the Phase II Study Group.

The research proceeded in four stages, each shaped by the ones that preceded it. I began by conducting a series of in-person interviews with experienced lawyers who specialized in one of the four fields I had selected.[88] Some of the interviews were one-on-one; others included small groups of lawyers practicing in a particular city. These discussions advanced the inquiry in several ways. They yielded valuable insights into the role of precedent in the lawyering process. They gave me a general sense of how lawyers viewed conflicts. And they provided information that helped me to frame questions that would be addressed to a broader population of practitioners.

Partly on the basis of the interviews, I made one change in the scope of the research: one of the four areas—labor and employment law—was omitted from further investigation. Although the number of conflicts in that area was substantial, the conflicts themselves were generally among the weakest in the Study Groups. Not surprisingly, even experienced labor and employment lawyers had paid little attention to them. In that situation, I saw no more than a small likelihood of securing the kind of specific information I wanted about the effects of the conflicts on the practice of law.

I was more optimistic about the prospect of obtaining useful responses from specialists in maritime law, antitrust, and ERISA. However, resources would not permit extensive in-person interviewing. I therefore decided to try a different approach: examining published materials written by lawyers for the guidance of other lawyers. Included in this category are such works as course outlines for continuing legal education (CLE) programs and practice-oriented treatises. The value of these materials lies in the combination of authorship and purpose. The authors are individuals whose background and stature would have made them likely candidates for interviews or surveys if I were to continue with the method of posing questions to experienced lawyers in the three areas of the law. The purpose of the materials is to assist practicing attorneys

---

[88] I began with specialists for two reasons. First, they were more likely to have encountered the conflicts in their own practice. Second, they could speculate knowledgeably about how other lawyers would deal with the conflicts they had not personally experienced.

in counseling and litigation.[89] Thus, to the extent that the existence
of an intercircuit conflict would affect those activities, whether
positively (as opportunities) or negatively (as pitfalls), we would
expect the experienced authors to call attention to them.[90] If, in
this context, nothing is said, or if there is no suggestion that
lawyers should modify their behavior to take account of the conflict, this is evidence that the conflict will not give rise to any
of the consequences that concerned the Federal Courts Study
Committee.

Two of the three fields that I was investigating—antitrust and
ERISA—have generated numerous CLE outlines, treatises, and
other practice-oriented materials. As a first step, student assistants
used conventional tools of legal research to search those materials
for discussions of the conflict issues identified in Phase I and II.
I then analyzed the materials to see what each author had to say
about each conflict. Did the writer mention the conflict at all? If
so, did the text elaborate, even minimally, on the consequences of
the conflict for lawyers or their clients?[91] Was there any suggestion, direct or indirect, that the difference in circuit law would
warrant litigating in one forum rather than another?[92] Was there
any indication, direct or indirect, that the advice to be given a
client, or the course of action to be taken, would vary depending
on which circuit's law was controlling?[93]

---

[89] See, for example, Carla A. Hills, ed, *Antitrust Adviser* v (3d ed 1985) ("The *Antitrust
Adviser* was written to assist the practitioner who represents business clients to circumvent
antitrust problems . . . and to respond appropriately to antitrust controversy when it does
arise.").

[90] For illustrations, see authorities cited in notes 91–93.

[91] For example, a lawyer might warn that structuring a transaction in accordance with
the law of the circuit poses risks because other courts of appeals have ruled differently.
See, for example, Gregory C. Yadley and Kent Schenkel, *Shareholder Guaranties of Corporate
Debt: Considerations in Drafting and Structuring*, Fla Bar J (Oct 1991) at 39, 42 (suggesting
different approach to borrowings because of the "uncertainty [that] reigns in this area").
Or a writer might simply note that the conflict creates problems for a particular class of
individuals. See, for example, Ralph C. Losey, *Bruch Creates Split in Circuits on Standard of
Appellate Review*, Natl L J (Nov 4, 1991) at 20 ("The conflicting interpretations of 'de novo'
[in reviewing benefit claim denials] cause headaches for insurance companies and ERISA
plan administrators."). The author does not elaborate on the nature of these "headaches."

[92] See, for example, Jed S. Rakoff and Howard W. Goldstein, *RICO: Civil and Criminal
Law and Strategy* § 7.03[2][a] (1992) ("A RICO plaintiff should consider the receptivity of
the district court and circuit to private civil RICO."). This suggestion, of course, directs
the lawyer's attention to the totality of circuit law, not its position on one particular issue.

[93] See, for example, R. Quincy White and Sandy L. Koropp, *Circuits Split on Color Trade-
marks*, Natl L J (May 5, 1993) at S17 (until Supreme Court resolves the issue of whether
color can serve as a trademark, "those wishing to protect color as a trademark in the 7th

The research yielded voluminous material, with half a dozen or more references for some of the issues that we investigated. However, we found very little evidence to indicate that the Study Group conflicts influenced lawyers' decisions or shaped advice to clients.

For some of the conflicts we could find no mention at all in the materials we examined. Some conflicts were discussed only in passing, suggesting that the point of difference did not loom large even in the eyes of specialists. By far the most common form of discussion was what might be called the academic reference: the author would cite the Study Group case and note the conflict, but would not elaborate in any way on the significance of the conflict for the practice of law. These references did not describe how an experienced practitioner might act in the face of conflicting authority, nor did they allude, even in general terms, to any difficulties that the existence of the conflict might create.

We did find some references that went beyond citation or description. For example, a compliance guide to price discrimination, prepared for a CLE program held early in 1994, took note of the conflict on what constitutes below-cost pricing, then added, "Thus, counsel should check the caselaw in its circuit to find out which measure [of cost] governs."[94] A discussion of asset reversions under ERISA explicitly noted the possibility of "successful forum shopping."[95] But these were exceptions.

What conclusions could we draw from this body of evidence? One possible explanation is that conflicts that have the potential for harming multicircuit actors or encouraging forum shopping among circuits generally do not do so. That conclusion would have been consistent with the overall thrust of the interviews up to that

---

Circuit should attempt to protect the color only in connection with a symbol or design"). The question whether color can be protected as a trademark gave rise to one of the conflicts in the Phase I Study Group. See *NutraSweet Co. v Stadt Corp.*, 917 F2d 1024 (7th Cir 1990), cert denied, 499 US 983 (1991) (RN 664). The Supreme Court resolved the conflict in the 1994 Term. See *Qualitex Co. v Jacobson Prods. Co.*, 514 US 159 (1995).

[94] Barbara A. Reeves, *Price Discrimination: A Compliance Guide*, in *33rd Annual Advanced Antitrust Seminar: Distribution, Marketing, and Joint Ventures* at 471, 479 (Practicing Law Institute, 1994). The author was actually referring to pricing claims under the Robinson-Patman Act, rather than Section 2 of the Sherman Act, which was the subject of the Study Group conflict. However, the two issues often overlap.

[95] Michael S. Gordon, *Asset Reversion Litigation—the Plaintiff's Perspective*, in *Employee Benefits Litigation*, C507 ALI-ABA 593, 596 (1990) (available on Westlaw). The comment is quoted in full in text accompanying note 118.

point, and indeed the lawyers I interviewed had pointed to a number of reasons why conflicts might play a smaller role in practice than an academic perspective might suggest.[96]

Notwithstanding the strong pattern that was emerging, I was reluctant to treat negative evidence as conclusive. A high proportion of the material consisted of outlines for CLE programs, and I could not exclude the possibility that more extended discussion of the conflicts took place in the oral presentations. To provide a check on inferences drawn from the absence of affirmative evidence, I embarked on another series of interviews. This time I talked to attorneys who had served as faculty for CLE programs or who had written practice-oriented treatises or guidebooks in the field of antitrust.[97] The interviews were conducted by telephone.

Overall, the interviews tended to confirm the impressions given by the written materials: intercircuit conflicts simply do not loom large in the decisions and actions of the practicing bar. I recognized, however, that the number of lawyers interviewed was small, and that their responses might not represent an adequate range of experiences. For that reason, I decided to conduct a survey that would reach a somewhat broader sample of the bar. The survey was designed and carried out with the assistance of the Federal Judicial Center.

The survey was limited to two fields of practice: maritime law and antitrust. Maritime law was chosen because it is the only federal "specialty" in which the organized bar has expressed concern about unresolved intercircuit conflicts.[98] Antitrust was selected primarily because our interviews indicated that the Study Group cases included a high proportion of conflicts that were familiar to the bar. In addition, I felt that there would be value in comparing responses from maritime lawyers with responses from members of

---

[96] For discussion, see Section D.

[97] I did not limit the survey population to lawyers who had written about the specific conflicts I was investigating. Much of the written material was coauthored, and some dated back several years. Thus, identifying the authors of particular sections of an outline or article would have taken time and effort that I did not think would be worthwhile.

[98] In 1989, the Maritime Law Association of the United States submitted a report to the Federal Courts Study Committee that discussed nine intercircuit conflicts on maritime law issues. A copy of the report is on file with the author. See also Michael F. Sturley, *Observations on the Supreme Court's Certiorari Jurisdiction in Intercircuit Conflict Cases*, 67 Tex L Rev 1251 (1989) (arguing that the Supreme Court has erred in failing to resolve conflicts involving COGSA).

a specialty bar that has not viewed conflicts as a significant problem.[99]

For the maritime survey, we obtained a mailing list from the Maritime Law Association of the United States. The list was limited to "proctor members"—members with at least four years' experience who have demonstrated "proficiency" in admiralty.[100] For the antitrust survey, we used a list drawn from the leadership group of the Antitrust Section of the American Bar Association. We mailed a total of 505 surveys to maritime lawyers; the number returned was 162. The rate of return on the antitrust surveys was lower—only 82 out of 447.

Although the survey instrument included some general questions, our primary interest was in ascertaining the respondents' experience with the specific conflicts identified in the earlier phases of the study. Drawing on information gained in interviews, we selected eleven conflicts in maritime law and eleven in antitrust. For each conflict, a booklet included with the survey instrument provided a statement of the issue and a citation to the cases on both sides. We asked the lawyers to select the three conflicts with which they were most familiar and then to answer two sets of detailed questions about those conflicts. One set of questions focused on the particular conflict's effect on the practice of law generally; another set asked about the respondent's most recent encounter with the conflict in litigation or counseling. The survey instrument also gave the participants a chance to comment on the issues or expand on their answers.[101]

The survey responses substantially augmented the data obtained through interviews. The analysis that follows is based on both bodies of material.

C. FINDINGS

When the field research for this project began, there were 68 conflicts that I planned to investigate: 14 in antitrust, 32 in labor

---

[99] ERISA too would have served this purpose, but investigating the ERISA conflicts would have required surveying the several specialty bars that regularly handle ERISA matters. Resource limitations precluded such an undertaking.

[100] See Robert M. Jarvis, *Admiralty: 1991 Survey of Florida Law*, 16 Nova L Rev 127, 134 n 50 (1992) (describing qualifications for proctor membership).

[101] Copies of the survey materials are on file with the author and with the Federal Judicial Center.

and employment law, 10 on ERISA issues, and 12 in maritime law.[102] As the research proceeded, however, the pool of conflicts shrank considerably.

The first dropouts were the conflicts on labor and employment law. As noted in the preceding section, interviews with lawyers led me to conclude that the conflicts in that field had such a low level of visibility that it would not have been fruitful to seek detailed information about practitioners' experience with them.

No other area was dropped entirely from the research. However, some individual conflicts were omitted because they appeared, on the basis of the initial interviews and the practice materials, to be too narrow or unimportant to warrant further investigation. Thus, in the final stages of the field research I was concentrating on 30 conflicts: 11 each in maritime law and antitrust, and 8 on ERISA issues. The surveys, interviews, and practice materials shed light on six aspects of those conflicts: their incidence, their effects on outcomes, the extent to which they led to forum shopping, their other effects on litigation, their effects on primary activity, and the legal context of the conflicts. The most useful information came from the surveys of the maritime and antitrust bars; thus, in this section, I rely primarily on the survey responses as the basis for analysis.

Incidence of the conflicts. To put the more specific responses into context, we must know how frequently the conflict issues arose in practice. Reported decisions give us valuable clues, but they do not tell the whole story. Some issues may generate judicial opinions on a scale disproportionate to their incidence in life. Others may be important in primary activity even though they do not often appear in judicial opinions.

The maritime and antitrust surveys included several questions that shed light on the incidence of the 22 conflicts in those areas. First, we asked the participants whether they had personally encountered the conflicts either in counseling or in litigation. A single encounter would have sufficed for an affirmative response, but for seven of the maritime conflicts and three in antitrust, affirmative answers came from fewer than half of the participants. Three maritime conflicts and one in antitrust had response rates under 30 percent.

---

[102] As explained in the discussion of methods, these numbers include some conflicts from the Phase II Study Group.

Next, we asked the respondents to select the three conflicts with which they were most familiar, or with which they had had the most experience. Three maritime conflicts and three in antitrust were selected by fewer than 15 lawyers. Not surprisingly, the six conflicts selected least often were, with one exception, the same ones that drew the smallest number of positive responses to the earlier question.[103]

Taking both sets of replies into consideration, we may reasonably conclude that five of the survey conflicts did not arise very often. The antitrust conflicts in this category are those involving price squeezes in regulated industries[104] and jurisdiction over foreign entities.[105] In maritime law, the conflicts involved preemption by the Longshore and Harbor Workers' Compensation Act (LHWCA)[106] and the penalty wage statute.[107] The six conflicts that were selected by fewer than 15 lawyers for detailed responses will not be further discussed here.

The remaining conflicts—a total of 16—will be referred to as the "core group" of antitrust and maritime conflicts.[108] This designation reflects a relative ranking. It does not necessarily mean that the conflicts in the core group arose with great frequency, and indeed there is evidence that most of them did not. One of the questions we posed to the lawyers about the conflicts they had chosen for detailed consideration was, How often had the conflict issue been relevant to the resolution of a dispute in the lawyer's area of practice? The respondents reported their experiences on a

---

[103] The exception occurred in antitrust. Although more than half of the respondents said they had encountered the conflict on the role of intent in predatory pricing, only eight selected it for detailed discussion.

[104] The conflict case was *Town of Concord v Boston Edison Co.*, 915 F2d 17 (1st Cir 1990), cert denied, 499 US 931 (1991) (RN 659). See Hellman, *By Precedent Unbound* at 717 (cited in note 8).

[105] The conflict case was *Timberlane Lumber Co. v Bank of America*, 749 F2d 1378 (9th Cir 1984), cert denied, 472 US 1032 (1985) (Phase II case; RN 844). See Hellman, *By Precedent Unbound* at 788 (cited in note 8).

[106] The conflict case was *Crater v Mesa Offshore Co.*, 539 So2d 88 (La), cert denied, 493 US 905 (1989) (RN 176). See *Lewis v Modular Quarters*, 487 US 1226 (1987) (White, J, joined by Blackmun, J, dissenting from denial of certiorari) (noting conflict).

[107] There were two conflicts involving the penalty wage statute. Both are noted in *Hibernia Nat'l Bank v Chung*, 475 US 1147 (1986) (White, J, dissenting from denial of certiorari) (RN 935 and RN 963; Phase II case).

[108] Four of the eight antitrust conflicts were selected by fewer than 20 lawyers. Further, some respondents did not answer all questions about the conflicts they had chosen. The antitrust results are thus less reliable than those based on the maritime survey.

scale of 1 ("rarely or never") to 5 ("very often"). For convenience, I shall refer to 1 and 2 as the "low end" of the scale; 4 and 5 will be referred to as the "high end."[109]

For all but two of the antitrust conflicts, responses at the low end outnumbered responses at the high end. For the other two antitrust conflicts, the numbers at both ends were equal. In the maritime survey, responses at the low end outnumbered responses at the high end for three of the eight conflicts in the core group. These patterns suggest that all of the antitrust conflicts and three of the eight in maritime law may have come into play less often than the initial data imply.

The field research did not furnish a sufficient basis for assessing the incidence of the eight ERISA conflicts. As already noted, resource limitations precluded use of the survey technique in that area of law. Case reports, commentaries, and interviews provided some information about the frequency with which the conflicts arose, but not enough to warrant confident estimates.[110]

Effect on outcomes. As emphasized throughout this article, a conflict is unlikely to give rise to any of the consequences that concerned the Federal Courts Study Committee unless it affects (or can be expected to affect) the outcome of a litigation. We therefore asked the survey respondents whether, in cases where the conflict issues were relevant, application of one circuit's law rather than another's determined the result.

The perception that conflicts were outcome-determinative was strongest within the maritime bar. Of the eight conflicts in the core group, five produced more responses at the high end of the frequency scale than at the low end. Yet even here the evidence was by no means one-sided. For each conflict, at least 30 percent of the responses were at the low end of the scale.

On antitrust issues, the survey responses indicate that the conflicts generally were not outcome-determinative. Seven of the eight core conflicts drew more responses at the low end of the scale than at the high end. For the remaining conflict (involving dealer termination as a per se violation of Section 1 of the Sherman Act), the numbers at both ends were the same.[111]

---

[109] This convention will be used throughout this article.

[110] Two of the ERISA conflicts were resolved shortly after the denial of review in the Study Group cases. See Section E.

[111] For discussion of this issue, see text accompanying notes 153–56.

Forum shopping. When an intercircuit conflict remains unresolved, a federal judge has written, "attorneys [will] take their cases
to the forum most favorable."[112] That is a plausible supposition.
But is it an accurate description of lawyers' behavior? To find out,
we asked the survey respondents how often the specific conflicts
led lawyers to file suit in one circuit rather than another.

In the field of antitrust, the results indicate that conflict-based
forum shopping is not a common litigation tactic. Of the eight
conflicts in the core group, only one produced more responses at
the high end of the frequency scale than at the low end. This was
the conflict over whether a plaintiff can prevail on a tying claim
without showing power over price in the relevant market by showing the uniqueness of the tying product.[113] One other conflict, involving dealer termination as a per se violation, generated a substantial number of high-end responses, though not as many as
those at the low end.

In the field of maritime law, the survey data provide strong evidence that conflicts generally do *not* lead lawyers to file suit in one
circuit rather than another. For every one of the eight core conflicts, responses at the low end of the frequency scale substantially
outnumbered responses at the high end. Indeed, high-end responses rose above the 20 percent mark for only three of the conflicts.

Of particular interest is the pattern of responses on conflicts involving the Carriage of Goods by Sea Act (COGSA). Professor
Michael F. Sturley, a prominent maritime law scholar, has stated
that "[c]onflicts under COGSA are precisely the type most likely
to be intolerable, because litigants can easily exploit them through
forum shopping."[114] The conflicts in the questionnaire included
three COGSA issues, two of which were discussed by Professor
Sturley.[115] However, the evidence of forum shopping is meager in-

---

[112] Roger J. Miner, *Federal Court Reform Should Start at the Top*, 77 Judicature 104, 106
(1993).

[113] The Study Group case was *Will v Comprehensive Accounting Corp.*, 776 F2d 665 (7th
Cir 1985), cert denied, 475 US 1129 (1986) (Phase II case; RN 931).

[114] Sturley, 67 Tex L Rev at 1268 (cited in note 98). Professor Sturley contrasts COGSA
with the LHWCA, saying, "LHWCA itself prevents most forum shopping." Id at 1260.

[115] Professor Sturley discussed the conflict on the effect of a deviation from the carriage
agreement (RN 951) and the conflict on the burden of proof on the "fire" defense (RN
713). Id at 1266–68.The third COGSA issue involved the "inherent vice" defense (RN
715).

deed. For two of the issues, responses at the low end outnumbered responses at the high end by a ratio of 6 to 1. For the third issue, the ratio was almost 3 to 1.

Why do lawyers not take advantage of the venue options that Professor Sturley describes? One probable explanation is that the conflicts are not perceived as outcome-determinative. But it is also likely that when lawyers decide where to file suit, differences in circuit law pale in importance when weighed against other considerations.[116] Finally, venue options in commercial litigation may be limited by forum selection clauses in the bill of lading.[117]

One of the most explicit discussions of forum shopping in the practice materials dealt with a conflict involving ERISA. The subject was asset reversions. The author stated:

> Obviously, jurisdictions which are clearly inhospitable to plaintiffs' theories on asset reversions should be avoided where possible. An asset reversion in a nationwide or multistate pension plan may lend itself to successful forum shopping. Close attention should be paid to relevant circuit court opinions that will govern the federal district courts where the asset reversion action may lie.[118]

We have no way of knowing whether, and to what extent, lawyers paid heed to this suggestion. However, the responses to the antitrust and maritime surveys strongly point to the conclusion that, for the most part, intercircuit conflicts do not lead to forum shopping.

This conclusion is also supported by the interviews. The predominant attitude among lawyers was nicely captured by an experienced litigator in the field of antitrust. The lawyer characterized the survey conflicts as "good examples, but narrow," and said that they would not be dispositive in choosing a forum. The lawyer added, "I can't remember an instance where we're down to our last conference call and someone has said, 'If we file there, we'll lose!' "

---

[116] See Section IIID.

[117] Although some courts have refused to enforce forum selection clauses in contracts subject to COGSA, others have found such clauses to be valid, especially when the designated forum was one within the United States. See generally C. Andrew Waters, *The Enforceability of Forum Selection Clauses in Maritime Bills of Lading: An Update*, 15 Tulane Maritime L J 29 (1990). The Supreme Court recently held that COGSA does not invalidate foreign forum selection clauses. *Vimar Seguros Y Reaseguros, S.A. v M/V Sky Reefer*, 515 US 528 (1995). Presumably the holding applies a fortiori to clauses designating a domestic forum.

[118] Gordon at 596 (cited in note 95).

Other effects on litigation. Even if conflicts do not generally lead to forum shopping, they may add to the complexity or cost of litigation in the forum that is chosen. The survey responses indicate that, to some extent, this does occur.

We asked the survey participants how often additional cost or complexity had resulted from the conflicts they had selected for detailed discussion. Four of the maritime conflicts and five of those in antitrust engendered more responses at the high end than at the low end. Thus, some conflicts that seldom influenced the choice of forum did have some effect on the shape or course of the lawsuits that were filed.

This result is contrary to what I would have expected. Nevertheless, its significance should not be overstated. High-end responses remained below the 50 percent mark for all of the maritime conflicts and for all but two of those in antitrust. In other words, conflicts may result in added cost or complexity more often than they lead to forum shopping, but that does not necessarily mean that the former occurs often in absolute terms. To find out whether it did, we must delve further into the survey responses.

In addition to the frequency question, I asked the lawyers to think back to the last time they had encountered each of the selected conflicts in a litigation situation and to state whether the existence of the conflict had affected the litigation (other than by influencing the choice of forum). Among the maritime conflicts, only one generated more "yes" than "no" answers. This was the conflict on recovery for economic loss in admiralty.[119] Among the antitrust conflicts, "no" answers outnumbered "yes" responses for all eight core conflicts. Many of the antitrust participants did not answer this question at all.

These patterns cast doubt on the hypothesis that unresolved conflicts frequently result in added cost or complexity in litigation. However, we need not rely solely on a tally of one-word answers. When participants said "yes" to the question about effect on litigation in the most recent encounter, we asked them to explain their

---

[119] The conflict was presented to the Court in the 1984 Term and again in the 1989 Term. The later case was *Texas Eastern Transmission Corp. v McMoRan Offshore Exploration Co.*, 877 F2d 1214 (5th Cir), cert denied as *Marathon Oil Co. v McMoRan Offshore Exploration Co.*, 493 US 937 (1989) (RN 286). For discussion of the issue see Hellman, *By Precedent Unbound* at 791 (cited in note 8).

response. We received a total of 165 such comments from the maritime lawyers and 36 from participants in the antitrust survey.[120]

About 20 percent of the comments shed no light on whether the conflict had added to the cost or complexity of the particular litigation. The respondent simply recited the procedural history, described the result, or identified the aspect of the suit that was affected. Included in this category are responses that referred to settlement or settlement discussions but did not explain further.

Another, somewhat larger, group of explanations focused on consequences distinct from added cost or complexity. For example, some lawyers representing maritime defendants reported that plaintiffs had filed suit in state court. Other respondents simply noted the effect of applying the particular rule in force in the circuit or argued that the court had interpreted the law erroneously. Some of the maritime respondents said that the existence of the conflict had facilitated or encouraged settlement.

The remaining comments indicated, with varying degrees of explicitness or clarity, that the conflict had indeed added to the cost or complexity of the particular litigation. Some of the respondents spoke in general terms of increased expense or difficulty. Others referred to more specific consequences. Here are some representative examples from the maritime survey:

- "Opposing counsel used conflict to urge change of law in my circuit." (Conflict on punitive damages for injuries incurred by seamen.)[121]
- "Substantial amount of research time; briefing [and] preparation of jury charges." (Conflict on definition of "seaman" under Jones Act.)
- "Increased risk of appeal and made settlement more difficult." (Conflict on punitive damages.)
- "It affected the amount and structure of evidence (and its cost) in the effort to vitiate the conflict." (Conflict on shipowner's liability for injuries arising out of defective stowage.)

---

[120] The comments are brief and generally conversational in style. They are useful for discerning broad patterns, but they should not be viewed as a source of hard quantitative data.

[121] The same lawyer said of another conflict, "The conflict allowed me to argue for a change in the law." (Conflict on effect of deviation under COGSA.)

Here are some responses from the antitrust participants:

- "Required to brief both possibilities [to] demonstrate why requested result should not be changed." (Conflict on definition of "sham" under *Noerr-Pennington* doctrine.)
- "Ambiguity on law 'encourages' clients on both sides of issue. Tougher to settle or otherwise quickly resolve." (Conflict on business justification defense under section 2.)
- "Uncertain state of law made settlement discussions difficult." (Conflict on essential facilities doctrine.)

Other comments, however, were considerably more ambiguous. For example, a substantial number of respondents spoke of uncertainty or unpredictability, but did not say that this uncertainty had resulted in increased cost or other tangible consequences. Other participants referred to "bad jury instructions" or to results adverse to the client, but did not point to added cost or complexity en route.

On balance, the explanatory comments indicate that conflicts do sometimes add to the cost or complexity of litigation. However, the survey data as a whole suggest that the phenomenon is not a common one. The survey responses encompass more than 500 encounters with the 16 core conflicts. But the total number of affirmative answers to the question focusing on the respondent's most recent encounter was less than 200. And little more than half of those alluded, even ambiguously, to added cost or complexity.

Effect on primary activity. Thus far the discussion has focused on the effect of conflicts on litigation. We also attempted to determine how the conflicts affected lawyers in counseling and the structuring of transactions. We did this in two ways. For each of the issues selected for detailed response by the survey participants, we asked, in general terms, how often the existence of the conflict added to the difficulty of advising a client in a counseling situation. In addition, we asked the lawyers to focus on their most recent encounter with that conflict. The questions then were: "Did the existence of the conflict affect the advice that you gave to the client? If Yes, please explain."

The picture that emerged was a complex one. Of particular importance, when we looked at the explanatory comments, we discovered that the antitrust and maritime lawyers approached the "counseling" questions from very different perspectives. The antitrust lawyers responded primarily by describing advice they had given in the context of primary conduct and the structuring of transactions.[122] The maritime lawyers generally talked about particular incidents that had led, or might have led, to the filing of a lawsuit.[123] The two groups will therefore be discussed separately.

In antitrust, the answers to the more general question strongly indicated that the conflicts did make counseling more difficult. Responses at the high end of the frequency scale outnumbered responses at the low end for all eight of the core conflicts. For all but two of the conflicts, the ratio was 2 to 1 or higher.

When we turned to the query about the effect of the conflicts on the lawyers' most recent encounters, we found that the evidence was more equivocal. Affirmative answers outnumbered negative answers for only three conflicts. For three other conflicts, the numbers were almost the same.

But what sorts of effects were the lawyers referring to? And how closely did their experiences correspond to the Federal Courts Study Committee's concept of harm to multicircuit actors? To find out, we looked at the explanatory comments that accompanied the affirmative responses. The most frequent comment was that the lawyer recommended a more conservative course of action. One attorney elaborated upon this point:

> As a practitioner who mainly counsels large corporations operating nationally, which are only rarely involved in antitrust cases, staying out of court is a major goal. The existence of intercircuit conflicts, like any other uncertainty in antitrust law, results in counseling advice based on conservative assumptions (i.e., that the most restrictive view will be followed). Obviously, this most conservative advice is not always followed by clients. However, when it is not followed and a more aggressive position is taken, it is done so conscious that the risk is [increased].

---

[122] Among the 71 antitrust comments in response to the question on counseling, 41 focused, explicitly or implicitly, on counseling in the context of primary conduct. Twenty-four responses were ambiguous as to context. Only five comments clearly dealt with claims or litigation.

[123] Of the 147 maritime comments in response to the question on counseling, only 12 were concerned with primary conduct; 99 referred to particular claims or incidents. The remainder were ambiguous as to context.

This theme was sounded in more than one-third of the explanatory comments offered by the antitrust lawyers in response to the counseling question. For example:

- "Advised client (a likely target defendant) that conflict created ambiguity and therefore risk. Led to more conservative conduct." (Conflict on uniqueness of tying product.)
- "Had client use the higher 'total cost' number, as a safety net." (Conflict on proper measure of cost in predatory pricing.)[124]

Other antitrust lawyers referred to "recognizable" or "excessive" risk (without explicitly saying that they had recommended a more conservative course of action) or said only that the conflict had made it more difficult to give definitive advice.

These comments reinforce the conclusion that, in the realm of antitrust, conflicts sometimes added to the difficulty of counseling clients on pricing policies or other matters arising in the conduct of business. What is not so clear is how frequently this occurred in absolute terms. The survey responses encompass more than 150 encounters with the eight core conflicts. Within this group, negative answers to the question about effect on counseling slightly outnumbered the positive.

On this particular point, however, we need not rely entirely on lawyers' after-the-fact descriptions; we also have some direct contemporaneous evidence of the conduct of a sophisticated multicircuit actor. The area of law most likely to be analyzed on a circuit-by-circuit basis is predatory pricing.[125] As it happens, we have access to extensive internal documentation of an aggressive pricing campaign by a major national firm. This comes about because the firm, the Brown & Williamson Tobacco Corporation, was sued by a competitor, Liggett, in a case that ultimately went to the Supreme Court.[126] In response to Liggett's discovery requests,

---

[124] Similar comments were made in interviews. One antitrust lawyer, discussing the conflict over the "sham" exception to *Noerr* immunity, recalled that he once gave a client very conservative advice "by asking the client to put himself in a witness box and see if the practice could be defended to a jury."

[125] See, for example, 3 Julian O. Von Kalinowski et al, *Antitrust Laws & Trade Regulation* § 21.03[3] (1993) (case law summaries for individual circuits).

[126] *Brooke Group Ltd. v Brown & Williamson Tobacco Corp.*, 509 US 209 (1993). "Brooke Group" is the new corporate name of the entity formerly known as the Liggett Group,

Brown & Williamson disclosed internal documents that were described by the district judge as "more voluminous and detailed than [in] any other reported decision."[127] These documents indicate that the Brown & Williamson executives did consider "legal risks" in formulating their pricing strategy.[128] But nothing in the memoranda even hints that the company considered anything other than a national approach.[129] If, in this setting, intercircuit differences did not affect planning by a national corporation, one must wonder how salient the phenomenon really is even for well-counseled multicircuit actors.

In maritime law, the frequency question yielded mixed results. For four of the conflicts, responses at the high end of the scale outnumbered those at the low end. For the other four, the pattern was reversed. But when we move to the question about the respondents' most recent encounters with the selected conflicts, we find that affirmative answers outnumbered negative answers for all but two of the core conflicts.

Once again, the explanatory comments shed light on the nature of the experiences that underlay these responses. Like their antitrust counterparts, maritime lawyers often spoke of hedging their advice, but, other than that, the pattern of responses was quite different. Only two participants said that they had counseled a

---

and practitioners often refer to the case as *Liggett*. In some sources the petitioner's new name is spelled as "Brook."

[127] *Liggett Group Inc. v Brown & Williamson Tobacco Corp.*, 748 F Supp 344, 354 (MD NC 1990), aff'd, 964 F2d 335 (4th Cir 1992), aff'd, 509 US 209 (1993).

[128] In an internal memorandum that "provide[d] the pros and cons for two potential Brown & Williamson price offerings," the writer listed "[p]ossibly greater legal risks" "as one of the 'Cons' of the 'Black and White' and Private Label Offerings" approach. Joint Appendix at 105, *Brooke Group Ltd. v Brown & Williamson Tobacco Corp.*, 509 US 209 (1993) (No 92-466). A later version of the document referred simply to "Legal risks." Id at 113.

[129] The portion of the "pros and cons" document that elaborates on the "legal risks" is not included in the Supreme Court record. However, the complete document is reproduced in the record on appeal in the Fourth Circuit. The discussion of legal risks is only one sentence in length, and it may not even refer to predatory pricing. See Joint Appendix at A-1707, *Liggett Group Inc. v Brown & Williamson Tobacco Corp.*, 964 F2d 335 (4th Cir 1992) (Nos 90-1851, 90-1854) ("To the extent that Brown & Williamson's offering will be similar to L&M, we risk legal actions by that company."). One might surmise that full discussion of the point was contained in material that was withheld from discovery on the grounds of privilege. However, the record in *Liggett* included "several dozen documents" which Brown & Williamson claimed were subject to attorney-client privilege or work-product protection, but which were "inadvertently" produced during discovery. See *Liggett Group Inc. v Brown & Williamson Tobacco Corp.*, 116 FRD 205, 207 (MD NC 1986) (denying motion to "recall" documents). In any event, I found no further references to the prospect of "legal risks" in any of the later memoranda.

more conservative approach to primary activity. None referred to the risks engendered by a proposed course of conduct. Rather, the maritime lawyers described their handling of claims triggered by accidents that had already occurred. Some said that the conflicts had affected litigation strategy. More often, the lawyers reported that the conflict had influenced their evaluation of a claim or the amount to be paid in settlement.[130]

The comments by the maritime lawyers thus indicate that the conflicts generally had little impact in matters involving the conduct of business. However, the conflicts did sometimes contribute to the difficulty of advising clients when incidents occurred that might be the basis for a legal claim. Further, and in contrast to the antitrust survey, affirmative answers represented a majority of the encounters reported by the participants in the context of counseling. Yet, as noted at the outset, the responses to the frequency question did not bespeak a phenomenon of significant proportions.

To make sense of the data, we must look at the conflicts separately. The key fact is that more than two-thirds of the encounters that elicited affirmative responses to the counseling question were generated by three conflicts—those involving seaman status under the Jones Act, punitive damages for injuries to seamen, and recovery for economic loss. The survey thus provides evidence that those conflicts did make counseling more difficult, albeit not in the context of primary activity. As for the other conflicts, the impact appears to have been relatively minor.

The legal context of the conflicts. As already noted, it will often be difficult to distinguish between the consequences flowing from the existence of a conflict and those generated by other sources of uncertainty in the law. To shed light on this point, we invited the survey respondents to consider the conflict issues in their larger context. Specifically, the lawyers were asked to choose one of five possible characterizations for each of the selected conflicts:

> 1. The conflict is a major source of uncertainty in an
> area of law that would otherwise be clear.

---

[130] The difference between the antitrust and maritime responses probably reflects the different characters of the two kinds of practice: maritime practice is far more litigation-oriented than is antitrust. In statistical year 1994, more than 5,000 maritime cases were filed in the federal courts alone. Antitrust cases—which are exclusively within the jurisdiction of the federal courts—numbered fewer than 700. Director of the Administrative Office of United States Courts, *Annual Report*, table C-2A (1994).

2. The conflict is a major source of uncertainty, but is only one element of an area of law that is lacking in definitive rules.

3. The conflict is a minor source of uncertainty in an area of law that is otherwise clear.

4. The conflict is a minor source of uncertainty in an area of law that is lacking in definitive rules.

5. The conflict issue described does not create any serious legal uncertainty.

In antitrust, the survey evidence indicates that the conflicts generally did not play a central role in creating uncertainty. Only one conflict was viewed as "a major source of uncertainty in an area of law that would otherwise be clear" by more than 25 percent of the respondents; this was the conflict on the proper measure of cost for a predatory pricing claim. Six of the eight core conflicts were characterized by a substantial majority of the respondents as arising in areas of law that were lacking in definitive rules, not areas of law that were otherwise clear. From this we may infer that resolution of the conflicts would not have significantly diminished whatever effects the conflicts had on lawyers' ability to advise clients and conduct litigation.

The pattern of responses in maritime law was quite different. For all but one of the eight core conflicts, a majority of the lawyers said that the area of law would have been clear if it were not for the conflict. Five of the conflicts were viewed as major sources of uncertainty by two-thirds or more of those discussing the particular issue. Included among these were the three conflicts that appear to have made counseling more difficult;[131] the other two were the conflicts on the fire defense and the effect of deviation on limitation of liability under COGSA.

D. SUMMARY AND EVALUATION

The object of the field research was to determine whether conflicts that had the potential for affecting the work of lawyers actually did so. The findings suggest several conclusions.

The most clear-cut finding is that lawyers seldom file suit in

---

[131] These were the conflicts involving seaman status under the Jones Act, punitive damages for injuries to seamen, and recovery for economic loss.

one circuit rather than another in order to take advantage of favorable circuit law or to avoid an unfavorable precedent. Thus, the Federal Courts Study Committee's concern that conflicts "encourage forum shopping among circuits" appears to be misplaced. Further, to the extent that forum shopping signals unfairness or harm to multicircuit actors, those consequences too would not materialize.

This conclusion comports with what we know of litigation practice generally. As Professor Edward A. Purcell has pointed out, litigating in a distant forum can involve "substantial . . . costs, risks, delays, and uncertainties."[132] The disincentives to filing suit in any place but the client's home forum (and that of counsel) are numerous and strong.[133] To overcome these disincentives, a lawyer would have to be convinced, not only that some other circuit's law was substantially more favorable, but that the difference would remain in existence long enough to control the disposition or settlement of the case. That will not happen very often.

Beyond this, the effect of conflicts appears to vary from one area of practice to another. The survey responses indicate that conflicts in the field of antitrust had their greatest impact when lawyers were counseling clients about the possible legal ramifications of a proposed course of conduct. In maritime law, conflicts came into the picture when lawyers were considering litigation or settlement of claims for incidents that had already occurred.

The most difficult task is to determine how often these situations occurred and how serious the consequences were. We do have some clues. To begin with, the number of conflicts that merited full-scale field research is quite small. In four major areas of federal practice, the residue from five Supreme Court Terms after the initial lawyer interviews consisted of only 30 conflicts. Even if every one of those conflicts proved to be a frequent impediment to efficient litigation or effective counseling, I doubt that we would view this as a major problem in the legal system.

In fact, the research suggests a more limited impact. This conclusion emerges most clearly in the survey participants' descrip-

---

[132] Edward A. Purcell, Jr., *Geography as a Litigation Weapon: Consumers, Forum-Selection Clauses, and the Rehnquist Court*, 40 UCLA L Rev 423, 445 (1992).

[133] See id at 445–49 (analyzing "deterrent effects of geography"); see also Michael E. Solimine, *The Quiet Revolution in Personal Jurisdiction*, 73 Tulane L Rev 1, 56 (1998).

tions of their most recent encounters with the core conflicts. We asked separately whether the conflicts affected litigation and whether they affected counseling. In antitrust, only three conflicts elicited more "yes" than "no" answers to either question. In the maritime survey, six conflicts fit this pattern; however, for all but one of those, at least one-third of the lawyers reported that the conflict had had no effect.

It is also important to note that what the maritime numbers represent, as revealed by the explanatory comments, is something quite distant from the concerns articulated by the Federal Courts Study Committee. Of particular relevance, in elaborating on the concept of "harm to multi-circuit actors," the Study Committee spoke of "adverse consequences [that] are felt in the planning and execution of business transactions, or their avoidance."[134] Although the maritime lawyers' comments vary widely in their specificity, what stands out is that very few of them refer to the planning and execution of business transactions at all. Rather, as noted earlier, they deal with liability for incidents that had already occurred.

Why do conflicts that have the potential for affecting the selection of the forum or interfering with planning by multicircuit actors so seldom do so? Drawing on the interviews and practice materials, as well as the more general comments from survey participants, I have identified five factors that tended to diminish the impact of the Study Group conflicts on the work of lawyers.

First, few of the conflicts involved rule choices that were likely to control outcomes. Sometimes the law in one or both circuits contained elements of indeterminacy. Often the conflict issue was only one part of a network of rules that would be brought to bear in advising clients on primary conduct or the possibility of litigation. Seldom would lawyers conclude that the point on which the circuits differed would determine whether a transaction was lawful or a lawsuit winnable.

Second, as hypothesized earlier, lawyers generally view federal decisions as constituting a single body of law. Indeed, practice materials sometimes described the "conflict" cases in a way that signaled harmony rather than inconsistency.

Third, experienced lawyers give less weight to individual prece-

---

[134] Federal Courts Study Committee, Tentative Recommendations for Public Comment (Dec 22, 1989) at 119.

dents and specific holdings than a doctrinally focused perspective might suggest.[135] They are well aware of the techniques that enable a court of appeals panel to distinguish prior cases and of the differences in judicial philosophy that may lead a panel to do so.[136] They are cognizant, too, of the hierarchical structure that allows the Supreme Court to overrule circuit law. Of particular importance, if lawyers perceive a trend or pattern in the actions and rationales of courts nationwide, they will often discount decisions that appear to be aberrations.[137]

Fourth, federal appellate decisions are only one source of the legal rules that lawyers consider in litigation and counseling. In many situations, rules emanating from other sources may be given more weight. For antitrust lawyers, Department of Justice and Federal Trade Commission guidelines may set the bounds of permissible activity. For maritime lawyers, nonpreempted state law may offer support for particular claims irrespective of federal law.[138]

---

[135] This theme was sounded by many of the practitioners I interviewed; it can also be seen in a number of published works. For example, an overview of antitrust counseling by a practicing attorney acknowledges the existence of unresolved conflicts, but goes on to say that "perhaps the only way . . . to counsel clients in the antitrust area is to ignore . . . the results of specific cases and to concentrate instead on five basic factors that have historically been involved in establishing liability under the antitrust laws." Donald E. Knebel, *Antitrust Counseling: The Five Factors of Antitrust Liability*, 9 J Corp L 359, 364 (1984).

[136] As one participant in the maritime survey put it, "While precedent is very important, hope does spring eternal. Bright minds and judicial identity render precedent often secondary." Another participant was more acerbic: "The author of a panel opinion can justify almost any result by disregarding certain established fact, creating evidence, or ignoring established precedent."

[137] As one antitrust lawyer said in responding to our survey, "I find I can advise comfortably as long as I believe any court will continue to strive for decisions that make sense from an economic perspective. In general, 'bad' precedent for my clients is usually distinguishable, and this is a better climate for antitrust than if apparent conflicts were resolved too hastily." A prominent example of an aberrational decision is *Lessig v Tidewater Oil Co.*, 327 F2d 459 (9th Cir 1964), in which the Ninth Circuit adopted a relatively lenient standard for attempted monopolization under Section 2 of the Sherman Act. One of the lawyers I interviewed said, "When *Lessig* was the law I ignored it because I thought it was bad law and wasn't likely to survive long." Other lawyers spoke in a similar vein. Although *Lessig* survived longer than might have been expected, it has now been overruled. See note 140 and accompanying text.

[138] State law plays a role in antitrust counseling as well. One survey participant wrote, "In counseling, it is often difficult to factor in how various state laws will affect the outcome if the matter were litigated. The area of distributor and dealer termination is particularly tricky due to [the] interplay of contract, tort, dealer laws and federal laws on antitrust. In some states like Wisconsin, it is virtually impossible to terminate a dealer due to the Wisconsin Fair Dealership Law even where poor performance is habitual. Even though [Supreme Court decisions have] clarified the federal law, the state laws have kept things very muddy in the dealer termination area."

Finally, legal rules of any kind are only one of the elements that lawyers consider in counseling and litigation, and they are not necessarily the most important. Especially where ongoing relationships are involved, those who operate within the framework of the law may not insist on enforcing the full measure of their legal rights.

E. THE STUDY GROUP CONFLICTS AND THE SUPREME COURT

The picture that emerges from the field research is very different from the one suggested by the Federal Courts Study Committee report. Seldom do unresolved intercircuit conflicts lead to forum shopping. Harm to multicircuit actors is somewhat more common, but still infrequent. What we do find is uncertainty that adds to the difficulty lawyers have in counseling clients.

There will be differences of opinion about how serious a problem this kind of uncertainty presents. Before we can evaluate it, however, we must consider one additional factor: the effect of intervening decisions by the Supreme Court. These decisions can be divided into two groups: those that resolved Study Group conflicts, and those that addressed closely related issues.

Of the 30 conflicts that remained in the field research program after the initial lawyer interviews, six have been resolved.[139] These include two conflicts in antitrust, two in maritime law, and two on ERISA issues.

In antitrust, the Court rejected the Ninth Circuit's *Lessig* rule and established uniformity on the elements of a claim of attempted monopolization.[140] The Court also clarified the "sham" exception to *Noerr* immunity, thus resolving another long-simmering conflict.[141]

The two maritime law decisions also involved issues that had

---

[139] In the explanatory materials we sent to the survey participants, we acknowledged that some of the conflicts had been resolved. We asked the lawyers to describe their experiences as of the time certiorari was denied.

[140] *Spectrum Sports, Inc. v McQuillan*, 506 US 447 (1993). The issue was presented to the Supreme Court in *Mobil Oil Corp. v Blanton*, 471 US 1007 (1986) (White, J, dissenting from denial of certiorari) (Phase II case; RN 806).

[141] See *Professional Real Estate Investors, Inc. v Columbia Pictures Indus.*, 508 US 49 (1993). Among the cases cited by the Supreme Court as illustrating the "inconsistent and contradictory" definitions adopted by the courts of appeals was *South Dakota v Kansas City So. Indus., Inc.*, 880 F2d 40 (8th Cir 1989), cert denied, 493 US 1023 (1990) (RN 450).

been the subject of extensive litigation in the lower courts. The Court resolved the conflict over the validity of an "aid in navigation" requirement for seaman status under the Jones Act.[142] More recently, the Court clarified the circumstances under which a shipowner can be held liable under the LHWCA for injuries arising out of defective stowage.[143]

In the realm of ERISA, the Court took up two issues within a year of the denial of certiorari in the Study Group cases. One decision resolved the conflict over coverage of insurance agents.[144] The second dealt with the interplay of ERISA and the bankruptcy code.[145] Both were described as important by the lawyers whom I interviewed.

In addition to these decisions, Supreme Court rulings on related issues have cast five of the Study Group conflicts in a new light. This phenomenon was particularly significant in antitrust.

The Study Group included two conflicts on the elements of a predatory pricing claim under Section 2 of the Sherman Act. One involved the proper measure of cost; the other dealt with the role of intent. The Supreme Court has not resolved either of these issues; however, in *Brooke Group Ltd. v Brown & Williamson Tobacco Corp.* (the *Liggett* case),[146] the Court made clear that a plaintiff cannot prevail on a predatory pricing claim without showing a dangerous probability that the defendant would recoup its investment in below-cost prices.[147] This recoupment requirement makes the cost and intent issues largely irrelevant in most cases. Indeed, some prominent attorneys view *Liggett* as having delivered the coup de grace to all predatory pricing claims.[148]

Another decision of the same Term, *Hartford Fire Insurance Co.*

---

[142] *McDermott Int'l, Inc. v Wilander*, 498 US 337 (1991).

[143] *Howlett v Birkdale Shipping Co.*, 512 US 92 (1994).

[144] *Nationwide Mut. Ins. Co. v Darden*, 503 US 318 (1992).

[145] *Patterson v Shumate*, 504 US 753 (1992).

[146] 509 US 209 (1993), discussed in text accompanying notes 126–29.

[147] *Brooke Group*, 509 US at 224.

[148] This view has been expressed by both plaintiffs' and defendants' lawyers. See, for example, Kenneth L. Glazer, *Predatory Pricing and Beyond: Life After Brooke Group*, 62 Antitrust L J 605, 605 (1994) (article by counsel for plaintiffs in *Liggett* case); Mark E. Weber, *Developments: Practical Effects of Liggett on Predatory Pricing Litigation*, Antitrust (Fall 1993) at 38 (article by counsel for defendants in American Airlines antitrust suit). The point was also made by several of the lawyers I interviewed.

v California,[149] addressed the extraterritorial reach of the antitrust laws. The problem of extraterritoriality gave rise to one of the Study Group conflicts;[150] however, the Court virtually ignored the case that was the focus of the conflict and, instead, decided *Hartford Fire* on narrow grounds.[151] But the conflict had never played a central role in litigation over extraterritoriality;[152] thus, in that respect, the Court left the law largely where it had been.

The issue of dealer termination as a per se violation of Section 1 of the Sherman Act, which the Court declined to consider in the 1984 Term, presents a more complex picture.[153] The 1988 decision in *Business Electronics Corp. v Sharp Electronics Corp.*[154] went a great distance toward rejecting the application of a per se rule, to the point where one survey participant could describe the issue as "largely moot." Nevertheless, the conflict was selected by more lawyers for detailed discussion than any other in the antitrust survey. Moreover, most of the lawyers who offered explanatory comments gave no indication that they viewed the issue as defunct.[155]

At first blush, it seems rather odd to find so much concern about an issue that had been resolved, at some level of generality, several years before the survey was conducted. A partial explanation may be that some lawyers believe that the Third Circuit, whose rule was rejected in *Business Electronics*, has continued to march to its own drummer.[156] Whether or not that characterization is persua-

---

[149] 509 US 764 (1993).

[150] The issue was presented to the Supreme Court in *Timberlane Lumber Co. v Bank of America*, 749 F2d 1378 (9th Cir 1984), cert denied, 472 US 1032 (1985) (Phase II case; RN 844).

[151] See Andreas F. Lowenfeld, *Conflict, Balancing of Interests, and the Exercise of Jurisdiction to Prescribe: Reflections on the Insurance Antitrust Case*, 89 Am J Intl L 42, 45 (1995).

[152] See Hellman, *By Precedent Unbound* at 788 (cited in note 8).

[153] The Study Group case was *Malley-Duff & Associates, Inc. v Crown Life Insurance Co.*, 734 F2d 133 (3d Cir), cert denied as *Agency Holding Corp. v Malley-Duff & Associates, Inc.*, 469 US 1072 (1984) (Phase II case; RN 766).

[154] 485 US 717 (1988).

[155] As a general matter, I do not think the lawyers adhered strictly to our request that they discuss their experience with the conflicts as of the time certiorari was denied. Perhaps this was just as well.

[156] Among the cases cited in support of this view is *Alvord-Polk, Inc. v F. Schumacher & Co.*, 37 F3d 996 (3d Cir 1994), cert denied, 514 US 1063 (1995). One CLE author described Alvord-Polk as "completely contrary to the trend indicated by Supreme Court opinions." Alan H. Silberman, *Vertical Price, Customer and Territorial Limitations*, in *36th Annual Antitrust Institute* (Practicing Law Institute, 1995), vol 1 at 727.

sive, the lawyers' responses suggest two other conclusions. First, the conflict that the survey respondents were discussing is not the same conflict that the Supreme Court declined to resolve in the 1984 Term. The issue may be framed in similar language, but beneath that similarity lie important differences in the legal propositions that are taken as given and those that are viewed as litigable. Second, Supreme Court decisions that resolve conflicts may end up reshaping lines of argument or advice rather than placing an issue outside the range of uncertainty.

Maritime law offers an example of what might be regarded as a correlative phenomenon. The conflict is the one over the availability of punitive damages for injuries suffered by seamen.[157] The Supreme Court has never addressed that issue; however, in *Miles v Apex Marine Corp.*,[158] the Court held that the damages recoverable in a general maritime cause of action for the wrongful death of a seaman do not include either loss of society or lost future earnings. Although *Miles* said nothing about the conflict issue,[159] every court of appeals to consider the question has now concluded that, under the analysis in *Miles*, punitive damages may not be recovered for injuries suffered by seamen.[160] These courts include the Fifth Circuit, whose decision in *Complaint of Merry Shipping*[161] was the leading pre-*Miles* authority supporting the availability of punitive damages.[162] Moreover, the Louisiana appellate court, whose position was cited by several survey respondents as contrary to that of the Fifth Circuit,[163] has also overruled its precedent and held that punitive damages are unavailable.[164] Thus, it seems un-

---

[157] The issue was presented to the Court in the 1989 Term. See *McMonagle v Northeast Women's Center, Inc.*, 493 US 901, 902 (1989) (White, J, dissenting from denial of certiorari) (citing *Kidd v F/V St. Patrick*, 493 US 871 (1989), denying cert to 816 F2d 1345 (9th Cir 1987) (RN 101)).

[158] 498 US 19 (1990).

[159] The only mention of punitive damages comes in the Court's statement of the facts, which notes that the district court granted the defendant's motion to strike the claim for punitive damages. See id at 22.

[160] See, for example, *Horsley v Mobil Oil Corp.*, 15 F3d 200, 203 (1st Cir 1994).

[161] 650 F2d 622 (1981).

[162] In *Guevara v Maritime Overseas Corp.*, 59 F3d 1496, 1507 (5th Cir 1995) (en banc), the court said, "After *Miles*, it is clear that *Merry Shipping* has been effectively overruled."

[163] One lawyer said, "Plaintiffs routinely file in state court in Louisiana, where *Miles v Apex* has been interpreted in a more limited fashion."

[164] See *Bridgett v Odeco, Inc.*, 646 So2d 1249 (La App 1994). The court noted that the "anomalous interpretations of *Miles*" in prior Louisiana cases served "no purpose other than

likely that lawyers in the future will continue to experience the difficulties reported by so many survey respondents in counseling on this issue, even though no nationally binding precedent explicitly resolves it.[165]

F. RECAPITULATION

Of the 30 conflicts that remained for field research after the initial attorney interviews, 10 have been significantly affected by intervening Supreme Court decisions. Six or seven have been resolved by decisions squarely addressing the conflict issue.[166] One conflict has been eliminated by circuit overruling in light of a Supreme Court decision on a related issue.[167] Two have been made largely irrelevant by the Court's endorsement of a high hurdle for the underlying cause of action.[168] In short, 10 of the conflicts no longer exist in anything resembling the form that they took at the time the Court denied review. Included in this group are several of the conflicts that most often affected the work of the lawyers who participated in the survey.[169]

At the least, this history cautions against interpreting the survey responses as evidence that unresolved intercircuit conflicts constitute a problem of major proportions in the practice of law. But it also suggests a broader point about conflicts, one that is best discussed as part of an overall assessment of the implications of the research.

IV. IMPLICATIONS

One mystery has always attended the debate over "national appellate capacity" generally and the "problem" of unresolved

---

to encourage plaintiffs to engineer arguments in favor of invoking jurisdiction in [Louisiana] courts." Id at 1254. *Bridgett* was reaffirmed in *Brodtmann v Duke*, 708 So2d 447, 452–53 (La App 1998).

[165] Pockets of uncertainty may remain on related issues. See, for example, *CEH, Inc. v F/V Seafarer*, 70 F3d 694, 701–02 (1st Cir 1995) (allowing punitive damages "for reckless or willful destruction of property"; distinguishing cases involving personal injuries to seamen).

[166] The debatable case is *Business Electronics*.

[167] This is the conflict on the availability of punitive damages for injuries to seamen.

[168] These are the conflicts on predatory pricing in antitrust.

[169] The major exception is the conflict over recovery for economic loss in admiralty. See Hellman, *By Precedent Unbound* at 791 (cited in note 8).

conflicts in particular. If the Supreme Court has largely given up on maintaining uniformity in the federal system[170] and conflicts are accumulating faster than they are being resolved,[171] why is there no outcry from the rank-and-file of the bench and bar? One possible explanation, favored by some academics, is that lawyers prefer a regime of uncertainty because it "generates a huge business" for them and their firms.[172] But even if that is true for some litigation-oriented practitioners, surely it does not explain the indifference of the many lawyers who engage primarily in counseling or of the busy trial judges confronted with motions and pleadings that require immediate decision.

The answer suggested by this study is that the problem of unresolved conflicts exists only if you look for it—and look for it in a certain way. If you concentrate your attention on individual court of appeals decisions that create conflicts and on individual denials of certiorari in conflict cases, you will see "a judicial 'darkling plain' where ignorant armies [clash] by night."[173] But if you look at the conflict issues over a period of time and in context, you will find, if not certitude, a landscape in which courts build upon and reexamine one another's decisions in the untidy but constructive tradition of the common law.

The field research suggests a broader point. The very language that we use to talk about conflicts may convey a misleading picture of what is going on. We say that an "issue" gives rise to a "conflict" that the Supreme Court "resolves" (or does not "resolve"). This language implies that the dimensions of the "issue" remain unchanged from the first decision through consideration by two or more courts of appeals and ultimate resolution by the Supreme Court. The implication is probably correct when the issue is binary and discrete, like the one involved in *United States v Cartwright*.[174]

---

[170] See Kenneth W. Starr, *The Supreme Court and the Federal Judicial System*, 42 Case Western L Rev 1209, 1212 (1992).

[171] See note 10 and accompanying text.

[172] See Panel Discussion I, 38 SC L Rev 463, 484 (1987) (remarks of Prof. Paul M. Bator).

[173] See *Northern Pipeline Construction Co. v Marathon Pipe Line Co.*, 458 US 50, 91 (Rehnquist, J, concurring). Justice Rehnquist was of course quoting Matthew Arnold's "Dover Beach": "[F]or the world . . . /Hath really neither joy, nor love, nor light,/ Nor certitude, nor peace, nor help for pain;/ And we are here as on a darkling plain/Swept with confused alarms of struggle and flight,/ Where ignorant armies clash by night."

[174] 411 US 546 (1973). The question in *Cartwright* was whether mutual fund shares in a decedent's estate were to be valued at the bid price or the asked price. No one argued that

For other issues, however, the reality will not be so straightforward. Judges and lawyers may continue to frame the issue in the same words, but beneath the verbal identity may lie important differences in the propositions that are accepted as part of the legal landscape and those that are viewed as litigable. Similarly, when the Supreme Court does intervene, its decision may end up reshaping the framework for litigation and counseling about an issue rather than closing a chapter in the particular area of the law.[175]

The conflict on dealer termination under Section 1 of the Sherman Act provides a good example.[176] What was the "issue" that gave rise to the conflict? Did the Supreme Court resolve it in the *Business Electronics* case? If so, why is there so much continued uncertainty about the law governing the termination of price-cutting dealers and distributors? If not, how could the Supreme Court come so close and not resolve a matter of so much importance to a large segment of the economy?

Perhaps these are the wrong questions. Perhaps we should simply recognize that the further we move from *Cartwright*-type conflicts, the more likely it is that a Supreme Court decision will recast the framework for litigation and counseling about an issue rather than relegate the issue to the realm of the defunct. By the same token, the Court's failure to resolve such conflicts will add only marginally to the uncertainty that is inherent in our system of precedent.

In this light, there is a certain irony in Justice Scalia's comments about the cases in which the Supreme Court denied review over Justice White's dissent. Justice Scalia said, "If it's really an important issue, it's going to be back . . . ."[177] But when "it" comes

---

there were any other possibilities. The question thus involved a choice between two perfected rules—rules that required for their application no more than a finding of historical fact. The rules were self-contained in operation and dispositive in all disputes in which the issue arose. See Hellman, *By Precedent Unbound* at 760–61 (cited in note 8).

[175] This pattern can be viewed as a departure from the traditional model of lawmaking by appellate courts. In that model, the law "works itself pure from case to case." Graham Hughes, *Are Justices Just?* New York Review of Books (Nov 19, 1981) at 41, 42 (quoting Lord Mansfield on the common law); see Hellman, 23 Ariz St L J at 917 and n 13 (cited in note 78). In the situation described in the text, the law never "works itself pure"; rather, uncertain boundaries and gray areas characterize the legal landscape as long the issue, in some form, remains alive. In future work I shall explore the origins and implications of this development.

[176] See text accompanying notes 153–56.

[177] See text accompanying note 34.

back, it may not be quite the same issue. And the Court may deny
review once again, implicitly agreeing with Justice Brandeis that
sometimes "the most important thing we do is not doing."[178]

---

[178] Conversations Between L.D.B. and F.F. [Louis D. Brandeis and Felix Frankfurter],
Typescript at 15 (conversation of June 23, 1923), in *The Louis Dembitz Brandeis Papers, Part
II: United States Supreme Court, October Terms, 1932–1938*, Reel 33, Frame 464 (University
Publications of America microfilm collection). See also Alexander M. Bickel, *The Unpub-
lished Opinions of Mr. Justice Brandeis* 17 (Chicago, 1957) (quoting Brandeis-Frankfurter
Conversations). Bickel does not give the context of the remark. As recorded in Frankfurter's
notes, Brandeis was talking about his colleagues' indifference to issues of federal jurisdiction.
Justice Holmes, he said, "likes to decide cases where interesting questions are raised." But
"Holmes is beginning to learn—intellectually he is beginning to appreciate our responsibility, though not emotionally. I tell him, 'the most important thing we do is not doing.' "

MICHAEL J. KLARMAN

THE PLESSY ERA

The Supreme Court confronted four principal issues involving
race and the Constitution in the period from 1895 to 1910—the
Plessy era, as I shall call it. First, on two separate occasions, the
Court sustained the constitutionality of state-imposed racial segregation. *Plessy v Ferguson*[1] raised the issue of state-mandated segregation in the context of railroad transportation and *Berea College
v Kentucky*[2] in the context of private higher education. Second, the
Court heard numerous challenges to southern state schemes for
disfranchising their black citizens. In several cases the Court declined to reach the substantive merits of the dispute, rejecting the
discrimination claim on procedural grounds such as mootness. In
other disfranchisement cases, the Court offered narrow interpretations of the scope of the Fifteenth Amendment, holding that it
forbade none of the following: facially neutral legislation adopted
for a racially discriminatory purpose, open-ended grants of discretion to voter registrars that created ample opportunity for racial
discrimination in administration, or racially motivated interfer-

Michael J. Klarman is James Monroe Professor of Law & F. Palmer Weber Research
Professor of Civil Liberties and Human Rights, University of Virginia School of Law.

AUTHOR'S NOTE: This article, in revised form, will appear as chapter 1 of my book, provi-
sionally entitled *Neither Hero nor Villain: The Supreme Court, Race, and the Constitution in
the Twentieth Century* (Oxford University Press). I am grateful to Barry Cushman, Pam
Karlan, J. Morgan Kousser, Andrew Kull, Andrew Schroeder, and Bill Stuntz for helpful comments on an earlier draft. I also benefited from discussions at a faculty workshop
at the University of Texas School of Law and at the 1998 University of Virginia Constitutional Law conference. Andrew Schroeder provided outstanding research assistance. Comments from readers would be welcomed and should be directed to mklarman@lawl.law.
Virginia.edu.

[1] 163 US 537 (1896).
[2] 211 US 45 (1908).

ences with the right to vote by private individuals. In one extraordinary decision, *Giles v Harris*,[3] the Court candidly conceded that even if southern disfranchisement devices were unconstitutional, the Court was powerless to provide adequate remedies for the violation.

Third, the Court heard about ten cases in which southern black defendants sought to overturn their criminal convictions on the ground that members of their race had been systematically excluded from jury service. In these decisions the Justices reaffirmed their ruling in *Strauder v West Virginia*[4] that excluding blacks from juries because of their race, either by statute or through the deliberate exercise of administrative discretion, violated the Fourteenth Amendment. Yet nearly all of these cases rejected the constitutional challenge, imposing stringent standards of proof on defendants alleging race discrimination in jury selection and announcing a broad rule of deference to state court findings on the question of discrimination. Only on the rare occasions when state officials admitted the deliberate exclusion of blacks from juries or when state courts refused black defendants the opportunity to present evidence of race discrimination in jury selection did the Court find a constitutional violation and reverse the conviction. Fourth and finally, the Court in *Cumming v Richmond County Board of Education*[5] rejected a Fourteenth Amendment challenge to a scheme of separate and *un*equal in education on the ground that inequality was not unreasonable in light of the circumstances.

Recent legal scholarship tends to vilify the Court for its *Plessy*-era performance and especially for the *Plessy* decision itself. Commentators have called *Plessy* "ridiculous and shameful," "racist and repressive," and a "catastrophe." The principal purpose of this article is to shed light on why the *Plessy*-era Justices did what they did. One cannot begin to understand the Court's racist decisions without first understanding the racist times in which they were rendered. Indeed, I intend to go so far as to suggest that, given the background state of race relations at the turn of the century and the limited capacity of the Supreme Court generally to frustrate dominant public opinion, it may be implausible to think that

---

[3] 189 US 475 (1903).

[4] 100 US 303 (1880).

[5] 175 US 528 (1899).

the Justices realistically could have reached different results in these cases. Most people understand that the Supreme Court was not about to protect women's rights before the rise of the women's movement or gay rights before the rise of the gay rights movement. I want to suggest, similarly, that it may be fanciful to expect the Justices to have defended black civil rights when racial attitudes and practices were as abysmal as they were at the turn of the century.[6]

This article proceeds on the basis of certain methodological assumptions, the validity of which I hope to verify along the way. First, the Constitution frequently is indeterminate on pressing questions of social policy. For example, the Equal Protection Clause does not resolve whether racial segregation—separate but *equal*—is permissible, or indeed even whether racial classifications should be treated differently than others. Nor, as we shall see, did the original understanding of the Fourteenth Amendment or precedent construing it provide much guidance for the Court when confronting the various racial issues presented during the *Plessy* period. Moreover, to the extent these traditional sources of constitutional law did provide insight, they generally pointed in the direction of rejecting the civil rights claim. It is not my contention that the constitutional text or other legal sources are never determinate. For example, the Fifteenth Amendment expressly forbids disfranchisement based on race. Southern states understood this and thus almost universally refrained from adopting explicit racial qualifications on the suffrage, for fear that courts would invalidate them. However, there was no similar constitutional clarity with regard to the race issues that actually were litigated in the Supreme Court during the *Plessy* era.[7]

---

[6] Michael J. Perry, *The Constitution in the Courts: Law or Politics?* 145 (1994) (first quotation); Judith Baer, *Equality Under the Constitution: Reclaiming the Fourteenth Amendment* 112 (1983) (second quotation); Paul Oberst, *The Strange Career of Plessy v. Ferguson*, 15 Ariz L Rev 389, 417 (1973) (third quotation). I have sought to describe, explain, and criticize this tendency to ahistorically condemn some of the Court's past failures to defend civil rights and civil liberties in Michael J. Klarman, *Rethinking the Civil Rights and Civil Liberties Revolutions*, 82 Va L Rev 1 (1996).

[7] I have elaborated on this argument about the Constitution's general indeterminacy and provided numerous examples in Michael J. Klarman, *Fidelity, Indeterminacy and the Problem of Constitutional Evil*, 65 Fordham L Rev 1739 (1997). On the other hand, I have suggested that it was the relative clarity of the constitutional violations that enabled the Court to render several civil rights victories during the Progressive era, when race relations reached a post–Civil War nadir. See Michael J. Klarman, *Race and the Court in the Progressive Era*, 51 Vand L Rev 881 (1998).

Second, in light of the general indeterminacy of traditional legal sources, the Court's constitutional interpretations are likely to reflect the personal values of the Justices. Those values, in turn, are likely to be broadly reflective of popular opinion, because the Justices are part of contemporary culture. This is not to say, of course, that the Court precisely mirrors public opinion; it plainly does not. Court decisions invalidating school prayer or criminal prohibitions on flag burning, as well as protecting the procedural rights of criminal defendants, plainly have contravened majority opinion. Yet these countermajoritarian decisions themselves simultaneously reveal the limits of the potential gap between public opinion and judicial outcomes. The Court did not invalidate school prayer until after the demise of the nation's unofficial Protestant establishment. The Court did not revolutionize criminal procedure until after the civil rights revolution, the War on Poverty, and revulsion against totalitarian excesses had altered popular attitudes toward criminal defendants. And the Court did not invalidate flag burning prohibitions until after a dramatic post–World War II transformation in popular conceptions of free speech.[8]

Moreover, many of the Court's most countermajoritarian decisions have involved issues upon which a gap exists between elite opinion, as represented by the Justices, and mass opinion, as represented in legislation. This was true, for example, about both school prayer and flag burning. It also was true about the Court's race decisions from roughly World War II until 1970. However, during the *Plessy* era, there was no evident disparity between elite and popular attitudes on issues like racial segregation, black disfranchisement, and black jury service. Such a gap may have existed on issues like lynching, but not on the race questions that became subjects of Supreme Court litigation.[9]

---

[8] For scholarship embracing the general conception of judicial review described in this paragraph, see Robert G. McCloskey, *The American Supreme Court* (2d ed. 1994); Robert A. Dahl, *Decision-Making in a Democracy: The Supreme Court as a National Policy-Maker*, 6 J Pub L 279 (1957); Barry Friedman, *Dialogue and Judicial Review*, 91 Mich L Rev 577 (1993); Girardeau A. Spann, *Pure Politics*, 88 Mich L Rev 1971 (1990). See also Gerald N. Rosenberg, *The Hollow Hope: Can Courts Bring About Social Change?* (1991). The particular examples noted in the text are considered at some length in Klarman, 82 Va L Rev (cited in note 6).

[9] This paragraph borrows from my discussion of the culturally elite bias of judicial review in Michael J. Klarman, *What's So Great About Constitutionalism?* 93 Nw U L Rev 145, 189–91 (1998).

This article takes no normative stand on how we ought to regard public actors who performed egregiously bad deeds that were consistent with the general tenor of their times. My goal, rather, is to render more explicable to a later generation the race decisions of the *Plessy* era—decisions that appear virtually unfathomable unless one has an intimate familiarity with their background racial context. Thus, it is necessary to begin this exploration of the Constitution and race in the *Plessy* era by canvasing the state of American race relations at the turn of the century. Without understanding this broader context, we cannot hope to appreciate why the Justices behaved as they did during this period, rejecting constitutional challenges to segregation, disfranchisement, race-based jury exclusion, and separate and *un*equal.

I. THE EXTRALEGAL CONTEXT

The decade of Reconstruction that followed the Civil War witnessed extraordinary changes in American racial attitudes and practices. Slavery was abolished. The 1866 Civil Rights Act and the Fourteenth Amendment guaranteed to blacks protection in their basic civil rights. The Reconstruction Act of 1867 and the Fifteenth Amendment enfranchised blacks for the first time in most of the nation. Additional civil rights legislation enacted in the 1870s solidified protection for the suffrage, as well as forbidding race discrimination in jury selection and guaranteeing blacks equal rights of access to common carriers and public accommodations. In the South, blacks turned out to vote in extraordinary numbers, returning hundreds of black officeholders. Large numbers of blacks served on southern juries; local streetcar transportation generally was desegregated; and for the first time blacks were extended the benefits of the public school system. Similar changes also took place in northern racial practices during Reconstruction. In most states, blacks voted for the first time. Restrictions on black testimony in court were removed. Public education was extended to blacks in states that previously had excluded them, and several states forbade racial segregation in public schools.

The official end to Reconstruction in the mid-1870s did not suddenly eradicate the advances of the preceding decade. Republican presidents and congressmen remained committed to the protection of black voting rights, though northern opinion was increasingly divided on the efficacy of federal intervention, and the use of military force to protect black suffrage was no longer politically practicable. Prominent southern Democrats like Wade Hampton of South Carolina and L. Q. C. Lamar of Mississippi continued to endorse the legitimacy of black political participation and vouchsafed its protection under their Redeemer governments.[10] With blacks still voting in substantial numbers, black officeholding persisted well past the end of Reconstruction, in some states not peaking until the 1880s. Blacks continued to serve on southern juries, at least through the 1880s and sometimes into the 1890s, though in smaller numbers than during Reconstruction. Some racial integration persisted in southern public accommodations, and more in railroad travel. While public schools remained completely segregated, the enormous racial disparities that would later characterize public spending on education had not yet begun to develop by the early 1880s.[11]

---

[10] C. Vann Woodward, *Origins of the New South 1877–1913* at 78–81, 209, 321 (1951); Eric Anderson, *Race and Politics in North Carolina 1872–1901: The Black Second* 130, 137, 159, 319–20 (1981); George Brown Tindall, *South Carolina Negroes 1877–1900* at 12, 20–30, 38–39, 61–64, 66–67 (1952); Vernon Lane Wharton, *The Negro in Mississippi 1865–1890* at 181, 202–03 (1947); Joseph H. Cartwright, *Triumph of Jim Crow: Tennessee Race Relations in the 1880s* at 49–50 (1976); Stephen Cresswell, *Multi-Party Politics in Mississippi, 1877–1902* at 17, 89 (1995); Roger A. Fischer, *The Segregation Struggle in Louisiana 1862–1877* at 134–35 (1974); Paul Lewinson, *Race, Class, and Party: A History of Negro Suffrage and White Politics in the South* 37–39 (1932).

[11] Most historians have followed Woodward in portraying a dramatic deterioration in southern race relations beginning in the late 1880s. C. Vann Woodward, *The Strange Career of Jim Crow* 32–44, 65–65 (3d rev ed 1974); Sheldon Hackney, *Populism to Progressivism in Alabama* 180–84 (1969); Cartwright, *Tennessee Race Relations* at 175–76, 198 (cited in note 10); Tindall, *South Carolina Negroes* at 306 (cited in note 10); Dale A. Somers, *Black and White in New Orleans: A Study in Urban Race Relations*, 40 J Southern Hist 19, 20–21 (1974); George C. Wright, *Life Behind a Veil: Blacks in Louisville, Kentucky 1865–1930* at 7, 50–51 (1985); Charles E. Wynes, *Race Relations in Virginia 1870–1902* at 149 (1961); Anderson, *North Carolina* at ix, 331–32 (cited in note 10); Fischer, *Segregation Struggle in Louisiana* at 134–36 (cited in note 10); Henry C. Dephloff and Robert R. Jones, *Race Relations in Louisiana, 1877–98*, 9 La Hist 301, 322 (1968). Dissenters from the Woodward thesis have emphasized greater continuity in southern racial practices, denying the existence of a more permissive environment from which relations could deteriorate. Howard N. Rabinowitz, *Race Relations in the Urban South, 1865–1890* passim, esp. 331–34 (1978); Joel Williamson, *After Slavery: The Negro in South Carolina During Reconstruction, 1861–1877* at ch 10 (1965); John W. Cell, *The Highest Stage of White Supremacy: The Origins of Segregation in South Africa and the American South* ch 4 (1982); Neil McMillen, *Dark Journey: Black Mississippians in the Age of Jim Crow* 3–5 (1989). Yet even Woodward's critics, while accusing him of painting too rosy a picture of the post-Reconstruction decade, concede that "something highly significant happened in southern race relations during the 1890s." Howard N. Rabinowitz, *More Than the Woodward Thesis: Assessing "The Strange Career of Jim Crow,"* 75 J Am Hist 842, 849 (1989). See also William Cohen, *At Freedom's Edge: Black Mobility and the Southern White Quest for Racial Control 1861–1915* at 202, 246 (1991); C. Vann Woodward, *"Strange Career" Critics: Long May They Persevere,* 75 J Am Hist 857, 862 (1989).

By the late 1880s southern race relations had commenced a long downward spiral. The annual number of black lynchings rose dramatically, peaking early in the 1890s. The same Democratic politicians who in the early 1880s had actively campaigned for the black vote were by the 1890s demanding black disfranchisement and white political supremacy. Beginning around 1890, southern states adopted legal measures such as poll taxes and literacy tests to supplement the substantial de facto disfranchisement of blacks already accomplished through violence and fraud. Integration in railroad travel became less prevalent through the 1880s, and beginning in 1887 southern states enacted statutes mandating segregation. Blacks largely had disappeared from southern juries by around 1890, while black political officeholders also declined in number until finally being eliminated around the turn of the century. Racial disparities in public spending on education first became significant in the 1890s and then became enormous in the first decades of the twentieth century. Southern state legislatures in the 1890s and early 1900s enacted a new generation of more restrictive labor control measures aimed at coercing black agricultural labor. Racial practices likewise deteriorated in settings untouched by formal legal enactment. For example, New Orleans in the 1880s had witnessed interracial labor solidarity on the docks and in organizations like the Knights of Labor, an interracial clientele among black and white prostitutes, interracial boxing matches and baseball games, as well as black jockeys at the horse races. Virtually all of this integration had disappeared by the early to mid-1890s.[12]

The perception of contemporary southern blacks that race relations were deteriorating was evidenced by a renewed interest in African migration in the 1890s as well as the growing popularity of separate black cities. The rising acceptance among southern blacks of Booker T. Washington's philosophy of racial accommo-

---

[12] W. Fitzhugh Brundage, *Lynching in the New South: Georgia and Virginia, 1880–1930* at 7–8 (1993); Tindall, *South Carolina Negroes* at ch 12 (cited in note 10); Anderson, *North Carolina* at 146, 245–47, 252–79 (cited in note 10); Cartwright, *Tennessee Race Relations* at 52, 60 (cited in note 10); Cohen, *Freedom's Edge* at 211 table 9, 246 (cited in note 11); Daniel A. Novak, *The Wheel of Servitude: Black Forced Labor After Slavery* 36 (1978); James McPherson, *The Abolitionist Legacy: From Reconstruction to the NAACP* 138, 300–06 (1975); Somers, 40 J Southern Hist (cited in note 11); Fischer, *Segregation Struggle in Louisiana* at 148–51 (cited in note 10); Wright, *Blacks in Louisville* at 50, 59–62, 70–74 (cited in note 11); Wharton, *Negro in Mississippi* at 230–33 (cited in note 11); sources cited in notes 34–35, 84–89, 121, 143.

dationism likewise testified to contemporary perceptions of deterioration. It was only the absence of genuine alternatives that inclined so many southern black leaders temporarily to acquiesce in segregation and disfranchisement, focusing their energies instead on economic advance and industrial education. It was thought preferable to "adopt a policy of self-effacement" than to incite white violence, as in the murderous race riots that ensued after white supremacy political campaigns in Wilmington, North Carolina, in 1898 and in Atlanta in 1906.[13]

The causes of this notable worsening of race relations can be divided into internal and external factors. The former altered the inclinations of white southerners with regard to their racial practices. The latter relaxed outside constraints on those practices, thus freeing the white South to implement racial policies that might have been preferred all along but would have been too risky to adopt when national intervention remained possible.[14]

Let us consider internal factors first. Economic hard times for southern farmers in the 1880s led to the rise of protest movements, most notably the Farmers' Alliance. By 1890 the Alliance was beginning to translate its enormous membership into political power, first within the Democratic Party, and then in the creation of a Populist Party, which played an important role in many southern

---

[13] Kelly Miller, *A Negro's View*, 60 Outlook 1059, 1060 (Dec 31, 1898) (quotation); August Meier, *Negro Thought in America 1880–1915* at 100–18, 146–48, 218–19 (1963); McMillen, *Dark Journey* at 186–90 (cited in note 11); John Dittmer, *Black Georgia in the Progressive Era 1900–1920* at 168–69, 172, 175–79 (1977); August Meier and Elliot Rudwick, *Along the Color Line: Explorations in the Black Experience* ch 9 (1976); Woodward, *New South* at 350, 355–60 (cited in note 10); McPherson, *Abolitionist Legacy* at ch 19 (cited in note 12). It is revealing how many southern black leaders, including Washington, were prepared to endorse literacy tests and property qualifications, so long as fairly enforced. Their perception plainly was that, in light of existing circumstances, fairly enforced suffrage restrictions, even though certain to greatly reduce black suffrage, were the best available option. Woodward, *New South* at 337–38 (cited in note 10); August Meier, *Negro Thought* at 38–40, 109, 173, 196, 214–15; William Alexander Mabry, *Disfranchisement of the Negro in Mississippi*, 4 J Southern Hist 318, 329 (1938); Edward L. Ayers, *The Promise of the New South: Life After Reconstruction* 289 (1992); McMillen, *Dark Journey* at 50–51 (cited in note 11). In his private actions, as opposed to his public statements, Washington was more inclined to challenge segregation, disfranchisement, and other denials of black civil and political rights. Meier, *Negro Thought* at 111–14.

[14] Historians disagree about the relative importance of internal and external causes for changes in racial attitudes and practices around the turn of the century. Woodward emphasizes both, while Rabinowitz focuses on the removal of external constraints. Woodward, *New South* at chs 8, 9, 12 (cited in note 10); Woodward, *Jim Crow* at 69–82 (cited in note 11); Rabinowitz, *Urban South* at 135–36, 167 (cited in note 11); Howard N. Rabinowitz, *The First New South 1865–1920* at 140 (1992).

elections between 1892 and 1896. The rising political power of poor white farmers did not bode well for southern blacks, since the former's precarious social and economic status inclined them toward adopting measures that highlighted their supposed racial superiority. More affluent, higher status whites often were more concerned with class than with race demarcations, and frequently had displayed paternalistic attitudes toward blacks that were, in part, a relic of slavery days. These racial paternalists, men like Lamar and Hampton, had been genuinely committed to protecting (qualified) black rights in their states' post-Reconstruction governments. By the 1890s, however, these men were being increasingly supplanted by racial demagogues who campaigned for unmitigated white supremacy—men like Pitchfork Ben Tillman of South Carolina and James Vardaman of Mississippi.[15]

Moreover, the political empowerment of lower-class whites impelled the conservative paternalists to invoke the theme of "negro domination" as a stratagem for disrupting prospective economic and political alliances between lower-class blacks and whites. Populists in some southern states made earnest appeals to black voters in their efforts to unseat the Democrats from power. In North Carolina mostly white Populists successfully fused with mostly black Republicans to seize control of the state government in the mid-1890s. Even where such interracial alliances were unrealistic, though, Democratic appeals to race loyalty and to memories of "black domination" under Reconstruction proved an effective strategy for coercing white political unity within the Democratic Party.[16]

---

[15] Woodward, *New South* at 185–204, 209–11, 235–62 (cited in note 10); Ayers, *New South* at chs 9–10 (cited in note 13); Cresswell, *Multi-Party Politics* at chs 4–5 (cited in note 10); Lewinson, *Race, Class, Party* at ch 4 (cited in note 10); Anderson, *North Carolina* at 171–72, 193 (cited in note 10); George M. Fredrickson, *The Black Image in the White Mind: The Debate on Afro-American Character and Destiny 1817–1914* at 90–92, 226, 262 (1971); Ray Stannard Baker, *Following the Color Line: American Negro Citizenship in the Progressive Era* 84, 87, 252 (1908); Tindall, *South Carolina Negroes* at 20–21, 306 (cited in note 10); Woodward, *Jim Crow* at 48–50 (cited in note 11); Rabinowitz, *First New South* at 109, 118, 169–70 (cited in note 14); Cartwright, *Tennessee Race Relations* at 166–68 (cited in note 10).

[16] Anderson, *North Carolina* at 145, 214–17, 222, 239, 252–79 (cited in note 10); Greg Cantrell and D. Scott Barton, *Texas Populists and the Failure of Biracial Politics*, 55 J Southern Hist 659, 683 (1989); Fredrickson, *Black Image* at 202–03, 264, 266 (cited in note 15); Lawrence C. Goodwyn, *Populist Dreams and Negro Rights: East Texas as a Case Study*, 76 Am Hist Rev 1435, 1447 (1971); Frederic D. Ogden, *The Poll Tax in the South* 11, 17 (1958); Woodward, *Jim Crow* at 76–80 (cited in note 11); Roger L. Hart, *Redeemers, Bourbons, and Populists: Tennessee 1870–1896* at 194–95 (1975); note 89.

The inclination of southern whites to further subordinate blacks was a necessary, but not a sufficient, condition for the deterioration in American race relations that began in the 1890s. Without northern acquiescence, southern racial practices could not have become as oppressive as they did. Several factors explain the diminishing northern commitment to racial equality and the growing willingness to extend the South a free hand in ordering its race relations.

First, a significant increase in southern black migration to the North in the 1890s apparently induced many northern whites to adopt characteristically southern racial attitudes. Fears among northern whites of such a black exodus from the South had been widespread at the time of the Civil War, but diminished after a sizable black migration in the 1860s tapered off in the 1870s and 1880s. However, black migration northward increased appreciably in the 1890s. Whereas southern black migration to the North had been about 49,000 in the 1870s and 62,000 in the 1880s, it rose to roughly 132,000 in the 1890s and 143,000 in the 1900s. This growing black presence in northern states brought increased discrimination in public accommodations, occasional efforts to introduce racial segregation into the public schools, a rash of black lynchings, and a general hardening of racial attitudes. Even former bastions of abolitionism and racial egalitarianism like Boston or Cleveland witnessed increasing racial prejudice and discrimination in the 1890s.[17]

Another factor inclining northern whites toward southern racial practices was the immigration of millions of southern and eastern Europeans, beginning in the 1880s and accelerating dramatically around 1900. Northerners concerned about the dilution of

---

[17] Cohen, *Freedom's Edge* at 92–93 (cited in note 11); Allan H. Spear, *Black Chicago: The Making of a Negro Ghetto 1890–1920* at 7–8, 12 table 1, 23, 44–45, 201 (1967); Gilbert Osofsky, *Harlem: The Making of a Ghetto* 35, 40–42 (1963); McPherson, *Abolitionist Legacy* at 309–11 (cited in note 12); David A. Gerber, *Black Ohio and the Color Line, 1860–1915* at 28–29, 249–63, 276, 295 (1976); Emma Lou Thornbrough, *The Negro in Indiana Before 1900: A Study of a Minority* 184–91, 206, 207 n 2, 265, 279–82, 332, 392 (1957); David M. Katzman, *Before the Ghetto: Black Detroit in the Nineteenth Century* 93 (1973); Kenneth Kusmer, *A Ghetto Takes Shape: Black Cleveland, 1870–1930* at 30–31 (1976); Baker, *Color Line* at ch 6 (cited in note 15); Leslie H. Fishel, Jr., "The North and the Negro, 1865–1900" at 57, 363, 396–424, 489–90 (Ph.D. diss, Harvard University, 1953); August Meier and Elliott M. Rudwick, *Early Boycotts of Segregated Schools: The Alton, Illinois Case, 1897–1908*, 36 J Negro Educ 394 (1967); August Meier and Elliott M. Rudwick, *Early Boycotts of Segregated Schools: The East Orange, New Jersey, Experience, 1899–1906*, 4 Hist Educ Q 22 (1967); John Spencer Bassett, *Stirring up the Fires of Race Antipathy*, 2 So Atl Q 297, 298 (1903); 58 Nation 439 (June 14, 1894); New York Age (Oct 1, 1908), p 1.

"Anglo-Saxon racial stock" by Italian Catholics and Russian Jews found themselves attracted to southern racial policies. Henry Cabot Lodge, who in 1890 introduced in the House legislation to secure the suffrage rights of southern blacks, was in 1896 the leading Senate spokesman for literacy tests to restrict European immigration in order to preserve Americans' racial superiority. One women's suffragist from Mississippi nicely captured the connection between the southern commitment to white supremacy and the northern commitment to Anglo-Saxon supremacy:

> [J]ust as surely as the North will be forced to turn to the South for the nation's salvation [on account of the purity of its Anglo-Saxon blood], just so surely will the South be compelled to look to its Anglo-Saxon women as a medium through which to retain the supremacy of the white race over the African.

Racial nativist sentiment was strongest in New England, where six of the *Plessy* Court Justices had been either raised or educated.[18]

America's imperialist adventures of the 1890s also contributed to the convergence of northern and southern racial attitudes. Beginning with the clamor for the annexation of Hawaii early in the decade and culminating with the acquisition of Puerto Rico and the Philippines after the Spanish-American War of 1898, supporters of imperialism argued their case partly in the racial terms of Manifest Destiny—the "white man's burden." Most proponents of territorial acquisition rejected the notion of extending full citizenship rights to persons thus incorporated into the United States—a position that the Supreme Court conveniently accommodated early in the twentieth century. It was difficult for northerners defending imperialism and limited self-government for acquired territories in white supremacist terms to criticize southern racial practices such as black disfranchisement. Thus one delegate to Alabama's disfranchisement convention of 1900 observed that territorial acquisition "has forced the race problem to the attention

---

[18] Carl Degler, *In Search of Human Nature: The Decline and Revival of Darwinism in American Social Thought* 48–49 (1991) (first quotation); Aileen Kraditor, *The Ideas of the Woman Suffrage Movement, 1890–1920* at 201–02 (1965) (second quotation); Charles A. Lofgren, *The Plessy Case: A Legal-Historical Interpretation* 98–99 (1987); John Higham, *Strangers in the Land: Patterns of American Nativism 1860–1925* at chs 3–4, 6 (1955); Otto H. Olsen, ed, *The Thin Disguise: Turning Point in Negro History, Plessy v. Ferguson: A Documentary Presentation (1864–1896)* at 21 (1967); McPherson, *Abolitionist Legacy* at 125, 322–23 (cited in note 12).

of the whole country and in the wise solution of this question we have the sympathy instead of the hostility of the North."[19]

Manifest Destiny and the Spanish-American War heightened the growing desire for sectional reconciliation, which also contributed to the deterioration in race relations at the end of the nineteenth century. The ferocious human toll extracted by the Civil War had incited feelings of vindictiveness and resentment, which blocked any prospects for immediate reconciliation. Over the long term, though, many forces pulled the sections back together—common ancestry, history, religion, economic ties. A principal issue keeping them apart was the political and civil status of southern blacks. A pressing question for the remainder of the nineteenth century was which force would prove stronger over time—the desire of both sections for national reconciliation or the commitment of northerners to protecting the rights of southern blacks.

As Civil War antagonisms receded into the distance, the sectional rift gradually was healed, usually at the expense of southern blacks. By the early 1870s, Confederate political leaders were receiving amnesty and Confederate soldiers were being invited to participate in Memorial Day demonstrations. In 1876 the Republican presidential candidate, Rutherford B. Hayes, won on a platform of sectional reconciliation and then put a white southerner back into the Cabinet while taking federal troops out of the South. In 1887–88 President Grover Cleveland appointed a former Confederate officer, L. Q. C. Lamar, to the Supreme Court. The "deepest and sincerest expression" of this reconciliation sentiment took place in joint processions and battle commemorations by Union and Confederate veterans—events that multiplied in the 1880s.[20]

National reconciliation quickened in the 1890s, as northerners increasingly acquiesced in southern "home rule" on the race ques-

---

[19] Hackney, *Populism to Progressivism* at 159–61 (quotation) (cited in note 11); Clarence H. Poe, *Suffrage Restrictions in the South: Its Causes and Consequences*, 175 North Am Rev 534, 542 (1902); Woodward, *New South* at 324–26 (cited in note 10); Paul Gordon Lauren, *Power and Prejudice: The Politics and Diplomacy of Racial Discrimination* 64–70 (1988); *Downes v Bidwell*, 182 US 244 (1901); Woodward, *Jim Crow* at 70–74 (cited in note 11); Alfred Holt Stone, *Studies in the American Race Problem* 379–80 (1908); Willard B. Gatewood, Jr., *Negro Troops in Florida, 1898*, 49 Fla Hist Q 1, 15 (1970).

[20] Paul H. Buck, *The Road to Reunion 1865–1900* passim (quotation at 236) (1937); Woodward, *Jim Crow* at 70 (cited in note 11); William Gillette, *Retreat from Reconstruction, 1869–1879* at 72 (1979); Eric Foner, *Reconstruction: America's Unfinished Business* 500–05, 567, 580–82 (1988); Vincent P. DeSantis, *Republicans Face the Southern Question: The New Departure Years, 1877–1897* at 32–33, 54–56, 74 (1959).

tion. National organizations like the League of American Wheel-
men (bicyclists) or the National American Woman's Suffrage Association preserved sectional peace by capitulating to the demands
of white southern members for the exclusion or segregation of
blacks. The sectional issue played less of a role in the 1896 presidential election than in any other since the Civil War. After his
victory that year, President William McKinley declared that "the
north and the south no longer divide on the old [sectional] lines."[21]

The Spanish-American War of 1898, which afforded the first
opportunity since the Civil War for soldiers to demonstrate national solidarity on the battlefield, appreciably advanced the cause
of sectional reconciliation. The *Atlanta Constitution* proclaimed
that the death of the first white southerner in the war "seals effectively the covenant of brotherhood between the north and south
and completes the work of reconciliation which commenced at Appomattox." A black editor cautioned, though, that "the closer the
North and South get together by this war," the more difficult it
was for blacks "to maintain a footing." In 1899 President McKinley spoke before the Georgia House of Representatives, where just
fourteen months earlier he had been denounced for appointing a
black postmaster against the wishes of the local community, and
affirmed that the care of Confederate soldiers' graves was a national responsibility. In his second inaugural address in 1901, Mc-
Kinley spoke of sectional reconciliation—"We are reunited. Sec-
tionalism has disappeared"—and neglected entirely the subject of
black rights.[22]

Last but not least, the demise of the Republican Party's historical commitment to protecting black rights contributed to the na-

[21] Buck, *Road to Reunion*, at 282 (cited in note 20) (quotation); Letter to the editor, 54
Nation 227 (March 24, 1892); 62 Nation 391–92 (May 21, 1896); Somers, 40 J Southern
Hist at 40 (cited in note 11); Fishel, "The North and the Negro" at 411–12, 415–16 (cited
in note 17); Kraditor, *Woman's Suffrage Movement* at 170–72, 199–200, 213 (cited in note
18); McPherson, *Abolitionist Legacy* at 319–22 (cited in note 12); Stone, *American Race Problem* at 293 (cited in note 19).

[22] Ayers, *New South* at 329–33 (first quotation at 332) (cited in note 13); Gatewood, 49
Fla Hist Q at 10 (second quotation) (cited in note 19); Gerber, *Black Ohio* at 361–62, 364
(third quotation) (cited in note 17); Piero Gleijeses, *African Americans and the War Against
Spain*, 73 NC Hist Rev 184, 199, 204–06 (1996); Buck, *Road to Reunion* at 118, 283, 306–
07 (cited in note 20); Miller, 60 Outlook at 1060 (cited in note 13); New York Times (Nov
13, 1898), p 18; Stone, *American Race Problem* at 293–97 (cited in note 19); William McKinley, Second Inaugural Address (March 4, 1901), in Davis Newton Lott, ed, *The Presidents
Speak: The Inaugural Addresses of the American Presidents, from Washington to Clinton* 207–
12 (1994).

tion's acquiescence in southern racial practices. This factor may be especially significant, given that the Republican Party dominated the national government, including the Supreme Court, during the entirety of the period discussed in this article (1896–1908). The Republican Party had committed itself to the protection of black civil and political rights during Reconstruction. Partly, this was a genuine ideological commitment, and partly it was a partisan strategy for building the Republican Party in the South on the backs of black voters. Republicans did not abandon the cause of southern black suffrage in 1877 when the withdrawal of federal troops from the South marked the formal end of Reconstruction. While President Rutherford B. Hayes did pursue a sectional reconciliation policy that significantly departed from Republicans' Reconstruction strategy, he remained genuinely committed to securing the constitutional rights of southern blacks. As a strategic matter, Republicans could not yet afford to renounce protection for southern black suffrage. The Democrats frequently controlled the House of Representatives after 1874, and every presidential contest from 1876 to 1888 was decided by a razor-thin margin. Many Republicans attributed these electoral results to the rampant fraud and violence that southern whites employed to nullify the black vote. Since several northern states—New York, Connecticut, Ohio, Indiana—still were not reliably Republican in the 1870s and 1880s (as they would later become), party leaders calculated that to secure control of the national government, they must remain competitive in the South. With blacks comprising 40–60 percent of the population in most southern states, and the vast majority of the freedmen supporting the party of emancipation, the Republicans' best hope of remaining competitive in the region lay in protecting the black vote.[23]

Moreover, well past the end of Reconstruction, northern Repub-

---

[23] DeSantis, *Southern Question* at 19–132, 158, 168, 196 (cited in note 20); Buck, *Road to Reunion* at ch 4 (cited in note 20); LaWanda Cox and John Cox, *Negro Suffrage and Republican Politics: The Problem of Motivation in Reconstruction Historiography*, 33 J Southern Hist 303 (1967); Foner, *Reconstruction* at 228–31, 282–307 (cited in note 20); William Gillette, *Right to Vote: Politics and the Passage of the Fifteenth Amendment* 46–49 (1965); Xi Wang, *The Trial of Democracy: Black Suffrage and Northern Republicans, 1860–1910* at 91–92, 105–06, 109, 134–79 (1997); Robert M. Goldman *"A Free Ballot and a Fair Count": The Department of Justice and the Enforcement of Voting Rights in the South 1877–1893* at 65–108, 190 (1990); Michael Les Benedict, *The Politics of Reconstruction*, in John F. Marszalek and Wilson D. Miscambel, eds, *American Political History: Essays on the State of the Discipline* 54, 80–81, 86 (1997).

licans continued to find political profit in waving the "bloody shirt," which included condemnation of southern white outrages against blacks. While after the mid-1870s northern public opinion no longer endorsed federal military intervention to protect southern black voters, many northerners continued to disapprove of the fraud and violence used to nullify the Fifteenth Amendment in the South. Southern electoral tactics remained a politically profitable issue for northern Republicans well into the 1880s and helped to unite a party divided over economic and fiscal issues. Thus post-Reconstruction Republican administrations continued to enforce the 1870s civil rights legislation in voting cases, and President Hayes vetoed seven times the efforts of a Democratic Congress to repeal that legislation in 1879–80. Republican Party leaders such as James Blaine and James Garfield reiterated powerful rhetorical commitments to black suffrage in the late 1870s, as did party platforms throughout the 1880s.[24]

By the 1890s, though, three important changes combined to transform the Republican Party's posture toward protecting black voting rights. First, it had become clear that Republican efforts to construct a viable party in the South had failed. Attempts to build the party principally on black votes during Reconstruction had succumbed to ferocious resistance by southern whites. Policies by President Hayes of appealing to southern white conservatives and by President Chester Arthur of appealing to southern white independents also had proven miserable failures. By the late 1880s, the Republican vote in most southern states was declining significantly, as whites suppressed the black vote and the few remaining white Republicans deserted the party in the midst of rising racial tensions. After winning a consistent 40–41 percent of the southern presidential vote between 1876 and 1884, the Republican total fell to 37 percent in 1888 and then to just under 30 percent in 1896.

---

[24] Buck, *Road to Reunion* at ch 4 (cited in note 20); Gillette, *Retreat from Reconstruction* at 1–16, 179–85, 230–35, 366–70, 374–75 (cited in note 20); Wang, *Trial of Democracy* at 138–40, 163–215 (cited in note 23); Goldman, *Voting Rights* at chs 3–4, 6 (cited in note 23); DeSantis, *Southern Question* at chs 1–5 (cited in note 20); Republican Platform of 1880, plank no. 7, in Donald Bruce Johnson and Kirk H. Porter, eds, *National Party Platforms, 1840–1972* at 62 (5th ed 1975); Republican Platform of 1884, in ibid, 74; Republican Platform of 1888, in ibid, 80; President James Garfield, Inaugural Address (March 4, 1881), in *Inaugural Addresses* 163–70 (cited in note 22); *Ought the Negro to Be Disfranchised? Ought He to Have Been Enfranchised?* 268 North Am Rev 225 (1879) (James Blaine); ibid, 244 (James Garfield).

In 1894, for the first time since black enfranchisement, every one of the twenty-eight southern congressional districts containing a majority black population returned a Democratic representative.[25]

Moreover, by the 1890s the electoral dividends returned by bloody shirt tactics in the North had declined appreciably, as a new generation of voters seemed less concerned about southern suppression of the black vote. The best evidence of this transformation in northern sentiment is the fate of the Republicans' proposed elections bill in 1890–91 (known as the Lodge bill, or the Force bill, depending on one's sectional and partisan affiliation). The Republican Party platform in both 1884 and 1888 had promised a stronger electoral law to safeguard the rights of southern voters. When Republicans in 1888 won control of both houses of Congress and the presidency for the first time since 1874, the bill's passage seemed a genuine possibility. Yet the elections bill apparently was a good deal more popular with Republican politicians than with their constituents, and even Republican congressmen proved willing to sacrifice the bill in exchange for legislative action on economic issues deemed to be of greater urgency—namely, the tariff and the currency. The elections bill died of insufficient Republican commitment. In retrospect, it should be seen as the party's last gasp of civil rights ardor for decades to come.[26]

Finally, the Republicans in 1894 won one of the largest victories in congressional history and in 1896 the largest presidential victory in a quarter century. These were transitional elections. Some formerly contested northern states were converted into secure Republican bastions—a political equilibrium that remained largely intact until the New Deal resurrection of the northern Democratic Party in the 1930s. Moreover, Republicans in the mid-1890s proved competitive for the first time in border states such as Kentucky

---

[25] DeSantis, *Southern Question* at 19–181, 190–93, 246, 261–62 (cited in note 20); Gillette, *Retreat from Reconstruction* at 335–62 (cited in note 20); Wang, *Trial of Democracy* at chs 4–5 (cited in note 23); Goldman, *Voting Rights* at chs 3–4 (cited in note 23); J. Morgan Kousser, *The Shaping of Southern Politics: Suffrage Restrictions and the Establishment of the One-Party South, 1880–1910* at 12 table 1.1, 92–93 (1974); 59 Nation 475 (Dec 27, 1894).

[26] Buck, *Road to Reunion* at ch 11 (cited in note 20); Wang, *Trial of Democracy* at 224–27, 242–52, 263 (cited in note 23); Richard E. Welch, Jr., *The Federal Elections Bill of 1890: Postscripts and Prelude*, 52 J Am Hist 511 (1965); DeSantis, *Southern Question* at ch 5 (cited in note 20); 61 Nation 162 (Sept 5, 1895); 51 Nation 141, 144 (Aug 21, 1890); ibid, 161, 164 (Aug 28, 1890).

and Maryland. After the mid-1890s, it was apparent that the Republican Party could maintain national control without any southern electoral support. The party's electoral incentive to defend the suffrage rights of southern blacks was gone. Meanwhile, Republican hegemony in northern states reduced the party's need to bid for the votes of northern blacks, which in the 1870s and 1880s occasionally had represented the balance of power in tightly contested elections.[27]

These transitional elections produced a marked change in Republican Party policy. *The Nation* in 1896 observed a "striking" shift from four years earlier in "the entire absence of any allusion" to black political rights in Republican Party state conventions. The party's national platform likewise diluted its usual demand for a "free ballot and a fair count" in the South. William McKinley, who had voted for the federal elections bill in the House in 1890, failed to mention it in his letter accepting the Republican Party's presidential nomination in 1896 or in his inaugural address in 1897. Northern state Republican parties became less eager to run black candidates after the mid-1890s, and black representation at party conventions declined.[28]

* * *

This is the general racial context within which the Supreme Court at the turn of the century considered the constitutionality of segregation, disfranchisement, racial jury exclusion, and separate and unequal educational facilities. Had the text, original under-

---

[27] DeSantis, *Southern Question* at 21 (cited in note 20); Gerber, *Black Ohio* at 338 (cited in note 17); Gillette, *Retreat from Reconstruction* at 372–76 (cited in note 20); Goldman, *Voting Rights* at 254–55 (cited in note 23); Margaret Law Callcott, *The Negro in Maryland Politics 1870–1912* at ch 4 (1969); Walter Dean Burnham, *The Changing Shape of the American Political Universe*, 59 Am Pol Sci Rev 7, 12–14, 23–24 (1965); 61 Nation 162 (Sept 5, 1895); 62 Nation 370–71 (May 14, 1896); Richard E. Welch, Jr., *The Presidencies of Grover Cleveland* 40–41, 97, 110–11, 212 (1988).

[28] 62 Nation 391–92 (May 21, 1896) (quotation); 61 Nation 162 (Sept 5, 1895); Gerber, *Black Ohio* at 338, 361–62 (cited in note 17); Kousser, *Southern Politics* at 22 n 12, 31 (cited in note 25); DeSantis, *Southern Question* at 231, 255 (cited in note 20); Leslie H. Fishel, Jr., *The Negro in Northern Politics, 1870–1900*, 42 Miss Valley Hist Rev 466, 475 (1955); Wang, *Trial of Democracy* at 261–62 (cited in note 23); Thornbrough, *Negro in Indiana* at 315 (cited in note 17); Republican Party Platform of 1892, in *National Party Platforms* at 93 (cited in note 24); Republican Party Platform of 1896, in ibid at 109; William McKinley, First Inaugural (March 4, 1897), in *Inaugural Addresses* at 198–207 (cited in note 22).

standing, or Court precedents clearly resolved these issues, perhaps the background racial context would have been less significant in shaping the Court's decisions. But, as we shall see, the traditional sources of constitutional law failed to provide conclusive, or even particularly suggestive, answers. Accordingly, the Justices' own racial sentiments inevitably guided their resolution of these issues.

Moreover, the relatively little we know about the racial views of the *Plessy* Court Justices suggests no reason to doubt that their predilections roughly mirrored those of the general population. Justice (later Chief Justice) Edward D. White was a former Confederate soldier from Louisiana. At a minimum, White had helped redeem his state from Republican rule during Reconstruction; possibly, he had been a member of Klan-type organizations at that time. Chief Justice Melville Fuller had been a prominent Democratic state legislator in Illinois during the Civil War. There he had led the opposition to Lincoln's Emancipation Proclamation, supported state constitutional provisions barring further black emigration to Illinois and rejecting black suffrage, and helped enact a school segregation law for Chicago. Justice David Brewer, a Kansas Supreme Court justice in the early 1880s, had dissented from a decision invalidating school segregation under state law. It is tempting to read Brewer's opinion as indicative of his own personal views regarding the desirability of school segregation.[29]

As we shall see, the performance of these Justices on race cases during the *Plessy* era was consistent with this meager evidence of their personal racial views. Only Justice John Marshall Harlan, the sole dissenter in *Plessy*, seemed to defy his past. Harlan had been a slaveowner in antebellum Kentucky. While he fought for the Union, he opposed emancipation. As a Kentucky politician after the war, he opposed the Thirteenth Amendment as well as the Civil Rights Acts of 1866 and 1875. While Harlan's judicial opinions suggest a *partial* transformation in his racial views after his

---

[29] Robert B. Highsaw, *Edward Douglass White: Defender of the Conservative Faith* 19, 23–24 (1981); Benno C. Schmidt, *Principle and Prejudice: The Supreme Court and Race in the Progressive Era. Part 3: Black Disfranchisement from the KKK to the Grandfather Clause*, 82 Colum L Rev 835, 883–84 (1982); Robert L. McCaul, *The Black Struggle for Public Schooling in Nineteenth Century Illinois* 61–63 (1987); James W. Ely, *The Chief Justiceship of Melville W. Fuller 1888–1910* at 7–8 (1995); *Board of Education v Tinnon*, 26 Kan 1, 23 (1881) (Brewer, J, dissenting); Michael J. Brodhead, *David J. Brewer: The Life of a Supreme Court Justice, 1837–1910* at 107 (1994). See also Robert J. Glennon, Jr., *Justice Henry Billings Brown: Values in Tension*, 44 U Colo L Rev 553 (1973).

ascent to the High Court, he plainly was the exception, not the rule.[30]

II. THE CASES IN THEIR CONTEXT

A. SEGREGATION

1. *Plessy v Ferguson*. *Plessy v Ferguson* rejected an equal protection challenge to a Louisiana statute requiring railroads to provide separate and equal accommodations to black and white passengers. The Court denied that the Fourteenth Amendment's purpose had been "to abolish distinctions based upon color, or to enforce social, as distinguished from political, equality." Further, the Court denied that "the enforced separation of the two races stamps the colored race with a badge of inferiority" and insisted that if blacks thought otherwise, this was "solely because [they] cho[se] to put that construction upon it."[31]

Railroad segregation had first become an issue around 1840 in Massachusetts, when some carriers imposed it by regulation or custom. While pressure from abolitionists narrowly failed to convince the state legislature to forbid the practice, it succeeded at inducing railroad companies to do so. Massachusetts eventually did become the first state to enact public accommodations legislation forbidding racial discrimination, but not until 1865, the year the Civil War ended. In the absence of legislative regulation, antebellum courts confronted the segregation issue under the common law. Common carriers such as railroads were subject to a common law requirement that they take all comers, subject to the imposition of reasonable rules and regulations for the comfort and convenience of the traveling public. While only a few cases raised the issue before the Civil War, the prevailing view was that racial segregation qualified as a reasonable policy.[32]

---

[30] Tinsley E. Yarbrough, *Judicial Enigma: The First Justice Harlan* 55–59, 62, 77–78, 84, 109–10, 138–39 (1995); Loren P. Beth, *John Marshall Harlan: The Last Whig Justice* ch 5 (1992); *Civil Rights Cases*, 109 US 3, 26 (1883) (Harlan, J, dissenting); *Plessy v Ferguson*, 163 US 537, 552 (1896) (Harlan, J, dissenting); *Berea College v Kentucky*, 211 US 45, 58 (1908) (Harlan, J, dissenting).

[31] *Plessy v Ferguson*, 163 US 537, 544 (first quotation), 551 (second and third quotations) (1896).

[32] Patricia Minter, "The Codification of Jim Crow: The Origins of Segregated Railroad Transit in the South, 1865–1910" at 9–14 (Ph.D. diss, University of Virginia, 1994); Wil-

Railroad segregation was mandated by several of the black codes adopted by southern state legislatures to restrict the freedmen's rights immediately after the war. These codes remained in force, however, for only a year or two. As black enfranchisement enabled Republicans to gain control of southern state legislatures, several enacted public accommodations statutes forbidding common carriers from making racial distinctions. Yet these laws were notoriously underenforced and generally were repealed once Democrats regained ascendancy through the 1870s. Congress enacted civil rights legislation in 1875 which arguably forbade racial segregation in common carriers, but the Supreme Court invalidated that law in 1883. Most northern states responded to the Court's decision by enacting their own public accommodations laws, which included bans on racial discrimination and segregation by common carriers.[33]

Historians have disagreed about the extent to which southern railroad travel actually was integrated in the period from the end of Reconstruction through the adoption of railroad segregation statutes beginning in the late 1880s. While no systematic measure is possible, travelers' accounts, court cases and newspaper reports demonstrate at least some, and possibly much, integration on first-class railroad cars. Integration certainly prevailed in second-class smoking cars. Railroad travel probably was more racially integrated in the eastern seaboard states, owing to their deeper racial paternalist traditions. Local streetcar transportation, which had been integrated in most southern cities after the Civil War, generally remained that way through the turn of the century.[34]

---

liam S. McFeely, *Frederick Douglass* 92–93 (1991); Leon Litwack, *North of Slavery: The Negro in the Free States, 1790–1860* at 106–09 (1961); Joseph William Singer, *No Right to Exclude: Public Accommodations and Private Property*, 90 Nw U L Rev 1283, 1374 (1996); Gilbert Thomas Stephenson, *Race Distinctions in American Law* 112 (1910); note 44.

[33] Fischer, *Segregation Struggle* at 31–41, 62–63, 69, 78–79 (cited in note 10); Catherine A. Barnes, *Journey from Jim Crow: The Desegregation of Southern Transit* 2–3 (1983); Stephenson, *Race Distinctions* at 115, 208–10 (cited in note 32); Somers, 40 J Southern Hist at 23–24, 28 (cited in note 11); Wharton, *Negro in Mississippi* at 175, 230–31 (cited in note 10); Lofgren, *Plessy* at 18–19 (cited in note 18); Foner, *Reconstruction* at 369–71, 421–22 (cited in note 20); note 55.

[34] Woodward, *Jim Crow* at 23–24, 27–29, 38–41 (cited in note 11); Wynes, *Race Relations in Virginia* at 69, 71–73, 150 (cited in note 11); Minter, "Jim Crow" at 90–91, 136–37, 171, 193–95 (cited in note 32); Stephen J. Riegel, *The Persistent Career of Jim Crow: Lower Federal Courts and the "Separate but Equal" Doctrine, 1865–1896*, 28 Am J Leg Hist 17, 27 (1984); Barbara Y. Welke, *When All the Women Were White, and All the Blacks Were Men: Gender, Class, Race, and the Road to Plessy, 1855–1914*, 13 L & Hist Rev 261, 266–67, 276

It also seems likely that the extent of railroad integration was declining even before the first railroad segregation statutes were enacted. That is, de jure segregation largely replaced de facto segregation rather than integration. The railroad segregation statutes generally came in two waves. Florida enacted the first in 1887, followed by eight other states by 1892. A second wave carried along the eastern seaboard states beginning in 1898. Streetcar segregation statutes and ordinances swept the South between 1900 and 1906. The new segregation laws provided for separate but equal railway accommodations, imposed criminal penalties on violators, and afforded certain limited exceptions (such as nurses accompanying patients).[35]

Ascertaining the causes of these statutes is difficult. On one view, they reflect the deteriorating race relations described earlier. Railroad segregation laws can be seen as a product of the rising political power of lower-class whites, for whom the subordination of blacks was important to elevating their own social status. More affluent, higher-status whites tended to be preoccupied more with class than racial differentiation. Thus, for example, upper-class white neighborhoods in Atlanta actually preferred blacks for their

---

n 40 (1995); Cartwright, *Tennessee Race Relations* at 168, 185 (cited in note 10); Somers, 40 J Southern Hist at 28 (cited in note 11); Fischer, *Segregation Struggle* at 31–41, 148–49 (cited in note 10); Williamson, *Negro in South Carolina* at 281–83 (cited in note 11); Meier and Rudwick, *Color Line* at 268–69, 309–10 (cited in note 13); Wright, *Blacks in Louisville* at 52–54 (cited in note 11); *Heard v Georgia Railroad*, 1 ICC 719, 720–22 (1888); Letter to the editor, 50 Nation 219 (March 13, 1890): Charleston News & Courier (Nov 5, 1883), p 2; *South Carolina Society*, 39 Atlantic Monthly 670, 676 (June 1877).

Woodward and the other sources noted above document substantial railroad integration. Others have doubted whether much integration really existed prior to the imposition of de jure segregation. Williamson at 283–85; Rabinowitz, *First New South* at 133–34, 138 (cited in note 14); Rabinowitz, *Urban South* at 182 (cited in note 11). The debate is usefully summarized in Lofgren, *Plessy*, at 9–17 (cited in note 18). See also Cell, *White Supremacy* at ch 4 (cited in note 11). Woodward later conceded there probably was less integration than he had earlier suggested. Woodward, 75 J Am Hist at 862 (cited in note 11).

[35] Somers, 40 J Southern Hist at 29, 38 (cited in note 11); Woodward, *Jim Crow* at 31–35, 97–105 (cited in note 11); Lofgren, *Plessy* at 17, 22 (cited in note 18); Charles S. Mangum, Jr., *The Legal Status of the Negro* ch 8 (1940); Stephenson, *Race Distinctions* at ch 9 (cited in note 32); Cartwright, *Tennessee Race Relations* at 103–07 (cited in note 10); Stanley J. Flomsbee, *The Origin of the First "Jim Crow" Law*, 15 J Southern Hist 235–47 (1949); Minter, "Jim Crow" at 51–67, 161 (cited in note 32); Barnes, *Southern Transit* at 7–11 (cited in note 33); Meier and Rudwick, *Color Line* at ch 12 (cited in note 13); Jennifer Roback, *The Political Economy of Segregation: The Case of Segregated Streetcars*, 46 J Econ Hist 893 (1986). See also note 166.

Tennessee's 1881 railroad segregation law was an exception to the general trend noted in the text; it was attributable to an unusual set of political circumstances. See Flomsbee (cited in this note).

postal carriers, rather than lower-class whites. The rising political power of less affluent whites, on this view, forced higher-status whites to acquiesce in the demand for formalized railroad segregation. Several of these statutes were enacted by state legislatures dominated by the Farmers' Alliance.[36]

Other explanations also have been offered for the passage of railroad segregation laws. Many historians have attributed these statutes to the greater assertiveness of a younger generation of blacks not schooled in the norms of racial deference inculcated under slavery. One manifestation of this assertiveness was an increased number of black lawsuits in the 1880s challenging inferior railroad accommodations. Since railroad companies generally preferred neither to pay the sizable damage awards resulting from lawsuits successfully challenging inferior accommodations nor to shoulder the expense of providing genuinely equal (but separate) accommodations, some of them may have opted to permit integration, thus propelling state legislatures into action. Alternatively, the segregation laws may be more a product of changed circumstances than of changed racial attitudes. On this view, the greater penetration of southern railroads in the 1870s and 1880s brought black and white strangers into greater proximity, thus necessitating some novel measure of racial control. Finally, one might attribute the timing of the railroad segregation statutes simply to the removal of external constraints. Before the Supreme Court invalidated the 1875 Civil Rights Act in 1883, southern legislative efforts to mandate railroad segregation might have been preempted by federal law.[37]

Whatever the causes of these statutes, the question in *Plessy* was

---

[36] Riegel, 28 Am J Leg Hist at 27 (cited in note 34); Woodward, *Jim Crow* at 48–50 (cited in note 11); Wharton, *Negro in Mississippi* at 231–32 (cited in note 10); Lofgren, *Plessy* at 24 (cited in note 18); Baker, *Color Line* at 29–30 (cited in note 15); Woodward, *New South* at 211–12 (cited in note 10); Hart, *Redeemers* at 164–65 (cited in note 16); Minter, "Jim Crow" at 62, 83, 114–15, 128, 132, 144 (cited in note 32); Clarence A. Bacote, *Negro Proscriptions, Protests, and Proposed Solutions in Georgia, 1880–1908*, 25 J Southern Hist 471, 472–73 (1959).

[37] Minter, "Jim Crow" at 83, 193 (cited in note 32); Welke, 13 L & Hist Rev at 277, 295, 312 (cited in note 34); Lofgren, *Plessy* at 25–26 (cited in note 18); Rabinowitz, *Urban South* at 333–39 (cited in note 11); Ayers, *New South* at 140–41, 145, 247, 520 n 74 (cited in note 13); James C. Cobb, *Segregating the New South: The Origins and Legacy of Plessy v. Ferguson*, 12 Ga St U L Rev 1017, 1018–19, 1022–23 (1996); Bassett, 2 So Atl Q at 300–01 (cited in note 17); Cell, *White Supremacy* at 55–58, 103–04, 131–35, 142–43 (cited in note 11); Valeria Weaver, *The Failure of Civil Rights 1875–1883 and Its Repercussions*, 54 J Negro Hist 368, 370 (1969).

whether they were constitutional. The text of the Fourteenth Amendment does not answer that question. It says nothing specifically about the permissibility of racial classifications. Nor does "equal protection of the laws" plainly bar a statute requiring "equal but separate" facilities.

It is no accident that the Fourteenth Amendment fails explicitly to mandate legislative color-blindness. Proponents of a constitutional ban on racial classifications proposed language suitable to that purpose during congressional debates. It was rejected. Indeed, some Radical Republicans opposed ratification because the amendment's failure to forbid all racial classifications rendered it "a party trick designed only for electioneering purposes." Other Republicans continued to support the amendment, while lamenting their inability to command the votes necessary to ban all racial classifications.[38]

Nor is it particularly surprising that Congress in 1866 would have rejected a ban on color-consciousness. Northern racism remained strong in the postbellum period. It is true that the egalitarian ideological implications of a war to end slavery had helped eradicate northern laws barring black immigration and black testimony in court. But white racial attitudes had not changed sufficiently to induce most northern states to enfranchise blacks, desegregate public schools, or legalize interracial marriage. In 1866 most northerners were committed to protecting only the *civil* rights of blacks—the rights to contract, property ownership, court access, and protection of the law. These were the rights guaranteed against race discrimination in the 1866 Civil Rights Act, for which the Fourteenth Amendment was designed to provide a secure constitutional foundation.

Many northern Republicans in 1866 continued to resist the extension to blacks of either equal political rights, such as voting or jury service, or social rights, such as interracial marriage or school integration. Thus Republican congressmen made a conscious decision not to guarantee black suffrage in the Fourteenth Amendment. They feared alienating enough northern voters to cost their

[38] Andrew Kull, *The Color-Blind Constitution* 3–4, 58–87 (quotation at 64) (1992); Earl M. Maltz, *Civil Rights, the Constitution and Congress, 1863–1869* at 6, 82–92 (1990); Raoul Berger, *Government by Judiciary: The Transformation of the Fourteenth Amendment* 143–44 (1977); Alexander M. Bickel, *The Original Understanding and the Segregation Decision*, 69 Harv L Rev 1, 42–45, 60 (1955).

party its veto-proof majorities in Congress. The question of de jure segregation arose only occasionally in congressional debates on the 1866 Civil Rights Act or the Fourteenth Amendment. Democratic opponents would enumerate a parade of horribles to which the measure's adoption inevitably would lead, including compulsory racial integration of public schools and public accommodations. Republican proponents responded by vehemently denying such broad ramifications.[39]

On the other hand, unlike with regard to public education, where blacks were pervasively excluded or segregated at the time, a significant amount of racial integration existed in railroad travel when the Fourteenth Amendment was adopted. The North had largely eliminated Jim Crow transportation by then, and many southern cities had desegregated their streetcars. On the reasonable assumption that constitutional amendments generally seek to reinforce rather than to alter predominant social mores, the Fourteenth Amendment arguably rejected de jure railroad segregation.[40]

Moreover, again in contrast with the issue of school integration, Congress evinced some commitment to integration of railroad travel at the time the Fourteenth Amendment was drafted. While the same Congress that wrote the Fourteenth Amendment continued to segregate schools in the District of Columbia, it also imposed on local railroads charter requirements that plausibly could be construed to forbid racial segregation. Indeed, the Supreme Court in 1873 interpreted one such ambiguous railroad charter— "no person shall be excluded from the cars on account of race"—

---

[39] James E. Bond, *The Original Understanding of the Fourteenth Amendment in Illinois, Ohio, and Pennsylvania*, 18 Akron L Rev 435 (1985); Fishel, "The North and the Negro" at 56–57, 66, 97–100 (cited in note 17); Litwack, *North of Slavery* at ch 3 (cited in note 32); Foner, *Reconstruction* at 25–26, 226–27, 244–45 (cited in note 20); Maltz, *Civil Rights* at 6, 71, 74–76 (cited in note 38); Kull, *Color-Blind Constitution* at 60, 76–77, 85–86 (cited in note 38); Cong Globe, 39th Cong, 1st Sess 541 (1866) (Rep. John L. Dawson); ibid, App 183 (Sen. Garrett Davis); Bickel, 69 Harv L Rev at 11–29 (cited in note 38); Lawrence Grossman, *The Democratic Party and the Negro: Northern and National Politics, 1868–1892* at 1–14 (1976); Alfred Avins, *Social Equality and the Fourteenth Amendment: the Original Understanding*, 4 Houston L Rev 640 (1967); Berger, *Fourteenth Amendment* at chs 3, 4, 9 (cited in note 38); Gillette, *Right to Vote* at 21–45 (cited in note 23); Charles Fairman, *Reconstruction and Reunion, 1864–1888 pt I* ch 20 (1971).

[40] Barnes, *Southern Transit* at 2 (cited in note 33); Gerber, *Black Ohio* at 46 (cited in note 17). On the view that constitutional amendments generally reflect an existing consensus, see David Strauss, "Do Constitutional Amendments Matter?" (unpublished manuscript, 1997); Klarman, 93 Nw U L Rev at 171–72 (cited in note 9).

to require integration, not simply equality within a segregated system. Of course, such charter provisions are not conclusive as to
the bearing of the Fourteenth Amendment on the question of de
jure railroad segregation. Congress frequently mandated racial solutions for the District of Columbia that it was not yet prepared
to impose on the rest of the nation. Nor is the Supreme Court's
pro-integration decision of 1873 particularly reliable evidence as to
how most Republican congressmen would have felt about railroad
integration when they passed the Fourteenth Amendment in 1866.
The year 1873 was a high water mark for Reconstruction; several
southern states adopted public accommodations laws that year, and
the Senate passed a strong civil rights bill the next.[41]

The 1875 Civil Rights Act also offers ambiguous evidence as to
whether the original understanding of the Fourteenth Amendment
permitted railroad segregation statutes. On the one hand, it seems
significant that less than a decade after the Fourteenth Amendment
passed, a substantial majority of Republican congressmen endorsed
legislation requiring "full and equal enjoyment" of public convey-
ances, "applicable alike to citizens of every race and color"—language that most supporters interpreted to forbid segregation. On
the other hand, Republicans became more racially egalitarian after the mid-1860s, rendering dubious any attempt to infer the
Fourteenth Amendment's original understanding from legislation
adopted many years after its passage. Moreover, in debates over
the civil rights bill, some Republicans expressly stated that Congress possessed broader power under Section 5 of the Fourteenth
Amendment—authorizing congressional enforcement "by appropriate legislation"—than did courts interpreting Section 1, which
forbids states from denying equal protection. On this view, the
fact that Congress believed it possessed constitutional authority to
legislate against railroad segregation does not prove that a court
had power to invalidate the practice on its own. Finally, at least
some congressional Republicans believed that the "full and equal

---

[41] Lofgren, *Plessy* at 65, 124, 146 (cited in note 18); Earl M. Maltz, *"Separate but Equal"
and the Law of Common Carriers in the Era of the Fourteenth Amendment*, 17 Rutgers L J
553, 558–68 (1986); Michael W. McConnell, *Originalism and the Desegregation Decisions*, 81
Va L Rev 947, 982–84, 1117–19 (1995); *Railroad Company v Brown*, 84 US 445 (1873);
Kull, *Color-Blind Constitution* at 91–93 (cited in note 38); Maltz, *Civil Rights* at 124 (cited
in note 38); Foner, *Reconstruction* at 437–39 (cited in note 20).

enjoyment" language of the 1875 Civil Rights Act barred only racial exclusion, not segregation.[42]

In light of the evidence just canvased, one plausibly might conclude that there is no definitive original understanding of the Fourteenth Amendment with regard to railroad segregation. Unlike original intent, however, legal precedent strongly supported the constitutionality of de jure railroad segregation. The Justices in *Plessy* were not writing on a blank slate simply because the Supreme Court had yet to consider the permissibility of racial segregation under the Fourteenth Amendment. Roughly three decades worth of lower court decisions tilted strongly toward sustaining de jure racial segregation. Two lines of precedent were particularly relevant: cases sustaining the railroad *practice* of racial segregation against various legal challenges, and those upholding state laws mandating public school segregation against Fourteenth Amendment attack.[43]

Railroad segregation policies had been subject to three different sorts of legal challenge before the enactment of segregation statutes converted the issue into a Fourteenth Amendment one by supplying the state action that Section 1 seems to demand of any successful constitutional challenge. First, the question arose whether the common law permitted racial segregation. The common law required common carriers to afford access to all who paid the fare, but permitted them to adopt reasonable regulations for the convenience of the traveling public. For example, nobody believed that railroad companies violated their common law obligations by establishing separate "ladies" cars, from which all unaccompanied males were excluded. Beginning with landmark northern cases in the 1850s and 1860s, courts generally sustained railroad segregation as reasonable. They opined that "repugnancies" between the races arising from natural differences created friction that could

---

[42] Compare McConnell, 81 Va L Rev at 1120–31 (cited in note 41) with Michael J. Klarman, *Brown, Originalism, and Constitutional Theory: A Response to Professor McConnell*, 81 Va L Rev 1881, 1884–1914 (1995); Earl M. Maltz, *Originalism and the Desegregation Decisions—a Response to Professor McConnell*, 13 Const Comm 223 (1996).

[43] Lofgren, *Plessy* at 47, 67, 79 (cited in note 18); Maltz, 17 Rutgers L J at 568 (cited in note 41); Kull, *Color-Blind Constitution* at 88–89, 96, 116 (cited in note 38); Riegel, 28 Am J Leg Hist at 20, 39–40 (cited in note 34); Welke, 13 L & Hist Rev at 296 (cited in note 34); Minter, "Jim Crow" at 23 (cited in note 32). But see Barton J. Bernstein, *Case Law in Plessy v. Ferguson*, 47 J Negro Hist 192 (1962).

be reduced through segregation. But to be reasonable, separate facilities had to be equal.[44]

Likewise, all reported lower federal court decisions interpreted the "full and equal enjoyment" language of the 1875 Civil Rights Act to forbid racial exclusion or inequality, but not segregation. These decisions are especially revealing for two reasons. First, the congressional debates on the statute had evinced much greater support for eradicating segregation than had the Fourteenth Amendment debates. Yet courts interpreting the Act were nonetheless reluctant to construe ambiguous statutory language to forbid segregation. Second, these judicial decisions were delivered around 1880, when public opinion was far more supportive of integration than it would later become.[45]

Finally, the Interstate Commerce Commission consistently interpreted the provision in its enabling legislation barring "undue or unreasonable prejudice or disadvantage" to permit segregation so long as equal facilities were provided. The commission reasoned that segregation was a reasonable policy and that public sentiment demanded it. It is revealing that courts and agencies interpreting three different texts that dealt generally with equality but were ambiguous on the segregation issue overwhelmingly reached the conclusion that separate but equal was permissible because reasonable. It is difficult to imagine why a court construing the Equal

---

[44] *Day v Owen*, 5 Mich 520 (1858); *West Chester and Philadelphia v Miles*, 55 Pa 209 (1867); *Gray v Cincinnati Southern Railroad*, 11 F 683 (CCSD Ohio 1882); *Murphy v Western & Atlantic Railroad*, 23 F 637 (CCED Tenn 1885); *Houck v Southern Pacific Railway*, 38 F 226 (CCWD Tex 1888); Thomas M. Cooley, *Treatise on the Law of Torts* 282–84 (1879); Lofgren, *Plessy* at ch 6 (cited in note 18); Maltz, 17 Rutgers L J at 553–58 (cited in note 41); Minter, "Jim Crow" at 14–23, 31–33, 41–42, 74–83, 107–08 (cited in note 32); Welke, 13 Law & Hist Rev (cited in note 34); D. H. Pingrey, *A Legal View of Racial Discrimination*, 30 Am L Reg 69, 92 (1891); Stephenson, *Race Distinctions* at 211–14 (cited in note 32).

[45] *United States v Dodge*, 25 Fed 882 (WD Tex 1877); *Smoot v Kentucky Central Railway*, 13 F 337 (CCD Ky 1882) (dicta); *United States v Washington*, 20 F 630 (CCWD Tex 1883) (dicta); *Hall v DeCuir*, 95 US 485, 504 (1878) (Clifford, J, concurring); Lofgren, *Plessy* at 134–35, 238 n 45 (cited in note 18); Riegel, 28 Am J Leg Hist at 25, 32–35 (cited in note 34); Singer, 90 Nw U L Rev at 1384 (cited in note 32); Minter, "Jim Crow" at 42–46 (cited in note 32).

McConnell presents impressive evidence that most Republicans understood the 1875 Civil Rights Act to forbid segregation. McConnell, 81 Va L Rev at 990–97, 1002–04, 1013–14, 1022–23, 1073–77, 1099–1100 (cited in note 41). Compare Earl M. Maltz, *The Civil Rights Act and the Civil Rights Cases: Congress, Court, and Constitution*, 44 Fla L Rev 605, 620–26 (1992). For reasons noted below, however, I believe he overstates his claim that the original understanding of the Fourteenth Amendment rejected segregation. See note 68.

Protection Clause would have felt constrained to reach a different conclusion.[46]

Because state law had segregated public schools much longer than railroads, many lower courts had confronted the Fourteenth Amendment issue in the education context well before *Plessy*. We shall consider these decisions in greater detail below. For now, it is sufficient to note that they almost unanimously held that the Fourteenth Amendment permitted public school segregation. Perhaps the Supreme Court in 1896, if inclined, could have identified reasons for why railroad but not school segregation statutes were unconstitutional (e.g., some version of the rights/privileges distinction). Yet the consistent body of lower court precedent rejecting Fourteenth Amendment challenges to school segregation would have made it difficult for the Court to adopt the "color-blindness" approach espoused by Justice Harlan in his *Plessy* dissent. Indeed, the Court, with Justice Harlan's acquiescence, had squarely rejected the color-blindness interpretation in 1883 when it unanimously sustained an Alabama statute imposing heavier penalties on interracial than intraracial fornication. The Court in *Pace v Alabama*[47] reasoned that so long as both parties to the fornication were subjected to similar criminal penalties, the races were being treated equally, and thus the Equal Protection Clause was satisfied. Analytically, *Plessy*'s endorsement of separate but equal was a straightforward application of *Pace*.[48]

Finally, the Supreme Court by the turn of the century plainly had established in its Fourteenth Amendment jurisprudence involving nonrace issues that legislation impinging on individual property and liberty interests was constitutional if reasonable. For example, in *Holden v Hardy*,[49] decided just two years after *Plessy*, the Court rejected a Fourteenth Amendment challenge to a state maximum-hour law for miners. The Justices stated that the constitutional question was "whether the legislature has adopted the

---

[46] *Council v Western & Atlantic Railroad*, 1 ICC 638 (1887); Lofgren, *Plessy* at 141–44 (cited in note 18); Riegel, 28 Am J Leg Hist at 30–31 (cited in note 34); Minter, "Jim Crow" at 112 (cited in note 32).

[47] 106 US 583 (1883).

[48] Earl M. Maltz, *Only Partially Color Blind: John Marshall Harlan's View of Race and the Constitution*, 12 Ga St U L Rev 973, 992 (1996); Kull, *Color-Blind Constitution* at 116 (cited in note 38); Lofgren, *Plessy* at 78 (cited in note 18); note 69.

[49] 169 US 366 (1898).

statute in exercise of a reasonable discretion, or whether its action be a mere excuse for an unjust discrimination, or the oppression, or spoliation of a particular class." Thus, for *Plessy* to hold that racial segregation was permissible because reasonable was simply to align the Court's interpretation of the Equal Protection Clause with the remainder of its Fourteenth Amendment jurisprudence. Given dominant public opinion regarding race at the time, it is hardly surprising that most of the Justices would have considered separation of the races a valid exercise of the state police power to promote the public health, safety, and morals.[50]

Thus the constitutional case for sustaining railroad segregation statutes was strong, probably much stronger than the opposing case. While the original understanding of the Fourteenth Amendment was ambiguous, the *Plessy* Court was correct to state that segregation has been "generally, if not universally, recognized as within the competency of state legislatures." Reasoning from precedent, most contemporary legal commentators already had concluded that racial segregation was permissible. Given the powerful legal case for upholding railroad segregation, the Court was unlikely to resist public opinion that strongly favored the practice. Indeed, given the deterioration in race relations at the turn of the century, it seems doubtful whether the Court would have invalidated railroad segregation even had the legal materials more strongly supported such a result.[51]

Most southern whites, other than those employed by or invested

---

[50] *Holden*, 169 US at 398 (quotation); Charles Wallace Collins, *The Fourteenth Amendment and the States* 109 (1912); Lofgren, *Plessy* at 79–80, 84–88, 92, 94, 183–84 (cited in note 18); Owen M. Fiss, *Troubled Beginnings of the Modern State, 1888–1910*, Vol 8 of *History of the Supreme Court of the United States* 363–64 (1993); Nelson Lund, *The Constitution, the Supreme Court, and Racial Politics*, 12 Ga St U L Rev 1129, 1137, 1143–44 (1996); Howard Gillman, *The Constitution Besieged: The Rise and Demise of Lochner Era Police Powers Jurisprudence* ch 2 (1993); William E. Nelson, *The Fourteenth Amendment: From Political Principle to Judicial Doctrine* 121–22, 150–51, 175–96 (1988).

[51] *Plessy*, 163 US at 544 (quotation). For scholars regarding *Plessy* as a clear repudiation of the Reconstruction amendments, see Benno C. Schmidt, Jr., *Principle and Prejudice: The Supreme Court and Race in the Progressive Era. Part 1: The Heyday of Jim Crow*, 82 Colum L Rev 444, 461 (1982); Olsen, *Thin Disguise* at 5–7, 17 (cited in note 18); Robert Harris, *The Quest for Equality: The Constitution, Congress and the Supreme Court* 101 (1960); Oberst, 15 Ariz L Rev at 389, 410–11 (cited in note 6). Others have taken a view nearer to the one espoused in the text. Riegel, 28 Am J Leg Hist at 20, 37–40 (cited in note 34); Lofgren, *Plessy* at 92, 200 (cited in note 18); Kull, *Color-Blind Constitution* at 88–89, 116 (cited in note 38); Cobb, 12 Ga St U L Rev at 1035 (cited in note 37). Contemporary legal commentary on *Plessy* is collected in Lofgren, *Plessy* at 145, 242 n 68 (cited in note 18).

in railroad companies, strongly favored segregation by the 1890s. The dramatic increase in racial violence and lynching made segregation increasingly appear to be "the embodiment of enlightened public policy"—a progressive strategy for reducing interracial conflict. Moreover, northern opinion had grown increasingly receptive toward racial segregation. A Boston newspaper, commenting on the exclusion of a black bishop from a white hotel the same year that *Plessy* was decided, observed that social equality "appears more unthinkable today than ever." Northerners not only had become more supportive of segregation, but they also were more inclined to accommodate white southerners in their racial preferences. Finally, by the time of *Plessy*, the Republican Party had grown increasingly indifferent toward black rights. Supreme Court Justices, as products of the larger culture, were likely to reflect these changes in racial attitudes.[52]

It bears emphasis that the point just made is one about the Justices' *inclination*, not about the Court's *capacity*. I shall suggest later that the Court, had it been inclined to invalidate racial segregation in the 1890s, probably would have lacked the power to enforce such a decision. Yet the Justices probably had no such inclination; they likely approved of racial segregation as a policy matter. And if they endorsed the policy, and the legal materials supported its constitutionality, why would they have invalidated it?

Two principal pieces of evidence might be cited to rebut this argument. First is Justice Harlan's dissent in *Plessy*. If Harlan could conclude that railroad segregation statutes were unconstitutional, why not the rest of the Court? It is true that public opinion in the 1890s did not unanimously favor racial segregation. Some remnants of abolitionist thought continued to nurture integrationist ideals. Not all judges had agreed that the common law permitted racial segregation on common carriers or even that the Fourteenth Amendment allowed public school segregation. That this recessive

---

[52] Stone, *American Race Problem* at 64 (cited in note 19) (first quotation); Fishel, "The North and the Negro" at 396–97 (cited in note 17) (second quotation); Baker, *Color Line* at 305 (cited in note 15); Brundage, *Lynching* at 126–27, 156, 200, 209 (cited in note 12); Cell, *White Supremacy* at 19, 30–31, 174–80 (cited in note 11); Ayers, *New South* at 432 (cited in note 13); Fredrickson, *Black Image* at 293–94 (cited in note 15); J. Newton Baker, *The Segregation of White and Colored Passengers on Interstate Trains*, 19 Yale L J 445 (1910); note 17.

strand of integrationist opinion would find some, albeit slender, representation on the Supreme Court is not astonishing. What is more surprising is the identity of its representative—John Marshall Harlan, the former slaveowner and emancipation opponent. That the vote in *Plessy* was 7–1 rather than 8–0 hardly reveals that the issue was genuinely in doubt.[53]

Second, most northern states responded to the Supreme Court's invalidation of the public accommodations provision in the 1875 Civil Rights Act by enacting their own similar laws, which plainly were constitutional under the Court's rationale in the *Civil Rights Cases*.[54] Moreover, most northern state courts interpreted these laws, where ambiguous, to bar racial segregation as well as exclusion. Yet the existence of these statutes does not indicate that *Plessy* was in tension with dominant northern white opinion. Northern public accommodation laws were largely symbolic. Writing the principle of nondiscrimination into law was an important symbolic victory for black constituents, whose votes were much prized by Democrats and Republicans battling for control of closely contested northern states in the 1880s and early 1890s. To actually enforce such statutes, however, would have alienated far larger blocs of white voters who strongly opposed "social equality" for blacks. A combination of low statutory penalties, the inability of most black victims of discrimination to afford litigation, the unwillingness of white-dominated juries to convict violators or to impose significant sanctions, and the omnipresent threat of physical coercion confronting blacks testing their rights of access ensured that the statutes were, at best, lightly enforced. This probably explains why enactment of the statutes was not actively resisted, and indeed often was supported, by northern state Democratic parties, home to those voters with the most unmitigated white supremacist

---

[53] *Allen v Davis*, 10 Weekly Notes of Cases 156 (Crawford County, Pa 1881); *Coger v North Western Union Packet Co.*, 37 Iowa 145 (1873); *King v Gallagher*, 93 NY 438, 457 (1883) (Danforth, J, dissenting); Kull, *Color-Blind Constitution* at 99–100, 108 (cited in note 38); Yarbrough, *Judicial Enigma* at 55–59, 62, 77–78, 84, 109–10, 138–39 (cited in note 30); Beth, *John Marshall Harlan* at ch 5 (cited in note 30). Explaining why Justice Harlan took the pro–civil rights stand he did is difficult. His biographer offers some interesting speculation, but I am not certain that he has solved the mystery. Yarbrough at 141–43.

Justice Brewer was absent in *Plessy*, but there is reason to believe that he would have voted with the majority. See note 29.

[54] 109 US 3 (1883).

convictions. Accordingly, these laws probably did not evince any significant northern commitment to integrated public accommodations.[55]

Moreover, it was one thing for white northerners voluntarily to impose a requirement of railroad integration on themselves, but quite another to force it on a fiercely resistant white South. Many white northerners candidly acknowledged that they would have favored segregation had blacks constituted the same percentage of northern state populations as they did of southern. In addition, even northerners whose support for integration was not contingent on the size of the black population might have been reluctant to coerce the white South into adhering to such a policy. Indeed, the state public accommodations laws had been widely supported by northern Democrats, the vast majority of whom favored allowing white southerners a free rein in ordering their own race relations, both for electoral and federalism considerations. For these reasons the existence of northern statutes barring railroad segregation does not suggest that most white northerners would have opposed the outcome in *Plessy*.[56]

The strongest evidence that *Plessy* coincided with northern white opinion is the generally indifferent reaction to the decision. Most northern newspapers either gave *Plessy* routine notice or none at all. The *New York Times*, which reported several other Court decisions on its front page that day, relegated its report of *Plessy* to a page 3 column on railway news. Thus, one leading student of *Plessy* concludes that the decision "embodied conventional wisdom," and

---

[55] Mangum, *Legal Status of Negro* at ch 3 (cited in note 35); Stephenson, *Race Distinctions* at 121–24, 129–30, 132 (cited in note 32); Grossman, *Democratic Party* at 63–106 (cited in note 39); Gerber, *Black Ohio* at 41, 45, 49, 57–58, 236, 459 (cited in note 17); Thornbrough, *Negro in Indiana* at 259–66 (cited in note 17); Katzman, *Black Detroit* at 91, 96–97 (cited in note 17); Fishel, "The North and the Negro" at 4, 278–79, 380–84, 433 n 268, 501 (cited in note 17); Singer, 90 Nw U L Rev at 1374–77 (cited in note 32); Weaver, 54 J Negro Hist at 374–77 (cited in note 37); Stanford K. McCoy, "False Promises: Public Accommodations Statutes in the North after the Civil Rights Cases" (unpublished student paper, University of Virginia School of Law, 1998); Alfred Avins, *De Facto and De Jure School Segregation: Some Reflected Light on the Fourteenth Amendment from the Civil Rights Act of 1875*, 38 Miss L J 179, 236–37 (1967); McPherson, *Abolitionist Legacy* at 115–16 (cited in note 12). But see Olsen, *Thin Disguise* at 8 (cited in note 18).

[56] McPherson, *Abolitionist Legacy* at 314 (cited in note 12); Stone, *American Race Problem* at 5–10, 13, 52, 346–48 (cited in note 19); Fishel, 42 Miss Valley Hist Rev (cited in note 28); Grossman, *Democratic Party* at 154–55 (cited in note 39); Gerber, *Black Ohio* at 235–36 (cited in note 17); Thornbrough, *Negro in Indiana* at 302 (cited in note 17).

another that it so closely "mirror[ed] the spirit of the age . . . that the country hardly noticed."[57]

2. *Berea College.* The Court had one other opportunity during this period to consider the constitutionality of racial segregation, this time in the context of private higher education. In 1904 the Kentucky legislature enacted a statute (known as the Day law, named for its sponsor), forbidding interracial instruction at all schools and colleges within the state. The law plainly was directed at Berea College, which had been founded in 1855 as a college for Appalachian whites and former slaves and was one of only two integrated institutions of higher education in the South at the turn of the century. The other was Maryville College in Tennessee, which recently had become the target of similar legislation.[58]

The segregation law at issue in *Berea College* posed a more difficult constitutional question than had the Louisiana railroad segregation statute at issue in *Plessy.* The *Plessy* era of constitutional law was also the *Lochner* era. During this period, the Court afforded the greatest constitutional protection to individual rights of property and contract. Even at the zenith of its commitment to protecting economic liberty, however, the Court clearly distinguished between government regulation of quasi-public entities such as common carriers and other more private enterprises. For example, the *Lochner* era Court sustained government regulation of railroad rates, so long as nonconfiscatory, but invalidated state regulation of prices and wages in areas not "affected with a public interest." State regulation was more easily justified for entities like common carriers, which frequently enjoyed a monopoly position, largely insulating them from the competition of the marketplace.

The same monopoly status that would enable a railroad company to set unreasonably high rates also would allow it to ignore the preference of white travelers for segregated seating. Thus, railroad segregation statutes were not difficult to justify even for those

---

[57] Lofgren, *Plessy* at 197 (cited in note 18) (first quotation); Schmidt, 82 Colum L Rev at 469 (cited in note 51) (second quotation); Ely, *Melville W. Fuller* at 158 (cited in note 28). But see Olsen, *Thin Disguise* at 25, 123–30 (cited in note 18).

[58] *Berea College v Kentucky*, 211 US 45 (1908); Scott Blakeman, *Night Comes to Berea College: The Day Law and African-American Reaction*, 70 Filson Club Hist Q 3, 4–5, 26 n 45 (1996); Paul David Nelson, *Experiment in Interracial Education at Berea College, 1858–1905*, 59 J Negro Hist 13, 23 (1974).

committed to a generally libertarian approach. By way of contrast, if a private college chose to integrate its student body, segregationists were free to take their custom elsewhere. For the state to demand segregation from a private institution enjoying no monopoly position thus raised distinct issues of liberty (rather than equality). Indeed, language in *Plessy* strongly suggested that the state had no business interfering with voluntary integration of the races, which is precisely what the Day law accomplished. At a time when most of the Justices questioned the constitutional legitimacy of state interference with private contractual arrangements that created no traditional third-party harms, the Day law should have posed a more serious constitutional question than did the Louisiana railroad segregation statute.[59]

On the other hand, racial attitudes and practices had continued to deteriorate in the years between *Plessy* (1896) and *Berea College* (1908). The sectional reconciliation sentiment furthered by the Spanish-American War of 1898 and the accelerating black migration northward early in the twentieth century further inclined white northerners toward adopting southern white racial attitudes. Specifically, support for school segregation increased appreciably in the North. School boards introduced racial segregation in Alton, Illinois, in 1899; East Orange, New Jersey, in 1905–06; Wichita, Kansas, in 1906; and Oxford, Pennsylvania, in 1909. Whites in Chicago made several unsuccessful attempts to secure a school segregation ordinance during this decade. Several midwestern medical

---

[59] *Munn v Illinois*, 94 US 113 (1877); *Ribnik v McBride*, 277 US 350 (1928); *Tyson & Brother v Banton*, 273 US 418 (1927); Gillman, *Constitution Besieged* at 68–69, 180 (cited in note 50); Barry Cushman, *Rethinking the New Deal Court: The Structure of a Constitutional Revolution* 48–52, 57 (1998); Brief for Plaintiff in Error, *Berea College v Kentucky*, at 9–10, 24–26; *Plessy v Ferguson*, 163 US 537, 544 (1896); *Berea College v Kentucky*, 211 US 45, 68–69 (1908) (Harlan, J, dissenting). The legal aspects of *Berea College* are discussed in Schmidt, 82 Colum L Rev at 447–49 (cited in note 51); Stephenson, *Race Distinctions* at 154–59 (cited in note 32); Fiss, *Troubled Beginnings* at 370–72 (cited in note 50); David E. Bernstein, *Philip Sober Controlling Philip Drunk: Buchanan v. Warley in Historical Perspective*, 51 Vand L Rev 799, 830–32 (1998); Louis Michael Seidman, *Brown and Miranda*, 80 Cal L Rev 673, 695–97 (1992). For factual background, see Blakeman, 70 Filson Club Hist Q (cited in note 58); Robert Allen Heckman and Betty Gene Hall, *Berea College and the Day Law*, 66 Register Ky Hist Soc'y 35–52 (1968); Nelson, 59 J Negro Hist (cited in note 58); McPherson, *Abolitionist Legacy* at ch 14 (cited in note 12). Gillman, *Constitution Besieged* (cited in note 50) is the best general discussion of the *Lochner* era. See also Charles W. McCurdy, *Justice Field and the Jurisprudence of Government-Business Relations: Some Parameters of Laissez-Faire Jurisprudence*, 61 J Am Hist 970 (1975); Michael Les Benedict, *Laissez-Faire and Liberty: A Re-evaluation of the Meaning and Origins of Laissez-Faire Constitutionalism*, 3 L & Hist Rev 293 (1985).

schools expelled their black students upon the demand of their white classmates. The San Francisco city council passed an ordinance in 1906 segregating the Japanese in public schools (fomenting a foreign policy crisis for President Roosevelt). In a widely noted speech in 1907, Harvard President Charles Eliot stated with regard to Berea College that "perhaps if there were as many Negroes here as there we might think it better for them to be in separate schools."[60]

If Supreme Court Justices shared this growing public disillusionment with school integration, they might have been reluctant to invalidate the Day law. Indeed, the generally indifferent reaction of the northern press to the Court's decision upholding Kentucky's statute apparently confirms that the result was consonant with prevailing public opinion.[61]

The stated rationale in *Berea College* makes the case difficult to interpret. The Justices declined to decide whether a state government possessed the power to compel segregation in private schools. Rather, the Court held that because Berea College was a corporation owing its existence to a state charter, restrictions could be imposed upon it that might have been unconstitutional if applied to an individual. This was a classic application of the rights/privileges distinction: One might have a constitutional right to attend or teach at an integrated school, but one had no constitutional right to a state-granted corporate charter. While the scope of the Day law was broad enough to forbid private individuals from attending or teaching at an integrated school, the Court did not have to resolve the constitutionality of that aspect of the statute, because the case involved only a criminal prosecution of Berea College, a corporate entity.

Several commentators have argued that the Court's "ducking"

---

[60] Schmidt, 82 Colum L Rev at 451 (cited in note 51) (quotation); Stephenson, *Race Distinctions* at 159–64, 184 (cited in note 32); Gerber, *Black Ohio* at 266–67 (cited in note 17); Davison M. Douglas, *Limits of Law in Accomplishing Racial Change: School Segregation in the Pre-Brown North*, 44 UCLA L Rev 677, 684–97, 701–04 (1997); Meier and Rudwick, 36 J Negro Educ (cited in note 17); Meier and Rudwick, 4 Hist Educ Q (cited in note 17); Meier and Rudwick, *Color Line* at 310 (cited in note 13); Randal M. Jelks, *Making Opportunity: The Struggle Against Jim Crow in Grand Rapids, Michigan, 1890–1927*, 19 Mich Hist Rev 23 (1993); Spear, *Black Chicago* at 23, 45, 85–86 (cited in note 17); Baker, *Color Line* at 123, 229 (cited in note 15); Lewis L. Gould, *The Presidency of Theodore Roosevelt* 257–61 (1991).

[61] Blakeman, 70 Filson Club Hist Q at 21, 23–24 (cited in note 58); Schmidt, 82 Colum L Rev at 449–50 (cited in note 51); Indianapolis Freeman (Dec 5, 1908), p 6.

of the broader constitutional issue indicates the Justices' reluctance to approve the extension of racial segregation to private institutions. These commentators surmise that the Justices, if forced to take a position, would have barred prosecutions of persons under the Day law. In support of this argument, they note that the corporate charter rationale was invoked almost as an afterthought by the Kentucky Court of Appeals and had not even been argued in the Supreme Court. Moreover, the rationale seems contrived, given the numerous state laws already invalidated by the Court for interfering with the constitutional rights of corporations.[62]

It is impossible to say whether this argument is correct. If the Justices really were inclined to invalidate segregation in private education, all they had to do was rule that the Day law was nonseverable, and thus its constitutional applications to corporations must fall along with its unconstitutional applications to individuals. Such a ruling would not have been a stretch. Thus the most one justifiably can infer from the Justices' contrived rationale is that they preferred to avoid the underlying constitutional question. This conclusion sheds no light on which result they would have reached if forced to confront the issue.

It is perfectly conceivable that the Justices in 1908 would have seen racial segregation as a sufficiently important public policy to justify subordinating the individual liberty interest in private contractual exchanges. Even those Justices most committed to a libertarian perspective acknowledged that valid police power objectives could trump individual liberty interests. After *Plessy*, racial segregation plainly qualified as such. According to the dominant contemporary understanding, segregation served the state interest in removing occasions for interracial friction and violence. It also furthered the state's supposedly important objective of preventing miscegenation and thus maintaining racial integrity. President Roosevelt himself proclaimed in 1905 that "race purity must be maintained," and numerous state and federal courts had concurred

---

[62] Ely, *Melville W. Fuller* at 159 (cited in note 28); *Ho Ak Kow v Nunan*, 5 Saw 562 (CCD Cal 1879) (Justice Field on circuit); *Berea College*, 211 US at 62–67 (Harlan, J, dissenting); Gillman, *Constitution Besieged* at 106–09 (cited in note 50). For commentators suggesting that the Court probably would have invalidated the Day law as applied to individuals, see Bernstein, 51 Vand L Rev at 832–33 (cited in note 59); Fiss, *Troubled Beginnings* at 370–71 (cited in note 50); Schmidt, 82 Colum L Rev at 447, 452 (cited in note 51).

by rejecting Fourteenth Amendment challenges to miscegenation bans. Moreover, the Justices likely would have perceived a more urgent state interest in maintaining educational than railroad segregation. Interracial contact in education was of greater duration and involved younger persons.[63]

For these reasons, if the Justices had been compelled to express an opinion, they might well have sustained the Day law as applied to individuals. As I have said, one cannot know for sure. But the legal materials would not have compelled a contrary result, and if the Justices' personal predilections mirrored contemporary public opinion on race, they would not have been inclined to forbid segregation even in private education.

3. *Public school segregation.* The Supreme Court had no occasion to consider the constitutionality of public school segregation during the *Plessy* period. Earlier efforts to appeal such cases to the Court had failed for lack of funds. The absence of such a case, however, should raise no doubt as to what its outcome would have been. It is virtually inconceivable that the *Plessy*-era Court would have invalidated public school segregation.[64]

Nineteenth-century public education was more racially segregated than railroad transportation. In the antebellum North, most states either segregated blacks or else excluded them entirely from the public schools. Only in a few states along the Canadian border, with tiny black populations, was the law silent about black public education, and thus integration was implicitly permitted and apparently practiced. Massachusetts was the only state in the antebellum period that formally barred public school segregation. After the Civil War, a handful of additional northern states—Rhode Island, Connecticut, and Michigan—integrated their public schools, partially as a result of the war's ideological repercussions. Yet most northern states continued to segregate blacks by law. Indeed, a

---

[63] Seth M. Scheiner, *President Theodore Roosevelt and the Negro, 1901–1908*, 47 J Negro Hist 169, 181 (1962) (quotation); *Muller v Oregon*, 208 US 412 (1908); *Holden v Hardy*, 169 US 366 (1898); Lofgren, *Plessy* at 110 (cited in note 18); Mangum, *Legal Status* at 239–40 (cited in note 35); Brief for the Defendant in Error, *Berea College v Kentucky*, 2, 4, 6–12, 39; *Berea College v Kentucky*, 94 SW 623, 624–27 (Ky Ct App 1906); Note, *Constitutionality of a Statute Compelling the Color Line in Private Schools*, 22 Harv L Rev 217, 218 (1909).

[64] J. Morgan Kousser, *Dead End: The Development of Nineteenth Century Litigation on Racial Discrimination in Schools* 21 (1986); *Reynolds v Board of Education*, 72 P 274, 281 (Kan 1903).

couple of midwestern states continued to exclude them altogether from public education.[65]

Slaveholding states almost universally excluded blacks from public education before the war. It became clear during Reconstruction that a Republican Congress would require southern states to provide for black public education as a price of readmission to the Union. At this point, segregation replaced exclusion. The only public school integration occurring anywhere in the South during Reconstruction was in New Orleans, an experiment that lasted for about six years, involved at most 20 percent of the city's blacks, and ultimately was destroyed by ferocious white resistance and the end of Reconstruction.

Elsewhere in the South, school integration simply was not practicable, in light of intense white resistance and the shallow roots of public education. State constitutional provisions inserted by Radical Republicans in Louisiana and South Carolina explicitly barred school segregation, yet were almost universally ignored in practice. While many southern blacks supported integration in principle, they recognized the futility of overcoming intense white resistance and generally pursued instead an equal division of the public school fund. After Reconstruction, many southern states formally segregated their public schools, confirming in law what already existed in fact. Thus school segregation in the South was far more pervasive than railroad segregation. It had been enshrined into law much earlier. And it generated less resistance among blacks.[66]

---

[65] Thornbrough, *Negro in Indiana* at 161–66, 317–23 (cited in note 17); David Martin Ment, "Racial Segregation in the Public Schools of New England and New York, 1840–1940" at chs 3–4 (Ph.D. diss, Columbia University, 1975); Litwack, *North of Slavery* at ch 4 (cited in note 32); Leonard Levy, *The Law of the Commonwealth and Chief Justice Shaw* 116 (1956); Fishel, "The North and the Negro" at chs 4–5 (cited in note 17); Gerber, *Black Ohio* at 190–91 (cited in note 17); Eugene H. Berwanger, *Reconstruction on the Frontier: The Equal Rights Struggle in Colorado, 1865–1867*, 44 Pacific Hist Rev 313, 318, 326 (1975); Carleton Mabee, *Long Island's Black "School War" and the Decline of Segregation in New York State*, 58 NY Hist 385 (1977); Edward J. Price, Jr., *School Segregation in Nineteenth-Century Pennsylvania*, 43 Pa Hist 121 (1976); Roger D. Bridges, *Equality Deferred: Civil Rights for Illinois Blacks, 1865–1885*, 74 J Ill St Hist Soc'y 83, 87, 96 (1981); Kousser, *Dead End* at 20 (cited in note 64).

[66] Foner, *Reconstruction* at 96, 320–22, 332, 365–68, 553–54, 592–93 (cited in note 20); Louis Harlan, *Desegregation in New Orleans Public Schools During Reconstruction*, 67 Am Hist Rev 663 (1962); Fischer, *Segregation Struggle* at chs 5, 6 (cited in note 10); William Preston Vaughn, *Schools for All: Blacks and Public Education in the South, 1865–1877* at 55, 57, 85–102 (1974); John Hope Franklin, *Jim Crow Goes to School: The Genesis of Legal Segregation in Southern Schools*, 58 So Atl Q 225, 230–31, 233–34 (1959); Tindall, *South Carolina Negroes*

Most northern states formally abolished school segregation in the 1870s or 1880s. Yet, as we shall see, segregation remained prevalent in regions of those states where the largest percentage of the black population resided. Moreover, by the 1890s, accelerating black migration northward resulted in the resegregation of schools in some localities that had formerly enjoyed integration.[67]

This is the historical background of public school segregation. Now we shall consider the legal background. The original intent argument against public school segregation is much weaker than with regard to railroad segregation. Given the underdeveloped status of public education in 1866–68, many contemporaries would have considered it more of a privilege than a right, and thus subject to whatever conditions the state chose to attach to it. Access to common carriers, on the other hand, was a well-established common law right. Moreover, the same Congress that wrote the Fourteenth Amendment persisted in segregating the schools in the District of Columbia, while simultaneously forbidding local railroads from segregating their passengers. It seems unlikely that Congress would have understood the Fourteenth Amendment to forbid school segregation when it continued to segregate the District's public schools, over which it exercised plenary control.

Furthermore, the vast majority of states that ratified the Fourteenth Amendment in 1866–68 either excluded blacks entirely from public education or else segregated them. It seems highly improbable that in ratifying the amendment these states would have, without protest, knowingly rendered their own public education practices unconstitutional. More plausibly, the contemporary understanding was that the amendment permitted public school segregation. Finally, the issue of public school segregation occasionally arose in the congressional debates on the 1866 Civil Rights Act and the Fourteenth Amendment. Opponents sought to score rhetorical points by exaggerating the scope of the measure

---

at 211 (cited in note 10); Horace Calvin Wingo, "Race Relations in Georgia, 1872–1908" at 194–95 (Ph.D. diss, Emory University, 1962); Cartwright, *Tennessee Race Relations* at 18, 107, 182 (cited in note 10); Wright, *Blacks in Louisville* at 65 (cited in note 11); Anderson, *North Carolina* at 329 (cited in note 10); Michael W. Homel, *Two Worlds of Race? Urban Blacks and the Public Schools, North and South, 1865–1940*, in David N. Plank and Rick Ginsberg, eds, *Southern Cities, Southern Schools: Public Education in the Urban South* 239–40 (1990).

[67] McConnell, 81 Va L Rev at 967–71 (cited in note 41); Kousser, *Dead End* at 38 n 28 (cited in note 64); notes 17 and 74.

under consideration, arguing that it would lead to a parade of horribles, including school integration. Republican proponents, whose opinion seems more weighty for original intent purposes, responded by denying that school segregation was prohibited.[68]

In sum, solid evidence suggests that the original understanding of the Fourteenth Amendment permitted public school segregation. To circumvent that evidence, it is necessary either to reject originalism as one's theory of constitutional interpretation or to focus one's originalist lens at a higher level of generality, attending to the Framers' general conceptions of equality rather than to their views about the permissibility of particular social practices. Ultimately, the Supreme Court would pursue both strategies in expanding the constitutional rights of black Americans. At the turn of the century, however, the existence of compelling originalist evidence supporting the constitutionality of public school segregation would have weighed heavily with the Justices.

Lower court precedent was equally unequivocal. More than a dozen decisions by state supreme courts and lower federal courts rejected Fourteenth Amendment challenges to public school segre-

---

[68] McConnell, 81 Va L Rev at 960, 962, 965–67, 1036–40 (cited in note 41); Alfred H. Kelly, *The Congressional Controversy Over School Segregation, 1867–1875*, 64 Am Hist Rev 537 (1959); Fairman, *Reconstruction and Reunion* at 1177–79, 1193 (cited in note 39); Berger, *Fourteenth Amendment* at ch 7 (cited in note 38); Bickel, 69 Harv L Rev at 56, 59 (cited in note 38); Avins, 38 Miss L J at 244–46 (cited in note 55); Maltz, 17 Rutgers L J at 567 (cited in note 41); Maltz, 44 Fla L Rev at 616 (cited in note 45); Maltz, 13 Const Comm at 228–31 (cited in note 42); Cong Globe, 39th Cong, 1st Sess 500 (1866) (Edgar Cowan); ibid, 1117, 1118 (James Wilson); ibid, 1121–22 (Andrew Rogers); ibid, 1268 (Michael Kerr).

Michael McConnell recently has defended *Brown* on originalist grounds. He argues that the debates on the 1875 Civil Rights Act are the most extensive congressional discussion of school segregation during Reconstruction and thus shed important light on the Fourteenth Amendment's original understanding. McConnell argues that in the mid-1870s a majority of both houses of Congress evinced support for a ban on school segregation. McConnell's argument is subject to a number of objections. First, given that Republicans often became more racially egalitarian over the course of Reconstruction, antisegregation views expressed in the mid-1870s may not be reliable evidence of sentiment in 1866–68. Second, at least some congressional Republicans supported ambiguous "full and equal enjoyment" language because they thought it permitted segregation. Third, at least some Republicans believed that Congress had broader power under Section 5 of the Fourteenth Amendment than a court had interpreting Section 1. Thus, even had the 1875 Civil Rights Act explicitly barred school segregation, this would have provided only limited originalist support for *Brown's* invalidation of the practice. Finally, McConnell fails adequately to defend the view that congressmen enacting legislation should be understood as expressing constitutional interpretations rather than mere policy preferences. For these criticisms, see Klarman, 81 Va L Rev at 1884–1914 (cited in note 42); Maltz, 13 Const Comm (cited in note 42). See also Avins, 38 Miss L J (cited in note 55). Originalism understandably suffers as a constitutional theory if it cannot justify *Brown*. Professor McConnell's heroic efforts to supply an originalist justification for *Brown* must be understood in that light.

gation. Frequently these courts observed that the same Congress that proposed the Fourteenth Amendment continued to segregate the schools in the District of Columbia. Many decisions invoked the notion of natural racial differences, which were said to be more powerful than law. Further, courts rejecting challenges to public school segregation reasoned that the Equal Protection Clause could not possibly forbid all group classifications, since everyone acknowledged that state legislatures could impose gender segregation in education. Since some group classifications were assumed to be permissible, the relevant question had to be whether a particular classification was reasonable. On the prevailing view, racial classifications plainly qualified as such.

There were numerous late nineteenth-century court decisions ordering the admission of black plaintiffs to formerly all-white schools. But these almost invariably involved either instances of inequality in the separate black schools or else *state* statutory or constitutional bars on segregation. The only two nineteenth-century decisions invalidating public school segregation under the Fourteenth Amendment were issued by lower court state judges in Pennsylvania and Kansas, both in 1881. The precedents construing the Fourteenth Amendment were sufficiently uniform that contemporary legal commentators generally took it as settled that the federal constitution permitted racial segregation in public schools. Congress seemed to share a similar assumption. Throughout the 1880s, it was prepared to accept southern school segregation in the context of the Blair bill, which would have provided federal funding for public education to be apportioned among the states according to rates of illiteracy.[69]

---

[69] *Allen v Davis*, 10 Weekly Notes of Cases 156 (Crawford County Pa 1881); *Tinnon v Board of Education*, 26 Kan 1 (1881) (affirming the trial court on state law grounds). Other state court decisions invalidating public school segregation under state law include *Clark v Board of Directors*, 24 Iowa 266 (1868); *Workman v Detroit*, 18 Mich 400 (1869); *Longress v Board of Education of Quincy*, 101 Ill 308 (1882). The more numerous decisions rejecting Fourteenth Amendment challenges include *Bertonneau v Board of Education*, 3 F Cas 294 (CCD La 1878); *United States v Buntin*, 10 F 730 (1882); *King v Gallagher*, 93 NY 438 (1883); *Garnes v McCann*, 21 Oh St 198 (1871); *Cory v Carter*, 48 Ind 327 (1874); *Lehew v Brummell*, 103 Mo 551 (1891), *Stoutmeyer v Duffy*, 7 Nev 342 (1872); *Ward v Flood*, 48 Cal 36 (1874). For discussion of these various decisions, see Kousser, *Dead End* (cited in note 64); Kull, *Color-Blind Constitution* at 95–112 (cited in note 38); McConnell, 81 Va L Rev at 971–77 (cited in note 41); Mangum, *Legal Status* at 78–119 (cited in note 35); Stephenson, *Race Distinctions* at 177–90 (cited in note 32). On the Blair bill, see Allen J. Going, *The South and the Blair Education Bill*, 44 Miss Valley Hist Rev 267 (1957); Willard B. Gatewood, Jr., *North Carolina and Federal Aid to Education: Public Reaction to the Blair Bill, 1881–1890*, 40 NC Hist Rev 465 (1963). Kousser is correct that relying on mere

With original intent and lower court precedent so overwhelmingly in support of the constitutionality of public school segregation, only a dramatic shift in public sentiment could have led the *Plessy*-era Court to invalidate the practice. Yet, if anything, dominant public opinion had become even more supportive of school segregation. Integration of public schools had been inconceivable to most southern whites in the mid-1860s and remained so in 1900. Indeed, as we shall see, by the turn of the century white southerners increasingly resisted even separate but equal education for blacks.

Nor would there have been much support in the North for compelling southern school integration. The growing northern commitment to sectional reconciliation translated into deference to white southerners' resolutions of their own race issues. Most white northerners at the turn of the century were not even committed to integrating their own schools. It is probably a mistake to infer substantial northern support for school integration during the *Plessy* era from the enactment in many northern states in the 1870s and 1880s of laws barring school segregation. The timing of these enactments seems attributable primarily to three factors: the slow growth during these decades of the northern black population, the highly competitive political situation, and the desire to avoid the inefficiencies inherent in a dual school system populated by relative handfuls of sparsely distributed black students. None of these conditions held true nearly to the same extent by the end of the century.[70]

The Civil War decade had witnessed a substantial black migration to the North, sparking race riots in southern Ohio and Indiana and renewed efforts to enforce the black exclusion laws of Indiana and Illinois. But this Civil War migration tapered off in the

numbers of decisions to establish the dominant view is misleading, given that state courts invalidating segregation under state law would not have reached the Fourteenth Amendment question. Kousser, *Dead End* at 10–12 (cited in note 64). Still, Kousser understates the extent to which there was a settled understanding that the Fourteenth Amendment permitted public school segregation.

[70] On these northern state laws, see Fishel, "The North and the Negro" at chs 4, 5, 7 (cited in note 17); Grossman, *Democratic Party* at 66, 70, 75, 81, 87–92 (cited in note 39); Gerber, *Black Ohio* at 45, 56–57, 190–244 (cited in note 17); Douglas, 44 UCLA L Rev at 684–97 (cited in note 60). McConnell argues that the passage of these laws indicates a widespread understanding that the Fourteenth Amendment barred school segregation. McConnell, 81 Va L Rev at 970 (cited in note 41); see also Ment, "Racial Segregation" at 145–46 (cited in note 65). I think the laws probably reflect the factors noted in the text more than any perceived constitutional imperative.

1870s and 1880s, leading to greater white tolerance, which manifested itself in the widespread adoption of public accommodations and anti-school segregation laws. As black migration northward accelerated in the 1890s, northern white racial prejudices reignited, producing demands for the reintroduction of school segregation.[71]

Nor did the intense party competition that had fostered these school segregation bans last until the end of the century. From roughly 1874 to 1894, neither political party enjoyed a secure advantage in most of the lower North. Even a black population as small as 1–2 percent of a state's electorate potentially represented the balance of power. With both parties possessing an electoral incentive to bid for the black vote, in some states it was Republicans and in others Democrats who engineered passage of civil rights legislation. After the transitional Republican victories of the mid-1890s, however, many of these northern states no longer remained politically competitive. With Republicans commanding secure majorities, they no longer needed the black vote. Many of the northern school boards that introduced segregation around the turn of the century were Republican-controlled.[72]

Finally, many northern communities had voluntarily desegregated their schools before the enactment of state laws forbidding segregation, because they found a dual school system prohibitively expensive. Relatively small black populations spread over sparsely populated rural districts exacerbated the cost inefficiencies of a dual school system. In these rural northern school districts, per capita spending on black children was sometimes two or three times that on white, owing to such inefficiencies. In the economic hard times that commenced with the Panic of 1873, many northern communities determined that segregated schools were too expensive. This condition also failed to hold true through the end

[71] *People v City of Alton*, 54 NE 421, 428 (Ill 1899); Foner, *Reconstruction* at 31–32 (cited in note 20); Gerber, *Black Ohio* at 26–30, 41 (cited in note 17); Thornbrough, *Negro in Indiana* at 184–91 (cited in note 17); Fredrickson, *Black Image* at 133–34 (cited in note 15); Bridges, 74 J Ill St Hist Soc'y at 84 (cited in note 65); Spencer R. Crew, *Black Life in Secondary Cities: A Comparative Analysis of the Black Communities of Camden and Elizabeth, New Jersey 1860–1920* at 125–27 (1993); Grossman, *Democratic Party* at 100–01 (cited in note 39); note 55.

[72] Gerber, *Black Ohio* at 211–12, 230–31, 235–43, 331, 333–34, 338 (cited in note 17); Grossman, *Democratic Party* at ch 3 (cited in note 39); Katzman, *Black Detroit* at 180 (cited in note 17); Bridges, 74 J Ill St Hist Soc'y at 104–08 (cited in note 65); Meier and Rudwick, 4 Hist Educ Q at 25, 31 (cited in note 17); Meier and Rudwick, 36 J Negro Educ at 395 (cited in note 17); notes 27–28.

of the century. As more southern blacks migrated northward and more northern blacks migrated from countryside to city, black population densities increased, thus reducing the cost inefficiencies of operating a dual school system.[73]

The commitment of white northerners to school integration not only eroded over time, but also was of dubious intensity in the first place. Much like the public accommodations laws discussed earlier, school segregation bans represented symbolic commitments that were largely ignored in practice without penalty. Such laws meant little in those regions inhabited by the largest number of blacks and the most racially intolerant whites: New York City and Brooklyn, Philadelphia, Cincinnati, southern New Jersey cities, and downstate counties in Ohio, Indiana, and Illinois. Thus, it probably would be mistaken to infer from these antisegregation laws a commitment by white northerners to impose school integration on themselves, much less to impose it on a more fiercely resistant white South.[74]

The Justices who formed the majority in *Plessy* certainly would have thought public school segregation constitutional. Even Justice Harlan, the lone dissenter in *Plessy*, probably shared that view. This conclusion is an inference from Harlan's opinion for the Court in *Cumming* (discussed below), upholding separate and *un*equal in education where reasonable, and the careful qualification in his *Berea College* dissent that *public* school segregation naturally posed a different question. Not a single *Plessy*-era Justice likely would have thought public school segregation unconstitutional.[75]

---

[73] Douglas, 44 UCLA L Rev at 687–89, 694–95 (cited in note 60); Fishel, "The North and the Negro" at chs 4, 5 (cited in note 17); Gerber, *Black Ohio* at 41, 53, 56, 190–97, 271, 274–76 (cited in note 17); Irving G. Hendrick, *Approaching Equality of Educational Opportunity in California: The Successful Struggle of Black Citizens, 1880–1920*, 25 Pacific Hist 22, 24–25 (1981); Ment, "Racial Segregation" at 78–81, 99–101, 136–37, 158 (cited in note 65); Cleveland Gazette (Feb 16, 1884), p 2; ibid (June 7, 1884), p 2; *Chase v Stephenson*, 71 Ill 383 (1874).

[74] Price, 43 Pa Hist at 135–37 (cited in note 65); Ment, "Racial Segregation" at 49, 153, 169–70, 180, 183, 282, 286 (cited in note 65); Douglas, 44 UCLA L Rev at 684–97 (cited in note 60); Gerber, *Black Ohio* at 57, 265–66 (cited in note 17); Fishel, "The North and the Negro" at 183–84, 317–25 (cited in note 17); Meier and Rudwick, 4 Hist Educ Q at 29 (cited in note 17); Meier and Rudwick, 36 J Negro Educ at 395 (cited in note 17); W. E. B. DuBois, *The Philadelphia Negro* 349 (1899); Homel, "Two Worlds of Race?" at 242 (cited in note 66); 58 Nation 112 (Feb 15, 1894).

[75] Yarbrough, *Judicial Enigma* at 228 (cited in note 30); Schmidt, 82 Colum L Rev at 472 (cited in note 51); Fiss, *Troubled Beginnings* at 369 (cited in note 50); *Berea College v Kentucky*, 211 US 45, 58 (1908) (Harlan, J, dissenting); Earl M. Maltz, 12 Ga St U L Rev at 990–91 (cited in note 48). But see Kull, *Color-Blind Constitution* at 124–29 (cited in note 38).

B. DISFRANCHISEMENT

Slaves naturally were not permitted to vote in the antebellum South. Free blacks had enjoyed the suffrage in some southern states, but not after the 1830s. In the late antebellum North, only five New England states imposed no racial restriction on the right to vote. The trend in the North was toward restricting black suffrage. Pennsylvania and Connecticut once had permitted blacks to vote, but no longer by the Civil War.[76]

White resistance to black suffrage did not suddenly evaporate after Appomattox. It is true that the war augmented support for black suffrage and that the Republican Party gradually concluded it was an imperative. Yet most white southerners remained adamantly opposed, as did many white northerners. Between 1865 and 1867, half a dozen northern states voted down referenda that would have extended suffrage to blacks. Republican congressional leaders rejected proposed versions of the Fourteenth Amendment that would have enfranchised blacks for fear of a northern political backlash. The dominant understanding of Section 1 of the Fourteenth Amendment was that it protected only civil, not political, rights. Even Republican leaders who favored black suffrage acknowledged that they lacked the votes necessary to secure it under the Fourteenth Amendment.[77]

Republicans in the late 1860s faced a conundrum. If they forced black suffrage on resistant northern constituents, they risked sacrificing the party's tenuous majorities in several northern states. If they permitted the status quo of black disfranchisement in

---

For a fascinating discussion between Justices Felix Frankfurter and John Marshall Harlan (the first Justice Harlan's grandson) over whether the *Plessy* dissent indicates that the elder Harlan would have endorsed *Brown*, see Tinsley E. Yarbrough, *John Marshall Harlan: Great Dissenter of the Warren Court* 121–23 (1992).

[76] Litwack, *North of Slavery* at 75, 263 (cited in note 32); Grossman, *Democratic Party* at 16 (cited in note 39); Woodward, *Jim Crow* at 20 (cited in note 11).

[77] Gillette, *Right to Vote* at ch 1 (cited in note 23); John N. Mathews, *Legislative and Judicial History of the Fifteenth Amendment* 11–14, 17–18, 22 (1909); Bond, 18 Akron L Rev at 445–53 (cited in note 39); Leslie H. Fishel, Jr., *Northern Prejudice and Negro Suffrage, 1865–1870*, 39 J Negro Hist 8 (1954); Fredrickson, *Black Image* at 183–86 (cited in note 15); Gerber, *Black Ohio* at 35–37 (cited in note 17); Thornbrough, *Negro in Indiana* at 239–41 (cited in note 17); Berwanger, 44 Pac Hist Rev (cited in note 65); Amy H. Hiller, *The Disfranchisement of Delaware Negroes from the Late Nineteenth Century*, 13 Del Hist 124, 125–27 (1968); Foner, *Reconstruction* at 223–24 (cited in note 20); McMillen, *Dark Journey* at 36–37 (cited in note 11); Vikram David Amar, *Jury Service as Political Participation Akin to Voting*, 80 Cornell L Rev 203, 223–26 (1995).

the South to continue, however, they faced the prospect that a politically resurgent South would enable the Democratic Party to reassume its accustomed control over the national government. Republicans in 1866 pursued the politically expedient strategy of pressuring southern states to enfranchise blacks while leaving northern states free to continue disfranchising them. This approach was embodied in Section 2 of the Fourteenth Amendment, which provided that states denying the suffrage to adult males for reasons other than criminal offense would suffer a proportionate reduction in their congressional representation. Since blacks in 1866 constituted majorities in three southern states, and more than 40 percent of the population in five others, Section 2 represented a powerful inducement for the South to enfranchise blacks. But its force depended on the amendment's ratification. With southern states refusing to ratify in 1866–67, the amendment could not secure passage in three-fourths of the state legislatures, as required for ratification under Article V.[78]

Thus Republican leaders pursued a different tack in 1867, after the party had preserved its enormous congressional majorities at the 1866 election, partly by avoiding the suffrage issue. The Republican Congress now forced black suffrage upon the South as an exercise of the congressional war power and deployed federal forces to register the freedmen to vote for delegates to constitutional conventions that Congress required southern states to hold. The result was a mass black voter turnout and Republican domination of the conventions as well as of the state legislatures elected under the new constitutions. This strategy, while successful in its immediate objective, lacked permanency as a solution. The Reconstruction Act was an exercise of the war power. Most contemporaries doubted that Congress had constitutional authority permanently to impose black suffrage on the states by statute. Moreover, while the recent state constitutional conventions had written black suffrage into state law, Democrats mights easily repeal such provisions once they regained local control. Finally, Congress had extracted from southern states seeking readmission to the Union

---

[78] Foner, *Reconstruction* at 251–69 (cited in note 20); Maltz, *Civil Rights* at 36–37, 50, 122–23 (cited in note 38); Joseph James, *The Ratification of the Fourteenth Amendment* 24, 42–43, 47–48 (1984); Fairman, *Reconstruction and Reunion* at 253–58 (cited in note 39); Fishel, 39 J Negro Hist (cited in note 77).

promises not to add future qualifications to the suffrage. Yet these conditions of readmission were of dubious constitutionality, since they deprived southern states of equal rights within the Union.[79]

For these reasons, most Republicans by 1868 favored a constitutional amendment to permanently protect black suffrage. But such an amendment would have to be national in scope for the party to avoid charges of rank hypocrisy. This simply recreated the party's dilemma. Many northern Republican voters continued to resist imposing black suffrage on themselves, as evidenced by the defeat of several black suffrage referenda in 1867. The party's solution to the dilemma was to be deceitful. The Republicans' national platform in 1868 endorsed black suffrage in the South under the Reconstruction Act, while committing to state control of the suffrage in the rest of the nation. Most northern Republican candidates ignored the suffrage issue in their campaigns that year. After the election, though, the Republican Congress immediately introduced a constitutional amendment to bar disfranchisement based on race throughout the nation. Over Democratic charges of deceit, Republicans rammed the Fifteenth Amendment through Congress and the requisite number of state legislatures, often by slender party line divisions. In a couple of northern states, voters retaliated against Republicans for their electoral bait-and-switch tactics, returning Democratic majorities at the ensuing state elections. The Republican-dominated Congress, however, ignored efforts by these now Democratic state legislatures to rescind their states' earlier ratification of the Fifteenth Amendment. Four southern states, not yet restored to congressional representation, were required to ratify the amendment as a condition for their readmission to the Union.[80]

---

[79] Fairman, *Reconstruction and Reunion* at 259–309 (cited in note 39); Maltz, *Civil Rights* at 124–41 (cited in note 38); Foner, *Reconstruction* at 271–80 (cited in note 20).

[80] Foner, *Reconstruction* at 315, 445–49 (cited in note 20); Fishel, "The North and the Negro" at 104–24 (cited in note 17); Gerber, *Black Ohio* at 38–40 (cited in note 17); Thornbrough, *Negro in Indiana* at 241–49 (cited in note 17); Gillette, *Right to Vote* passim (cited in note 23); Maltz, *Civil Rights* at 121–56 (cited in note 38); Cox and Cox, 33 J Southern Hist (cited in note 23); Mathews, *Fifteenth Amendment* at 20–21, 60–63, 73 (cited in note 77); Bridges, 74 J Ill St Hist Soc'y at 90–93 (cited in note 65). Historians have disagreed about the Republicans' principal motive in passing the Fifteenth Amendment. The conventional view is that the party was trying to solidify its southern electoral base. Gillette, in his revisionist book, argued that Republicans were trying to enhance their position in northern and border states, where black voters might provide the margin of victory. LaWanda and John Cox responded to Gillette by stressing principle rather than partisan

With their suffrage now secured in the South, black voters turned out in huge numbers, with the ballot constituting an important symbol of the freedmen's liberation. As anticipated, the party of emancipation was the principal beneficiary of this black voter turnout. Since blacks constituted 40–60 percent of the population in most southern states, Republicans won resounding victories everywhere. Black voters also elected large, though never proportionate, numbers of black officeholders. For example, at particular moments during Reconstruction, blacks constituted nearly half the representatives in the lower houses of the Mississippi and Louisiana legislatures and a majority in South Carolina's. As many as sixteen southern blacks were elected to Congress during Reconstruction. Numerous blacks held state executive offices, and a black justice sat on the South Carolina Supreme Court. There were also hundreds of local black officeholders during Reconstruction— sheriffs, magistrates, county council members.[81]

This potent display of black political power was short-lived, however. Southern whites, even where a minority of the population, continued to possess a majority of the economic, social, and physical power. Through a combination of fraud, intimidation, and violence, whites gradually reduced the black vote in one southern state after another, enabling Democrats to "redeem" the South from Reconstruction. Where necessary—as in Alabama in 1874, Mississippi in 1875, and South Carolina in 1876—whites conducted extraordinary campaigns of intimidation and murder to overthrow Republican rule. The euphemistically named "Mississippi plan" of 1875 was in fact a campaign of unparalleled political violence and intimidation that left scores of blacks dead throughout the state. The Grant administration had used military intervention to suppress such violence in the past, but was no longer prepared to do so. The President and his Cabinet calculated in the autumn of 1875 that deploying the military to protect the party's southern base would alienate voters in critical northern states, where support for military Reconstruction had faded. Freed from the threat

---

advantage as the Republicans' animating purpose. The debate is summarized in Goldman, *Voting Rights* at 6–10 (cited in note 23).

[81] Foner, *Reconstruction* at 291, 294, 351–58 (cited in note 20); Wharton, *Negro in Mississippi* at 167–69, 176, 179 (cited in note 10); McMillen, *Dark Journey* at 37 (cited in note 11); Tindall, *South Carolina Negroes* at 8–9 (cited in note 10); Williamson, *South Carolina Negroes* at 330 (cited in note 11); Rabinowitz, *First New South* at 75–76 (cited in note 14).

of outside intervention, southern whites took whatever steps they deemed necessary to reassume political control.[82]

Southern black political power, while reduced, did not suddenly disappear with the end of Reconstruction. A majority of eligible blacks were still voting in most southern states in 1880. Blacks continued to sit, often in significant numbers, in several state legislatures and occasionally in Congress. There were nine blacks in South Carolina's legislature and eleven in Mississippi's in 1882, and eighteen in Louisiana's in 1890. Indeed, in states like Tennessee and North Carolina, the number of black officeholders peaked in the 1880s, not during Reconstruction, as blacks began demanding their share of the spoils of office in return for providing the vast majority of the party's electoral support. Black congressmen continued to represent Mississippi into the 1880s, South Carolina and Virginia into the 1890s, and North Carolina until 1901. Perhaps more significantly, in many black belt counties, blacks continued to hold important local offices through the 1880s and, less frequently, into the 1890s. In North Carolina's majority black congressional district, there were literally hundreds of black local officeholders under the Republican-Populist fusion regime of the mid-1890s.[83]

A more dramatic decline in black political participation took place in the late 1880s and early 1890s. Majority black counties that had voted Republican or Independent in the early 1880s were, by the end of the decade, controlled by Democrats who had intimidated or defrauded black voters. Part of this change may be attributable to the Democrats' control of the presidency from 1885 to 1889. For the first time since passage of enforcement legislation

---

[82] Foner, *Reconstruction* at 422–44, 550–63 (cited in note 20); Gillette, *Retreat from Reconstruction* at 104–65, 306–23 (cited in note 20); Wharton, *Negro in Mississippi* at ch 13 (cited in note 10); Williamson, *South Carolina Negroes* at 266–73, 343, 357, 360 (cited in note 11); Cresswell, *Multi-Party Politics* at 14–17 (cited in note 10); Benedict, "Politics of Reconstruction" at 57, 70–71 (cited in note 23).

[83] Anderson, *North Carolina* at 4–5, 43, 64, 66, 106–07, 187, 238, 245, 247, 250–51, 276, 333, 340–41 (cited in note 10); Cartwright, *Tennessee Race Relations* at 65–66, 71–72, 78–80, 83, 101 (cited in note 10); Lawrence D. Rice, *The Negro in Texas 1874–1900* at ch 6 (1971); Kousser, *Southern Politics* at 15 table 1.2, 28, 106–07, 130 (cited in note 25); Woodward, *Jim Crow* at 32–33 (cited in note 11); Cresswell, *Multi-Party Politics* at 17, 42–43 (cited in note 10); Tindall, *South Carolina Negroes* at 54, 58–59 (cited in note 10); Wharton, *Negro in Mississippi* at 202 (cited in note 10); Fischer, *Segregation Struggle* at 152–53 (cited in note 10); Wynes, *Race Relations in Virginia* at 42–43 (cited in note 11); Meier, *Negro Thought* at 37 (cited in note 13); Donald G. Nieman, *Black Political Power and Criminal Justice: Washington County, Texas, 1868–1884*, 55 J Southern Hist 391, 395–96 (1989).

in 1870, white southerners were largely immunized from potential criminal prosecution for disfranchising blacks through fraud and violence. Another factor may have been the perception by 1890, even after Republicans had reassumed control of Congress and the presidency, that northerners had grown sympathetic to the southern white view of black political participation and thus would not intervene against disfranchisement. The rising power of the Farmers' Alliance in the South by the late 1880s, which threatened to sow political divisions among whites along economic lines, also might have furthered the cause of black disfranchisement.[84]

While the timing and the method of formal disfranchisement varied from state to state, the general pattern was consistent. First, black political participation gradually was reduced through force and fraud. Then, Democratic-controlled legislatures enacted new electoral laws, such as complex voter registration requirements, which further reduced the black vote and, concomitantly, Republican Party representation in state legislatures. This enabled implementation of state constitutional changes, primarily poll taxes and literacy tests, which consummated black disfranchisement. In most southern states, however, black political participation already had been drastically reduced before the final constitutional capstone was put in place.[85]

Formal disfranchisement took many forms. Complex voter registration requirements conferred broad discretion on white Democratic registrars and disadvantaged the illiterate as well as those who were most mobile—both groups assumed to be disproportionately black. Residency requirements for voting, generally longer in the South than elsewhere, similarly penalized more itinerant blacks. Secret ballot laws operated as surrogate literacy tests by requiring voters to read and mark their ballots by themselves. Conviction for certain crimes resulted in disfranchisement. The

---

[84] Kousser, *Southern Politics* at 36, 99, 107–08, 153–54, 157 (cited in note 25); Wynes, *Race Relations in Virginia* at 41 (cited in note 11); DeSantis, *Southern Question* at 191 (cited in note 20); Anderson, *North Carolina* at 145 (cited in note 10); Cartwright, *Tennessee Race Relations* at 95–97, 199–202, 216, 237 (cited in note 10); Cresswell, *Multi-Party Politics* at 215 (cited in note 10).

[85] Kousser, *Southern Politics* at 3, 39–40, 50, 99, 127, 147, 161–62, 174–75, 189–90, 203, 243, 246 (cited in note 25); Anderson, *North Carolina* at 185, 296 (cited in note 10); Cresswell, *Multi-Party Politics* at 220 (cited in note 10); Tindall, *South Carolina Negroes* at 68–71, 88–89 (cited in note 10); Rice, *Negro in Texas* at 113–14, 130–39 (cited in note 83); Cell, *White Supremacy* at 185 (cited in note 11). See also notes 177–79.

list of disfranchising offenses was gerrymandered to reflect white perceptions of black criminal propensities—"furtive offenses [rather than] the robust crimes of the whites," as the Mississippi Supreme Court explained. For example, arson and obtaining money under false pretenses, as well as fornication and wife beating, would result in disfranchisement, but murder would not.

Most of the disfranchising states adopted literacy tests, which would have disproportionately impacted blacks even if applied fairly, given much higher black illiteracy rates (still over 50 percent in most southern states in 1900). But it was never contemplated that the tests would be fairly applied. Determinations of literacy required discretionary judgments by voter registrars, who were appointed by Democratic officials committed to preserving white political supremacy. Moreover, most literacy tests were accompanied by "understanding clauses," which permitted illiterates to register if they could satisfy registrars of their ability to understand a state constitutional provision that was read to them. Grandfather clauses performed a similar function by exempting from the literacy test those who had been eligible to vote before 1867 (when blacks were first enfranchised in the South) or were descended from such persons, as well as, in some states, former soldiers and their descendants. Every southern state adopted a poll tax as a requirement for voting. These required prospective voters to pay an annual tax ranging from $1.00 to $2.00, in some states cumulating over years of nonpayment. Poll taxes disparately affected blacks, who were generally poorer than whites, and were responsible for disfranchising many prospective voters at a time when most people were farmers or farm laborers, living mainly on credit and earning annual incomes averaging less than $100. Finally, most southern states adopted white primaries, effectively excluding those blacks still registered to vote from participating in the only southern elections that made any practical difference—the Democratic primary.[86]

[86] *Ratliff v Beale*, 74 Miss 247, 266 (1896) (quotation); Stephenson, *Race Distinctions* at ch 11 (cited in note 32); Kousser, *Southern Politics* at chs 2–3 (cited in note 25); Ogden, *Poll Tax* at chs 1–2 (cited in note 16); Hackney, *Populism to Progressivism* at ch 9 (cited in note 11); Tindall, *South Carolina Negroes* at ch 5 (cited in note 10); John C. Rose, *Negro Suffrage: The Constitutional Point of View*, 1 Am Pol Sci Rev 17 (1906); Woodward, *New South* at 330–38 (cited in note 10); Callcott, *Negro in Maryland Politics* at ch 5 (cited in note 27); Lewinson, *Race, Class, and Party* at chs 4–5 (cited in note 10).

The timing of disfranchisement varied widely. Georgia enacted a poll tax after Redemption in 1871 and made it cumulative in 1877. In 1882 South Carolina adopted a draconian registration law and its infamous eight-box law, which operated as a surrogate literacy test by requiring voters to place their ballots in the correct box. Many southern states adopted secret ballot laws and more complex voter registration requirements in 1889–90, and Mississippi blazed a new trail with its disfranchising constitutional convention in the latter year. South Carolina followed suit in 1895, but most of the other disfranchising conventions and constitutional amendments did not take place until the turn of the century— Louisiana in 1898, North Carolina in 1900, Alabama in 1901, and Virginia in 1901–02. Texas, with a smaller black population and less bitter memories from the Civil War and Reconstruction, did not adopt its disfranchising poll tax until 1903. Georgia did not finally disfranchise blacks by constitutional amendment until 1908.[87]

The causes of formal disfranchisement were complex, and the electoral dynamics varied from state to state. Most southern whites never had accepted the legitimacy of the Fifteenth Amendment. These people probably would have supported formal elimination of the black vote as soon as the decline of Republican representation in southern legislatures and the threat of northern intervention had rendered this possible. The informal suppression of the black vote by the late 1880s, and the concomitant demise in Republican Party strength in southern state legislatures, rendered possible the adoption of formal disfranchisement measures. Ironically, the threat of outside intervention proved greatest in the moment before it precipitately declined. In the 1888 election, Republicans regained secure control of the presidency and both houses of Congress for the first time since 1874. The Republican Party platform and President Benjamin Harrison's inaugural address both promised stronger legislation for the supervision of federal elections, thus jeopardizing the southern black disfranchisement that already had been achieved through force and fraud. These national political developments inspired several southern states im-

---

[87] Kousser, *Southern Politics* at 32, 41–42, 67 table 3.2, 91 table 4.3, 196–97, 210–11, 238, 239 table 9.1 (cited in note 25); Cohen, *Freedom's Edge* at 205 & table 8, 209 (cited in note 11); Tindall, *South Carolina Negroes* at 69–70 (cited in note 10).

mediately to enact voter registration laws, secret ballot requirements, and other devices to "legally" disfranchise blacks and thus
negate the proposed federal legislation. Moreover, the Republicans' failure to enact the proposed elections bill in 1890–91 was
widely interpreted by white southerners as an invitation to proceed
with formal disfranchisement.[88]

Internal political developments in the South in the 1890s also
explain the success of the disfranchisement movement. The rise
and fall of Populism in the 1890s probably played some role,
though it is difficult to say precisely how much. The spate of new
electoral laws passed in 1889 and the Mississippi constitutional
convention of 1890 occurred before the creation of the Populist
Party, and thus cannot be attributed to this political phenomenon.
The high tide of southern Populism came between 1892 and 1896
and probably explains the relative absence of disfranchisement activity during these years. Conservatives feared holding a constitutional convention with radical Populism afoot. Moreover, with the
temporary reinvigoration of partisan competition in the South, all
parties had an incentive to compete for the black vote, which made
a disfranchisement campaign all but impossible.

With southern Populism largely extinguished after 1896, the
disfranchisement movement accelerated. White former Populists
often supported disfranchisement, blaming blacks for their electoral defeats. Indeed, especially in Georgia, Alabama, Louisiana,
and Texas, fraudulent manipulation of the black vote probably did
enable Democrats to cheat Populists out of significant electoral
victories. Moreover, some former Populists now endorsed black
disfranchisement because their political tribulations had taught
them the difficulty of establishing a viable alternative to the Democratic Party so long as the presence of black voters could be used
as a rhetorical whip to maintain white political unity. Conservative
white Democrats likewise supported disfranchisement, and indeed
usually led the crusade. They were anxious to avoid a repetition

---

[88] Kousser, *Southern Politics* at 32, 140, 152, 238 (cited in note 25); Wharton, *Negro in
Mississippi* at 182, 197–98, 208–09 (cited in note 10); Lewinson, *Race, Class, and Party* at
86–87 (cited in note 10); Cresswell, *Multi-Party Politics* at 102 (cited in note 10); Anderson,
North Carolina at 145, 165 (cited in note 10); Cartwright, *Tennessee Race Relations* at 91 n
69, 208 (cited in note 10); Fredrickson, *Black Image* at 262 (cited in note 15); Welch, 52
J Am Hist at 512, 526 (cited in note 26); Goldman, *Voting Rights* at 190 (cited in note 23);
Ogden, *Poll Tax* at 29–30 (cited in note 16); Dephloff and Jones, 9 La Hist at 321 (cited
in note 11); 51 Nation 86–87 (July 31, 1890).

of the interracial, class-based movement that had won control of the North Carolina government in the mid-1890s and had come perilously close to evicting Democrats from power in several other southern states. Such recent displays of black political power recalled Reconstruction memories (often imagined) of "negro domination." Many whites resolved to eliminate forever the threat posed to white supremacy by black suffrage. In addition to disfranchising blacks, many conservative Democrats were eager to disfranchise as many of the poor white farmers who had voted Populist as possible, and they privately said so.[89]

It is impossible to say how much black disfranchisement resulted from formal as opposed to informal methods, or which among the formal devices was most effective. Yet the bottom line result is apparent: Black voter registration and turnout fell dramatically in the 1890s and was substantially eliminated by the beginning of the twentieth century, except in the largest southern cities where a few hundred blacks continued to vote. In Louisiana black voter registration fell from 95.6 percent before the 1896 registration law went into effect to 9.5 percent immediately thereafter, and then to 2.9 percent in 1902 and 1.1 percent in 1904. In Alabama black voter registration plummeted from 180,000 in 1900 to 3,000 in 1903 after new constitutional suffrage provisions were implemented. Registration figures undoubtedly overstated voter turnout by a substantial margin. In Mississippi black voter turnout was an

---

[89] Woodward, *New South* at 261–62, 275–77, 322, 343–44 (cited in note 10); Kousser, *Southern Politics* at 16–17, 36–37, 40, 43, 68–70, 91, 131, 157–59, 175, 203, 215–16 (cited in note 25); Anderson, *North Carolina* at chs 11, 12, 14 (cited in note 10); Hackney, *Populism to Progressivism* at 22, 36, 42–43, 47, 62–63, 151–52, 177 (cited in note 11); Rice, *Negro in Texas* at ch 5 (cited in note 83); Goodwyn, 76 Am Hist Rev (cited in note 16); Cantrell and Barton, 55 J Southern Hist at 660, 683, 687–91 (cited in note 16); Ogden, *Poll Tax* at ch 1 (cited in note 16); Cell, *White Supremacy* at 119–22, 152–54, 170 (cited in note 11); Ayers, *New South* at 269–76, 304 (cited in note 13); Lewinson, *Race, Class, and Party* at 74–76 (cited in note 10); Rabinowitz, *First New South* at 101–12 (cited in note 14); William Alexander Mabry, *Louisiana Politics and the "Grandfather Clause,"* 13 NC Hist Rev 290 (1936); Joseph H. Taylor, *Populism and Disfranchisement in Alabama*, 34 J Negro Hist 410 (1949); William Alexander Mabry, *Ben Tillman Disfranchised the Negro*, 37 So Atl Q 170, 171–73, 182 (1938). On southern memories of Reconstruction and horrors of black domination, see Stone, *American Race Problem* at 261–71 (cited in note 19).

In states such as Tennessee and Virginia, Populists made little effort to appeal to black voters. But in other states—principally Texas, Alabama, and Georgia—the appeal to black voters was genuine. Populists in those states gave blacks positions in the party and promised them protection for their rights to serve on juries and to vote, an equal share of the school fund, an end to convict lease, and legal action against lynching. For differing assessments of the extent of the Populists' appeal to black voters and of the success of interracial alliances, see the sources noted above.

estimated 29 percent in the 1888 presidential election, 2 percent in the 1892 presidential contest, and 0 percent in the 1895 gubernatorial election. Florida implemented election law changes after the 1888 elections, including a poll tax, eight-box law, and more stringent voter registration requirements. Black voter turnout fell from an estimated 62 percent in Florida's 1888 gubernatorial election to 11 percent in 1892 and just 5 percent in 1896.[90]

Disfranchisement was a momentous event in the history of southern race relations. Conditions for southern blacks could not have deteriorated as much as they did without political disempowerment. As black voters disappeared, so did black officeholders. No blacks sat in the Mississippi legislature after 1895, down from a high of sixty-four in 1873. In 1896 just one black representative remained in the South Carolina lower house, where during Reconstruction there had been a black majority. The last black congressman to represent any southern state until the early 1970s, George White of North Carolina, relinquished his seat in 1901. Perhaps more importantly, black disfranchisement meant an end to black officeholding at the local level. Sheriffs, justices of the peace, jurors, county commissioners, and school board members played the most crucial governmental role in the lives of late nineteenth-century southerners. These officials exercised tremendous discretion in the administration of law. The most important method of depriving southern blacks of their constitutional rights was to vest broad administrative discretion in local governmental officials and then trust them to further the ends of white supremacy.

Disfranchisement was essential to the success of this strategy. During Reconstruction, when blacks voted in large numbers and Republicans controlled most state governments, many of these local officials either were black or were white Republicans beholden to the black vote. Even after Reconstruction, black officeholders remained abundant in states and counties where blacks continued to vote in large numbers, at least through the 1880s. After disfran-

---

[90] Lewinson, *Race, Class, and Party* at 81, 104, 106, 123, 144 (cited in note 10); Kousser, *Southern Politics* at 101 table 4.10, 145 table 6.3, 163 table 6.6, 223 (cited in note 25); Rabinowitz, *First New South* at 114, 115 (cited in note 14); Woodward, *Jim Crow* at 342–44 (cited in note 11); Dewey W. Grantham, Jr., *Georgia Politics and the Disfranchisement of the Negro*, 32 Ga Hist Q 1, 20 (1948); Earl Lewis, *In Their Own Interests: Race, Class, and Power in Twentieth Century Norfolk, Virginia* 21 (1991); Cresswell, *Multi-Party Politics* at 109, 220 (cited in note 10); Ogden, *Poll Tax* at 115–17 (cited in note 16).

chisement, though, these local offices were occupied entirely by whites, most of whom were committed to a race-conscious administration of the law. Thus, for example, disfranchisement facilitated the exclusion of blacks from juries, which removed a significant impediment to racially biased administration of the law. Similarly, disfranchisement eroded the ability of blacks to safeguard their fair share of the public school fund, leading to enormous disparities in educational spending.[91]

This is the historical background to black disfranchisement. The legal question confronting the Supreme Court was whether the various disfranchisement measures violated the Fifteenth Amendment, which provides that the right of U.S. citizens to vote "shall not be denied or abridged by the United States or by any State on account of race, color, or previous condition of servitude." White southerners were careful not to openly nullify the amendment by imposing express racial conditions on the suffrage. They assumed that such measures would induce federal intervention, either in the form of judicial invalidation or reduction in congressional representation under Section 2 of the Fourteenth Amendment. Thus, many southern politicians were alarmed by Maryland's disfranchisement proposal in 1910–11, which expressly denied the binding force of the Fifteenth Amendment and sought to impose an explicit racial qualification on the suffrage. Southern critics of Maryland's efforts feared that the nation would "not submit without a protest to the barefaced nullification" of the Fifteenth Amendment, and they predicted that Maryland's scheme would incite a backlash against their own more subtle disfranchisement measures. Indeed, one might surmise that even southern state courts would have felt compelled to invalidate laws that explicitly barred black political participation, much as they reversed criminal convictions in cases where jury commissioners admitted racially

---

[91] Michael J. Klarman, *The Puzzling Resistance to Political Process Theory*, 77 Va L Rev 747, 789–807 (1991); Wharton, *Negro in Mississippi* at 134, 176 (cited in note 10); Tindall, *South Carolina Negroes* at 58–59 (cited in note 10); Cresswell, *Multi-Party Politics* at 142 (cited in note 10); Anderson, *North Carolina* at 4–5, 54, 187, 245, 248–51, 315–19 (cited in note 10); Foner, *Reconstruction* at 355–57, 362–63, 590–92, 595 (cited in note 20); Rabinowitz, *Urban South* at 36–42, 266, 277 (cited in note 11); Rice, *Negro in Texas* at 86–112, 240–41 (cited in note 83); Nieman, 55 J Southern Hist (cited in note 83); Wharton, *Negro in Mississippi* at 167–68 (cited in note 10); Wynes, *Race Relations in Virginia* at 25–26, 29–30 (cited in note 11); Cartwright, *Tennessee Race Relations* at 119, 128–30, 147–50 (cited in note 10); Samuel N. Pincus, *The Virginia Supreme Court: Blacks and the Law 1870–1902* at 47 (1990); notes 126, 142.

motivated exclusion of blacks. Thus, in 1904 a Georgia court invalidated a state law limiting the right to vote in municipal elections to whites.[92]

Most white southerners saw the wisdom in avoiding measures that formally nullified the Fifteenth Amendment. Yet they persisted in viewing that amendment as entirely illegitimate. The president of the Louisiana disfranchisement convention of 1898 stated the prevalent view when he referred to the Fifteenth Amendment as "the greatest crime of the Nineteenth Century." On this view, a crazed Republican Congress bent on partisan gain had imposed "black domination" by ignorant freedmen on the South. Deterred by the threat of outside intervention from explicitly nullifying the amendment, white southerners generally felt "morally justified in evading and defeating [its] admitted purpose." Accordingly, the disfranchisers were not subtle about their objectives. They openly stated their purpose to disfranchise blacks to the extent permitted by the Fifteenth Amendment. Thus Carter Glass at the Virginia disfranchisement convention of 1901–02 acknowledged that the convention's mission was "to discriminate to the very extremity of permissible action under the limitations of the Federal Constitution, with a view to the elimination of every negro voter who can be gotten rid of, legally."[93]

The Supreme Court had little to draw upon in terms of original intent or legal precedent in determining the constitutionality of suffrage restrictions that fell short of express racial qualifications yet had the effect of disfranchising most blacks and few whites. However, the original understanding of the Fifteenth Amendment

---

[92] US Const, Amend XV, § 1 (first quotation); 90 Nation 334 (April 7, 1910) (second quotation); George B. Tindall, *The Question of Race in the South Carolina Constitutional Convention of 1895*, 37 J Negro Hist 277, 283 (1952); Kousser, *Southern Politics* at 45–46 (cited in note 25); Stephenson, *Race Distinctions* at 319–20 (cited in note 32); Callcott, *Negro in Maryland Politics* at 130–32 (cited in note 27); *Porter v Commissioners of Kingfisher County*, 51 P 741 (Okla 1898); *Howell v Pate*, 119 Ga 537 (1904).

[93] Amasa M. Eaton, *The Suffrage Clause in the New Constitution of Louisiana*, 13 Harv L Rev 278, 281–82, 288, 289 (1899) (first quotation); Rose, 1 Am Pol Sci Rev at 19 (cited in note 86) (second quotation); Buck, *Road to Reunion* at 287 (cited in note 20) (third quotation); *Ratliff v Beal*, 74 Miss 247, 266 (1896); Poe, 175 North Am Rev at 534–37 (cited in note 19); Callcott, *Negro in Maryland Politics* at 122 (cited in note 27); Collins, *Fourteenth Amendment* at 141–44 (cited in note 150); Hackney, *Populism to Progressivism* at 190–91 (cited in note 11); Mabry, 4 J Southern Hist at 329 (cited in note 13); Tindall, *South Carolina Negroes* at 85–86 (cited in note 10); Mabry, 13 NC Hist Rev at 309 (cited in note 89); Baltimore Sun (Feb 3, 1908), p 12; 61 Nation 199 (Sept 19, 1895); 8 Nation 124 (Feb 18, 1869).

seemed clearly to permit suffrage restrictions that simply had a disparate impact on black voters. Many congressional Republicans in 1869 favored a broader version of the amendment that would have forbidden suffrage qualifications based on property and education as well as race. One prominent Senate Republican warned that a simple ban on race-based disfranchisement would permit southern states to establish property and literacy tests that would "cut out forty-nine out of every fifty colored men in those States from voting." At different points during the debates on the Fifteenth Amendment, both houses of Congress had passed a broader measure. Yet a consensus proved difficult to achieve in the limited time available, and the conference committee fastened upon the most limited version of the amendment, which was plainly understood to permit disfranchisement based on property or literacy qualifications. Too many New England Republicans intent on disfranchising illiterate Irish immigrants and California Republicans intent on disfranchising Chinese aliens had opposed the broader versions of the Fifteenth Amendment. Given this evidence of original intent, it would have been a stretch for the *Plessy*-era Court to have invalidated literacy tests or poll taxes simply because of their disparate racial impact. At a time when southern black illiteracy was still roughly 50 percent and most southern blacks remained impoverished tenant farmers and sharecroppers, even fairly administered literacy tests and poll taxes would have disfranchised most blacks.[94]

Even setting aside a pure disparate impact claim, however, there remained several possible grounds for challenging the constitutionality of southern disfranchisement measures. First, the grandfather clause could be challenged as a surrogate racial classification. That is, the criterion selected to determine voter eligibility— whether one had voted before 1867 or had ancestors who did— was not simply motivated by a racially discriminatory purpose but actually was a stand-in for race. Second, even if literacy tests, poll taxes, and other disfranchising devices were not per se invalid under the Fifteenth Amendment, they might be unconstitutional be-

---

[94] Cong Globe, 40th Cong, 3d Sess 863 (1869) (quotation); Maltz, *Civil Rights* at 142– 56 (cited in note 38); Gillette, *Right to Vote* at 46–78 (cited in note 23); Mathews, *Fifteenth Amendment* at 24, 32–36, 41–46 (cited in note 77); Rose, 1 Am Pol Sci Rev at 23–24 (cited in note 86); *Stone v Smith*, 34 NE 521 (Mass 1893) (rejecting a constitutional challenge to a literacy test).

cause adopted with a discriminatory racial motive. (This is roughly what the law would be today.) Third, the procedure for administering the literacy tests might be unconstitutional. Specifically, empowering registrars to determine whether prospective voters possess "good character" and an adequate "understanding" grants unbridled administrative discretion that invites discriminatory exercise, and thus arguably violates the Constitution. Fourth, disfranchisement methods such as the literacy test could be challenged because of the race-conscious way they were actually administered (rather than simply because of their *potential* for discrimination). Suits challenging disfranchisement in Virginia, South Carolina, Alabama, and Mississippi raised all of these claims.[95]

The law applicable to resolving these constitutional challenges was virtually nonexistent at the turn of the century. No precedent determined whether a facially race-neutral classification was in fact a racial surrogate. Still, the grandfather clause was about as patent an evasion of the Fifteenth Amendment as one could imagine. Many contemporary observers predicted that courts would invalidate these devices, and the Supreme Court ultimately proved them right, though the ruling came too late to negate their effectiveness.[96]

The Court first considered whether a racially discriminatory motive could invalidate an otherwise constitutional suffrage qualification in *Williams v Mississippi*.[97] A black criminal defendant challenged his indictment for murder on the ground that blacks had been unconstitutionally excluded from Mississippi grand juries. He argued that Mississippi law required that jurors be qualified voters, but that the suffrage qualification requirements in Mississippi's 1890 constitution unconstitutionally excluded blacks. Williams raised essentially two challenges to Mississippi's suffrage requirements—that they had been adopted for the impermissible purpose

---

[95] Brief of Plaintiff in Error, *Williams v Mississippi*, 4–6, 15–17; Brief for Appellant, *Giles v Harris*, 10–13; *Yick Wo v Hopkins*, 118 US 356, 373–74 (1886).

[96] *Guinn v Oklahoma*, 238 US 347 (1915); Mabry, 13 NC Hist Rev at 301, 304, 306, 309 (cited in note 89); Poe, 175 North Am Rev at 542 (cited in note 19); Eaton, 13 Harv L Rev at 289–90 (cited in note 93); Rose, 1 Am Pol Sci Rev at 29–30 (cited in note 86); Stephenson, *Race Distinctions* at 307, 315–16 (cited in note 32). For further discussion of the grandfather clause and how one might interpret the Court's invalidation of it, see Klarman, 51 Vand L Rev at 917–21 (cited in note 7).

[97] 170 US 213 (1898).

of disfranchising blacks and that they conferred unbridled discretion on voter registrars to administer an understanding clause.

Williams rejected both challenges. As to motive, the Court drew upon a dominant tradition in constitutional law that held legislative motive to be irrelevant. For example, in *Fletcher v Peck*,[98] Chief Justice John Marshall had denied that allegations of bribery could justify rescission of a legislative land grant on the ground that the Court could not properly consider questions of legislative motive. More recently, and closer on point, the Court in 1885 unanimously had rejected an equal protection challenge to a San Francisco ordinance imposing a curfew on laundry operation. The city council's discriminatory animus toward the Chinese, who operated most of the city's laundries, was not a well-guarded secret. Yet the Justices implicitly denied the relevance of legislative motive and considered only whether the ordinance had a reasonable relationship to a permissible police power objective. Further, nothing in the congressional debates on the Fifteenth Amendment suggested that facially neutral but racially motivated suffrage restrictions were prohibited. Indeed, a couple of passing references to the issue implied the contrary view.[99]

However, this tradition rejecting judicial inquiries into legislative motive was not the only one available to the Court. Chief Justice Marshall had seemed to contradict his own dictum from *Fletcher v Peck*. In *McCulloch v Maryland*,[100] Marshall first articulated an extraordinarily broad formula for defining congressional power, but then qualified it by cautioning that the Court would invalidate laws enacted by Congress "under the *pretext* of executing its [enumerated] powers." This sounds suspiciously like a motive inquiry. Similarly, the Court in a couple of post–Civil War decisions invalidated under the ex post facto clause statutes imposing the ironclad oath as a professional qualification. These decisions, too, are difficult to understand except in terms of the Court's will-

---

[98] 6 Cranch 87 (1810).

[99] *Williams v Mississippi*, 170 US 213 (1898); *Fletcher*, 6 Cranch at 130; *Barbier v Connolly*, 113 US 27 (1885); Cong Globe, 40th Cong, 3d Sess 863 (1869) (Oliver P. Morton); id at 1009 (Jacob M. Howard and William M. Stewart). See also *McCray v United States*, 195 US 27, 56 (1904); *Ex parte McCardle*, 7 Wall 506, 514 (1868); Thomas M. Cooley, *Treatise on Constitutional Limitations* 257–59 (7th ed 1903).

[100] 4 Wheat 316 (1819).

ingness to inquire into legislative motive. The majority opinion invalidated the oath requirement because it found an unconstitutional purpose to impose punishment, while the dissenters saw only a bona fide occupational qualification. Finally, Justice Stephen Field, sitting on circuit, expressly employed motive analysis to invalidate the infamous San Francisco "queue ordinance," which required prisoners to cut their hair short and plainly had been motivated by anti-Chinese animus.[101]

Thus, in 1898 there was some precedent on both sides of the question whether legislative motive was relevant in constitutional law. Still, it seems fair to say that the tradition rejecting such motive inquiries was preponderant and that *Williams* had more law behind it than would have a contrary ruling. Indeed, if it seemed probable in the 1890s that discriminatory racial motive could invalidate otherwise constitutional legislation, the southern disfranchisers likely would not have been quite so open about their objectives.

As to the constitutionality of vesting voter registrars with broad discretion, the relevant precedent was *Yick Wo v Hopkins*.[102] There, the Court struck down a San Francisco ordinance that required persons seeking to establish a laundry in a wood, but not a stone or brick, building to secure a permit from the board of supervisors. The Court invalidated this ordinance on two grounds. First, it contained no standard to guide the discretion of the board of supervisors in granting laundry permits. Second, in practice, the board had granted permits to essentially all Caucasian applicants, while denying them to every one of the 200 or so Chinese petitioners. Both aspects of the *Yick Wo* holding were potentially relevant to the issue of black disfranchisement.

Literacy tests with "good character" and "understanding" clauses granted broad discretion to voter registrars. The vagueness of these standards seemed to invite discriminatory application, which of course had been the purpose behind their creation. Op-

---

[101] *McCulloch*, 4 Wheat at 422; *Cummings v State of Maryland*, 4 Wall 277 (1866); *Ex parte Garland*, 4 Wall 333 (1866); *Ho Ah Kow v Nunan*, 12 Fed Cas 252 (CCD Cal 1879); Charles J. McClain, *In Search of Equality: The Chinese Struggle Against Discrimination in Nineteenth-Century America* 47, 53–54, 73–76 (1994). See also *Hammer v Dagenhart*, 247 US 251 (1918); *Powell v Pennsylvania*, 127 US 678, 695 (1887) (Field, J, dissenting).

[102] 118 US 356 (1886).

ponents had criticized understanding clauses as the shams they were—creating officials "who are expected to perform questionable or dishonest acts." Numerous warnings were issued that courts would consider them fraudulent and invalidate them. Yet the good character and understanding clauses at least supplied standards of some sort, which is more than the ordinance in *Yick Wo* had done. Moreover, the good character clause had been patterned explicitly after a similar requirement for alien naturalization under federal law. Whether "good character" and "understanding" are standards definite enough to meaningfully cabin administrative discretion is not a question susceptible to objective measurement. To the current day, the Court continues to wrestle with the question of when legislative standards are so vague as to pose constitutional difficulties. Thus it is hard to see how *Yick Wo* constrained the *Williams* Court in either direction. *Williams* distinguished *Yick Wo* with the uninspired observation that it was not this case.[103]

Broad grants of administrative discretion also can be challenged on the basis of how they are administered in practice. The *Williams* Court rejected this claim with the observation that "it has not been shown that their [Mississippi's voter requirements] actual administration was evil, only that evil was possible under them." It is unremarkable for the Court to reject an as-applied challenge for which no supporting evidence exists in the record. The more interesting question is what standard of proof the Court would have imposed had the issue been adequately presented. *Yick Wo* again would have been the most relevant precedent. Yet the facts there established an irrefutable case of discriminatory administration. Had the standard for proving racially motivated disfranchisement been set this high, it would have been nearly impossible for black litigants to meet. The *Plessy*-era Court never resolved this question in the disfranchisement context, though it did shed some light on it in the analogous area of black exclusion from juries. There, as we shall

---

[103] Mabry, 13 NC Hist Rev at 300, 304, 309 (first quotation, from *New Orleans Daily Picayune*) (cited in note 89); *Williams v Mississippi*, 170 US at 223–25; McMillen, *Dark Journey* at 42 (cited in note 11); 51 Nation 183–84 (Sept 4, 1890); Kousser, *Southern Politics* at 58 n 29, 59 n 31 (cited in note 25); Woodward, *New South* at 332–33, 341 (cited in note 10); Mabry, 37 S Atl Q at 180 (cited in note 89); Benno C. Schmidt, Jr., *Juries, Jurisdiction, and Race Discrimination: The Lost Promise of Strauder v. West Virginia*, 61 Tex L Rev 1401, 1469 (1983).

see, the standard set by the Court for proving racial discrimination
proved virtually impossible to satisfy.[104]

The Court's failure to resolve the standard-of-proof question in
the disfranchisement context was not owing to the absence of an
appropriate case raising the issue. In *Giles v Harris*,[105] plaintiff alleged race discrimination in the administration of a "good character and understanding" clause and sought an injunction compelling
the registrar to enroll him and others in his county who were similarly situated. The Court held that even if the allegations of fraudulent administration were true, plaintiff was not entitled to his requested relief. Justice Oliver Wendell Holmes offered two reasons
for this result. First, if plaintiff's allegation of rampant fraud in
Alabama's voter registration scheme were true, then for the Court
to order him registered would make it a party to the sham. Second,
for the Court to order plaintiff's enrollment on the voting lists
would be "an empty form" if a conspiracy truly existed among
Alabama whites to disfranchise blacks. The Court would be powerless to enforce an injunction in that context, and thus plaintiff's
remedy must come, if at all, from the political branches of the
U.S. government. Holmes left open the possibility of an action for
money damages, but such a suit would have to be heard before a
jury (unlike a request for an injunction). With blacks almost completely excluded from southern juries by this time, the prospects
for such a lawsuit succeeding were not promising, to say the least.
In any event, when Giles did bring a legal action for damages, the
Supreme Court in *Giles v Teasley*[106] rejected his claim again on very
similar grounds. First, if the registration board were patently unconstitutional, then it could do Giles no damage. Second, in any
event, the Court could provide no effective relief against this sort
of political action by the state.[107]

The two extraordinary *Giles* opinions are among the most candid
confessions of limited judicial power to appear in the U.S. Reports.
The only analogous expressions appear in cases where the Court

---

[104] *Williams*, 170 US at 225 (quotation); *Yick Wo*, 118 US at 373–74; Mangum, *Legal Status* at 395 (cited in note 35).

[105] 189 US 475 (1903).

[106] 193 US 146 (1904).

[107] *Giles v Harris*, 189 US at 486–88 (quotation at 488); *Giles v Teasley*, 193 US at 164–66.

confessed its inability to safeguard civil liberties during wartime. In *Ex parte Milligan*,[108] the Court conceded that it had not been possible to calmly consider the constitutionality of martial law as applied to civilians in a non-war zone during the Civil War. In *Korematsu v United States*,[109] Justice Jackson's dissenting opinion admitted that the Court was powerless to interfere with military operations during World War II, including the order evicting Japanese-Americans from their West Coast homes. The *Giles* results suggest that where public opinion is sufficiently strong, even a plain constitutional violation may go unredressed. The Court had declared its unwillingness to enforce the Fifteenth Amendment even on the assumption that Alabama was violating it.[110]

In several other suits challenging disfranchisement, the Court also failed to reach the merits. Suits seeking to enjoin voter registration and vote tabulations under the Fifteenth Amendment were dismissed as moot, because the elections already had taken place. Viewing these cases in juxtaposition with the *Giles* decisions, contemporary observers noted the Court's tendency to dispose of disfranchisement challenges "on some technical or subsidiary point, leaving the merits of the real issue untouched."[111]

The Court during this period issued one additional decision friendly to disfranchisement. *James v Bowman*[112] finally resolved in the affirmative the question of whether the Fifteenth Amendment contained a state action requirement. Specifically, the issue was whether Congress under the Fifteenth Amendment could criminalize racially motivated interferences with the right to vote by private individuals. The text of the amendment appears to provide a clear negative answer—"The right of citizens of the United States to vote shall not be denied or abridged by *the United States or by any state* on account of race, color, or previous condition of servitude." Moreover, the Court decades earlier had interpreted

[108] 71 US (4 Wall) 2, 109 (1866).

[109] 323 US 214, 242 (1944) (Jackson, J, dissenting).

[110] Fiss, *Troubled Beginnings* at 376–79 (cited in note 50); Rose, 1 Am Pol Sci Rev at 39 (cited in note 86); Schmidt, 82 Colum L Rev at 847, 849–50 (cited in note 29).

[111] 90 Nation 334 (Apr 7, 1910) (quotation); 87 Nation 480–81 (Nov 19, 1908); Blakeman, 70 Filson Club Hist Q at 23–24 (cited in note 58); *Mills v Green*, 159 US 651 (1895); *Jones v Montague*, 194 US 147 (1904); *Selden v Montague*, 194 US 154 (1904); Mangum, *Legal Status* at 400 (cited in note 35).

[112] 190 US 127 (1903).

similarly explicit language in the Fourteenth Amendment to impose a state action requirement and invalidated congressional legislation punishing private interferences with black civil rights.[113]

On the other hand, lower court decisions and dicta in a famous Supreme Court case from Reconstruction had suggested the absence of a Fifteenth Amendment state action requirement. Several lower federal court decisions, mainly from the early 1870s, had rejected constitutional challenges to criminal prosecutions of private individuals under the Force Acts for interfering with black political and civil rights. Justice Joseph Bradley in his circuit court opinion in *United States v Cruikshank*[114] plainly had rejected in dicta a Fifteenth Amendment state action requirement. On appeal the Supreme Court in dicta strongly had intimated the same, declaring in the context of a criminal prosecution of private individuals that the right to be free of race discrimination in voting was a privilege of U.S. citizenship (and thus within Congress's power to protect). Moreover, the Court in other decisions had held that Congress, under its Article I power to regulate the time, place, and manner of federal elections, could criminalize *individual* interferences with the right to vote in *congressional* elections. Thus some significant support existed for a contrary result in *James v Bowman*, though precedent hardly compelled it. Other lower federal court decisions had anticipated the Court's ruling, invalidating Force Act prosecutions of private individuals for racially motivated interferences with the right to vote. Considering the strong textual basis for inferring a state action requirement from the Fifteenth Amendment and the dramatic decline in popular support for black suffrage by 1903, the result in *James* was predictable.[115]

Thus the Court rejected all constitutional challenges to black

---

[113] *United States v Cruikshank*, 92 US 542 (1875); *Civil Rights Cases*, 109 US 3 (1883); *United States v Harris*, 106 US 629 (1883).

[114] 25 Fed Cas 707, 713–14 (CCD La 1874).

[115] *Given v United States*, 25 F Cas 1324 (CCD Del 1873); *United States v Canter*, 25 F Cas 281 (CCSD Ohio 1870); *United States v Hall*, 26 F Cas 701 (CCSD Ala 1871) (Judge Woods); *United States v Crosby*, 25 F Cas 701 (1871) (by implication); *United States v Cruikshank*, 92 US 542, 556 (1875); Mathews, *Fifteenth Amendment* at 104–14 (cited in note 77); Mangum, *Legal Status* at 381 (cited in note 35); Michael Les Benedict, *Preserving Federalism: Reconstruction and the Waite Court*, 1978 Supreme Court Review 39, 71–75; *Ex parte Yarbrough*, 110 US 651 (1884); *Ex parte Siebold*, 100 US 371 (1880). The lower court decisions imposing a state action requirement under the Fifteenth Amendment were *Karem v United States*, 121 F 256 (6th Cir 1903) and *United States v Amsden*, 6 F 819 (DCD Ind 1881).

disfranchisement during the *Plessy* period. *Giles v Harris* suggests that one reason was the Court's candid recognition of its own limited power. Yet it would be mistaken to read *Giles* to suggest that the Justices would have been inclined to invalidate Alabama's disfranchisement scheme had they only possessed the power to make such a ruling stick. The Justices probably possessed no greater commitment to protecting black suffrage than did the rest of the nation.

By 1900 most white southerners were intensely committed to eliminating blacks from politics. That commitment encompassed a willingness to use mass violence and murder, as evidenced by the race riots in Wilmington, North Carolina, in 1898 and in Atlanta in 1906, both of which concluded electoral campaigns dominated by the issue of black disfranchisement. Indeed, the determination to disfranchise southern blacks was so great that many of them decided to abandon politics as the course of least resistance. Likewise, both northern and southern Progressives increasingly viewed black disfranchisement as an enlightened solution to the problems of rampant southern electoral fraud and violence. Solving the "Negro question" would, as one southern Progressive put it, remove "the most fruitful source of bitterness between the races."[116]

Similarly, the northern commitment to black suffrage had greatly eroded in the decades since Reconstruction. The ideal of universal manhood suffrage that many northerners had espoused a generation earlier was undermined by concerns about the political participation of the flood of (often illiterate) immigrants entering the country around the turn of the century. Northerners' reluctance to permit political participation by recent immigrants rendered them increasingly sympathetic to white southerners' unwillingness to tolerate black suffrage. The nation's imperialist adventures of the 1890s furthered the erosion of northern support

---

[116] Poe, 175 North Am Rev at 537–41 (quotation at 541) (cited in note 19); Kousser, *Southern Politics* at 258, 262–63 (cited in note 25); Fiss, *Troubled Beginnings* at 379 (cited in note 50); Stone, *American Race Problem* at 420 (cited in note 19); Mangum, *Legal Status* at 388, 394 (cited in note 35); Gleijeses, 73 NC Hist Rev at 199–200 (cited in note 22); Meier, *Negro Thought* at 35–36, 214–15 (cited in note 13); Hackney, *Populism to Progressivism* at 175–77, 186 (cited in note 11); Dittmer, *Black Georgia* at 99–101 (cited in note 13); Mabry, 4 J Southern Hist at 319–20 (cited in note 13); Woodward, *New South* at 326–27, 347–48 (cited in note 10); Lewinson, *Race, Class, and Party* at 88–89 (cited in note 10); 61 Nation 199 (Sept 19, 1895).

for universal manhood suffrage. *The Nation* noted in 1898 the temporal coincidence of the Supreme Court decision in *Williams v Mississippi*, sanctioning southern black disfranchisement, and the country's efforts to figure out what to do with the "varied assortment of inferior races in different parts of the world, which must be governed somehow, and which, of course, could not be allowed to vote." If Americans were not prepared to permit Filipinos to vote, why should southern whites be coerced into permitting southern blacks to do so? The sectional reconciliation sentiment of the McKinley years, accelerated by the Spanish-American War, further reduced northern willingness to contest southern black disfranchisement. Finally, the Republican Party's commitment to protecting black suffrage had virtually disappeared. The willingness of Republicans in 1890–91 to abandon the federal elections bill in favor of congressional action on the tariff and silver purchase signified the erosion of that commitment. The electoral realignment of the mid-1890s rendered Republicans less dependent upon, and thus less committed to defending, southern black suffrage.[117]

For these various reasons, by the turn of the century many white northerners shared the nearly universal view of white southerners that the Fifteenth Amendment had been a mistake and that black suffrage was "the greatest self-confessed failure in American political history." This shift in public opinion was evident in *Congress*'s posture toward disfranchisement. In 1893–94, Democrats took advantage of the fact that they controlled Congress and the presidency for the first time since the 1850s to repeal most of the voting rights guarantees in the 1870s enforcement legislation. When Republicans reassumed control of the national government from 1896 to 1910, they made no effort to reenact these provisions. Moreover, Congress was confronted with a patent violation of Section 2 of the Fourteenth Amendment. Section 2 *requires* Congress to reduce a state's congressional representation if its adult male citizens are disfranchised for any reason other than the commission

---

[117] 66 Nation 398–99 (May 26, 1898) (quotation); 53 Nation 46–47 (July 16, 1891); 61 Nation 302 (Oct 31, 1895); Kousser, *Southern Politics* at 251–54 (cited in note 25); Kraditor, *Woman's Suffrage* at 126–32 (cited in note 18); McPherson, *Abolitionist Legacy* at 125 (cited in note 12); Hackney, *Populism to Progressivism* at 159–60 (cited in note 11); Woodward, *New South* at 324–25 (cited in note 10); Stone, *American Race Problem* at 412–13 (cited in note 19); Poe, 175 North Am Rev at 542 (cited in note 19); notes 23–28.

of crimes. The disfranchisement need not be racially motivated for the penalty to be applicable. Thus the difficulty of establishing racial motivation that confronted litigants seeking to prove Fifteenth Amendment violations in court was not an obstacle to congressional enforcement of Section 2 of the Fourteenth Amendment. Yet Congress took no enforcement action, and the Republican Party barely made noises in that direction.[118]

The Supreme Court, like Congress, is broadly reflective of national opinion. If Congress was unwilling to enforce Section 2 of the Fourteenth Amendment against black disfranchisement, it is hardly surprising that the Court would be reluctant to order remedies for somewhat less transparent violations of Section 1 of the Fifteenth. Only blatant constitutional violations, such as an explicit racial restriction on the suffrage, could have induced the Court to resist preponderant national sentiment sympathetic toward black disfranchisement. Indeed, *Giles* inspires doubt as to whether the Court would have intervened even in the face of a patent Fifteenth Amendment violation. A contemporary legal commentator accurately captured the situation at the turn of the century: With both Court and Congress reflecting "the apathetic tone of public opinion," the Fifteenth Amendment, while still part of the Constitution "in the technical sense," was "already in process of repeal . . . as a . . . rule of conduct."[119]

C. JURY EXCLUSION

In the antebellum period, blacks were excluded from jury service in all southern and most northern states. Even after the Civil War, black jury service was staunchly resisted by many whites, including

---

[118] Stone, *American Race Problem* at 351 (quotation), 353, 415–20 (cited in note 19); Baker, *Color Line* at 240, 302–03 (cited in note 15); Morton Keller, *Regulating a New Society: Public Policy and Social Change in America, 1900–1933* at 255–56 (1994); McPherson, *Abolitionist Legacy* at 112, 313, 354–55 (cited in note 12); Wang, *Trial of Democracy* at 254–57, 261 (cited in note 23); Republican Platform of 1904, in *National Party Platforms* at 139 (cited in note 24); Eugene Sidney Bayer, *The Apportionment Section of the Fourteenth Amendment: A Neglected Weapon for Defense of the Voting Rights of Southern Negroes*, 16 Case W L Rev 965, 965–66, 974 (1965); James Wilford Garner, *The Fourteenth Amendment and Southern Representation*, 4 So Atl Q 209 (1905).

[119] Mathews, *Fifteenth Amendment* at 126 (quotation) (cited in note 77); Cobb, 12 Ga St U L Rev at 1030 (cited in note 37); J. W. Garner, *Commentary*, 13 Am J Soc 828, 831 (1907–08).

through much of the lower North. Many southern states during presidential Reconstruction (1865–66) continued to bar black jury service by statute. These laws were repealed, however, during congressional Reconstruction. Once enfranchised, blacks used their political power to secure both state and federal statutes forbidding race-based exclusions from jury service. During Reconstruction, and in some places well into the 1880s, southern blacks served on juries in large numbers, especially in counties with substantial black populations. However, in those former slave states where the black population was not large enough to produce Republican state control—Maryland, Kentucky, West Virginia—state law continued to bar black jury service until the Supreme Court intervened in 1880.[120]

As southern black voting was gradually suppressed, blacks disappeared from juries. Black jury service, conceived to be a form of political officeholding, was even more anathema to most southern whites than was black voting. Moreover, with racial segregation spreading through most public areas of southern life, the jury box could not resist the pressure for racial separation. Other than in North Carolina, where black jury service rebounded under the fusion regime of the mid-1890s, blacks became noticeably less present on southern juries by the late 1880s and generally disappeared in the 1890s. Through the first three decades of the twentieth century, essentially no blacks sat on southern juries.[121]

The original understanding of the Fourteenth Amendment was much less supportive of black jury service than the Fifteenth Amendment was of black suffrage. While the latter expressly forbade abridgement of the suffrage based on race, the framers of the former consciously had eschewed a general bar on color-consciousness and had repeatedly denied their intention to safe-

---

[120] Litwack, *North of Slavery* at 94, 96 (cited in note 32); Rabinowitz, *Urban South* at 38–39 (cited in note 11); McCaul, *Black Struggle* at 100 (cited in note 28); Thornbrough, *Negro in Indiana* at 271 (cited in note 17); Gerber, *Black Ohio* at 40 (cited in note 17); Mangum, *Legal Status* at 311 (cited in note 35); Wharton, *Negro in Mississippi* at 135–37 (cited in note 10); Nieman, 55 J Southern Hist passim, esp. 399 table 1 (cited in note 83); Wynes, *Race Relations in Virginia* at 25–26 (cited in note 11); Tindall, *South Carolina Negroes* at 263–64 (cited in note 10); Callcott, *Negro in Maryland Politics* at 61–63 (cited in note 27); *Strauder v West Virginia*, 100 US 303 (1880); *Bush v Kentucky*, 107 US 110 (1883).

[121] Anderson, *North Carolina* at 317–19 (cited in note 10); Stephenson, *Race Distinctions* at 253–71 (cited in note 10); Cartwright, *Tennessee Race Relations* at 176–77 (cited in note 10); Wynes, *Race Relations in Virginia* at 138 (cited in note 11); Rice, *Negro in Texas* at 255–57 (cited in note 83); Nieman, 55 J Southern Hist at 400–01 (cited in note 83).

guard from race discrimination political rights, such as voting and jury service. When Democratic opponents charged that the 1866 Civil Rights Act and the Fourteenth Amendment would require integration of juries, Republican backers denied any intention to protect political rights.

When Republicans returned a few years later with the Fifteenth Amendment, the question arose whether to extend the proposed ban on racial discrimination in voting to include political officeholding. The issue had immediate practical significance because the Georgia legislature had recently excluded duly elected black representatives, on the ostensible ground that the state constitution did not affirmatively sanction black officeholding. An early version of the Fifteenth Amendment prohibiting race-based exclusions from political office passed the Senate but not the House. Too many northern Republicans feared that their racially prejudiced constituents, while perhaps willing to bear black voters, were unwilling to countenance black elected officials. This legislative history makes it difficult to argue that the Fifteenth Amendment forbade race-based exclusions from juries. Even a Radical Republican like Henry Wilson conceded that the amendment left states free to exclude blacks from jury service.[122]

However, Republican attitudes toward black jury service changed over the course of Reconstruction. Moreover, enactment of national legislation protecting black jury service did not require the two-thirds majority in both houses of Congress that a constitutional amendment does. In 1875 Congress criminalized race-based exclusions from jury service. Democrats objected that Congress lacked power to protect political rights under section five of the Fourteenth Amendment. Supporters responded that the right to a jury selected without regard to race was a *civil* right of black criminal defendants. The 1866 Civil Rights Act, after all, had guaranteed blacks the same right as whites to "full and equal

---

[122] Bickel, 69 Harv L Rev at 62 (cited in note 38); Schmidt, 61 Tex L Rev at 1423–24 (cited in note 103); Maltz, *Civil Rights* at 67–68, 147–55 (cited in note 38); Bond, 18 Akron L Rev at 446–47 (cited in note 39); Maltz, 44 Fla L Rev at 623–25 (cited in note 45); Gillette, *Right to Vote* at 50, 60–61, 68, 71, 77–78 (cited in note 23); Foner, *Reconstruction* at 423–24 (cited in note 20); Cong Globe, 40th Cong, 3d Sess 1296 (Feb 17, 1869) (Henry Wilson); *Ex parte Virginia*, 100 US 339, 365–68 (1880) (Justice Field, dissenting); New York Times (Feb 15, 1869), p 4. But see Amar, 80 Cornell L Rev at 228–34 (cited in note 77).

benefit of all laws and proceedings for the security of persons and property."[123]

The Supreme Court first confronted this question of race-based exclusions from jury service in *Strauder v West Virginia*. Notwithstanding any original intent difficulties, the *Strauder* Court, dividing along partisan lines, invalidated by a 7–2 vote state statutes barring blacks from jury service. The Court emphasized that the Fourteenth Amendment, unlike the 1866 Civil Rights Act, did not enumerate a limited category of protected rights. The purpose of that amendment, the Justices boldly declared, had been "to strike down all possible legal discriminations against [blacks]." The Court also highlighted the civil rights of black defendants, rather than the political rights of excluded black jurors. With its broad language ostensibly condemning any race-conscious legislation and its holding apparently in tension with the original understanding of the Fourteenth and Fifteenth Amendments, *Strauder* can be seen as the product of an era in which many northerners, and especially Republicans, remained committed to the protection of black civil and political rights. Just the previous year, Republicans had successfully fended off Democratic efforts to repeal the congressional ban on race-based exclusions from jury service. The Hayes administration filed a brief in support of Strauder's position, and press reaction to the Court's decision followed partisan lines.[124]

Strauder's precise holding was of limited import, since only a few border states in 1880 retained express statutory prohibitions on black jury service. The pressing question after *Strauder* was what rules the Court would develop to handle allegations that blacks had been excluded from jury service not by state law, but through the discriminatory exercise of administrative discretion. A typical state jury selection statute of this era provided that jurors be of "good intelligence, sound judgment, and fair character." The year after *Strauder*, the Court in *Neal v Delaware*[125] employed some

---

[123] Maltz, 13 Const Comm at 227–28 (cited in note 42); McConnell, 81 Va L Rev at 1024 n 365 (cited in note 41); Schmidt, 61 Tex L Rev at 1427–28 (cited in note 103); Cong Globe, 42d Cong, 2d Sess 843 (Feb 6, 1872) (Sen. Carpenter); ibid, 844 (Sen. Sherman).

[124] *Strauder v West Virginia*, 100 US 303, 306–10 (1880) (quotation at 310); Schmidt, 61 Tex L Rev at 1414, 1422–29, 1450–54 (cited in note 103); Bickel, 69 Harv L Rev at 64–65 (cited in note 38). See also Stephen Cresswell, *The Case of Taylor Strauder*, 44 W Va Hist 193 (1983).

[125] 103 US 370, 397 (1881).

broad dicta implying that the complete absence of blacks from
Delaware juries notwithstanding their sizable percentage of the
state's population constituted a prima facie case of race discrimination. The actual holding in *Neal* was more limited, however. The
Court reversed the defendant's criminal conviction on the ground
that Delaware had conceded the existence of race discrimination
in jury selection. *Yick Wo*, the Chinese laundry case, had established in 1886 that racially discriminatory administration of the
law was just as unconstitutional as explicit statutory discrimination.
The facts in *Yick Wo*, however, revealed an irrefutable case of race
discrimination. By the dawn of the *Plessy* era, the Court had yet to
provide guidance on the standard of proof for establishing racially
discriminatory administration of the law.[126]

Already operating beyond the charted boundaries of original intent, and lacking any precedential guidance, the Court's resolution
of this critical standard-of-proof question inevitably would be influenced by public sentiment regarding black jury service. By the
1890s southern white opinion had become intensely hostile toward
black officeholding. While a southern black had sat in every U.S.
House of Representatives but one between 1869 and 1901, not
another would be elected from 1901 until 1972. Blacks sat in significant numbers in southern state legislatures through the 1880s,
but none was elected to the Virginia legislature after 1891, the
Mississippi legislature after 1895, or the South Carolina legislature
after 1902. A principal theme of North Carolina's white supremacy
campaign in 1898 was the necessity of ending black officeholding,
which had been widespread in the eastern counties under the fusion regime of 1894–98. Federal patronage appointments of southern blacks as local postmasters and customs collectors became
increasingly controversial through the 1890s, leading to mass protests by disaffected whites, the lynching of a black South Carolina
postmaster in 1898, and two celebrated battles between Mississippi
and South Carolina whites and President Theodore Roosevelt in
1902–03.[127]

[126] Miss Code Ann § 2358 (1892), reproduced in *Williams v Mississippi*, 170 US 213, 218–
19 (1898); *Eastling v Arkansas*, 62 SW 584, 587 (Ark 1901); Schmidt, 61 Tex L Rev at
1457–58 (cited in note 103).

[127] Anderson, *North Carolina* at 168–69, 242–48, 310–11 (cited in note 10); Wynes, *Race
Relations in Virginia* at 45 (cited in note 11); Tindall, *South Carolina Negroes* at 58–67, 255

Southern white opinion hostile to black officeholding met with
little resistance from white northerners or the Republican Party.
Most northern whites never had been enthusiastic about black officeholding, which is why the practice was not explicitly protected
in the Fifteenth Amendment. By the turn of the century, fewer
blacks were holding office in the North. There was a lengthy hia-
tus in black state legislative representation in Indiana after 1897,
Massachusetts after 1902, and Ohio after 1906. The Republican
Party likewise accommodated the preferences of white southerners
with regard to black officeholding. President McKinley ceased antagonizing white southerners with black patronage appointments
after the Spanish-American War of 1898. During his second administration, President Roosevelt largely refrained from appointing southern blacks to federal patronage positions, and President
Taft completely ended federal patronage for southern blacks and
reduced that of northern blacks as well. There is little reason to
doubt that Supreme Court Justices shared the general disillusionment of most white Americans with black officeholding or at least
the willingness to accommodate southern whites in their fierce opposition to the practice.[128]

Amidst this growing opposition toward black officeholding generally and jury service specifically, it is noteworthy that the *Plessy*-
era Court reaffirmed *Strauder*'s prohibition on race-based exclusions from jury service. Further, the Court reaffirmed *Neal*'s ruling
that racially discriminatory jury selection could be proven by the
admissions of state officials. Indeed, the Court in 1900 slightly extended these rulings in *Carter v Texas*,[129] where it quashed an indictment on the ground that black criminal defendants had been

---

(cited in note 10); Henry Litchfield West, *The Race War in North Carolina*, 26 Forum 578,
581–82, 590 (1899); William Alexander Mabry, *"White Supremacy" and the North Carolina
Suffrage Amendment*, 13 NC Hist Rev 1, 2, 17 (1936); Cresswell, *Multi-Party Politics* at 142,
185 (cited in note 10); Gould, *Theodore Roosevelt* at 118–22 (cited in note 60); Stone, *American Race Problem* at ch 7 (cited in note 19).

[128] Thornbrough, *Negro in Indiana* at 395 (cited in note 17); Gerber, *Black Ohio* at 215–
17, 338, 365 (cited in note 17); Crew, *Black Life in Secondary Cities* at 136–37 (cited in note
71); Katzman, *Black Detroit* at 204 (cited in note 17); Kusmer, *Black Cleveland* at 64–65
(cited in note 17); Meier, *Negro Thought* at 163, 165 (cited in note 13); Scheiner, 47 J Negro
Hist at 175–78 (cited in note 63); Dittmer, *Black Georgia* at 94, 106–07 (cited in note 13);
Woodward, *New South* at 462 (cited in note 10); New York Times (Nov 22, 1898), p 6;
76 Nation 21 (Jan 8, 1903).

[129] 177 US 442 (1900).

denied the opportunity to present evidence of alleged race discrimination in jury selection.[130]

In its other jury cases, however, the Court largely nullified *Strauder* by making such discrimination virtually impossible to prove. Once the Court had rejected constitutional challenges to disfranchisement, black exclusions from jury service could be defended, in jurisdictions where jurors were selected from voter lists, on the ground that few blacks were registered to vote. Moreover, *Yick Wo* notwithstanding, the Court refused to invalidate jury selection statutes specifying vague criteria such as "good intelligence, sound judgment, and fair character." In several cases, the Court ruled that a criminal defendant was entitled to a hearing on his motion to quash an indictment on the grounds of racially discriminatory jury selection only if he produced evidence, not mere allegations. What evidence the Court had in mind is uncertain. Rejecting dicta in *Neal*, the Court ruled that the absence of blacks from juries in the county where the defendant had been prosecuted raised no inference of discrimination. The Court also rejected as an inadequate proffer of proof an attempt to compel the testimony of state jury commissioners. Nor is it certain that those officials could have been forced to testify, because of the risk of self-incrimination under the 1875 Civil Rights Act, which criminalized racial discrimination in jury selection. Further, the Court reaffirmed the rule that state officials were presumed to have done their constitutional duty. Criminal defendants bore the burden of overcoming that presumption with positive proof of discrimination. Yet, as one contemporary legal commentator observed, "the motives of the county officers in selecting persons for jury service are too subtle, too subjective, to admit of positive proof."[131]

Moreover, where the defendant offered proof of discrimination but the state court found it inadequate, the Supreme Court deferred to these findings unless clearly erroneous. Since the Court

[130] See also *Smith v Mississippi*, 162 US 592 (1896); *Rogers v Alabama*, 192 US 226 (1904); Schmidt, 61 Tex L Rev at 1470–71 (cited in note 103).

[131] Miss Code Ann § 2358 (1892), quoted in Schmidt, 61 Tex L Rev at 1462–63, 1469 (cited in note 103) (first quotation); Collins, *Fourteenth Amendment* at 76 (cited in note 50) (second quotation); *Smith v Mississippi*, 162 US 592 (1896); *Gibson v Mississippi*, 162 US 565 (1896); *Tarrance v Florida*, 188 US 519 (1903); *Brownfield v South Carolina*, 189 US 426 (1903); *Martin v Texas*, 200 US 316 (1906); *Thomas v Texas*, 212 US 278 (1909); *Franklin v South Carolina*, 218 US 161 (1910).

had interpreted federal law to authorize removal of jury discrimination claims to federal court only when a state statute imposed facial discrimination, and since federal habeas corpus review of state criminal convictions generally was unavailable at this time, state courts always made the initial findings as to race discrimination in jury selection. Thus the Court's decision to extend broad deference to state court findings of no discrimination made it virtually impossible to secure a hearing on the jury exclusion claim in a forum that was not openly committed to preserving white supremacy. While southern state courts conceded they were bound by *Strauder*, they nonetheless denied that administration of the law should be "in the hands of a people assumed to be inferior to the white race." Accordingly, these courts were reluctant to second-guess denials of race discrimination by jury selection officials, requiring "very strong and convincing testimony" to prove discrimination. The fact that no blacks had served on juries in a particular county for decades, notwithstanding the presence of hundreds of qualified black voters, was ruled insufficient to overcome the jury commissioners' denial of discriminatory motive.[132]

The *Plessy*-era jury discrimination cases illustrate how formal constitutional rights can be largely nullified through the use of "subconstitutional" rules bearing on standards of proof, standards of appellate review, and access to federal court. While the Court reaffirmed *Strauder* on numerous occasions, these decisions left southern state courts free to exclude blacks entirely from juries. Conceding that they were bound by *Strauder*, these courts routinely rejected Fourteenth Amendment challenges to criminal convictions of black defendants obtained from all-white juries in counties with large black populations where no blacks had served on juries for years. Between 1904 and 1935, the Supreme Court failed to reverse a single criminal conviction of a black defendant on the basis of race discrimination in jury selection, notwithstanding the nearly universal practice in the South of intentionally excluding

---

[132] *Smith v State*, 77 SW 453, 454 (Tx Ct Crim Apps 1903) (first quotation); *Royals v State*, 75 So 199 (Fla 1917) (second quotation); *Thomas v Texas*, 212 US 278 (1909); *Virginia v Rives*, 100 US 313 (1880); Schmidt, 61 Tex L Rev at 1430–40, 1455, 1462–75, 1498 (cited in note 103); Mangum, *Legal Status* at ch 12 (cited in note 35); Stephenson, *Race Distinctions* at ch 10 (cited in note 32); Collins, *Fourteenth Amendment* at 73–75 (cited in note 50); *Thompson v State*, 74 SW 914 (Tex Ct Crim Apps 1903); *Tarrance v Florida*, 30 So 685 (Fla 1901); *State v Daniels*, 46 SE 743 (NC 1904); *Haynes v State*, 72 So 180 (Fla 1916).

blacks from juries. Only beginning in the 1930s, when the Court's formal commitment to nondiscrimination in jury selection flowered into a genuine substantive resolve, did the subconstitutional rules begin to change. The Court then became willing to infer discriminatory purpose from the long-term absence of blacks from juries and to independently determine disputed facts rather than deferring to state court findings. The adoption of more efficacious subconstitutional rules clearly reflected the Court's heightened commitment to the underlying constitutional right. Thus the Court's willingness during the *Plessy* era to employ subconstitutional rules that effectively nullified the *Strauder* right must be partially attributable to the Justices' relative indifference toward racial discrimination in jury selection.[133]

D. SEPARATE AND UNEQUAL

Plessy v Ferguson sustained the constitutionality of a statute mandating "equal but separate" railroad accommodations. However, segregation in practice, whether in public education or railroad travel, rarely afforded blacks anything approaching equality. "Scarcely fit for a dog to ride in" is how one black Marylander described southern Jim Crow railway cars. The *Plessy*-era Court heard only one challenge to the inequality aspect of segregation. In *Cumming v Richmond County School Board*,[134] the Court rejected an inequality challenge to the administration of the public school fund on the ground that the allocation at issue was reasonable.[135]

The antebellum South almost universally excluded blacks from public education. After the war, southern whites accepted black education only with great reluctance. Freedmen's Bureau schools, established by the War Department to educate newly freed slaves,

[133] Schmidt, 61 Tex L Rev at 1413, 1458, 1476–81 (cited in note 103); *Eastling v State*, 62 SW 584 (Ark 1901); *State v Baptiste*, 30 So 147 (La 1901); *Welch v State*, 236 P 68 (Okla 1925); *Commonwealth v Johnson*, 78 Ky 509 (1880); John R. Gillespie, *The Constitution and the All-White Jury*, 39 Ky L J 68–71, 74–75 (1950); *Norris v Alabama*, 294 US 587 (1935); *Pierre v Louisiana*, 306 US 354, 358 (1939). Schmidt fails to sufficiently acknowledge that the Justices' commitment to federalism principles was not independent of their attitudes toward race. Schmidt at 1482–95.

[134] 175 US 528 (1899).

[135] Callcott, *Negro in Maryland Politics* at 135 (quotation) (cited in note 27); Barnes, *Southern Transit* at 15 (cited in note 33); Bettye C. Thomas, *Public Education and Black Protest in Baltimore 1865–1900*, 71 Md Hist Mag 381, 387–88 (1976); Mangum, *Legal Status* at 221–22 (cited in note 35); Minter, "Jim Crow" at 144 (cited in note 32).

frequently were physically attacked, as were the northern teachers employed in them. Under presidential Reconstruction in the South, and in the border states that escaped Reconstruction altogether, public schools were created for blacks, but their revenue was limited to that raised from black taxes—ordinarily a paltry sum. This state of affairs likely reflected dominant white opinion in the South. Had it not been for external pressure from Congress and internal pressure from black voters after enfranchisement, southern black education probably would have been either entirely neglected or else drastically underfunded.[136]

Reconstruction Republicans wrote southern state constitutions that extended public education to blacks on equal terms with whites, while generally refraining from expressing a commitment either way with regard to racial segregation. In practice, though, public schools were segregated nearly everywhere in the South, even in the two states that had written explicit prohibitions on public school segregation into their Reconstruction constitutions. Southern whites were so fiercely resistant to "mixed schools" that most southern blacks resigned themselves, at least temporarily, to pursuit of equality within a segregated system.[137]

Before black political power began to decline appreciably in the 1880s, public funding for black and white education was almost equal. In North Carolina and Alabama, per capita spending on black education actually exceeded that on white until around 1880. In South Carolina, where Wade Hampton and his Redeemers had pledged to improve black schools, per capita spending on black and white education was nearly identical from 1876 to 1879, before diverging slightly thereafter. Under Readjuster rule in Virginia in the early 1880s, when black political power was at its zenith, discrepancies between state funding of black and white schools narrowed. However, as black political power declined with the overthrow of the Readjusters in 1883, so did public funding for black

---

[136] Richard Barry Westin, "The State and Segregated Schools: Negro Public Education in North Carolina, 1863–1923" at 5, 32–33, 39 (Ph.D. diss, Duke University, 1966); Fischer, *Segregation Struggle* at 13, 27–28, 44 (cited in note 10); Victor B. Howard, *The Struggle for Equal Education in Kentucky, 1866–1884*, 46 J Negro Educ 305, 307, 309, 315 (1977); Vaughn, *Schools for All* at 27–37 (cited in note 66); Rice, *Negro in Texas* at 211–12, 214 (cited in note 83); Wharton, *Negro in Mississippi* at 245 (cited in note 10); Wright, *Blacks in Louisville* at 35 (cited in note 11); Foner, *Reconstruction* at 207–08 (cited in note 20); Callcott, *Negro in Maryland Politics* at 63–64 (cited in note 27).

[137] See sources cited in note 66.

schools. In Nashville, Tennessee, black teachers received equal pay until the first formal disfranchisement measures passed in the late 1880s. As the threat of external pressure from Congress and the reality of internal pressure from black voters dissipated, southern whites were freed to follow their own predispositions with regard to black education. In the view of most, black schooling spoiled good field hands, foolishly encouraged competition with white labor, and rendered blacks dissatisfied with their subordinate position in life.[138]

Not only were southern whites by the end of the century freer to implement derogatory views toward black education that they might have held all along, but also their attitudes toward black instruction apparently were deteriorating. During and after Reconstruction, at least some southern whites accepted that blacks eventually would attain full-fledged citizenship and must be educated for its responsibilities. By the turn of the century, however, whites almost universally rejected black political participation, and with it the importance of equal black education. Thus many prominent white southerners had concluded by 1900 that the post–Civil War experiment in black tutelage had proven a failure. Georgia's governor privately expressed this view: "God made them negroes and we cannot by education make them white folks. We are on the wrong track. We must turn back." Some of this attitude change may be attributable to growing popular acceptance of "scientific" evidence purportedly indicating that the black race was in a deteriorating condition, on the road to extinction. On this view, blacks were losing the Darwinian struggle for the "survival of the fittest," and efforts to ameliorate their condition through education were futile owing to the superior force of biological destiny. It seems

---

[138] J. Morgan Kousser, *Progressivism—for Middle Class Whites Only, North Carolina Education, 1880–1910*, 46 J Southern Hist 169, 173, 178–79 (1980); Franklin, 58 So Atl Q at 227–28, 235 (cited in note 66); Tindall, *South Carolina Negroes* at 210–14 (cited in note 10); Homel, "Two Worlds of Race?" at 247, 249 (cited in note 66); Rabinowitz, *Urban South* at 170, 176, 178–81 (cited in note 11); Jane Dailey, *Deference and Violence in the Postbellum Urban South: Manners and Massacres in Danville, Virginia*, 63 J Southern Hist 553, 568 (1997); Carl Harris, *Stability and Change in Discrimination Against Black Public Schools: Birmingham, Alabama, 1871–1931*, 51 J Southern Hist 375, 378 (1985); Vaughn, *Schools for All* at 43–48 (cited in note 66); Mangum, *Legal Status* at 133 (cited in note 35); James D. Anderson, *The Education of Blacks in the South, 1860–1935* at 22, 25, 96–97 (1988); Baker, *Color Line* at 84–86, 247–48 (cited in note 15); Lewis R. Harlan, *Separate and Unequal: Public School Campaigns and Racism in the Southern Seaboard States 1901–1915* at 40, 69–70 (1958); Westin, "Negro Public Education" at 100, 208 (cited in note 136).

fair to conclude that by 1900 some southern whites opposed black education entirely, while others supported rudimentary education to achieve literacy, as well as perhaps basic industrial and agricultural training. Very few whites supported genuinely equal educational opportunities for blacks.[139]

Yet southern state law, wholly apart from whatever constraints existed under the federal Constitution, required equality within a segregated system. A typical southern state constitution, while mandating public school segregation, also forbade racial distinctions in the distribution of the common school fund. In 1883 North Carolina enacted legislation that permitted localities to supplement their state educational allocation by levying additional taxes that were to be segregated by race. That is, local taxes raised from whites would be devoted to white schools, and vice versa. The state courts promptly invalidated the law under the state constitution, which forbade "discrimination in favor of or to the prejudice of either race" in public education. Likewise, Kentucky's practice of funding black education solely from black taxes was invalidated by state and federal courts in the mid-1880s.[140]

By the turn of the century, demand was growing in every southern state for formal segregation of the public school fund. Whites complained that it was unfair for black education to be so heavily subsidized by white taxes. Notwithstanding powerful political campaigns, the movement failed in every state. Opponents noted that courts surely would declare such a scheme unconstitutional, which on the basis of the earlier Kentucky and North Carolina litigation seems probable. Critics also predicted that a formal racial division of the school fund would incite congressional retaliation. Perhaps

---

[139] Wingo, "Race Relations" at 185–92, 199–203 (quotation at 202) (cited in note 66); Woodward, *Jim Crow* at 93–94 (cited in note 11); Wynes, *Race Relations in Virginia* at 122, 132, 134 (cited in note 11); Tindall, *South Carolina Negroes* at 213–14, 223 (cited in note 10); Wharton, *Negro in Mississippi* at 246 (cited in note 10); Harlan, *Separate and Unequal* at 40, 137–38 (cited in note 138); John S. Haller, Jr., *Outcasts from Evolution: Scientific Attitudes of Racial Inferiority, 1859–1900* at ch 2 (1971); Fredrickson, *Black Image* at ch 8 (cited in note 15); Anderson, *Education of Blacks* at 100–01 (cited in note 138).

[140] *Puitt v Commissioners,* 94 NC 709, 715 (1886) (first quotation, from NC Const, Art IX, § 2); *Riggsbee v Town of Durham,* 94 NC 800 (1886); *Claybrook v Owensboro,* 16 Fed 297 (D Ky 1883); *Dawson v Lee,* 83 Ky 49 (1885); Anderson, *North Carolina* at 329 (cited in note 10); Howard, 46 J Negro Educ at 321–23 (cited in note 136); Stephenson, *Race Distinctions* at 196–99 (cited in note 32); Westin, "Negro Public Education" at 61–66 (cited in note 136); Frenise A. Logan, *The Legal Status of Public School Education for Negroes in North Carolina, 1877–1894,* 32 NC Hist Rev 346 (1955).

most significantly, opponents emphasized that the school fund already had been racially divided by less direct methods. Why formalize the policy and risk its invalidation? [141]

Beginning in the 1890s, southern states subverted the educational equality provision in their constitutions by reposing discretion over the allocation of school funds to local boards of education. For example, an Alabama statute passed in 1891 provided that the state public school fund should be apportioned to counties according to the total (black and white) number of resident schoolchildren, but then should be distributed to township trustees to allocate to particular schools in a manner they "deem just and equitable." Frequently, the only formal constraint imposed on the exercise of discretion was the requirement that black and white schools enjoy the same length school term. Teacher salaries, teacher qualifications, student/teacher ratios, the grading of schools, spending on physical plant and equipment were all left to the discretion of local educational officials. School officials then invariably exercised that discretion to divert funds from the black to the white schools. This technique for sabotaging black rights was nothing new, of course. Black suffrage and jury service were nullified in precisely the same way. [142]

Black disfranchisement essentially extinguished any political constraints on racially discriminatory administration of the public school fund. Soon thereafter (and not unrelatedly), the Progressive educational campaigns that swept the South from 1900 to 1915 poured much larger sums of money into public education, which administrative officials were now largely free to divert to white

---

[141] Harlan, *Separate and Unequal* at 61, 102–08, 139–40, 158–59, 174, 201, 228–29 (cited in note 138); Westin, "Negro Public Education" at ch 4 (cited in note 136); Wingo, "Race Relations" at 206–08, 215–16 (cited in note 66); Dittmer, *Black Georgia* at 116, 142–43 (cited in note 13); Tindall, *South Carolina Negroes* at 212 (cited in note 10); McMillen, *Dark Journey* at 75–76 (cited in note 11); Woodward, *New South* at 405 (cited in note 10). Contemporary observers like W. E. B. DuBois and many subsequent historians have denied that black education received more than the proportionate share of taxes paid by blacks. Harlan at 19; McMillen at 77–79; Ayers, *New South* at 419–20 (cited in note 13); J. Morgan Kousser, *Separate But Not Equal: The Supreme Court's First Decision on Racial Discrimination in Schools*, 46 J Southern Hist 17, 25–27 (1980).

[142] Glenn N. Sisk, *Negro Education in the Alabama Black Belt, 1875–1900*, 22 J Negro Educ 126, 128 (quotation) (1953); Westin, "Negro Public Education" at 67–71, 116–17, 138, 182 (cited in note 136); Harlan, *Separate and Unequal* at 15–16, 108, 140–44, 158–59, 175, 235–36 (cited in note 138); Mangum, *Legal Status* at 127–28 (cited in note 35); Logan, 32 NC Hist Rev at 352 (cited in note 140).

schools. This temptation to "rape the Negro school fund" was great and scarcely was resisted. The result was enormous disparities in black/white educational spending, especially in black belt counties. By 1915, per capita spending on white education was roughly three times that on black in North Carolina, six times in Alabama, and twelve times in South Carolina. In some majority black counties, the disparity grew as high as thirty or forty to one. Incredibly, disparities in per capita annual spending generally were mild in comparison with other inequalities, such as spending on physical plant, equipment, and transportation. Formal segregation of the public school fund scarcely could have been more effective in diverting educational resources to whites. Yet these racial disparities in public educational spending were largely immune from legal challenge, for the same reason that black exclusion from juries had been permitted notwithstanding *Strauder*. School officials had been empowered to exercise their discretion in the allocation of public funds, and courts refused to presume that those officials had acted in racially discriminatory ways.[143]

The Supreme Court heard only one challenge during this period to racial inequality in education. In *Cumming v Richmond County Board of Education*, a Georgia county ceased funding a black high school while continuing to provide high school education for some whites. The school board's defense was that the limited funds available for black education were better spent on a larger number of black children at the primary school level (400) than a much smaller number at the secondary level (fifty or sixty). The Court rejected the Fourteenth Amendment challenge to this separate-and-*un*equal scheme, reasoning that the board's action had not been motivated by racial animosity and that it was reasonable to redistribute scarce funds among black schools so as to maximize the educational opportunities of the black community as a whole. The author of the Court's unanimous opinion was Justice Harlan,

---

[143] Harlan, *Separate and Unequal* at 11, 14–15, 69, 74, 95, 106, 130–32 (quotation at 131), 162, 166–67, 176, 204–07, 246, 248–50, 254–55, 265, 269 table 17 (cited in note 138); Westin, "Negro Public Education" at ch 4 (cited in note 136); Tindall, *South Carolina Negroes* at 221–23 (cited in note 10); McMillen, *Dark Journey* at 72–74 (cited in note 11); Franklin, 58 So Atl Q at 235 (cited in note 66); Sisk, 22 J Negro Educ at 129 (cited in note 142); Dittmer, *Black Georgia* at 143 (cited in note 13); Wingo, "Race Relations" at 212–15 (cited in note 66); *Lowery v Board of Graded School Trustees*, 52 SE 267, 272 (NC 1905); *Smith v Board of Trustees*, 53 SE 524, 530 (NC 1906).

the sole dissenter in *Plessy* and the Fuller Court Justice most sympathetic toward black civil rights.[144]

To analyze *Cumming*, it is useful to begin with the question of whether the Court in 1899 would have invalidated a statute expressly providing that only whites should receive a high school education. The answer is not clear. While it seems hard to fathom today, for the *Cumming* Court to have sustained such a statute would not have been inconsistent with existing law. The Fourteenth Amendment forbids states from denying persons "equal protection of the laws." To read this language to require that everyone be treated the same would be nonsensical, since the very nature of legislation is to differentiate. Rather, the Equal Protection Clause must mean that persons can be treated differently only when justified by relevant differences. Yet that formulation delegates to judicial discretion the determination of whether differences among individuals or groups are sufficient to justify differential treatment. The Justices in 1899 likely believed that natural racial differences justified disparate educational opportunities.[145]

Nor is this approach to equal protection inconsistent with anything said in *Plessy*. The Court there did *not* hold that the Constitution required that racially separate facilities be equal. The Louisiana statute under review, not the Court, imposed the equality requirement. *Plessy* had no occasion to decide whether separate and *un*equal could be constitutional. Language in the decision suggested, however, that the Constitution required reasonableness, not equality. The Court in 1899 might well have thought it unreasonable to provide blacks with inferior railroad accommodations, but not with inferior educational facilities. They certainly would have thought this with regard to women, for example.[146]

On the other hand, when the Court in 1883 had rejected an equal protection challenge to a statute punishing interracial forni-

---

[144] *Cumming v Richmond County Board of Education*, 29 SE 488 (Ga 1898); aff'd, 175 US 528, 544–45 (1899); Kousser, 46 J Southern Hist (cited in note 141); Schmidt, 82 Colum L Rev at 470–72 (cited in note 51).

[145] Kull, *Color-Blind Constitution* at 3–4, 81–82, 114–15 (cited in note 38); *King v Gallagher*, 93 NY 437, 448–50 (1883); Joseph Tussman and Jacobus tenBroek, *Equal Protection of the Laws*, 37 Cal L Rev 341, 343–44 (1949).

[146] *Cumming*, 29 SE at 490–91; Lofgren, *Plessy* at 190 (cited in note 18); Schmidt, 82 Colum L Rev at 468–70 (cited in note 51); Mark V. Tushnet, *The NAACP's Legal Strategy Against Segregated Education, 1925–1950* at 22 (1987); Kousser, *Dead End* at 27–28 (cited in note 64); Seidman, 80 Cal L Rev at 692 (cited in note 59).

cation more severely than intraracial, it had emphasized the equality with which the law treated both races. Likewise, the Court in 1914 would declare unconstitutional in dicta a statute authorizing racial inequality in luxury railroad accommodations. Moreover, a much-cited speech by a Republican Senator in 1866 had declared that the Fourteenth Amendment would forbid a state's supporting white public schools from all taxes and black schools only from a special tax imposed on blacks. Finally, as we have seen, state and lower federal courts in the 1880s had invalidated state laws providing expressly for racially unequal educational expenditures. These various legal data suggest that the Court in 1899 possibly would have invalidated a statute providing for only white high school education.[147]

Cumming did not have to resolve this question, though, because the inequality there derived not from the face of the statute but from the discriminatory exercise of administrative discretion. The Georgia statute creating county boards of education left to their discretion the establishment of high schools. We know from the jury cases that the Court was unwilling to presume a discriminatory exercise of administrative discretion or to infer racially discriminatory purpose from disparate racial impact. Thus, even if the Court in 1899 would have deemed unconstitutional an explicit statutory command for racially unequal educational expenditures, that did not commit the Court in *Cumming* to invalidate an exercise of administrative discretion that accomplished the same unequal result.

Thus existing law did not compel, or even predispose, the Court to invalidate the inequality in *Cumming*. In the absence of determinate law, the legal outcome probably turned on the Justices' policy views, which in turn were likely to reflect general societal attitudes. At the turn of the century, public opinion generally accepted that black and white education served very different purposes. We have seen that many southern whites opposed black education altogether, while others favored only minimal literacy or industrial training. Very few white southerners endorsed secondary educa-

---

[147] *Cumming*, 175 US at 542; Schmidt, 61 Tex L Rev at 1497–98 (cited in note 103); Cong Globe, 39th Cong, 1st Sess App 219 (June 5, 1866) (Sen. Timothy O. Howe); Mangum, *Legal Status* at 89 (cited in note 35); Kousser, 46 J Southern Hist at 35–36 (cited in note 141); note 140.

tion for blacks. Reflecting this white resistance to equal black education, Booker T. Washington's accommodationist philosophy emphasized industrial, rather than liberal arts, education for blacks. Thus even the nationally recognized leader of southern blacks did not publicly support equal black education.

Public high school education as we know it today was virtually nonexistent for southern blacks at this time. In 1890 only 0.39 percent of eligible southern black children attended high school, and in 1910 just 2.8 percent. The black high school at issue in *Cumming* was the only one in the state of Georgia, and one of only about four existing in any of the eleven former Confederate states. By 1916 Georgia still had fifty-four times as many whites enrolled in public high school as blacks, and the deep South states of Mississippi, South Carolina, and Louisiana still did not have a single four-year black public high school.[148]

Northern whites, while more committed to black literacy, frequently accepted the southern white view of the limited education appropriate for southern blacks. Thus, northern philanthropic organizations such as the Peabody and Rosenwald funds, which heavily subsidized southern black education, agreed that southern blacks should receive an industrial, not a liberal arts, education. This would prepare them for the same "negro jobs" held by their parents, mainly manual labor and service positions. Likewise, the Southern Education Board, which combined northern philanthropists and southern educators in a public schools crusade that lasted from 1901 to 1915, refrained from endorsing equal education for blacks, partly from lack of conviction and partly from fear of alienating southern white supporters. President William McKinley, visiting Tuskegee during his southern tour in 1898, praised the school's industrial education mission and its managers, who "evidently do not believe in attempting the unattainable." President William Howard Taft likewise favored principally industrial training for southern blacks.[149]

---

[148] Anderson, *Education of Blacks* at 33–78, 186, 188, 196–98 (cited in note 10); Harlan, *Separate and Unequal* at 133, 247, 256 (cited in note 138); Meier, *Negro Thought* at ch 6 (cited in note 13); Westin, "Negro Public Education" at 196, 198 (cited in note 136); Homel, "Two Worlds of Race?" at 251 (cited in note 66); Dittmer, *Black Georgia* at 146 (cited in note 13); Ayers, *New South* at 322–23 (cited in note 13).

[149] Anderson, *Education of Blacks* at 92–94, 226–29 (first quotation at 226) (cited in note 10); Hackney, *Populism to Progressivism* at 163 (second quotation) (cited in note 11); Baker, *Color Line* at 304 (cited in note 15); Harlan, *Separate and Unequal* at ch 3 (cited in note

Supreme Court Justices in 1899 likely would have shared this prevalent societal view of the appropriate limits for black education. Thus it is unsurprising that the Justices would have agreed with the Richmond County School Board's conclusion that it was reasonable to close a black high school and reallocate its funds to the education of a much larger number of black primary school students.

* * *

This article has considered Supreme Court decisions from the turn of the century in four areas involving race and the Constitution: segregation, disfranchisement, black jury service, and separate-and-unequal education. In all four contexts the Constitution was sufficiently malleable to accommodate southern white racial practices. Moreover, the Court's rulings tracked dominant national opinion, which had become increasingly sympathetic toward those practices.

The Court acquiesced in railroad segregation at a time when deteriorating southern race relations convinced many southern blacks of the futility of protesting such practices, and racial violence and lynching made segregation increasingly appear to be a reasonably progressive policy. Moreover, accelerating black migration northward rendered racial segregation more acceptable to white northerners, and a growing commitment to sectional reconciliation inclined them to extend to white southerners a free rein in ordering that region's race relations. Likewise, the Court tolerated southern black disfranchisement at a time when the degeneration of southern race relations made the political exclusion of blacks seem an attractive alternative to the interracial violence and killings that characterized southern elections. Moreover, changing northern racial attitudes led many to conclude that the Fifteenth Amendment had been a mistake, and the Republican Party lost both its ideological and strategic commitment to protecting black suffrage. Finally, Congress by this time had repealed the core of the Reconstruction-era voting rights legislation and implicitly acquiesced in disfranchisement by declining to reduce southern con-

---

138); Meier, *Negro Thought* at 85–99, 164–65 (cited in note 13); William Howard Taft, *Southern Democracy and Republican Principles*, in *Present Day Problems: A Collection of Addresses Delivered on Various Occasions by William H. Taft* 221, 225–26 (1908).

gressional representation under Section 2 of the Fourteenth Amendment.

The Court permitted black exclusion from jury service at a time when black officeholders were completely disappearing in the South and becoming noticeably less present in the North as well. Republican presidents had reduced, and soon would eliminate entirely, southern black patronage appointments for fear of antagonizing southern whites. Moreover, the national government was sufficiently unconcerned about the administration of criminal justice with regard to southern blacks that it did not even seriously consider enactment of proposed antilynching legislation. Lastly, the Court approved of racial inequality in educational spending at a time when the most prominent black leader of his generation refrained from openly advocating liberal arts education for blacks, and northern opinion generally acquiesced in the southern white view that blacks were not fit for higher education.

All of the Court's *Plessy*-era race decisions were broadly consistent with national opinion and not inconsistent with the text of the Constitution and existing legal precedent. A contemporary legal commentator could accurately conclude in 1911 that the Fourteenth Amendment had placed no practical restraint on the ability of southern states to deal with the "race problem" as they desired.[150]

III. Consequences

With the exception of a couple of unimportant jury discrimination cases, the Supreme Court during the *Plessy* era rejected all civil rights claims. That is, these decisions legally validated the status quo engineered by white southerners. By ruling against the claims of black litigants, the Court eschewed two other options that were at least theoretically available—ruling in favor of those claims and declining to rule on them at all.

Assessing the significance of decisions affirming the status quo would appear more difficult than measuring the effect of rulings that mandate change. When the Court orders an alteration in current practices, it is possible to observe whether they do in fact

---

[150] Charles Wallace Collins, *The Fourteenth Amendment and the Negro Question*, 45 Am L Rev 830, 853 (1911) (quotation).

change, and thereby assess the significance of the Court's decision. (Even here, though, one must be careful to avoid the fallacy of assuming that changes in social practices that follow a Court decision are a product of that decision, rather than of the underlying social forces that themselves rendered the Court's ruling possible.) Yet when the Court affirms the legal status quo, how does one measure the decision's impact?

Judicial affirmation of the status quo, as opposed to a judicial refusal to decide, arguably further entrenches existing arrangements by placing the Court's imprimatur on them. If one believes that the Supreme Court performs an important educational function in American society—providing moral instruction through its constitutional interpretations—then the Court's validation of a particular practice lends important legitimacy to it. Clearly, measuring this sort of intangible effect of Supreme Court decisions is no easy task.

Furthermore, a Court decision affirming the legal status quo, by definition, refrains from ordering a change thereto. Thus, measuring the effect of such decisions also requires an assessment of how effective a contrary decision would have been. That is, could it have been enforced, and what changes in the status quo would its enforcement have entailed? Concretely, one consequence of *Plessy* is that the Court failed to invalidate de jure railroad segregation. To measure *Plessy*'s complete effect requires hypothesizing the consequences of a counterfactual decision invalidating railroad segregation laws. But how can one know with any certainty how efficacious an imaginary judicial decision would have been?

For these reasons, assessing the consequences of Court decisions affirming the status quo is anything but scientific. Still, the effort is worthwhile because of the question's importance. To fully understand *The Supreme Court, Race, and the Constitution in the Twentieth Century*,[151] we need to develop some sense of how important a role the Supreme Court has played in shaping American racial attitudes and practices. While the conclusion is open to much dispute, it seems to me that with regard to neither of the measures noted above did the *Plessy*-era race decisions have much consequence.

---

[151] Michael J. Klarman, *Neither Hero nor Villain: The Supreme Court, Race, and the Constitution in the Twentieth Century* (forthcoming, Oxford University Press).

A. SEGREGATION

Many commentators have suggested that *Plessy* legitimized racial segregation and encouraged its expansion. For example, one historian has written that *Plessy* "invited the pervasive spread of legally imposed Jim Crow," and another that *Plessy* "gave further impetus to the case for segregation." An eminent federal judge recently concluded that *Plessy* "unleashed forces of ignorance, evil and hate," and that segregated schools "were the direct result of *Plessy*."[152]

There is no direct evidence that *Plessy* affected the spread of southern segregation laws. Most southern states enacted railroad segregation statutes between 1887 and 1892, without perceiving the need for antecedent Supreme Court validation. It is true that the Atlantic seaboard states did not follow suit for several years—South Carolina in 1898, North Carolina in 1899, Virginia in 1900, and Maryland in 1904. But the delayed timing in these states is easily explicable without invoking *Plessy*. In South Carolina, for example, railroad segregation bills had been introduced in the state legislature repeatedly since 1890, but the railroad companies were politically powerful enough to defeat their enactment until 1898. Moreover, North Carolina and Maryland were governed in the mid-1890s, respectively, by a Populist-Republican fusion regime and a Republican one, rendering Jim Crow railroad legislation politically impracticable. Similarly, the spread of de jure segregation to other areas of southern life after the turn of the century is more plausibly attributable to other factors than to *Plessy*'s validation of the practice. Jim Crow possessed an internal logic that made its extension difficult to resist. If jails were segregated, why not courtrooms; and if courtrooms, why not the Bibles upon which witnesses swore? Moreover, the politics of white supremacy disabled politicians from resisting any plausible proposed extension of Jim Crow without risking electoral retaliation. In sum, during the Jim Crow era white southerners generally were content to write their

---

[152] Olsen, *Thin Disguise* at 1 (first quotation), 17, 25 (cited in note 18); Wynes, *Race Relations in Virginia* at 76 (second quotation) (cited in note 11); Nathaniel R. Jones, *The Harlan Dissent: The Road Not Taken—an American Tragedy*, 12 Ga St U L Rev 951, 951–54 (third quotation) (1996). See also Schmidt, 82 Colum L Rev at 470 (cited in note 51); Ely, *Melville W. Fuller* at 158 (cited in note 28); Fischer, *Segregation Struggle* at 154 (cited in note 10); Bruce A. Glasrud, *Jim Crow's Emergence in Texas*, 15 Am Stud 47, 52 (1974).

racial preferences into law first and then test the courts' willingness
to accommodate them, not vice versa.[153]

Even if *Plessy* did not provide a crucial green flag to the spread
of racial segregation, one could argue that it legitimized the practice and thus delayed its eventual destruction. On this view, *Plessy*
taught the nation that racial segregation comported with the Constitution and therefore, implicitly, was not immoral. As one prominent historian puts the point, after *Plessy* separate but equal "bore
the imprimatur of the national government." *Plessy*'s significance
in this regard depends on the weight one generally ascribes to the
Court's educational function. Many scholars have emphasized this
pedagogic role, especially in the context of decisions such as *Brown
v Board of Education*.[154]

Yet there is much reason to believe that Americans make up
their own minds on the pressing moral issues of the day, heedless
of the Court's instruction. Many landmark constitutional decisions
are as noteworthy for the backlash movements they inspired as for
their legitimizing effect. After *Prigg v Pennsylvania*[155] invalidated
northern states' personal liberty laws as inconsistent with the Fugitive Slave Clause, those same states evaded or even defied the
Court's ruling by enacting increasingly aggressive laws to frustrate
rendition of fugitive slaves. *Dred Scott v Sandford*[156] failed to persuade many northerners that Congress lacked constitutional power
to bar slavery from the federal territories. Quite to the contrary,
the Republican Party grew stronger after the decision, achieved
majority status in the North, and during the Civil War simply ig-

---

[153] Lofgren, *Plessy* at 203 (cited in note 18); Linda M. Mathews, *Keeping Down Jim Crow: The Railroads and the Separate Coach Bill in South Carolina*, 73 So Atl Q 117, 119–24 (1974); Tindall, *South Carolina Negroes* at 300 (cited in note 10); Minter, "Jim Crow" at 174–75 (cited in note 32).

[154] Ayers, *New South* at 327 (quotation) (cited in note 13). On the Supreme Court as educator, see Alexander Bickel, *The Least Dangerous Branch* 26 (1962); Eugene V. Rostow, *The Democratic Character of Judicial Review*, 66 Harv L Rev 193, 208 (1952); Christopher L. Eisgruber, *Is the Supreme Court an Educative Institution?* 67 NYU L Rev 961 (1992). On the legitimizing effect of the Constitution and Court interpretations, see J. M. Balkin, *Agreements with Hell and Other Objects of Our Faith*, 65 Fordham L Rev 1703 (1997); Seid-man, 80 Cal L Rev (cited in note 59). On *Brown*'s educational effect specifically, see David J. Garrow, *Hopelessly Hollow History: Revisionist Devaluing of Brown v. Board of Education*, 80 Va L Rev 151, 152–53 (1994); Mark Tushnet, *The Significance of Brown v. Board of Education*, 80 Va L Rev 173, 175–77 (1994).

[155] 41 US (16 Pet) 539 (1842).

[156] 60 US (19 How) 393 (1857).

nored the Court's ruling. Far from educating doubters to believe that racial segregation was immoral, *Brown v Board of Education*[157] crystallized southern white resistance to changes in the racial status quo and rendered racial extremism profitable for southern politicians. Similarly, it seems doubtful that *Roe v Wade*[158] educated many Americans out of their right-to-life position or that *Bowers v Hardwick*[159] convinced many who were not already convinced of the immorality of homosexuality. It is unclear why *Plessy* should have had a more significant educational effect than these other landmark constitutional decisions. The reason it produced no political backlash against segregation is that, unlike with regard to these other rulings, there existed no intensely committed, politically powerful minority group aggrieved by the decision. (Black political power already had been largely nullified by the time of *Plessy*.)[160]

To fully assess *Plessy*'s effect, we also must consider the likely consequences of a contrary decision, invalidating de jure railroad segregation. Courts are, as Alexander Hamilton famously observed in *Federalist No. 78*, the "least dangerous branch" of government. They lack the executive power of the sword and the legislative power of the purse. Court decisions do not enforce themselves. Unless supported by the political branches, courts possess limited capacity to compel recalcitrant parties to conform to their rulings.[161] White southerners would not have voluntarily complied with a hypothetical Court decision in 1896 invalidating de jure railroad segregation. The Fourteenth Amendment, imposed

---

[157] 347 US 483 (1954).

[158] 410 US 113 (1973).

[159] 478 US 186 (1986).

[160] Thomas D. Morris, *Free Men All: The Personal Liberty Laws of the North, 1780–1861* (1974); Arthur Bestor, *State Sovereignty and Slavery: A Reinterpretation of Proslavery Constitutional Doctrine, 1846–1860*, 54 J Ill Hist Soc'y 122, 137–38 (1961); Paul Finkelman, *Prigg v. Pennsylvania and Northern State Courts: Anti-Slavery Use of a Pro-Slavery Decision*, 25 Civil War Hist 5, 21–35 (1979); Don E. Fehrenbacher, *The Dred Scott Case: Its Significance in American Law and Politics* 561–67 (1978); Michael J. Klarman, *Brown, Racial Change, and the Civil Rights Movement*, 80 Va L Rev 7, 75–150 (1994); John C. Jeffries, Jr., *Justice Lewis F. Powell, Jr.* 354–59 (1994); Rosenberg, *Hollow Hope* at 188, 341–42 (cited in note 8); Ruth Bader Ginsburg, *Speaking in a Judicial Voice*, 67 NYU L Rev 1185, 1205 (1992); Klarman, 93 Nw U L Rev at 175–79 (cited in note 9).

[161] See generally Rosenberg, *Hollow Hope* (cited in note 8). For useful criticism of Rosenberg, as well as his response, see David A. Schultz, ed, *Leveraging the Law: Using Courts to Achieve Social Change* (1998).

against the will of most white southerners in 1866–68, commanded
little independent moral authority among them. A judicial interpretation of that amendment invalidating railroad segregation laws
would have commanded little more, especially because issued by
a northern- and Republican-controlled Supreme Court. Thus enforcement of a hypothetical contra-*Plessy* decision would have required the exercise of the federal government's coercive power.
Moreover, the white South's commitment to racial segregation was
sufficiently intense that more than token efforts would have been
required to overcome it.

The question, then, is whether the national government would
have possessed the will and the power to overcome that resistance.
These are two separate points. First, would the national political
branches have possessed the *inclination* to enforce a hypothetical
contra-*Plessy* decision against the South? Second, would they have
had the *capacity* to make that ruling stick? Congress and the president likely would have been reluctant to enforce such a decision
for essentially the same reasons that the Justices were disinclined
to issue it. We already have explored at some length the relevant
factors and need not repeat that discussion here. It is true that
Congress in 1875 had enacted a law that arguably forbade railroad
segregation. But this was during Reconstruction, when Republican
civil rights ardor was at its zenith. Moreover, the statute contained
ambiguous language that permitted a segregationist interpretation,
which is what most courts gave it. By the 1890s, Congress would
not have dreamed of enacting such a statute, as confirmed by the
Republicans' tepid efforts to pass the elections bill in 1890–91.
Congress and the president probably would have been no more
eager to enforce a court decision that would have been the rough
equivalent of such a statute.[162]

Even had the inclination existed, however, the national government likely would have lacked the capacity to enforce a contra-
Plessy decision. The unhappy fate of earlier public accommodations
laws makes this clear. The 1875 Civil Rights Act was widely seen
to be a dead letter before the Supreme Court invalidated it in

---

[162] Gillette, *Retreat from Reconstruction* at chs 10–11 (cited in note 20); Foner, *Reconstruction*
550–52 (cited in note 20); James S. Valone, "Prejudice and Politics: The Civil Rights Act
of 1875" at 66, 81 (master's thesis, Pennsylvania State University, 1958); Avins, 38 Miss
L J (cited in note 55); note 26.

1883. Blacks seeking to enforce their statutory right of access frequently met with such hostility and even violence that the law was easily nullified in practice. Southern state public accommodations laws passed during Reconstruction, which either explicitly or implicitly barred racial segregation in transportation, also went almost completely unenforced. In most southern communities, a black person seeking to enter a white hotel or restaurant would have suffered either economic retaliation or physical violence. It is noteworthy that these southern state laws proved ineffective even when Republicans controlled both state and federal governments, and federal military forces still occupied portions of the South. It would have been that much more difficult for the national government to enforce a contra-*Plessy* ruling in 1896, when Democrats controlled every southern state but one and federal troops had long ceased policing southern race relations.[163]

Even the northern state public accommodations laws, most of which either explicitly barred railroad segregation or were construed by courts to do so, generally proved inconsequential in practice. Blacks often could be intimidated from exercising legal rights through threats of violence. And when the laws were put to the test, enforcement required either private or public lawsuits. Litigation by individual blacks was sporadic at best, owing to general poverty. State enforcement, while more practicable in this regard, still required juries willing to convict and to impose significant penalties. Such verdicts were difficult to come by in unsympathetic regions, where black rights were most likely to be violated.[164]

If the northern public accommodations laws proved difficult for state governments to enforce, it would have been that much harder

---

[163] McPherson, *Abolitionist Legacy* at 21–22 (cited in note 12); Valone, "Civil Rights Act of 1875" at 88–94, 105 (cited in note 162); Weaver, 54 J Negro Hist at 368 (cited in note 37); Fischer, *Segregation Struggle* at 69–70, 81–85, 145 (cited in note 10); Fishel, "The North and the Negro" at 373, 376–77 (cited in note 17); Gerber, *Black Ohio* at 48–49 (cited in note 17); Wright, *Blacks in Louisville* at 56–59 (cited in note 11); Wynes, *Race Relations in Virginia* at 77–78 (cited in note 11); Wharton, *Negro in Mississippi* at 230–31 (cited in note 10); Foner, *Reconstruction* at 370–72 (cited in note 20); Williamson, *Negro in South Carolina* at 287 (cited in note 11); Mangum, *Legal Status* at 33 (cited in note 35); Charleston News & Courier (Nov 5, 1883), p 2.

[164] Gerber, *Black Ohio* at 258–62 (cited in note 17); Thornbrough, *Negro in Indiana* at 260–65 (cited in note 17); Fishel, "The North and the Negro" at 378–82 (cited in note 17); Weaver, 54 J Negro Hist at 374–77 (cited in note 37); New York Times (June 30, 1895), p 20; note 55.

for the national government to render effective a contra-*Plessy* decision. Black plaintiffs would have been harder to locate in the South, where blacks were more likely to be economically dependent upon whites. Perhaps more significantly, for black litigants in the 1890s to challenge segregation in much of the South would have been to invite physical violence and perhaps even lynching. It is no accident that the *Plessy* litigation emanated from New Orleans, where a uniquely tolerant racial atmosphere enabled a black person to seek admission to a white railway car without incurring personal danger. It is for these reasons that the southern public accommodations laws of Reconstruction vintage almost never were enforced. Moreover, resistance to integration would have been greater in the South given the much larger black percentage of the population and the concomitantly deeper commitment to racial separation. And because segregation was not an issue that divided southern whites, the federal government could have expected little assistance from state judges, juries, prosecutors, or law enforcement officials in implementing a court decision invalidating de jure railroad segregation.

Finally, state governments would have enjoyed greater leverage to secure compliance with public accommodations legislation than would have the federal government to compel submission to an antisegregation Court decision. This was an era in which federalism restrictions on national power remained hugely important. For example, state governments in 1896 plainly possessed constitutional authority to criminalize individual violations of a public accommodations law, whereas Congress almost certainly lacked the authority, under the *Civil Rights Cases*, to criminalize individual interference with a hypothetical right against de jure railroad segregation. Similarly, in an era of minimal national government spending, state authorities possessed greater financial leverage to secure compliance by local government entities than the federal government possessed to compel obedience by the states. For all these reasons, a contra-*Plessy* decision would have been even more difficult to enforce than were northern public accommodations laws. Yet, as we have seen, those northern statutes went largely unenforced at the time.[165]

---

[165] Lofgren, *Plessy* at 32 (cited in note 18); Riegel, 28 Am J Leg Hist at 21 n 19, 24 n 31 (cited in note 34); Fischer, *Segregation Struggle* at 69–71, 82–87 (cited in note 10); Som-

Lastly, even an enforceable contra-*Plessy* decision would have had only the effect of restoring the status quo ante *Plessy*. Yet in the years before southern state legislatures adopted railroad segregation statutes, the increasingly prevalent norm was one of de facto segregation—that is, segregation resulting from railroad company policy or custom, rather than from state coercion. Thus it would be mistaken to assume that railroad segregation laws were necessary to achieve segregated railroad travel. In numerous other contexts, statutory intervention was unnecessary to secure rigid segregation of the races. Steamboat travel, for example, was even more racially segregated than railroad transportation, even though only three states bothered to compel such segregation by statute. Similarly, after the turn of the century, southern courtrooms were universally segregated, although no state statute compelled that practice. Segregation likewise was pervasive in southern theaters, hotels, restaurants, and other places of public accommodation, even though only rarely compelled by statute.[166]

It seems unlikely that legislative intervention would have been essential to accomplishing segregation in the railroad transportation context when it was not in so many others. It is true that some railroad companies staunchly resisted statutory segregation mandates because of the expense associated with providing separate but equal accommodations. Yet even in the absence of a statutory command, public pressure on railroads to provide segregated seating would have been enormous as race relations deteriorated in the 1890s. Thus, for example, southern railroads after the turn of the century universally segregated interstate passengers, even after the Supreme Court had made it clear that for a state to compel such segregation by law would violate the dormant commerce clause of the Constitution. In sum, a hypothetical Court decision

---

ers, 40 J Southern Hist at 25 (cited in note 11); Dittmer, *Black Georgia* at 166–67, 172–74, 206–07 (cited in note 13); Mangum, *Legal Status* at 113 (cited in note 35).

[166] Williamson, *Negro in South Carolina* at 274–99 (esp. 298–99) (cited in note 11); Somers, 40 J Southern Hist at 38 (cited in note 11); Woodward, *New South* at 212 (cited in note 10); Stephenson, *Race Distinctions* at 5, 214–15, 238, 350–51 (cited in note 32); Mangum, *Legal Status* at 57, 215 (cited in note 35); Wharton, *Negro in Mississippi* at 232 (cited in note 10); McMillen, *Dark Journey* at 8–9 (cited in note 11); Rabinowitz, *Urban South* at 182 (cited in note 11). The debate among historians over whether de jure railroad segregation replaced de facto segregation or integration is summarized in Lofgren, *Plessy* at 9–17, 201 (cited in note 18), which espouses the former view.

invalidating railroad segregation laws likely would have only replaced de jure segregation with de facto.[167]

This conclusion naturally raises the question why southern state legislatures bothered to enact these railroad segregation laws if they were so unimportant to actually securing segregation. Apparently the explanation lies in some combination of the symbolic value of legislated white supremacy and the incentives of politicians. That state regulation was unnecessary to secure segregation does not show that it bore no significance. Statutes may possess a symbolic value even if they lack functional significance. It is hard to understand, for example, why so many southern states today retain their statutory bans on adultery, fornication, and sodomy other than for their symbolic value; in practice, these laws go almost completely unenforced. A great deal of Jim Crow was concerned with exactly this sort of symbolism—the omission of courtesy titles for blacks, rules of sidewalk etiquette, and expectations of black submissiveness. Many aspects of legislated Jim Crow, including railroad segregation statutes, may have performed a similar symbolic function. These laws represented white political supremacy, whether or not they were actually necessary to securing segregated seating arrangements.

Moreover, once blacks were disfranchised, there existed virtually no political resistance to whatever Jim Crow measures some opportunistic politician proposed. Much as politicians today bid against one another to prove their toughness on crime, politicians in the Jim Crow South sought to outdo each other in demonstrating their commitment to white supremacy. Moreover, once a proposal to extend the reach of racial segregation had been introduced, most politicians found it difficult to resist without jeopardizing their political futures. Candidates who opposed the spread of legal segregation were easily tarred with the label "nigger lover." Only such a political dynamic can explain, for example, the

---

[167] *Chiles v Chesapeake & Ohio Ry.*, 218 US 71 (1910); Mangum, *Legal Status* at 206–07 (cited in note 35); Barnes, *Southern Transit* at 12 (cited in note 33); Joseph R. Palmore, *The Not-So-Strange Career of Interstate Jim Crow: Race, Transportation, and the Dormant Commerce Clause, 1878–1946*, 83 Va L Rev 1773, 1804–07 (1997). But cf Jones, 12 Ga St U L Rev at 955 (cited in note 152); Roback, 46 J Econ Hist (cited in note 35); Mathews, 73 So Atl Q (cited in note 153); Walter E. Campbell, *Profit, Prejudice, and Protest: Utility Competition and the Generation of Jim Crow Streetcars in Savannah, 1905–1907*, 70 Ga Hist Q 197 (1986).

impassioned campaigns conducted by southern politicians early in
the twentieth century for repeal of the Fifteenth Amendment—at
a time when southern blacks already had been almost universally
disfranchised.[168]

These same points are relevant to assessing the consequences of
a hypothetical contra-*Berea College* decision. In 1900 only two private institutions of higher learning in the South permitted integration. So a hypothetical Court decision barring state-mandated segregation of private education obviously would have been of limited
import. Yet there is reason to believe that even such a narrow decision would have been inefficacious. William G. Frost, the president of Berea College, admitted in 1906 that the pending Supreme
Court decision was irrelevant to the college's future because "the
dominant element in Kentucky, though it may be defeated on this
special issue, can find other ways to prevent the reestablishment
of the ideal conditions of the past, for many years to come."[169]

The experience of Berea College also demonstrates how Jim
Crow law generally reflected rather than produced Jim Crow practice. The college's student body, which had been majority black
for much of its history, had a white/black ratio of greater than six
to one by the time the Day law was enacted in 1903. Moreover,
in the 1890s the college on its own initiative had dismissed its one
black faculty member, barred interracial dating, and segregated
students in dorms, dining halls, and sports teams. President Frost's
principal argument against the proposed Day law was that it was
unnecessary because the college already was segregated. The Day
law also illustrates how opportunistic politicians could not resist
an opportunity to score points with white supremacist voters by
enacting largely symbolic legislation. Once the bill was introduced
in the Kentucky legislature, representatives who privately conceded that the state had no business meddling with a private college's race relations could not afford to publicly oppose the bill

---

[168] McMillen, *Dark Journey* at 23–28 (cited in note 11); Dailey, 63 J Southern Hist (cited
in note 138); Ayers, *New South* at 432 (cited in note 13); Somers, 40 J Southern Hist at
41–42 (cited in note 11); Schmidt, 82 Colum L Rev at 866 (cited in note 29); Garner, 13
Am J Soc at 830 (cited in note 119); Bassett, 2 So Atl Q at 302–04 (cited in note 17);
Baker, *Color Line* at 246, 254–59, 266 (cited in note 15); Charles E. Wynes, *The Evolution
of Jim Crow Laws in Twentieth Century Virginia*, 28 Phylon 416, 417, 420 (1960); John
Hammond Moore, *Jim Crow in Georgia*, 66 So Atl Q 554, 561 (1967).

[169] Heckman and Hall, 66 Register Ky Hist Soc'y at 47 (quotation) (cited in note 59).

and thereby invite use of the race question against them for the remainder of their political careers.[170]

Finally, to imagine the truly unimaginable, what would have been the likely consequences had the *Plessy*-era Court invalidated public school segregation? White southerners always had resisted school integration more fiercely than railroad integration. Thus hostility to such a ruling would have been even greater than to a hypothetical contra-*Plessy* decision. Southern white resistance to *Brown* in the 1950s truly was massive. However, by that date World War II and a variety of other factors already had begun to work a change in the racial attitudes of white southerners. One can only imagine how much more intense opposition to a school desegregation ruling would have been before that liberalization of racial attitudes had commenced. A handful of southern communities closed their schools rather than integrate in the wake of *Brown*. Court-ordered school desegregation in the 1890s likely would have destroyed the public school system in the South, had it even been possible to implement such a decision.[171]

In the face of such impassioned white resistance, it seems doubtful that many blacks could have been induced to bring lawsuits enforcing such a hypothetical Court decision. Black litigants seeking to enforce *Brown* in the 1950s often suffered economic retaliation and sometimes physical violence. But by the post–World War II period, lynchings had become a rarity. By way of contrast, well over a hundred southern blacks were lynched annually in the 1890s, and often in response to behavior far less insurrectionary than challenging school segregation. It seems likely that prospective black litigants seeking to enforce a school desegregation decision in the South at the turn of the century would have put their lives in jeopardy.[172]

The unenforceability of northern state laws barring school seg-

---

[170] Blakeman, 70 Filson Club Hist Q at 10 (cited in note 58); Heckman and Hall, 66 Register Ky Hist Soc'y at 37–38, 42–43 (cited in note 59); Nelson, 59 J Negro Hist at 17–24 (cited in note 58); 87 Nation 480–81 (Nov 19, 1908).

[171] Williamson, *Negro in South Carolina* at 217–18, 290 (cited in note 11); Wynes, *Race Relations in Virginia* at 124–25 (cited in note 11); 19 Nation 180 (Sept 17, 1874). On massive resistance to *Brown*, see Numan V. Bartley, *The Rise of Massive Resistance: Race and Politics in the South During the 1950s* (1969); Klarman, 80 Va L Rev at 75–150 (cited in note 160).

[172] Kousser, *Dead End* at 5 (cited in note 64); Somers, 40 J Southern Hist at 20 (cited in note 11); Brundage, *Lynching* at 25, 111–13 (cited in note 12); Wharton, *Negro in Mississippi* at 225 (cited in note 10).

regation speaks volumes as to the likely inefficacy of a hypothetical *Brown* decision in the 1890s. Most northern states barred de jure school segregation, and northern courts in the late nineteenth century awarded victory to black litigants able to prove deliberate segregation by public officials. Yet, in practice, neither the laws nor the lawsuits made much difference. One reason is the relative sparsity of such suits. A court victory meant at most that a particular black litigant was admitted to a white school. These lawsuits were not treated as class actions, and thus repeated litigation would have been necessary to produce significant integration. Yet a leading authority has unearthed only one such lawsuit in Pennsylvania in the twenty-five years after the statutory ban on school segregation was enacted in 1881, and just two in New Jersey in the thirty years after passage of its 1881 desegregation law. The sparsity of such suits was attributable to a variety of factors: the poverty of prospective black litigants, black concerns about inciting retaliatory white violence or economic retribution, ambivalence in the black community about the benefits of integrated schools (which almost never hired black teachers and often offered hostile learning environments for black students), the mild or nonexistent statutory penalties provided for violations, and a recognition by blacks of the limited efficacy of legal victories in the face of determined community resistance. Segregationist school boards and parents possessed many options to evade judicial orders compelling the admission of particular black students to white schools—including gerrymandered attendance zones, discriminatory transfer policies, segregated classrooms within officially integrated schools, and the use of economic retribution and physical violence against black integrators.[173]

For example, in Alton, Illinois, determined black parents carried their school segregation challenge to the state supreme court five times over a ten-year period beginning in 1899, on each occasion securing a reversal of jury verdicts against them. But, in the end,

---

[173] Kousser, *Dead End* (cited in note 64); Douglas, 44 UCLA L Rev at 681–704 (cited in note 60); Price, 43 Pa Hist at 135 (cited in note 65); *Longress v Quincy*, 101 Ill 308 (1882); *Dove v Keokuk*, 41 Iowa 689 (1875); *Pierce v Burlington*, 46 NJL 76 (1884); McConnell, 81 Va L Rev at 975–76 (cited in note 41); Meier and Rudwick, 36 J Negro Educ at 400 (cited in note 17); Fishel, "The North and the Negro" at 193–94, 207–08 (cited in note 17); Gerber, *Black Ohio* at 200–02, 205–06, 265 (cited in note 17); Meier, *Negro Thought* at 48–49 (cited in note 13); Ment, "Racial Segregation" at 156–58, 172, 282–83 (cited in note 65).

Alton schools stayed segregated and remained that way until 1950. No further black litigation against school segregation took place in Illinois for forty years. Southern Illinois shared many of the racial attitudes of the South. But southern blacks were poorer and more economically dependent on whites for their livelihood; southern whites were more committed to white supremacy and prepared to use violence to sustain it; and the South had no analogue to northern Illinois which was, at least rhetorically, committed to racial integration. Thus, if northern laws barring school segregation were so ineffective, it is difficult to imagine a hypothetical *Brown* decision rendered around 1900 making any difference at all. Indeed, if the two southern state constitutions from the Reconstruction era that explicitly barred school segregation had been all but completely ignored in practice, even while Republicans dominated at the state and national levels, why should one expect a Court decision at the turn of the century barring school segregation to have been more efficacious?[174]

B. DISFRANCHISEMENT

It seems implausible that Supreme Court decisions like *Williams v Mississippi* (1898) were significant in encouraging southern black disfranchisement. Numerous southern states had adopted disfranchising electoral laws and two already had conducted disfranchising constitutional conventions (and a third was underway) by the time *Williams* gave a green light to the enterprise. Disfranchisement in other states came later not because they were awaiting advance Supreme Court approval, but rather because of divergent local circumstances, combined perhaps with something of a copycat effect. Mississippi (1890) and South Carolina (1895) probably held disfranchisement conventions first because they were the two states with the largest black populations, the most vivid recollections of black political power during Reconstruction, and the earliest eviscerations of the state Republican Party after Redemption. Peripheral South states like Virginia (1901–02), with a smaller black population and a Reconstruction experience rela-

---

[174] *People ex rel. Bibb v Alton*, 54 NE 421 (1899), 193 Ill 309 (1901), 209 Ill 461 (1904), 221 Ill 275 (1906), 233 Ill 542 (1908); Meier and Rudwick, 36 J Negro Educ (cited in note 17); Kousser, *Dead End* at 36–37 n 23 (cited in note 64); Douglas, 44 UCLA L Rev at 702–04 (cited in note 60); New York Age (Oct 1, 1908), p 1; note 66.

tively free of "black domination," were slower to call disfranchisement conventions. In other states, most notably North Carolina (1900) and Alabama (1901), disfranchisement was delayed by the strength of Populism in the mid-1890s. The decision of many southern states to attach grandfather clauses to their literacy tests, notwithstanding widespread doubts about their constitutionality, attests to the willingness of disfranchisers to act without advance judicial approval.

Nor is it likely that *Williams* played a significant role in legitimizing disfranchisement. The white South did not need the Court's imprimatur to validate its efforts at undermining the Fifteenth Amendment. The vast majority of white southerners already regarded that amendment as a product of illegitimate external coercion. Had the Court invalidated disfranchisement, the white South almost certainly would have regarded such a ruling as no more legitimate than the amendment it was interpreting. It is possible that *Williams* had greater influence on northern white attitudes toward disfranchisement. But the ruling would not have been possible in the first place unless many white northerners already sympathized with the southern white perspective on black suffrage, for reasons already considered at some length.

The likely impact of a hypothetical contra-*Williams* decision would have depended on the national government's inclination and capacity to enforce such a ruling. From our earlier discussion, it seems unlikely that the national government would have had much inclination to enforce such a decision. Republicans controlled both houses of Congress and the presidency from 1896 to 1910, yet took no steps to reenact the voting rights provisions that the Democrats had repealed in 1893–94 or to enforce Section 2 of the Fourteenth Amendment, which seemed to require a reduction in southern congressional representation as a penalty for disfranchisement. The latter omission is especially revealing. Section 2 would have been a great deal easier to enforce than a Court decision invalidating formal disfranchisement methods. Implementation lay entirely within Congress's control, since the Constitution requires Congress to reapportion representation among the states every ten years. Enforcement of a Court decision invalidating disfranchisement measures, by way of contrast, depends largely on the cooperation of local public officials—judges, juries, prosecutors, sheriffs—all of whom possessed ample opportunity and incentive

for nullification. Thus, if Congress was unwilling to invoke a constitutionally mandated remedy for disfranchisement, the implementation of which lay entirely within its control, what reason is
there to expect that it would have been enthusiastic about enforcing a hypothetical contra-*Williams* ruling?

Nor is it obvious how the political branches could have made
such a decision stick, even if inclined to enforce it. If the hypothetical Court decision had invalidated the discriminatory administration of literacy tests and ordered the registration of individual
black litigants, the ruling would have had little systemic effect. Few
southern blacks commanded the economic resources or independence necessary to support litigation. Moreover, at the turn of the
century, there was no NAACP or similar organization that could
spread the costs and risks of litigation over the black community.
Finally, the demonstrated willingness of southern whites to use
violence to defeat black suffrage would have deterred most blacks
from litigating against disfranchisement.[175]

One can hypothesize a Court decision that went further and invalidated literacy tests and poll taxes on their face, either on the
ground that they had been adopted with a racially discriminatory
purpose or that they conferred unfettered discretion on administrative officials. It is hard to see how the national government
could have checked southern white defiance of such a ruling. After
all, southern black voting rights, protected in theory by the 1870s
enforcement legislation, had been substantially nullified in practice
by the late 1880s through force and fraud. Over time, it had become all but impossible to secure criminal convictions against
persons who violated the voting rights of southern blacks. Such
prosecutions had been generally successful in the early 1870s at
suppressing Klan violence directed against black political participation, especially in North Carolina, South Carolina, and Mississippi.
But these criminal prosecutions were dependent upon an unusual
financial commitment by the national government, a particularly
committed attorney general (Amos Akerman), the presence of
large numbers of blacks on juries, and the assistance of federal
military authorities in rounding up defendants and protecting
prosecutors and witnesses from intimidation.

---

[175] Miller, 60 Outlook at 1061 (cited in note 13); Mangum, *Legal Status* at 394 (cited in
note 35); notes 118, 163–64.

These conditions did not outlast the early 1870s. Attorney General Akerman was replaced in late 1871 by George H. Williams, who lacked the former's commitment to protecting black voting rights. The Department of Justice was understaffed and could pursue only a relative handful of meritorious cases. After the Panic of 1873, the department lacked the financial resources necessary to continue its aggressive prosecutorial stance. In any event, mounting successful voting rights cases was difficult in light of the harassment, open intimidation, and even murder of prosecution witnesses and, occasionally, prosecutors themselves. Further, successful prosecutions required cooperative juries, which were uncommon after 1879, when Congress removed the ironclad oath as a condition of jury service and provided for bipartisan selection of jurors. Securing convictions or even indictments became exceedingly difficult at this point, given that "almost every Democrat in the [South] approves and sanctions the frauds committed, believing that the end justifies the means." In the few cases in which convictions were obtained, federal judges generally imposed trivial fines ($5–$10) and no prison sentences.[176]

Moreover, a hypothetical contra-*Williams* decision, even if enforceable, only would have restored the status quo ante, which by the 1890s increasingly was one of black disfranchisement through force and fraud. A contra-*Williams* decision would have had no effect on such informal black disfranchisement. Yet it was precisely these measures that inspired the prominent New South spokesman, Henry Grady, to observe in 1890, when formal disfranchisement had barely begun, that "the Negro as a political force has dropped out of serious consideration." For example, in Mississippi, a majority black state, disfranchisement through fraud and intimidation had virtually eliminated the black vote before any formal suffrage restrictions were imposed. Many white southerners

---

[176] Goldman, *Voting Rights*, passim (quotation at 88) (cited in note 23); Wang, *Trial of Democracy* at 93–133 (cited in note 23); Rose, 1 Am Pol Sci Rev at 41 (cited in note 86); Everette Swinney, *Enforcing the Fifteenth Amendment, 1870–1877*, 28 J Southern Hist 202 (1962); Kermit Hall, *Political Power and Constitutional Legitimacy: The South Carolina Ku Klux Klan Trials, 1871–1872*, 33 Emory L J 921 (1984); Stephen Cresswell, *Enforcing the Enforcement Acts: The Department of Justice in Northern Mississippi, 1870–1890*, 53 J Southern Hist 421 (1987); David Lyons, "Federal Enforcement of Civil Rights: *United States v. Shotwell* and the Ku Klux Klan Trials in North Carolina, 1871" (unpublished student paper, University of Virginia School of Law, 1991); Schmidt, 61 Tex L Rev at 1408–09, 1417–18, 1450–54, 1495–96 (cited in note 103); Gillette, *Retreat from Reconstruction* at 42–45 (cited in note 20); Tindall, *South Carolina Negroes* at 72, 256–57 (cited in note 10).

acknowledged that formal disfranchisement measures were simply a means of "purifying" the southern electoral system. That is, rather than disfranchising blacks through force and fraud, methods that were "debauching the morals and warping the intellect" of whites, "legal" methods would now be employed to accomplish similar results.[177]

While fraud and violence were critical to black disfranchisement, one must not unduly minimize the significance of legal restrictions. Extralegal suppression of the black vote undermined Republican Party strength in state legislatures sufficiently to enable enactment of electoral devices such as complex registration requirements and secret ballot laws, which further reduced black suffrage. There is no denying the significant impact such devices had on the black electorate in at least some southern states. For example, black voter turnout in South Carolina declined from an estimated 70 percent in 1880 to 35 percent in 1884, after the adoption in 1882 of a complex voter registration requirement and an eight-box law. Yet it seems unlikely that a contra-*Williams* ruling would have affected these instruments of legal disfranchisement. Registration requirements and secret ballot laws were too prevalent in the North by the 1890s for the Justices to have been disposed to rule them unconstitutional.[178]

The disfranchisement provisions most susceptible to Fifteenth Amendment challenge were those implemented by state constitu-

---

[177] Lewinson, *Race, Class, and Party* at 67 (first quotation) (cited in note 10); Wynes, *Race Relations in Virginia* at 56 (second quotation) (cited in note 11); Ogden, *Poll Tax* at 8, 29–31 (cited in note 16); James P. Coleman, *The Origin of the Constitution of 1890*, 19 J Miss Hist 69, 81–82 (1957); Cohen, *Freedom's Edge* at 207 (cited in note 11); McMillen, *Dark Journey* at 8, 39 (cited in note 11); 51 Nation 87 (July 31, 1890); 61 Nation 199 (Sept 19, 1895).

[178] Cohen, *Freedom's Edge* at 205 & table 8 (cited in note 11). Kousser argues persuasively that law was not irrelevant to disfranchisement, as Key's fait accompli thesis would suggest. V. O. Key, Jr., *Southern Politics in State and Nation* 535–36 (1949). But Kousser mainly emphasizes statutory provisions such as secret ballot and registration requirements rather than constitutional provisions such as literacy tests. See Kousser, *Southern Politics* at 3, 41, 43, 83, 139, 151, 208, 241 table 9.2 (cited in note 25). Recent historians generally have endorsed Kousser's position. See Ayers, *New South* at 309 (cited in note 13); Anderson, *North Carolina* at 185 (cited in note 10); Cartwright, *Tennessee Race Relations* at 239 (cited in note 10); Cresswell, *Multi-Party Politics* at 108–09 (cited in note 10). An earlier generation of historians was more sympathetic to Key's perspective. Woodward, *New South* at 343 (cited in note 10); Ogden, *Poll Tax* at ch 5 (cited in note 16); Wynes, *Race Relations in Virginia* at 53–54 (cited in note 11). The debate is usefully summarized in Rabinowitz, *First New South* at 115–16 (cited in note 14) and Cresswell, *Multi-Party Politics* at 19–20 (cited in note 10).

tional amendment—namely, the literacy tests with grandfather and understanding clauses. Ironically, these were probably the least important instruments of black disfranchisement at the time. Force, fraud, and electoral devices like secret ballot laws were far more important to black disfranchisement than were literacy tests. Indeed, it is not much of an exaggeration to say that blacks already had been effectively disfranchised before state constitutional suffrage restrictions were implemented. For example, in South Carolina the Republican vote (mostly black) had been largely eliminated through force, fraud, and the 1882 electoral laws before constitutional restrictions were enacted in 1895. Likewise, fewer than 10 percent of black males of eligible age were voting in Georgia even before the implementation of state constitutional disfranchisement measures in 1908. This is the status quo ante that a contra-*Williams* decision would have restored.[179]

For these reasons, a hypothetical contra-*Williams* decision likely would have had little effect on black suffrage. At bottom, black disfranchisement depended on the discriminatory exercise of administrative discretion and, ultimately, the omnipresent threat of white violence. Effective protection of black voting rights thus required either federal military intervention, as during the Klan trials of the early 1870s, or a federal takeover of the state voting apparatus, as under the 1965 Voting Rights Act. The former option ceased to be politically viable after the demise of civil rights ardor in the North by the mid-1870s. The latter was not practicable in the nineteenth century in light of the underdeveloped capacity of the national bureaucracy. Yet the only alternative strategy—federal court review of state administration of the electoral system—was powerless to check passionate resistance to black suffrage by state officials and private citizens in the South. That system simply afforded too many opportunities for local nullification.[180]

---

[179] Grantham, 32 Ga Hist Q at 6, 9–11, 16, 21 (cited in note 90); Lewinson, *Race, Class, and Party* at 92–93 (cited in note 10); Dittmer, *Black Georgia* at 94 (cited in note 13); Kousser, *Southern Politics* at 211, 218 table 7.13 (cited in note 25); Tindall, *South Carolina Negroes* at ch 5 (cited in note 10).

[180] DeSantis, *Southern Question* at ch 1 (cited in note 20); Gillette, *Retreat from Reconstruction* at chs 5, 7 (cited in note 20); Goldman, *Voting Rights* at xxiv–v (cited in note 23); Foner, *Reconstruction* at 603 (cited in note 20); Mangum, *Legal Status* at 393–94 (cited in note 35); McMillen, *Dark Journey* at 44, 47–48 (cited in note 11).

C. JURY EXCLUSION

The only civil rights victories during the *Plessy* era came in jury exclusion cases. The Court reversed a couple of criminal convictions where southern black defendants had been denied adequate opportunities to prove allegations of race discrimination in jury selection. Now, then, we finally can measure the effect of the Court's invalidation of a southern racial practice. Plainly, such decisions had no impact whatsoever on southern black jury service. Blacks continued to be entirely absent from southern juries through the 1930s, *Strauder* notwithstanding. So much for the notion that civil rights victories would educate white southerners to accept the legitimacy of black constitutional rights. Southern states easily evaded the *Strauder* right through the fraudulent exercise of administrative discretion in the selection of jurors. By refusing to presume unconstitutional motivation on the part of state administrative officials, to infer discriminatory motive from disparate impact, or to closely scrutinize state court findings of fact, the Court effectively invited nullification of the right.

What would have been the likely consequence had the Court resolved these subconstitutional issues differently? As with segregation and disfranchisement, there is little reason to expect that white southerners would have happily acquiesced in such decisions. But the capacity for federal enforcement of a nondiscrimination right in the jury context seems much greater. This is true for two reasons. First, the Supreme Court has greater capacity to review what goes on in southern courtrooms than on railroads or in voting booths. Court proceedings take place on the record, and blacks contesting jury selection methods do not bear the onus of initiating litigation themselves. Second, the Court possesses a remedy for race-based jury exclusion that does not depend, at least directly, on the cooperation of either the political branches of the national government or officers of the state legal system. Specifically, the Supreme Court has the theoretical power to continue reversing state court criminal convictions indefinitely if state officials persist in defying Court decisions requiring color-blind selection of jurors. It is true that one scarcely can imagine the *Plessy*-era Court implementing such a remedy. But that is attributable to the Justices' lack of inclination to invoke dire remedies for black jury exclusion, not their lack of power. (Whether the Court had the manpower to review every criminal conviction of a southern black defendant who alleged racial discrimination in jury selection is another question.)

It is true that southern states might have defied such a remedy by executing sentences even after the Court had reversed them. Such a step would not have been entirely unprecedented. Georgia had defied the Marshall Court in this manner in 1830 during their famous confrontation over the issue of Cherokee removal. But such a step would have required a greater willingness to openly defy federal authority than did the evasive measures generally adopted by southern states to nullify federal rights during this period. That is not to say that such open resistance would have been out of the question. Southern courts and politicians took precisely such steps during the period of massive resistance to *Brown*. But such blatant state defiance possibly would have inspired the national political branches to take a stand in defense of national supremacy, much as President Dwight Eisenhower was impelled to do in 1957 in response to Governor Orval Faubus's defiance of a federal court school desegregation ruling in Little Rock. Whether such federal executive enforcement would have been forthcoming in the wake of state defiance of hypothetical Court decisions overturning criminal convictions of southern blacks on the ground of racial discrimination in jury selection is, again, a question more of inclination than of capacity. We have seen considerable reason to doubt whether such an inclination would have existed, though it doubtless would have been greater had the issue been posed in the stark terms of a direct state challenge to national supremacy.[181]

D. SEPARATE AND UNEQUAL

Southern whites hardly required antecedent Supreme Court approval to legitimize their campaign for separate and unequal in public education. The trend in this direction was well advanced before *Cumming*. Racial inequalities in public education were justified, in the minds of white southerners, by natural differences between the races that dictated different sorts of education for each

---

[181] Charles Warren, *The Supreme Court in United States History.* Vol 1: *1789–1835* at 729–36 (1922); Jill Norgren, *The Cherokee Nation Cases of the 1830s,* 1994 Yearbook Sup Ct Hist Soc'y 65, 70–71; notes 127–28.

and by the belief that blacks paid less in taxes to support the educational system. No Court decision was necessary to validate these beliefs. Growing racial disparities in educational spending after 1900 were not a result of *Cumming*'s endorsement of the practice, but rather of the culmination of black disfranchisement and the Progressive school campaign of the early twentieth century that raised the stakes of depriving blacks of their proportionate share of the public school fund.

Racially disparate educational expenditures were, as we have seen, a product not of state statutory or constitutional command, but rather of the discriminatory exercise of administrative discretion. Thus for a Court decision to have been effective in ending such racial disparities, it would have had to either eliminate that discretion or else closely supervise its exercise. Suppose the Supreme Court had been willing to take such an unprecedented step in 1899. Could it have made the decision stick?

There is no reason to expect that white southerners would have voluntarily complied with such a decision, given their nearly universal opposition to equal educational spending for blacks. North Carolina state court decisions in the 1880s invalidating statutory authorization for local school taxes to be allocated on a racial basis had been widely defied and evaded. Similar state and federal court decisions in Kentucky in the 1880s seem to have been entirely disregarded, as that state continued to raise "segregated" public school taxes well into the twentieth century. A Supreme Court decision mandating equal educational expenditures for the races would have encountered even stauncher resistance among white southerners as a form of "outside interference."[182]

Nor would the national political branches likely have been sympathetically inclined toward enforcement of such a hypothetical ruling. A general northern willingness to accommodate white southerners in their racial practices, combined with a specific concurrence in the view that black southerners did not need or deserve equal educational opportunities, would have disinclined the national government to enforce such a Court decision.

---

[182] Anderson, *North Carolina* at 329 (cited in note 10); Harlan, *Separate and Unequal* at 47 (cited in note 138); Mangum, *Legal Status* at 121 (cited in note 35); *Trustees of Colored Schools v Trustees of White Schools*, 203 SW 520 (Ky 1918); *Crosby v City of Mayfield*, 117 SW 316 (Ky 1909).

Even had the inclination existed, however, the capacity probably would have been lacking. Racial discrimination in jury selection can be redressed by reversing criminal convictions of black defendants, but there is no analogous remedy for persistent diversion of the public school fund to white education. Criminal and civil litigation against recalcitrant public officials who persist in flouting the Constitution is always a possibility. But this option is unattractive in light of the ample opportunities for nullification by unsympathetic prosecutors, judges, and juries, which we have seen undermined enforcement of the 1870s voting rights legislation. Civil litigation, moreover, places the onus of enforcement on generally impecunious blacks, who also were susceptible to economic and physical intimidation. Theoretically, the hypothetical contra-*Cumming* decision could have ordered the closing of recalcitrant school districts. But such a remedy is both difficult to imagine and would have been impossible to enforce without federal military intervention. Congress lacked the most efficacious enforcement mechanism—the threat to cut off federal funding for school districts that persisted in violating the hypothetical Court ruling. In 1900 the national government did not generally subsidize public education. It is plausible that southern blacks' recognition of the futility of legal remedies explains the almost complete absence of lawsuits challenging the enormous racial disparities in educational funding that existed in southern black belt counties by the early decades of the twentieth century.[183]

* * *

It is possible to imagine one further consequence of the *Plessy* Court's rulings in civil rights cases: blacks victimized by Jim Crow practices might have ceased bothering to litigate. If civil rights claims rarely succeeded in Court, and were successfully evaded even when formally vindicated, at some point blacks might have reasoned that the costs of litigation exceeded the benefits. Had this been an effect of the *Plessy*-era race decisions, it might have been significant, depending on how crucial a role one believes litigation

---

[183] Mangum, *Legal Status* at 78 (cited in note 35). On the importance of threats to cut off federal funding to school desegregation in the 1960s, see Rosenberg, *Hollow Hope* at 50, 97–100 (cited in note 8); Stephen C. Halpern, *On the Limits of the Law: The Ironic Legacy of Title VI of the 1964 Civil Rights Act* ch 3 (1995).

played in the subsequent success of the civil rights movement. Yet the many Court defeats (and the few Pyrrhic victories) of the *Plessy* era plainly did not discourage blacks from litigating. Notwithstanding the dismal Court record on civil rights, litigation may have remained the most promising protest strategy available to southern blacks at the time. Litigation, unlike a political protest movement, does not require mass popular support to succeed. And litigation, unlike direct action protests, was *relatively* safe, since it took place in the courtroom rather than on the streets—not an insignificant consideration in a period when black lynchings were commonplace. Whatever the explanation, the *Plessy* era defeats did not inhibit blacks from continuing to challenge the racial status quo in the courts. Beginning in 1909, they frequently had the assistance of the NAACP when doing so. And, as it turned out, Court victories lay just around the corner, in the second decade of the twentieth century.[184]

IV. Conclusion

It is possible to draw some tentative lessons from the *Plessy*-era race cases. First, the Justices' performance confirms the limited capacity of the Supreme Court to play the heroic role of rescuing minorities from majoritarian oppression. The Justices are too much a part of majoritarian culture for them to possess the inclination to resist dominant public mores. The significant overlap between their views and prevailing social practices disables them from seeing the oppression that might be apparent to observers inhabiting an external vantage point. For example, most of the Justices in 1896 would have seen segregation as a reasonable response to interracial friction and violence, and thus would have been loath to rule it inconsistent with the Fourteenth Amendment.

Second, the text of the Constitution and legal precedent construing it were sufficiently indeterminate to accommodate the Justices' racial inclinations. The Equal Protection Clause, for example, does not plainly bar racial segregation. While the Fifteenth Amendment does expressly forbid disfranchisement based on race, it does not clearly prohibit literacy tests and poll taxes, regardless

---

[184] For discussion of these Progressive era civil rights victories, see Klarman, 51 Vand L Rev 881 (cited in note 7).

of the motivation for their enactment. Nor were the Justices at the turn of the century constrained by constitutional text or legal precedent in defining the standards of proof for allegations of racially discriminatory exercise of administrative discretion. When the traditional sources of constitutional law do not point clearly toward a result that the Justices disfavor as a policy matter, it is natural for them to avoid that outcome.

Third, "subconstitutional" rules are as important to the effective enforcement of constitutional rights as are their formal declaration. Constitutional law in the *Plessy* era plainly had established that the right to vote and to serve on juries could not be denied based on race. Yet the Court's unwillingness to examine legislative motive, to invalidate broad grants of discretionary authority, to presume unconstitutional motive in state administrative action, to infer illicit purpose from the fact of racial exclusion, or to seriously review state court findings of fact virtually invited nullification of the underlying rights.

Moreover, the content of these subconstitutional rules cannot be divorced entirely from substantive views about the importance of the underlying rights at issue. When the Justices became more genuinely committed to protecting the underlying constitutional rights, beginning in the 1930s and culminating in the 1960s, the subconstitutional rules changed. Uncabined grants of discretionary authority were invalidated. Access to federal court for constitutional claims was substantially broadened. States were put to the burden of justifying hugely disparate racial impacts. And state court findings of fact were no longer immunized from federal court review. Thus, while it might be mistaken to treat the invocation of these subconstitutional rules to undermine the underlying constitutional rights as a mere pretext to camouflage the *Plessy* Court's racism, it also would be wrong to deny the connection between the content of these rules and the shallowness of the Court's commitment to the underlying rights.[185]

Fourth, the content of these subconstitutional rules was especially important in the race context. This is because in three of the four settings canvased in this article—every one but racial segregation—nullification of the constitutional right at issue was

---

[185] Schmidt, 61 Tex L Rev at 1440, 1472, 1475 (cited in note 103); Robert Jerome Glennon, *The Jurisdictional Legacy of the Civil Rights Movement*, 61 Tenn L Rev 869 (1994).

achieved not by formal repudiation but rather by the discriminatory exercise of administrative discretion. White southerners quickly learned how to nullify constitutional rights that they viewed as illegitimate. Rather than inviting federal intervention through open repudiation, they delegated broad enforcement discretion to administrative officials. Especially after suppression of the black vote, these state officers could be trusted to exercise that discretion in the service of white supremacy. To effectively deal with this problem of pervasive fraud in the administration of ostensibly race-neutral statutory schemes required a different set of subconstitutional rules than the Court employed at the turn of the century.

Fifth, even had the *Plessy* Court been more committed to the pursuit of racial equality than were most Americans at the time, clear limits exist on how much judicial intervention could have accomplished. At the turn of the century, the national government would have had little inclination to enforce aggressive pro–civil rights interpretations of the Constitution for pretty much the same reasons that the Justices were not inclined to render them. Moreover, southern whites were fierce in their opposition to black civil and political rights, and suppression of the black vote had disabled the beneficiaries of such hypothetical rulings from providing any significant political support. Further, most methods of federal enforcement required some cooperation by government officials at the local level—judges, juries, sheriffs, prosecutors. Thus unified opposition by southern whites could effectively nullify whatever constitutional rights the Court deemed blacks to possess. The national government in 1900 lacked the administrative capacity necessary to effectively secure black rights in the South by bypassing the local enforcement apparatus. There was no Federal Bureau of Investigation, and the Justice Department possessed inadequate funding and staffing to prosecute all civil rights violations. There were few federal grant-in-aid programs that could have been used as a lever to coerce southern compliance with civil rights rulings. There was inadequate federal bureaucratic capacity to enable an assumption from the states of the administration of spheres, such as elections, where black rights had been nullified. Such a capacity would exist by the time of the second Reconstruction, though for reasons that were largely independent of race. Yet the sort of national bureaucratic power that proved crucial to the enforcement of landmark civil rights legislation and Court rulings in the 1960s would have been quite inconceivable during the *Plessy* era.[186]

Finally, even if the Court somehow could have defied dominant public opinion by broadly defining the constitutional rights of blacks, and found some way to enforce such rulings, it remains unlikely that much would have changed in practice for southern blacks. Most of Jim Crow's legal apparatus reflected rather than produced a social reality of white supremacy. Formal disfranchisement and de jure railroad segregation, for example, played relatively minor roles in disfranchising and segregating southern blacks. Deeply rooted social mores, reinforced by economic power and ultimately the threat and reality of physical violence, dictated the terms of the southern racial hierarchy. Legal confirmation of these antecedent social norms often was more symbolic than functional. Thus judicial invalidation of Jim Crow legislation alone would not have made much difference in alleviating the oppression of southern blacks. A great deal more would be required.[187]

---

[186] Schmidt, 61 Tex L Rev at 141 (cited in note 103); Foner, *Reconstruction* at 603 (cited in note 20); Gillette, *Retreat from Reconstruction* at 363 (cited in note 20); Stephen Skowronek, *Building a New American State: The Expansion of National Administrative Capacity, 1877–1920* at 46, 161–62 (1982).

[187] Williamson, *Negro in South Carolina* at 298–99 (cited in note 11); McMillen, *Dark Journey* at 4, 9–10, 23–32 (cited in note 11); Stephenson, *Race Distinctions* at 351–52 (cited in note 32); Wharton, *Negro in Mississippi* at 216–33, 274 (cited in note 10); Gerber, *Black Ohio* at 49 (cited in note 17); Glasrud, 15 Am Stud at 56 (cited in note 152); Moore, 66 So Atl Q at 554–57 (cited in note 168). Compare Woodward, *Jim Crow* at 68–69, 97, 102, 105 (cited in note 11), which emphasizes more the significance of law. As should be clear from the text, I strongly disagree with the claim of several libertarian commentators that Jim Crow practices could not have flourished without formal state backing. See, for example, Richard A. Epstein, *Forbidden Grounds: The Case Against Employment Discrimination Laws* 91–115 (1992); David E. Bernstein, *The Law and Economics of Post–Civil War Restrictions on Interstate Migration by African Americans*, 76 Tex L Rev 781, 831–39 (1998); Roback, 46 J Econ Hist at 893–94, 916–17 (cited in note 35).